THE ACADEMY OF FISTICUFFS

The Academy of Fisticuffs

POLITICAL ECONOMY AND
COMMERCIAL SOCIETY IN
ENLIGHTENMENT ITALY

Sophus A. Reinert

Harvard University Press

Cambridge, Massachusetts
London, England
2018

Frontispiece. Alessandro Magnasco, *Il Mercato del Verziere,* 1733.
Raccolte d'Arte Antica, Pinacoteca del Castello Sforzesco, Milano Raccolte.
Copyright © Comune di Milano—All rights reserved.

Library of Congress Cataloging-in-Publication Data
Names: Reinert, Sophus A., author.
Title: The Academy of Fisticuffs : political economy and commercial society
in Enlightenment Italy / Sophus A. Reinert.
Description: Cambridge, Massachusetts : Harvard University Press, 2018. |
Includes bibliographical references and index.
Identifiers: LCCN 2018006858 | ISBN 9780674976641 (alk. paper)
Subjects: LCSH: Accademia dei Pugni. | Verri, Pietro, 1728–1797. | Beccaria,
Cesare, marchese di, 1738–1794. | Enlightenment—Italy—Lombardy. |
Socialism—Italy—Lombardy—History—18th century. | Lombardy
(Italy)—Economic conditions—18th century.
Classification: LCC B802 .R434 2018 | DDC 945/.07—dc23
LC record available at https://lccn.loc.gov/2018006858

Til Erik August

Er der nogen nærmere, end Fader og Søn?
—Henrik Ibsen, *De unges Forbund* (1869)

Lions, wolves, and vultures don't live together
in herds, droves or flocks. Of all animals of prey,
man is the only sociable one.

—John Gay, *The Beggar's Opera*, 1728

CONTENTS

Europe at the Time of
the Academy of Fisticuffs

0 — 500 km

0 — 500 miles

Inset map labels:

SWITZERLAND
Tyrol
Savoy
Turin
Piedmont
Milan
Milan
Parma
Modena
Venice
Isria
Venetian Republic
Dalmatia
Republic of Genoa
Lucca
Florence
Tuscany
Papal States
Corsica
Rome
Naples
Sardinia
KINGDOM OF NAPLES AND SICILY
Palermo
Tunis

Main map labels:

N

Christiania (Oslo)
Bergen
SWEDEN
Stockholm
St. Petersburg
RUSSIA
KINGDOM OF NORWAY AND DENMARK
Duchy of Courland
Copenhagen
Lithuania
Edinburgh
IRELAND
Dublin
GREAT BRITAIN
Bristol
London
United Netherlands
Amsterdam
Berlin
PRUSSIA
Poland
Warsaw
Hanover (Br.)
SAXONY
Leipzig
Dresden
Bautzen
Austrian Neth.
Ensdorf
SMALL GERMAN STATES
Prague
BOHEMIA
Galicia
Paris
HOLY ROMAN EMPIRE
AUSTRIAN DOMINIONS
ATLANTIC OCEAN
FRANCE
Baden
Ettal
Bavaria
Milan
Budapest
Hungary
Moldavia
Bordeaux
Siena
Wallachia
PORTUGAL
Lisbon
Madrid
SPAIN
Naples
OTTOMAN EMPIRE
Cadiz
Ceuta
Melilla
Oran
Casbah (Algiers)
Mediterranean Sea
see inset
Athens
Greece
MOROCCO
ALGERIA
TUNIS
CRETE

— xi —

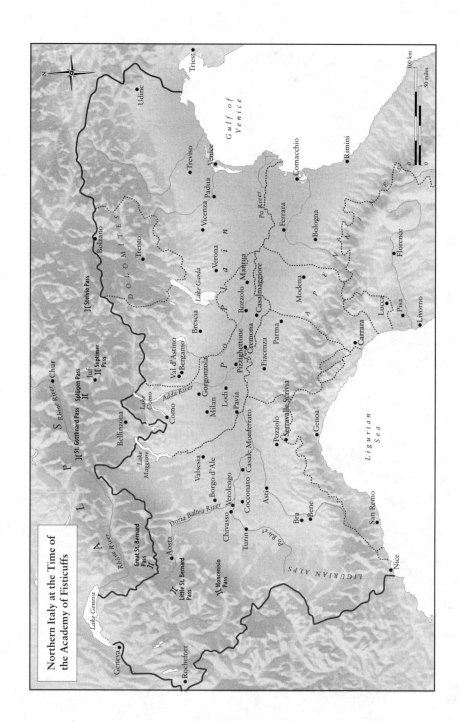

Northern Italy at the Time of
the Academy of Fisticuffs

THE ACADEMY OF FISTICUFFS

Introduction: *Lupi sacri*

⟫⟨

"Now everyone speaks of Public Economy as if it were Religion," the Vallumbrosan monk Ferdinando Facchinei lamented in a 1764 manuscript held in the Venetian state archives.[1] His fear was that while the lives of individuals and the ideals of societies alike traditionally had been understood and evaluated in theological terms, what we might call an "economic turn" was in the process of dramatically recasting how Europeans conceived of themselves and of their polities. The present volume can be considered an extended meditation on the emergence of political economy and what was called "commercial society" in Enlightenment Italy. At its heart, it is a story of theorists and practitioners, but it is also a saga of monks and major-generals, lovers and lawyers, bandits and bureaucrats. The tension between the worldly and the otherworldly identified by Facchinei lay side by side with similar tensions between the gradual and the revolutionary, states and markets, the individual and the social—all of which emerged amid ruthless economic and territorial competition on the Italian peninsula and, indeed, across an increasingly globalized world.

The specific object of Facchinei's critique was a recently published work by the better-known Milanese writer and soon statesman Cesare Beccaria, whose text *Dei delitti e delle pene,* or *On Crimes and Punishments,* many today would argue, "changed Western civilization."[2] In his own time, Beccaria was one of the most prominent members of the Accademia dei pugni, the "Academy of Fisticuffs," a caffeinated think tank of aristocratic intellectuals and reformers that did much to put Milan on the intellectual map of mid-eighteenth-century Europe. Baron Friedrich-Melchior Grimm dubbed the Academy of Fisticuffs the "coterie de Milan"; Voltaire referred to them as the "École de Milan."[3] Because of Beccaria's book, however, the group was soon known throughout the European world, from St. Petersburg to Philadelphia. As its English translator put it in 1767, "perhaps no book, on any subject, was ever received with more avidity, more generally read, or more universally applauded" than *On Crimes and Punishments*.[4] But Facchinei's criticism was a telling one to level against what is best known as a work condemning the cruel punishments of Old Regime Europe, and suggests that the stakes of their disagreement revolved around something even deeper than the logistics of penal reform. In fact, Facchinei's censure of the rise of political economy as an organizing discipline of worldly existence went hand in hand with his equally intriguing charge that Beccaria was a "socialist," in what marked the term's earliest known vernacular appearance. What follows will seek to shed light on this moment, the context of *On Crimes and Punishments* (and the larger pugilistic project of which, however influential, it was only a limited expression), and what invectives against the Academy of Fisticuffs entailed at the time. All of this is to explore how the episode can help us recast the longer histories of commercial sociability, human rights, and worldly melioration, and of the period and movement commonly referred to as "The Enlightenment," on which so much of "modernity" is seen to rest.[5]

Specifically, the broader context of Facchinei's engagement with Beccaria and his colleagues opens fruitful new perspectives on the intertwined trajectories of socialism and capitalism as originally conceived; the history of marketization across expanding territories; the changing nature of international competition in such a context; the early codification of political economy; and, of course, the tension between secularism and political theology in early modern Europe—perspectives that, though anchored in the North Italian Po Plain in the eighteenth century, widen far beyond it. For what their quarrel ultimately revolved around was nothing less than the role of Providence in earthly affairs and the capacity of human beings to peacefully coexist and purposefully improve their individual and collective conditions in the world through economic means. The pugilists were, in the end, theorists, architects, and builders of a world that cannot but look familiar to us, for the planet we inhabit is still very much characterized by varying and competing forms of economic integration, on the one hand, and sometimes violent political partitioning, on the other; and some of our greatest challenges remain—like in the eighteenth century—those of safeguarding sociability, domestically as well as internationally, all the while negotiating the *just* roles of inequality, individual rights, and religion in civic life.

Indeed, of the ceaseless debates animating early modern Europe, few were more vocal, or more consequential, than that which raged over the vexing question of human sociability—the question, in other words, of why people could or could not *just get along*.[6] The nebula of anxieties and assumptions motivating this debate is often crystallized in a famous Manichean opposition, popularized centuries earlier by the Renaissance humanist Erasmus of Rotterdam, between the Roman playwright Plautus's trenchant observation that "lupus est homo homini" (man is a wolf to man) and the Stoic philosopher Seneca's more hopeful "homo, sacra res homini" (man is something sacred to man).[7] Were men wolves to one another, or were they sacred? Was humanity really characterized by an "appetitus socialis" or "Desire of Society," as the Baroque Dutch jurist Hugo Grotius had argued, or should one rather put one's faith in the English political philosopher Thomas Hobbes's vision of life in the "state of nature" as "solitary, poore, nasty, brutish, and short?"[8] Similarly, was the subsequent "civil state" of "society" the fragile result of a hard-fought victory to be vigilantly defended against man's predatory passions, or was it the orderly and blessedly spontaneous result of either instinctive camaraderie or countervailing self-interests? Was humanity social before it became political, or vice versa, and how, if at all, did economic forces play into this relationship between sociability and politics?[9]

Though the term "society" is remarkably polyvalent, by the early modern period it had come to represent an array of related meanings in European languages similar to those with which we operate today, signifying varying degrees of union between individuals through relations of community, similarity, friendship, allegiance, association, partnership, and / or participation, with emotive, economic, but also political connotations.[10] By the mid seventeenth century, Hobbes could argue in his *De Cive,* or *On the Citizen,* published at the very beginning of the blood-drenched English Civil War (1642–1651), that the emergence of states had made "citizens" sacred to each other in "societies," whereas the relationship between such "commonwealths" remained lupine.[11] To use the vocabulary of the American political philosopher John Rawls for the occasion, time had socialized "people" within polities, but not yet the relations between different "peoples," intended as "actors in the Society of Peoples, just as citizens are the actors in domestic society."[12]

Leviathans had arisen from the depths of time and taken the form of modern states, socializing individuals and saving them from the fearsome brutality of their natural condition, but they remained terrible to behold. As Hobbes put it in *On the Citizen*, "Kingdoms and empires, armed and garrisoned, with the posture and appearance of gladiators, look across at each other like enemies."[13] Strikingly, however, in his later *Leviathan*, first published in 1651, he elaborated on the metaphor of the gladiator to make an important, if often neglected, further point about the role of states in the world:

> In all times, Kings, and Persons of Soveraine authority, because of their Independency, are in continuall jealousies, and in the state and posture of gladiators; having their weapons pointing, and their eyes fixed on one another; that is, their Forts, Garrisons, and Guns upon the Frontiers of their Kingdomes; and continuall Spyes upon their neighbours, which is a posture of War. But because they uphold thereby, the Industry of their Subjects; there does not follow from it, that misery, which accompanies the Liberty of particular men.[14]

The state of nature between individuals was, then, not quite like the state of nature between polities, and Hobbes did not suggest that reciprocal fears might give rise to anything like a global leviathan or world state to match the formation of individual societies.[15] He did, however, indicate something quite extraordinary, something that also happens to speak to one of the gravest tensions of modern world history: in his eyes, it was precisely the jealousy of sovereigns that safeguarded the welfare and competitive industry of their respective citizens. The civil and commercial state of polities, as Hobbes, with different phrasing, emphasized in what amounts to one of his most explicitly *economic* passages, ironically depended on the state of nature and therefore ruthless struggle for supremacy between them.[16] Yet the economic lives of these disparate and jealous polities remained inexorably intertwined through trade and travel, leading to a seemingly insurmountable tension between the political and economic spheres of sovereignty in international affairs, between, in short, states and markets.[17] Or, as a tradition of thought drawing its inspiration from Roman law has put it, between *imperium,* "rule over people," and *dominium,* "rule over things."[18] A divided world could be prosperous but also inherently dangerous, and the deeper question of whether prosperity with time would neutralize or galvanize said danger still remains unresolved.

Was Hobbes right? If so, how durable might a political society be, and what, if anything, could one do to expand the thresholds of sociability even further, perhaps one day even aligning the world's political and economic interests altogether? Many writers at the time, of course, suggested that something akin to a "fatherland common to all," a "general Society of Mankind," or a "Union of distinct Societys" already existed, maintained, for example, by "commerce" or by the "similarity" of humans; but it was increasingly evident that the bonds of sociability weaving these ideal "societies" of *peoples* together remained treacherously evanescent compared to those supporting *people* in a polity, and that even these latter could break down.[19] In short, and regardless of whether one believed in the primacy of society or of politics, an overarching question remained as to what extent, and how, competing and often warring states themselves could be brought together in a process of peaceful improvement—not unlike what, building on an august tradition, the Königsberg philosopher Immanuel Kant soon would call the project for "perpetual peace."[20]

This challenge of human sociability, seemingly perennial in nature, had long been the domain of theology and political philosophy. As Facchinei's critique of Beccaria made clear, however, economic affairs had undeniably risen to a position of prominence in domestic policy and international relations alike in the early modern period, and the politics and sociology of commerce increasingly claimed the attention not only of the likes of Hobbes but of sovereigns, laymen, and particularly the reformers that so profoundly characterized the European Enlightenment.[21] The substantial incongruity at the time between competing and territorially solidifying states, on the one hand,

and increasingly expansive and international markets, on the other, and the ways in which economic and political concerns affected one another, offered concrete challenges and opportunities but also fertile grounds for intellectual debate.[22] Not fortuitously, it was at the intersection of these worlds—the divine and the secular, the ideal and the practical—that the neologisms "socialists" and then "socialism" made their first appearances, in debates around the nature and future of human sociability in the European Enlightenment.[23]

In Mazdak's Wake

The early twentieth-century Chicago economist Jacob Viner once noted that "most abstract terms ending in 'ism,'" among which we perforce must count both "capitalism" and "socialism," "inevitably accumulate about them a haze of uncertainty and imprecision."[24] Indeed, if the term "socialism" ranks among both the most inspiring and the most bloodcurdling words in recorded history, its meaning is made even more uncertain by the fact that it has undergone noticeable denotational drift since it was first invented.[25] For the terms "socialist" and "socialism"—quite distinct from the countless proto-socialist (in our current, still contested sense) writings and regimes populating the historical record, dating back at least to the teachings of the Zoroastrian prophet Mazdak, who lived in present-day Iran around 500 BCE[26]—did not originate, as is often argued, in British and French Utopian Socialism of the 1820s, among the religious Owenites, the Fourierists, and the Saint-Simonian apostles of socio-industrial civilization.[27] Rather, they emerged more than half a century earlier in theological debates over secularization and sociability in the tumultuous smaller states of Germany and, particularly, the Italian peninsula. The word "socialists" made its first appearance in dusty Latin tomes written against the Leipzig-trained jurist and political philosopher of natural law Samuel von Pufendorf and his followers, who were criticized for sidelining religion through their emphasis on humanity's quintessentially social nature and ends.[28] "Socialists" and eventually "socialism" were originally rare and derogatory terms in the intellectually effervescent decades following the global Seven Years' War (1756–1763)—famously dubbed "the first world war" by Winston Churchill—and the subjects of the abuse never referred to themselves as such.[29] None of the eighteenth-century "socialists" here discussed ever claimed to be one, or even really acknowledged being called one in print.

From the perspective of intellectual history, it is hard to deny that the term at first was something of a nonstarter. Precisely by virtue of its very rarity, however, we are forced to consider how and why it breached, however obliquely, what Hans Robert Jauss might have called the "Erwartungshorizont" or "horizon of expectations" of the time (not to mention ours when considering "Enlightenment" texts).[30] As an anomaly, it demands explanation, and one might even say that the very unexpectedness of Enlightenment "socialism," its rareness in the vocabulary of the eighteenth century, offers an opportunity to approach contemporary theories of political economy and commercial society from a new perspective. As an example of Hans Ulrich Gumbrecht's "single word or small detail" that "hints at a different tone or rhythm," the surprising appearance of the term "socialism" suggests that something new was afoot at the time.[31] Indeed, the word can help illuminate an important period—and rupture—not only in a particular Italian past, but also in the broader histories of marketization and what we today know as capitalism, the subject of one of the most thriving historiographical renaissances of recent years.[32] But precisely because the words appear only exceptionally and intermittently, a broad contextualization is necessary to appreciate what the terms "socialists" and "socialism" originally meant and the work they were intended to do in Enlightenment debates over political economy and commercial society.[33]

Though only in unassuming notes, the Cambridge historian and political philosopher Istvan Hont identified the original meaning of the term "socialists" with "society-ists," later calling them "market socialist[s]."[34] In effect, the word was coined to describe a cluster of positions and proposals regarding the pursuit of worldly melioration in secularized commercial societies united by laws and founded on individual rights in a world of interlocked yet economically competing states—a worldview that many today would identify, however hazily, with "capitalism."[35] These first "socialists" were, in very real terms, prophets of the modern world as we know it, and explicitly sought to make their polities hospitable to "capitalists," also a neologism of the time, albeit one the meaning of which would prove somewhat more consistent over time, at least if one accepts Beccaria's own description of "capitalists" as those "who employ their money in commerce."[36] But it is important to note that

these terms remained arguable even then, perhaps resisting definite definition altogether. What they can do, however, is help us delineate shifting areas
of meaning, theoretical arguments, and practical policies during a crucial
moment in the venerable and ongoing debate over the prospects of peace
and prosperity in a divided world.

In engaging with eighteenth-century usages of the term "socialism," this
volume thus principally looks back to its origin in early modern debates about
natural law, human nature, public happiness, state sovereignty, international
trade, and commercial society in Enlightenment Europe rather than forward
to its usages in nineteenth-century labor movements or, through its tortuous
transformation into ostensible iterations of communism, in the contexts of
Karl Marx, the Gulag Archipelago, and today's "Socialism with Chinese Characteristics."[37] The differences between Enlightenment socialisms and
Romantic socialisms (or, as some may wish to argue, "false" and "true"
socialism), and the paths the term began to take between the second half of
the eighteenth century and the first half of the nineteenth century, is a largely
neglected chapter in the history of political economy during the first great
period of economic globalization, and offers a timely sounding board for
some of the most pressing concerns of our own time.[38] This is not to say that
these socialisms were entirely unrelated (and it is anyway worth emphasizing
that, as Gareth Stedman Jones recently argued, it is always a question of
"varieties of socialism"), only that the term was protean enough when first
conjured to justify, in Reinhart Koselleck's elegant phrase, multiple "futures
past."[39]

Evangelists of Reason

Within this larger perspective, in what follows I will seek to explain why the
term "socialist" was used to criticize the Milanese coterie of mostly noble
writers and reformers active in the mid-1760s known as the Academy of Fisticuffs, the leading members of which were the Counts Pietro (1728–1797) and
Alessandro Verri (1741–1816) and the Marquis Beccaria (1738–1794), whom the
British utilitarian philosopher Jeremy Bentham dubbed "the first evangelist
of reason."[40] And, as noted, it was the initially anonymous publication of
Beccaria's On Crimes and Punishments that first merited the label "socialist" in
the vernacular in print.[41] The short pamphlet remains one of the most famous

and influential publications of its age, and certainly the most lionized work to emerge from the Italian Enlightenment, constituting nothing less than "the most widely read text on penal reform in the western world."[42] In the eyes of many, even popular publications, Beccaria was the "father" of modern criminology, and his *On Crimes and Punishments* "revolutionized" penal law in the Western world and eventually for humanity as such.[43] Both learned and beautifully written (though, as the Turinese historian Franco Venturi put it, Beccaria's learning was more "enthusiastic" and "youthful" than "the culmination of a deep, well-founded culture"), the treatise engaged with a wide array of sources and intellectual traditions to present an impassioned plea for penal reform, most distinctively against torture and capital punishment.[44]

Through his chosen lens, however, Beccaria touched upon diverse aspects of human life, from morality to commerce, from religion to the origins of societies and political communities. Indeed, he suggested a new interpretation of the so-called social contract in which individuals were never forced to give up their right to life—from which most of his proposals derived—as

Marquis Cesare Beccaria (1738–1794). Jean-Baptiste-François Bosio, *Cesare Bonesana, Marquis of Beccaria*, no date.

well as a guiding definition of justice as sociability that underscored the practical limits of the material inequality viable in a polity.[45] In turning his attention to crimes and punishments, Beccaria theorized about civilization itself, about the just, the good, and the useful in civic life, and in this regard he was a prominent participant of a long tradition of political and economic thinking that emerged out of the ideals and aspirations of the republican city-states of medieval and Renaissance Italy, often known as "civic" or "civil economics."[46] Simultaneously, however, some scholars today remember eighteenth-century "socialists" like Beccaria as forerunners of an economic paradigm centered on "free trade," on the precocious usage of mathematics in economics, and on an analytical trajectory in political economy, jurisprudence, and utilitarian moral philosophy known as "Law and Economics."[47] And if one accepts the vague, if commonplace, equation of the eighteenth-century idiom "commercial society" with the modern concept of "capitalism"—an assumption on which much scholarship on the phenomena, rightly or wrongly, rests and by which it frequently justifies itself—then an inescapable proposition emerges: the first "socialists" were also among Enlightenment Europe's greatest proponents of "capitalism."[48] From this perspective, Enlightenment "socialists" were those bold enough to believe that political economy trumped theology as a matrix for social organization.[49] Yet in terms of our current debates, it is, on the surface, not much of an exaggeration to observe that the "socialists" of the 1760s and those of the mid-nineteenth century figure at the theoretically and conceptually opposite extremes of the spectrum of political economy as commonly understood.

This seeming paradox of eighteenth-century theories of commercial society—and some related ones—lies at the core of this book. The richness, complexity, and contradictions of these "socialists" is precisely what makes them so intriguing, for they precociously engaged with some of the core questions still faced by opponents and proponents of what we have come to know as global capitalism: How are polities, their laws, and their policies successfully territorialized? How can competitive economic development be achieved? What does a world system connected by economic forces look like, and how does it relate to its *inevitably* social, cultural, and political counterparts? What are market societies ultimately about, and is commerce really a source of moral order apart from politics and the law? And how, methodologically, should one theorize about these questions in the first place? To what extent, specifically, could the extraordinary achievements of contemporary natural sciences, and particularly its formal instruments, be brought to bear on "social science," that third great neologism of the late eighteenth century?[50]

Many of the underlying preoccupations in these discussions, however subterranean and inchoate, bottomed out in the most uncreative of New Year toasts: "world peace."[51] Peace was an important goal of many of these early modern debates over political economy, and an explicit purpose of socialism and social science as the terms were first employed revolved around the central preoccupation of transcending humanity's violent past and present to achieve a secular, man-made, and global system of peaceful relations between peoples bound by social norms and mutual interest.[52] And, though not always explicitly, such preoccupations also informed quotidian reforms and the practical, applied aspects of political economy. But one must be wary of projecting more-recent normative preferences regarding capitalism and globalization onto these early economic thinkers, for they differed and dissented over crucial questions such as what faith should be invested in providential powers and mechanisms; the right tools of political economy; the nature and politics of commercial sociability; the role of government and the state in economic life; and, ultimately, just how artificial, gradual, and precarious such a commercialized future perforce would have to be. They differed, in other words, over what the triumph of the economic in the world eventually might look like. And though many "hoped" for a better future at the time, they fiercely disagreed over whether it should be actively strived for or trusted to result on its own.[53]

Markets and Societies

Societies had, of course, long contained markets, understood as geographical sites of periodic exchange. But as the Austro-Hungarian historical economist Karl Polanyi observed toward the end of World War II, the brave new world of early modern Europe had increasingly (and arguably again) seen the emergence of market societies per se—that is, societies which, in Steven L. Kaplan's terms, did not merely harbor "markets" as "sites" but were themselves organized according to a "market principle," becoming what contemporary writers began referring to as "commercial societies."[54] Similarly, Paolo Malanima has observed how the institution of intermittent "economic fairs" tends to dominate economic life only in societies in which "exchanges are the exception rather than the norm."[55] And, tellingly, many observers at the time noted that such fairs were becoming less and less important as the reach, frequency, and modalities of trade expanded in eighteenth-century Europe.[56] As Aldo Carera has argued, "market" understood in the traditional sense "was a moment, as well as a site," and eighteenth-century Europe witnessed the gradual dislocation of exchange both temporally and geographically.[57] Today, at the frontiers of the world economy, this normalization and territorial expansion of exchange is often referred to as a process of "marketization."[58] Yet even as these new forms of societies emerged historically, the nexus of the social, the economic, the political, and the spiritual out of which the term "socialism" arose remained deeply contentious—as contentious as the market societies themselves. Historiographically, the subsequent debate over "commercial society" in the eighteenth century has most often been approached in relation to the writers of the so-called Scottish Enlightenment, and more particularly by reference to the works of the military man and historian Adam Ferguson and, of course, the moral philosopher and political economist Adam Smith.[59]

The latter's epochal 1776 *Inquiry into the Nature and Causes of the Wealth of Nations* presents readers with the concept of a "commercial society" as the presumed final era of his "four stages" theory of history, charting mankind's supposed progression through eras defined on the basis of its primary means of subsistence—from hunting and gathering through pastoralism to agriculture and finally commerce, in which, as Smith put it, "every man thus lives by exchanging, or becomes in some measure a merchant, and the society itself grows to be what is properly a commercial society."[60] In furthering this argument, Smith was indebted to a "sect" of *économistes* who adhered to the doctrine of Physiocracy, literally meaning the "rule of nature," that flourished in France in the 1760s and 1770s. The Physiocrats, led by the court physician and at the time renowned theoretician of bloodletting François Quesnay (1694–1774), are often identified as the world's first economists and best remembered for their doctrinaire insistence on the virtues of laissez-faire and the unique ability of agriculture to create wealth. They spearheaded a program of radical liberalization of the grain trade in France that brought them fame at first but subsequently, as their experiment floundered in the face of real conditions and the country descended into bread shortages and subsistence

trauma, widespread infamy.[61] Years before achieving policy influence, however, Quesnay had argued in the authoritative pages of the *Encyclopédie,* "No
man who lives in society provides for all of his needs with his own labor;
rather, he obtains what he lacks through the sale of the produce of his labor.
Thus everything becomes tradable, everything becomes wealth through a
mutual traffic between men."[62] The point, for Quesnay as for Smith, was not
merely that a lot of trade took place in a commercial society; rather, the point
was that the very sociology of the polity had become commercialized, with
people depending on *each other* for their subsistence (even survival) and engaging socially in, and crucially *on,* mercantile terms through what eventually would become known as "the cash nexus," an endless array of human
activities rendered commensurate by the abstractions inherent to monetized
exchange.[63] In the Scottish formulation, this process fostered and encouraged a
number of civic virtues as well. "Commerce and manufactures," wrote Smith,
paraphrasing his friend David Hume, "gradually introduced order and good
government, and with them, the liberty and security of individuals, among
the inhabitants of the country, who had before lived almost in a continual
state of war with their neighbours, and of servile dependency upon their
superiors."[64]Although he went on to warn of certain dangers inherent to the
division of labor, particularly as related to the stupefying consequences of
endlessly repeating the same tasks over and over again, his vision relied on
commerce to do some remarkably heavy lifting.[65] Far from merely supporting the "wealth" of a nation, trade and industry were active sources of
social and moral order, of good government, political empowerment, civic
equality, and, under certain circumstances, even world peace.[66]

   This Scottish variant of the theory of commercial society has undoubtedly received the most sustained attention in recent historiography, also for
the simple linguistic reason that English increasingly is the language of international scholarship and of graduate education alike.[67] But there were
many such visions regarding the nature, opportunities, and challenges of an
economic age circulating in the European world at the time. Across Germany
and the United States well into the nineteenth century, for example, the final
stage of human development was long thought to be, not one of "commerce,"
with "manufactures" in a secondary role, but instead one of "commerce and
manufacturing" with an emphasis on the latter, a surprisingly consequential divergence from its idealized Scottish counterpart, which gave political

and moral justification to industrializing policies as a means of societal and indeed civilizational progression.[68] Sometimes commercial society was not related to stages of development at all, but was instead thought to be descriptive of a specific kind of polity or the culmination—momentarily, at least—of mankind's temporal development through the ages, regardless of underlying productive structures or primary means of subsistence; and sometimes it simply spoke to the nature of sociability and how individuals approached each other and their surroundings. Decades before Smith's *Wealth of Nations* was published, for example, Italy's first professor of political economy, Antonio Genovesi, hoped, through his teachings in Naples, to bring about a society in which everyone approached the world "with the eyes of a merchant." Abandoning Latin and aiming to reach as many "youths" as possible, he believed that only such a shift in popular attitudes could result in individual and ultimately social "surplus." Only a veritable commercial society in this sense, he argued, where citizens actively were taught how to flourish in material terms, could lead to anything like economic development and worldly betterment. It was an attitude very similar to that which, in those precise years, drove the American founding father Benjamin Franklin to pen a best-selling self-help essay that eventually would become known as *The Way to Wealth*, an essay that the German sociologist Max Weber later would see as embodying nothing less than the "the spirit of Capitalism."[69]

But if the definitions of such commercial societies were conflicting at times, they were nonetheless fundamentally aligned in attempting to make sense of how economic factors influenced human history and social relations, and how one might overcome the tension between spatially demarcated political communities and a seemingly seamless economic domain; how, in short, to best address the incongruity of states and markets in a world characterized by competition between people as well as peoples. Though the institution of private property would come to dominate "socialist" discourse in the Romantic period, and certainly was a cause of debate during the Enlightenment, this potentially lethal tension between states, markets, and human welfare and sociability really gripped the first socialists. In these chapters I explore and analyze one of the most sophisticated, if also one of the most neglected, traditions of considering the emerging international system of commercial societies in eighteenth-century Europe, and I approach it not from the provincial and latecoming, if more famous, Scottish vantage point, but from that of the city-states of Northern Italy, the historical fountainhead of what we have come to define as capitalism, institutionally as well as intellectually.[70] As Vincenzo Ferrone recently has argued, "The Enlightenment" was a *"laboratory of modernity"*—and there were few places where experiments were quite as varied, or had been going on for quite as long, as on the Italian peninsula.[71] Even more specifically from the perspective of the history of political economy broadly conceived, however, Italy's long and tumultuous history truly offers a unique and underappreciated perspective on the dynamics of economic ideas and policies, greatness and decline, state building and commercial society.[72]

Lay of the Land

Principally, therefore, in this volume I focus on the extraordinary homonymous coterie of thinkers and civil servants united, however briefly, around these challenges of sociability and political economy in Habsburg Milan during the 1760s and 1770s, prime among them the Marquis Cesare Beccaria, the Count Pietro Verri, and their frequent visitor Henry Lloyd, who was a Welsh major-general, an international spy, and a quixotic economic theorist. And though I concentrate on the territories of Northern Italy, and the Lombard city of Milan in particular, I also consider the area in a larger international context increasingly characterized by the circulation of people, goods, and ideas across frequently contested borders. Though many members of the group continued their intellectual and administrative activities well beyond the French Revolution, the emphasis will be on their activities in the 1760s and early 1770s, by most accounts their period of greatest intellectual fervor and creativity, and how their works related to the contemporary questions of criminal law, commercial sociability, economic development, international competition, and world order. Arguably, the problem of Enlightenment "socialists" is far more interesting for what it helps elucidate about eighteenth-century European political economy and the complex histories of capitalism and of commercial society than for what it tells us regarding the etymological history of more recent ideologies, and this book turns to the historical phraseology of "socialism" both as a subject of analysis in its own right and as a lens through which to focalize important aspects of our collective past.

Although the following is primarily an intellectual history of political economy and commercial society in eighteenth-century Milan, it is not intended as a straightforward history of ideas, nor simply as a search for "origins." The "socialists" and "capitalists" of the Enlightenment emerged from distinct debates triggered by specific socioeconomic realities, inflected and animated by particular cultural, political, and military changes taking place in certain parts of eighteenth-century Europe, and the purpose and import of those debates cannot be appreciated outside of these diverse contexts.[73] And though the chapters are informed by a generally sequential chronology, they also offer different perspectives—at times at some length—on the essential problem of theorizing and practicing the political economy of commercial society. If one is now forced to defend digressions, which Laurence Sterne famously called the "soul of reading," or to at least caution the reader that they will appear, there is no better place than here.[74] This is a book capacious enough to make room for fourteenth-century civic art, sixteenth-century bandits, nineteenth-century historical economists, and even the empty market stalls of contemporary East Timor. It is also, I hope, a book persistent enough in its lines of argument to trust its readers to understand the function of these passages as lenses or mirrors of distance, of anticipation, of inversion, and of clarity.

As such, though the central subject aims at excavating the historical challenges of sociability in relation to the political economy of commercial society in early modern Italy, it invites analyses that venture past the strictly philological, at times through close readings of manuscript notes and learned texts, at other times through art history, at others yet again through the archival reconstruction of events, reforms, and social networks. As such, parts of what follows may read like the intellectual biography of a group of economic writers and administrators, but I also seek to place them in their due time and space, as well as a larger thematic frame of reference. In a previous study I approached the constellation of European political economy holistically, considering the emergence of political economy in Europe as a coherent discourse from a bird's-eye perspective. Though paradoxically broader in scope, the chapters in this volume offer a more sustained engagement with the particulars of a far tighter orbit.[75] And though this is a "contextual" study, I have endeavored to place texts in relation to not merely other texts but also a broader range of material, symbolic, and interpersonal conditions. The larger history in which the protagonists of this story were embedded, in short, and the relations between them, influenced their writings no less than the words that they read. As such, a study of the Academy of Fisticuffs forces us to consider what the late Michael O'Brien poignantly called "the role of the heart" in intellectual history.[76]

Yet, though focused in this way, this book in many ways remains a global study, as its protagonists often thought in planetary terms and saw their quotidian existences influenced by an emerging worldwide web of commerce and communication. "The society of the late Enlightenment," as Emma Rothschild has argued, "was as wide as the world."[77] But, to be clear, the challenges practically faced by Beccaria and his colleagues very much belonged to the period of so-called proto-globalization, what Charles S. Maier recently defined "Leviathan 1.0"—that is, the period of state building that preceded the "political modernity" inaugurated by "new technologies of communication and transportation" that "allowed for a decisive intensification of state ambition and governmental power" in the late nineteenth century.[78] What the anarchist writer Hakim Bey calls "the closure of the map" had not yet taken place, and parts of the globe remaining "open," "unpoliced [and] untaxed."[79] Yet "the markets," as Karl Marx and Friedrich Engels rightly wrote of the period in *The Communist Manifesto,* "kept ever growing," eventually giving way to a true "world market."[80] The governmental challenges of this period were thus not merely international, as polities had to contend with other powers in an ever-expanding world, but also national, as they continued to struggle with the internal territoriality of their solidifying states. Tarun Khanna and Krishna G. Palepu have argued that "emerging markets reflect those transactional arenas where buyers and sellers are not easily or efficiently able to come together," and called the missing intermediary linkages in an economy "institutional voids."[81] From this perspective, the present work is also a story about "modern" market societies when they first emerged, and the complex realities that once filled institutional voids even at the original core of the world economy.

Fernand Braudel's dream of writing a "total history" was of course no less a chimera than a truly "objective" account of the past, but to discuss the rise of "commercial society," and theories of it, in a manner entirely divorced from the practical realities of the time is at best misleading.[82] The period here under analysis, the "Enlightenment," is particularly resistant to treatment in a purely idealized fashion, for even among its contemporary exponents it was conceptualized in deeply operational terms. The eighteenth century was a period of extraordinary intellectual effervescence, yes, but also one of dramatic practical and institutional reform—and the main champions of Enlightenment justified the former squarely in terms of the latter.[83] Indeed, though the historiography of the elusive and often challenged temporal category "The Enlightenment" remains a thing in constant flux, among its most striking changes over the past few years has been the rise to prominence of the history of political economy, not understood in the reductionist—if oftentimes illuminating—terms of the Austrian Harvard economist Joseph A. Schumpeter's technical "history of economic analysis," but as the careful reconstruction of past economic ideas and policies in their historical contexts.[84] This scholarship frequently draws inspiration from contemporary problems, increasingly picking up on Hont's suggestion that in order to understand our current predicaments, it might be worthwhile returning to the time when, as Hume put it, "trade" first became an "affair of state."[85] This new trend we are observing, however, is less a revolution or a U-turn than the gathering of momentum of a historiographical movement long in the making. Already in his 1969 Trevelyan Lectures at the University of Cambridge, Venturi argued provocatively that "an *Aufklärung* [Enlightenment] which does not touch upon the state, the land, or commerce, is clipped in at least one of its wings."[86] Five decades later, such an *Aufklärung* would be the historiographical equivalent of a dodo—utterly flightless, not to mention extinct.[87]

Echoing Venturi, John Robertson has again defined "The Enlightenment" primarily in terms of the emergence of "political economy," *the* science of worldly melioration, and it was precisely in this domain that some of the most imaginative and powerful arguments regarding the nature and future of human society took form, were debated, and even were implemented in the eighteenth century.[88] Venturi opened his multivolume *Settecento riformatore,* or *Reformist Eighteenth Century,* by noting that the "Enlightenment reformist movement" was driven by the emergence of "economic science" and a related "empirical will to understand, investigate, and dominate the reality of social and political life."[89] Although the etymology of the word "reform" would indicate the return to an original condition, by the eighteenth century the word had become a broad call to do precisely the opposite: to change the world, to strategically alter laws and habits, to inflect hearts and minds to make the world "better," to "improve" it, according to a contemporary vogue.[90] The dominating debates of the age revolved around regulation, understood broadly as adjustment or control—of people, passions, territories, measures, and so on—by laws to structure socioeconomic conditions, and increasingly whether what we now call "development" resulted best from directed attempts to achieve it or from unintended mechanisms or even divine providence.[91] The Enlightenment was the original site of the world's "economic turn," the century of regulatory reform par excellence.[92]

In engaging with these world-historical changes, this volume focuses on the neglected theater for the intellectual and economic history of Europe that was Austrian Lombardy. Though recent decades have witnessed substantial interest in early modern Italy, not all parts of the peninsula have received due attention from scholars. Of the polities contained in Petrarch's "Italia mia," Florence, Naples, Rome, and Venice remain the unrivaled focuses of Anglophone research.[93] And states like Genoa, Milan, and Turin remain largely overlooked. In this study, I therefore seek to introduce and better integrate Lombard debates and scholarship with the mainstream historiography of the Italian and European Enlightenment.[94] This integration will underscore Enlightenment's transnational dimension but will also reveal highly consequential ways in which the Milanese Enlightenment was unconventional if not sui generis. Where British intellectual historians have noted that, though an "emphasis on material inequality seems unremarkable in our time . . . , in historical perspective it is extraordinary," a Milanese viewpoint will forcefully remind us that inequality, already in the eighteenth century, was a foundational concern for some of commercial society's foremost theorists and legislators.

Although my ambitions are clearly grander, I will have succeeded if at least some readers are convinced that, far from being a mere ancillary "periphery" of the phenomenon, dimly reflecting and refracting the lights of Paris or Edinburgh, not to mention Naples or Königsberg, Milan was a beacon at the very core of Enlightenment political economy, offering a new and illuminating outlook on the phenomenon and on the longer history of commercial societies and of capitalism. For though Facchinei's charge of "socialism" is undeniably imbued with retroactive gravitas by virtue of the word's tumultuous afterlife, my argument is that, even taken on its own terms, in its own complex context, the challenge of Enlightenment socialism helpfully elucidates problems and promises still haunting us to this day.

In Lieu of a Road Map

Chapter 1 begins with an execution and ends with coffee, two poles of repulsion and attraction around which the Academy of Fisticuffs revolved in Austrian Lombardy. If the former could be considered sociability's terminal failure at the time, the latter was its most fashionable new vehicle. The chapter opens by examining the complex role of capital punishment in eighteenth-century Milan, and what it said about relations between the state, society, and the Catholic Church, as a means of better understanding the world that Beccaria and his allies sought to reform, and why. From there, it sketches the remarkable history of the city of Milan itself, once at the very center of the world economy, and charts Milan's changing fortunes and degrees of political and economic independence across the centuries. It then turns to Pietro Verri and explains his founding of the Academy of Fisticuffs in light of his disillusionment with army life during the Seven Years' War, as well as of his discovery, under the influence of his companion-in-arms Henry Lloyd, of the "new science" of political economy around 1760, at a time that Peter Groenewegen and others rightly have argued to be "perhaps the most important period in the history of economic thought."[95] Returning to Milan, Verri set up the Academy as a café society think tank, inviting a number of young men of promise to further the cause of "enlightened" reformism and the ideals of patriotism and cosmopolitanism—two agendas that, I will argue, ultimately would be harder to square than scholars so far have maintained. Finally, the chapter analyzes the pugilists' famous if short-lived journal, *Il Caffè*, published between 1764 and 1766, and the imaginary coffee shop in which Verri situated the group's activities.

Chapter 2 focuses on the Fisticuffs' twin preoccupations with political economy and penal reform. It analyzes the early work of Verri and his circle and situates the group in relation to older traditions of approaching the interrelated challenges of trade, crime, sociability, inequality, development, and international relations. Though, with few notable exceptions, the historiographies of criminology and political economy today are generally separated, a deeper understanding of the group's project shows how their economic and juridical works were facets of the same overarching project for secular sociability, reform, and improvement.[96] This is clearest in the case of Beccaria, whose *On Crimes and Punishments* was by far the most influential product of

Count Pietro Verri (1728–1797).
Anonymous, *Portrait of the Young
Pietro Verri Pointing to a Political
Maxim of the Philippicae,* no date.

the group's coffee shop and, indeed, of the Italian Enlightenment. Though
ostensibly devoted merely to the question of penal reform, Beccaria's treatise adumbrated nothing less than a bold and holistic vision of secular sociability based on inalienable individual rights that crucially were not given *by*
society, but held *against* it; far from conformist or collectivist, his theory
of sociability was deeply anchored in an intrinsic and unbending belief in
individual human dignity. More broadly with regard to the history of political economy, Chapter 2 also begins to problematize the common assumption that the Academy of Fisticuffs drew extensively on the teachings of the
Physiocrats. Although the pugilists had divergent approaches to political
economy that only intensified with the passing of time, I will argue that both
Verri and Beccaria, though familiar with and responsive to Quesnay's work,
adopted—like so many thinkers and writers in the European world—distinctly
and durably Antiphysiocratic stances early on.[97]

Chapter 3 turns to the group's most influential foreign acquaintance, the
marauding Welsh Jacobite military officer Henry Lloyd, and his pivotal contributions to the Academy's evolving political economy and methodology of

reform, particularly in terms of its precocious embrace of formal mathematical models. Much like other members and colleagues of Verri's coterie, Lloyd developed a materialist moral philosophy, but he went farther than them in imbuing this with a republican political ethos. By emphasizing a mechanistic view of humanity, he furthermore disenchanted the great questions of war, wealth, and human sociability, opening them to a mechanical science of social affairs to be approached with tools and languages borrowed from the natural sciences. Several members of the group subsequently turned to algebra and even differential calculus to further their analytical aims, theorizing, like Lloyd, that a mechanical approach to the sciences of man best fit their deist or possibly even atheist cosmologies, and more specifically a secular "enlightened" approach to reformism. That said, the pugilists never explicitly joined the "radical" arm of the Enlightenment recently lionized by Jonathan Israel.[98] And, though sometimes overlooked by scholars, both Verri and Beccaria ultimately reneged on the mathematical projects of their youths when they turned to more practical policy pursuits, with significant consequences for their legacies.[99]

Chapter 4 changes gears, considering the group's work to further commercial society in light of the practical exigencies of political economy and criminal law at the time, and particularly in light of the chronic challenge of banditry in Renaissance and early modern Northern Italy. Far from being an abstract and philosophical category, "commercial society" was an eminently practical project for the Academy of Fisticuffs and the age-old tradition of "civic" or "civil economics" on which it drew, the technicalities of which in turn influenced its theoretical payload. Chapter 4 analyzes the polyvalent concept of "banditry" in the history of the region from the perspectives—social, political, economic, and even artistic—offered by different case studies across the centuries. In particular, an explosion of banditry in the northern Apennines and Ligurian Alps, which threatened trade and diplomatic relations between the Republic of Genoa, Savoy Piedmont, and Austrian Lombardy, obsessed statesmen and legislators in Northern Italy around the time of the pugilists' main work and served as a neglected backdrop for their economic theory and for Beccaria's *On Crimes and Punishments*. I will argue that this outbreak was a symptom at the frontiers of a larger process of state formation taking place in early modern Europe, a tortuous and complex process by which the spatial sovereignties of different political communities that had interacted, competed, and coalesced as city-states gave way to territorial states, nation-states, and empires, simultaneously socializing expanding polities and threatening relations between them. Wars on banditry were acute symptoms of, and vehicles for, the gradual territorialization of commercial society, of what we today would call "marketization."

Soon after the publication of the Academy of Fisticuffs' main pamphlets and articles, an anonymous tract appeared proclaiming that Verri and Beccaria were "socialists." Chapter 5 explores and analyzes this neologism, which was first incubated in the networks of the Benedictine international as a term to critique those who believed in the possibility of a secular human society bound by laws and commerce rather than divine intervention. A number of variations of this criticism developed over the course of the eighteenth century, most notably by Beccaria's nemesis, the Vallumbrosan monk Ferdinando Facchinei of Forlì. Chapter 5 engages with the published and unpublished works of this frequently misunderstood scholar to analyze what his violent critique of the group ultimately was about, focusing particularly on the explicit tension he delineated between theology and political economy as principles of worldly organization. It then traces the numerous echoes of this polemic and the changing uses of the term "socialism" in eighteenth-century Italy, with particular emphasis on the work of the Celestine General Appiano Buonafede. In so doing, the chapter also offers new light on the theoretical origins of arguments for an "invisible hand" ordering economic affairs. In the case of the debates surrounding the Academy of Fisticuffs, at least, the concept was quite literally meant to denote direct divine intervention in markets and a providential ordering of economic life in opposition to the secular political economy adopted by contemporary "socialists" like Beccaria.

Chapter 6 turns to the relationship between economic theory and practice in these debates over political economy and commercial society. The Academy of Fisticuffs dissolved at the very peak of its fame following a disastrous journey Beccaria and Alessandro Verri undertook to Paris in 1766, amid acrimonious disputes resulting from its engagement with Facchinei as well as from internal jealousies both sexual and professional. Verri continued theoretical work on political economy into the early 1770s, at which point his approach had begun to deviate in significant ways from those of his former colleagues. Soon, however, he grew tired of economic theorizing, and devoted the rest of his life to practical work in the Milanese administration. Beccaria too, though adulated across Europe, retired from the public eye to teach political economy in Milan, eventually, like Verri, dedicating himself to the quotidian work of Lombard economic policy. In spite of their important early works, both would, in Schumpeter's economic taxonomy, spend the majority of their lives as "consultant administrators."[100] And although Beccaria did begin work on a larger volume, *The Refinement of Nations*, to address the gradual expansion of human sociability and culture, in many ways to parallel for the international order of polities what *On Crimes and Punishments* had done for individuals, he ultimately only left us a sketch of this plan for the melioration and socialization of mankind. Again like Verri, however, he stopped at the threshold of utopia, staunchly remaining a reformer within the existing institutional structure of his polity rather than invoking revolutionary change. Nonetheless, careful engagement with the twenty years or so of his policy work amply demonstrates the extent to which the pugilists successfully translated economic theories into practical reforms and, over time, contributed to the territorialization of an expanding market society in Northern Italy.

Chapter 7 turns to the complex ways by which "socialism" became "social science" in late eighteenth-century Italy, and how what originally had been a criticism was turned into a positive and widely embraced project for secular societal reform. Although scholars have hardly ever paused to consider the works of the renegade Franciscan Giacomo Giuliani of Padua, he was a liminal figure in the gradual transformation of eighteenth-century discourses in the wake of the French Revolution and the rise of Napoleon, and his 1803 *L'antisocialismo confutato*, or *Antisocialism Refuted*, and later lectures on political economy can serve to bridge the gap between Enlightenment and Romantic socialism. There were parallels but also dramatic differences between the two usages of the term, and Chapter 7 begins the perhaps never-ending project to, to quote Keith Tribe, "disentangle similarity from difference."[101] As will be clear, the two broad traditions of "socialism" aligned in their preoccupation with secularism and the nature and importance of sociability in commercial societies, but according to contemporary criteria, important aspects of Enlightenment "socialism" would today instead be equated with the term "capitalism." Both terms, in short, emerged from a broader debate over the nature of market societies and international peace in eighteenth-century political economy that is still worth revisiting.

Unsurprisingly, the conclusion to Chapter 7 recapitulates the main arguments made in the earlier chapters. In particular, it retraces the paths taken
by the main protagonists and their contributions to penal law, to the discipline of political economy, and to the progress of commercial society in
eighteenth-century Lombardy. But it also emphasizes the human element of
these larger processes; as Marci Shore put it regarding the protagonists
she portrayed in her *Caviar and Ashes:* "The story of these individuals and
their relationship is a story of a journey from the cafés to the corridors of
power, a story of faith and betrayal."[102] Like the Warsaw Marxists of the
early twentieth century whom she so beautifully depicted and interpreted, so
Verri, Beccaria, and their contemporaries provide an extraordinary window
upon the lived experience of past ideas, and of what some of the grand slo-
gans of historiography and more recent ideologies actually looked like on
the ground when they first took form. In this light, the Academy of Fisticuffs must be counted as one of the premier intellectual ateliers of the European Enlightenment and, in important ways, of our "modernity" more
broadly considered.

Some concerns—the problem of inequality, the politics of punishment,
the role of religion in civic life, the task of socializing *people* as well as
peoples—are, if not timeless, both ancient and urgent. Though historical books
by definition are about something past, they are invariably written in a
present. The Afterword briefly contemplates this volume, *The Academy of Fisticuffs,* in light of the particular present in which it was written, the past with
which it engages, and the time that divides the two. The gulf between us
and eighteenth-century political economy or Enlightenment commercial society is surely enormous, but many of the challenges of twenty-first-century
economics and postmodern global capitalism would have been sensible to
the pugilists, and, more importantly, all of them are more sensible to us
because of the pugilists and their perspectives. We can still benefit from their
insights, but we also need, and perhaps all the more, their pugnacious spirit.
"Don't count the days," urged the greatest pugilist of all, "make the days
count."[103]

CHAPTER ONE

Hard Knocks Café

O N   T H E   M O R N I N G   O F   June 6, 1767, one Giovanni Battista Torriggia
was executed in the Piazza Maggiore of Milan, a prize possession of
the Habsburg Empire then under the formidable rule of Austria's Maria Theresa.[1] As is the case with so many people born before the nineteenth century,
we really only know of Torriggia because of how he died, the historical record
being far more prone to memorialize deviance than conformity.[2] He was
condemned to death for the "barbarous" and violent murder of his wife,
Giovanna, whom he ostensibly had mowed down with "repeated strikes of
a scythe," and the ferocity of his crime was more than matched by the cruelty of his punishment: Torriggia was "dragged behind a horse" through the
city before ending his days "on the wheel on a stage," his cadaver displayed
until sundown for the moral and legal education of the Milanese citizenry.[3]

Breaking on the wheel, in Torriggia's case ominously referred to as simply
"the wheel," has been called "the most prolonged and agonizing of Old
Regime capital punishments," though in competition with being burned alive
and being drawn and quartered, the accuracy of this statement remains hard
to assess.[4] It was, in any case, a truly terrible way to go. A frequently quoted
eyewitness account from Hamburg in 1607 described breaking on the wheel
with transcendent gruesomeness: during his long-drawn-out execution, the

culprit was transformed "into a sort of huge screaming puppet writhing in rivulets of blood, a puppet with four tentacles, like a sea monster of raw, slimy and shapeless flesh mixed with splinters of smashed bones."[5]

While the precise modalities of deaths such as Torriggia's could be almost endlessly creative, symbolic genres of execution remained relatively uniform throughout early modern Europe. As a form of capital punishment, for example, hanging was usually reserved for thieves, burning being set aside for arsonists, heretics, and alleged sodomites. Torriggia's "wheel" was reserved for aggravated murders and more complex cases where statements had to be made regarding the rule of law and the real locus of sovereignty, whether in the case of wife-murderers, poachers, smugglers, bandits, or sundry outlaws.[6] Though the actual procedure of execution on the wheel was somewhat fluid at the time, essential tropes and instruments recurred. Victims could be bound to a cross, their bones slowly broken and their internal organs burst with strategic strikes from a cudgel or iron rod before they were intertwined with an elevated wooden wheel for public spectacle until death, sometimes days later; they could be bound to a cross on the ground, their bodies slowly broken with a wooden "breaking" wheel, sometimes called a "St. Catherine's wheel" in remembrance of the eponymous if apocryphal saint (according to her hagiography the wheel broke when the emperor tried to kill her with it and so she was decapitated instead); they could be bound directly to the wheel for cudgeling and subsequent exposure; or, more prosaically, they could just be repeatedly run over by a horse and cart. The cruelty was sublime and, though bound by institutionalized practices and a complex and sedimented body of law, the particulars of it were often left to the imagination of the civil authorities who determined just how to cause death with blunt objects and wooden wheels.[7]

Torriggia's punishment was memorialized through a broadside promulgated by the Milanese Confraternity of the Beheaded St. John the Baptist to advertise the event of his execution. This was one of a number of similar societies devoted to the "good death" in medieval and early modern Italy, lending succor to the condemned and tending to the rigorously ritualized logistics of execution, including the attainment of a confession (through carefully scripted scenarios involving everything from simple prayer to deception and the painfully ironic threat of bodily harm); ensuring publicity for the event; planning the accompanying parade; taking care of a cluster of

Jacques Callot, *The Wheel*, ca. 1633.

symbolic ceremonies around the event itself to *"ensure the eternal health of the poor person to be executed"*; and of course organizing burials after the fact.[8] Milan had at least two such confraternities, one for nobles and the other for commoners, and between 1471 and 1763 the books of the latter recorded 3,241 executions in the city of Milan, though there, as elsewhere, the absolute frequency of capital punishments decreased over the course of the seventeenth century and dramatically so in the eighteenth.[9] This moment of reduction in what by today's standards would be considered legal cruelty coincided with a conscious policy by Habsburg authorities to alleviate the suffering of prisoners and to take the charge of their provisioning off private hands—to bring the lives as well as the deaths of the imprisoned and condemned fully into the sphere of state control and embrace what Michel Foucault centuries later would dub "biopolitics."[10]

Generally speaking, early modern criminal law was in many ways the inverse of what has become the norm in more recent eras; whereas "the determination of guilt" is now a public affair and subsequent punishments are largely private, in early modern Europe the determinative part could be private, even secret to almost everyone, including the condemned, and the punishment was rigorously public.[11] The publicity of the event was, for secular authorities, the very point of it all, and one of the principal reasons why it had to be so terrible in the first place. So why then did the members of the Confraternity of the Beheaded St. John the Baptist, who themselves worked to publicize executions, rely on gothic iconographies depicting the opposite, rather suggestive of Giovanni Battista Piranesi's haunting etchings in his coeval *Carceri d'invenzione* (Imaginary prisons)?[12] Why invoke this frightening imagery of skulls, dark dungeons, and cloistered deaths? Perhaps because John the Baptist himself was beheaded in prison, but perhaps also for the very same reason actual executions were so publicized: to incite moral behavior through fear, horror, and, importantly, the awareness of the deadly and terrifying relationship between crimes and punishments.[13]

Members of the Confraternity cared for criminals' souls and the longer continuum of their voyages through eternity—hence the iconographical presence of silver platters on their seals connecting the beheaded St. John the Baptist on top of the frame with the depicted decapitee in the middle and, through the former's prefiguration of Christ, to Eucharistic redemption for the criminal[14]—and were, in this, joined by a number of

Giovanni Battista Piranesi, *The Pier with Chains*, from *Imaginary Prisons*, 1761.

The seal under which the Milanese Confraternity of the Beheaded St. John the Baptist circulated its fliers around the time of the Academy of Fisticuffs.

other similar societies in Milan, including the *Protectores aut defensores captivorum vel carceratorum,* or simply the Protectors of Prisoners. But they were also allies of secular authorities who sought to keep the proverbial peace and society as such afloat, safeguarding it against internal and external enemies.[15] That Torriggia escaped eternal damnation by giving in to the Confraternity on the scaffold was fine and good under the lens of eternity. Whether or not the exigencies of "this life" were hierarchically subsidiary to those of "the next," however, society would still collapse if everyone went around murdering their partners. The law was assumed to be all that stood between society and the abyss: authority was seen as the fundamental source of sociability, and punishment, often emblematically cruel, as the means by which order, tragically, had to be scaffolded. As E. P. Thompson put it, "It is not possible to conceive of any complex society without law."[16] The question was how to make it respected and efficient.

However grisly to modern sentiments, Torriggia's execution was a surprisingly commonplace occurrence in urban Italy at the time. Commonplace but not trivial, the very routine and ritualization of execution was meant to enforce its ceremonial importance. Codifiers and architects of baroque criminal law like the Roman judge and lawyer Prospero Farinacci and the Piedmontese lawyer and statesman Giulio Claro, still influential in the eighteenth century, had suggested such inspired executions only in the case of "extremely atrocious offenses [*atrocissimis delictis*]," with particularly horrifying public displays of suffering "to terrorize others [*ad aliorum terrorum*]" and set a memorable example to deter future misconduct.[17] Thomas Hobbes had followed such thinking candidly, stating in his 1651 *Leviathan* that "the aym of Punishment is not revenge, but terreur."[18] Montesquieu would argue much later that "severity in penalties suits despotic government, whose principle is terror, better than monarchies and republics, which have honor and virtue for their spring," but by those standards penal law suited despotism throughout the known world.[19] To prevent unlawfulness and maintain society and morality, the argument went, states themselves had to commit terrible acts and, in Foucault's phraseology, adopt a "policy of terror."[20] As the influential French jurist Pierre-François Muyart de Vouglans could still put it in his 1780 *Les loix criminelles du Royaume dans leur ordre naturelle* (The criminal laws of the kingdom in their natural order), "punishment" was "vengeance," and

> the power to inflict penalties is the most essential element of Legis-
> lation, because that power alone can give strength to the Law and
> ensure, by such means, peace and tranquility within a State. . . .
> That power, known as the Right of the Sword [*Droit de Glaive*],
> because it extends onto the lives of men . . . can only belong to the
> supreme authority that Divine Providence confers on Sovereigns.[21]

Prolonged, flamboyant executions were public spectacles of ritualized retribution. Although, as Paul Friedland has argued, executions served as ceremonies of civic vengeance and social regeneration, they were frequently
theorized primarily as vehicles of terror and therefore, paradoxically, deter-
rence and legal empowerment, tangibly manifesting that highest expression
of sovereign authority which some have come to call "Necropower."[22] Punishments both mended the social ruptures caused by crimes and, supposedly, counteracted future misbehavior by encouraging respect for the laws
of society by "terrorizing" people into sociability.[23] As such, they were obviously regulatory and disciplinary in nature, not to mention dependent on a
functioning and increasingly unchallenged state apparatus under the aus-
pices of which capital punishment was the supposedly successful culmination of a complex chain of social administration: from the codification of
law through the identification of deviance, criminal investigation, arrest,
imprisonment, court proceedings, verdict (whether "just" or not), parade,
and execution.[24]

    At the same time, however, early modern punishments, and particularly
capital ones, could be notoriously carnivalesque.[25] They were, sometimes
even explicitly, presented and experienced as festive "sacrifices" through
which a community could purge its pollution.[26] The carnivalesque elements
of such ceremonies are evidenced also by fliers encouraging often rambunc-
tious gatherings in public squares to witness executions (the boilerplate
ending of many Confraternity broadsides was an insistent "*si prega a non
mancare*"—"please do not miss it") and the overturning of the quotidian, reflected not only in the victim's inversion of civic roles but in that ultimate
binary switch of earthly existence itself.[27] Publicity, of course, also facilitated
a sense of popular complicity in the execution—of partaking, as Friedrich
Nietzsche would put it, "*in the right of the masters*"—and thus a socialization

of the law.[28] And authorities knew how to put on a good show. Sometimes, perhaps, they were too good. On February 9, 1760, for example, when one Francesco Manuelli was executed for murder in the Piazza del Popolo in Rome on the first Saturday of Carnival, the gathering was so vast and unassailable that the local members of the Confraternity of the Beheaded St. John the Baptist were unable to even retrieve his corpse from the teeming scaffold until the vast crowd, the "folla del popolo," had finally dispersed.[29] Truly exemplary punishments of bandits and brigands, however, like that of the great French smuggler Louis Mandrin, "the Robin Hood of France" slowly broken on the wheel after confessing and begging for forgiveness in front of 6,000 spectators in 1755, were so outrageous precisely because they involved the execution of someone who, by remaining outside the law for so long, had undermined the authority, not only of God, but of the state as such, endangering its territorial control as well as its socializing mission and justification.[30]

Scholars, particularly following German sociologist Norbert Elias's controversial thesis regarding a "civilizing process" that gradually altered people's emphatic reactions to human misery during the early modern period, have long observed that popular sensibilities toward death and suffering changed dramatically during the eighteenth century.[31] Working in this tradition, Pieter Spierenburg has argued that the publicity and brutality of early modern punishments reflected the "instability" of contemporary state formation, weak monopolies on violence and authority, and the persistence of real territorial threats not only international but also internal in the form of "bandits and armed vagabonds." The decline of executions, their brutality, and their publicity, observable around Europe at the time, could therefore convincingly be explained by increases in the territorial consolidation of states and the ensuing changes in popular "sensibilities."[32] The gallows may long have been a scaffold of state formation, the argument goes, but polities were eventually both solidified and socialized to the point where public executions became counterproductive.[33] The geographical shift, observable around Europe, of capital punishments themselves from the place of the crime, seemingly haphazard but indicative of the need to set localized examples, to a centralized site of public execution in different cities and regions, and finally in the nineteenth century to behind prison walls, similarly suggests expanding and strengthened state structures, as well as the increasing saturation of territory by sovereignty.[34] That said, crimes and punishments would continue to be spatially related in the eighteenth century, the decapitated heads of criminals, for example, being put on display at the "place of their crime" in Hapsburg Mantua at the time of the Academy of Fisticuffs.[35]

Truth be told, Adam Smith had already explained, in his so-called *Lectures on Jurisprudence* (1762–1763), a similar relationship between "the progress of government and the punishment of crimes." When a "government is very weak," he told his students, "no crimes are punished," because it lacks the capacity to do so. When "society gathers greater strength," however, "punishments" are "always the most severe imaginable," until, "when society made a still greater progress and the peace and good order of the community were provided for, and tranquillity firmly established, these punishments would again be mitigated and by degrees brought to bear a just proportion to the severall crimes." As time passed, in short, and "progress" brought greater "strength" but also "civility" to "society," punishments became more clement.[36]

The question that still begs to be asked, and which perhaps never can be satisfactorily answered, however, is why punishments became progressively *crueler* in the wake of the Middle Ages, only to become more humane again in the late eighteenth century. Although evidence on a continental scale would be hard to amass, the trauma involved in the regime change from city-states and decentralized authorities to solidifying, if still relentlessly competing and often mutually hostile, territorial state structures—and the countless wars, both civil and international, that complicated this process—may have played a decisive role. Legal and political writers from Jean Bodin to Thomas Hobbes certainly justified their sometimes ruthless theories in precisely these terms, and many practical cases seem indicative of the same underlying logic.[37] The vast majority of executions in early modern Florence, for example, took place during the turbulent Republic of 1494–1512 and the early, more fragile Medici principate, precisely as one would have expected from this angle of interpretation. Similarly, executions were far, far more frequent in urban contexts than in rural, often still "feudal" regions of Italy.[38] From this perspective, exemplary punishments were both consequences of, and remedies for, periods not only of state building but also of governmental vicissitudes more generally, of adjustment, territorial instability, and consequent lack of social cohesion in polities.[39] They served as legal reminders that the great problem of human sociability remained unresolved as regimes changed and civic spheres shifted and expanded, from feudal rurality to urban republics, from city-states to nation-states.[40]

As such, legal cruelty can be seen as merely one manifestation of a timeless axiom of political philosophy that has found eloquent champions from antiquity through St. Thomas Aquinas to the lawyers of U.S. president George W. Bush: *necessitas non habet legem*—"necessity knows no law."[41] And, as a powerful tradition of interpretation would have it, this dictum was all the more true in unconsolidated or besieged polities. During one of the many fateful storms in the first-century Roman poet Virgil's *The Aeneid,* for example, tempest-tossed Trojans are barred from safe harbor in Carthage on the express order of its ruler, Dido. To their grievances she eloquently responded, "Severe conditions and the kingdom's youth / constrain me to these measures, to protect / our long frontiers with guards." The moral of Virgil's anecdote was simple and of a perennial pertinence: extreme tribulations demand radical measures in vulnerable realms. Machiavelli might have been one of Virgil's most ardent acolytes, quoting this very passage favorably when he decreed in chapter 17 of *Il Principe* (The prince), that *Fortuna* put *new* princes in contexts where they could not escape being "called cruel."[42] The more vulnerable a polity felt, this Machiavellian line of interpretation would thus argue, the more eagerly it would sanction cruelty; or, to put it in the late conservative columnist Charles Krauthammer's more recent terms, the more it would feel *"morally compelled—to do terrible things."*[43]

Whatever secular decline might be observable in early modern Europe as a whole, capital punishments, many elaborate in their infliction of pain and, in the parlance of penal law, their strategic and political invocation of "terror," remained on average a monthly occurrence in Milan during the middle decades of the eighteenth century, yet with a rather uneven chronological distribution. From four capital sentences in 1764, for example, the number suddenly rose to twenty-three the following year before returning to four the next.[44] This peak in capital punishments happened to coincide with the most famous Milanese attack on the institution itself. For the complex world in which Torriggia died—to atone for his sins and safeguard his eternal salvation, to heal the body politic, to reinforce the authority of the state, and to encourage social cohesion—was about to irrevocably change, not merely in its Milanese incarnation but in its various inflections in the European world, arguably also because of a short pamphlet recently penned by one of Torriggia's compatriots.

Cesare Beccaria's "notoriously misunderstood" *Dei delitti e delle pene* (1764), or *On Crimes and Punishments,* was in effect destined to become one of the most influential books of its century, and though rightly addressed to "humanity," it was very much the fruit of its Milanese soil—of the Confraternity of the Beheaded St. John the Baptist, of executions made into "spectacles" and "futile excess of punishments," and of distant Habsburg rulers.[45] And *On Crimes and Punishments* would produce a holistic vision of enlightened and enlightening reform that stretched from the technicalities of penal law to the very future of world order—a project to socialize people as well as peoples, and ultimately to transcend the Erasmian dichotomy and render human wolves themselves sacred.[46] For Milan was a privileged vantage point from which to analyze the historical dynamics of sociability, the commerce of human affairs, and the seemingly inevitable transition from city-states to empires that so dominated political, legal, and economic thinking in the long eighteenth century.

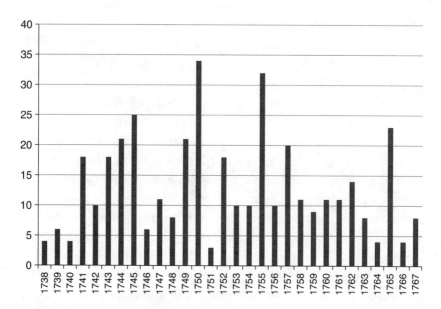

Capital sentences in the Duchy of Milan, 1738–1767.

Beccaria Redivivus

Frequently mentioned yet rarely engaged with at length by English-language historians, Beccaria has achieved a canonical status matched by no other Italian thinker born in the eighteenth century, except perhaps Giacomo Casanova (whose intellectual achievements were overshadowed by conquests of another kind).[47] As Schumpeter so succinctly put it in his *History of Economic Analysis,* "A[dam] Smith's life work contains no match for *Dei delitti e delle pene."* But in addition to being a great theorist, Beccaria was also an eminent practitioner, and, though "almost certainly more richly endowed by nature" than his Scottish counterpart, Schumpeter continued, Beccaria eventually "gave to the public service of the Milanese 'state' what A[dam] Smith reserved for mankind."[48] It is also a remarkable coincidence that Beccaria, like better-known contemporaries such as the Genevan firebrand Jean-Jacques Rousseau and Adam Smith, never managed to bring his final project to fruition.[49] Following the staggering success of his earlier works, Rousseau never completed his long-intended *Institutions politiques* (Political institutions), which, informed by a "historical study of morality" and aimed at discovering the "best" form of "Government" available to man, he considered "of the various writings I had in progress, the one which I meditated about for the longest time, which I attended to with the most relish, which I wanted to work on for my whole life, and which in my opinion ought to put the seal on my reputation."[50] Similarly, Smith never finished (and indeed burned most of) his historical work on "the general principles of law and government, and of the different revolutions they have undergone in the different ages and periods of society, not only in what concerns justice, but in what concerns police, revenue, and arms, and whatever else is the object of law."[51] Beccaria too would embark on a massive project on the history of what he called "civilization," of law, politics, trade, and human sociability, very much mirroring the concerns of his even more famous contemporaries, and he too ultimately failed at bringing together all the different pieces of his projected *Ripulimento delle nazioni* (The refinement of nations).[52] Adding his Milanese perspective to the well-known dialogue between the Scotsman Smith and the Genevan Rousseau on these problems, however, allows us to better triangulate some of the core concerns of the Enlightenment and the often widely divergent visions for political-economic reform that resulted from contemporary inquiry into the potent nexus of history, law, government, economic affairs, and international politics, an overlapping cluster of preoccupations the analysis of which Beccaria's friend and later nemesis Pietro Verri late in life would refer to by the neologism "social science."[53]

Born on March 15, 1738, into a noble lineage past its prime, and the eldest of four siblings, the Marquis of Beccaria experienced the same traumatic generational conflict that plagued contemporaries like the brothers Pietro and Alessandro Verri. The reasons for these conflicts were many and varied, but largely resulted from the punitive and authoritarian child-rearing traditions of Milanese family patriarchs, the repeated abuses of which served as a common backdrop for these theorists' reformist fervor against the excesses of "despotism," suffering," and "violence" they experienced in their childhoods and in their polities alike.[54] Following his early training at the Jesuit Collegio Farnesiano in Parma ("eight years of fanatical and servile education," as he later would reminisce to his French translator, the *philosophe* and liberal political economist André Morellet), where he first met Pietro Verri, Beccaria studied jurisprudence at the university of Pavia.[55] Following his studies there, Beccaria joined the Accademia dei trasformati, or "Academy of the Transformed," a salon-like gathering of the upper crust of Milanese literary society at the time, including the renowned poet Giuseppe Parini (1729–1799) and Pietro Verri himself, who was a full decade older than the young Marquis and the scion of a much wealthier family of greater patrician status in Milan than the Beccarias. It was under Verri's influence that Beccaria turned from literary to more purposefully reformist endeavors.[56]

Much to the surprise of friends and family, the quiet Beccaria soon proved himself willing to sacrifice fame and fortune for the woman he loved: the pulchritudinous young Teresa Blasco, whom he had first met in Milan, then courted in the countryside of nearby Gorgonzola; "I promise you constancy in all tribulations," he declared to her in furtive notes, "I will love you forever."[57] Temperamentally, they were nothing alike; whereas she has been called both "minute and peppery" and "very attractive and very bubbly," as well as being an ambitious and extrovert social climber, Beccaria himself was "corpulent" and "introspective," of a melancholy disposition, and prone to inertia and ennui, and has been described, in something of a flight of fancy, as having "a good deal in common with the surly, canonical investigator in the style of Sherlock Holmes or Salvo Montalbano."[58] Although she was of much lower social rank than him and prone to carnal misadventures, Beccaria was tempted to accept her proposal to marry in secret, against his parents' wishes, in 1760, when he was twenty-three and she barely sixteen.[59] "I greatly fear the high-handedness of my parents," he wrote to her, and rightly so.[60] Friends soon convinced them not to go through with their plans for a clandestine matrimony, but their intentions alone made their union a cause célèbre in Milan and well beyond it, reaching even the attention of the Habsburg administration in Vienna. Beccaria was disowned by his parents, who refused to ever see them again and even appealed to Duke Francesco d'Este, then governor of the Duchy of Milan, to arrest and imprison the young Marquis. Both families wrote supplications to Empress Maria Theresa of Austria, and, at the end of the day, Beccaria was put in house arrest while the authorities sought to mediate a solution to secure the familial—and urban—peace.[61] He drafted two letters to Teresa in January 1761, intent on leaving her, but eventually had a change of heart.[62] The couple married a mere month later, much to the consternation of Beccaria's family, and were forced to living marginalized and in relative poverty until Pietro Verri, who had recently returned from the Seven Years' War and whose father in the past had also sought to put him under house arrest over relations with a woman, engineered a rapprochement more than a year later. Verri's plot was for the star-crossed lovers to surprise the Beccaria clan at lunchtime and thus provoke a public catharsis. This proved melodramatically successful, and, in a tempest of tears, between a kneeling Cesare begging for forgiveness and a pregnant Teresa swooned in a chair, the elder Beccarias could not but forgive the two on the memorable afternoon of 19 May 1762.[63]

During these emotional times, the details and consequences of which will be explored in Chapter 6, Pietro Verri also invited Beccaria to became a founding member of what soon would be known as the Accademia dei pugni—the "Academy of Fisticuffs"—alongside Verri's brother Alessandro and less-known contemporary figures like Sebastiano Franci (1715–1772), future Habsburg inspector of the mints of Milan and Mantova, and the Istrian erudite scholar, reformist civil servant, and political economist Gian Rinaldo Carli (1720–1795). Pietro Verri himself was living through a period of great familial discord following his return from Vienna, including his father accusing him of an incestuous relationship with his younger sister Francesca, and his younger brother Alessandro feeling that the legal studies that he had recently finished had been forced upon him.[64] Beccaria was the worst off of the group, and clearly in need of financial support during the period in which he was disowned by his family (even "lacking bread," Verri noted). Beyond providing mutual support and a forum to discuss the ideas of the age, their hope was that, together, they might secure government employment through their projects and find ways out of their personal predicaments.[65]

The group wove an imagined community of pugilistic reformers, and their short-lived *Il Caffè—The Coffee* or *The Coffeehouse,* modeled on Joseph Addison and Richard Steele's *The Spectator*—remains one of the Enlightenment's intellectually preeminent journals. Yet the group's intellectual fervor was not to last, as the publication of *On Crimes and Punishments* led to Beccaria's almost overnight apotheosis on the European stage and the beginning of a vitriolic falling out with the companions of his youth as jealousy and bitter rivalries, no less intense than the familial ones they had sought to escape, overcame the once tight coterie.[66] After an aborted journey to Paris, the details of which will also be discussed in Chapter 6, Beccaria even declined an invitation by none other than Catherine the Great to rewrite Russia's legal code, decidedly dedicating himself to his homeland.[67] By this time the Verri brothers had begun an explicit smear campaign against their former friend, and other members of the group found themselves taking sides in their quarrel. The pugilists turned on themselves. Painfully, however, Pietro Verri and Beccaria continued to serve the Milanese state in similar and often competing capacities for the following decades, frequently even sitting on the same councils and having to sign the same documents. And for personal as well as theoretical reasons, Verri would gradually come to crystallize a position opposed to those of Beccaria and particularly Carli in the administration, with consequences for debates over political economy in eighteenth-century Italy.

Actively soliciting the patronage of Wenzel Anton von Kaunitz, chancellor of state and minister of foreign affairs under the Habsburg empress Maria Theresa, under whose sovereignty the Milanese state lay, Beccaria presented himself during the summer of 1765 as someone who "always delighted in and occupied [him]self with those sciences which appertain to the regulation and the economy of the state," adding that he would consider himself "ever so fortunate were I able to employ my efforts and my entire person in the service of Your Majesty."[68] It was a telling self-description, particularly in the context of the overarching project of which *On Crimes and Punishments* had been the major published expression. But this was the context in which his colleague Carli, himself about to embark on a meteoric rise through the Austrian administration, wrote in a memorandum on Lombard economic reform of the need to "balance commerce and the application of public economy with jurisprudence [*livellare il Commercio e l'applicazione della Pubblica Economia con la Giurisprudenza*]," and in which considerations regarding legal and economic matters came together as the basis for large-scale institutional reform.[69]

Beccaria's efforts were rewarded in 1768 when he was appointed Professor of Cameral Sciences—the second chair devoted to something like political economy in Italy, after the appointment of Antonio Genovesi to such a chair in Naples in 1754—at the Scuole Palatine in Milan, a dignified educational institution that, in a previous incarnation, counted St. Augustine among its faculty members.[70] Beccaria's lectures would soon be designated "economy and commerce" (later again they would take the name of "public economy" and "civil economy"), and shortly afterward, in 1771, he would be made member of the Supreme Economic Council of the Habsburg administration in Milan.[71] Beccaria devoted the rest of his life to the daily management of the Milanese state, including stints in the Societá Patriotica (Patriotic Society) as well as on the official Magistrato Camerale (Cameral Magistrature), devoted to strictly economic concerns. And when in 1786, after he had consolidated a number of institutions, including the Magistrato Camerale, into a unified Consiglio di Governo (Governing Council), Joseph II was able to, as the Habsburg emperor himself put it, "govern Lombardy," Beccaria was asked to head the "IIIrd Department" (out of VII), which was devoted to questions of industry, trade, and provisioning. Similarly, Beccaria was recruited in 1791 to be part of the council established to reform its penal system, the cause that first had made his name in the European world.[72] He died in late 1794, on the eve of the Napoleonic invasions and the establishment of the Cisalpine Republic in Northern Italy, still eulogized everywhere in the European world, from St. Petersburg to Philadelphia, as one of the greatest reformers of the Enlightenment almost solely on the merits of his youthful polemics and his personal reputation as paladin of "the empire of humanity."[73]

Beccaria's project, though, was far grander than his short pamphlet *On Crimes and Punishments*. And just as the origins and orientation of his

best-known work cannot be understood outside of the matrix offered by
the Academy of Fisticuffs, neither can the problem of Enlightenment socialism and all that it represents. The pugilists have long served as a locus
for one of the cardinal questions of eighteenth-century studies, intrinsically
bound to the larger problem of Enlightenment sociability between people
and peoples, regarding the vexing relationship between "patriotism" and
"cosmopolitanism" in the so-called age of reason—how, in short, historical
actors mediated between local loyalties, transnational allegiances, and often
ostensibly universalist ethics during the Enlightenment.[74] Scholars have
frequently conflated the two categories of "patriotism" and "cosmopolitanism" as twin expressions of an "enlightened" spirit based on "doux
commerce" (sweet commerce) supposedly championed by these Milanese
reformers. That is, it has been argued that they followed an idealist, rather
impractical, and toothless political project based on faith in the supposedly
universally civilizing and peaceful consequences of domestic as well as
long-distance trade.[75] Yet the Academy's project was forged not only in the
context of a cosmopolitan coffee-shop culture but also in the crucible of international competition, in light of Lombardy's complex economic past
amid rival zones of foreign influence and of Milan's place in the larger projects of the House of Habsburg in the wake of the Seven Years' War. For
though the Academy has often been mentioned as a preeminent example of
the forces at play in the emergence of a "public sphere" in eighteenth-century
Italy, and political economy has often been discussed as the science of Enlightenment par excellence, the two issues are seldom considered organi-
cally. Yet contemporaries saw them as deeply entangled; as Pietro Verri
summarized the Academy's position on the matter in the short introduction
to an article on growing tobacco, that other great vehicle of sociable consumption in eighteenth-century Europe:

> I believe it is a good thing that many write and think about the true
> interests of a nation, about finance, trade and agriculture. Mist and
> mystery serve the impunity of the few and the wretchedness of the
> many. It is a good thing for the facts of political economy to be
> known, hence it is a good thing that many think about them, for
> from the ferment of various opinions the truth will increasingly be
> separated out and made simple.[76]

It is precisely to this nexus of sociability and political economy that one must turn to understand not only the backdrop of *On Crimes and Punishments,* but the early history of commercial "socialism" and some of the ideological origins of modern capitalism as we know it.

The Academy of Fisticuffs

To be clear, the Academy of Fisticuffs was not a scholarly society or academy in the sense of the term inaugurated by the seventeenth-century establishment of the Royal Society of London or the Académie des sciences (the Academy of Sciences) in Paris, though the Milanese endeavor had certainly been inspired by them, while simultaneously drawing on a far older tradition of smaller Italian learned academies.[77] The Fisticuffs did not enjoy in-house research facilities like an anatomical theater or a botanical garden on the model of Frederick II's Königliche Akademie der Wissenschaften (Royal Academy of Sciences) in Berlin or the Accademia dei Fisiocritici (better known as the Academy of Sciences) in Siena, nor did it offer essay prize contests like that of the Académie des Sciences, Arts, et Belles-Lettres de Dijon (Academy of Sciences, Arts, and Literature of Dijon), which lionized and in turn was lionized by Jean-Jacques Rousseau. It certainly did not read reports pertaining to sightings of the mythical Kraken, as would the Royal Society of Edinburgh.[78] In effect, the Academy of Fisticuffs did not even enjoy a proper physical existence, and it left no traces of such with the exception of a 1766 group painting by the Milanese portraitist Antonio Perego, sundry collections of manuscripts, and the two volumes of the aforementioned journal *Il Caffè.*[79] It was, at best, a virtual academy, unburdened, but also unprotected, by official fixtures.

With no material fetters constraining its members' wills or providing institutional grounding, the same autonomy that empowered the Academy intellectually soon precipitated its dissolution. Its flame burned brightly but quickly, leaving a more lasting mark on Italian history through two years of activities than many other academies would do over centuries of existence. The issue of defining the Fisticuffs institutionally is not simplified by the fact that the name *Il Caffè*—in Italian literally signifying both "the coffeehouse" and "the coffee," as established by Venice's very first, and eponymous, coffeehouse in 1683—served as a shorthand for several disparate but interconnected

Antonio Perego, *The Academy of Fisticuffs*, 1766. From left to right: Alfonso Longo, Alessandro Verri, Giambattista Biffi, Cesare Beccaria, Luigi Lambertenghi, Pietro Verri, Giuseppe Visconti di Salicento.

concepts: for the group of people congregating and the imaginary place in which they met, but also for their means of communicating with the world and, importantly, what they were drinking while so doing. As one survey of the phenomenon has asserted, the Academy of Fisticuffs embodied "the whole concept of the coffee-house revolution."[80]

The group consisted of a group of leading noble and upper-class Milanese and, to a lesser extent, other Northern Italian statesmen and intellectuals. Led by the indominable Count Pietro Verri, then in his early thirties, the coterie included, in addition to Beccaria, Carli, and Franci, Verri's restless younger brother Alessandro, Count Gian Battista Biffi (1736–1807), the internationally renowned professor of mathematics Paolo Frisi (1728–1784), Count Luigi Lambertenghi (1739–1813), Marquis Alfonso Longo (1738–1804), and Beccaria's cousin Count Giuseppe Visconti di Salicento (1731–1807). Some were closer to the group's core than others, and some, like Frisi, did not even live in Milan.[81] Nearly all were aristocrats, members of a conflicted upper stratum of Lombard society that, in a partial process of "embourgeoisment" over the course of the century, would cling to traditional privileges while increasingly embracing "capitalist" forms of rent extraction. And all would, extraordinarily, with time come to play major roles in the Habsburg adminis-tration, where, as later chapters will show, their complex loyalties deeply in-flected their work on political economy.[82] Verri first wrote about the group—"a select company of talented youths is gradually taking shape in my house"—on April 6, 1762, about six weeks before orchestrating Beccaria's forgiveness with his parents, and in private correspondence referred to this "society of friends" as a "Coffeepot Society."[83] Their humorous choice for the official name of their group mirrored those of many more-famous institutions in Italy, from the Renaissance on, and derived specifically from gossip circulating around Milan in the summer of 1763, according to which Verri and Beccaria had re-solved an intellectual dispute by resorting to "powerful punches"; hence the idea of a school of hard knocks, or Academy of Fisticuffs.[84]

Though the group shared similar sources of influence—particularly Hobbes's *Leviathan,* David Hume's *Essays,* Francis Hutcheson's *Inquiry,* Mon-tesquieu's *Spirit of the Laws* and equally importantly his earlier *Persian Let-ters,* Emer de Vattel's *The Law of Nations,* and the emerging authorities on political economy, all in French originals or translations—Beccaria in par-ticular was, earlier and with greater fervor, struck by two authors in partic-ular: Jean-Jacques Rousseau and the Elizabethan English philosopher and statesman Francis Bacon.[85] He was so taken by Rousseau's *Julie, or the New Heloise* that he named his first daughter Giulia; and he introduced Pietro Verri to Rousseau's *Social Contract.* Verri told Biffi,

> [Beccaria] read me some of Rousseau's *Social Contract* and I was en-chanted. I believe that he is the first who has dealt with the true source of the principles of the duties one man owes to another. The book cannot fail to be proscribed by Rome and to pass on to posterity.[86]

Beccaria himself wrote to Biffi,

> I am entirely absorbed in copying some works of Bacon of Verulam, who not only ranks among the most sublime geniuses, but may also be considered the legislator of the intellect.[87]

Though, in short, the group formed a coherent discursive community in the early to mid 1760s, its individual members appropriated, connected, developed, and invented in personalized ways, and Beccaria's dual, perhaps eclectic embrace of Bacon and Rousseau would profoundly come to mark his thinking.

Different members of the Academy of Fisticuffs thus had different areas of specialty, and the interdisciplinary reformist fervor they propagated depended entirely on the group's internal, if at times overlapping, division of labor. In the realm of political economy, the group's pioneers were Pietro Verri, Gian Rinaldo Carli, and Sebastiano Franci; the area of jurisprudence was covered by Beccaria, Luigi Lambertenghi, Alfonso Longo, and particularly Alessandro Verri, who, in addition to having studied law like many of his other colleagues, also served as one of Milan's Protectors of Prisoners during the years 1763–1765 (a post previously held by his older brother Pietro in 1751–1752); the Academy's most advanced mathematicians were Beccaria, Lamberthengi, and Paolo Frisi, the latter of whom also was one of Europe's foremost astronomers; erudition was covered by Carli and Alessandro Verri; Beccaria undoubtedly had the most felicitous pen; and finally, all of them shared a common interest in questions of political philosophy and institutional reform. Indeed, given recent research in organizational and behavioral science by the likes of Teresa Amabile and Toby Egan, it is not surprising that the Academy of Fisticuffs manifested such creativity. Its members held diverse but synergetic forms of expertise, they volunteered their contributions toward a common goal based on intrinsic motivations, and they shared a physical space conducive to caffeinated interactions with access to newspapers, journals, extensive private book collections, and, of course, nearby Milanese libraries.[88]

Additionally, its members took on names from antiquity to fit their personalities and aspirations; Beccaria adopted that of Titus Pomponius Atticus to reflect his contemplative inclination, while Pietro Verri chose the name of Lucius Cornelius Sulla, a Roman general and dictator who also received backhanded praise in *On Crimes and Punishments,* in honor of his preference for enlightened despotism.[89] Their image fit their project, however, in that the Academy and its journal were simultaneously entertaining and deadly serious, a reflection and vehicle of solidifying forms of consumption-based polite sociability as well as an incubator of ideas regarding power politics, institutional reform, and the technologies of international competition.[90] The

Fisticuffs spoke to supposed universals of human nature, yet were deeply embedded in Lombard lands and the "Milanese state" of their time.

Mediolanum

The name Lombardy derived from the sixth-century Germanic Langobard conquerors of the Italian peninsula, and was long used as a name for Italy as such throughout Europe. London's Lombard Street, for example, at the heart of the city's financial district and long home to Lloyd's Coffee House, one of the most mythical locations in the history of global capitalism, still derives its name from Italian merchants and pawnbrokers who had worked there since before the reign of Edward II (1284–1327).[91] Eventually, however, Lombardy came to designate only a shifting territory south of the Alps centered on the Po River between Piedmont in the west and the Veneto in the east, more or less equated with the political state centered on the city of Milan.[92] Originally founded around 600 BCE by people known as Insubres or Insubri—of Celtic, Etruscan, Gaulish, and Ligurian origins—Milan, or "Mediolanum," would eventually become the capital of the Western Roman Empire before being conquered during the Gothic War by a Germanic tribe known as Longobards or Lombards descending from southern Scandinavia. An independent polity from the 1183 Peace of Constance, by which the Hohenstaufen Holy Roman Emperor Frederick Barbarossa was forced to recognize the independence and authority of the Northern Italian city-states united in the Lombard League, and briefly a republic in the mid-fifteenth century, Milan emerged to become one of the great city-states of the Renaissance. It hosted the likes of Leonardo da Vinci and, under the leadership of the redoubtable Giangaleazzo Visconti, almost conquered Florence.[93] Lombardy also witnessed a precocious process of state formation and territorial centralization under the subsequent Sforza dynasty, importantly including the early elimination of most "feudal" fiefs and the establishment of a political system for thinking about and acting upon the economy. This included not merely measures to ensure provisioning, but also active industrial policies to promote the domestic manufacturing of high-value added goods in competition with neighboring as well as distant polities.[94]

Few Italian cities reflect the changing faces of foreign influence on the peninsula better than Milan.[95] Louis XII claimed Milan for France in 1499, and it was incorporated into the fledgling House of Habsburg after the 1525 Battle of Pavia only to soon pass to the Spanish line of that family, remaining under the Crown of Spain until the War of Spanish Succession. The Treaty of Utrecht, which ended this conflict in 1713, gave sovereignty over the Milanese state back to the Austrian Habsburgs, and it remained part of their dominions until Napoleon's invasion in 1796, when it became capital of the short-lived Cisalpine Republic, in turn absorbed by the Napoleonic vassal state of the Italian Republic from 1802 to 1805.[96] In the 1760s, then, Milan with its rich Lombard hinterland was one of the premium possessions of the Austrian Empire, a multinational concatenation of states (ranging from the Low Countries in the west to Transylvania in the east, with an imperial capital in Vienna) rather than a coherently consolidated territorial and political organism, which many "Italians" eyed with pained diffidence.[97]

The first half of the eighteenth century saw dramatic changes to the Milanese state, as Vienna, in order to secure the rest of its empire during a period of near-constant warfare, found itself forced to alienate half of its Lombard dominions to neighboring polities, including not only prime agricultural land, but also major cities and important mountain passes alike. The controversial 1743 Treaty of Worms had, in particular, given large parts of historical Lombardy to Savoy Piedmont, territorial transitions that were confirmed at the 1748 Treaty of Aix-la-Chapelle that ended the War of Austrian Succession.[98] Not only were international lines of communication and taxation jeopardized, but Lombardy found itself internally dismembered by administrative fragmentation and an increasingly untenable infrastructure, including poor roads that could literally dissolve during periods of heavy rain, failed canalization projects, and a terrain that often became unpassable during the cold winter months.[99] At midcentury the "Stato di Milano" hosted a little over one million inhabitants, about 120,000 of which lived in Milan, in a total territory of less than 8,000 square kilometers.[100] Though productivity and agricultural techniques in the region, specializing in high value-added processed products and activities such as silk, cheese, wine, and cured meats for domestic and international markets, were comparatively advanced by European standards, manufacturing was believed to have declined since its Renaissance heyday in the face of international competition, in some eyes precipitously.[101] The great British agronomist and political economist Arthur Young proclaimed after his travels there, "Lombardy is one of the richest plains in the world; for fertility of soil united with the use that is made of it by watering, it much exceeds every other in Europe."[102] And though the region remained one of the most heavily urbanized in the world, its urbanization ratio was nonetheless lower than it had been in the late thirteenth century and again in the sixteenth century.[103]

Around 1 percent of the population controlled about half of the land in the middle of the eighteenth century—not unlike how around 1 percent of the world's population controls about half of global household wealth today—and though their wealth was partially "feudal," real power lay in the privileged urban centers and particularly in the hands of the three hundred or so patrician families of Milan, from which many members of the Academy of Fisticuffs descended.[104] About 85 percent of the population was employed in agriculture, and while the hilly regions of Lombardy frequently were cultivated through sharecropping until the late eighteenth century, the plains were largely worked by large-scale wage labor organized by professional "middle tenants" and owned by the urban patriciate, which Verri in his private correspondence referred to as the "oligarchs." However, given that as the century progressed the nobility collectively drew less of their income from political mechanisms, dues, and tax privileges and ever more from investments, rents, and business ventures, Alexander I. Grab has argued that they became "more of a capitalist" class over time, remaining "partially a feudal class, and partially a capitalist class."[105]

As Carlo Capra and others have shown, this period was also characterized by a marked tendency toward centralization throughout the Habsburg dominions, by which Vienna sought to rationalize the functioning of its culturally heterogeneous dominions in what aptly has been called a "revolution from above," a rapid and wide-ranging reform—at times an overthrow—of Old Regime institutions with few equals in contemporary Europe.[106] Ultimate jurisdiction over Milan changed when the Austrian monarchy's Italian-Spanish Council was disbanded in 1757 and replaced by an Italian Department within the Austrian Chancellery of State run by Empress Maria Theresa's confidant von Kaunitz, one of the grandest statesmen in an era of great statesmen. Officially, and it is worthwhile to remember that the Seven Years' War was raging at the time—pitting Austria, France, and their allies against Hanoverian Britain, Prussia, and their associates—this structural transformation of Austria's relationship with its Northern Italian dominions was justified in relation to "the existing connection between foreign policy and the domestic affairs of these two lands."[107] It was a conscious attempt by Kaunitz to wrest control of Italian affairs from local institutions and to increase the tax burden on key lands such as Lombardy. And his means of so doing was by undermining traditional forms of "fiscal feudalism" and establishing close connections to local elites to improve the effectiveness of metropolitan management over the growing possessions of the Habsburg Empire, one of numerous episodes in the process of absolutist consolidation of sovereignties in eighteenth-century Europe.[108] Political-economic concerns were high on Kaunitz's list during these reforms, and he explicitly sought to rationalize the economic management of the Habsburg Empire and empower the government's ability to measure, assess, promote, and control economic life and resources in its domains, with the ultimate, and successful, goal of economic development and increased revenues, even instituting a central Hofrechnungskammer (Court Accounting Office) in 1761.[109]

Very much in emulation of the meritocratic reforms recently instituted in Prussia by Frederick the Great, Austrian authorities approved new regulations for the Italian Department toward the end of 1762, explicitly citing merit rather than pedigree, nepotism, or venality as the only means of careerism in the administration. As a whole, Lombardy soon became nothing less than a "testing ground" for Habsburg reformism.[110] The value of "merit" in commercial contexts was a common trope at the time though, intrinsically bound to the ongoing process—more or less conscious—of legitimizing the ideals of a competitive market society, not unlike what Thomas Piketty calls the "meritocratic hope" underpinning modern ideals of capitalist democracy.[111] The Venetian painter Giovanni Battista Tiepolo rendered the idea beautifully in his 1757 *Allegory of Merit Accompanied by Nobility and Virtue,* commissioned for the Rezzonico family in Venice, and the image can serve to highlight some of the complexities involved in the ideal and its role in the eighteenth-century imagination.

Taking the form of an elderly bearded man, "Merit" is captured in the moment of ascension toward the "Temple of Glory," accompanied by a lance-wielding embodiment of "Nobility" and an elegant female "Virtue." The winged figure of "Fame" sounds a celebratory trumpet above it all, and one of the many plump little *putti* or cherubim fluttering around the scene can be seen leafing through the so-called *Libro d'Oro* (Golden book) of Venetian

Giovanni Battista Tiepolo, *Allegory of Merit*, 1757.

nobility, in which the Rezzonico had been inscribed as patricians in 1687. Surrounding the painting, along the upper parts of the supporting walls, are images depicting the sea as well as a cornucopia spewing forth coins.[112] With Venetian finances in jeopardy following one of many wars against the Ottomans, the nouveau riche had been able to buy their way into the patriciate in the second half of the seventeenth century, joining families that had held the privilege of sitting on the Grand Council since the late thirteenth century.[113] Among these newcomers were the Rezzonico, a family from Como, on Lake Como in northern Lombardy, that had made a fortune in commerce and finance and was admitted for the princely sum of 100,000 ducats—or around 350 kilograms of gold, enough to buy almost 2.5 million cups of coffee in a mid-eighteenth-century Venetian neighborhood coffeehouse at 5 soldi each.[114] Tiepolo's frescoes were, appropriately, commissioned by the patriarch Giambattista Rezzonico the year before his son Carlo was elected Pope Clement XIII, in many ways the family's historical apex, and though his vision of familial virtue, fame, glory, and, strikingly, martial nobility on the basis of a merit conceptualized as commercial success certainly reflected both self-fashioning and wishful thinking, it nonetheless depicted a worldview that increasingly was championed by European authorities and intellectuals alike, and that, importantly, had deeper roots on the Italian peninsula than anywhere else on the continent.[115]

In line with such meritocratic ideals, Kaunitz initiated a gradual realignment of the employee base of the Italian Department, away from Spanish and Southern Italian political protégés and toward professionals selected for their actual abilities. Similarly, these reforms were aimed at, and resulted in, a forceful rolling back of the power base of the Milanese state's old patrician oligarchy and a resultant escalation of metropolitan control over provincial government.[116] The nature of the Milanese Enlightenment, and of the activities of the Academy of Fisticuffs in particular, can be understood only in light of this generational shift, which in the 1760s was both personal, as young patricians such as Pietro Verri and Cesare Beccaria seemingly turned their backs on their familial loyalties, and institutional, as the structures and nature of government in Milan were restructured.[117] Pietro Verri himself thought his familial conflicts originated in his father's fear of being "eclipsed" by him, and certainly felt similarly about his group's relation to contemporary Milanese society.[118]

The crucial institutional figure in these reforms, and in many ways Kaunitz's gatekeeper in Milan with regard to local intellectuals, was the historiographically enigmatic Habsburg plenipotentiary Count Karl Joseph von Firmian (1716–1782). Born in the Tyrolese capital of Trento to a noble family that would count a future archbishop of Vienna among its members, Firmian traveled widely in his youth, from his childhood studies at Ettal, in Bavaria, and formal enrollment at the University of Leiden to an aristocratic grand tour through France and Italy.[119] He frequented Masonic circles in Florence in the early 1740s, where he also devoted himself to erudite studies—of everything from the Etruscans, Tacitus, and "ancient martyrologists" through the Renaissance humanists Angelo Poliziano and Pico della Mirandola to the French philosopher Pierre Bayle—and partook in the contemporary republican reinterpretation of Niccolò Machiavelli.[120] Strikingly, he showed the keenest interest in "le precieux morceau de l'Histoire de dix aneés [sic]," that "precious piece" by "the great Florentine secretary"—that is, in Machiavelli's explicitly republican *Discourses on Livy*, as well as his "entirely divine" letters.[121] While Firmian was ambassador to Naples in the 1750s, after seven years of successfully serving at the Habsburg court in Vienna, he actively sought to familiarize himself with the new science of political economy, becoming interested in the geopolitics of trade and befriending both Antonio Genovesi and Ferdinando Galiani, two of the greatest economic thinkers of eighteenth-century Europe. So impressed was the Bourbon de facto prime minister of Naples, Bernardo Tanucci, by Firmian that he wrote to a friend in Florence, then under Habsburg-Lorraine dominion,

> Oh if only you could have as your Governor Count Firmian, who here represents your Sovereign! He is the most philosophical knight of all who have walked this planet, and the kindest philosopher that a nation could wish for as conductor of the chariot, to which Virgil compared the republic.[122]

Trusted and respected by both Empress Maria Theresa and her right-hand man Kaunitz, and interested in what he called "the vicissitudes of mankind," Firmian was subsequently sent to Milan in 1757, where, in Verri's damning words, he ruled as if in his own "kingdom," implementing reforms, encouraging cultural life, and amassing an extraordinary collection of fine art and rare books.[123]

Firmian's influence on Lombardy's political economy was both direct, through his dutiful implementation and development of Kaunitzian reform programs in the region, and indirect, through his purposeful patronage of local talent. Preoccupied with the secular economic decline of the region and the means of reversing it, during his tenure Firmian led numerous successful projects to encourage industry and, importantly, infrastructure and thus domestic communication and territorial unification. Under his watch, new and improved roads connected urban centers and rural hinterlands, and long-dormant canal projects were completed, improving navigability on crucial rivers such as the Adda and the Po, thus increasing market access for Lombard goods and manufactures both regionally and internationally.[124] These projects were very much in the spirit of contemporary measures elsewhere in Europe to "improve" territories and unify them culturally and economically through technological developments, the vogue for and effectiveness of which would explode with the coming of the steam engine and the telegraph.[125] Similarly, there can be no doubt that Firmian's active patronage contributed greatly to the intellectual climate in which the Academy of Fisticuffs would flourish. Just as Firmian, while ambassador to Naples, had sustained the young art historian Johann Joachim Winckelmann, by many considered the founder of modern archaeology, so he eventually took Beccaria under his wing in Milan. Firmian's relationship with Verri was far less friendly, but it remains that Firmian gave foundational institutional support for what eventually would be known as the "Lombard Enlightenment."[126]

The story of the Academy of Fisticuffs, however, must start with that of the restless young Verri and his turn to the "new" discipline of political economy that was conquering the salons and government offices of Europe in the mid-eighteenth century. Verri officially entered Habsburg civil service with Firmian's blessing in 1764, but had already served under Austrian command during the Seven Years' War, even before he took it upon himself to edit and publish *Il Caffè*. And though his wartime experiences seldom are found relevant for his later development as a political economist, his time on the field of battle, not to mention his own later musings on the matter, eloquently set the stage for the emergence of his Academy and help explain its core preoccupations with political economy and, importantly, the challenge and promise of human sociability.

Modern Warfare

Unlike many of the great *philosophes* of the European Enlightenment, who wrote extensively about war, peace, and the future of world order from the safety of their studies, Pietro Verri and some of his colleagues remarkably practiced what they preached. As behooved a young member of the provincial aristocracy in the Habsburg Empire, Verri entered the armed services as captain in the Austrian army during the Seven Years' War, eventually with deployment to Field Marshal Leopold Joseph von Daun's campaigns of 1759–1760. The road there had been far from straight, however. He had greatly suffered from his relations with his father, and long resisted the legal studies that he was encouraged to pursue. Late in life Verri would credit his "love of books" not to juvenile studies but to his first love, the older and more experienced Roman noblewoman Maria Vittoria Ottoboni Boncompagni (long married to Duke Gabrio Serbelloni), whom he had "frequented" for four years in the mid-1750s.[127] It was she who first introduced him to the life of theater and foreign literature, of salons and sentiments, and, of course, the pleasures of female company. Yet, as lovers go, she went, suddenly moving on to her cousin during the summer of 1758. Heartbroken, Verri sought succor not in his studies, as his family had hoped, but instead in the young and newlywed Countess Barbara Corbelli, married to his friend Francesco d'Adda. But this was not to last either. She quickly became pregnant, and, increasingly "desperate" for release from the complexities of his situation, Verri went to war. "My poor treatment at home," he confided in his uncle, "has forced me to become a soldier."[128] It was, in any case, a good time to join the Austrian side, still energized by the August massacre at Kunersdorf, during which Frederick the Great lost half of his army and was driven to the brink of suicide, and Verri partook in successful battles and skirmishes on the northern frontier in Central and Eastern Europe, in Prussia, Bohemia, Lusatia, and Silesia.[129] Soon, however, he received news that Barbara d'Adda had died during childbirth at only twenty-one years of age, a shock that he would claim inspired him to seek death on the field of battle and, as his friend and hagiographer Isidoro Bianchi put it, to rethink the very "tenor of his life."[130]

Having ventured into the field at the age of thirty to escape domestic troubles and a burgeoning world-weariness, and in hopes of finding "plenty of libertinism, plenty of partying and merriment, and plenty of camaraderie among men," Verri soon discovered that "this union of men which forms the army is the aggregate of the refuse of other societies." As a body of individuals, the army was an interesting example of what a "society" might be—that is, a "union" of the "discontent" held together by inertia and by force, by "tedium" and the "slavery" of not being able to leave one's regiment, not to mention by ignorance. For, to Verri's great surprise, members of this martial "society" were "neither informed of the events of the present war, nor of the theory of the art of war in general."[131] Obviously Verri belonged to a cultivated elite in the world of eighteenth-century warfare, and his romantic vision of battling philosopher-kings fit poorly with the cruel realities of contemporary conflict. Yet his intellectual formation was not without its benefits. For example, under heavy fire from charging Prussian hussars at Żary, in what today is Western Poland, and admitting that the "feral" sound of cannonades caused him "terror," he found strength, he wrote, in "following my Ruggiero," a reference to the mythical hero in Ludovico Ariosto's Renaissance masterpiece *Orlando furioso* (Raging Roland).[132]

In light of Verri's fears, it was an appropriate reference, given Ariosto's precocious insight into the ways in which the arquebus—"il cavo ferro e il fuoco" (iron tube and fire)—would spell the end of chivalry, turning the noblest of knights into a wild boar to be felled by its simple hunters.[133] The art of war had for millennia romanticized the ancient emphasis on valorous personal confrontations engrained in the Western tradition by the Homeric epics, but now any novice with a rifle could kill the greatest warrior from a safe distance. Modern warfare, in short, would develop in the sign of cowardly Paris and his bow, not of heroic Achilles with his vulnerable heel.[134] It was, perhaps, with similar sentiments that Verri referred to his manservant as "Sancio [sic] Panza," Don Quixote's companion in Cervantes's eponymous obituary for the chivalrous genre, killed by "those devilish instruments."[135] For, as Rabelais had argued, "artillery was inspired by diabolical suggestion," just as the printing press was inspired by the "divine."[136] Indeed, Verri soon discovered he had been tilting at windmills with his sentimentalized conception of warfare, a grim disenchantment that nonetheless would have profound consequences for his later theoretical developments. Whereas the more academic Scotsman David Hume would soon refer to the arquebus as a "furious engine, which, though it seemed contrived for the destruction of mankind, and the overthrow of empires, has in the issue rendered battles less bloody, and has given greater stability to civil societies," Verri was less sanguine about the civilizing consequences of modern combat and the horrors that might be unleashed by military technologies once polities realized that the international competition over land, trade, and resources could take on existential importance.[137] Once warfare had become a question of technology and resource management, of economics broadly put, it quickly ceased to be the domain of epic champions facing each other as representatives of their respective sides. International competition and, in a more focused manner, war now risked being a total civilizational experience.[138] And though wars of citizen soldiers could further merits such as discipline, patriotic sociability, community, self-sacrifice, and "virtue," in the classical sense of political philosophy—and many Britons, Frenchmen, and even American colonials experienced the Seven Years' War in precisely such a way—not everyone involved did. Many in effect fought for conglomerated imperial armies, in lands far from their own, for causes they might not have fathomed in languages they frequently did not understand.[139] And these poor souls, rather than their virtuous alter egos, constituted the antisociety that Verri encountered during his military service.

Following in the footsteps of Machiavelli by presenting "men as they are," Verri himself believed he had gained greater insight into the nature of human passions, pleasures, and pains from his experiences on the field of battle.[140] Surprisingly, given the canons of political philosophy, he observed that war fundamentally upset the structure of authority and the resilience of sociability in a polity or community, no matter whether one found oneself on the winning or losing side of a conflict. Even "Royal Princes," Verri mused, had to bow before great generals, for *"war takes men back to the state of nature; the strongest commands, those in need seek benevolence."*[141] In Adam Smith's contemporary vocabulary, wars turned the proverbial clock back on whatever softening progress that might have resulted from the gradual strengthening of government and society.[142] As the campaign progressed, the romantic nobility of war became an ever more distant memory for Verri, who ultimately came face to face with the "inhumanity" of it all. The worst of two worlds, martial "society" united "the feral aspects of a savage people with the falseness and baseness of a corrupt people"; war in his eyes came to be nothing less than a universal solvent of sociability.[143] But this was not to suggest that the armies he observed were bad at what they did. Indeed, their very vileness gave them strength; from the perspective of Verri's experiences on the Austrian front, it was not really "virtue" that helped win battles, but instead a certain fearlessness born from ignorance and destitution. It was true, he thought, that "a more wretched, cruder, more mistreated nation will win in war against a nation that is happier, cultivated, and well governed," but this was not because the simpler nation had maintained its virtuous patriotic courage as a shield against corruption and effeminacy, as an ancient tradition of republican political philosophy would have it, but simply because, "caring less for their lives, they expose themselves with greater indifference to the chance of bettering it or ending it."[144]

Toward the end of his last days in the field, Verri employed a powerful anecdote in his diary to exemplify how war made life itself lose all value. Laughing uncontrollably, an officer had entered his tent after having seen one of the indigent women trailing the supply wagons of their army. What happened, Verri asked? "She had a boy in the barrel she had on her back, another she held by the hand, and the third that she was breast-feeding had died on her," the captain explained mirthfully, "she held him dead in her arms and, instead of thanking the heavens for freeing her from that tedium, the stolid woman despaired!" The officer, Verri reminisced, then continued to laugh himself silly, to the point of nearly "dislocating his jaw." Far from being an agent of civil society and a school of patriotic virtue, he decided, war was the most horrible vehicle of "inhumanity."[145] The expansion of human sociability, it seemed, would require a different agent.

But the experience of war had not been a complete loss for young Verri, for in addition to seeing the world's darker aspects firsthand, he accumulated practical insights that would contribute to his subsequent theoretical works. In his much later 1771 *Meditazioni sulla economia politica* (Meditations on political economy), for example, he noted how truly poor countries could be breeding grounds of "conquering armies of men who despise life because they know so few of its pleasures," and, in the face of Napoleon's conquering Grande Armée in the wake of the French Revolution, he compared "armies," in which he strikingly did not differentiate between officers and ordinary troops, to "a cesspool that collects all the most deformed vices and all the refuse of society."[146] Even more formatively, he befriended the slightly older and mysterious Henry Humphrey Evans Lloyd on the fields of Bautzen, in Saxony, current-day Germany. A Welsh soldier, military theorist, and adventurer of Münchausen-like temperament, the burly Lloyd soon became a "mentor" able to "instruct" Verri in the ways of the world.[147] It was during the time they were defending Dresden against Prussian forces in the winter of 1759–1760, in particular, that the two men bonded, and Verri himself came to describe this period as one of the most formative of his life. In the mornings, the two men would survey the battlefields, assist with logistics, and engage enemy skirmishers, but the rest of the day Verri insisted they should spend "my way." This meant a "good lunch" with "excellent" pastries and "exquisite wines from Champagne and Burgundy," an afternoon spent browsing bookshops, and evenings dedicated to "Rhine wines," "coffee," and, of course, "women," for the "the ones that have remained in Dresden, and there are many, are all at the command of whoever offers them a gold coin. *Libertinism is so easy*."[148]

A New Niche

This was, quite plausibly, the turning point in Verri's life. Grieving over his lost love, disillusioned with the modes and ambitions of the Old Regime status quo supported by the Milanese patriciate, and thoroughly disenchanted with war both as a career and as a medium of positive change in the world, his sentiments turned him to the contemporary discipline of societal reform par excellence: political economy—to the novelties, as he put it in 1763, of "commerce" but also the exciting "new language of *natural law, law of peoples, social contract*" that had come to fill the salons and bookstores of the continent.[149] In this, Verri was very much participating in the "economic turn" observable throughout mid-eighteenth-century Europe.[150] As Voltaire famously explained in a short article on *"Bled ou Blé"* (Grain) in the wide-ranging 1770–1774 *Questions sur l'Encyclopédie* (Questions on the Encyclopédie), "Around the year 1750, the nation, satiated with verses, tragedies, comedies, opera, novels, fantastical stories, even more fantastical moral reflections, and theological disputes about grace and convulsions, finally turned to reasoning about grain."[151] Though frivolities frequently flowed from Voltaire's pen, one should not automatically presume that something is false merely because he claimed it to be true. The eighteenth-century French craze for agromania, and more generally for political economy, has been widely substantiated since. To speak of grain and of provisioning (and, indeed, of bread) was to address the pulsing heart of society, politics, and economic life, especially in France but to a certain extent throughout continental Europe. From the perspective of book history, French publications on economic subjects exploded around 1750, to the extent that new works in the genre were outpacing even the publication of new novels by the 1760s.[152] But this was not merely a French phenomenon. Internationally, too, the publication and translation of works in political economy came to occupy a markedly larger share of the European book trade in the same period, from Italy in the south to Sweden in the north.[153] And grand tourists increasingly came to travel in order to familiarize themselves with foreign economic theories and practices, further contributing to a continent-wide process of cumulative emulation.[154] This fashion for the "economic" was observable across a variety of spheres and activities, from the birth of "economic milling" and the foundation of agricultural societies to the experience of new forms of journalism such as business news and, to summon a rather basic metric, simply the number of times variations of the term "economic" appeared in printed sources in the various languages of Europe, including Italian.[155] Rulers and subjects in a growing number of European countries became convinced that governance, in its most ambitious as well as its most quotidian senses, had to be "economic," and not just narrowly by doing proper accounting and being accountable.[156] Just as in Cervantes's *Don Quixote* the eponymous hero discussed "the subject that is sometimes called reason of state" with his barber, thus ridiculing its popularity, so one of Pietro Verri's probably pretend anonymous reader's letters to *Il Caffè* made fun of the Fisticuffs' infatuation with the theme by complaining "damned *commerce*, nowadays it is spoken of everywhere!"[157] Many a true word is spoken in jest.[158]

There are few, if any, references to economic affairs in Verri's writings prior to his stay in Dresden, but gradually, and undoubtedly under Lloyd's influence, he began to engage with them in his memoirs as a possible new focus for his life once he returned to his Lombard homeland. Evidence suggests he stayed in Vienna for nearly a year, also to familiarize himself with the new discipline.[159]

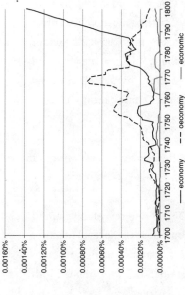

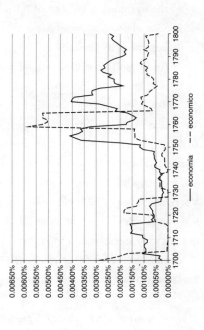

Google Ngrams of the words "économie" and "économique" in French publications; "economy," "oeconomy," and "economic" in English publications; and "economia" and "economico" in Italian publications, 1700–1800.

In Milan everything is left to the Doctors [of Law], yet commerce, finance, money, etc. do not seem to me to be subjects for lawyers; it could perhaps help my purpose if the Count Firmian had an inclination to refine the country . . . however a time of ruinous war like this is not one in which one thinks of reforms; I myself have not really read the authors on the subject that could give me a niche; I need to prepare; here there is an important library open in the morning, it would be worthwhile for me to frequent it and after lunch visit various houses and remain alert.[160]

Then, on the eve of his return to what he referred to as "Italy" in late December of 1760, Verri pondered,

So I shall be employed. But in what? Now I will reveal my plan. In Milan there are no other lights [*lumi*] but those of the legal practice. The mint, provisioning [*annona*], waters, manufacturing, and commerce are all in the hands of the Doctors [of Law], who, imbued with the opinions of the age of Bartolus [of Sassoferrato], truly have no idea of political economy or they have such ideas that it would be better not to have any. . . . This is the path that I would like to open for myself. But it is not without due consideration that I have decided so.[161]

Verri was careful in constructing his literary persona, and so it is perhaps not surprising, given his well-documented and often emphasized Oedipal conflicts, that he would have liked to highlight his break with the past and with Milanese traditions. Yet his surviving correspondence with his father Gabriele Verri, a renowned Milanese senator, makes it clear that his "new niche" was less novel than he might have liked, also in his homeland, and that he was not entirely alone in making his bold choice. Replying to a letter from Pietro in Vienna as early as September 1760, in which his son evidently had proposed his new project, Gabriele intriguingly responded:

The work that you design is not of a narrow extension. The *Dictionary of Commerce* by the French Savary collected in six volumes in folio will give you the sources of the entire subject. The difficulty consists in escaping the abstract and digging into the concrete, so that the work is useful.[162]

In a subsequent letter two weeks later, after he had been sent some of Pietro's early notes on political economy, Gabriele reiterated:

> I have read the articles which you propose to examine with regard to commerce with pleasure, and it seems to me that, theoretically speaking, you have exhausted the subject matter. The point is, [however], that Princes will enjoy only those things, from which they can profit, and which are conducive to practice, to which any speculation must aim in order to be useful.[163]

Interestingly, he continued by offering his son one final bibliographical suggestion:

> The renowned Roman banker Belloni has written a little work full of flair, in which he compendiously treats everything regarding the theory and the practice of commerce and of money. The work is worthy of the enlightened author.[164]

Gabriele Verri's suggestions to his son are important for several reasons. First of all, they show that Pietro Verri's break with his past was, in intellectual if not emotional terms, less totalizing than he and others have argued.[165] Had his father's reading recommendations stopped at Jacques Savary's famous seventeenth-century manual, which remained deeply influential throughout the world of the European Enlightenment and inaugurated a genuine tradition in the history of economic and business literature, it would have been easy to dismiss it as a mere rococo survival.[166] But his having encouraged Pietro to read the "enlightened" Girolamo Belloni's now-forgotten best seller *Del commercio* (On commerce), which between 1750 and 1850 was published in at least twenty editions in a number of European languages—including Latin, Italian, French, English, German, Russian, and Spanish—shows that he was attuned to the coming of the economic turn and the rise of political economy in Enlightenment Europe.[167] And it cannot be ignored that his insistence on the subject's utility and practicality would echo powerfully in the world and work of the Academy of Fisticuffs.

And so, under the influence of foreign ideas but very much in dialogue with his literal fatherland, Pietro Verri came to embrace a discipline à la mode, seeking to make a career of this ostensibly new field of political economy and the possibilities that it offered. Returning to Milan, he set about recreating the best that his experience in the war had taught him. Lloyd might have gone his own way for the moment, but Verri actively sought the company of similar "souls," soon issuing his report that "a select company of talented youths" was "taking shape" in his house, among them Beccaria, "whose extremely lively creativity and imagination united with an intense understanding of the human heart make for a man of singular merit." At this early stage Verri already noted his young colleague's gloomier side. "He is a profound algebraist and a good poet," Verri wrote of Beccaria, "his head made to explore new ways, unless he drowns in inertia and discouragement."[168] At the opposite end of the spectrum of initiative and aspiration, Verri's own modest life goal was, as one his biographers put it, by then nothing less than "immortality" in the "opinion of mankind," and political economy became his chosen vehicle for achieving glory by reforming his own life, the state of Milan, and, perhaps given his growing ambitions, the European world itself. And what soon would become the Academy of Fisticuffs was conceptualized precisely to unite companions and accomplices in this pugnacious enterprise.[169]

His project nearly floundered at the outset, as the problem remained of finding a space for his "new niche" within the baroque architecture of the Old Regime. Having finally returned to Milan in early January 1761, Verri began courting Firmian, seeking to impress him with varied manuscripts on the Milanese economy, when Firmian also returned to Lombardy later that spring. Beccaria too joined these efforts in 1762, composing a brief meditation on the ongoing monetary disorders in Milan, *Del disordine e de' rimedi delle monete nello stato di Milano* (On the disorder and remedy of the coinage in the State of Milan).[170] Very much in line with Verri's mission at the time, Beccaria stated that his "purpose" was to be "useful to the fatherland" and to contribute to widespread "enlightenment." Though hardly influential, his largely unknown piece went on to sketch out some of the major themes that would be expounded by the Academy of Fisticuffs.[171] He conjectured, for example, that money first had been invented haphazardly, from "need and utility"; he used a formal mathematical language to rhetorical effect; he warned of the dangers of unthinking emulation of foreign ideas and practices; and he championed the standardization of coinage as a means of facilitating commercial interactions.[172] More specifically, Beccaria drew upon, and contributed to, the contemporary obsession with the secular decline of the Italian economy, now "left in a corner, whereas before it was the center of all trade and the fatherland of all nations," and highlighted the increasing incongruity of states and markets at the time. The politically "diverse nations of Europe" had, he observed, become a "single nation" in terms of trade, though one wrecked by intestinal violence:

> That state of war in which Hobbes believed people found themselves shows itself in trade and in currency, where every nation seeks to enrich itself by impoverishing others, and fights with industry more than with arms. Opening the history books, one finds the most flourishing nations transformed by indolence into deserts and solitudes.[173]

Beccaria's work inspired a local polemic in Milan, in which the Verri brothers came to the defense of their friend.[174] The group's overtures had few tangible results, however, until Verri contacted Luigi Giusti at the Italian Department in Vienna directly, after which he was invited to join a new council established to reform taxation. Emboldened by this, Verri went even further. Soon he penned and circulated an analysis of Milan's balance of trade that shed light on issues regarding the "power and weakness of the state" that many believed should remain hidden from public scrutiny within the gothic vaults of reason of state—among Tacitus's *arcana imperii* (secrets of power). The result was a severe chastisement by Milan's authorities.[175] Kaunitz himself intervened as a result of Verri's "capriccio," which he could only explain as being an episode of "youthful levity."[176] Thus reprimanded, Verri and his colleagues thenceforth developed their economic niche in the service of "public happiness" with greater respect for the enduring architecture of the Old Regime.[177]

Verri's resulting pamphlet, entitled *Meditazioni sulla felicità* (Meditations on happiness), in many ways serves as the group's clarion call. Not only did it present a coherent argument for society emerging from a utilitarian, sensationist calculus of pleasures and pains, it emphasized the central importance of clarifying "the duties and rights of all men" and identified "public happiness," and thus the aim of "society" and the goal of "legislators," with "the greatest happiness divided with the greatest equality possible."[178] Because happiness ultimately depended on the relationship between "desires" and the "power" to satisfy them, and "wealth" was "one of the most common desires," political economy by necessity emerged as a cardinal discipline of human welfare for Verri.[179]

What exactly "economy" meant at the time of course remains a matter of some debate, though already in early modern Italy it clearly had come to refer also to the aggregate economic phenomena—activities and interactions— of regions and polities.[180] The word "economy" of course changed over time, much like "socialism" or, for that matter, "coffee"—the ingredients, preparation, taste, and appearance of the brew also continue to undergo remarkable transformations.[181] Etymologically, the original term for "economics," alternatively spelled "oeconomics," derived from the ancient Greek terms for household, *oikos*, and law, *nomos*, and would, for millennia, convey the idea of effective management with regard to familial estates, not unlike the once-vibrant tradition of "home economics" did. Economy in many ways looked inward, to the sphere of the domestic and its relation to other hearths and *people*, not out toward territorial concerns, distant lands, and foreign *peoples*. In his travel diaries from the early decades of the 1600s, for example, the indefatigable Roman pilgrim and aristocrat Pietro della Valle could claim he was made "not . . . for oeconomics [*l'economia*]" but instead for "political things, big things."[182] And Giovanni Domenico Civinini's *Della storia e natura del caffè* (On the history and nature of coffee) employed the term metaphorically to explain how the recently imported caffeinated drink affected the contained and systemic physical harmony of the consumer, what he called "the economy of the body."[183] But the term gradually changed to refer to wider material, political, and social concerns as well, translating "economy" from the microcosm of individuals to the macrocosm of communities. In the Austrian-Italian context, the Lorraine cleric and diplomat Lotharius Vogemonte (Lothar Vogemont), then based in Vienna, built on a well-established tradition of cameralism to argue in the early eighteenth century that "it is not at all good economy [*Economia buona*] to transfer raw, and unprocessed, the natural products of this Country a hundred and more leagues away from here, where they are then worked, and subsequently sent back at ten times the price," the exact same sentiment and strategy that the Neapolitan diplomat and political economist Ferdinando Galiani later would call "the economy of states."[184] Economy had now come to describe the theoretical and practical management of a political and social community, and resolutely not merely of the "estate" of a prince or ruler (though, to complicate matters, it was *also* used in such contexts). Galiani's fellow countryman Genovesi would write at length about "the art and science, which is said of commerce, a term which contains all that science, which we call economic philosophy."[185] By the time of the Academy of Fisticuffs, "economia" had, depending on context, come to designate both the material system of a polity or other unit of analysis and the art, craft, or science of managing it—what Alessandro Verri called "la scienza della economia"; economy was, as such, both a subject and an object of reform.[186]

When, upon his return from the front, Verri set out to write "the history of the economy of the country [*storia della economia del paese*]," which he also referred to as an "economic history [*storia economica*]," he was referring to many of the basic connotations of the term as currently used today—to the changing system of Lombardy's lands, resources, inhabitants, activities, and commercial exchanges, internally as well as internationally. Not only did there exist an "economy" that did not simply refer to an extended sovereign household, but the term could also be used in adjectival form, and Verri similarly thought nothing of referring to an administrative post in political economy as a "career of the economy [*carriera dell'economia*]," or to writing about "economic things."[187] His "economic" agenda was, however, deeply informed by personal experiences during the Seven Years' War; by his new insight into the frailty of social relations and the horrors of international rivalries; by the necessary relationship between theory and practice he learned with and from Lloyd; and of course by coffee and women. And if the journal he founded reflected the aims of the Fisticuffs' patriotic reforms within this larger Habsburg project of imperial restructuring, it remained intimately linked to the traditional ceremonies and exhilarating qualities of its namesake's consumption.

The $C_8H_{10}N_4O_2$ Enlightenment

The nineteenth-century French historian Jules Michelet once traced the origins of the Enlightenment, and really much of what he liked about Western Civilization, to "the advent of coffee."[188] It is a sentiment that still seems eminently justifiable when visiting Caffè Florian, a rococo time capsule of refined Enlightenment coffee culture that first opened its doors on Venice's St. Mark's Square in 1720. With its period glass walls, marble tables, and fulvously foamy ristretti, it is not surprising to think that the number of such cafés in Venice alone—admittedly scattered across a wide spectrum of lavishness from Florian level to what were essentially brothels serving broth— would reach two hundred by the time of *Il Caffè*'s publication.[189] If the Academy of Fisticuffs incarnated a movement, it was rather more its culmination than its institution, much like Verri and Beccaria contributed to rather than sparked the ongoing economic turn. An integral part and medium of the early modern consumer revolution, coffee consumption would increase in Europe from 2 million to 120 million pounds over the course of the eighteenth century, taking its place alongside tea and tobacco as a fashion, a dietary necessity, and a locus of "respectability" and sociability, first among the elites and then swiftly throughout broader social strata with the institutionalization of commercial coffeehouses in a gradually urbanizing Europe.[190]

Though European merchants had tasted and traded coffee for centuries, one of the very earliest descriptions of the drink by a Christian observer appeared in 1573, in the merchant metropolis of Aleppo, a Polanyian port of trade in what remains of present-day Syria. From the outset the enjoyment of this drink was understood to be a quintessentially social activity. For, as the European spectator noted, coffee was habitually imbibed in "an open Shop" where "you sit down . . . and drink together."[191] As it were, the first merchants vending coffee to Europe brought not only the beans but, quickly, also many (though significantly not all, such as a nearly obligatory musical accompaniment) of the institutions and rituals structuring its traditional consumption in the Middle East.[192] Coffee itself had long been an Ottoman monopoly, a particularly Islamic alternative or antithesis to wine, but the Ottoman stranglehold on the commodity was definitively broken once the Dutch brought a living coffee plant home from Aden in 1616. That single plant would in many ways serve as a milestone of globalization, simultaneously symbol and medium of the dramatic changes affecting world commerce and communication at the time. Domesticating a plant from one continent, the Dutch went on to replant it on two others for the economic benefit of a fourth, their original plant seeding the Dutch East India Company's vast plantations across Sri Lanka (then Ceylon), Malabar, Java, Bali, Sumatra, and the smaller islands of the East Indies, as well the Dutch colonies in the Western Hemisphere, such as Dutch Guiana, to satisfy new needs in Europe. Through French mediation, Dutch coffee plants would similarly be planted throughout the Caribbean and, after about 1727, in Brazil, establishing the still-extant "Bean Belt" stretching around the world between the latitudinal Tropics of Capricorn and Cancer—the area of the globe over which the sun at its zenith can appear directly overhead.[193]

As such, strains of the *Coffea* genus of evergreen flowering seed plants, originally indigenous to the Ethiopian highlands of Africa, were among the prime movers of early modern globalization in the wake of the so-called Columbian Exchange of flora, fauna, and disease following the intensification of transoceanic travel after 1492. The globalization of coffee is one of the most momentous cases of biological transplantation on record, from a cultural as well as an environmental standpoint; not only did it change societies and the trading patterns between them worldwide, it changed the very face of the planet.[194] In terms of its impact on Italian history, in particular, the assimilation of coffee—in cultural, social, and economic terms—can only be compared to the Greco-Roman domestication of the wine grape and the late Renaissance embrace of the tomato.[195] Like the tomato, coffee came to influence quotidian life and gastronomy in Italy, and, like wine, coffee did more than simply provide calories (in the case of coffee, depending mostly on what one added to it) or shape rituals of consumption and sociability. Like wine, coffee was also an addictive psychoactive substance that could fundamentally alter its consumers in sometimes permanent ways; but unlike wine, coffee was not a part of the religious culture of the time.

In his clarion call to explore the interrelation of history and biology, Daniel Lord Smail has suggested that "in the world of neurohistory, the long eighteenth century, the Enlightenment, has a peculiar distinction" for the unprecedented explosion of "autotropic mechanisms available on the market," thus providing a "gold mine of case studies that could benefit from the adoption of neurohistorical perspectives." Mine is decidedly not such a case study, but it remains that the Academy of Fisticuffs was inspired by, and organized around, the ritualized consumption of one of recent history's most formative "tropismatic mechanisms"—engaging, that is, in "human cultural practices that alter or affect brain-body chemistry."[196] Given what we are beginning to learn regarding the complex interaction of biology and culture, neurohistory and civilization, it seems insufficient to consider the practical and theoretical histories of the caffeinated pugilists entirely separately as so often has been done in the past.[197] Neither, however, would it be satisfying to go to the opposite extreme of considering human history as exclusively reflective of dynamic drinking habits—a liquid lens through which the drunken, squat, rash, and hallucinogenic Middle Ages gave way to the shapely, rational, ironic, and hyperactive age of reason and Enlightenment.[198]

Caffeine, which is produced by the coffee plant as a protective insecticide, is a stimulant that countless experiments have shown to improve the performance of a wide spectrum of cognitive functions, particularly related to alertness and the speed of processing information, which can alter the architecture of the human brain itself. Caffeine also directly affects a consumer's personality, usually triggering forms of impulsiveness as well as "improved moods, a better social disposition, and more self-confidence and energy." Some studies even suggest that it can "significantly ameliorate long-term depression and even make life worth living for some people."[199] Although on less empirical grounds, most of these effects—from increased alertness and work efficiency to serving as a temporary cure for melancholy—were well attested to already in the eighteenth century, and their cumulative effects made coffee the ideal drink for, well, most people, but particularly for intellectuals. "It is by lashing the imagination," the materialist doctor and philosopher Julian Offray de La Mettrie wrote in his radical 1747 L'homme machine (Machine man), "that coffee, the antidote to wine, dissipates our headaches and our sorrows without, like wine, saving them up for the morrow."[200] Or, as an eighteenth-century Italian treatise put it, "Coffee is so temperate that it can benefit every person, and every temperament," though it was known that in Aden, on the eastern approach to the Red Sea, "scholars" drank it "to reflect longer." So it was in the end quite appropriate that the contemporary term for the liquid extracted from coffee beans in Italy was *tintura,* a term at the time also used for "ink."[201] As Verri saw it, "coffee cheers the soul and arouses the mind," being therefore "particularly useful to those who practice the sciences."[202] The focused effects of coffee and the comparatively low potency of its mind-altering effects in contrast to those of other drugs, such as opium, that were becoming available on European markets, go a long way toward explaining its near-universal appreciation and deregulation.[203] And interestingly, given that the globalizing world concomitantly produced and was produced by European coffee culture, further increases in the consumption of coffee were justified in Italy by the very fact that its use already was so widespread in "so many, and so diverse parts of the world."[204] Nothing succeeds like success.

Yet coffee's legacy in Europe had two sides. Although it immediately was understood, as it is today, to be an "intellectual lubricant" that, as a sixteenth-century Arab source put it, made the "brain nimble," the fear was that it would similarly stimulate other parts of the body.[205] On the one hand, influential political economists took a view like that of merchant-economist John Cary of Bristol, who warned in 1695 that the contemporary vogue for herbal hot drinks led people to loiter in coffeehouses that kept "lusty Servants," which he held would "breed them up to nothing whereby they may be profitable to the Kingdom," and Venetian coffeehouses were renowned for catering to the widest range of carnal proclivities.[206] This was a common preoccupation at the time, fueled by orientalist myths of a distant, sybaritic East and its potentially corrupting influences on Europe.[207] On the other hand, the faux "oriental" trappings of many cafés could also remind patrons of, and attract them with, the novelty and exoticism of their consumption and the changing world of trade and international relations, as well as of increasing toleration and communication. As such, cafés were, for a while, both hotbeds of debauchery and new loci of sociability both individually interpersonal and culturally cosmopolitan, however idealized and abstract; "Caffés," the *Encyclopédie* argued, were "manufactories of mind [*d'esprit*], as much good as bad."[208] They became sites of commercial as well as cultural mediation, places in which, for ever-larger parts of particularly urban populations, foreign goods and institutions were adapted for local consumption—which, as soon will be clear, was precisely the role intellectually adopted by the Academy of Fisticuffs.[209]

Coffee shops would eventually crystallize as primary vehicles for the establishment of a learned and politicized "public sphere," to follow Jürgen Habermas's categorization.[210] They were, as numerous studies by now have demonstrated, privileged centers for the polite dissemination and digestion of information, the favorite place to read newspapers, debate, and, of course, engage in espionage.[211] As the Seven Years' War dawned in Italy, it was therefore natural to find a Venetian spy reporting that "all that is done in coffee shops and meeting places is discussing the present war between the King of Prussia and the Empress."[212] Coffee drinkers were generally understood and expected to have a penchant for politics, leading to decades of attempts by governments to monitor and control public debates in cafés.[213] But coffee shops were not only premier institutions for disseminating and channeling information, voluntarily or not. They were, as the *Encyclopédie* recognized, also institutions for its creation, not unlike what Bruno Latour called "centres of calculation."[214] And though it has recently been argued that "the characteristic form" of Enlightenment "café knowledge" was "satire," many contemporaries identified coffee with the pursuit of rather more applicable expertise.[215] Particularly, scholars have long acknowledged coffee's crucial role in shaping new forms of business behavior in early modern Europe, with coffeehouses serving, for example, as havens for looser associations based on insurance and brokering as well as formal banking.[216]

But just as coffee stimulated economic affairs on the level of individuals, so writers soon began to see it assisted in such matters on the aggregate level as well. As a cerebral lubricant facilitating both business acumen and more academic pursuits, identified not only with respectability but also sociability of a political kind, and taken to be a symbol of economic globalization and rising European global hegemony, it should, for both cultural and tropismatic reasons, not be surprising that coffee quickly came to be representative of the newly fashionable science of political economy. The Venetian libertine and economic writer Giacomo Casanova, for example, met with the adventurer and writer Ange Goudar in coffee shops to compose many of the fictitious letters making up their celebrated *The Chinese Spy,* an acute vivisection of domestic conditions and international relations in contemporary Europe. And both thought that there was an intrinsic link between these new institutions of sociability and public debate, on the one hand, and the emergence of political economy as a science of public happiness and international competition, on the other. It was in the coffeehouses of London, they wrote, that the English "genius for public oeconomy" was located, and whence "they settle the affairs of Europe."[217]

The Fisticuff Republic

Casanova and Goudar's idealized encounter of coffee culture and political economy was comparable to that through which Verri's coterie sought to shape the Milanese Enlightenment. Energized and optimistic to the core, they set about changing the world—leaflet by leaflet—with almost exhausting brio. "Everything," as one of the group's members put it, "can be improved."[218] The immediate motivation for the publication of their journal *Il Caffè* was explicitly Verri's wish, echoing the penchant for libertine reformism he had refined in the army, to "spread some useful notions among our fellow citizens and entertain them, in much the same way as, elsewhere, on [Richard] *Steele* and [Jonathan] *Swift* and [Joseph] *Addisson* [*sic*] and [Alexander] *Pope* and others have done."[219] Addison and Steele's extraordinarily influential daily paper *The Spectator,* originally published in the 1710s, reached Italy through French translations and inaugurated there, as it did everywhere, a wildly popular genre of reporting on fictitious encounters and debates in often imaginary spaces.[220] Not only was the "plan" of the *Spectator* "laid and concerted (as all other Matters of Importance are) in a Club," meeting twice a week "for the Inspection of all such Papers as may contribute to the Advancement of the Publick Weal," precisely as Verri hoped the Academy of Fisticuffs would, but among the many places habitually visited by the anonymous Spectator was a special coffee shop: "I appear on Sunday Nights at St. James's Coffee-House," the "Spectator" character announces in his first dispatch, "and sometimes join the little Committee of Politicks in the Inner-Room, as one who comes there to hear and improve."[221]

The virtual Academy and the journal they published seem to have drawn their principal inspiration from *The Spectator*'s weekly debates over political issues in London's St. James's Coffee House as well as the more learned Grecian in Devereux Court, a hybrid space of politicized knowledge that, in translation, became their whole world.[222] In the words of Alessandro Verri, "it seems an enterprise most worthy of this age of enlightenment that, after having discovered the laws of gravity and of motion, and having almost subjugated nature to human inquiry, we should think, however tardily, of making laws for ourselves."[223] Indeed, *Il Caffè* revolved entirely around a romanticized Milanese coffee shop, Caffè del Greco, supposedly owned by a Greek immigrant named Demetrius (plausibly also an inside reference to London's Grecian or to the famous Caffè Demetrio in Pavia, or, for that matter, both), who, as was appropriate given the exotic tastes and expectations of contemporary coffee consumers, was dressed in "oriental" garb and had seen "entire fields covered in coffee" in "Arabia." The historically existing Caffè del Greco, situated centrally on the Piazza del Duomo in central Milan, was fictionalized and memorialized by Verri and, much like Caffè Florian, was tastefully "decorated with the greatest riches and elegance," serving "a coffee truly worthy of the name."[224] "A truly authentic [*vero verissimo*] coffee from the Levant, scented with aloeswood. Anyone who tastes that coffee, no matter how grave the man or leaden in his spirit, will necessarily come alive and for half an hour at least become a reasonable person."[225] Coffee was the drink of innovation, reason, and of knowledge, of melioration and of communication—and *Il Caffè* was a drink and a site through which their generation found an identity and a voice in opposition to their patrician origins, as well as an exhilarating if momentary sense of the world's inherent malleability, not unlike what rock music gave the 1960s in large parts of Europe and North America.[226]

"A coffeehouse," the imaginary Demetrius himself wrote in the article that concluded the first volume of *Il Caffè*, "is a true encyclopaedia on occasion, so very universal [*universalissima*] is the series of things that happen to be discussed." To facilitate reasoned intercourse, Demetrius's coffee shop had "comfortable chairs," and the air was, implicitly in opposition to the ostensibly rowdy vulgarity of alcoholic drinking establishments, filled with a scent that "always consoles."[227] The German philosopher Georg Wilhelm Friedrich Hegel would later equate the coercive seductiveness of "the enlightenment" with a "perfume."[228] In Milan, enlightenment was the aroma of freshly ground coffee, suggested also by Beccaria's playful early essay "Fragment on Smells" for *Il Caffè*, which amid satirical reveries and a vague sentiment of science fiction pointed to how rare it was to find sanctuaries of refined and pleasant smells in eighteenth-century urban life. He even emphasized the contribution of fragrances to "public happiness" and the "public good," identified, in a deeply utilitarian but also egalitarian fashion he shared with

Pietro Verri, as "the greatest sum of pleasures divided equally among the greatest number of men." Not only were refined smells to be popularized and rendered democratic in light of a utilitarian and sensationist moral philosophy, they were a cardinal aspect of civilization once men left the state of nature:

> After having ceased to do battle with the necessities of life and having overcome the barriers that savage nature placed in the way of their pleasures, all men turned to cultivating the body and transforming it in some way, seeking to multiply agreeable sensations and giving new life to their senses.[229]

Strikingly also in the context of contemporary symbolic usages of light and darkness as metaphors of civility, progress, or barbarity, the café at night was "lit [*illuminata*], so the Iris sparkles everywhere, reflected in the mirrors and crystal hung from the walls and in the centre of the room."[230] *Il Caffè*, to return to Michelet's dictum, was literally Enlightenment.[231]

Like a beacon of civilization, the center, the essence of the coffee shop itself illuminated and enfragranced its patrons, shielding them from the putrid darkness outside. As Verri had envisioned the goal of *Il Caffè*'s publication in a diary entry of October 31, 1764, it was to "increase the enlightenment [*i lumi*] and the culture of our countrymen [*de' nazionali*]."[232] Or, as he put it in private correspondence the following year, "In our coffeehouse we will always make every effort to attack the nation's barbarism with the most powerful weapons at our disposal."[233] The materials they discussed though, he maintained, "interest humanity" entire.[234] Appropriately, the coffeehouse also offered its customers a multitude of newspapers bringing information from around the continent, "thanks to which people who were formerly Romans, Florentines, Genoese or Lombards are now all, more or less, Europeans." And in order for patrons to follow the consequences of the information they gathered, there was, "moreover, a good atlas" there, "to settle the questions that arise from the new politics [*politiche*]."[235] It was in this vein that Verri, in his later work on political economy, would insist on keeping the movement of printed books on the subject free of tariffs.[236]

Among Demetrius's many virtual customers was the Academy of Fisticuffs, "a small society of friends" driven by the "ambition" to "promote and increasingly induce the Italian people toward the spirit of reading, toward an esteem for the sciences and the fine arts and, more importantly, toward the love of virtue, honesty and a sense of duty." The patriotic group was animated by *"self-love, but a self-love useful to the public."*[237] The notion of self-love was one of the most zealously debated ideas in Enlightenment Europe, and often in light of a widespread and largely French-inspired dichotomy between "amour de soi," or self-preservation, and "amour propre," or self-love.[238] Different theorists, from seventeenth-century French Jansenist theologians through the Dutch émigré physician Bernard Mandeville to Rousseau and Adam Smith, made the interplay of these definitions central parts of their theoretical constructs, paving the way for what scholars have dubbed "Enlightened self-love," or essentially the notion that "egoism" could be "directed through reason to selfless ends."[239] Mandeville had emphasized the need for "Dextrous Politicians" to not merely "turn and divert the Course of Trade which way they please," but also, in his famous phrase, turn "Private Vices" into "Publick Benefits."[240] Verri frequently referred to Mandeville's paradox in his early writings, and though there can be no doubt that he generally put his regulatory faith in legislation, his piece in *Il Caffè* at least suggests that he conceived of private agencies contributing to this process of socialization and fruitful channeling of self-love toward the common good.[241] In his later *Meditations on Political Economy,* he would reiterate that "the private interest of each individual, *when it coincides with the public interest,* is always the surest guarantor of public happiness."[242]

The members of the Academy of Fisticuffs, in short, were well aware of ongoing European debates over the the role of self-interest in sociability, but never truly engaged with it in a sophisticated manner beyond the point of acknowledging that there were private interests as well as public interests, that the two did not always coincide, and that one of the principal tasks of politics but also of civil society therefore was to ensure their synergy. That said, they clearly formulated a preference for what Charles L. Schultze with time would come to call "the public use of private interest"—that is, a regulatory preference for harnessing the incentives of regulatees to further regulatory goals.[243] For, as *Il Caffè* put it, "What is certain is that self-interest, that is, the hope of riches and greater pleasures, is what drives all worldly action."[244] However, none of the Academy's members ever suggested that individual self-interest *automatically* might contribute to or tend toward social welfare. Their "faith" in the positive aggregate consequences of unrestrained individual actions was, as such, weaker than that of many of their more famous Scottish contemporaries.[245]

This might also be explained in relation to their censorial context, as it was difficult to explore questions of self-interest and sociability in eighteenth-century Europe without eventually touching upon problems of theology or upsetting political authorities. Verri himself had suffered Kaunitz's ire in the early 1760s, and he therefore explained that the "pen" with which the Fisticuffs' debates were recorded was guided by "an honest liberty worthy of Italian citizens," which kept a "total silence on sacred matters," and which "never neglected the respect that every prince, every government, and every nation deserves."[246] This was pretty much all the liberty that it was legal to pursue in Austrian Lombardy, with the aim of procuring "what good we can for our fatherland." And the group was not afraid to act on this principle, self-censoring a number of articles and leaving some entirely unpublished.[247] Though *Il Caffè's* authors were careful readers of Montesquieu, for example, they rarely touched upon their master's favored subject of how to compare and contrast forms of government.[248] And as for the ever-vexing question of defining "political liberty," Verri argued guardedly, and only during the second year of publication, "By the term *'political liberty'* I mean the belief that every citizen has of possessing their person and that which is theirs, and being able to dispose of them as they wish, insofar as they do not transgress laws enacted by legitimate authority."[249]

Yet Pietro Verri's anonymous character nonetheless defined himself as "born and raised in *Italy*."[250] Already from the outset, then, the Academy of Fisticuffs was an institution of multiple allegiances: to its local home of Milan; to a cultural ideal of "Italy" encompassing its various polities; to Austria and more specifically the Habsburg Empire; to Europe and, farther afield, to the quickly developing network of intercontinental trade to which it ironically owed its precious elixir of reason; and of course ultimately to humanity itself, to what the famous Swiss jurist and diplomat Emer de Vattel so aptly had called "the universal society of the human race."[251]

Commercial Societists

In the wake of Gianni Francioni's careful reconstruction, we know that *Il Caffè* was published in short periodical pamphlets every ten days between

June of 1764 and May 1766, collected in two volumes published during the summers of 1765 and 1766 respectively. The first year saw the publication of 36 pamphlets, the second 38, for a total of 74, containing nearly 140 different pieces of writing of dramatically varying lengths, the vast majority signed with a not always coherent cypher that, at the time, was meant to be anonymous ("A." for Alessandro Verri, for example, and "C." usually for Cesare Beccaria). Although the journal's contributors were many, it is undeniable that the Verri brothers did most of the actual work. In purely quantitative terms, Beccaria wrote a total of 7 identified articles, Alessandro Verri 31, and Pietro Verri at least 53. At a time when few books saw print runs of more than a few hundred, *Il Caffè* had an initial run of five hundred, with a yearly subscription cost of one Milanese scudo for the periodical pamphlets. Given this coin's official equivalence with the Conventionsthaler of the Holy Roman Empire, this would mean that the cost weighed in at an ideal 23.39 grams of silver. At a time when, as Robert C. Allen has shown, nominal daily wages for a building craftsman in Milan averaged about 5.4 grams of silver, a manual laborer would have had to work for four days and a morning to afford a subscription to the Fisticuffs' journal, and more than a week for the whole run.[252] By contrast, the previously mentioned cup of coffee in a neighborhood coffe shop in Venice at the time cost 5 soldi, of which there were 120 to the scudo.[253] A year's subscription to *Il Caffè*, in other words, came to no more than 24 such cups of coffee, or two cups a month. Taking Beccaria's own yearly salary of 3,000 lire, or 500 scudi, as professor of political economy in 1768 as a point of comparison, his daily wages would have been slightly more than 32 times that of a building craftsman. Even discounting his title and familial resources, his was a class of society for whom the cost of accessing the journal *Il Caffè* hardly would have been noticed in the larger economy of coffee shop sociability and consumption.[254]

Although the group wished to reform their polity *in toto* then, to "enlighten the multitude," the price of their publication suggests that the "people" to which they addressed themselves nonetheless belonged to wealthier segments of Milanese society.[255] *Il Caffè* often referred to "Italians," but also to subgroups including "the people," "the simple masses," "the multitude," and, perhaps revealing their most preferred audience of all, the "non-manual citizen," who, Beccaria claimed in justification of the journal, "should *least* ignore" their writings on "agriculture, the arts, commerce and politics."[256] But even though they used a mercantile metaphor to fit the theme of their new niche, the group made it clear that, whoever its immediate readership was, *Il Caffè's* "spreading of enlightenment" and of "useful knowledge" was intended to be universal:

> In the sciences and in letters, and ultimately in every field of human understanding, all sorts of coins are needed: big, small, gold and silver. For just as in a state it is necessary to descend from large gold coins to those of copper or silver so that everyone is included in commerce, such that whoever cannot spend a gold dobla can spend a silver papal coin instead, so it should be in the sciences. Let all men, if it be possible, participate in the sciences; let the commoner know one tenth of what the enlightened man knows; let the craftsman know three times as much as the commoner; let the merchant know more than the craftsman; and, finally, let every living being know something more than just eating, drinking, sleeping, yawning and bothering his neighbor, the gifts of which mostly come quite marvelously with a life free of misery and need.[257]

Everyone, in short, should benefit from "enlightenment," though different classes of society would do so to different degrees and at different times. And, however empowering in principle, the patriarchal, even patronizing tenor of Verri's agenda was hard to miss: "One should be more humane toward that so great, so despised and so unhappy part of men called the common people [*volgo*]."[258]

Not surprisingly, one of the central preoccupations of the Academy of Fisticuffs in the early 1760s was what they called "the spirit of society," which they hoped to strengthen and promote through political economy, penal reform, and cultural work alike. A number of their essays pondered the exact meaning of the term "society," along with how to reform society, and these and related questions are some of the recurring themes that gave unity to the entire enterprise of *Il Caffè*. To begin with, the group clearly believed humanity to be imbued with what, in a discussion of Pufendorf, Alessandro Verri called a "propensity for society" or peaceful association, though in a far weaker form than what had been suggested by many previous theorists of natural law. Verri ridiculed the notion that "man" could be considered "a social animal," for "society," his argument echoed Hobbes, was essentially "united" by "force and fear."[259] Sociability therefore had to be carefully learned, nurtured, and scaffolded even after the state of nature was overcome, for "men" never truly transcended the "tigers" they harbored inside.[260] Left to their own devices, people would kill not merely each other but, strikingly, their very environment:

> Is man civilized, is man tame? He is savage, carnivorous, a depopulator of the earth to prepare extravagantly exquisite feasts that shorten his very short life. Governments are compelled to prohibit, by penal laws, hunting and fishing at times when animals procreate because tame, civilized man would otherwise eat everything.[261]

So negative was his idea of human nature that, he argued, "being a spectator of humankind is to watch a tragedy unfold; there is who most rightly said that the history of men is the history of their crimes."[262]

Chapter 2 will turn more explicitly to the group's work on penal and economic reform, but it may be valuable to first shed light on what sort of "society" the Fisticuffs in the end envisaged operating in and, importantly, *upon*. Quintessentially, the group saw itself inhabiting and championing a "commercial" and "modern" form of society that furthered "prosperity" and "sociability" through "communications, trade and freedom of enterprise." Indeed, work lay at the very core of their "society." As an imaginary dialogue about China published in *Il Caffè* put it,

> Far from providing men with a free subsistence, the principles of healthy government advise not to remove the need to work for a living and to leave them the constant spur of industry. Filling individuals' grain stores and dispensing them from work is not the best thing to do; rather abundance should be kept firmly in their sight, so that to work for a living is always necessary, but never futile.[263]

As such, sociability resulted not from charity but from the belief, or hope, that individuals could improve their condition through meritocratic engagements in the labor nexus. Again it must be emphasized that there was nothing automatic about this. Dark passions had to be channeled toward constructive pursuits; legislators had to ensure that popular hopes of economic improvement were feasible. As later chapters will elucidate, reforms had to set the stage for the process of commercial sociability to take hold and grow by legal and economic means. It was toward this aim that Count Alfonso Longo published one of the most damning contemporary critiques of Old Regime primogeniture laws in *Il Caffè*, arguing in favor of a more mobile and meritocratic economic system in which labor was freer and in which nobility would be acquired on the basis of excellence alone and cease to be hereditary. In short, he argued, in clear opposition to Montesquieu's influential thesis regarding the need for a separation of powers to secure "liberty," that the absolute monarchy had to be cleansed of ancestral privileges and corrupting intermediary bodies alike.[264] Longo's vision could serve as a thesis statement for the Academy of Fisticuffs itself, and is worth quoting at length:

> The sole aim of the lawmaker is, of course, public happiness . . . It must be assured that pleasure is enjoyed not only by the few, but rather should be spread as much as possible among all subjects, just as wealth and comfort must not be concentrated in the hands of the few, thus abandoning the most necessary and numerous part of the population to pitiful destitution. I know that, in a civil society, distinctions of rank and condition ought to be admitted, but I also know that the provident lawmaker will act so that money passes from the hands of the rich to those of the poor, so as to ensure that even the lowliest commoner can share in the goodness of government, in the abundance of wealth, and in the profits of commerce. *The inequality of humans, so loathsome to the poor, may well be the terrible though necessary outcome of civil society, but the law must make such differences more tolerable, protect the common people, and induce them to work in the hope of attaining wealth and a life of greater comfort.* Indeed, the wheels of government should be so well oiled that only the idle are left poor, that is, those who are completely useless and only a burden on society. To achieve this end, it is indispensable that all honors and riches are given as rewards for industriousness, so that only those who are of service to the country, by their virtue or by commerce, are distinguished from the common people.[265]

Only through such reforms could the virtues of commercial society truly be unleashed, but *Il Caffè* remained adamant that, for the sake of sociability and public happiness, there had to be limits to the material consequences of "trade and freedom of enterprise," that is, to economic inequality. As Pietro Verri put it in his "Considerazioni sul lusso" (Considerations on luxury), "Public happiness means the greatest possible happiness divided among the greatest possible number of people. If, therefore, wealth and land can be owned, then the first and foremost of human rights demands that wealth and land be divided amongst the greatest possible number of people in a nation."[266] Historically, he thought, "the Israelite's Jubilee year and the agrarian laws of Ancient Rome," two of the perhaps most important historical *exempla* of economic redistribution, "were a direct emanation of these enlightened principles," but though they had found "their origin in the very nature of human society," he did not wish to "imply that those laws continue to be institutions good and worthy of being adopted in the circumstances in which Europe finds itself at present."[267] Ancient Israel and Rome had sought, for different reasons, to limit "commerce," falling back on "theocracy" and a "republican, religious and warrior spirit," respectively, to sustain their societies. In contemporary Europe, however, where "enlightenment finally, day by day, is distancing humans from their ancient savagery," there was no doubt that "industry" was "increasingly important as the only driving force remaining to stop the souls of languorous Europeans from sliding into that mortal lethargy that leaves the provinces barren and depopulated."[268] Now, property had to be simultaneously defended and delimited. The fundamental dilemma in commercial societies, in short, was how to encourage meritocratic economic incentives without allowing structural inequality to undermine the very sociability on which the process depended; economic forces were both the lifeblood of commercial society and, possibly, its fatal flaw.[269]

Good Company

A similar tension also informed *Il Caffè*'s articles on individual social relations. For there could indeed, as Rosalind put it in Shakespeare's *As You Like It,* be "too much of a good thing."[270] A right balance had to be struck between individuality and sociability, self-regard and public happiness, and one should be weary of the "two extremes" of any such spectrum. "Perhaps," Alessandro

Verri even mused, "the moderns are too sociable."[271] Indeed, beyond juris-prudence and political economy, sociability also had to be encouraged cul-turally, through new norms and habits befitting of society as it evolved through time. The members of the Academy went about this in various ways—partly, and almost by default, through their adopted genre and style of presentation. Several of their contributions proclaimed the virtues of "po-liteness," "civility," "urbanity and social law," not to mention the need for a "certain jargon shared by all sociable beings" to minimize conflicts and socialize "people in the place of fear." And, of course, their very mode of writing, their coffeeshop phantasmagoria, and their frequent appeals to "wit" served precisely this purpose.[272] The literature on the importance of polite-ness and wit in eighteenth-century salon culture is vast and expanding, but the Academy of Fisticuffs offers a remarkable example of what this project ultimately could be about, and what it sought to achieve.[273] It is worth noting that, drawing on the group's utilitarian inclinations in an analysis of "good company," Pietro Verri obliquely approached questions related to forms of government after all:

> However, for us to form a universal and clear idea of the essence of good company, let us first look at the purpose for which it is formed. Men obey the need to spend some hours of the day in company in order to have a good time. Thus, it follows as a consequence that *good company* is that from which the greatest number of men part feeling content. Good company, therefore, must resemble demo-cratic government more than any other; perhaps it can also exist under the aspects of a clement aristocracy, perhaps it can be found in the form of a moderate monarchy, but if despotism or anarchy are introduced, good company cannot be hoped for.[274]

Such "democratic" and relatively egalitarian "good company" was, of course, bound to include not merely men but also women, and several ar-ticles in *Il Caffè* touched upon what, by the 1760s, had become a sustained discourse in Italy about the appropriate role for women in society.[275]

In broad terms, the group was at the progressive forefront of women's rights at a time when such rights were few and women were subject to vio-lence of every type, from the rhetorical to the physical.[276] As Alessandro Verri observed, "we must be very proud if we believe that women are inferior to men in reason."[277] At the same time, there is little evidence that the pugilists themselves lived up to this ideal in a sustained fashion. Women were clearly an important part of the everyday life of the Academy of Fisticuffs, and Verri declared that he owed his "love of books" to his first lover, Maria Vittoria Ottoboni Boncompagni. But there is no trace of any intellectual exchange at all in the epistolary leading up to his marriage to his niece Maria Castiglioni, which instead conveyed a sense of restrained sexualized paternalism. Verri vacillated between lengthy expositions about her future allowance ("for your wardrobe I will pay 2,500 lire a year"), complaints about his family, and declarations that "you are and will be my delight," where she, often with notable orthographic errors, would write only short missives along the lines of

> Dear Pietro your Marietta does not live for anything but you, and desires nothing but your affection, my dear tell me that you will love me forever, I will have the happiness of being liked by you until I die, yes I do because you already know me intimately, and if I have the fortune of not being disliked by you presently, I can hope that you will always have the same feelings for me. My dear soul I hug you I desire for you all the happiness that a soul like you deserves.[278]

Their relationship would be worthy of a separate study, but, whatever it was, equal it was not.

The Fisticuffs' longest engagement with the issue of the role of women in society, in Sebastiano Franci's article "Difesa delle donne" (A defense of women), sheds light on some of these tensions.[279] Repeating a tired litany of grievances about the opposite sex, Franci noted that "endless complaints are made in Europe against women and their idle and lax lifestyles that are completely useless to human society."[280] This "negative" portrait, he admitted, "does, in truth, closely resemble the original," but the fault lay not with "the sex itself," but rather with "ourselves," that is with men: "because we are the ones who point them in that gloomy way and compel them to walk down that muddy path."[281] If only "we took the trouble of educating their minds and presenting them good ideas," he argued with well-intentioned paternalism, "they would perfectly match our wishes and become that noble half which they were intended to be."[282] This, in his eyes, would have consequences well beyond education in arts and the natural sciences, for "adjustment of mind will persuade women that management and the household economy are within their competence; that work, being a universal necessity, is not beneath them, whatever their rank." Not only would such efforts improve the lives of women themselves; women "would be of eminent utility to the state."[283]

Women, Franci argued, were "organized more delicately" than men, seemingly underscoring their essential difference, but he also believed that "their delicateness is accidental," the product of a male-dominated society. Under different circumstances the female sex would be "perfectly capable of surpassing men" even in the "sphere of heroic virtues," including those "which belong to the virile soul, such as great generosity and military valor."[284] Looking back into the annals of "history," he gave copious examples of women of all ages demonstrating the most virile forms of virtue, including a memorable one involving "a young girl of tender age" who, during an Ottoman siege of the Hungarian city of Eger, saw her mother "struck and put to death by a cannonball," only to lift a "stone, warm with her mother's blood," and turn it against the assailants.[285] But, Franci concluded sycophantically, why "look to the histories for illustrious examples of female virtue" when Maria Theresa of Austria, "her most august imperial majesty," offered "a compendium of all the most eminent virtues—a compendium that is all the more effective for how enlightened and illustrious it is in the eyes of the universe?"[286]

The tone of Franci's essay was resolutely patronizing, expressing many of the patriarchal sentiments against which leading members of the Academy of Fisticuffs had rebelled, but nonetheless, and very much in line with the group's larger worldview, it also imbued men and women with an equal *potential*—for virtue, productive economic work, and even imperial leadership. Perhaps, as Rebecca Messbarger has argued, women were ultimately forced to "serve an economy not of their design" in *Il Caffè*, but, instead of being a problem unique to the female sex, this was true for most people united in society. Indeed, the challenge may be inexorably intertwined with the Milanese reformers' gradualist vision of transforming the "unjust" nature of Old Regime society from above, and demarcates some of the limits of contemporary "enlightenment" in social terms.[287] For sociability to expand, though, and worldly melioration to ensue, it remained that the relations between men and women, and more profoundly between human *beings,* had to be reformed.

Lice of the Universe

Pleasurable socialization, through politeness, wit, and humor, was a key to *Il Caffè*'s goal of transforming society by educating and entertaining its readership, but at first reading the journal seems to have emphasized education over entertainment. This may simply be because, as Robert Darnton and others have reminded us, it can be dastardly to "get" a historical joke, but all the same, as an anonymous letter from a probably fictional reader complained, most of the contributions were indeed "desperately serious" (itself, of course, being a rather droll observation).[288] Nonetheless, some of the pugilists' jocularity successfully transcended their historical moment. Letter sections, for example, would alternate between readers with exactly opposite suggestions; and in a half-joking piece on the virtues of the workaholic Alessandro Verri insisted, "It shall be forbidden to say that 'the desk kills the man'—something I cannot grant if not in the sense of hitting someone over the head with a desk."[289]

Some of the most amusing pieces, however, were more cosmological in nature, demonstrating the complexity both of the Fisticuffs' sense of humor and of the interconnection between the various articles published in their journal. On the surface, a series of technical contributions about Milanese climate, meteorology, and astronomy are among the drier pieces in *Il Caffè*.[290] Yet together they portray a deeply mechanistic view of the universe and of the role of human society in it—a view that, though rarely touching upon issues of religion explicitly, except through relentless critiques of "prejudice" and "superstition," nonetheless resolutely provincialized theology and even humanity as such through a flurry of natural observations, equations, and planetary vistas. In a context in which many still believed they were influenced by celestial phenomena, the Academy of Fisticuffs could not have been more explicit with regard to "the ills caused to society as a whole by this prejudiced belief," by "these feculent remnants of ancient barbarisms." For, beyond its costs for individuals, superstition also had profound economic consequences on a structural level:

Agriculture especially suffers the damage of such prejudices, and often the harvest of both silk and grains is ruined, because instead of considering the season and the mild or humid air, instead of observing atmospheric phenomena, which have a physical and no small influence on the good budding and blooming of agricultural produce, very often rural tasks are performed at the wrong time so as to obey the wishful influences of the moon.[291]

This cosmic and materialist approach to political economy culminated in Alessandro Verri's simultaneously humorous and harrowing critique of "man" as a "rational animal" in *Il Caffè*'s second year of publication:

Were these the trifles, wretched man, imbecilic man, to be learnt from the sight of an immense sky, of an endless host of worlds and from an interminable aggregate of universes? Mud worm—for it is in the mud that you crawl, in comparison, wretch!—this mean figure of yours, *louse of the universe, with the vastitude and magnificence of nature, how dare you draw the clever conclusion that it is all concerned with you?* And that the sun, animator of the world and wonder of the sky, a million times vaster than this ball of yours on which you revolve around it, how could you believe that it was concerned with protecting your right eye when smallpox, cataract, a drop of gout, a pin, a punch leave you half blind? Perhaps it was the persuasion that the universe always watched over humankind that gave the sun and the moon eyes, nose and a mouth, almost as though they were always staring at us benignly from the vault of heaven, with their big faces. Yet every time one turned one's gaze towards them disillusionment was at hand. Such highly amusing notions live in the pineal gland, or in the brain, or in the cerebellum, or in the meninges, or in the pia mater, or in the dura mater, or in the blood, or in the heart—in substance, in the seat of what exists, sure, but which cannot reside or lie in any place, namely, in the fine mind of the admirable human race with the universal applause of the public, for which I declare myself to be the devoted and respectful servant of that self-same race.[292]

Whatever Providence might be, if anything, it could be terrifyingly insouciant about the earth and humanity's fate, and "fortune," as Pietro Verri repeatedly emphasized, was merely "ignorance of the concatenation of the objects that have an immediate influence on men." In his eyes, one of the principal tasks of the Academy of Fisticuffs was therefore to fight ignorance and superstition, for "the more man is enlightened, the lesser the number of events he attributes to fortune."[293]

This conflict between reason and superstition, and the former's vindication in experience, was one of the unifying themes of all of the group's work, and was evident at the outset. The second issue of Il Caffè contained a powerfully symbolic prose poem by a "Petrarchan" poet who visited Demetrius's virtual coffee shop. It described the "Temple of Ignorance," the very antithesis of the group's home, an immense "gothic" structure the entrance of which was flanked by two statues turning their backs on each other in spite; their names were "Teorica" and "Pratica," "Theory" and "Practice." The walls of the Temple were "covered with various paintings and extravagant implements," including "racks and torture instruments of all kinds" as well as "depictions of shipwrecks and civil wars." Inside its harlequinesque halls, a shriveled old hag proclaimed incessantly: "Youth, youth, listen to me, do not trust yourselves, what you feel inside you is nothing but illusion. Mark the words of the old, and trust their deeds"; a "decrepit old man" shrieked, "Youth, youth, reason is a chimera!" And in a large cavern underneath, "those unshaven and unwashed learned scholars [eruditi]" performed rote memorization, "believing themselves to be alone in the world in possessing an intimate knowledge of the true science" and burning, in a yearly ritual, the works of Francis Bacon, Galileo Galilei, Isaac Newton, Montesquieu, and the French philosophe Étienne Bonnot de Condillac, something akin to an Enlightenment all-stars lineup.[294]

Cosmicism and the Fatherland

The first of many probably fictitious letters to the editors published in Il Caffè, which appeared right after the "Temple of Ignorance," underlined Verri's point by praising the Academy for benefiting the "patria," or "fatherland," because the project of presenting "the public with useful truths, stripping them of all magisterial tedium, is an enterprise worthy of true philosophers

and upstanding citizens." The members of the Fisticuffs replied to this by encouraging their readers to submit articles for *Il Caffè*, emphasizing that "talented youths," the very phrase by which Verri had described his fledgling
group two years earlier, should "come forward, and they will not be judged
by their audacity, or their name, or their dress."[295] As in Kaunitz's contemporary meritocratic reforms for Austrian Lombardy, what ultimately
mattered was talent freely employed in the cause of the common good, in as
open a competition as possible.

Hence the coterie's ruthless war on some of the ostensibly stymying
institutions of Italian economic and literary culture, and particularly the
habit of rejecting foreign vocabularies in an attempt to maintain the purity
of a Dantean language. As Alessandro Verri argued on the pages of *Il Caffè*,
"For if by Italianizing French, German, English, Turkish, Greek, Arabic,
and Slavonic words we can render our ideas better, we shall not refrain
from doing so out of fear."[296] And this was explicitly not a merely Milanese
or Lombard program: "We declare that we shall use in our paper the language that is understood by learned men from Reggio di Calabria to the
Alps, such are the borders that we have set ourselves, with full discretion
to fly on occasion across seas and mountains to take what is good wherever
it is," including, of course, coffee. The group may have been eminently
grounded in its local context, but it identified with the Italian peninsula
and embraced exchanges with the world entire. This because the members
of the Academy of Fisticuffs, in their own words, were "extremely jealous
of what little liberty left to a social given all the laws, all the duties, and all
the chains with which he is burdened"—that is, in the political state after
humankind had left the state of nature. To encourage what liberty they
could, they therefore gave "the broadest permission to every kind of living
being, from the insect to the whale, to express their good or bad opinion of
our writing," a statement that echoed in the group's several critiques of
anthropocentrism.[297]

At the time, then, the group sought to convert, not merely the few and
the erudite, but instead an ever-growing class of meritocratic educated young
citizens—men and remarkably women—intimately bound, with cultural and
economic bonds, not only to their immediate "fatherland" and to their Austrian masters, but also to a system of international commerce exemplified
by their drink of choice: coffee.[298] The Fisticuffs' justification for engaging

with a wide, freely debating public through the medium of political economy, the primary means of renewing the fatherland, was penned by Pietro Verri:

> I believe it is a good thing that many write and think about the true interests of a nation, about finance, trade, and agriculture. Mist and mystery serve the impunity of the few and the wretchedness of the many. It is a good thing for the facts of political economy to be known, hence it is a good thing that many think about them, for from the ferment of various opinions the truth will increasingly be separated out and made simple. Anyone who provides us with reasonable writings on these matters will always find an honored place in this journal.[299]

Unlike traditional forms of reason of state, to which, as Kaunitz had made clear to Verri, parts of the Habsburg administration still adhered, and which, like contemporary criminal law, drew power from the secrecy of its theory and practice, eighteenth-century political economy increasingly found its identity in being a publically debated science of economic life.[300] As an enterprise, the Academy of Fisticuffs contributed to the fulfillment of all the "institutional criteria" outlined by Habermas for the emergence of a "public sphere" during the Enlightenment.[301] But when one then considers that authoritative voices have defined, as Verri himself had, political economy as the principal preoccupation of "the Enlightenment," some questions beg to be answered: What relation did these two driving concerns have to one another?[302] In short, how did a coffee culture fomenting sociability and public debate interact with the development of political economy in Austrian Lombardy? And how, one might further ask, did this interaction in turn play into the tangible tensions between patriotism and cosmopolitanism, between universal ideals and local constraints, that so vexed eighteenth-century Europe? Scholars have, of course, offered answers to these questions before, for the cases of Europe in general as well as for Lombardy in particular, but the following discussion will diverge from common avenues of interpretation and simplification colored by the experiences of the Cold War. Rather than subject them to the Procrustean bed of more recent ideologies, with their Manichaean conception of planning and laissez-faire, autarky and cosmopolitanism, Chapter 2 will embark on a more rigorous archaeology of the economic, legal, and political ideas actually propagated by the Fisticuffs in the mid-1760s to excavate the substance of their theories, policy proposals, and administrative efforts.[303]

Beyond the almost universal wish of scholars to locate antecedents of current economic ideals in the eighteenth century, recent historiography has at length emphasized the importance in early modern Europe of self-fashioning, whether autobiographically, sartorially, or gastronomically.[304] This makes for often colorful (literally) and theoretically sophisticated stories, but it also risks weaving histories that—if one cares at all about history's disciplinary pretensions to understand what the past was *like*—may sideline pertinent aspects of the historical record. Emma C. Spary's fascinating work *Eating the Enlightenment,* to take merely one recent and very fine example, marshals the current historiography of science to offer an insightful "poststructuralist reading of the ways in which individuals employ foods for self-fashioning," but neither dearth, nor famine, nor grain, to mention three of the cardinal exits on the foodways of the Enlightenment, make more than a fleeting appearance in her text, let alone in her index.[305] Given what we know of *Il Caffè*'s publication schedule, Verri and Beccaria probably spent less than an afternoon, however caffeinated, writing the self-fashioning pieces on their imaginary coffee shop; yet they would literally spend thousands of hours, over several decades, anxiously calibrating the measures by which the Milanese state regulated economic life within its borders and ensured its citizenry's subsistence in relation to the cultivation, production, marketing, and processing of grain under dynamic and often highly unpredictable conditions of dearth, abundance, and contraband.

Coffee certainly transformed from an exotic novelty into a formative if complex and segmented staple of consumption in eighteenth-century Europe, and though it was indubitably *thought* to be somehow representative of, even foundational for, the age, its importance in the economic and gastronomic imagination of Enlightenment Europe can all too easily be exaggerated. Self-fashioning and political economy were clearly related for the Academy of Fisticuffs, most obviously through the group's wildly successful efforts to ingratiate themselves with Habsburg authorities in pursuit of posts in the civil administration through their journal, but it cannot be ignored that its members' careers mostly would be dedicated to historiographically far less interesting—and far harder to survey—questions of bureaucratic routine and legislation. And a sustained engagement with their sometimes-conflicting economic ideas and policies make it clear that none of them embraced an ideology of cosmopolitan laissez-faire or, in its modern shorthand, "free trade," any more than they heralded a planned economy.[306] They were indeed prophets of commercial society and with time even criticized as "socialist" and praised as "capitalist," but the granularity of their project to bring such a thing about amply testifies to the nuance and complexity of their criminological visions and political economies alike. And if the members of the Academy of Fisticuffs at times relied on satire as a weapon, their aims and intentions in wielding it were deadly serious. *Qua* drink and *qua* journal, *Il Caffè* was a means to an end, not an end in itself.

CHAPTER TWO

Capital (and) Punishment

—————⟶⟫●⟪—————

T HE FIRST AND BEST-KNOWN ARTICLE of political economy published in *Il Caffè* was Pietro Verri's "Elementi de Commercio" (Elements
of Commerce), the bibliographical history of which has been obfuscated by
the author's aggressive autobiographical revisionism. Too proud to acknowledge his influences, Verri pretended to have composed the short piece "in
Vienna before reading the authors active in the field" in spite of his evident
familiarity with, among others, a number of works recently published in
Paris—partly original compositions, partly translations of prominent English and Spanish authors—by the circle of Jacques Claude Marie Vincent de
Gournay, Intendant du Commerce under Louis XV, and of course conversations with his companion-in-arms Henry Lloyd.[1] His encounter with the
latter, in particular, and the formative friendship that followed, provided
Verri not only with new armaments in the ongoing generational conflict
with his father and the institutions of Old Regime Milan, but significantly
with new theoretical tools for economic theorizing derived from mathematics and military science. While Verri's "Elements" drew on a broad
European tradition of thinking about the relationship between commerce,
welfare, and independence to a far greater extent than he was willing to confess, his friendship with Lloyd and personal wartime experiences allowed

him to inflect contemporary theories with powerful results. The short essay would in fact propose, in embryonic form, many of the key theorems and preoccupations of Milanese political economy over the next few decades.[2]

Verri introduced the article to the readers of *Il Caffè* as a contribution sent in by one of their readers, who tellingly signed himself "Filantropo" (Philantropist); and it was, in the spirit of the Fisticuffs' endeavor, presented as "even more populist [*popolari*] than those of Mr. Forbonnai[s], since those of the illustrious Frenchman are greater and more philosophical than mine."[3] He thus mentioned François Véron Duverger de Forbonnais, an acolyte of Gournay and one of Europe's most celebrated political economists, in the metatext of the "Elements" to highlight the Academy's resonance with the new transalpine fashion for political economy, without undermining the originality of the Italian contribution.[4] *Il Caffè* consciously partook in the economic turn that was affecting all of Europe, but it is worth resting briefly on the specific works that influenced it. The members of Verri's group did not, for example, draw on the increasing output of the Parisian "sect" of economic writers known as Physiocrats.[5] Rather, reconstructing Verri's readings at the time, it is clear that, though aware of the work of Quesnay and his followers, he engaged with a far broader, more pragmatic, and historically informed set of texts from across Europe. Most of them reached him in French editions or intermediary translations. Verri's authorities ranged from the Physiocrats' nemesis, Forbonnais, in Paris through the London merchant Charles King and the best-selling merchant-pamphleteer John Cary in Bristol, who he read in the epic edition prepared by Antonio Genovesi (which readers of *Il Caffè* were warmly encouraged to read), to Jacob Friedrich von Bielfeld in Berlin, Bernardo de Ulloa and Jerónimo de Uztáriz in Madrid, and David Hume in Edinburgh.[6] From a book-historical perspective, this was as close to a canonical reading list of contemporary best-sellers of political economy as one can imagine, though it deviated greatly from the texts long emphasized by the historiography of economics.[7]

Not surprisingly, given its sources, Verri's piece provided a densely argued case for the importance of the new economic science, beginning with a basic taxonomy. He adopted a number of categories for distinguishing between goods and phenomena, in particular differentiating neatly between the "absolute" and "artificial" spheres of economic life. "Absolute needs" belonged to the "natural order of things" and were those required for sheer survival, whereas "relative needs" were the fruits of "belief and wealth," imaginary constructs of commercial society on which the international economic system and his own coffeepot society had come to depend. In a parallel fashion, the concept of "abundance" similarly had two aspects for Verri, one "absolute" and one "relative." A country enjoyed "absolute abundance" when it could trade on the basis of a real economic "surplus," whereas it would only have "relative abundance" if it found itself in a situation in which it had to "surrender" a "lesser need" to a "greater need"— that is, when it had to exchange something it needed for something it needed relatively more. In this latter sense, Verri argued, there was "no nation in contact with others that is without an abundance [of something]." Though far from "anticipating" a theory of comparative advantage, he nonetheless presented a model of the world in which all countries could have *something* to gain from international trade.[8] Employing the same vocabulary of "active" and "passive" trades—"trade in surplus" and "trade in deficit"—harnessed by practicing merchants as well as some of the best-selling political economists of the eighteenth century, Verri subsequently explained that an "active" trade could only come from a position of "absolute abundance." This, in turn, depended on policies to encourage domestic economic activities, particularly in high-value-added sectors, along the lines of the time-tested European tradition of (1) encouraging the importation of raw materials and the exportation of manufactured and refined goods, and inversely (2) discouraging the exportation of raw materials and the importation of manufactured and refined goods.[9] It was a scheme that reflected centuries-old Italian as well as English policy, and that had been defended by authors Verri knew well.

In explaining how trade could still flourish in a country not technically in need of anything in "absolute" terms, and why more manufactures would always be beneficial, Verri even came to propose a simple theory of a balance of payments:

> When a nation has more to give than to receive, the remaining difference to its credit is compensated for by money, that standard by which we measure, by the universal consent of nations, human dealings with regard to goods. The remaining difference to be settled in money is called the "balance of trade."[10]

Until the recent sixth edition of the International Monetary Fund's *Balance of Payments Manual,* the "current account" of goods being exchanged was balanced by a corresponding "financial account" in terms conceptually similar to, even if far more technically sophisticated than, Verri's take on the concept of the "balance of trade."[11] International trade, in short, allowed all participating countries to achieve "relative abundance" through "passive" commerce, but only a select few to relish in "absolute abundance" through an "active" trade with the world; and political economy was the science to make this happen.

But more was at stake in international trade for Verri than mere profit margins, for, as he had learned from his readings, economic power had become an existential concern for modern polities:

> A nation that predominantly enjoys an *active commerce* will become, each year by multiplication, master, if not *de jure* then *de facto,* of the nations that have a less vigorous commerce. It is in that way that the nation becomes truly wealthy. . . . Such benefits are, instead, progressively lost to the nation that preponderantly has a *passive commerce,* leading it to destruction. Such trouble will grow exponentially, as the harmful effects become the causes of others, until the nation, reduced to a perfect state of dependence upon its neighbors, and lacking in inhabitants, becomes no good for anything except colonization.[12]

Unlike earlier political paradigms that equated a country's liberty with direct participation in government and freedom from arbitrary power, Verri's readings in the canon of political economy had convinced him that these political exigencies were ultimately trumped by international economic conditions. "When a nation comes to have, on its own, all it requires to satisfy its needs," he therefore argued, "then it will be completely independent from other nations, and need not fear the effects of ruinous commerce."[13]

To truly achieve independence, however, a country had to be either "extremely small" and thus, like ancient Sparta, able to control its people's wants, or "extremely vast" and thus, like the China of his day, able to embrace all necessary resources and labor within its expansive boundaries.[14] Although such independence by necessity would remain an unrealizable ideal for most polities, Verri's preoccupation with geography translated into a very clear preference for concentrated wealth and populations, and a geometric language for expressing it, which would have significant consequences for later developments in Milanese political economy: a "king who commands two million people, scattered across an area of a thousand miles," he argued, "will be at least ten times weaker than a king who commands twenty million people in an area of five hundred miles."[15]

As the principal means of achieving this goal, Verri followed an influential English viewpoint in arguing that one should encourage the development of domestic manufactures even when this would mean that local consumers—at least until costs of production fell with improved skills, technology, and productivity—paid more for their goods than they would have with open access to international suppliers.[16] It was all too easy to exaggerate trade's actual importance, however, and given "the current system in Europe," necessary goods should be secured domestically, in which case "foreign trade would be at a minimum, as the need that drives such trade would be at a minimum." Until nations reached this "perhaps chimerical degree of universal perfection," however, some countries would continue to "profit from the indolence of others, and become wealthy, populous and prosperous at their expense." Not all trade was sweet and civilizing in the eighteenth century, for "every advantage enjoyed by a nation in commerce is a disadvantage for other nations. The study of commerce, which today is spreading, is a true war, waged quietly by the peoples of Europe."[17]

What was needed, this central article in *Il Caffè* argued, were "gradual" reforms aimed at strengthening the industries of Austrian Lombardy, relying on "tariffs" rather than on "prohibitions" to reduce the importation of foreign manufactures and foster domestic ones, thus moving up the proverbial value chain. Quoting the same slogan by Jean-François Melon—who was a French political economist and longtime secretary to John Law, best known for his role in the so-called Mississippi Bubble, a Scottish adventurer-economist, and eventually controller general of finances for France—about commerce requiring "liberty and competition," around which Italy's first professor of political economy Genovesi had written at length, Verri similarly justified tariffs as a premier institution of political economy, for "liberty and competition are the soul of commerce—the liberty, that is, that comes from law, and not from license."[18]

How to Temporize

Theoretical dogmas set aside, what mattered to Verri was the pragmatic success of a policy. As long as laws were clear and not arbitrary, any successful economic policy would be not only acceptable but indeed desirable, regardless of its theoretical venerability or, for that matter, novelty. As Verri put it in a contemporary treatise on tariff reform, "I believe that a reasonable man, when he is tasked with organizing a system, should adopt things not because they are old, or because they are new, but solely because they are true and good."[19] Given the importance of laws and regulations for Verri, not to mention his faith in dictatorial authorities on the model of Sulla as well as in the capacity of young and caffeinated idealists to make a difference in the world, it should not be surprising that his early writings on political economy revolved around the capacity of "good government" and "enlightened legislators" to "direct commerce wisely" and the possibility of bringing qualified experts into the administration, nor that he saw the "natural first step" to reform as the "deputation of zealous, intelligent people" for such tasks. "A million in the hands of an imbecile," he remarked confidently in what might, to suspicious eyes, be thought of as something of a job application with the Habsburg administration, "will do less good to a nation than a mere pen in the hands of a wise minister." He had no doubts that "the great art of the lawmaker" lay in "skillfully directing human greed," fostering "industriousness" by encouraging "emulation" and countervailing the threat of "smuggling"; but if this was not difficult enough, it further required remarkable insight into the local conditions of a polity.[20] For, given the inherent fragility of commercial societies, much could go wrong in matters of political economy:

> Everything in nature happens by degrees. The body politic is a machine, whose various, complicated wheels are not perceivable by the many, nor are they immune to the risk of running awry. Every jolt can be fatal, with the dire consequences revealing to the unwary interrelations of which they were previously unaware. The hand of who is acquainted with the entire machinery is needed. Of the most immediate and universal of plans, the more they dazzle us, the more difficult and dangerous they are to put into practice, and the happi-

ness of a nation is all the more stable when the edifice is built gradually, by degrees.[21]

Verri here placed himself in a very specific tradition of political thought favoring gradual reforms and cumulative improvements over sudden, revolutionary politics.[22] During the eighteenth century, the position was often referred to by the shorthand "nil repente" or "nihil repente," meaning "nothing
suddenly." It would be rendered famous by the Neapolitan political economist Ferdinando Galiani's extraordinarily popular and wide-reaching condemnation of the Physiocrats, his 1771 *Dialogues sur le commerce des bleds*
(Dialogues on the grain trade), in which he repeatedly had urged *"nil repente,* rien tout-à-coup," or "nothing suddenly, nothing all-of-a-sudden."[23]
His point was that one should not rush in matters of economic administration and reform, plausibly drawing inspiration from the Neapolitan historian and philosopher Giambattista Vico, with whose work he was familiar.
In his 1708 *De nostri temporis studiorum ratione,* better known as *On the Study
Methods of Our Times,* Vico had elaborated on a lengthy medical allegory,
concluding "ut dicere audeam, cum nihil repente maximum fiat, vel repen-
tina morte" ("so that it may be said that just as no great event happens all of
a sudden, so nobody really dies of a sudden death").[24] This was, of course,
something of a timeless proposition, and Vico had probably in turn drawn on
the Latin translation of the classical Greek physician Hippocrates of Kos's
Aphorisms II.51, which, utilizing variations of "repente," argued that "Excess
and suddenness . . . is dangerous; in fact all excess is hostile to nature. But
'little by little' is a safe rule, especially in cases of change from one thing
to another."[25]

By the late eighteenth century, however, the phraseology "nil repente"
popularized by Galiani had become explicitly equated not with medicine but
with the "maxims" of Niccolò Machiavelli, plausibly because of, and contributing to, the diminutive Neapolitan's well-known nickname "Il Machiavellino."[26] The Florentine secretary had indeed emphasized throughout his
works, although not always, the need for "temporality" and "prudence," particularly in light of the examples of the "Warrior Pope" Julius II (1443–1513)
and, in his *Dell'arte della guerra* (The art of war), of the Roman dictator Quintus
Fabius Maximus (ca. 280 BCE–203 BCE), whose actions appropriately informed the adjective "Fabian," meaning gradual or cautionary.[27] And it was

in this context that the French consul to the recently established United States, Philippe Joseph Létombe, asked whether it was "suitable to imitate the wisdom of Fabius" in knowing "how to temporize," and informed the French minister of foreign affairs Charles Maurice de Talleyrand-Périgord that then-vice-president Thomas Jefferson "repeats to me incessantly that Machiavelli's maxim 'Nil repente' is the soul of great affairs."[28]

Whatever the ultimate source of Verri's position in the 1760s, he undoubt-edly aligned himself with this careful, measured medico-Machiavellian tradition of political reformism in opposition to the more revolutionary argu-ments, as well as with fundamental trust in the course of nature, of the French Physiocrats. His insistence on the fragility and contingency of political economy rested uneasily alongside its cardinal importance in the modern world, and in Verri's vision only powerful legislators seemed to stand between a polity and outright despair. Clearly, his writings at this point also reflected ambitions to find a post in the Habsburg administration not unlike the one he described so heroically, but whether disingenuously or not, there was no doubt in the "Elements" what the purpose of Verri's new "niche" might be: political economy, even commerce in general, was ultimately about "the pop-ulace" and the cardinal aim of "public happiness," at the expense of which "humanity" did not "permit experiments," and in the name of which "nothing new should ever be attempted if we have no prior evidence of the good out-come of our enterprise."[29] Economic science might be a relative novelty, but it had to be deeply grounded in historical experience and resolutely abstain from dramatic gambles with the economies of polities and the lives of people, not unlike Genovesi's earlier proposition that "economic philosophy" was to be a "harmonious connection" of "recipes" born from accumulated "experi-ence."[30] Verri may not have deployed the phrase "nil repente" itself, but he embraced its principles and spelled out its meaning at great length.

The foundational text in the Academy of Fisticuffs' political economy, in short, laid out a blueprint for development—understood in terms of the com-petitive increase of wealth and happiness for a polity—that contained many of the key architectural characteristics of the group's later work, including a subterranean engagement with the best that Europe had to offer on the sub-ject; the basic differentiation between the natural and the "artificial" (what depended on changing conventions) in social and economic affairs; a clear insight into the dark side of international trade and the Janus-faced nature of commerce; an intrepid trust in the progressive power of legislative reform to navigate these treacherous waters; an insistence on the absolute superiority of manufacturing for economic improvement and political emancipation alike, and the trenchant belief that tariffs and subsidies functioned better than prohibitions to this end; a penchant for mathematical and geometric conceptualizations fused with a deep-seated mistrust of theoretical flourishes not grounded in historical experience; an attempt to bridge the financial sphere and the real economy through a theoretization of money as a form of "universal" good; a preoccupation with smuggling and the connectedness of populations; and a transcendent belief that what ultimately mattered were humanity and public happiness with little if any consideration for the afterlife. All these elements would, in different constellations and with different emphases, profoundly shape the coming decades of Milanese intellectual life and, indeed, some of the central debates of Enlightenment Europe.

Greatness and Decline

While working on this simultaneously despondent and heroic vision of international trade, Verri had composed another, largely overlooked contribution to contemporary debates about political economy, entitled *Considerazioni sul commercio dello stato di Milano* (Considerations on the commerce of the state of Milan), which in its earliest incarnation was titled *Saggio sulla grandezza e decadenza del commercio di Milano sino al 1750* (Essay on the greatness and decline of the commerce of Milan up to 1750), which by virtue of its local focus spoke more directly to his loyalties and those of his group than his *Elements* had. Crucially, it also had a tangible influence on how Verri's collaborators in the Academy mediated the exigencies of patriotism and cosmopolitanism in formulating their political economies. This manuscript, which saw integral publication only in the twentieth century, was divided into three parts. The first part mapped out the economic history of Milan from the fifteenth century to 1750; the second explored the "present state of Milan's commerce"; and the third suggested "means" by which the Milanese economy could be "restored."[31] As a whole, Verri's manuscript sought to map "the fate of this Province from the point of its ancient opulence up until its present depression," echoing what in effect was nothing less than a contemporary obsession with the changing fortunes of the Italian peninsula.[32]

The main point Verri sought to convey in the first part of his unpublished *Considerations* was that Italy, uniquely among European powers, twice had declined from a state of absolute supremacy on the continent, with the fall of Rome and with the rise of unified nation-states at the end of the Renaissance.[33] And it had achieved dominion both through conquest and through commerce. In fact, "Italy's sovereignty over Europe through commerce in the fifteenth century was perhaps greater and more peaceful than it it had been before through arms." The laws of Italy, and of his "fatherland" Milan as part of it, had been extremely conducive to economic development up through the sixteenth century. "With such domestic laws, and with the vicinity to the great commerce of the Venetians, Lombardy was bound to prosper, were it not for the shackles on it, and equally on all of Italy, that were forming, which keep our commerce in a total dependency on the commerce of other Nations." Since that time, the primacy of commerce had migrated around Europe, from the Portuguese to the English via the Dutch and the French, "but it suffices us solely to observe that, *as the commerce of the Italian cities gradually was weakened, Italy, too, was reduced to that dependence in which it formerly kept the rest of Europe.*" Commerce, liberty, and power were in the end one and the same thing in a world of international economic competition, and no hegemony in such a system could be everlasting.

The outcome for Milan was predictable. "While the Portuguese advanced with great strides to take away from the Italians the dominion over Europe's commerce, internal troubles were brewing for Lombardy, destined through the loss of its natural Princes to become the Province of a vast monarchy," a monarchy under whose "bad government" Lombardy was debilitated by excessive contributions to the misadventure of Spanish imperialism. In matters of commerce, Verri decried from his historical studies, laying down the blueprint of the Academy of Fisticuffs' program of political economy in the process, "the gain of one Nation is the loss of another: this war is indeed more humane, but the Power of Principates is no less disputed in it, nor is it blind fortune, but the conduct of who presides over it, which has the principal influence on the outcome."[34] Trade might soften the mechanisms of interstate competition, but it resolutely did not solve the problem of international rivalry as such, or, for that matter, necessarily socialize relations between polities. From having been at the very core of the European economy, Lombardy's declining fortunes meant it now was losing out in this new commercial war; once an economic sovereign, it had become subject to a "declining" empire that, though "master of the treasures of Potosì"—a common shorthand for the mineral riches of the New World—"found a way to depend increasingly by the day on the other Nations of Europe."[35] Thus oppressed, the Lombards could not "think of manufacturing," that all-important activity in the history of Italy and in Verri's own political economy, and things only deteriorated until 1720. At that point, under the leadership of an abler foreign ruler and assisted both by high tariffs on industrial imports and a plague striking French competitors, Lombardy's textile manufactures, which for Verri were the cornerstone of the region's economy, finally began to recover, and with them the state itself. "This example proves," he put it poignantly, "that when fine cloths do not reach us from France, our internal manufactures prosper."[36] Political economy could, as such, emulate nature by strategically recreating natural inflections of trade by legislative means.[37]

One of the most important events in Verri's account of Milanese economic history, however, to which he would return often throughout the rest of his *Considerations,* was the plan for an economic recovery formulated by "Court Chancellor Count Sizzendorff [Philipp Ludwig Wenzel von Sinzendorf]" (1671–1742) on behalf of the Holy Roman Emperor Charles VI.[38]

> That Minister planned to avert French textiles from all His Majesty's States, and to grant free access to ours in the Hereditary States of Germany, proposing compensation in copper, wax, cloth, iron, and common fabrics: *thus full internal circulation was allowed among the subjects of the same Monarch, all members of one political body,* and the way was opened for us to enter most of Germany with our manufactures.[39]

What Sinzendorf had suggested, in other words, was the equivalent of a customs union or free-trade area to encourage intra-imperial economic development not at all unlike the *Zollverein* that eventually would be established under Prussian leadership in the mid-nineteenth century.[40] Timothy H. Breen has demonstrated how choices of consumption habits—whose goods one consumed and whose markets one relied on—were understood to be, and exercised as, signs of political allegiance in colonial America, similarly to how numerous nationalist calls to "buy American" and "buy Chinese" in the respective countries have been considered patriotic in more recent times.[41] Verri's take on the political dimension of markets hints at a similar resolution in light of his earlier analysis of the bellicosity of international trade. Milan's ultimate economic interest, he in essence argued, was to embrace its political allegiance to the Habsburgs in a context of merciless economic competition with France and England. A sense of patriotism to the local economy could flourish—even survive—only in submission to a political patriotism toward the House of Habsburg.[42]

Sinzendorf's plan was eventually corrupted by the interests of merchants, however, which, Verri argued, echoing an already common trope, were "not always those of the Nation," as well as by the stymying "ancient system left by the Spanish." In effect, "the most effective orders of the Sovereign" and "the most salutary institutions for the Nation" could go nowhere as long as the specters of Spanish oppression haunted the institutions of Milan's government. Yet, Austrian economic policies of 1725 were "among the best writings" Verri had "seen on the present subject," proposing tax exemptions on "raw materials" and "what is needed for domestic factories," "permission for Nobles to engage in commerce," "lowering the tariffs on the export of domestic manufactures," and attempts to attract workers from abroad. These decrees too, however, were ineffectual because of "the tenaciously bad establishment of [the Milanese] system." In 1732 tariffs were yet again removed on imported raw materials and reduced drastically on exported manufactures "produced in the State," but these praiseworthy efforts were once more thwarted by the inefficient remnants of Spanish misrule. Maria Theresa of Austria "renewed the project of Count Sizzendorff [sic]" for an imperial system of economic development yet again in the wake of the War of Austrian Succession in 1748, but even her best efforts continued to be trumped by local, shortsighted interests. If nothing else, though, a still-extant sovereign financial fund for the encouragement of commerce had emerged from her attempts.[43] Such, in Verri's narrative, was the miserable potted history of Milan under foreign administration, the forlorn narrative of its second decline and the many failed attempts at turning things around.

In an often-quoted analogy, Verri then went on to compare the relationship between the states of Europe to that between "private families" inside a "state" rather than "different nations." But whereas this might be taken to be an undiluted expression of the *doux commerce* thesis of international trade socializing relations and bringing peace and betterment for all, he was, from personal experience, all too aware of the Hobbesian ruthlessness of familial rivalries, and the "meek devotion to peace" between nations was hardly any better in his eyes.[44] Historically, Milan had lost out in this competition, in terms not merely of its political independence but of its relative economic prosperity, and its present state rendered meaningful reforms exceedingly complicated. Dexterously, Verri saw himself bound to decry the negative consequences of subjection to foreign powers while simultaneously praising Habsburg rule. "Milan remained direly and shamefully dependent on foreign nations," he argued, "in spite of the generous assistance and providential help of the extremely clement Sovereigns of Austria." The pivotal importance of institutions for the process of economic development was all too clear for Verri from studying the political mosaic that was the Lombard region. For whereas the nearby valleys of Bergamo, which had remained the westernmost outpost of the Venetian Empire throughout the period he considered, harbored sixty-five textile factories in 1763, neighboring Milan, so long subject to Spain, had only two. This was obviously not an issue of cultures, resources, peoples, climate, or technologies, but rather of policies and politics. Milan had lost "the envy of emulating Nations," and the survival of Spanish practices and institutions was the root of the problem.[45]

So what could be done? In private correspondence, Verri realistically noted that while "to think of returning [Milan's] ancient splendor would be a chimera, to diminish many branches of the ruinous commerce which we pursue would not." Principally, now that Milan was becoming an integral part of the Austrian monarchy, legislation would have to establish a functioning economic policy, and one had to "begin with a reform of the tariffs."[46] This would remain a crucial question for Verri, and his contemporary memoirs discussed at length the political and social consequences of tariffs. The Milanese "state" was still divided into different regions representing the historically independent urban centers of the region—Casalmaggiore, Como, Cremona, Lodi, Milan, and Pavia—each delineated by tariff barriers that now had become internal to the state, a unfortunate situation that "conserves the schism between the [other] five Provinces that make up the State, the way it was when every city supported itself independently." What was necessary now was to continue the process of territorial integration by ensuring "free internal communication" between the constituent parts of the now unified polity, with a "uniform tariff on all goods upon entering the State or exiting it," on Sinzendorf's model. This way, Verri argued in a passage that is striking in light of the overarching preoccupations of the Academy of Fisticuffs with problems of sociability, *"the State becomes a single society."*[47] Only through territorial marketization could the political community and administrative entity that was Lombardy be successfully socialized. As he put it in his *Considerations* at the time,

> "Tariffs," which we call "Dato della Mercanzia," are the primary mover deciding the direction taken by commerce; in the eyes of those who reflect on public matters, they are the most precious part of political economy, and the masterpiece of legislation, because whether the commerce of a Nation is useful or ruinous depends largely on Tariffs . . . and with many thorny and delicate operations the expert hand of legislation must draw the line between dependence on foreigners, the Nation's competitiveness, and the danger of smuggling, which increases with duties.[48]

In Verri's eyes, this was an altogether new way of conceiving of the wealth and power of nations. "The Romans, sons of Mars, thought themselves born to forcefully subjugate emulating Nations and to enrich themselves with their spoils, and never descended to competing industriously in commerce, the name of which they barely understood." That a government had to shepherd the economy was fully realized in the modern world by Louis XIV's finance minister, Jean-Baptiste Colbert, one of Verri's enduring political icons, and the massive encouragements and tariffs adopted by the English demonstrated the way to greatness.[49] The main problems were thus political and territorial, in defining the spatial extensions of economic policy and their relation to competing interests, as well as legal and cultural, in terms of overcoming the survival of Spanish practices and institutions.

Massive reforms were needed, not only of laws but also of people's minds and cultural attitudes toward the organization of material life. Chief among them, Verri thought in the wake of Sinzendorf's plan, of the Gournay circle's publications in the 1750s, and of Kaunitz's own recent meritocratic agenda, elites had to be actively encouraged to engage in commerce and be absolved of any negative social consequences of so doing; not only were nobles to engage in trade, trade itself was to be ennobled.[50] This argument would make its way into a number of the Academy of Fisticuffs' publications in subsequent years, presenting a coherent case for a truly commercial society fundamentally structured around the economic interactions of ideally equal members rather than theological strictures, military actions, or aristocratic notions of rank and honor.

The principal instrument of reform for Verri, however, even in terms of directing the cultural and political dimensions of the local Lombard economy, remained the tariff:

> As for the "Dato della Mercanzia," it will have to aim to make du-
> ties on foreign luxury goods heavier, and proportionally lower those
> on goods that are used by the common people [plebe]; it must also
> burden goods which compete with our domestic factories, and pro-
> mote in preference the manufactures of States subject to the August
> [Austrian] Sovereign . . . and it would also be desirable that that fra-
> ternity which was benignly proposed, or rather ordered, first under
> the reign of the August Charles VI [by Sinzendorf], then under the
> felicitous current reign, in this occasion could establish itself, so that
> the Hereditary States and Lombardy reciprocally protected their
> manufactures, lightening the duties in tariffs to their mutual
> benefit.[51]

A tariff was the territorial demarcation of economic policy, its effective-ness a mirror of the state's mastery of its dominion and the threshold of sovereignty.

Verri's political economy had all the characteristics of a hydra in the early 1760s. Economically, its head was resolutely buried in Milanese soil; cultur-ally and historically, it spoke to the heart and mind of *Italia*, Petrarch's be-loved peninsula betwixt ocean and Alps; yet politically, its gaze was fixed across those very mountains, toward Vienna and the Hungarian heartland of the Habsburg monarchy.[52] In terms of ideas, however, in spite of these conflicting loyalties, it moved in a land of no borders, its ears open to the news, innovations, and institutions of the world. And paradoxically, it was precisely by marauding around a cosmopolitan everyman's land that Verri's hydra found the means for its local prejudices to flourish:

Now that the true interests of States, and their real and physical force can be seen in bookshops; now also that governing a Nation is no longer a magical art, but rather a public science and subject to the laws of reason; now that the universal light has warmed the souls of the Europeans; now finally that every State is on guard and active in profiting from the somnolence of their neighbors, nothing remains for us to do but to wake up too, to contemplate, to meditate on the true causes of happiness in the Provinces, or instead placidly present our neck to that yoke which industrious peoples impose on the slothful, and no longer complain about the dependency or the misery we ourselves have sought.[53]

Political economy, in short, presented states with a simple choice; be industrious and emulative of foreign ideas and practices, or accept poverty and dependence in international affairs. Throughout numerous articles in *Il Caffè*, members of the group cumulatively enforced the message that the key to improvement lay in the competitive emulation, adoption, and even physical transplantation and "planting" of foreign ideas, practices, industries, and even products of the soil. However provocative and experimental, this approach nonetheless had history on its side.

Who knows how many laughs that innovator received who first proposed the farming of mulberries in his country? Nowadays those mulberries form one of the main products of Italian trade through the silk that we farm thanks to them. How much buffoonery did that innovator have to hear who first proposed the farming of maize here last century? . . . It is, I believe, a sure sign of a good Italian patriot that of persuading us that our opinions on matters of agriculture can be changed for other, more rational ideas of greater benefit to the nation.[54]

Although related in shifting ways, then, patriotism and cosmopolitanism were not the same for Pietro Verri, just as they were not the same for the other members of the Academy of Fisticuffs, something that was made remarkably clear in the most pugnacious article on political economy to be published in *Il Caffè*. This was Abbé Sebastiano Franci's undervalued and understudied "Alcuni pensieri politici," or "Some Political Thoughts," the most succinct theorization of political economy to be based on Verri's narrative of Italian and Milanese economic history.[55]

The Bloodless War

We know little of Franci (1715–1772), except that he was born to a noble dynasty on the Piedmontese side of the Lago Maggiore and would become the oldest member of the Academy of Fisticuffs. In spite of their noble title, his family was involved in the wool and silk trades, and he himself became a not inconsiderable landowner through marriage. His education remains a mystery, but he had already turned to Milanese economic concerns relating to the coinage by 1757, before Verri even joined the army, and would contribute several articles on economic matters for *Il Caffè*. After the group's eventual dissolution, he would become the Habsburg-appointed inspector of the mints of Milan and Modena in 1771, passing away suddenly in Milan in 1772.[56]

Originally Franci intended "Some Political Thoughts" to be a dialogue entitled "La guerra senza sangue," or "The Bloodless War," but Verri insisted on changing the title and form while editing the manuscript for publication. This was only one of several serious editorial interventions underlining the group's torn loyalties and complex internal dynamics.[57] The piece's principal preoccupation was with the "much praised balance of power among the nations of Europe." Once upon a time, Franci began, one feared nations overpowering others with only "military glory," Verri's "sons of Mars." This was because for millennia "a sovereign wishing to have a greater number of subjects was compelled to conquer land to enlarge the country."[58] That was the old model. But Italian history had changed all that—not just through one of its regions, but through a galaxy of commercial societies stretching from the far south to the far north of the peninsula:

> Around the thirteenth century the Florentines, Pisans, Amalfitans, Venetians, and Genoese began adopting a different policy for enhancing their wealth and power because they noticed that the

sciences, the cultivation of land, the application of the arts and of industry, and the introduction of extensive trade could produce a large population, provide for their countless needs, sustain great luxury and acquire immense riches, without enlarging their territories.[59]

Italians had been the first among Europeans—and by extension in the world in the Academy of Fisticuffs' eyes—to discover the principles of political economy and to circumvent what eventually would be known as the Malthusian trap of poverty by nurturing activities yielding increasing returns to scale.[60] More people, economic writers of the Italian Renaissance had begun observing, could be supported on a given piece of land by manufactures and trade than by sheer agricultural surplus alone, on the basis of which they theorized economic development and codified economic practices that were widely emulated in early modern Europe.[61] Precisely like Verri in his *Considerations*, Franci demonstrated that Italy had twice risen to dominate the world, with the iron legions of Rome and with the golden trade of the Renaissance. "They achieved all this with such great success that they drew the eyes of the world on Italy for a second time in history. Their example was soon imitated." Indeed, "today, all of educated Europe agrees that it is from these principles that the power of kings and the happiness of peoples must be derived, and it would appear improper to seek one's own greatness and the equilibrium of others in sources other than those mentioned."[62] The world, in short, had changed, and the means of achieving supremacy depended more on economic prowess than on military might. But had this revolution really pacified international relations? The answer, Franci thought, was no, not necessarily.

> If an indolent people are unable to provide for their own needs, industrious nations will rush to them and with feigned mercy present them with all that they may need. They give them food and clothing and relieve them of the need to work, and if they see that they are inclined to luxury, they parade before them thousands of trifles, so as to fuel and satisfy that inclination. Such enormous damage must be remedied at once and the nation defended vigorously from such pernicious enemies by the most effective of weapons, which are the sciences, the arts, industry and commerce.[63]

Economic policies had become the only "weapons by which to defend a nation from its enemies." It was, thus, "not impossible to eradicate poverty from a nation and hold back the enemies that trouble it," but this required a properly political understanding of international trade and of what was at stake in its right development. Nations, Franci argued forcefully, had to actively choose their partners in trade to ensure future welfare and defend themselves against dependence in international relations.[64]

> Generally speaking, a weak nation with little wealth never does well to sell its raw materials to rich and powerful states. As such states are full of industry, they will use those materials for manufacturing, thereby doubling their value many times over and, by supporting a large part of their population with such fine crafts and earning immense profits, they will continue to maintain their superiority.[65]

What a nation traded, in short, was of truly existential importance. But political economy was not simply a means of defending oneself against hostile forces in the modern world; it was also a means of attacking them.

> Once its most formidable enemies are defeated, a nation can then attempt to make its own conquests. The surest way to do so is to reduce the price of its manufactured goods, perfected as much as possible, to a level that cannot be matched by others, and then diligently find the way to penetrate the markets of foreign countries, through trade and through appropriate treaties with their rulers.[66]

This was "how important conquests" could be made, Franci argued, this was the "guerra d'industria," the "war of industry." And only success in said "war of industry" could prepare one for the inevitable real wars that forever would plague the interactions of nations.[67] Franci's original manuscript, however, suggested that although inherently agonistic, commerce was in any case a preferable alternative to conquests as a means of international competition. As the opening passages of "The Bloodless War" observed, "It would by now be about time that one thought of a new kind of war in Europe, which did not demand the destruction of humanity, and which promoted the interests of states more effectively."[68] Whereas, for reasons of political prudence, Franci's published essay never engaged with the actual economic conditions of contemporary Milan, one of the characters in his manuscript dialogue asked his interlocutor explicitly to "descend to give me all of this in more minute detail and teach me how we Milanese can make agriculture, the arts, industry, and commerce assert themselves." Having praised Verri's *Considerations,* mentioning "the registers of Milanese customs, diligently examined by a great citizen," and realizing that a minute account of the Lombard economy would be too voluminous a subject for discussion, he simply implored, "Tell me how one can weaken the enemy without a bloody war"—how, in short, to achieve greatness and dominion as a political community without offending humanity as such. Much like the question itself, the dialogue's answer did not bode well for cosmopolitanism.[69]

Most importantly, Franci repeatedly argued, Milan should not export any raw materials in exchange for manufactured goods. Not only did such asymmetrical relations of trade cause an outflow of funds, create poverty in one's fatherland, and subject it to a state of dependence on other nations, but they would further encourage the "superiority of heretics over Catholics"—that is, Northern over Southern Europeans. The spiritual dimension of contemporary international competition—perhaps simply an expression of political interests in liturgical guise—was even more evident in Franci's discussion of the herring trade. "Our rituals" such as the institution of not eating meat on Fridays and other special occasions ["giorno magro"], he lamented, every year brought new gold to Protestant coffers. "If the Church came to the opinion of prohibiting fish fished by heretical hands, our critical century [*il nostro secolo critico*] could call this ban an excessive scruple, and it would certainly be that in the face of religion itself; but to the eyes of politics it would be considered a reasonable precaution."[70] Finally, the listener intervenes,

> All this is well, I too know that this sort of bloodless war is the most necessary and useful, but it does not suffice, I think, to keep bloody wars at bay. The interests of princes, always tricked by a great number of sterile treaties that every now and then are brought back

onto the scene, produce discords which do not permit any other decision but that of war [*quella delle armi*].[71]

In a modern world system characterized by a multiplicity of sovereign political communities perpetually connected by movements of goods and people, the nature of international rivalry was shifting from sporadic explosions of reciprocal violence to a commercially competitive continuum. This "war of industry," the "bloodless war," was a form of conflict characteristic of the age of commercial societies that, unlike its older and purely military incarnations, could never find respite. If certain economic activities—and more specifically, at the time, technology-intensive manufacturing compared to the export of raw materials—were more conducive to wealth and greatness than others, an unremitting struggle for wealth and power was intrinsically embedded in the modern state system. And to make matters worse, Franci was certain that there was no better way of preparing for a bloody war than to successfully conduct a bloodless one. Trade was a parallel war, a companion and possible prelude to military conquests, and the way in which it perpetually intertwined competing polities meant lasting peace was even more elusive than before.[72] But he never seemed to consider the rather logical scenario in which, if all states adopted his proposed measures, international trade would simply grind to a halt.

Franci's manuscript was too explicit for Verri, who, in spite of the group's good relations with both Firmian and Kaunitz, rightly feared alienating Austrian censors and their friends in the administration.[73] His personal experience with discussing Milanese matters had resulted in a reprimand from Kaunitz, and he obviously did not wish to see this happen again through Franci's reference to his text.[74] Verri's caveat, in the introduction to the first issue of *Il Caffè*, that the Academy of Fisticuffs would keep a "total silence on sacred matters" similarly trumped Franci's hardly virulent observations on the relationship between religious life and economic might in the modern world.[75] Perhaps Verri also objected to its tenebrous tone, so at odds with the polished levity for which he strove. Although somewhat mellowed in the transition from manuscript to printed text, Franci's fundamental message about the importance and ruthlessness of economic competition survived unscathed, deeply problematizing received opinion regarding his group's loyalties and the nature of their cosmopolitanism.

Cosmopolitan Patriots

There can be no doubt that what we have come to call "The Enlightenment" was profoundly cosmopolitan in many ways, actively—perhaps even chiefly—shaped by international trade and cultural transfer, not to mention an ever more global understanding of natural and human affairs. Volumes of trade, of travel, and of translation exploded as the eighteenth century progressed, connecting regional debates and practices across the European world and increasingly beyond it. It was, in David Armitage's terms, an age of global-ization, if not yet a globalized age.[76] As Beccaria himself put it in a self-analyzing piece on "fogli periodici," or "Periodical Papers," for *Il Caffè*,

> News make us practically fellow citizens of all of Europe; it produces a continuous commerce between different nations and destroys the diffidence and the contempt with which solitary nations regard for-eigners. Everything in Europe tends to become closer and have more in common, and there is a greater impetus toward equality than there was in the past. All this is due to the communion of ideas and of enlightenment.[77]

Yet, it might be argued that excessive emphases on, and fusion of, the eighteenth-century buzzwords "cosmopolitanism" and, by some quirky default, "laissez-faire"—as if peaceful global interactions can only ever find libertarian expression—have served to obfuscate our understanding of the historical record and of the nature of Enlightenment reformism, in Milan and elsewhere. A variety of cosmopolitanisms existed in eighteenth-century Europe, not all of which related to economic concerns.[78] Though there has been a clear historiographical reaction to this in recent years, we long were led to believe that most eighteenth-century political economists were some-how members of the liberal Mont Pèlerin Society *avant la lettre,* an idiom that seldom enlightens much in intellectual history.[79] So dominant has this vision of peaceful, reasoned universalism been that most attempts to come to grips with the coexistence of "patriotism" and "cosmopolitanism" in the Academy of Fisticuffs alternatively have conflated the two—"this was a time of opti-mism, when the words 'patriot', 'cosmopolitan' and *'philosophe'* were, for Verri, one and the same"—or in fact presented the latter as a simple extension of the former, as in "cosmopolitanism only extends patriotism just as individual happiness finds its fulfilment in that of the public." This effectively emasculates "patriotism" and safeguards the Milanese Enlightenment from being associated with often demonized currents of political economy and philosophy, but it goes too far in projecting current ideals on unsuspecting historical actors.[80]

In the case of the Academy of Fisticuffs, scholars have located a unifying force toward perpetual peace in their ostensible embrace of an idealized logic of commercial societies—or even atomized individuals—bound together by the exigencies of peaceable international trade from which everone would benefit.[81] Known in the eighteenth century through variations of Montesquieu's "doux commerce" thesis (though the extent to which Montesquieu himself actually argued this, or that most of his readers understood him this way, is eminently debatable), and celebrated in modern historiography in the wake of the remarkable and eclectic Princeton economist Albert O. Hirschman, this ethereal line of analysis nonetheless fails to account for the reality of international economic competition at the time and of the Academy's explicitly "patriotic" solutions to the problem based on tariffs, subsidies, and other political interventions in economic life.[82] Their patriotism was not simply a more local manifestation of a greater love for humanity, but a torn allegiance divided between loyalties to the historical polity of Milan, to the Italian peninsula as a cultural entity, to the House of Habsburg as their worldly sovereign, and ultimately to European civilization and to humanity at large. The Fisticuffs' political economy was all too aware of the tensions between local needs and universal aspirations, the ideal dynamics of economic development and the cruel realities of international competition, so their most explicit engagement with the concept of "patriotism" confounds the principles of laissez-faire cosmopolitanism.

Gian Rinaldo Carli was one of the older members of the Academy, an Istrian nobleman whose earlier work had dealt both with economic matters and with the erudite controversies over witchcraft in early eighteenth-century Italy. A friend of Verri's since the mid-1750s, his only article for Il Caffè appeared in the second volume, and was entitled "La patria degli Italiani," "The Fatherland" or "Homeland of the Italians."[83] It tells the story of a stranger who one day entered Demetrius's coffee shop. The local patron Alcibiades, a character representative of common Milanese opinions in the dialogue, asked the stranger if he was a "foreigner," and the stranger replies negatively. "Are you Milanese, then?" replied Alcibiades. *"No, sir, I am not Milanese,"* the stranger retorted to everyone's bafflement. "I am Italian, replied the stranger, and an Italian in Italy is never a foreigner just as a Frenchman is not a foreigner in France, or an Englishman in England, or a Dutchman in Holland, and so on." Alcibiades sought to explain to him that anyone born outside of the city walls was a foreigner, but the stranger interrupted him.

> This might be called a mystic genius of the Italians, which makes them inhospitable and hostile to each other, and which, as a consequence, has led to the running aground of the arts and sciences and to great impediments to national glory, which never grows when a nation is split into many factions and schisms.[84]

Gradually the patrons of the coffee shop realized the stranger was "a good patriot," and decried "the misfortune with which such an irrational prejudice has condemned us to believe that an Italian is not a fellow citizen of other Italians" despite being born in "that space which *the Apennines divide and sea and Alps surround.*" Carli's learned reference was to Petrarch's previously mentioned *Canzoniere* CXLVI, one of the founding documents of Renaissance patriotism, by which Italy was understood to be a cultural rather than political unity.[85]

In the past, Italy had been one "nation . . . united . . . in a single body and bound in a single system," but this had been broken by the vicissitudes of history.[86] His conclusion drew on Galileo, a character often praised by the Academy of Fisticuffs for his "Italian" contribution to the world of learning, to explain the relationship between cultural patriotism and political life. "Let us transport," he says, Galileo's star system "to our national politics":

> Whether they are great or small, whether situated in one place or another, whether they follow particular laws in rotating on their axes, whether they are loyal to their natural sovereign or to the laws, whether they have subordinate bodies or not, our cities, though they are divided under different dominions and obey different sovereigns, should join together into a single system for the progress of the sciences and the arts. Let the love of patriotism, which is to say the uni-

versal good of our nation, be the Sun that enlightens them and
attracts them. . . . Let us all become, therefore, Italians once again,
so as not to cease being men.[87]

In the context of Carli's private correspondence at the time, it is evident that
this project of pan-Italian patriotism—which he himself practiced as an Istrian working in Lombardy and communicating with literati across the
peninsula—was one aspect of a larger vision of national regeneration. Only
as a whole could Italian individuals, and Italy as such, reclaim their lost
prominence on the European stage, and it would have to do so by emulating
the more successful nations across the Alps, particularly through the vehicle of translations of works on political economy, agriculture, and technology for popular dissemination.[88]

Historiographically speaking, Carli's eloquent conceptualization was
long taken as one of the principal textual antecedents of the *Risorgimento,* Italy's late nineteenth-century process of national unification, and through it
the Academy of Fisticuffs became a vehicle of nationalism by proxy.[89] Today
historians are more prone to place the article squarely outside of the Fisticuffs' agenda as a nationalist aberration disliked by the Verri brothers and
included in their journal only by some sort of mistake.[90] This literature often
returns to Verri's editorial critiques of Carli's article and to the fact that, in a
later letter to his brother, he was surprised to hear news that "The Fatherland of Italians" had been received so well in Paris. Verri indeed did convey
reservations to Carli, writing that "it is really beautiful, but I wouldn't want
our fatherland to undermine our impartiality as good cosmopolitans," and
wrote to his brother that though the *philosophe* André Morellet might "like"
the piece, "I don't." That said, his thoughts on the matter may have been more
favorable than recent historiography would suggest.[91] Processes of nation
building are seldom linear, and I will argue that the Fisticuffs ultimately occupied a position that cannot be reduced to either romantic nationalism or
libertarian cosmopolitanism.[92]

For there can be no doubt that, behind his self-fashioning cosmopolitan
façade, Pietro Verri himself relied on a very similar if not identical language
of competing national identities, even Italian "national hatred," in his private
writings. The long memoirs he composed around his military service during
the Seven Years' War, for example, were replete with references to national

categories of precisely Carli's sort. "Germans," which at times included Austrians in his national imaginary, were "robust, stocky," and quite crude, while "Italians" were both more sophisticated and polite. In a striking passage he rhetorically asked, "How many foreigners reside in Italy, in Tuscany, in Naples, in Rome, etc., for the pure pleasure of living in that society rather than elsewhere." Italy was his "patria" and "nazione," clearly including most of the polities on the peninsula, no less than "Milan" was, and this influenced him the same way the "Germanized" soldiers he encountered in the field reflected the mores of their new "nation." He was, he proclaimed, "Italian" through and through, and even his persona in Demetrius's coffee shop was "born and raised in Italy."[93] But it is worth emphasizing that, in spite of his justification for "national hatred," his cosmopolitan ideals usually inhibited such outright expressions of hostility. While Verri's "patriotism" may have been "burdened by a message of international antagonism," it was emphatically not, like that of later Polish nationalists studied by Brian Porter, "virtually defined by hate."[94]

And patriotism was far from an abstract category for the Academy of Fisticuffs; it was lived. Verri, for one, proudly wrote throughout his autobiographical writings of how he was happy to sacrifice Habsburg careerism for the good of both his Milanese and larger Italian "fatherlands": "In this country," he proudly wrote to his brother Alessandro later in life, "one knows and one says publically that I was the country's only support, and that I have had the courage to reject both rank and money rather than betray the fatherland."[95] Equally proudly, he would bewail the lack of "sentiment of fatherland and love of national glory" shown by the Milanese in not celebrating his achievements enough.[96] "It is a great glory to Italy," he would write in 1785, when "one of its children is crowned in Paris, Berlin, Copenhagen, or St. Petersburg, which certainly is not a bad thing."[97] Throughout his life, Pietro was quite a lot more patriotic than his brother Alessandro, who wrote an extremely friendly letter to Carli complaining, not about his use of the term "Italian" in the article, but instead about the implied positive aspects of such an Italian national character. He fully accepted that "Italians" existed and that they were united by common national characteristics across "this peninsula" just as identifiable Englishmen lived in a geographically delineated England and Frenchmen in France, he just did not happen to like them very much.[98]

The Verri brothers' own writings over a period of several decades, in short, presented Italy precisely the way Carli did in his article—as a suprapolitical nation both culturally and, strikingly, in terms of phenotypes—and the question arises what else might have been troublesome about "the Fatherland of the Italians." There are, after all, good reasons Pietro Verri might have been disingenuous in his critiques. Chief among them was simple prudence. It was one thing to express national pride or national generalizations in private writings and correspondence; to publish such in a journal was something else. In the wake of Kaunitz's recent "blazing letter" following the debacle of his *Considerations,* Verri had opted to lie low and "follow orders" to avoid upsetting the authorities; and though Carli's article expressed a cultural and geographical rather than explicitly political national sentiment, it nonetheless ventured into potentially dangerous territories, given Habsburg claims on the peninsula.[99]

In spite of the handful of sentences to the contrary in Verri's vast corpus of writings, it is difficult not to conclude that he and the other members of his group in effect shared many of Carli's central opinions with regard to the cultural unity of Italy already in the 1760s. And what were the Academy's proposed economic policies, if not partial? What did their arguments for a properly peninsular Italian language in opposition to the rarefactions of old do, if not contribute to the development of a cultural identity based on politicized geographical criteria? One answer to the problem, and the point at which Verri in the end came to a clear agreement with Carli, lies in their differentiation of allegiances and sovereignties.[100] There were, in the end, at least four different kinds of patriotism at play in the Academy of Fisticuffs, each of which found its more or less explicit and idiosyncratic resolution in respect to the actual institutional context of Austrian Lombardy. Religiously, as Franci's manuscript for "The Bloodless War" demonstrates, the group looked to Rome in opposition to the "heretic" commercial nations of northwestern Europe. Politically, they could not but turn to Vienna, the seat of the House of Habsburg for which Milan was a key province. Culturally, they actively and expressly sought to resurrect a Petrarchan ideal of peninsular unity, on the basis of Italy's peculiar history, in dominant opposition to the rest of Europe. This same national history, characterized by Italy's unique dual cycle of greatness and decline, informed the coterie's economic patriotism.

Because of their political loyalties, Verri and his group identified solutions to the challenges of international competition and material melioration in collaboration with Austrian authorities, and chief among them Sinzendorf's oft-praised plan for imperial economic development. Yet their eyes were always set on ways to make the Milanese province flourish within that sphere, primarily through the exports of its modernized agricultural system and through the pointed improvement of its manufactures.[101]

Although contributing to the political economy of a de facto empire, the Academy of Fisticuffs had in the end drawn nothing but warnings from the lessons of France and England. In clear opposition to the continental ideal of universal betterment envisaged for its dominions by the Austrian monarchy, the English and French texts reaching Milan primarily envisaged imperial economic systems as vampiric, drawing raw materials from the colonies to fuel metropolitan industries. The economically liberal writings of late seventeenth-century pamphleteers, like those of the English baron and merchant Dudley North, though famous in the historiography of economics, simply never made their way to Milan, where Verri and his friends instead engaged with far more cantankerous, some would say "mercantilist," writers such as Cary and Forbonnais.[102] In the Habsburg case, Milan was conceived of as a valuable manufacturing center in its own right, a center that could help enrich the empire synergetically. There was, as such, opportunity—in the form of larger markets—rather than sacrifice involved in Milan's submission to Habsburg authority, a fact that in turn must have greatly facilitated the Fisticuffs' complex mosaic of patriotic loyalties. Nor, for that matter, can these loyalties be reduced to a pristine blueprint for the *Risorgimento*—not without denying the very multiplicity of the group's express aims, and not without uprooting its members from their historical contexts and identities.

Numerous versions of cosmopolitanism of course coexisted in Enlightenment Europe, but in this context it might be useful to consider the *Encyclopédie*'s own definition of "cosmopolitanism," which, drawing on Montesquieu, went like this: "I put my family above myself, my country above my family, and the human race above my country."[103] The idea was clear. A cosmopolitan, as Kant and others would argue, had no particular loves, and thought of humanity before country or even family.[104] In this context, material concerns are preeminent litmus tests of loyalties, shaping, nurturing, and reflecting economic identities. Relative wealth was, in practical terms, not an infinite resource in an eighteenth-century world of ruthlessly partitioned empires, resources, and industries, any more than it is today. Wealth was instead, as many thinkers at the time began to reveal, the fiercely contested key to a flourishing political life. And if one accepted the widespread equation of wealth with power, it was very much a positional good.[105] Economic differences decided military and thus political and cultural hierarchies. Trade could not, as often has been argued in the secondary literature, be a universal solvent of patriotic commitments for the members of Verri's group. Through their explicit conceptual analogies of commerce with conquest, they were instead galvanized by it. "It is only natural," Franci explained in *Il Caffè*, "that every nation should seek, first and foremost, its own happiness rather than that of others."[106] Of course, complete cosmopolitanism looked good on paper, remained a praiseworthy aim in theory, and, as John Robertson has reminded us, offered a "comparative" framework for intellectual debates that would prove vital to the development of the Enlightenment's key discipline of political economy.[107] But as economic development proved to be an inherently uneven and competitive process, could the geographical distribution of wealth ever be immaterial in practice? In spite of their deeply utilitarian moral philosophy and their assurance that the goal of politics was "the greatest happiness possible divided as equally as possible," the Fisticuffs' answer was resolutely no.[108]

Verri and his collaborators had succeeded in founding an "imagined community," a wide public sphere of unified subjects of different polities, but though some of their interests overlapped in a Venn diagram of their cultural, political, and economic loyalties, large parts did not.[109] If their coffeepot community was cosmopolitan, it was, in Kwame Anthony Appiah's terminology, decidedly so in a "partial" manner, resistant to the "hard-core cosmopolitan who regards her friends and fellow citizens with icy impartiality"—in short, less a "matter of action" or a rigorous "ideology" than an indefinite "sentiment."[110] Ultimately, and arguably consciously, their reformist realism got the better of their more utopian rhetoric, which is why the only cosmopolitanism they ever adumbrated was something akin to the cosmopolitanism of nations later envisioned in the nineteenth century by the likes of the architect of the German customs-union Friedrich List and the Italian nationalist Giuseppe Mazzini, for whom the nation was a necessary stepping-stone toward cosmopolis.[111]

Though the Academy of Fisticuffs had no fixed physical presence, unlike the more famous learned societies of its age, it by no means defaulted into simply being a local embassy of the *Respublica literarum,* the truly cosmopolitan, meritocratic, and egalitarian "Republic of Letters" that first began to flourish in the sixteenth century. For even if the high-minded toleration professed by this earlier international community of scholars at times had run aground of practical concerns, its ideals nonetheless remained clear. As the French monk and literary figure Nöel d'Argònne, better known as Bonaventure d'Argonne, wrote in 1699, "The Republic of Letters . . . embraces the whole world and is composed of all nationalities, all social classes, all ages and both sexes."[112] Demetrius's coffee shop was certainly a "world made by words" in Anthony Grafton's apt phrase, but it was a world that mirrored the reality and practical exigencies of inter-state competition far more closely than the more arcadian "Republic of Letters" did.[113] If inclusive and remarkably appreciative of women, the imaginary world of the Academy nonetheless occupied an importunate landscape of contested borders and differential relations of power. When push came to shove and the cosmopolitan ideal risked threatening economic conditions in Lombardy, they happily shoved it aside. Indeed, Verri's agonistic approach to the world found expression even locally, as he was adamant that, far from being some emancipatory cosmopolitan concept, "public opinion" was just another weapon of dominion to "capture" the "popular vote."[114] Ultimately the Fisticuffs' cosmopolitanism and openness to foreign cultures and ideas informed a patriotic program of economic development in which international allegiances and global ideals were honored only as long as they contributed to local needs.

Ironically, Verri was far more of a localist than Carli was. Not only did he barely move from his Milanese homeland following his military service, but when the Supreme Council of the Economy was inaugurated by Austrian authorities in Milan in 1765, and the institution, however meritocratic, came to be dominated by non-Milanese appointees like Carli, Verri's choice was clear.[115] He did not embrace "Italianism," let alone cosmopolitanism. He turned on his heels and resolutely took sides with the local home interests he had previously scorned: the patrician class from which he descended and in which he participated.[116] Similarly, though he had been a long-term member of the Cameral Magistracy of Milan, Verri would resign from his post in

1780 in protest against the institution's increasing subjection to Vienna.[117] Cultural and intellectual cosmopolitanism was one thing, and Verri was the first to rejoice at how technology allowed fashions and ideas to travel and intermingle across borders; but his hopes were that such interactions would be conducive to comparative betterment locally. There was always the danger, in short, that cosmopolitan patriotism in practice meant little more than openness to foreign ideas and practices in the pursuit of greatness.[118]

Verri's "new niche" of political economy was, after all, meant to illuminate practical policy, not to derail it with chimeras.[119] This was why—as soon will be clear—both Verri and Beccaria explicitly abandoned their original faith in the mathematical modeling of economic concerns later in life, and why, despite claims of recent scholarship to the contrary, Verri never discarded his belief in the crucial importance of tariffs for demarcating allegiances and developing local manufactures.[120] As he echoed Hume even in the later editions of his 1770s masterwork *Meditations on Political Economy*, a work in which Verri supposedly "abandoned his old arguments in favor of state intervention": "A tax [*tributo*] on the export of a raw material can be a very strong incentive to increasing annual output by reducing it to a manufacture. A tax on a foreign manufacture can give vigor to a similar domestic manufacture."[121] In the Fisticuffs' reformist imagination, mathematical exuberance and theoretical dogmatism were both paths down which "Teorica" and "Pratica" would be forced to turn their backs on one another, paths that led out of the enlightened coffee shop, straight into the gothic halls of the "Temple of Ignorance."[122]

There were, in short, myriads of reasons why the Academy of Fisticuffs was not an agent of "market cosmopolitanism" in Pauline Kleingold's taxonomy of variations of the term "cosmopolitanism," however much its members maintained that commerce had socializing consequences under certain conditions. At the same time, though, the pugilists were undoubtedly some of the greatest proponents of what she identified as "moral cosmopolitanism" in the eighteenth century, and Beccaria himself made his name in the European world precisely by arguing that human beings were everywhere imbued with certain inalienable rights.[123] The relations the group envisioned between people as well as peoples, however, were deeply intertwined, and, as will be clear, they would essentially argue that "moral cosmopolitanism" trumped—and indeed could be antithetical to—"market cosmopolitanism." Their chosen niche ultimately enclosed the full architecture of human improvement and sociability, from the macrocosm of political economy to the microcosm of criminal law. Vast, as vast as a wholly material cosmos allows, and yet architectonically unified already at their inception, the structures of engagement that Verri eventually would call "social science" demanded, in the group's agenda, more effort than simply letting go.

Crimes and Punishments

It is perhaps fitting that the greatest achievement of the Academy of Fisticuffs—the publication of Beccaria's *On Crimes and Punishments*—would simultaneously mark its downfall. Demetrius's virtual coffee shop, which Verri first described taking shape in earnest in 1761–1762, was, for all intents and purposes, forced to close its doors in late 1766, overcome by sundry kinds of caffeinated anxieties.[124] Edginess was a two-faced phenomenon, creative yet contentious as the intensity of the group's social and intellectual collaboration inevitably fostered rivalries over fame, authorship, and, of course, women. Verri's complex role as the group's *primus motor* was doubtlessly at the problem's core. He took great pride in encouraging the ideas and guiding the career choices of his younger colleagues, but ultimately found himself too heavily invested, and too proud, to see them individually harvest the fruits of their common labors.[125] And, as later chapters will explain, personal rivalries as well as political and theoretical disagreements eventually resulted in years of hostilities, particularly between Verri on the one hand and Beccaria and Carli on the other, a situation aggravated by the fact that they all served on the same committees and councils in Habsburg Milan.[126] But there can be no doubt that Beccaria and other member benefited tremendously from, and contributed notably to, the workshop that was the Academy. A large part of *Il Caffè*'s success resulted from the variety of its articles, and the same multiplicity of perspectives also influenced the individual works produced by the group's core members, and few more so than Beccaria's short magnum opus.

The most coherent, if nonetheless partial, account of the genesis of *On Crimes and Punishments* appears in Verri's memoirs, composed after the fact and after his falling out with Beccaria:

Regarding the book *On Crimes and Punishments*. The book is by the Marquis Beccaria. I gave him the subject, and the majority of its ideas are the result of daily conversations between Beccaria, Alessandro [Verri], Lambertenghi, and myself. Our society spent the evenings with everyone working in the same room. Alessandro has the *History of Italy* between his hands, I my political economic works, others read; Beccaria was bored and bored the others. Out of desperation he asked me for a topic, and I suggested this [i.e., crimes and punishments], knowing it to be highly appropriate for an eloquent man with an extremely lively imagination. But he knew nothing of our criminal methods. Alessandro, who was Protector of Criminals, promised him assistance. Beccaria began to write some ideas on loose pieces of paper. We supported him with enthusiasm. We encouraged him so much that he wrote a great multitude of ideas. After lunch we went for a walk, we spoke of the horrors of criminal jurisprudence, we debated and went into the matter, and in the evening he wrote. But it is so difficult for him to write and it costs him so much effort that after an hour he collapses and cannot continue. Having amassed his materials, I wrote it and it was given an order, and a book took shape.[127]

Verri's description of the Academy's modus operandi is evocative of the intensity of the group's intellectual fervor and sociability, but also suggests the treacherous terrain they ventured into, for the careerism and personal ambitions underlying the individual members' commitment to the group—not to mention Verri's own in bringing them all together—aligned poorly with the authorial fluidity of their workshop-style compositions.[128] Beccaria cannot have been entirely unfamiliar with criminal procedures, being a lawyer trained by one of Italy's oldest universities, but Alessandro Verri was probably to a certain extent right, writing for *Il Caffè* in 1765, that one had to "unlearn" the "erudite jurisprudence" taught at the universities upon entering the courtrooms.[129] Yet, as always with the writings of the Verri brothers, reality was somewhat more complex than how they depicted it. In the end, Pietro Verri's admonition to "do Socrates's job, that of the midwife for others' thoughts, helping them to express themselves and adorning and ennobling others' expressions," was easier said than done.[130]

Alessandro Verri certainly brought to the Fisticuffs' debates his experience as a Protector of Prisoners, but the other members of the Academy in turn helped him fulfill his duties in the same collaborative way described in his brother's memoirs. Part of the Protector's task was to pen supplications to reduce the sentences of people found guilty of various crimes, in cases ranging from theft through incest to murder, and there can be no doubt that such practical engagements with the politics of criminal procedure in Habsburg Milan provided Beccaria with important perspectives on the subjects the group was discussing around the time when *On Crimes and Punishments* was written. Yet we know from surviving manuscripts that Alessandro Verri actively relied on his colleagues in his professional obligations, and that he trusted his brother, Longo, and interestingly Beccaria himself to correct and even compose many of his surviving supplications.[131] The majority of these collaborative supplications were written in Latin, with a select few composed in Italian. As an institution, such supplications often fell back on ideals of Christian charity, clemency, and compassion. In this context the Academy of Fisticuffs' contributions stand out for their inherent—if not always consistent—emphasis on questions of political economy, juridical principle, and the overarching goal and challenge of human sociability.

A few cases in particular are worth highlighting for their relevance to the group's project and approach to the problem of commercial sociability. One Giovanni d'Auregard of Brussels, for example, "a foreigner, without assistance, far from his fatherland" and unable to pay his debt because of "misfortune," had been sentenced to imprisonment, from which, being unable to earn a living, let alone pay his debt, he would never emerge. Yet it was "a principle that accords not only with humanity," Alessandro Verri argued, "but also with the most rigorous justice that a Debtor not be sentenced to life imprisonment, a punishment equal to death." Even the creditor would be better served by having the debtor work to pay his debts, maintaining him as a productive member of society; and, in general, "it is not a punishment what the law imposes on Debtors who are imprisoned if they do not pay [their debts]; *a punishment supposes a crime, and it is not a crime to be poor.*"[132] This would become one of Beccaria's principal points in his nearly coeval *On Crimes and Punishments*. Not only did economic development depend on a sort of risk-taking behavior that necessitated legal support, but the law had to take account of conditions of economic inequality and the uneven distribution

of power that could emerge from the pecuniary relationships quilting commercial societies.

A second, very different case is worth mentioning for the light it sheds on
the Academy of Fisticuffs' gradual articulation of an argument regarding the
just relationship between a crime and its punishment in a secular commercial
society. With regard to a crime of lesbian incest in urban Milan, in which a
mother was sentenced to seven years of prison and a day of public flagellation
and her daughter to imprisonment until further notice, Verri and his team put
together several interrelated arguments to make this central point. First of all,
a man was willing to marry the daughter, and marriage was the only way for
the young woman to "remedy" the "past events," but only if the crime was not
publically broadcast through the mother's flagellation. More generally though,

> public flagellation, intended to set an example, might still produce
> some scandal. The crime is still unknown to many; it would be so
> to nobody after such publicity. The revelation of such facts would
> perhaps not serve the ends to which punishment aims, that is the
> correction of customs. This is an offense [colpa] that by not being fre-
> quent seems to require such a solemn example all the less.[133]

The public example of corporeal crime for such an incestuous relationship
might paradoxically lead to the opposite result of what the judges were aiming
for. Rather than frightening people from committing such crimes, as Hobbes
had suggested, it would make them aware of its existence and therefore plausibly encourage imitators. Above all Verri pointed to the need for a political
weighing of the jurisprudence, the ultimate aim of which was not the law in
itself but what it sought to achieve—namely, the "correction of customs" in
society. What mattered—what was *just*—ultimately depended on what contributed to peaceful sociability, an argument that Beccaria would develop at
length and become uniquely affiliated with. For terror, the group maintained,
was not always the best vector of sociability.

Furthermore, and echoing the earlier argument regarding crime and poverty, Verri argued that although some jurists thought that "ignorance" was
not a valid excuse "when a wrong is committed [datur operam rei illicitae]," it
was not clear that this "poor, uncultured woman" was aware of the gravity of
her actions. Ignorance, like poverty, could not so easily be criminalized, for

they were themselves greater social ills in need of remedy, precisely the sorts of limits to social progress that "enlightenment" was meant to overcome. Finally, and most tellingly in terms of the group's legal arguments, there seemed to remain a "disproportion between the crime and the punishment" in the case of the incestuous woman. Verri cited previous cases to suggest that a mere "pecuniary" penalty would be more appropriate than corporeal punishment for such incest. The spirit of the law was inherently contextual, in that crimes and punishments, much like economic policies, had to be weighed in terms of their contributions to a progressive ideal of social betterment.[134]

Manuscript evidence similarly allows us to problematize Pietro Verri's above statement that On Crimes and Punishments was effectively his composition, based on Beccaria's rendering of ideas supplied to him by the Verri brothers. For reasons that will become clear in Chapter 6, Pietro Verri was already spreading these rumors in the late 1760s, much to Beccaria's consternation, yet not only do multiple embryonic "fragments" of the main arguments survive in Beccaria's hand, matching those Verri described as "pieces of paper" in his memoirs, but the first full and coherent ur-manuscript of the work—originally bearing the inverted title "Delle pene e delitti"—was entirely penned by the young Marquis.[135] This was the manuscript Beccaria gave Verri and which the latter subsequently edited for publication. Although Verri's textual interferences were numerous, and although the work had been conceptualized and composed in an intense dialogue with other members of the Academy of Fisticuffs, there can be no doubt that On Crimes and Punishments principally was Beccaria's work, and that he was its "author" in a modern sense of the term.[136] There will be time to return to Verri's editorial interventions later, but for the moment it suffices to say that he at times improved, and at times weakened, Beccaria's striking prose, that he toned down the numerous arguments for "literal" interpretations of the law as a plausible limit to magisterial abuses, and, perhaps most significantly, that he censored the young Marquis's clarion calls for truly widespread, one might even say "popular," enlightenment. Beccaria's statement in the original manuscript that "enlightenment restricted to the few is harmful, among the many it is not"—a clear idea animating many of the supplications he helped edit—is one example of what Verri's severe pen purged from the paper, even though the sentiment was common to the group.[137] Pietro Verri himself would, indeed, in private correspondence suggest that "we must expand sensibility, as it is all the more virtuous the more it tends to benefit a greater number, to all of society."[138] As it happened, however, the end result of *On Crimes and Punishments* was controversial enough.

Justice as Sociability

All too aware of the strictures of contemporary censorship, and, as the French writer Stendhal soon would put it, "traumatized" by the fear of persecution, Beccaria told his translator Morellet,

> In writing my work I had before my eyes Galileo, Machiavello and [Pietro] Gian[n]one. I heard the chains of superstition stir and the howls of fanaticism suffocate the whimpers of truth. This convinced me and forced me to be obscure and to wrap the lights of truth in a sacred fog. I have wanted to be a defender of mankind without being its martyr.[139]

With the examples of these persecuted and bedeviled thinkers in mind, Beccaria adopted various rhetorical strategies to avoid reprisals in his *On Crimes and Punishments* (including publishing it anonymously), generally in the spirit of Verri's careful caveat, in the opening pages of *Il Caffè*, that nothing "sacred" was to be discussed.[140]

His masterpiece nevertheless opened pugnaciously on the vexing question of inequality, criticizing the "tendency" for the "greatest power and happiness" to "accrue to the few while the rest are beset with weakness and misery." This, he learned from "our history books," was because

> laws, which are or should be pacts between free men, have been for the most part the instrument of the passions of the few or have arisen from a fortuitous and transient necessity. They have not been dictated by a calm student of human nature who has distilled the actions of a multitude of men and considered them from this point of view: *the greatest happiness shared among the greatest number.*[141]

Looking around him, and evidently to his group's writings, he saw reasons for hope, as in this "enlightened century" one had become aware of the true relations that obtain between sovereigns and their subjects and among different nations; commerce has become dynamic thanks to the philosophical truths made widely available by the printing press, and a quiet war of industry has broken out among nations, the most humane sort of war and the most worthy of reasonable men.[142]

But "very few," he noted, had "studied and fought against the cruelty of punishments" and "the irregularies of criminal procedures" complained about by contemporaries.

Yet the groans of the weak, sacrificed to cruel ignorance and wealthy indolence; the barbarous tortures multiplied with lavish and useless severity from crimes either unproven or imaginary; the squalor and the horrors of prison, intensified by uncertainty, the cruellest tormentor of the wretched—all of these should have roused those magistrates who guide human opinion.[143]

Beccaria thus took it upon himself to fight the proverbial good fight and change what increasing numbers of contemporaries across Europe were calling "public opinion," the same elusive yet powerful audience aimed for by Il Caffè.[144] And though he proclaimed to follow proudly in "the shining footsteps" of "the immortal President Montesquieu," he was clear from the outset to "distinguish my steps from his."[145] For a proper inquiry into the question of penal reform would demand nothing less than a rethinking of the social contract itself.

Like many of his contemporaries, Beccaria located the end of the state of nature and the origins of society in remotest antiquity. Though it often is assumed that the Scottish political economist Dugald Stewart coined the term "conjectural history" in his Life of Adam Smith to describe his master's endeavor, the term was already in use in English at the time, and the method, essentially what Rousseau had called "hypothetical history," had been applied for even longer:

To this species of philosophical investigation, which has no appropriated name in our language, I shall take the liberty of giving the title of *Theoretical* or *Conjectural History;* an expression which coincides pretty nearly in its meaning with that of *Natural History* as employed by Mr. Hume, and with what some French writers have called *Histoire Raisonée* [sic].[146]

Venturing to offer precisely such a philosophical investigation into the origins of human societies, Beccaria, like many before him, chose to emphasize the role of necessity in forming social relations. "The reproduction of the human species," he argued along economistic lines, "outstripped the means that sterile and uncultivated nature could offer to satisfy their increasingly intertwined needs, and brought together the earliest savages." Economic needs, in short, had first brought people together in the state of nature, a vision for the emergence of society that Beccaria would also have seen in Genovesi's translation of John Cary's *Essay on the State of England.* Ironically, however, whereas Genovesi in his annotations to Cary had argued that the Bristol merchant had "wished to delve into a subject which does not seem to be of his jurisdiction" and proven himself "poorly practiced in the history of humankind" for arguing that "all the orders of men that are now found in civilized nations were born from Commerce," Beccaria essentially agreed with the original.[147] Once some groups began banding together to fulfill their economic needs, others were forced to emulate them for reasons of security. "The first unions necessarily brought about the formation of others to oppose the former, and thus the state of war was transferred from individuals to nations," from people to peoples.[148] Seemingly closer to Hobbes than to Grotius or Rousseau on the question of human sociability, Beccaria saw no room for expansive sociability, let alone villages and settlements, in the state of nature, though humanity was characterized by the capacity to perfect it. The original challenge, however, was not simply that of sustaining complex societies; it was of going beyond even the orangutans.[149] Sociability, he had picked up from Hobbes and Pufendorf alike, was *learned,* depending on rigorous "discipline" and "training."[150]

But what did these social contracts entail for Beccaria?

Laws are the terms by which independent and isolated men united to form a society, once they tired of living in a perpetual state of war where the enjoyment of liberty was rendered useless by the

uncertainty of its preservation. They sacrificed a portion of this liberty so that they could enjoy the remainder in security and peace.
The sum of all these portions of liberty sacrificed for each individual's benefit constitutes the sovereignty of a nation, and the sover- •
eign is the legitimate keeper and administrator of those portions.[151]

Individuals, in short, invoked sovereignty by imbuing it with a part of
their liberty. The resultant authority was in turn devoted to defending the
liberties of its individual constituents and, importantly, sociability itself.[152] Yet
this partial sublimation of individual liberty into the greater political liberty
offered by subjection to their sovereign did not suffice to ensure sociability,
for wolves were not yet sacred; "men," as Beccaria's careful reader and American founding father James Madison soon would put it, were not "angels."[153]
The need for punishment arose for Beccaria, in a passage resonating with
echoes of Hobbes's *Leviathan* and Rousseau's *Social Contract,* not to mention
the earlier writings of the Academy of Fisticuffs, to combat "the despotic spirit
of every individual" and the universal instinct to "withdraw not only his own
share but also to usurp that belonging to others."[154] So pessimistic indeed was
the group's anthropology—which took criminal behavior to be almost
inevitable—that Beccaria resolutely rejected the idea that such a balanced
system could have emerged voluntarily for altruistic reasons: "No man ever
freely surrendered a portion of his own liberty for the sake of the public good;
such a chimera appears only in fiction," because "every man sees himself as
the center of all the world's affairs."[155]

Yet his was not a purely Hobbesian stance. In one of very few references
to specific authors in his entire work, Beccaria emphasized,

> It would be an error for someone speaking of a state of war prior to
> the establishment of society to understand it in a Hobbesian sense,
> that is, as entailing no duties or obligations prior to the establish-
> ment of society, rather than understanding the state of war as the
> outcome of the corruption of human nature and the lack of any
> express sanction.[156]

Like John Locke, Beccaria saw natural laws and a natural capacity for
sociability—however weak initially—binding humanity even before the ad-

vent of a social contract and of society as such, and considered the appearance of sovereignties and governments as driven by the necessary emergence of judicial power to sanction behavior and promote sociability. Quite unlike Locke, however, he identified the source of political authority squarely within the boundaries of a secular reality with no appeals to actual religious influences. A truly Hobbesian world only represented a past—and possibly future—absence of human justice.[157]

Though Beccaria and the Verri brothers agreed in practice about the logic of a social contract, one of Alessandro Verri's more philosophical articles in *Il Caffè* suggested the pertinent limitations of conjecture, and the importance of building political philosophy and what they soon would call the "social sciences" on "man and his principles":

> Would we need to establish whether men joined together in society out of fear, out of a love of their own kind or for their common defense, whether everyone originally gave up their natural freedom through certain contracts or for certain reasons? Would we deduce the law of nature and of nations from those ancient covenants? In what memoirs would we find them? These are arbitrary systems founded on what should or could have been, not on what was. Let us not posit hypothetical principles in matters in which we need sure and constant principles. Even if we could explain, so to speak, all moral phenomena and political cases by a hypothesis, just as we can explain all natural effects by a physical hypothesis, we would still not have reduced the rule of justice and injustice to likely principles. Let us not be Cartesians in morals; we have no vortices in these matters. Let us not substitute great and simple errors for the least ostentatious, though most certain truth. Let us start from man and his principles; let us take advantage of them and build on them. There can be no other foundation.[158]

Whatever the mysteries of primeval history, the role of the enlightened lawmaker, for the Academy of Fisticuffs, was to regulate the interaction of human passions to ensure the thriving not only of individual lives but of polities and, importantly, of humanity writ large. "Legislation," Beccaria wrote, was "the art of guiding men to the greatest happiness, or to the least unhappiness possible, to put it in terms of the total calculus of the goods and evils of life," what Verri would call the "calculus of pleasures and pains"; but to make any sort of headway in this discipline, one first had to accept that "it is not possible to reduce the turbulent activity of mankind to a geometric order devoid of irregularity and confusion."[159] This was quite plausibly a reference to the French physician and materialist philosopher Julien Offrey de La Mettrie's essay *L'homme machine* (Machine man), a work that had struck a chord with members of Verri's group and that, though expressing confidence that the universe was "geometrical" and mechanistic, strongly argued that evidence "teaches us never to draw general conclusions, even from all the most decisive experiments ever known."[160] Fittingly, Beccaria's favorite metaphor for legislation was architecture, in which a skilled legislator, like an architect, had to "counteract" the "ruinous" pull of forces, whether gravity or self-interest, "to align those forces that contribute to the strength of the building," constructing society on the paradoxical "foundation of self-love" and making "the general interest" the "product of the interests of each."[161]

Historically, this process had been anything but easy, and this insight gave Beccaria one of his clearest arguments against Rousseau's first *Discourse,* which had been devoted to how the arts and sciences had furthered corruption and inequality. Mankind had only been able to progress through its mistakes; what hurt society had, in Nietzschean terms, indeed made it stronger.

> It is not true that the sciences have always been harmful to humanity, and that when they have been so, it was an evil that man could not avoid. The multiplication of the human species across the face of the earth introduced war, the cruder arts, and the first laws, which were temporary pacts that arose and perished according to necessity. This was the first philosophy of men, whose few elements were just, because their indolence and their lack of wisdom saved them from error. But the needs of men multiplied as the number of men increased. Stronger and more lasting impressions were necessary, therefore, to discourage them from repeated returns to the original state of unsociability, which was becoming increasingly ruinous. Those first errors that populated the earth with false gods and created an invisible universe that regulated our own were, therefore, of great benefit to humanity (I mean a great political benefit).[162]

Only through such "errors," often superstitious in nature, had society gradually taken shape. "These were the first events of all nations that developed
from the savage peoples; this was the epoch in which great societies were
formed, and such was the nature of the bond necessary to bind them—
perhaps the only bond," to which he added that he was "not speaking of that
people chosen by God, for whom the most extraordinary miracles and the
most remarkable graces took the place of human politics."[163]

And so, countless polities cemented by ideals of "justice" arose from man's
unsocial origins, through trial and error as well as through vigilance and rigorous disciplining. In the opening dialogue of Plato's *Republic,* Thrasyma-
chus had suggested to Socrates that "justice" was "nothing other than the
advantage of the stronger." Beccaria's definition could not have been more
different, being "nothing but the bond required to hold particular interests
together, without which they would dissolve into the old state of unsociability." It was, as such, not a "real thing," merely a "human way of conceiving
things" that in no way was related to "that other kind of justice, which emanates from God and is directly concerned with the punishments and rewards
of life in the hereafter." There was a fundamental distinction between crime
and sin, and Beccaria considered justice a quintessentially secular concept related not to eternal values but to the basic needs of sociability in any given
moment. Justice in effect *was* sociability, and vice versa. And laws were good
or bad as they furthered or hindered just sociability.[164]

Of course, others before Beccaria had suggested something similar.
Vattel, in his best-selling *Droit des gens,* or *The Law of Nations,* a work with
which the Fisticuffs had engaged at length and that Stephen C. Neff has called
"the handbook of choice for statesmen and judges throughout Europe and
in the New World colonies as well," argued,

> Justice is the basis of all society, the sure bond of all commerce.
> Human society, far from being an intercourse of assistance and good
> offices, would be no longer any thing but a vast scene of robbery, if
> no respect were paid to this virtue, which secures to every one his
> own.[165]

But Vattel did not go as far as to reduce justice to sociability as such, a sentiment Beccaria might have elaborated on the basis of Samuel von Pufendorf's

dictum that "all that necessarily and normally makes for sociality is understood to be prescribed by natural law. All that disturbs or violates sociality is understood as forbidden."[166] The theologically rather radical nature of Beccaria's stance becomes clearly evident when compared to other popular conceptions of justice at the time, such as Rousseau's claim in *The Social Contract* that "all justice comes from God."[167] For Beccaria, justice was simply secular sociability, that which made peaceful human coexistence possible.

Justice *and* Fairness

The constant threat of societal collapse explained for Beccaria the need to defend justice with punishments, a secularized—in Weberian terms, "disenchanted"—conception of law and order that, by dispelling vengeance from the legal imagination, could focus on "prevention," the only acceptable "purpose of punishment." Sickened by the numbing and brutalizing spectacles of torture and execution he had grown up with in Milan, Beccaria urged the promulgation of laws in the vernacular and the domestication of unsocial passions through widespread enlightenment, the express purpose of *Il Caffè*.[168] "Do you want to prevent crimes?" he asked rhetorically. "Then see to it that enlightenment accompanies liberty." Yet he did not argue that one should set a stop to public displays of punishment entirely—far from it. Even petty crimes, Beccaria argued against the letter of Alessandro Verri's supplication in the case of the incestuous woman, should be punished in public to ensure the most transparent and public operation of the law imaginable, but, agreeing with the spirit of it, all punishments should be made milder, more humane, and "enlightened," measures that fostered sociability more effectively than terror.[169]

Equally importantly, legislators had to simplify and normalize the criminal code, ensuring the certainty of sentences and crucially establishing the right "proportion between crimes and punishments" in order to properly "deter men from committing crimes."[170] Though building on earlier suggestions by writers like Montesquieu and Vattel, Beccaria would be lionized throughout the European world for his rendering of this argument regarding the right proportionality of punishments. Jeremy Bentham might have dryly noted that Beccaria's advice ultimately was "more oracular than instructive" on this point, but, however vague, the principle of proportionality was eventually enshrined in Article XV of the 1793 Declaration of the Rights of Man and of the Citizen: "The law ought to impose only penalties that are strictly and obviously necessary: the punishments ought to be proportionate to the offense and useful to society."[171]

Everyone, Beccaria argued in an equally influential passage of *On Crimes and Punishments,* including nobles and the clergy, had to be equal before the law; for "to be legitimate, every distinction, whether it be in honor or wealth, presupposes an anterior equality founded on the laws."[172] This was part of a larger call for a more just and egalitarian society, one obvious fallout of which touched upon the ongoing European debate over whether the nobility should engage in economic endeavors. As part of the secular move away from "Gothic" or "feudal" political structures toward the full utilization of domestic resources both natural and human, Beccaria had no doubts that privileged people like himself should join the economy on an equal footing with everyone else, and saw a principal political challenge of commercial society to be precisely the task of maintaining such equality in legal and societal terms, as the fortunes—material and otherwise—of families and individuals by necessity diverged over time.[173] In fact, the very logic of a society structured and defined by commercial exchanges voided the idea of permanent economic segregation. This was a stance argued for forcefully by the members of the Academy of Fisticuffs, who were at the forefront of contemporary debates also in relation to the introduction of women to the workforce, which soon resonated in the inner sanctum of the Habsburg Empire.[174] As Maria Teresa's prime minister, Wenzel Anton von Kaunitz, praised the empowerment of business in a letter to Beccaria's friend Carli:

> Meanwhile I am delighted by the fact that the merchant class realizes the benefit dispensed to it by the clemency of Her Majesty, and that it appears intent on profiting from it. I hope that this fervor continues with corresponding effects, because from this must derive not only the public good but also the disillusionment of the nobility and the forceful convincing of the impassioned critics.[175]

Not only did Habsburg reforms facilitate and encourage the rise of the mercantile elements of the empire, but the hope was, for the sake of the "common good," that their success in turn would lead to further commercialization of society itself as more and more people emulated the "merchant class."

For Beccaria, such a social realignment and transformation based on the political support of fair economic pursuits could only occur on the basis of profound judicial reform; the ideal equality inherent to voluntary economic interactions would be possible only on the basis of an undisputed parity before the law. Given that "the true measure of crimes" was simply *the injury made to society,*" and given what ultimately mattered was the fragile sociability of mankind, "punishments should be the same for the highest as they are for the lowest of citizens."[176] The social contract itself demanded it:

> If every particular member is bound to society, society is likewise bound to every particular member by a contract that by its nature places both parties under obligation. This obligation, that descends from the throne to the hovel and equally binds the most elevated and the most wretched of men, means nothing other than that it is in the interest of all that the pacts useful to the greatest number be observed. The infringement of even one of them begins to legitimate anarchy.[177]

If the "political purpose of punishment" was to "instill fear in others," as argued by both Giulio Claro and Hobbes, Beccaria noted, then the "secret and private carnage" of torture was the antithesis of justice.[178] The ancient but perhaps rarely practiced ideal that pain might assist in the "purgation of infamy"—or, as an early eighteenth-century inquisitorial handbook intoned, "per mezzo del castigo salvino l'anime loro" ("through torture save their souls")—was similarly anathema to Beccaria on the basis of his strict differentiation between worldly and spiritual affairs, and evidence anyway suggested to him that "all differences between the guilty and the innocent disappear" in the crucible of pain.[179] Torture was an abomination because it failed twice. On the one hand, torture failed to consistently terrorize populations into sociability because it often was conducted in secret state spaces; on the other hand, the pain involved meant subjects were willing to say anything the torturer wished to hear in order to make it stop. "The impression of pain," he wrote, "may increase to such a degree, that, filling the entire sensory capacity, it leaves the torture victim no liberty but to choose the shortest route to relieve his pain momentarily . . . and thus the innocent and sentient man will declare himself guilty if he thinks that doing so will make the pain cease."[180] But it is worth noting that Beccaria and his followers at times seemed to conflate two very distinct practices of torture in early modern Europe: torture as punishment and torture as a device to discover truth in criminal proceedings—an example followed by numerous others, including Voltaire.[181] Though tenuous, this rhetorical move fell on fertile ground at a time when earlier conceptions of pain as useful and even salutary, inspired also by Christian concerns with cleansing and redemption, gradually were overturned.[182] Beccaria took his defense of bodily integrity farther than almost anyone before him, and his most revolutionary argument was against the institution of capital punishment itself.

The Right to Kill

Carli may have thought that "the ideas" expressed in *On Crimes and Punishments*, "to tell the truth, are Rousseau's," but though he was a very serious reader of *The Social Contract*, Beccaria eventually challenged the very foundations of the Genevan's vision with regard to the social contract and the state's right to kill.[183] "It is asked," Rousseau noted in *The Social Contract*, "how individuals who have no right to dispose of their own life can transfer to the Sovereign that same right which they do not have," but concluded that the question simply was "badly put," for "everyone has the right to risk his life in order to save it." Joining society was, as such, a form of Russian roulette for Rousseau, an all-or-nothing gambit in which an individual willingly sacrificed everything, including life itself, to an external judge of communal expediency:

> and when the Prince has said to him, it is expedient to the State that you die, he ought to die; since it is only on this condition that he has lived in security until then, and his life is no longer only a bounty of nature, but a conditional gift of the state.[184]

In effect, Rousseau echoed an established argument that was deeply entrenched in both Christian and natural law traditions: "Every evil-doer who attacks social right becomes a rebel and a traitor to the fatherland by his

Alessandro Magnasco, *The Inquisition or Interrogation in a Prison*, ca. 1710–1720.

crimes, by violating its laws he ceases to be a member of it, and even enters
into war with it." Having "broken the social treaty," he was no longer a
"member of the state" but its "enemy," fit for the abattoir "by right of war."
That said, he offered the caveat that "one only has the right to put to death,
even as an example, someone who cannot be preserved without danger." The
ultimate authority over life and death remained, however, in the subjective
will of the sovereign, the ultimate arbiter of what constituted "danger" to
the polity, why, and who deserved to die because of it.[185]

Beccaria took a radically different stance, but superficially appeared to
reach a similar conclusion. True, citizens had given up parts of their liberty
to imbue a sovereign entity with the power to maintain justice and thus
sociability, but they had not given it power over life and death. His very conception of sovereignty, of "the general will," simply lacked the "right" to
"slaughter" citizens subjected to it, who in crucial regards remained precisely
that even after having been convicted of crimes. Here a terminological point
is in order. Beccaria invoked the term *"volontà generale"* in his critique of capital punishment, but this was a far cry from Rousseau's concept of *"volonté
générale."*[186] In effect, Beccaria defined the "general will" as "the aggregate of
particular wills"—in other words, as what Rousseau called the *"volonté de
tous"* or "will of all" in exact opposition to his more alchemical notion of a
"general will."[187] Where the "general will," for Rousseau, revolved around
what he deemed the "common interest," the "will of all" focused merely on
the sum of all "private interest."

> There is often a considerable difference between the will of all and
> the general will: the latter looks only to the common interest, the
> former looks to private interest, and is nothing but a sum of partic-
> ular wills; but if, from these same wills, one takes away the pluses
> and the minuses which cancel each other out, what is left as the sum
> of the differences is the general will.[188]

It is striking that Beccaria, the far superior mathematician, refused to
quantify qualitative differences in the polity and thus diminish the primacy
of the individual in the collective. Tyrannies of the majority were, in short,
not his thing. "Who," Beccaria asked rhetorically before the age of state-
sanctioned and doctor-assisted euthanasia, "has ever willingly given other

men the authority to kill him?" His answer was nobody, for men did not even have the right to kill themselves in Beccaria's moral imagination—natural law itself was based on, and framed by, the rights of self-preservation. As such, the "death penalty is not a *right,* but," overturning Rousseau entirely, "the war of a nation against a citizen." The only case in which Beccaria could accept an execution was in the hypothetical case in which someone

> retains such connections and such power that he endangers the security of the nation even when deprived of his liberty, that is when his very existence can provoke a dangerous revolution in the established form of government. The death of such a citizen, then, becomes necessary when a nation is recovering or losing its liberty, or in time of anarchy, when disorder itself takes the place of laws.[189]

Necessity, it turned out, knew no law. And because of this Beccaria left a loophole in his otherwise passionate and adamant rejection of capital punishment, one that, though clearly meant for only the most extreme cases, remained remarkably capacious. If he had his way, however, the Confraternity of the Beheaded St. John the Baptist would face bleak times indeed. In fact, in the context of their activities in Milan, one of the central passages of the attack on capital punishment in *On Crimes and Punishments* takes on new meaning when it rails against "religion" that "comes into the mind of the scoundrel, who misuses everything, and, offering him an easy repentance and near-certainty of eternal happiness, greatly diminishes the horror of the final tragedy."[190] Not only would Torriggia's brutalizing death, described in Chapter 1, be a threat to the social fabric and to humanity itself, but what slight preventive justification it could have had would be entirely voided by the Confraternity's religious usurpation of an essentially political process. Just as the presumed virtues of torture were counteracted by the habitual secrecy of its implementation, so the virtues of public executions were undermined by theological promises of eternal salvation through repentence. As such, Beccaria in effect argued, religion actively assisted in the unraveling of sociability, divine law by definition becoming *unjust.*

In Beccaria's eyes this was not the only way in which capital punishment failed to live up to its policy expectations; the death penalty, he argued, was simply "useless."[191] Though political philosophers long had argued that "terror" was the principal justification for executions, Beccaria followed Montesquieu and Vattel in arguing that people's sensitivities eventually could be stunted to the extent that even the most horrible tortures failed to instill their intended psychological effect in witnesses, precisely the form of emotional curbing Verri had observed in the field during the Seven Years' War.[192] In a passage that would greatly inspire the twentieth-century French-Algerian philosopher and Nobel laureate Albert Camus, Beccaria noted that, given this calculus of impressionability,

> if it is important that men frequently observe the power of the laws, executions must not be separated by long intervals: they, therefore, require that crimes be committed frequently, and thus in order for this punishment to be useful, it is necessary that it not make the full impression on men that it should, that is, it must be useful and useless at the same time.[193]

Rather than being executed, he proposed that criminals instead should be condemned to hard work. This would not only offer the state free labor but also serve the pedagogical purpose of punishment better than the gallows, offering to perpetrators and the wider citizenry alike a constant reminder of the costs of crime.[194] "With the death penalty, every example given to the nation requires a crime," Beccaria noted in a curious appeal to both humanitarianism and utilitarianism; "with permanent penal servitude, a single crime provides many and lasting examples."[195] Although the circulation of printed accounts of executions to a certain extent must have counteracted this effect in practice, his point was that, given the finality of the judgment, an execution could be witnessed and learned from only once, whereas forced laborers could serve the citizenry as daily cues to the relationship between crime and punishment for the full duration of their sentences. The third edition of *On Crimes and Punishments,* published in Lausanne in 1765, included a frequently republished and reinterpreted allegorical frontispiece by the engraver Giovanni Lapi, based on a sketch by Beccaria himself, that illustrated precisely this point.[196] It played on many of the tropes of the work and of its context, and can fruitfully be juxtaposed with the imagery adopted by the Confraternities of the Beheaded St. John the Baptist at the time. A clear-sighted Justice looks away in disgust, refusing the gruesome tribute of severed heads offered by an executioner, and instead turns her gaze to a collection of work-related instruments, including shovels, hammers, and ploughs, that represented Beccaria's favored punishment of hard labor. In later variations, the rejection of the traditional dungeonesque iconography of punishment, as well as the site of forced labor, became even more explicit as the indoor scene was moved into an open glade, symbolizing, perhaps, the openness and clarity, not only of the criminal proceedings, but of the punishment and its moral lessons as well.[197]

Allegorical frontispiece by Giovanni Lapi for the third edition of Beccaria's *On Crimes and Punishments,* 1765.

Crime and Inequality in Commercial Society

The Königsberg philosopher Immanuel Kant famously dismissed Beccaria's argument against capital punishment as "moved by overly compassionate feelings for an affected humanity" and as being "all sophistry and juristic trickery." Justice, he would maintain, was a question of retribution, not sociability, a stance that helps elucidate important aspects of the Academy of Fisticuffs' approach to crime and punishment. Of course people could give up their right to life in the social contract, Kant maintained, for murder was, in accordance with the *ius talionis,* or right of retaliation, justly punished by murder, and, by virtue of being a hypothetical "co-legislator" of penal law, an individual in society by necessity authorized the use of punishment, including capital punishment, against itself.[198] It was a form of argument that the Fisticuffs frequently lambasted because it threatened sociability by relying on ideal concepts like "pure reason" and on a blindness to issues of context, social inequality, and ultimately hierarchies of power. For Beccaria, in fact, many crimes were neither expressions of evil nor errors of judgment, but instead, as the group's numerous supplications had reflected, acts of necessity, born from an imbalance in the architecture of the social world itself. You could not simply "abstract from all conditions of space and time."[199] Given man's undeniable passions, crime was even the logical outcome of extremes of inequality, and it was the task of the legislator to address structural inequities through levers both legal and economic in order to secure sociability and thus the possibility of worldly melioration. Laws, in short, currently failed to reflect the needs of *justice;* that is, they did not secure *sociability,* which depended on a great deal more social and material equality than Europe presently harbored:

> Who can fail to be deeply shaken by the sight of thousands of wretches whom poverty—whether willed or tolerated by the laws, which have always favored the few and abused the many—has dragged desperately back to the original state of nature . . . ?[200]

Poverty served the same unhappy function for Beccaria as war did for Verri: it was a social solvent and ultimately a decivilizing force to be fought and guarded against at all costs. And, like many of the Fisticuffs, Beccaria deeply feared the idea and reality of inequality before the laws. "The rich and powerful," he maintained,

> should not be able to make amends for assaults against the weak and the poor by naming a price; otherwise, wealth, which is the reward of industry under the tutelage of laws, becomes fodder for tyranny. There is no liberty whenever the laws permit a man in some cases to cease to be a *person* and to become a *thing*.[201]

Such injustice—and at its unadulterated apex, the commodification of persons perpetrated by the institution slavery—was literally dehumanizing. But beyond the needs to ensure legal equality to constrain and channel the profit motive within the "tutelage of laws," there was a point at which justice by definition had to be redistributive, and eighteenth-century Europe clearly found itself at precisely such a juncture in Beccaria's eyes. For, given present circumstances, the social contract itself seemed at risk. Ventriloquizing a hypothetical thief who was at the opposite end of the contemporary social spectrum from Demetrius's coffee shop, he spelled out the emotive logic of crime with maudlin clarity:

> What are these laws that I am supposed to respect, which leave such a great gap between me and the rich man? He denies me the penny I ask of him and justifies himself by ordering me to work, something with which he himself is unfamiliar. Who made these laws? Rich and powerful men who have never deigned to visit the squalid hovels of the poor, who have never broken mouldy bread amid the innocent cries of hungry children and a wife's tears. Let us break these ties, which are harmful to the majority and useful only to a few and to indolent tyrants; let us attack injustice at its source.[202]

Theft, in particular, Beccaria insisted, should be treated far less severely than it was, for it was "a crime born of poverty and desperation, a crime of that unhappy segment of men for whom the right to property (*a terrible and perhaps unnecessary right*) has left them nothing but a bare existence."[203] What one is to make of Beccaria's striking statement, which closely echoes similar ones in *Il Caffè*, is a question of debate, perhaps because it is one of the very few parts of his oeuvre that straightforwardly connects eighteenth- to nineteenth-century conceptions of "socialism."[204] Friedrich Engels would eventually write about the Enlightenment predecessors of "modern socialism" that their "kingdom of reason was nothing more than the idealized kingdom of the bourgeoisie," because they were unable to "go beyond the limits imposed upon them by their epoch" to really see the plight of the "proletariat."[205] But Beccaria's depiction of the forlorn thief challenging the very nature of justice in a commercial society that allowed for such material inequities to exist was far more inclusive than that. The question itself, however, which Hont called "the paradox of commercial society" and which in the nineteenth century would be addressed everywhere in the form of the "social question," was old.[206] Could economic inequality ever be *just?*[207]

Philosophers had, of course, wrestled with this question for millennia. Famously, the thirteenth-century Dominican theologian Saint Thomas Aquinas, in his question "whether it is lawful to steal in the case of necessity," defended the theft of bread by the poor and presented an uncompromising moral economy:

> According to the natural order instituted by divine providence, material goods are provided for the satisfaction of human needs. Therefore the division and appropriation of property, which proceeds from human law, must not hinder the satisfaction of man's necessity from such goods. Equally, whatever a man has in superabundance is owed, of natural right, to the poor for their sustenance. So Ambrose says, and it is also found in the *Decretum* of Gratian, the bread which you withold belongs to the hungry, the clothing you shut away to the naked, and the money you bury in the earth is the redemption and freedom of the penniless.[208]

A similar stance found its trumpet in early modern political philosophy when it was expounded by the seventeenth-century theorist Thomas Hobbes. The law, he argued, was invented to protect people's lives. Therefore, the moment one had to steal food to survive, laws against theft ceased to apply. As he put it in his *Leviathan:*

> When a man is destitute of food, or other things necessary for his life, and cannot preserve himself any other way, but by some fact

against the law; as if in a great famine he takes the food by force, or stealth, which he cannot obtain for money nor charity . . . he is totally excused.[209]

Few were willing to follow Hobbes all the way, though his sentiment echoed throughout the Enlightenment, also with regard to less terminal cases of economic inequality. On one end of the eighteenth-century spectrum, Rousseau had powerfully argued that there existed a "perpetual war" between "the rich" and the rest.

> The first man who, having enclosed a piece of ground, to whom it occurred to say *this is mine,* and found people sufficiently simple to believe him, was the true founder of civil society. How many crimes, wars, murders, how many miseries and horrors Mankind would have been spared by him who, pulling the stakes or filling in the ditch, had cried out to his kind: Beware of listening to this impostor; You are lost if you forget that the fruits are everyone's and the Earth no one's.[210]

A long tradition of pamphleteers and political economists had engaged with the question to reach a very different conclusion, however, and the perhaps best-known answer to the challenge posed by increasing material inequalities in commercial societies—and to Rousseau as such—was that of Adam Smith. His *Wealth of Nations* would acknowledge that, yes, inequalities were indeed greater than ever before in human history, but at the same time *everyone* was wealthier in absolute terms because of the virtuous circle set in motion by unconditional property rights and their incentive to improve one's conditions in a commercial society characterized by the division of labor. Inequality was quid pro quo for increased general welfare:

> Without the assistance and co-operation of many thousands, the very meanest person in a civilized country could not be provided . . . what we very falsely imagine [to be] the easy and simple manner in which he is accommodated. Compared, indeed, with the more extravagant luxury of the great, his accommodation must no doubt appear extremely simple and easy; and yet it may be true, perhaps,

that the accommodation of an European prince does not always so
'much exceed that of an industrious and frugal peasant, as the accommodation of the latter exceeds that of many an African king, the
absolute master of the lives and liberties of ten thousand naked
savages.[211]

The Scotsman's main retort to Rousseau's *Discourse*—and, one may add, to
Hobbes—in the *Wealth of Nations* thus relied on the fact that, materially
speaking, the institution of private property had made even the poorest segments of society better off. It mattered little to Smith that commercial societies made some individuals infinitely better off than others, because the
proverbial rising tide lifted all boats.[212] He explained this mechanism in his
earlier *Theory of Moral Sentiments*:

> The rich . . . consume little more than the poor, and in spite of their
> natural selfishness and rapacity, though they mean only their own
> conveniency, though the sole end which they propose from the
> labours of all the thousands whom they employ, be the gratification
> of their own vain and insatiable desires, they divide with the poor
> the produce of all their improvements. They are led by an *invisible
> hand* to make nearly the same distribution of the necessaries of life,
> which would have been made, had the earth been divided into equal
> portions among all its inhabitants, and thus without intending it,
> without knowing it, advance the interest of the society, and afford
> means to the multiplication of the species. When *Providence* divided
> the earth among a few lordly masters, it neither forgot nor aban-
> doned those who seemed to have been left out in the partition.
> These last too enjoy their share of all that it produces. In what con-
> stitutes the real happiness of human life, they are in no respect infe-
> rior to those who would seem so much above them. *In ease of body
> and peace of mind, all the different ranks of life are nearly upon a level,
> and the beggar, who suns himself by the side of the highway, possesses that
> security which kings are fighting for.*[213]

The passage is worth dwelling on. "Providence," in Smith's view, operated
actively through an "invisible hand" to ensure that material welfare would

trickle down from the richest in society to the poorest, who anyway were "nearly on a level," if not indeed superior, with regard to "the real happiness of human life," because, unencumbered by occupations, housing, and possessions, they could enjoy the pleasures of roadside tanning. Even St. Augustine, with whom a providential view of history is often associated, was wary, as R. A. Markus has shown, of seeing events and politico-economic systems within "the *saeculum,* the world of men and time," preceding the *eschaton* as guided by God or imbued with sacred significance.[214]

Nonetheless, Smith thought that the beggar's life was as good as it got, and himself never conceived of "market society" as being able to "guarantee anything more than strict justice," understood as "the rigid enforcement of 'to each his own'"—that is, of property rights.[215] "Charity" toward the starving and the hungry might round off the sharper edges of such a society, but only as an expression of "benevolence," not "justice." For Smith, drawing on an established tradition of natural law, "distributive justice" pertained to the realm of "imperfect" rather than "perfect" "rights"; it was voluntary, not necessary, and therefore did not belong "properly to jurisprudence."[216] Without property rights, without respect for "justice" thus understood, "the great, the immense fabric of human society, that fabric which to raise and support seems in this world, if I may say so, to have been the peculiar and darling care of Nature, must in a moment crumble into atoms."[217] There were, as by now is well known, numerous areas in which Smith saw a fruitful role for the state to intervene in economic life, but only in cases of "the most urgent necessity"—of manifest famine—could the state justly step in, under the rubrik of "reason of state," to save lives at the expense of private property. And it is worth noting that only states could violate the laws in these ways, and not, as in Hobbes's view, individuals, however starving they might be.[218] As Quesnay's acolyte Pierre-Joseph-André Roubaud similarly would emphasize in a context of deep subsistence trauma in France in the wake of the Physiocratic reforms, "needs are not rights."[219]

Needless to say, this definition of justice was very different from that of the Academy of Fisticuffs, who conceived of it much more broadly as sociability. From Smith's point of view, Beccaria's monologue would have been an affront to nature. Yet the Scotsman's praise of the roadside beggar betrayed precisely the sort of worldview against which the Milanese reformer rebelled, and for the same reason that, by unraveling the sociability on which commercial societies depended, it would encourage atomization. Even Smith's friend Hume had noted, in his *Essays*, that there *could* be such a thing as too much relative inequality, however much better off everyone was in absolute terms compared to the state of nature:

> A too great disproportion among the citizens weakens any state. Every person, if possible, ought to enjoy the fruits of his labour, in a full possession of all the necessaries, and many of the conveniencies of life. No one can doubt, but such an equality is most suitable to human nature.[220]

Hume's notion of "necessaries" was not far from Verri's concept of "absolute wants," and what everyone should have access to in a commercial society. But Hume's insistence that "too great disproportion" anyway "weakens any state," even if "equality" in terms of necessities was secured, opened up for a whole world of social policies for which he gave precious few guidelines. He did, however, suggest that states could intervene "even in less urgent necessities," a markedly weaker defense of property rights than Smith's, and generally argued that "rules of equity or justice depend entirely on the particular state and condition in which men are placed."[221]

Verri and Beccaria, and, as Chapter 3 will make clear, their friend Henry Lloyd, would all build on Hume's caveats to engage with the continuing problem, in spite of arguments by theorists of natural law for the sufficiency of "strict justice," of relative inequality *within* commercial societies. The Fisticuffs agreed that property was a "social convention," and not at all something justified by recourse to the wishes of some mystical "Nature" the way Smith would; but Beccaria only made his statement on the matter even stronger in later editions of the *On Crimes and Punishments*. Whereas the first edition had argued that property was a "terrible, but perhaps necessary right," Beccaria's revisions to the third edition ambiguously changed the phrase to "terrible, and perhaps unnecessary right."[222] Similarly, he would insert a striking passage in the section on "Debtors":

> Commerce and the ownership of goods are not the goal of the social pact, but they may be a means for achieving that end. To expose members of society to the evils to which so many circumstances give

rise, would be to subordinate the ends to the means—a paralogism in all of the sciences, especially in the science of politics. I fell into this error in earlier editions, in which I said that the innocent bankrupt should be imprisoned as a pledge of his debts or made to work like a slave for his creditors. I am ashamed of having written in this way. I have been accused of irreligion and did not deserve it. I have been accused of sedition and I did not deserve it. I have offended against the rights of humanity, and yet no one has admonished me for it.[223]

Beccaria's foreign critics quickly picked up on the ambiguity in *On Crimes and Punishments* with regard to property rights, with the Physiocrat Dupont de Nemours lambasting him in print for not according them sufficient importance, unequivocally stating that "the *right to property*" was *not* a "*terrible right*" at all, but instead the foundation of most things that mattered.[224] Even Verri maintained that Beccaria had gone too far, and in the wake of their fallout he criticized this specific argument repeatedly in private writings.[225] In a letter to his brother Alessandro, he joked that Beccaria, recently invited by Catherine the Great to rewrite the Russian legal code, would "begin the Code by abolishing the right to property; he will give you something fit for a novel [*ti farà un romanzo*]."[226] He, too, however, was vexed by the Janus-faced nature of inequality, and agreed, in his later economic writings, with Beccaria that "when the wealth of the nation is amassed in the hands of the few . . . no abundance and no civil liberty will be found in that nation." At the same time though, he warned that "direct laws" to ensure "careful adherence to the permanent uniformity of fortunes would remove emulation" to the extent that nobody would feel "the stimulus of need, everything would languish, and society would approach the state of isolation and savagery." Therefore, he concluded, when "there is too much inequality in the distribution of wealth, and equally when there is perfect equality, annual reproduction becomes restricted to bare necessity and industry is destroyed." The aim of a legislator was to reach a healthy "midpoint between these two extremes."[227]

Truth be told, Verri's stance was not very distant from Beccaria's. The latter himself never repeated the phrase about the "terrible right" in other contexts besides new editions of *On Crimes and Punishments,* and would, as soon will be clear, devote his life to the legislation of economic development in an increasingly commercialized society based on the institution of private property and its unique capacity to incentivize private interests for the common good. Indeed, the Fisticuffs aligned clearly with the mainstream of Italian political economy in explicitly and repeatedly arguing for state support for competitive individual initiatives rather than for the establishment of communal or state-owned enterprises or, for that matter, monopolistic privileges.[228] Their deep belief in meritocracy and individualism carried economic as well as social and political consequences, with a certain degree—always contextually dependent—of inequality serving to spur emulation and betterment for all.

So what should one make of Beccaria's infamous phrase? Perhaps, more than a concrete part of his policy proposal, it was simply a rhetorical flourish meant to empower the sentimental resonance of his argument against inhumanity and injustice. Or perhaps it was simply meant to give emphasis to this powerful "means" of achieving sociable "ends." Whatever the case, the creative tension between meritocracy and equality, property, and sociability that lay at the very core of his vision of commercial society would never—and perhaps *can* never—fully be resolved. Though the tone of Beccaria's argument at times mirrored that of a Rousseau, his qualifications of the institution were far more guarded than the Genevan's, if simultaneously much, much more expansive than Smith's.

Beccaria clearly fell somewhere between the two extremes proposed by Rousseau and Smith, and it is worth stating, for the record, that Rousseau and Smith represented rather radical arguments on opposite ends of the spectrum of Enlightenment political economy. One argued that the world would have been better off without *any* individual property at all; the other that the invisible hand of divine providence ensured that even the poorest beggars were *actually, literally* as happy as the wealthiest kings even though homeless, penniless, and, one can only assume, eventually hungry for more than sunlight and roadside dust.[229] Far more secular than both Rousseau and Smith, Beccaria ultimately put his faith in the capacity of human agency to navigate the imperfections of the universe on its own, championing a pragmatic world in which the productive tension between incentives and economic inequality did not break down at the expense of sociability. However serious Beccaria was at the time in questioning the limits of private property, it was clear to him that previous writers had confused society's ends with its means: "Commerce and the [private] ownership of goods," he stressed, "are not the goal of the social pact, but they may be a means of achieving that end." In fact, man had no "natural right" to property, merely a "social" one. Properly understood, a commercial society was a type of society based *on* commerce rather than a social organization *of* commerce.[230]

Where legal equality had to be absolute, economic equality had to be constituted broadly enough to permit, and even facilitate, the meritocratic incentives on which commercial forms of sociability rested. Understood as sociability, justice required, on the model of Hume but more forcefully, neither too much nor too little material equality. To make the exact opposite point, the Austrian economist and praxeologist Ludwig von Mises would, much later, argue that "society is not an end but a means, the means by which each individual member seeks to attain his own ends," based on an ideal of "reciprocity" of which "the wolf eats the lamb" was his best example.[231] In a world based on the utilitarian calculus of pleasure and pain, however, in which easy appeals to "Nature" and "Providence" were not an option, the prerogatives of sociability trumped property and propriety alike for Beccaria.[232]

A Penumbral Enlightenment

One of Beccaria's most incisive readers, the Pisan philosopher Giovanni Gualberto de Soria, observed that *On Crimes and Punishments* "travels farther than it seems, means more than it sounds like, and at times does not mean what it sounds like."[233] Penal law was, indeed, far from a minor aspect of "police" or public policy for Beccaria—it was the quiet lever of total societal reform.[234] "Laws," intended to be "pacts between free men," had historically taken the form of "instruments of the passions of the few" or been the result of "fortuitous and transient necessity," while what should have mattered was "guiding men to the greatest happiness, or to the least unhappiness possible, to put it in terms of the total calculus of the goods and evils of life." Humanity's final goal could only be *"the greatest happiness shared among the greatest number."*[235] The present was, in world historical time, the moment to act, and *On Crimes and Punishments* was in many ways the culmination of the Fisticuffs' reformist fervor. The coming of political economy—of competitive international regulation and "police"—had revolutionized everything, and as penal reforms could bring order to the microcosm of polities, so political economy could finally socialize the macro-relations between them. "Commerce," Beccaria argued on the backs of Verri and Franci, had "become dynamic thanks to the philosophical truths made widely available by the printing press, and a quiet war of industry has broken out among nations, the most humane sort of war and the most worthy of reasonable men." These were the "fruits that we owe to this enlightened century."[236] As such, Beccaria's On Crimes and Punishments can fruitfully be read in light of the great debate over the nature of "The Enlightenment," for he seemed to suggest that although an arduous process lay ahead, the tool of reform—the necessary enlightenment—lay ready for use. It was not only an age of enlightenment; it was, in this sense, also an enlightened age.[237]

But Beccaria was quite clear that certain kinds of political arrangements were more conducive to human sociability, and ultimately to world order, than others:

> If we look at history we will see that disorder grows with the expansion of the boundaries of empires and, as patriotic sentiment wanes in proportion, the motives for crimes grow according to the advantage each individual seizes from the disorder itself: for this reason, the need to implement more severe punishments continually increases.[238]

Perhaps inspired, like his friends, by the glorious history of the Italian city-states, Beccaria remained, while an architect of one of the world's greatest composite monarchies, very much a proponent of small, ideally highly populated states, whose existences were increasingly challenged in the eighteenth century.[239] Yet, though he was more convinced than some of his colleagues that there were civilizing consequences of trade, he also appreciated the evident but uncharted connections between commerce, conquests, and civilization at the time. In arguing for the abolition of torture as a form of punishment, for example, he looked both backward in time to the ancient Romans for inspiration and across the Alps toward England, recently victorious in the Seven Years' War, "whose glory in letters, *superiority in commerce and in wealth, and therefore in power,* and whose examples of virtue and courage leave no doubt as to the goodness of its laws."[240] But like the vast majority of Italian observers, Beccaria realized the constant care and attention for changing policies that served to support England's economic miracle, and he would devote the rest of his life to the careful management of Milan's economy and its external relations to the Habsburg monarchy and the world at large. What united his penal reform to his larger vision of political economy and adumbrated hopes for a pacified world order was his trust in the necessity of constant worldly administration to secure sociability of dynamic rather than doctrinaire regulations. This was as true in the sphere of crimes and punishments as it was in economic policy.[241]

Because it was "impossible to anticipate all the misdeeds engendered by the universal conflict of human passions," legislators had to abandon dogmatic faith in universal solutions. "In the arithmetic of politics," Beccaria argued in a passage that would inspire theorists like the French philosopher and mathematician Nicolas de Condorcet, "the calculus of probabilities must replace mathematical exactitude."[242] It was, in short, better to be "vaguely right," as the British logician Carveth Read would put it in the late nineteenth century, than to risk being "exactly wrong."[243] Out of necessity, and ironically so given his penchant for luminous metaphors, Beccaria had forged an approach to legislation that consciously abandoned clarity and certainty in favor of a penumbral and ambiguous world of grayscales. Rousseau had argued, in a passage of The Social Contract that aligned well with Smith's later faith in Providence, that "what is good and comfortable to order is so by the nature of things and independently of human conventions."[244] For Beccaria it was almost the exact inverse. For him there was no spontaneous order to the world, only spontaneous chaos, and he remained adamant, though the semantic nuance would have been meaningless to him, that genuine liberty demanded the curtailment of certain freedoms. A legislator, whether of penal law or economic policy, had to be eternally vigilant, ever haunted by the very real danger that man might "return to the original state of unsociability."[245]

In formalizing this approach, and with it the "scientific" tools of political economy, the Academy of Fisticuffs proved even more innovative than in its ideals for reform. The economic methodology developed in late eighteenth-century Milan looked beyond the mere quantifications of political arithmeticians toward analytical formalization, toward uncovering underlying mechanisms by means of selective abstractions that could be expressed in algebraic terms. "The geometric spirit," wrote Verri in *Il Caffè,* echoing a Cartesian postulate, "spreads over all the sciences . . . perfecting and embellishing them," adding, in a different piece, that "the men of today want analysis, proof and algebraic symbols everywhere."[246] But the group's first attempt at demonstrating how mathematics actually might help resolve problems of political economy and commercial sociability was appropriately penned by the young Beccaria. Before we turn to this algebraic appendix to *On Crimes and Punishments,* however, it is necessary to look more closely at one of the least known methodological influences on Verri and Beccaria, and perhaps the weirdest thinker in the pugilists' orbit. This will require returning to the formative fields of Bautzen, and to the marauding Welshman Henry Lloyd.

CHAPTER THREE

Cycloid Pudding

—————◦———

"I AM THE VERY MODEL of a modern Major-General," sings a character in Gilbert and Sullivan's Victorian comic opera *The Pirates of Penzance*. "I've information vegetable, animal, and mineral / I know the kings of England, and I quote the fights historical / From Marathon to Waterloo, in order categorical / I'm very well acquainted, too, with matters mathematical / I understand equations, both the simple and quadratical."[1] The famous duo ridiculed the mathematical exuberance and polymathic passions typical of military theorists in their comic opera, and historians have since located the personification of such theoretical impracticality in a major-general of an earlier century, Pietro Verri's dear friend Henry Humphrey Evans Lloyd.[2] In the early nineteenth century both the French emperor Napoléon Bonaparte and the Prussian general and military genius Carl von Clausewitz dismissed Lloyd as an idiot savant—a rather unhappy combination for a supposed expert on martial affairs—and his reputation never really recovered. Perambulating around St. Helena, the diminutive would-be-master of Europe in particular had passed the time in the wake of his defeat at Waterloo and his subsequent imprisonment at the ends of the earth by reading works ranging from the baroque dramatist Jean Racine to Adam Smith, as well as annotating Lloyd's chief military treatise. The surviving marginalia from his personal

copy convey Napoleon's verdict on the Welshman with redundant precision: "Ignorance . . . Ignorance . . . Ignorance . . . Absurd . . . Absurd . . .
Absurd . . . What absurdity. . . ."[3]

Economists have not been much kinder. Lloyd's principal publication in
the field of political economy, his anonymously published and now exceedingly rare *Essay on the Theory of Money* (1771), was criticized for being too much
the work of a *"theorist"* when it first appeared, and the same verdict was rather
ironically reached by the great Victorian economist William Stanley Jevons,
who himself was not entirely unfamiliar with the formalization of economics.
Disinterring the *Essay* as a "remarkable" example of applying "mathematical
theory" to economics, Jevons's epitaphic judgment of it—"sometimes crude
and absurd"—simultaneously served as a de facto reburial.[4] Scholarship on
Lloyd has therefore been limited, and his role in the historiography of the
Enlightenment and of political economy has been almost inconsequential due
to his treatment by his immediate successors.[5] In recent years, though, his
contributions have been reassessed by military historians, who have hailed
him as "the most important military thinker of the Age of the Enlightenment,"
and there are good reasons to reassess his thinking also from the perspective
of political economy.[6]

Lloyd's life and works were far from inconsequential.[7] He joined military
skirmishes across Europe to great acclaim, personally linked intellectual debates from London through Paris and Milan to St. Petersburg, produced numerous influential works on economic and military matters—acrimonious
Parisians even held one of his works responsible for Napoleon's Russian
gambit—and was nearly offered command of Loyalist troops in America
during the Revolutionary War.[8] There is no reason to doubt the verdict of
the great military historian, strategist, and Somme-veteran Basil H. Liddell
Hart that Lloyd "was better known in other countries during the eighteenth
century than any British soldier save perhaps Marlborough," and that "even
this illustrious exception might be questioned." And, given the extraordinary
achievements of John Churchill, the 1st Duke of Marlborough, during the
Nine Years' War (1688–1697) and as unofficial leader of the Grand Alliance
during the War of Spanish Succession (1701–1712), this was no mean praise.[9]

His Milanese friends reunited in the Academy of Fisticuffs counted counts
and marquises among their members, but Lloyd was the son of a clergyman
of Wrexham, in rural Wales, and would forever be haunted by the inequalities

Major-General Henry
Humphrey Evans Lloyd
(ca. 1718–1783). Nathaniel
Hone, *General Lloyd*,
1773.

of Old Regime society, particularly the aristocratic basis of higher military
service among the greater and lesser powers of Europe.[10] He matriculated at
Jesus College, University of Oxford, in the spring of 1740, but ended his
studies prematurely in wake of his father's death the following year.
Barred from a military career in England by his lack of a noble pedigree and
inability to buy a commission, Lloyd embarked on a continental career of
exile and rather extraordinary adventure. It would be neither the first nor
the last time that Lloyd suffered the ossified architecture of Old Regime careerism, and his repeated calls, throughout his various writings, for rewards
and promotions to be based on merit rather than pedigree doubtlessly reflected a wounded frustration.[11] Venturing first to Berlin in search of a commission, he bumped against the blue-blooded gates of the Prussian army and
instead fell for a local ballerina and, quickly, into debt. Hounded by creditors, he relocated to Venice, where Jesuits bought him out in exchange for
joining the order. They supported his studies for a year or two at the Pon-
tifical Gregorian University in Rome, the famous Collegio Romano, before
he returned to Venice to take the post of secretary to the Spanish ambassador

there. Soon journeying onward to Madrid, Lloyd came to briefly serve as secretary to Ricardo Wall, Irish cabinet secretary to the king.[12] He gained formal, if brief, military training at Madrid's School of Engineering before again decamping, this time to France, where he arrived in time to join the War of Austrian Succession. Fighting under the command of Herman Maurice, Comte de Saxe, he finally distinguished himself as a geometer at the decisive Battle of Fontenoy. Lloyd subsequently fought against the English as a Stuart partisan on the continent, scouted the British coast to identify plausible beachheads for a French invasion of the island, and fought in the Jacobite Uprising of 1745 for the Young Pretender Charles Edward Stuart.[13]

These eventful years marked the beginning of a singularly restless career. Though his education had been piecemeal, he had studied widely—in classics and mathematics, engineering and rhetoric, mapmaking and theology—at Oxford, Rome, and Madrid, and he would eventually come to serve, and not always at different times, Austrian, British, French, Portuguese, Prussian, and Russian armed forces. "I have never known a more restless man," Pietro Verri would eventually write to his brother.[14] Lloyd's endurance and temerity gained him the nickname "souffre-douleurs," or "punching bag," in the Austrian army, and indeed on his tireless campaigns he defied generals, dukes, kings, and even Catherine the Great. He apparently went rogue repeatedly during his frequent bouts of international espionage, negotiated a royal marriage, fought for Pasquale Paoli during the Corsican Revolt, routed Turkish Janissaries as general of a Russian division in the Balkans, and was nearly called on by Lord Shelbourne to take the "command in chief" of Loyalist troops in North America during the American Revolutionary War before quietly ending his days in Flanders in 1783. And though he would serve every major army in Europe during his career, Lloyd merged Jacobitism and republicanism to passionately profess love for his home country, Britain.[15]

Never satisfied with a life of mere action, Lloyd discussed philosophical matters even in the field, and as his manuscript *Essay on the Artillery* ("being now the soul of Military operations") bears witness to, his soberest ballistic reckonings were often interrupted by digressions on the nature of man and the philosophical problems of theory and practice. "Sometimes," Verri noted, Lloyd was "a Montesquieu, sometimes an Alexander," and the good Welshman was not above identifying with luminaries such as "Xenophon, Polybius, Cæsar, and Arian" as one "who had not only seen, but executed great things."[16]

His life, stretching across the entire geography of Franco Venturi's Enlightenment, from St. Petersburg to Philadelphia, reads, in Verri's words, like "a novel [*romanzo*]," the veracity of which must be taken with a grain of salt. Indeed, the Verri correspondence often delineates the unreliability of the major-general's stories, which repeatedly caused his Milanese hosts embarrassment.[17] Yet his inimitable intellectual formation and his direct exposure to, and engagement with, such varied debates and contexts ensured that his would be a singular voice in some of the premier discussions animating the European republic of letters. And it was while he was in Milan in the 1760s in intense dialogue with the Fisticuffs, and eventually as a British spy supporting the Corsican Revolt, that Lloyd began to compose his treatises on military theory, moral philosophy, and political economy, bringing his unique abilities and martial perspective to bear on the group's chosen challenge of formalizing what soon would be known as the social sciences.

In line with the other members of Verri's broader group, Lloyd emphasized the importance of fusing theory and practice. "Arts" and "sciences," he argued, were based "on certain and fixed principles, which are by their nature invariable; the applications of them only can be varied; but they are in themselves constant." The former, theoretical part of any "science" was "mechanical" and could be "reduced to mathematical principles"; the latter, operational part consisted in knowledge of the "just application" of such "principles and precepts" to "all the numberless circumstances" that might arise.[18] And, just as he made important contributions to the "geometrical" formalization of military theory at the time—his invention of the concept of a "line of operation" is a case in point—he similarly pushed the use of mathematical logic and argument in the discipline of political economy down a very different path from that envisioned, primarily in statistical terms, by political arithmeticians in the tradition of William Petty, not to mention by the mathematically less literate members of the so-called "Scottish Enlightenment."[19] The polymath Petty is often considered the "father of political arithmetic" for harnessing statistical data in his analysis and expressing himself in terms of "Number, Weight, or Measure," but Lloyd contributed instead to the Academy of Fisticuffs' project of applying more-complex mathematical instruments, such as algebra and differential calculus, to problems of political economy—to actual theoretical modeling and abstraction.[20]

Laputa Bound

Thanks also to Lloyd's influence, the Milanese pugilists in effect broke new ground already during the first year of *Il Caffè*'s publication, with the appearance, around the same time as *On Crimes and Punishments*, of Beccaria's short "Attempt at an Analysis of Smuggling." Not only the first, but arguably also the most thoughtful, piece of mathematical political economy to come out of the Academy of Fisticuffs' workshop, it sheds further light on his theory of human nature, the plan according to which he hoped mankind might be socialized, and the intrinsic limits of its realization. Equally importantly, it elucidates Beccaria's pathbreaking role in the coterie's methodological innovations.

> Algebra is a precise and quick method of reasoning about quantities, and as such it can be applied not only to geometry and the other mathematical sciences, but to everything which in any way grows or diminishes, and to everything that has comparable relations. Hence it can be applied even to the political sciences, up to a certain point. Those sciences look at the debits and credits of a nation, at taxes, and so on—all things that admit calculation and the notion of quantity. I said up to a certain point because political principles depend largely on many specific wills and a variety of different passions, which cannot be determined with precision. It would be ridiculous to have a politics made up entirely of figures and calculations, which would be more suitable for the inhabitants of the island of Laputa than for us Europeans. However, since the space I shall occupy in this paper is not of any great importance in the universe, and my attempt may please readers of a certain bent, I shall give a superficial idea of how the economic sciences can be considered analytically.[21]

What followed may have been the first-ever use of algebra to resolve an economic problem, and Beccaria's choice of the specific issue to analyze—smuggling—touched upon all levels of the larger question of sociability animating eighteenth-century debates: individual vice, its regulation by law in a polity, and the interaction of crimes and punishments with the larger, chaotic world of international trade and travel. As Michael Kwass has shown, smuggling, and the "global underworld" it helped spawn, was, and was understood to be, at the very core of the potentially revolutionary globalizing process during the eighteenth century.[22] Beccaria was at the forefront of surrounding debates, as the Fisticuffs' earliest work on tariffs and contraband testifies to, and his article suggested an "analytical" approach to the fostering of sociability in individuals in the context of the larger, still lupine world of competing polities. Yet he remained ever averse to utopias, political as well as methodological. There were no perfect methods, and his statement that a discipline of "politics," or an "economic science," constituted entirely of "figures and calculations" was worthy of Laputa is telling.[23]

The ribaldly named flying island of Laputa—a bastardized Spanish term for a woman of ill repute—was one of the most memorable lands invented by Jonathan Swift in his famous *Gulliver's Travels* (1726). From North Vietnam, Swift's hero Gulliver went trading in a geographical phantasmagoria where a "malicious Reprobate" Dutch pirate cost him his ship, goods, and crew. Swift offered coordinates of latitude 46° N, longitude 183° E for the piratical attack, a purposefully surreal location since longitude, by definition, operates on a spherical spectrum from −180° to 180°. Considering 183° E to be longitude 177° W, Gulliver's ship was boarded East of Japan, South of the Aleutian Islands, in what would have counted among the least probable hunting grounds for pirates anywhere on the planet, even for reprobate Dutch ones.[24] Adrift in uncharted oceans, Gulliver was eventually rescued by the "Floating Island" of Laputa, populated by a strange race of people whose "Ideas are perpetually conversant in Lines and Figures." There he ate "a Shoulder of Mutton, cut into an Æquilateral Triangle," and a "Cycloid Pudding," before learning of their strange ways.[25] For though they were "dextrous enough upon a Piece of Paper," they were, because of their "Contempt" for "practical geometry," the clumsiest, "awkward, and unhandy People" in the world when it came to "the common Actions and Behaviour of Life."[26] What surprised Gulliver the most, however, was

> the strong Disposition I observed in them towards News and Politics, perpetually enquiring into publick Affairs, giving their Judgments in Matters of State, and passionately disputing every Inch of

a Party Opinion. I have indeed observed the same Disposition among most of the Mathematicians I have known in *Europe*, although I could never discover the least Analogy between the two Sciences; unless those People suppose, that because the smallest Circle hath as many Degrees as the largest, therefore the Regulation and Management of the World require no more Abilities than the handling and turning of a Globe.[27]

Far from a throwaway reference, Swift's Laputa was a satirical, if deadly serious, way for Beccaria to state the purpose of his "politics" as well as his "economic science." He was averse to extremes and to dogmas, yet realized that rigorous analysis *could* improve the management of worldly affairs. The perpetual tension between utopia and reform elucidated by Venturi in his Trevelyan Lectures resolved itself in Beccaria's decision to draw on mathematics but not succumb to it, to adopt its principles without putting it on a pedestal.[28] Compared to the "political economy" of his contemporaries, however, what followed must have tasted decidedly of Cycloid Pudding.

> Our question is by how much, in terms of the value of a certain good, will merchants need to defraud the Treasury so that, even if the remainder is forfeited, their earnings from smuggling leave them with the same capital as before. The calculation of such a quantity generally can be enlightening for the setting of tariffs.[29]

So far, so good. But how, exactly, would one go about calculating this? Beccaria offered an answer, if not a solution, which is worth quoting at length not only for the argument offered but for the language in which it is couched.

> Let u be the intrinsic value of the goods; t the tax; x the portion of goods required; d the difference between the tax and the value. The ratio of the total value of the goods to the total tax will be the same as the portion of goods required to its corresponding tax, that is, $u \cdot t : x \cdot \dfrac{tx}{u}$ for the portion of tax corresponding to the part required x. The problem will therefore give us the equation $x + \dfrac{tx}{u} = u$, and by multiplication $ux + tx = uu$, and by division $x = \dfrac{uu}{u+t}$. However,

the tax can be equal to the value of the goods, that is, $t = u$; it can be greater than the value by an amount d, that is, $t = u + d$; or it can be less than the value by the same amount d, that is, $t = u - d$. By substituting, therefore, each respective value for t in the general equation $x = \dfrac{uu}{u = t}$, we will have in each case:

Where $t = u$, then $x = \dfrac{uu}{u + u} = \dfrac{uu}{2u} = \dfrac{u}{2}$.

Where $t = u + d$, then $x = \dfrac{uu}{u + u + d} = \dfrac{uu}{2u + d} < \dfrac{u}{2}$.

Where $t = u - d$, then $x = \dfrac{uu}{u + u - d} = \dfrac{uu}{2u - d} > \dfrac{u}{2}$.

Assuming that in the equation $ux + tx = uu$, t and x are indeterminate and u is constant, the equation will give a hyperbola between asymptotes, where the abscissae t taken on the asymptote at a distance of u from the asymptotic angle, plus that same distance again, will be at ordinates x parallel to the other asymptote at a constant rate, that is like the square of the power u. An inspection of the figure, for those willing to construct it, will show all the different cases of the equation.[30]

On the basis of this, Beccaria offered a "general theorem," according to which, ceteris paribus, "the amount required to balance the tax paid with goods smuggled" would be "the same as the square of the value of the goods, divided by the sum of the value and tax." In addition to facilitating the calculation of tariffs, the benefits of such an approach lay in "knowing what can be expected of smugglers, even after a certain number of reprisals."[31]

The short article is telling from the perspective of Beccaria's larger project. Firstly, to analyze a question of political economy, it deployed a technical mathematical language that had few equals, and that certainly was far more sophisticated than anything Verri could have mustered at the time. Secondly, it neatly exemplified his regulatory worldview: crime was not a sin, and human beings were perpetual criminals at their cores, even if regularly caught for their misdoings. Rousseau, in his infamous argument for the moral depravity of scientific and artistic progress delineated in his Discourse on the Sciences and Arts (1750), asked, "Without men's injustices, what would be the use of jurisprudence?"[32] While perhaps rhetorically pleasing, it amounted to little but a tautology inspired by a near angelic interpretation of the state of nature. For Beccaria, whose view of humanity was bleaker, "the Sciences and Arts" were the only means by which a legislator could calculate, as well as possible, measured responses to control individual misbehavior, strengthen the cohesive power of the state, and, ultimately, reinforce the social fabric. And where Rousseau had argued that the arts and sciences corrupted societies and human nature the more they progressed, Beccaria again took the diametrically opposite stance: the socialization of people and peoples depended entirely on a concomitant technological progress. He was simultaneously deeply pessimistic about human nature and, like Verri at the time, quietly optimistic about the legislator's ability to collect, process, and act upon information in order to regulate society. However imperfect and reflexive its application, mathematics held, for Beccaria and indeed for the entire Academy of Fisticuffs, the promise of helping solve the challenge of sociability. But other pugilists would take this project much farther than he was willing to go, and the question of why and with what consequences helps elucidate the complexities of contemporary debates regarding the nature of political economy and commercial society alike.

Rise of the Machines

Like Verri and Beccaria, Lloyd, too, felt that a science of society had to begin with a deeper understanding of humanity itself. "No object is so little known to us as Man," he began his manuscript *Essay on Man*, initiated in dialogue with the Academy of Fisticuffs sometime around 1766 and only published in fragments in his later works. Yet knowing human beings was essential for commanding them, whether as a major-general or an economic administrator.[33] "As we cannot form men to our wishes, and must take them as they are," he wrote later, repeating a Machiavellian mantra reiterated by a long line of thinkers from Hobbes through Spinoza and Rousseau to members of the Academy of Fisticuffs, "it is necessary to apply that motive which is analogous to their ideas of good and evil" in order to govern them.[34] What those ideas were was rather grim, and he in many ways shared Beccaria's negative anthropology by arguing that humans were "too much inclined" to the "pursuit of arbitrary measures" to get ahead in life.[35] Thus, the first question Lloyd asked was what precisely the "principle of motion or action in man" was, given that it was "impossible to regulate & watch" men's behavior without understanding its "spring and cause."[36]

Explicitly accepting the mechanistic conception of man proposed by Julian Offray de la Mettrie's "Machine Man" (1747) and Claude-Adrien Helvétius's *On the Mind* (1758), Lloyd quickly discarded the possibility of "internal" agency as against the observable rules of nature, deciding that the "cause" of all actions must be purely external and that human action is nothing but a "reaction" to outside stimuli.[37] Stimulus responses ultimately resulted in the formation of "ideas" that caused new sequences of action and reaction, ad infinitum. "I cannot see anything but matter and motion," he radically suggested, "in all the animal creation."[38] Like Hobbes in *Leviathan,* a work with which he was intimately familiar, Lloyd inferred his view of man from the Galilean postulate that motion was the natural state of all bodies. As such, man was "not free in his choice of acting or not acting," and "Life" was "nothing but motions; Death . . . but rest or total tranquility."[39] The same vocabulary similarly appeared in Lloyd's work on political economy: "Because in this as in mechanics, the celerity of motion will be in that proportion; the more therefore mankind is dispersed, the slower will be circulation, and the less will be their industry." Industry was life, and sloth literally the death of a body politic.[40]

If man were an animal machine, as de la Mettrie and Helvétius had suggested in line with the contemporary vogue for mechanical automata, a science of man would by default have to be mechanical in nature.[41] And like any other such form of mechanical knowledge, the social sciences of politics and political economy thus welcomed, even *required,* formal rigor. Historians have long studied the "mechanization of the world picture"—the gradual rise to prominence of numeracy and technology in Western culture in the wake of the Renaissance. In the early modern period this general preoccupation with measuring and mastering nature, often referred to with the shorthand "Scientific Revolution," concomitantly played into secular and sensationist currents in moral philosophy to provide all the necessary ingredients for a radical and deeply materialist philosophy of creation and of humanity's place in it.[42] Helvétius's flamboyantly atheist *On the Mind,* the forbidden best-seller of this literature, provided the argumentative bedrock for Lloyd's aggressive materialism. Drawing a blurred line between "Physical Man" and "Moral Man" that would become a leitmotif in his later writings and a key to understanding his political and economic philosophy, Lloyd argued that "physical man" was preoccupied solely with individual survival, and that "moral man" derived from sociocultural circumstances and from "an affinity between Man and some other Being," an artifact, in short, of sociability. Given man's mechanical nature, it was clear to Lloyd that "just and unjust" and "good & evil are relative to man & property and necessarily arise from society co-existing with man." As a result, man was neither inherently "bad & wicked" as "Hobbes [and] Spinoza" had claimed and his natural state was not "war," nor was he "naturally good" and accordingly in a natural state of "peace."[43] Man was, in the end, good or bad according to his "circumstances" and nothing else.[44]

Few more radical conclusions could be drawn from Enlightenment moral philosophy, and, given his inability or unwillingness to translate philosophical radicalism into social or political radicalism, one should not be surprised that Lloyd never published his mechanistic view of human nature.[45] On the basis of this viewpoint, however, he justified the hedonistic notion, discussed widely since Hobbes, that all actions could be measured in "Pleasure and Pain" and that the mainspring of all man's actions was "pain," which "solicits us to change our situation" and to assess "the principle of utility."[46] "After those principles," Lloyd concluded, "we must govern mankind since they are the only spring by which we are put in motion." But whereas the "wants" of physical man were finite, the "wants" of moral man were infinite, and consequently so was his capacity for pleasure and pain. Sociability was a human prerogative—for other animals could only "aggregate"—and depended on "reciprocal wants and succours."[47] And, as he explained in a fragment *On the Degrees of Sensibility*, which reflected many of the Academy of Fisticuffs' central propositions, the unfolding of what Lloyd already in the 1760s defined as "commercial society," with its concomitant refinements of the arts and sciences, also unfolded humanity's potential for both misery and happiness.[48] Put simply, the progress of civilization made good government necessary because so much more was at stake in terms of both pain and pleasure. And although he never seems to explicitly have mentioned the Anglo-Dutch philosopher Bernard Mandeville, in *The Fable of the Bees* (1714) Mandeville portrayed a society of hedonistic, self-interested individuals whose countervailing passions were judiciously balanced by "the dexterous management of a skillful politician" that was in profound concordance with these key elements of his moral philosophy.[49]

Lloyd shared this terminology and its sources with the Academy of Fisticuffs, but as always with that mercurial group, it is difficult to identify the arrows of causation. Drawing largely on Locke and Helvétius, for example, in 1763 Verri crafted a felicitous utilitarian framework for public policy to ensure "the greatest happiness possible divided as equally as possible."[50] Beccaria, who also found terms such as "political virtue" to be entirely "variable," elaborated a similar framework in his *On Crimes and Punishments* by examining the case of punishment from the perspective of utility.[51] And all of them would have agreed that something could "be lawfull, though at the same time it may be unjust."[52] None of them, however, seem ever to have come quite so close to the most radical wing of the Enlightenment as Lloyd did.

Lloyd never published the entirety of his *Philosophical Essays,* and it was Jeremy Bentham who, a generation later, drawing upon the same Milanese inflection of older European philosophies in his *Fragment on Government,* would eventually introduce the principles of utilitarianism in England. Bentham was quite frank about the origins of his thought in his correspondence: in the draft of a letter to Voltaire, dated November 1776, he explained, "I have built solely on the foundation of utility, laid as it is by Helvétius and Beccaria."[53] Although a letter from his younger brother Samuel in September 1790 does show that Bentham was reading Lloyd's work, the most explicitly utilitarian passages were still only in manuscript form at the time.[54] While Lloyd's largely unpublished mechanistic theory of human agency sheds light on the materialist origins of modern utilitarianism, for the present purposes it is more intriguing for the perspective it provides on the subterranean philosophical foundations of the Fisticuffs' reformism but also the profound ways in which they diverged from one another in their views.

For all of Lloyd's relativism, he still believed that the interaction between physical and moral man in his clockwork cosmology produced absolute truths about "justice" in human affairs, though he defined this term rather differently than Beccaria did. Some social and political structures erected by moral man, Lloyd argued, better served the needs of physical man. Certain elementary mechanic needs of physical man (and thus "just" by virtue of reflecting basic material nature rather than ideals of sociability) could, in other words, be satisfied only under specific forms of government. Like Helvétius, Lloyd argued that "preeminence," or status, was the "ultimate object of social action," but he abandoned the rationales of La Mettrie and Helvétius, derived from the Epicurean tradition, that preeminence satisfied "sensual pleasures," arguing instead it could "secure our independence." The hedonic calculus of sensibilities, of pleasure and pain, in the end, drove men toward liberty, not license.[55] Lloyd similarly modulated the sensationist foundations of his moral philosophy by stoically noting that "the great have such a facility in obtaining the objects of their wishes" that they "anticipate pleasure" and "destroy the powers of enjoyment," reducing them to a "state of apathy and insensibility" from which "ennui" and "suicide" would result.[56] Pleasure was, in short, not merely sensual gratification for Lloyd, but essentially a reflection of the degree to which individuals could safeguard and advance their authority and independence in the world.

It has been argued that Helvétius "marks a republican turning point in the French Enlightenment," but the interconnection of republicanism and a mechanistic utilitarian philosophy was even more expressive, if also paradoxical, in Lloyd's work, for his insistence on the continued importance of ancient civic virtue.[57] From his earliest philosophical manuscripts to his later published works, a "love of liberty and independence" remained the kernel of physical man's well-being for Lloyd. In fact, it was "inherent to all animals without exception," for "their existence depends on it."[58] Although man, in leaving the state of nature behind, forever had lost the grace of complete liberty, certain systems of political economy, such as England's "Monarcho-Aristo-Democracy"—which by virtue of being "mixed" was a "republic" based on "equality" (a pregnant term he refused to define)—allowed for light enough compromises that society's cultural and material achievements, along with the accompanying increase of passions and pleasure, more than made up for the loss.[59] The closest thing possible to the individual sovereignty offered by the state of nature, in other words, was the legal and political equality experienced in true republics, where even "the King" was "subject to the laws in civil matters."[60] Late in life Verri would muse that "Liberty is the greatest good that man can draw from the social condition," suggesting he disagreed with Lloyd and others about even the possibility of liberty in the state of nature. But he nonetheless came close to his old friend when insisting that, though one could enjoy "individual liberty" even under a "despotic government," understood as a physical freedom reminiscent of Isaiah Berlin's sense of "negative liberty," "*political liberty* can only be enjoyed under a *Constitution*."[61]

The French polymath Pierre Gassendi, who rehabilitated Epicureanism as a Christian philosophy in the seventeenth century and had influenced Lloyd early on, had also seen "virtue" as inseparable from a sensationist moral philosophy, but the two thinkers diverged in key ways. For example, "Of the several approved sorts of Government," Gassendi wrote, "the Monarchical seems to be the best" because, quoting Aristotle, "Government by many is inconvenient."[62] There were many ways of aligning moral and political philosophy in early modern Europe, and eclectic combinations abounded. Lloyd resolutely beat his own path, and there was nothing convenient about it. Instead, it was a path of paradoxes; man, for Lloyd as for the modern Epicureans, was a hedonistic machine built for individual affirmation that, as for the Stoics, thrived best in virtuous republics. And, improbably, Lloyd invested fetters of commerce with the task of binding the two parts of his incongruous philosophical construct together.

Wealth and Virtue

The German émigré philosopher Hannah Arendt once described "one of political science's oldest insights, namely that power cannot be measured in terms of wealth, that an abundance of wealth may erode power, that riches are particularly dangerous to the power and well-being of republics."[63] Today, this traditional historiographical trope of political philosophy is most often identified with the voluminous work of J. G. A. Pocock, and numerous historians have since stressed the near mutually exclusive relationship between wealth and virtue in classical republican thought and, somehow by proxy, in the early modern European world more generally.[64] The overall problem found numerous expressions across a variety of genres and contexts, and the exact mechanisms by which wealth supposedly led to the decline of virtue could be manifold. But it was far from the only way of conceptualizing wealth and virtue at the time, and in recent years scholars have expounded on the limitations of this framework at length.[65] What is more, the very definitions of *wealth* and *virtue* were far from uniform across time and space. "Wealth" could be understood to mean luxurious sloth, movable capital, even private property itself; and "virtue" could be taken to mean a whole array of con-

cepts and sentiments, from Pagan self-negation in favor of the civic good to
military valor and, increasingly, Christian rectitude. For some, the image of
"virtue" certainly found its purest incarnation in the *aretē* or "excellence" of
an ancient Spartan hoplite.[66] *Aretē* has the same etymological root as *aristos*,
itself both a term for superlative ability and, in plural form, a social denomi-
nator for the privileged nobility. Virtue similarly derived from the Latin *vir*
or "man," though the normative content of such "manliness" was almost infinitely protean. That St. Francis of Assisi, Cosimo de' Medici, Cesare Borgia,
and the raging Achilles of Homer's *Iliad* could all be avatars of "virtue" speaks
abundantly to the treacherous nebulosity of the term, which in other words
found expression in action as well as contemplation; in the most austere
form of self-imposed poverty and the highest expression of Renaissance
proto-capitalism; in transcendental pacifism and in the most blackguard
warmongering.[67]

   The main historiographical narrative according to which wealth and
virtue were antithetically opposed relies on a very specific definition of both
terms, according to which "wealth," understood to be politically mercenary
movable assets and sybaritic luxury, undermined "virtue," understood in
terms of military valor, self-denial, and the patriotic sentiment of landed citizens, to the point in which a polity was "corrupted" and conquered by purer
peoples.[68] This was one manifestation of the cyclical theory of time proposed
by the Hellenistic Greek historian Polybius, according to which all polities
were doomed to forever rise, prosper, and decline, only to rise again in a sequence of eternal recurrence.[69] Politically, such fears tend to reflect elitist,
agrarian, conservative positions favoring preexisting regimes and social
patterns of power.[70] As a paradigm of thought, it was attacked repeatedly
and from diverse angles throughout the early modern period, some seeking
to undermine the very validity of the problem posed. Mandeville, for one,
wrote his *Fable of the Bees* also to show the anachronism of virtuous ideals in
a world whose opulence depended upon hedonistic whims and vices, and by
the time of *Il Caffè* the language of political economy had largely moved on to
different pastures, though some would continue to debate the salience of
Epicurean and Stoic philosophical traditions for the formulation of economic
theory and practice.[71] Franci may have been the pugilist who most succinctly
criticized the claim that wealth corrupted virtue, arguing that commerce in
effect contributed to material improvement, military capacity, patriotic virtue,

and human sociability alike. Indeed, he noted with a certain sarcasm that it was hard to ignore the hypocrisy of Seneca and other ancients who proclaimed that wealth undermined virtue when they themselves had amassed "immense wealth."[72] And as Alessandro Verri observed in Il Caffè, "What definition is more important than that of virtue? And what, at the same time, is vaguer and more uncertain?" His own solution to the conundrum was to observe that times changed, and that, in his eyes at least, "the habit of being useful to society" should be "called 'virtue.'"[73]

In this context Lloyd was a rather late representative of the genre with respect to the mainstream of political economy, not to mention its cutting edge of utilitarian thinking spearheaded by Verri and Beccaria. His writings occupy a conceptual terrain not unlike that in which the Scottish social philosopher Adam Ferguson published his Essay on the History of Civil Society (1767) to defend the continued importance of martial conceptions of civic virtue in a world dictated by commerce.[74] While Lloyd, a Stuart partisan, might have fought with the French against Ferguson and the Hanoverian British at the battle of Fontenoy, the two agreed heartily on the need to "promote Virtue" and rehabilitate the ancient honor of the military professions: "As the influence of riches increases," Lloyd lamented, "that of honour and virtue declines."[75] Yet wealth and virtue could manifest themselves in many ways, and Lloyd's philosophy underlines the danger of too-rigid philosophical taxonomies by incorporating prevalent elements of Mandeville's Epicurean sensualism in the Stoic republican ideology he shared with Ferguson.

From the perspective of current interpretations of Enlightenment political and moral philosophy, Lloyd may have been a rather poor reader of contemporary texts, but his incongruent pastiche is itself enlightening with regard to the varieties, challenges, and preoccupations of eighteenth-century intellectual life.[76] Similarly, though Lloyd originally helped turn Verri's attention from the field of battle to that of political economy, not to mention to formal methods, the different members of the Academy of Fisticuffs would all bring divergent experiences, interests, and inclinations to the discipline in ways that eventually were not only mutually idiosyncratic, but that also fit poorly with our habitual labels for their collective endeavor.

Universal Theories?

Pietro Verri's economic thinking clearly developed between his early "Elements" (1760s) and his *Meditations on Political Economy* (1770s). In order to follow the thread of Lloyd's influence on this development, a brief thematic digression is required here, a leap ahead and back in time, outside the book's otherwise approximately chronological and narrative logic. There can be no doubt that the character of Verri's economic vision changes, particularly with respect to his theories of value and price formation and, crucially, the formality of his argumentative language. Yet one must nonetheless be wary, as foreshadowed in Chapter 2, of exaggerating the distance he traveled in this period in terms of concrete policy proposals. Indeed, he doubled down on many of his earlier arguments in the late 1760s and early 1770s. For example, he remained, in Milan as in Vienna, profoundly taken by the power of manufacturing to "multiply" wealth, by the crucial importance of industrial productivity in international competition, by the role of tariffs in calibrating industrialization and economic development, and by the need for a polity to produce more than it consumed.[77] Building on his earlier work but focusing on the role of output and productivity itself, he now observed how "the perfection of machines and instruments in a nation that has become wealthy through industry is such that a laborer in a day will work the manufactures that would take several days in a less industrious State."[78] Manufactures were also the context in which Verri's sustained antagonism toward Physiocracy became the clearest:

> Some writers have attributed reproduction solely to agriculture, and have called manufacturers a *sterile* class; I believe that to be an error, because no phenomena in the universe, be they produced by the hand of man or by the universal laws of physics, give us the idea of actual *creation*, but rather of a new modification of matter. *Joining* and *separating* are the only two elements which the human mind finds when analyzing the concept of *reproduction;* and it is just the same with the *reproduction of value* and of *wealth*, when earth, air and water in the fields are transformed into corn, or when the hand of man transforms the sticky fiber of an insect into velvet.[79]

More than simply worrying about the "balance of trade" in aggregate terms, Verri considered the more complicated question of *what* was being produced and traded. The key, he thought, lay in making the most of productivity differentials between countries, and he therefore continued to deem the importation of foreign goods a *"harmful trade,"* indeed the opposite of the *"useful trade"* of selling to foreigners.[80] Similarly, he noted how the "relative" wealth of nations had increasingly come to decide their standings in international relations, to the extent that "everyone" now "considers commerce a public matter."[81]

All of human history could, he now argued, be interpreted through such an economic lens, and, like many of his more famous contemporaries, Verri came to imagine a progression of ages of civilization based on how people acquired "the foodstuffs necessary for life," ranging from complete "savagery" through "pastoral, or hunting, or agricultural," until, outside of the savage state, "industry" finally came to "multiply annual reproduction" to produce an age of economic "surplus," the stage that Smith would call "commercial society."[82] More clearly than in the past, though, Verri now identified the galvanizing force in this process in the invention of money, through which

> societies were brought closer together, became acquainted, communicated with each other, from which it is evident that humankind owes far more than perhaps has been believed to the invention of money for the culture, for that artificial organization of needs, and for industry, which so greatly distance civilized societies from the wild and isolated ones of savages.[83]

The question of sociability thus remained at the core of Verri's political economy; and, much like Beccaria, he held that the "most meritorious inventions of mankind" were those that "bring man closer to man, and facilitate the communication of ideas, of needs, of sentiments, and reduce the human species to one mass"—those, in short, that furthered the eventual socialization of humanity entire, the creation of one global society out of all the peoples of the world.[84] In terms of politics and policy, too, Verri remained true to himself and *Il Caffè*'s vision of heroic administrators guiding a polity's political economy.

For, in spite of what many scholars have argued, it is difficult to ignore that Verri remained resolutely interventionist by today's standards. This is true both with regard to his historical vision and his practical proposals for contemporary reforms, forever torn between the need for active policy on the one hand, and the difficulties of undertaking it on the other. So if he warned against legislative hubris and the dangers of being "seduced by a poorly conceived spirit of order and symmetry" to "fathom and model that spontaneous movement of society," Verri continued to emphasize the virtues of skilled legislation and even enlightened despotism: "Wherever an essential change has been undertaken, wherever ancient disorders have been overcome with any speed and happy success, one will see that this was the work of a lone fighter against many private interests."[85] And though he believed that, when it came to the "execution of laws that already have been made," it was "indispensable" that decisions "depend on the opinions of many men," he maintained that "when it comes to organizing systems and directing the course [of things] toward a determinate end, overcoming interposed difficulties, all of which can never be foreseen, necessity demands that this impetus and this direction depend on a single driving principle," in other words on an enlightened and unfettered lawgiver.[86]

To bolster his claim, Verri pointed to the successes of "dictatorship" in ancient Rome, as opposed to the failures of the Decemviri, the fifth-century-BC council of ten commissioned to produce a code of law for the Roman Republic.[87] And he implicitly drew on another Roman episode, that of Cincinnatus's rule, to argue that once the necessary enlightened despot had done his job, once his "system" was erected, he should step back and allow virtuous people a say in the running of the polity—"because men die," as he put it in a phrase his brother Alessandro found worthy of Tacitus, "and systems remain."[88] "It is therefore best in political economy, especially when it comes to simplifying it and reforming old abuses, to create a despotism that lasts as long as necessary to get a providential system going regularly."[89] A reviewer in the *Giornale di Pisa* had no doubts about what the main message of Verri's book had been: "The enterprise of successful reform demands the power of an enlightened and despotic Dictator: the reform completed, the despotism must cease, and only the law, known to all, must decide the fate of a citizen."[90]

Verri himself, though claiming, "My soul has always been republican," had no qualms preaching the need for "beneficial despotism," nor did he see the need to reconcile his republican soul with his penchant for benevolent despotism.[91] His thinking on the matter is, in short, like Lloyd's moral philosophy not easily classifiable, or even particularly coherent by the standards of historiography; but perhaps an imaginary letter from a philosopher to an anonymous Monarch of clear Napoleonic demeanor, which Verri published on the very day of his death, might shed light on his moral and political compass. Encouraging the monarch to step down and establish a constitutional republic, he wrote, "Living is tedious whether one lives with superiors or inferiors; only equality allows for society, happiness, cordiality."[92] If what mattered was happiness and sociability, equality would have to be the long-term goal of moral philosophy and political economy alike, no matter the political regime in which they operated. Again, however, we may never know just how stringent his requirements for such equality were—or, for that matter, the degree to which they differed across overlapping legal, political, and economic domains.

Verri, in short, carefully distinguished between political and economic liberties, but, if his suggested economic policies remained interventionist by our standards, it is worth noting that his measured respect for spontaneous economic forces nonetheless was "liberal" in the eyes of his contemporaries. His former ally and, as mentioned before, eventual nemesis in the Milanese economic administration, Carli, for one criticized Verri at length for favoring "unlimited liberty."[93] Indeed, in a 1770 letter to Kaunitz, Carli explained that "the difference that lies between the opinion of said Minister [Verri] and myself can be reduced to this: he would like an *unlimited liberty* and I propose a reasoned regulation adapted to the conditions of the country and the nation." The problem, Carli wrote in the spirit of Neapolitan writers such as Genovesi and Ferdinando Galiani, was that

> as much as I have searched the ancient and current history of commerce and of peoples, I have not been able to find unlimited liberty anywhere except among Barbarians and in fiction; rather, I have observed that to the extent that nations have abandoned unlimited liberty with regard to manufacturing and trade to subject themselves to regulation, the much greater the progress they have made toward the perfection of crafts and universal prosperity.[94]

Kaunitz replied:

> It is certain that if the Councilor Count Verri were to intend an un-
> limited and unrestricted liberty, in that case he would be wrong
> and we would find ourselves in precisely that state which Your Ex-
> cellency calls barbarian, that is, full of disorder, arbitrariness, and
> inertia: but were he not to extend it beyond the limits of discrete
> regulation, that is, subject as little as possible to the obstacles of
> the laws, and to the cautions without which system one can never
> hope for a resurgence of crafts and manufactures; in this case, which
> I must assume, he would perhaps agree with Your Excellency's
> wise sentiment, that is, that it would have to be regulated by reason,
> and adapted to the circumstances of the Country and of the Nation.[95]

Odds are that Kaunitz was correct, for, though the Verri of the 1770s seemed to trust market forces to a greater extent than he had a decade earlier, Carli's charge of always championing "unlimited liberty" was certainly an exagger-ation. At the same time, the heightening formality of Verri's analytical language during the period had necessitated sharper statements on the matter, rendering his reasoning more dogmatic by default. Though I will return to their disagreements in Chapter 6, a specific point of dispute between Verri and Carli may usefully shed light on what their debate ultimately was about, and how it related to the problem of formalism.

In his *Meditations on Political Economy,* to take only one example, Verri had presented as a "primordial" principle of political economy that legisla-tors should "increase as far as possible the number of sellers of all goods, and diminish as far as possible the number of buyers." Such a market struc-ture would, he argued, reduce costs in comparison to competitors abroad and thus facilitate exports in a regime of open international trade. Carli dis-agreed with the universality of this claim, again warning that one had to consider said structures in context. "The trade of the barbarian nations of Africa," Carli wrote, after all seemed to fit Verri's proposals perfectly, yet "these are sellers without national buyers of gold and ivory to the European fleets, which benefit from the number of offers without competition from in-ternal buyers." The end result was simply that Africa exported treasured goods cheaply to foreigners. "The vaster the territory of a nation, and the more it sells without buyers," Carli thus retorted, "the more barbarian and savage it will be."[96] Depending on the context, an abstract economic theory could have diametrically opposite consequences when applied as policy.

From this perspective, what eventually divided the members of the Academy of Fisticuffs on the matter was less a specific question of "unlimited liberty," in favor of which none of them actually had argued, than a deeper issue of how far one could formalize and universalize political economy without undermining its real-world relevance. General debates over trade were simply one manifestation of this deeper challenge of theorizing and acting upon economic phenomena in a generalized manner to which Beccaria, Carli, Lloyd, and Verri all would offer different solutions at different times. Where Beccaria inaugurated the economic usage of algebra only to take a step back, Verri, like Lloyd, increasingly sought to look beyond the moment and consider how "isolated facts," historical experiences, and the local conditions of different states nonetheless could *"follow universal theories"* to be expressed in formal, even mathematical language.[97] But far from reflecting a Procrustean dichotomy of economic planning and laissez-faire, as Verri's disagreement with Carli might initially suggest, the pugilists all occupied shifting positions on a grayscale of quintessentially interventionist political economy, positions that, as Chapter 6 will make clear, would diverge ever further—and become ever more vexing to label—over the next few decades as they came to devote themselves to practical economic policy full time.[98] Few visions of political economy, however, would remain harder to categorize than Henry Lloyd's.

Pure Economics

Although his later writings essentially recast arguments he had begun formulating years earlier, Lloyd published the clearest expressions of his political economy first in his *Essay on the English Constitution* (1770), which applied his theories to contemporary England, and then in his more general *Essay on the Theory of Money* (1771). The opening chapters of the latter read like a submission to the Genevan essay-contest that rendered Rousseau famous, and a deep familiarity with Rousseau's work is evident throughout Lloyd's writings. How, he asked, did inequality arise, and should it—or could it—be banished again? As did Rousseau, Lloyd saw inequality as initially a physical phenomenon resulting from inborn differences, which was subsequently transplanted into the larger political, social, and cultural spheres.

The "Golden Age" when all men were independent and self-sufficient, living in tiny scattered communities before the "odious distinction of master and slave" arose, was now a distant memory. "Chance and curiosity" had resulted in the invention of "money," or, as both Lloyd and Verri preferred to call it, the "universal merchandize," which "by facilitating the communication between mankind [sic] gave birth to all the arts, manufactures, sciences, and forms of government, which we now see, and admire in the different parts of the globe."[99] Thus, perhaps with implicit recourse to Locke, Lloyd simultaneously refined Rousseau's earlier argument and rejected its essential thrust by blaming the instrument of economic exchange itself, or rather its "circulation," for the origins of civil society and the rise of inequality, rather than property rights per se—possessing "numerous flocks [of sheep] alone," he argued, could not give a man dominion over another, seemingly for practical reasons, but vast hoards of currency were another matter entirely.[100]

It is not clear whether it was Lloyd or Verri who first used the term "universal merchandize," but both were clearly indebted to Hume's essay "On Money" as well as Locke's earlier definition of "money" as a "universal Commodity."[101] In the draft of a letter intended for Monsignor Gaetani sent to Alessandro Verri on April 11, 1781, Pietro Verri reminisced about the origins of this term:

> I believe the definition of money is mine. I have debated at length this and other issues of political economy with the Englishman General Lloyd. . . . My friend [Lloyd] published his *An Essay on the Theory of Money* in London at the same time as me [i.e. simultaneously with Verri's *Meditations on Political Economy*] in 1771, and there defines money in the same way as I do. Whose definition is it? Which of the two of us found it first? In truth, I cannot remember. I know that Lloyd is a man of great integrity, that we discussed these matters for months, and that I would not at all be ashamed if I owed it to him; nevertheless, I believe it mine in good faith.[102]

This again raises the problem of assigning authorship to ideas in the context of the Academy of Fisticuffs. The twentieth-century Trinity College economist, librarian, and book collector Piero Sraffa (member of a rather different "cafeteria group" in Cambridge involving Frank Ramsay, John Maynard Keynes, and Ludwig von Wittgenstein), for one, believed Verri had plagiarized Lloyd, and it remains plausible that Lloyd had provided Verri with the original impetus to study political economy while the two were on military campaigns together.[103] On the other hand, Verri composed an article-length manuscript entitled "Axiom: Money Is the Universal Merchandize" already in 1768, years before it seems Lloyd first used the term in writing, though again the vastly different archival corpuses of the two men make such comparisons problematic.[104] Not unlike the case of Verri and Beccaria, the thematic and argumentative affinities between Verri and Lloyd simply serve to underline the caffeinated fervor of the Academy of Fisticuffs and the problems inherent in considering communal intellectual projects—on the model of an atelier or a workshop—from canonical perspectives of intellectual history that frequently highlight the Olympian achievements of individual thinkers.

As fate would have it, Lloyd's and Verri's approaches would come together in the most mathematically formal work of political economy published during the eighteenth century, the 1772 sixth edition of Verri's *Meditations on Political Economy,* which included a technical appendix (translating its discursive parts into a formal mathematical idiom) along with fellow pugilist Paolo Frisi's review and summary of Lloyd's *Essay on the Theory of Money.* Though exceptionally rare, one copy of it made its way into Sraffa's knowledgeable hands. He noted it represented "perhaps the first example of 'pure economics,' in other words of the mathematical method in economics, understood as a form of reasoning, and not as simple calculation."[105] In the new introduction, Verri argued that the right "method" and "organization of theorems" was all that was lacking to make "political economy" a "science" and "give it shape," and Frisi himself praised the two other authors for having "wanted to substitute vague expressions with the rigor of geometric proportions," further pointing out that "the Englishman" also had sought to demonstrate his theories with "algebraic symbols."[106] Though the alacrity of its members soon would fade, the Academy of Fisticuffs' faith in the power of mathematical abstraction peaked during the very years that Lloyd spent in Milan, forming an essential context for his thoughts on man, society, and political economy.

Both Lloyd and Verri would also emphasize at length the importance of "circulation" in an economy—identifying in money, its distribution, and what in today's terms would be known as the "velocity" of its flow as the origin as well as engine of meritocracy, justice, and social development.[107] Defining "circulation" as "the passage of a piece of money, or currency paper from the possession of one person, to that of another," Lloyd argued that "the Industry of a Nation" would "be in proportion to the quantity of circulation." As the "advantages" of money became evident, societies invented affiliated institutions (such as banks and paper money) to facilitate transactions, which gave further impetus to "trade" and "industry," again spawning more circulation, and ultimately people, in a virtuous circle: "the number of inhabitants will, *ceteris paribus*, be in proportion to the quantity of circulation."[108] Indeed, Lloyd ventured an "axiom" that he also represented mathematically: "*industry in general, and foreign and active commerce in particular* are in proportion to the quantity of paper circulation."[109] More specifically, and in accordance with his penchant for formal language, he joined Petty in arguing that "Industry in general, and arts, manufactures, commerce, and navigation in particular, will be in the *inverse ratio* to the space, which a given number of men occupy."[110]

It is worth noting here how Lloyd and Verri, though they engaged with parallel problems using analogous vocabularies, at times differed remarkably in their ultimate arguments. The Milanese patrician agreed with the Welsh soldier that the industry of a population, its demographical density, and the geographical extent of a polity were clearly related. But Verri warned that there could be too much of a good thing, and that a commercial city-state eventually would have to "principally turn its industry toward manufactures" for exports in order to feed its population. Even if exceedingly wealthy, a small polity would by necessity find itself in an "uncertain and precarious" situation, dependent on foreign markets, in which "everything can change very quickly." True "prosperity," he argued, could be found "between these two extremes" of size, when a state "does not occupy so much land as to keep people from communicating easily and not contracted so much as to be forced to seek food outside."[111]

Like Verri, however, Lloyd also modeled this vision of socioeconomic evolution on the four-stage theory of his day: from savage hunting and gathering through pastoralism to agriculture and, finally, to a commercial society based on manufacturing. Compared to contemporary attempts like that of Smith, his model remained remarkably coherent in its mechanisms of the stages of development. Once the institution of money had been discovered, subsequent stages of civilization simply embodied ever-increasing saturations of currency with accompanying innovations. "Circulation" was *the* source of civilization and the key to its mysteries.[112] Strikingly though, Lloyd went even farther than Beccaria in envisioning a limited degree of sociability existing already in the pre-economic and pre-political state of nature. Without money, "mankind" would doubtlessly have been "separated into very small societies, insomuch that scarce a considerable village would, in this hypothesis, be found upon the face of the globe," but the very fact that limited societies existed put Lloyd at odds with more dogmatic theories that resolutely put politics ahead of society, arguing no sociability at all could exist in the absence of a social contract. In this state of "almost perfect equality . . . societies would be very limited," he elaborated, "each small village would form a separate community, intirely [sic] unconnected with others."[113] Circulation was a progressive phenomenon, gradually socializing ever-larger regions and peoples through the establishment of economic interconnections. "As all Europe forms a chain," he therefore argued, "of which each nation is a link, it is evident that you cannot touch one without affecting all the others more or less."[114] Humanity was, as such, coming together in a single society, the "one mass" about which Verri had written, in the form of an ever-denser network of economic interactions, the lifeblood of which was the circulation of goods and capital.[115]

Salus Populi

As Locke had suggested almost a century earlier, "Money in its Circulation" drove "the Wheels of Trade."[116] Like Locke, Lloyd emphasized the positive political consequences of increased circulation. Venturing far beyond Locke, however, Lloyd insisted that money was a vector not merely of trade but of sociability and, possibly, of political liberty. This because circulating wealth, which had originally shackled humanity in chains of inequality, if encouraged to proliferate could have the counterintuitive consequence of liberating it. Banks, in particular, epitomized this trend for Lloyd, channeling the stagnant fortunes of the few into the hands of the many, facilitating commercial sociability and empowering the citizenry alike: banks "promote circulation and industry, equalise the fortunes of individuals, and form opulent bodies of citizens, who oppose an invincible barrier to the despotism of kings and their ministers."[117] His mechanistic moral philosophy rested on the peculiar postulate that movement equaled life, which at its kernel was characterized by a striving for liberty.[118] Now, the same relationship among movement, life, and liberty appeared in an economic context: circulation created a healthy economy that, in the end, served to produce individual freedom.

The problem was that, for the extraordinary gains to be had from a system of freer entrepreneurial enterprise and competition, the individual liberty Lloyd sought to safeguard risked undermining itself if simply unleashed in commercial society.

> Civil liberty, never fails to excite the subject of industry, being secured in the employment of its fruits. By freely following his own genius, he generally succeeds in the pursuits of riches: the concurrence of others, animated by the same motives, forces him to search new methods, which may entitle him to the preference. Arts therefore, and manufactures, are brought to a degree of perfection, no where else to be found.[119]

The essential problem was one of "preference" in political communities. The sort of civil liberty he saw enjoyed in commercial societies was extraordinarily conducive to wealth creation, yet the unequal accumulation of this very same wealth could ultimately destabilize the liberty that had caused it. One of the main points of Lloyd's 1771 *Essay*, much like Verri's contemporaneous *Meditations*, was to show that "the liberty of a nation is in proportion to the equality, and despotism to the inequality of circulation."[120] Lloyd was here modulating an idiom developed by Montesquieu and Rousseau, who wrote, "The more the State expands, the more freedom is diminished."[121] The *reason* political freedom increased with the concentration of people, Lloyd suggested, had less to do with the sociology of political communication than with the augmented economic circulation engendered by such aggregation, and the general empowerment resulting from widespread and more equi-tably distributed wealth. "There is no method so effectual to enslave a rich and free nation," Lloyd assured his readers in terms again similar to those of other members of the Academy of Fisticuffs, "as that of augmenting the luxury of individuals."[122] He defined "luxury," not in terms of wealth or fash-ions per se, but purely in terms of "an inequality of fortunes"—"the fewer are rich, and the more are poor."[123] As Verri put it, plausibly following Hume, great inequalities voided all "abundance" and all "civil liberty," "remov[ing] emulation" from society and driving it toward "the isolated and savage state." Both "too great inequality of fortunes," on the one hand, and "perfect equality," on the other—the extremes of a modern Gini-coefficient of national income inequality—would "annihilate industry," either because people "cannot hope for a better life" or because they "do not fear a worse one."[124]

And economic inequalities invariably produced imbalances of more dan-gerous sorts. Joining a long line of argument stretching back to Benjamin Franklin as well as Hobbes and Harrington, if not earlier, and forward to Adam Smith, Lloyd argued that "power always follows riches," and both were positional goods. The only way to maintain the necessary equilibrium in a polity, therefore, was to ensure a certain degree not only of legal and political but also of economic equality, otherwise a country's "constitution" would be dissolved, "and every man re-entered into his original right, which force may oppress, but can never destroy, or invalidate."[125] What was at stake in ques-tions of equality was nothing less than the social contract and the social fabric itself. Like Beccaria, in short, Lloyd maintained that extremes of inequality in commercial societies had desocializing and depoliticizing consequences, regardless of how much better off everyone was compared to the state of nature, but he was even more explicit about the political consequences of ma-terial inequality. History proved this both ways. Not only had "the cruel race of monopolizers" successfully "oppressed the poor" in the past, inducing them to commit "several violences" that disrupted "the peace of the nation," but in the longer history of commercial societies only Carthage could be seen to have endured for a substantial period, and then only because its "spirit of commerce maintained a certain equality of riches between the citizens."[126]

Perhaps to an even greater degree than in Beccaria, then, there was an unresolved contradiction at the core of Lloyd's and Verri's political econo-mies. On the one hand, they repeatedly warned that individual rights had to be protected. In Lloyd's words, if that "right, which every man has to his personal security as well as to his property, be openly, and wantonly, violated; his duty of obedience ceases."[127] Verri put it similarly, arguing that "*property*" was the "basis of justice in all civilized societies" and that inequality therefore had to be remedied "indirectly."[128] On the other hand, both Lloyd and Verri agreed with Beccaria that governments and legislators had to vigilantly maintain a certain degree of economic equality to conserve a polity against violent dissolution, indeed imbuing the executive with the power to do nearly everything in defense of what the Welshman called "that general law, which is the basis, and includes all others, *Salus populi suprema lex esto.*" Historically, this famous Ciceronian maxim—"let the health of the people be the supreme law"—had been used to defend vastly divergent viewpoints, and as we have seen, Hume and Smith would both use the very same principle to justify interventions in the case of famines. It was an appropriately deceptive idiom for Lloyd to employ. For if it historically had justified anti-tyranny attacks on the very idea of a sovereign emanating laws, and thus subjecting citizens to an "arbitrary" power in that they had no say in their formulation, it had also, and frequently, encapsulated the moral argument for states of exception, as they have come to be called, and absolutism in the language of "reason of state."[129] Lloyd put the "health" of a people at the core of all human organization very much as Beccaria had identified "justice" with "sociability." But where the latter had avoided creating tensions between individual and social rights by explicitly making the right to property secondary to that of life and, indeed, of sociability, Lloyd provided no logical exit from the friction between private property and societal welfare that haunted his contemporaries across the European world, from Franklin in Boston to Rousseau in Geneva. Lloyd's social contract would dissolve under too little as well as too much interference with the rights of life and property. But without guidelines for how to reconcile individual strivings for wealth and liberty in a social or political community, definitions of justice remained, by necessity, open to conflicting interpretations.[130]

Subterranean and partial, Lloyd's indebtedness to Beccaria is worth noting. Generally speaking, they shared preoccupations with "public enemies" and with "smuggling," not to mention with individual rights in political communities more broadly and the absolute need to secularize politics and ensure that the "clergy" had "no influence on the legislative power."[131] Lloyd's greatest fear also lay in the dissolution of sociability and the rise of "real anarchy, where force alone distinguishes the rights of mankind."[132] Yet his engagement with the young Milanese's ideas of the relationship between punishment and sociability went far deeper, amounting to one of the earliest and most profound engagements with Beccaria's work in the English language. Like *On Crimes and Punishments,* Lloyd affirmed that no country in the world displayed "more humanity towards criminals than England, who knows neither tortures, perpetual imprisonments, galleys, or slavery"; but while cherishing its example, he resolutely asserted it could not be enough.[133]

> The spirit of avarice, too natural in a commercial people, has carried the degree of punishments beyond the limits prescribed by humanity and natural equity. All ideas of distributive justice, are lost and confounded by the number and equality of punishments: death being almost a common penalty for all crimes, great and small. The manner of it makes little or no difference. The king's humanity has, indeed, saved many, but still the numbers which thus perish annually, is a real loss to a nation, and their example neither does nor will diminish the number of crimes.[134]

However lenient with regard to torture, English criminal law had become *unjust* by disregarding what for the Academy of Fisticuffs was the cardinal principle of proportionality between crimes and punishments. And not only was such indiscriminate reliance on capital punishment dehumanizing, it was also, as Beccaria so eloquently had argued, deeply uneconomic and detrimental to the goals of political economy. "Crimes," Lloyd similarly argued, were "essentially connected with the morals of the nation," and it was "vain to attempt diminishing the number of crimes by any penalty whatever: for, while the causes remain, the effects become necessary consequences of them." Like Beccaria, Lloyd directed the focus of legal thought away from individual sins toward underlying structural causes. By continuing down the current path, "punishments" would merely "destroy the inhabitants, without diminishing the evil." If punishments were necessary, they were so only "to hinder any future evil from a criminal" and to "render him an useful example to deter others; while he lives, the example lives, and his life may be rendered useful to the state." There was, ironically, no room for capital punishment in the major-general's moral imagination, for "an inanimate and dead being is useless, and soon forgot."

> The wants of man are immediate and strong. The fear of punish-
> ment is diminished by its distance and uncertainty, and must there-
> fore cede to the first, unless you diminish the sources from which
> the crimes proceed, the number of laws and punishments will only
> prove their impotency.[135]

Given the deeply mechanistic, geometrical premises of Lloyd's cosmology, capital punishments and judiciary ruthlessness were not even palliative measures—they were downright destructive to humanity and to a state's political economy.

Absolute Force

Lloyd's emphasis on the circulation of wealth and the health of political bodies led him from the abstractions of moral philosophy to more concrete issues of price formation, which though theoretically groundbreaking would become a target of severe criticism from his contemporaries. Lloyd and Verri were both avid readers of Montesquieu, who in his *Spirit of the Laws* had proposed that "prices will be fixed in a compound ratio of the total of things in commerce with the total of the signs [monies] that are also there."[136] Lloyd formalized this further by expressing the price (p) of merchandise as a function both of the quantity of it available on the market (M) and the quantity of circulation of currency (C). He presented this in the simple equation $\frac{C}{M} = p$. Assessing the impact on price of variations in the quantity of the merchandize (y), he presented a further equation $\frac{C}{M/y} = py$. The change in prices, in other words, depended on the ratio between available circulating currency and the change in the quantity of the good available—hardly a novel argument in anything but its algebraic formulation.[137] As one contemporary critic remarked, "All his calculations ultimately show no more than what we already knew, that is, that price increases the more buyers increase or sellers decrease and vice versa."[138]

Pietro Verri proposed a similar equation in his *Meditations on Political Economy*, written the same year as Lloyd's *Theory of Money*. For Verri, however, the price (p) was an even more straightforward function of the number of buyers (C for "compratori") and the number of sellers (V for "venditori"), that is, $p = \dfrac{C}{V}$. The fellow pugilist Frisi subsequently sought to formulate a compromise between Lloyd's and Verri's price equations in his 1772 mathematical appendix to the *Meditazioni*. Renaming Lloyd's variable for circulation (C) as (Q), presumably to avoid a terminological overlap, he suggested the equation $p = \dfrac{CQ}{MV}$:

> That is, generally speaking, prices are directly proportional to the numbers of buyers and to the quantity of circulation, and inversely proportional to the number of sellers and to the quantity of goods or manufactures.[139]

Frisi's methodological considerations regarding the use of mathematics, however, far superseded those of Verri or Lloyd. From the earlier equation $p = \dfrac{C}{V}$, he explained one could use differential calculus to derive the maximum and minimum price levels. If both variables changed simultaneously, one would have to calculate $dp = \dfrac{(VdC - CdV)}{V^2} = 0$, and, subsequently, $\dfrac{dC}{dV} = \dfrac{C}{V}$.[140]

Similarly, in order to determine graphically the maximum annual production of a country (R for "riproduzione" or reproduction) in terms of the work put in (T for "travaglio" or work)—an "isoperimetrical" question in the vocabulary of the time as it related to the establishment of perimeter areas between graphed variables—Frisi suggested that one could use "the differential equations of the problem $dT = 0$, $dR = 0$, and the integral equation $R + AT = B$."[141] This would reveal under what conditions the area of a curve of production projected on a Cartesian graph would be the greatest, and the national economy thus maximized. What this amounted to was a staggering application of the most avant-garde methods of contemporary mechanical physics—and importantly artillery science—to the study of political economy.[142] Sraffa in fact noted that "Frisi, in addition to being (perhaps) the first to have used a mathematical reasoning and, explicitly, abstraction, is perhaps also the first to have used trigonometry in economics."[143] It cannot be ignored, however, that the reception of Verri's and Lloyd's works at the time might have been hurt by Frisi's extreme analytical representation of them.

Mathematics aside, Lloyd thought that increased circulation had much wider implications than changing prices by opening the way for entirely new economic activities. Manufacturing, for example, depended on a certain level of circulation, of intensity and complexity of economic life in his model, and allowed even more men to share the same spaces, again increasing circulation and, according to Lloyd's calculations, the "arts and sciences," which were "in a compound ratio of the quantity of circulation and liberty."[144] Although unusually formal in its presentation, Lloyd's idea of a virtuous circle of wealth and liberty was not new at the time. For example, Voltaire's *Letters Concerning the English Nation* (1733), a collection to which Lloyd's own work is remarkably similar in tenor, noted that "as trade enriched the citizens in England, so it contributed to their freedom, and this freedom on the other side extended their commerce, whence arose the grandeur of the State" and, strikingly, that the pecuniary power of English merchants justified comparisons with "*Roman* citizens," evoking an array of sentiments that deeply problematize the previously mentioned historiographical obsessions with the supposed dichotomy between wealth and virtue.[145] Like the members of the Academy of Fisticuffs, Lloyd maintained that urbanization was viable only on the foundation of a solid agricultural sector and a flourishing export of manufactures, and his model showed how a self-reinforcing cycle could move a polity toward the stage of commercial society.[146] The process was neither necessary, nor permanent, however, and if the cycle were to break down prospects were frightful: "In such a city as London, every thing is to be dreaded from the despair of half a million of people reduced to want bread."[147] Quite tellingly, Lloyd's model of an "able minister" was the renowned promoter of agriculture Maximilien de Béthune, Duke of Sully, rather than *le Grand* Colbert, famous at the time for his emphasis on the importance of manufactures.[148] First things first.

In effect, Lloyd identified a number of ways in which this virtuous cycle of circulation and development eventually could come to an end in a state. It could, for example, topple under the weight of its own success, by virtue of internal inequalities, or because of relations with foreign powers. Particularly, as circulation increased and people grew wealthier, they could lose their competitive edge in international trade as costs of production increased. This problem was perhaps most famously articulated at the time by Montesquieu in the *Spirit of the Laws* and by David Hume in his essay on "The Jealousy of Trade," but it plagued thinkers and statesmen across the European world.[149] To circumvent this inescapable Polybian decline, seemingly programmed into the very nature of things, Lloyd suggested establishing industries in the countryside, where wages and rent (and thus the key variable of circulation) were lower. By actively investing in the general improvement of an entire country, good government could ensure a constant equilibrium between the wealth of individuals and the wealth of towns and cities, and keep output competitive.[150] His solution, in other words, was the diametrical opposite of that offered by Petty's political arithmetic, which ruthlessly argued for the forced relocation of the population of cities (and, in the case of Ireland, of entire countries) to increase England's density of population.[151] Lloyd might have drawn on an older tradition of formal political economy, but he resolutely went beyond it, both methodologically and argumentatively.

It is, however, impossible to divorce economics from the larger political and military elements of Lloyd's vision, as he considered bellicose pursuits intimately related to economic and political conditions. His "political economy" was in the end a science of creating, maintaining, and defending national welfare measured in the almost metric quantities of liberty and happiness manifested by the citizenry. Needless warfare, the major-general had learned during a lifetime in the field, spelled the end of all that, but he still maintained—against Verri—that only an army could pacify and thus socialize and territorialize a country, internally as well as externally.[152] Like money, armies could change the world for the better as well as for the worse, and Lloyd's definition of national power ultimately formalized more mercurial notions of wealth and virtuous soldiers circulating at the time, represented algebraically as population and circulation. In a rather extraordinary attempt to have his cake and eat it too, he utilized mathematics to adduce the superiority of a republic both mercantile *and* military, both wealthy *and* virtuous.

Although Lloyd joined Verri in acknowledging the potential for positive reform represented by enlightened despots, and though he concluded that monarchies were "singularly adapted" to offensive warfare, he claimed, with more tenacity than his Milanese friend, to remain a republican at heart.[153]

Elaborating upon his peculiarly mechanistic and utilitarian inflection of classical republicanism in his manuscript *Essay on Man,* Lloyd concluded that "commercial republics," while difficult to maintain, were uniquely able to promote the common good because they, alone among the possible systems of government, could fulfill both the "just" needs of physical man and the "arbitrary" needs of moral man.[154] The "natural" passions for "independence" and "preeminence" were, for Lloyd, only properly united, for the majority of the population, in republics, which by virtue of requiring active participation in political life most closely mirrored the individual agency and therefore liberty enjoyed by men in the state of nature.[155] His utilitarian demand for a general "equality" of "liberty" and of "circulation"—which produced more industrious citizens, more arts, commerce, and sciences— would furthermore refine men's pleasures and, similarly to what Montesquieu had argued before him, expand the pool of happiness beyond even that which had existed in the state of nature.[156]

In arguing for such an explicit synergy between wealth and virtue, Lloyd presented an ideal of commercial republicanism that synthesized ostensibly conflictual paradigms. In fact, he explicitly rejected a common historical assumption of the era, concluding that "the Asiatic and Roman empires were vanquished not because they were too rich, but too extensive."[157] Rome fell, not due to the corrupting and effeminate influence of wealth, and thus lack of virtue, he argued, but instead because it lacked the necessary manpower to defend effectively and territorialize its vast domains. In some senses wealth was even a precondition for virtue for Lloyd, because "virtue," as he argued in his manuscript *Philosophical Essays,* "is a vague term" and one could only love a country if invested in it.[158] Yet, while he did not think wealth explained the fall of Rome, for even "the Greek and Roman soldier" was animated "by the hopes of plunder," Lloyd agreed that rampant "luxury, vice, and folly" *could* lead to a situation in which "the influence of riches" spelled doom for "honour and virtue," and he did at times denigrate "effeminate" urban soldiers.[159] This may be explained by recourse to his vital distinction between wealth and luxury, which, following the examples of Montesquieu, Helvétius, and Verri, he repeatedly defined as the "inequality" of wealth.[160] Virtue and wealth were inseparable as long as fairly distributed, or "justly" in Beccaria's sense of promoting sociability.[161] Whereas Verri and Beccaria, however, who concerned themselves more with food supplies than with speculations about "virtue," joined authors of an Epicurean persuasion like Melon, Genovesi, and Helvétius in thinking that even "luxury" nonetheless could indirectly benefit the common good, Lloyd remained true to his reading of Rousseau by adamantly opposing such a compromise.[162] Taking the commercial emphasis on "exchange" from one side of the ideological divide and the need for egalitarian, "virtuous" representative government from the other, the internal architecture of his paradoxical political economy was in turn supplied by a radically mechanistic moral philosophy.

At deep odds with later historiographical tropes, Lloyd became an unlikely Enlightenment synthesis of the classical republican political theorist James Harrington, who described an egalitarian agrarian republic in his *Oceana,* and his opponent Matthew Wren, who, in his *Considerations* on Harrington's work, argued for a strong monarchy to domesticate the sea of commercial exchanges.[163] These authors form the two poles of Pocock's analysis of early modern English political economy, but Lloyd quixotically strove for an *Oceana* based on the circulation of monied wealth rather than on landed property. Pocock masterfully charted one trajectory of early modern political economy, arguing that "the effect of approaching the birth of political economy through the alternative paradigms of civic humanism, Addisonian morality, and natural jurisprudence is that it appears to have had far more to do with morality than with science."[164] One could say that the effect of approaching the birth of political economy through the prism offered by Lloyd's life and work is that it appears more scientific again, if by "science" one intends the so-called scientific method and the application of formal, including mathematical, methods of analysis.[165] Better still, it appears a *moral science* of wealth and virtue, of military power and public happiness. The key term for expressing this in Lloyd's political vocabulary is the theoretical and algebraic culmination of his thought: the concept of *absolute force.*

Whereas Montesquieu, an author upon whose shoulders Lloyd repeatedly sat, explicitly denied the possibility of an "absolute force," nothing that "all size, all force, all power is relative," Verri argued in his *Meditations* that the "forza" (power) of a nation depended on its "population" and output, or "annual reproduction," and noted further that the two were "always inseparable in societies civilized by lively industry and a rapid circulation."[166] Lloyd similarly, and repeatedly, presented the "axiom" that *"the absolute force of a nation, is in a compound ratio of the number of its inhabitants, and quantity of their industry,*" here understood as industriousness measured, by nearest proxy, in terms of a nation's tax returns.[167] The "Relative Force" of a nation was more accurate and depended on a variety of "circumstances," but as a baseline for comparisons, a simple equation sufficed: $\frac{P(opulation) + T(axes)}{1,000,000} = AF$, or *Absolute Force*. Because *P* in effect represented military manpower, which, for Lloyd, had better be virtuous, and *T* represented economic might as reflecting the capacity to finance military expenditures, the greatness of a nation and the "sinews of war" could, by recourse to the simplifying logic of mathematics, be seen to lie neither in wealth, nor in virtue; it lay, with algebraic certainty, in their addition.[168] Lloyd was, in short, formalizing Vattel's earlier statement to the effect that "the strength of a state consists in three things—the number of the citizens, their military virtues, and their riches."[169] Given the formula for absolute force, the looming war against France, with an AF of 34, looked bleak for England with a meager AF of 18, which still outshone Spain's AF of 10.5 and Portugal's measly AF of 4.[170] Though far more concrete, and technical, than either of them, Lloyd was in the end drawing on both Montesquieu and Vattel, who similarly had argued that "the power of a nation is relative, and ought to be measured by that of its neighbours, or of all the nations from which it has any thing to fear."[171] The magnitude of any given absolute force was, indeed, relative to what it was compared with, and, as such, hardly absolute at all.

From Lloyd's perspective, however, there would have been little doubt that France's numerical superiority—based essentially on demographic factors—would have carried the day in a war against Britain had the two countries been neighbors on a flat plain. This, however, is where the principal aim of his at first jarringly reductionist and mechanistic analysis of society emerges, for Lloyd after all understood well that simple calculations could not model complex realities. England's "circulation" was considerably higher than France's and divided with more equality among a population of half its size and with a heavier burden of taxation, so her "national industry" was higher than France's by a ratio of 20 to 9.375, the consequences of which Lloyd argued were "impossible to ascertain" properly. The keys to England's victory, though, were hidden in this very uncertainty. Indeed, Lloyd used his theory of absolute force to highlight England's main strengths: its relatively more equal wealth distribution, manufactures, and navigation, as well as its geography, "Monarcho-Aristo-Democratic" (that is, "republican") government, and the vigor with which clockwork individuals were willing—even programmed—to fight for their liberty in "free" states.[172] Drawing on the theoretical and emotive categories of both wealth and virtue, these were all factors safely outside his model, yet ultimately meant that in his eyes, England, barring the possibility of bad legislation, remained an impregnable fortress. Helvétius noted once that the reconciliation of "commercial" and "military genius" was "one of the most difficult problems in politics"; absolute force might be seen as Lloyd's algebraic solution to the conundrum.[173]

The principal arguments Lloyd contributed to the contemporary discourse of political economy in England were thus intriguingly *explicit* externalities to his own theoretical model; he summoned the Chimera of absolute force only to have it defeated by the Bellerophon of commercial republicanism. By first mathematically "proving" England's comparative weakness, Lloyd's logical conclusion that only commercial republicanism could save the day became all that more striking. Apart from uniting and formalizing vague and often mutually exclusive concepts of wealth and virtue, absolute force also served a rhetorical part of his grand call for reform, which, when examined out of its context, immediately becomes, as Jevons put it, "crude and ab-surd."[174] What Deirdre McCloskey has called the "rhetorical prestige of formality" has a long history in economics.[175] One of the interlocutors in Montesquieu's widely celebrated *Persian Letters,* beloved by the Academy of Fisticuffs and well known to Lloyd, spoke of "the mathematicians" who "oblige a man to be persuaded against his will, and override him tyrannically"; similarly, a critic of Verri sarcastically noted how "the intellect is forced to admit defeat" in the face of such mathematical flourish.[176] Lloyd's use of theoretical rigor was no different.

Shoveling formulas ahead of his ideological arguments, Lloyd indeed committed an *argumentum ad verecundiam* (argument based on authority) fal-lacy; only by an appeal to the authority of formal reasoning—of the "objec-tive" power of numbers—could he validate his normative concerns, no matter the paucity of his logic. This is not to pass judgment on him anachronisti-cally for adulterating his positive analysis with normative concerns, for, as scholars repeatedly have shown, the question is hardly between "rhetoric" and "non-rhetoric," but instead between awareness and unawareness of the rhetorical and of course social and cultural dimensions of all "science."[177] Lloyd was well aware of the advantages and disadvantages of formalism in political economy, but he never published his most lucid methodological caveats. His manuscript *On Artillery*, however, perhaps by virtue of dealing with a field where "accuracy" could be measured almost exactly (after all, it takes longer to know if you have hit the mark with political economy than with a twelve-pound howitzer), dealt with this problem explicitly:

> So many circumstances necessarily concurr . . . [that] every experiment, will forever render Theory, however exact intirely useless and all we can ever derive from it will only prove what cannot be done, but never show precisely what can be exactly put in practice.[178]

Pocock has argued that "the growth of commerce" in eighteenth-century England was "associated with the growth of oligarchy," but Lloyd envisioned a striking alternative: economic development could unchain liberty from the yoke of inequality and increase humanity's capacity for happiness without necessarily corrupting civic virtue and military prowess.[179] That Lloyd would theoretically achieve this vision justifies Pietro Verri's description of him in a 1769 letter to his brother: "I do not know any man more seductive and capable of organizing a system to reach his goal."[180] Indeed, Lloyd's formal and discursive languages of political economy intertwined to produce a uniquely coherent argument for commercial republicanism, while his idiosyncratic mosaic of influences provided him with a means of cutting the Gordian knot of wealth and virtue. In 1771 the *Giornale de' letterati*, or *Journal of the Literati*, of Pisa had declared "public virtue" to be a concern of the past, inserting "public wealth" in its place, and what tension between wealth and virtue remains in Lloyd's work, and indeed the fact that he still wielded such an anachronistic vocabulary through the 1760s and 1770s, reveals much about the ideological baggage he brought with him to Milan.[181] Verri, for one, felt that "virtue" and "glory" animated so few that only manipulating "personal interest" could serve as the lever of political economy.[182] Lloyd's proposed solution, however, and his vision of how to increase the absolute force of a commercial republic, speaks abundantly to the fertility of intellectual cross-pollination in the Enlightenment.

Economic Scholasticism

Even though Lloyd knew the limitations of his methodological abstractions and believed that privileging theory over practice was both "absurd and ridiculous," his failure to publish these most cogent reservations in this respect doubtlessly helped seal his quixotic legacy.[183] From the serious to the satirical, refutations of his attempt to formalize political economy appeared quickly in both Britain and Italy.[184] One of the most interesting retorts to the method adopted by the pugilists and their Welsh associate was perhaps the anonymous pamphlet *Meditazioni sulla economia stercoraria, ossia critica al libro intitolato Meditazioni sulla economia pubblica* (Meditations on the Stercoral Economy, or Rather Critique of the Book Entitled Meditations on Political Economy).[185] Alessandro Verri immediately suspected it might be the work of Ferdinando Facchinei, a vehement critic of the Academy of Fisticuffs—not only for their mathematical methods—to whom we soon will turn at length, whereas Parisian readers suspected the author had to be Ferdinando Galiani, which, given his sense of humor, his best-selling skewering of Physiocracy, and his general fame, made a certain sense. Pietro Verri insisted it had to be his growing nemesis Carli.[186] Centuries later, Franco Venturi demonstrated that Verri was right; their former friend and ally had indeed anonymously circulated copies of it to ridicule Frisi, Verri, and Lloyd's mathematical exuberance.[187]

To the extent that they have noted its existence, scholars have tended to rapidly dismiss Carli's short piece as a crude and ill-conceived joke. Yet *The Stercoral Economy* was not without merits. In effect, far from being vulgar in tone, its language was elegant and indeed quite formal, achieving comedic effect through the tension between its scholarly apparatus—which ranged from classical erudition to algebra—and its subject matter, excrement. It took the form of a summary of, and commentary on, a recently anonymously co-authored work (animated "only by love of dear humanity"), in which one writer had supplied the ideas, the other the mathematical method, precisely the case of Verri and Frisi's collaboration on the sixth edition of the *Meditations*.[188] A mathematical ode to the virtues and utility of "public stercoration," Verri was appalled to learn that it ridiculed his concept of "merce universale" by implicitly "changing the last two letters of the first word," that is turning "merce" into "merda"—turning "universal merchandize" into "universal shit."[189] As will be clear, however, Carli here took aim not merely at Verri's mathematical formalism but also at contemporary Physiocratic arguments regarding the singular importance of agriculture—all of which were, in his eyes, manure.

Carli began, with characteristic erudition, by discussing the Roman philosopher and consul Marcus Tullius Cicero's reproach (in the character of Cato the Elder) of the archaic Greek poet Hesiod, who in his didactic agricultural poem *Work and Days* had neglected the question of "Quid de utilitate loquar stercorandi" (What is the advantage of manuring?), continuing on to note:

> In this enlightened century applications and discoveries have been pushed to ensure the happiness, and wealth of nations to the highest point possible of human intellect, and as a consequence the kingdoms and provinces of Europe, and among them that of Our Italy, are so superabundant with comforts, pleasures, and contentedness, that there is no longer anyone among men who does not conclude it better to be alive, than to die. Yet nobody speaks of the greatest, and most secure source of the abundance, and wealth of peoples, and principally Mediterranean ones, which is public stercoration.[190]

Employing the same language of "surplus" and "reproduction" harnessed by Verri and others including the Physiocrats, Carli also played with their trope that agriculture was the sole source of the wealth of nations. "A Mediterranean country cannot count on anything but the product of the soil, given it has no industries except agriculture," Carli argued jokingly, and what way to better increase the fertility of the soil but manure?

> Fertility [of the soil] cannot be achieved without stercoration, and this stercoration increases the greater the number of stercorants, just like it diminishes the greater the number of people who are abstemious or on a diet. . . . *Fertility is in direct proportion to the number of stercorants and inverse to people who are abstemious or on a diet.*[191]

But this was only the beginning. Taking Frisi's models as a starting point, Carli argued that to express these relations analytically, one should call Fertility F; the number of stercorants S; and the number of abstemious A. If one then calls the number of stercorants s the number of abstemious a, and fertility f one will have the three following analogies:

$$I.\ I.\ F{:}f = \frac{s}{A} : \frac{s}{a}; \ II.\ S{:}s = \frac{A}{F} : \frac{a}{f}; \ III.\ A{:}a = F{:}S{:}f{.}s.$$

And so on, the end result tautologically proving the original assumption that fertility depended on defecation. "The intellect," Carli, concluded, "is forced to admit defeat" in front of such a flurry of logic and equations, and he could only suggest establishing huge public storehouses for the conservation and distribution of the excrement of different "classes" across the country.[192] With time, given this logic, the feedback mechanism of dung, grain, and population growth would create wonders, as more food meant more people, which in turn meant more excrement, or "universal merchandise," and thus greater fertility in turn leading to yet more food, and so on, "to infinity." The entire country would be filled with grain, people, and, needless to say, shit. Luckily, the authors had also composed "a table," plausibly a reference to Physiocracy's central *Tableau économique,* showing the country's "consumption" and "reproduction" as well as

> how many men will have to replace horses and oxen in pulling char-
> iots, carts, and plows, and how many cats and rats will be substi-
> tuted on tables because of the lack of calves, and how many people
> might be exposed [to the elements] every year, and how many killed,
> like in China, which thereby does not cease being the most popu-
> lous, and most virtuous Country in the World.[193]

What began as a sophisticated form of scatological humor here becomes something of a Juvenalian satire, which in taking to their logical extremes contemporary arguments—and particularly, fashionable infatuations with mathematics as well as Physiocracy's obsession with agriculture and all things Chinese—presented a deeply felt invective against current trends of political economy.[194] Finally, Carli argued, people would learn to "walk, get dressed, eat, digest, and stercorate geometrically, by way of which, in a profusion of *universal merchandise,* you can forever ensure yourselves complete happiness."[195]

More soberly, one contemporary Italian mathematician hoped the 1772 edition of the *Meditations* ultimately would

> serve as a shining example to everyone of the danger one runs in wanting to make use of Geometry outside the Realm of Nature and in claiming to express with lines and analytical symbols moral quantities, which depend on thousands factors and which are absolutely not at all susceptible to any exact measurement.[196]

The friendliest of these many critiques might have appeared in a private letter of 7 March 1772 to Paolo Frisi by the Piedmontese mathematician, and seasoned Grand Tourist, Count Ignazio Radicati di Cocconato, who wrote:

> I will not say a word [about the sixth edition of the *Meditations*] because I am not sure I have understood the meaning of the author: there is something obscure . . . one will make of political economy more or less what the scholastics have done with philosophy. By virtue of splitting hairs, one does not know what to hold on to.[197]

"Scholasticism" was defined—decidedly unjustly—in d'Alembert's article "Philosophie de l'École" for the *Encyclopédie,* as a canon that "substitutes words for things" and "frivolous and ridiculous questions for the grand objectives of true philosophy."[198] Radicati di Cocconato, in other words, warned of the inadequacy of mathematical instruments for analyzing complex social phenomena, fearing they might lead scholars down the slippery slope of impracticality and produce an economic science divorced from the reality it ostensibly sought to explain and affect. Lloyd's writings were soon ridiculed; Verri chose to never again republish the mathematical appendix to his works; and Beccaria, whose use of mathematics had been the most precocious, had simultaneously been the most careful in its application to political economy and would be most singularly devoted to practical administrative pursuits.

The charge that economics would become a "scholastic" pastime of theoretical hairsplitting has since frequently resurfaced. The Danish economist

L. V. Birch, for example, entitled his critical 1926 review essay of the Austrian economist Eugen von Böhm-Bawerk "Modern Scholasticism," but never has the term been applied to mainstream economics as frequently as in the past decades. From Robert Heilbroner and William Milberg's barrage against "soporific scholasticism" to both historical and analytical criticisms in recent years, this forlorn phrase has become a cornerstone of one of the most important methodological debates of modern economics.[199] And it lurks behind French rock star economist Thomas Piketty's critiques of his profession's "childish passion for mathematics."[200] Few, however, realize the full pedigree of their cause, whatever side of the field they occupy, and few appreciate just how long political economists have grappled with the promise and problems of theoretical formalization. The year before Verri and Lloyd first published their mathematical treatises, and seven years before Adam Smith published his unequivocally discursive *Wealth of Nations,* the Académie Royale des Sciences et Belles Lettres de Prusse in Berlin offered a prize essay contest on the self-consciously methodological question "Why has oeconomics [*Oeko-nomie*] so far gained so few advantages from physics and mathematics?"[201] More generally, the Accademia Virgiliana in Mantua offered similar prize essay contests, in both 1788 and 1790, devoted to the question of "Whether there is now some excess in the use that is made of calculus, what the reasons for this are, what damage can result from it, and which rules we have for establishing its proper confines."[202] With none of the submissions found prize-worthy, the question of establishing the right role for mathematics in political economy, not to mention the degree of its theoretical universality that had divided Carli and Verri, was left inconclusive—and remains so to this day.

In recent years, of course, there have been numerous and noteworthy attempts to chart the origins of economics as a mathematical science, ranging from the institutional importance of the Mathematical Tripos examinations at the University of Cambridge under Alfred Marshall to broader arguments regarding the "technocratic culture of rising American capitalism." Philip Mirowski has more generally argued that "machine rationality and machine regularities are the constant in the history of neoclassical economics; it is only the innards of the machine that have changed from time to time."[203] Long before neoclassical and even classical economics, the Academy of Fisticuffs developed their own form of mechanistic and algebraic political economy, not from earlier developments in statistics and political arithmetic, but from the amalgamation of practical military experience and an android moral philosophy informed by the materialism of Helvétius.

The theoretical and practical sources of formalization in economics are many and varied, and the discussions that such formalization invariably has engendered must be approached as an inherent tension in the science of political economy, and indeed in the very idea of social science itself. The mechanistic philosophy fueling intellectual developments in modern economics rests on the laurels of the Enlightenment, and, interestingly, so does the corresponding charge of scholasticism. Beccaria, Lloyd, and Verri chose—to different extents and with different caveats—to brave the risk of scholasticism in order to develop an analytical language with which to make sense of what factors counted in the great art of social administration, whether in relation to commerce or to conquests. Lloyd even relied on formal modeling to facilitate a fusion of vague but vexing concepts like wealth and virtue, mathematically incorporating Stoic and Epicurean elements that by all accounts should have precluded such a union. Perhaps the emotive force behind his mathematical exuberance can help us question our own. Lloyd himself, after all, never envisioned that the formal, quantitative language of political economy could exist without its qualitative twin, and it was indeed their synergistic interrelation that made his vision of commercial republicanism possible. So unlike Cassio in Shakespeare's *Othello,* whom Iago dismissed as a "great arithmetician" who "never set a squadron in the field," the pugilists and their allies in the end favored "practice" over "prattle."[204] For Lloyd, as for Verri and Beccaria, captains of industry and of cavalry alike had to master theory as well as practice; they had, in other words, to survey battlefields at dawn and browse bookshops in the afternoon.

It should be evident by now that the Academy of Fisticuffs and their Welsh comrade, Henry Lloyd, were far more preoccupied with the practical origins and consequences of their theories than were many canonical writers of the eighteenth century. Though deeply informed by recent developments in mathematics and radical mechanistic branches of moral philosophy, the group's efforts in the realm of political economy and institutional and cultural reform more generally were born from concrete experiences of war and trade, whether in relation to campaigns during the Seven Year' War or to the calculation and refinement of tariffs and budgets in Northern Italy. Though

addressed to humanity at large and engaged with ostensibly perennial problems of civilization, sociability, and economic competition, their works remained resolutely grounded in specific times and spaces. The Academy of
Fisticuffs might have inhabited the virtual world of mirrored salons, fresh
newspapers, and fragrant coffee, but its members enjoyed a unique *terroir* between the Alps and the Apennines, amid the mist-shrouded irrigations of
the Po Plain. And how its members theorized the nature of commercial society and the politics of international trade reflected that world of secular
commercial networks, canals, and mountain passes, in which "trade" was not
some abstract concept but a real activity involving particular people, goods,
and resources crossing often treacherous terrain to far-off destinations. The
early modern concern with perpetual peace was also a heartfelt reaction to
the constant wars that had torn the European continent apart for centuries—
Harper's Monthly Magazine reminded its readers in 1882 that, in spite of the
revolution in international trade, "war, not commerce, was the business of
the last century"—but the challenge of sociability was broader than even
that.[205] Beccaria and his colleagues had focused on the problem of crime and
punishment for a good reason, using the military analogies of external warfare to illuminate the struggle to socialize and pacify polities internally. And
it was at the intersection of people and peoples that the problems of political
economy and commercial sociability were both most manifest and most
acute.

CHAPTER FOUR

Achtung! Banditi!

———— ⟫●⟪ ————

I N ONE OF THE OPENING SCENES of Carlo Lizzani's 1951 neorealist masterpiece *Achtung! Banditi!*, the first great Italian World War II epic, the heroic *partigiani*, or antifascist partisans, descend from the northern Apennines and the Ligurian Alps to sabotage a munitions factory toward the war's end. Passing around a bombed-out and still smoldering farmhouse on their way down the mountainside, they come across one of the numerous road signs put up by the German army across Italy wherever it felt uncertain of its territorial control: *"Achtung! Banditen"* (Beware! Bandits). Defiantly, the partisans strike the sign with their weapons, tear it down, and throw it toward the cloud-shrouded valley below. The short scene encapsulates the movie's moral message by underlining the historical polyvalence of banditry; for who were really the bandits in the Apennines? The sign clearly referred to the partisans themselves, dubbed bandits by the occupying forces. In rejecting and inverting it, the partisans expressed a warning to the real bandits in the movie's moral economy: the Fascist regime itself. "Beware, bandits," their stern faces seem to say, "we are taking our rightful lands back."[1] One man's bandit, to repeat a tired yet eternally lucid cliché, is often another man's freedom fighter.[2]

In fact, though frequently marginalized or discussed from a "social" and frequently utopian perspective, bandits have historically occupied a space in the very core of political philosophy and political economy alike. And they naturally occupy, too, a fault line in Max Weber's classic definition of "the state" as "that human community which (successfully) lays claim to the *monopoly of legitimate physical violence* within a certain territory, this 'territory' being another of the defining characteristics of the state."[3] Not only do bandits by their mere presence threaten the success of governmental monopolies on violence, they destabilize territories and challenge the very legitimacy of states. Taking this argument one step further in light of recent scholarship on the historical development of commercial societies, bandits were by definition the nemeses of such societies. As scholars from a remarkably wide variety of theoretical, ideological, and empirical perspectives have argued, "markets" are eminently social and political historical constructions, not the teleologically necessary manifestations of behaviors immanent in human nature.[4] Annabel Brett has recently explored the tension between "nature and the city," in early modern political philosophy, arguing that the "civitas," meaning human "commonwealth" rather than simply built urban environment, was "a metaphysical, not a physical place," the borders between which were a site of "tense negotiation" at the time not merely between polities but also between polities and nature.[5] And though this undoubtedly is true, the metaphysical *civitas* itself in turn depended on the actual territoriality of civilizations and the borders between them.[6] Indeed, bandits played a significant yet often ignored role in the processes of early modern state formation and in concomitant debates of political economy during the so-called age of state-building "mercantilism."[7] Unveiling how requires a more careful excavation of what Henri Pirenne long ago called a "territorial economy," and Saskia Sassen more recently has referred to as "the political economy of urban territoriality," terms themselves closely related to Michael Mann's notion of a state's "infrastructural power."[8]

Few regions offer a richer history of banditry and state building than the Italian peninsula. And it is noteworthy, in light of this history, that Antonio Genovesi, Italy's first professor of anything like "political economy" and a man who is often referred to as a "mercantilist," never called his discipline by either of those names. Rather, the Neapolitan *abbé* first chose "commerce and mechanics," a decision doubtlessly influenced by his mentor Bartolomeo Intieri's statement that "physics is the foundation of the economy of politics," then "economia civile" or "civil economy," in more modern terms "civil economics."[9] Today the phrase "civil economics" has come to be identified largely with a tradition of Catholic economic thought focused on the importance—and ostensibly revolutionary possibilities—of a "Third Sector" of voluntary associations related to but distinct from states and markets. The expression was, however, rather more inclusive in Italy during the long eighteenth century, reflecting a historical context in which the discipline of political economy was still searching for an identity.[10] Consider the case of Enlightenment Lombardy, for example. There the terms "civil economics," "political economy," "public economics," "economics," "economics and commerce," "the sciences of Finance, Commerce, etc.," and "Cameralism," from a contemporary tradition of originally Germanic statecraft and economic administration, were all used, seemingly interchangeably, by the same historical actors, including our pugilists, to refer to essentially the same thing: aggregate analyses of what we today would understand to be the economic dimension of civic life.[11]

It is important to note, though, that "civil society" at the time seldom was contrasted to the state in the way Western political philosophy has habitually done since the works of Immanuel Kant and Georg Wilhelm Friedrich Hegel.[12] Because of Europe's unique developmental trajectory, in other words, analyses of the emergence of governmental state capacity that assume it to be something imposed on a presumed preexisting civil society are of only limited analytical relevance.[13] Historically, a civil society was often understood to be necessarily and essentially inseparable from its government and disciplined by an array of laws that, although weak by contemporary comparison, were upheld by recognizably statelike structures such as courts, legislators, and law-enforcing institutions. The meaningful contrast with civil society was less the state than the state of nature.[14] "Economia civile" was a political, legal, *and* social economy, in that it engaged with the economy of the *civitas,* Cicero's old concept of a "social body of citizens united by law [*concilium coetusque hominum jure sociati*]" that Thomas Hobbes would equate with "that great Leviathan called a Common-Wealth, or State (in latine [*sic*] *Civitas*)." And although grounded in, and expanding across, the natural world, such a civil society was dramatically distinct from it.[15] The "civile" part of eighteenth-century political economy was, in short, hardly a Catholic prerogative, though Catholicism of course deeply influenced thinking on the matter at the time, and was less antithetical to than synonymous with the state as such, however embryonic by modern standards. The "civilizing process," around which so much has been written in the wake of contentious German sociologist Norbert Elias's book *The Civilizing Process* (1939), can, after all, easily be seen to take form in the emerging communes of medieval Italy, where mercantile, classical, and religious influences came together to domesticate elite behavior and discipline urban life.[16] Civil society, as opposed to savagery in the state of nature, required the government of the self and of others, and *economia civile* was the discipline of its material organization.[17]

Yet the example of *economia civile* highlights the inherent problems of applying modern conceptions of political economy, such as "states" and "markets," to earlier historical periods. There were of course "states" in existence in the eighteenth century, theorized as such in terms remarkably similar to many of those we would use today. Similarly, the economic imagination of early modern Europe allowed for markets, not merely in the physical sense of marketplaces and fairs, but also along the lines of today's more abstract principle of exchanging goods as such, without immediate reference to people and places. Widely conceived, political economy operated on the tacit and sometimes explicit assumptions that states had territories in which there were marketplaces, that sovereignty over the former did not by necessity entail supremacy in the latter, whatever formal dominion might suggest, that both marketplaces and territories were actively competed for by states involved in shifting constellations of alliances, and that some greater commercial principle united these different locations through the production and exchange of goods across myriad borders still partitioning the European continent, not merely political but also of customs and religions.[18]

The state was far from the only locus of sovereignty at the time, however, and what Weber would have liked to be monopolistic claims to legitimacy and violence really took the form of competing spectrums of authority.[19] James Scott is certainly right to point out the extent to which "the premodern state" was "partially blind," in that it lacked the capacity to monitor, regulate, and administer the people, things, and concepts it would have liked to, in order to achieve, in his terms, the "legibility" necessary for social "manipulation."[20] States seldom had a crystalline idea of where their own borders were, of who lived within them, and what passed between them internally and with regard to other states, and a central concern of the tradition of *economia civile* lay precisely in remedying this situation—through everything from cartography to cadastres—in expanding the civil sphere of governance over ever larger areas and harness controlled resources to fruitful ends. As a Milanese cadastral instruction for surveyors put it as early as 1549, minute descriptions and assessments of the most varied terrains and people of the state were necessary to ensure "true news" of the "quality and quantity of goods" in the dominion, a strategic necessity guiding many of the key attempts to codify economic statecraft in early modern Europe, from French *économie politique* through German *Kameralismus* to English "political arithmetick."[21] As Emer de Vattel so poignantly put it, "a nation ought to know itself."[22] Cadastres had, of course, been part of political economy broadly conceived since antiquity, but it is undeniable that the eighteenth century gradually saw their increased sophistication, theorization, international emulation, and purposeful application for policy purposes.[23] Not surprisingly, Enlightenment cadastres were often justified in relation not merely to state power but to the "public good" of "peoples" in terms of how a more complete territorial awareness and assessment would improve revenues and the "dignity" of the "State" and thus "the administration of justice, defense, and the peace of all."[24] In Michel Foucault's words, "the administrative survey of populations" was "a requirement of any power."[25]

One of the founding works on the historiography of the phenomenon known as mercantilism, the Berlin don of economics Gustav von Schmoller's *The Mercantile System and Its Historical Significance,* remains remarkably helpful in illuminating this process.[26] Schmoller saw the origins of early modern political economy in the economic policies of medieval European towns, and discerned "the soul of that policy" in the nationalist or patriotic "putting of fellow-citizens at an advantage, and of competitors at a disadvantage." The period saw, in other words, the spatial demarcation of competing lines of exclusion, in which "territorial institutions" sought to "shut themselves off from the outer world, and to harmonize and consolidate their forces at home" to produce "an independent territorial unit" ultimately based on the "territorial harmonizing of production and consumption."[27] This territoriality of state power—and of the state–economy nexus as it was coming into being— eventually transcended its urban origins.[28]

What to each in its time, gave riches and superiority first to Milan, Venice, Florence, and Genoa; then, later, to Spain and Portugal; and now to Holland, France, and England, and to some extent, to Denmark and Sweden, was a *state* policy in economic matters, as superior to the territorial as that had been to the municipal.[29]

As this impulse of governance on behalf of internal economic and mercantile interests outgrew the medieval city-states and then superseded the "territorial state," only to align itself with the nation-state, Schmoller argued, it came to define European history in global terms, in relation to both the internal and external relations of states as they emerged and solidified. "Questions of political power" were essentially "questions of economic organization," and "what was at stake was the creation of real *political* economies as unified organisms, the center of which should be, not merely a state policy reaching out in all directions, but rather the living heartbeat of a united sentiment."[30] He was, in essence, speaking of nationalism, understood as *economic nationalism*.[31]

Only he who thus conceives of mercantilism will understand it; in its innermost kernel it is nothing but state making—not state making in a narrow sense, but state making and national-economy making at the same time; state making in the modern sense, which creates out of the political community an economic community, and so gives it a heightened meaning. The essence of the system lies . . . in the total transformation of society and its organization, as well as of the state and institutions, in the replacing of a local and territorial economic policy by that of the national state.[32]

Strikingly, in light of eighteenth-century debates, Schmoller emphasized the crucial importance of internal "circulation" and external "commercial competition" for the process of early modern national state building.[33] The need to defend circulation, and the seemingly uncontrollable escalation of competition, paradoxically gave rise to paragovernmental preoccupations with the nature and fate of humanity as such.

The very idea of international law is a protest against the excesses of national rivalry. All international law rests on the idea that the several states and nations form, from the moral point of view, one community. Since the men of Europe had lost the feeling of community that had been created by the Papacy and Empire, they had been seeking for some other theory which might serve to support it; and this they found in the reawakening "law of nature." But the particular ideas for which in the first instance men strove, and for which they sought arguments *pro et contra* in the law of nature, were mainly products of the economic and commercial struggle then proceeding.[34]

There was, then, a deep tension at the very core of early modern political economy in Schmoller's analysis. On the one hand, human circulation and communication depended on the expansion of civil spheres of government civilizing and pacifying ever-greater areas and bringing them under the ordering institutions born from urban life—the territorialization of civilization, no less. On the other, in the absence of the unifying sense of community previously offered by the Holy Roman Empire and the Papacy, these competitive regional projects of state expansion and spatial socialization ended up undermining the circulation and subsequent socialization of humanity as such. The great Renaissance realist Niccolò Machiavelli might, perhaps unsurprisingly, have encapsulated this mindset (likely common everywhere, always) when he instructed Iuliano Lapi in a Florentine chancellery dispatch of August 27, 1503, to *"have an eye on everything that regards the good of our city and the conservation of those places and of our men."*[35]

The paradigm of the "common good" was, contrary to what its semantics might suggest, rigorously circumscribed in spatial terms, and the sublimation of city-state good into territorial, and ultimately universal, good was by necessity a painful and ironically paradoxical process. And though less interested in the underlying philosophy of this mechanism than their Prussian predecessor, influential economists, sociologists, and historians along the lines of Edwin F. Gay, Eli F. Heckscher, Karl Polanyi, Henri Pirenne, and Fernand Braudel in the subsequent century adopted the basic historical process laid out in Schmoller's *The Mercantile System and Its Historical Significance.*[36]

Schmoller's account in many ways still represents our principal and most compelling way of understanding the nature and consequences of European state-formation in the early modern period and the nature of economic competition today.[37] This transformational juncture, this Schmollerian moment, has cast its long shadow over global history ever since. Schmoller saw "natural law" as the attempt to again impose coherence on this anarchic world, swaddling humanity with ideas rather than with empires of the sword or of the soul. Here he put his finger on a set of problems that had preoccupied early modern political philosophers and economists and that has again become a fixation of the historiographical mainstream—namely, the sociability question and the overarching problem of pacifying a world at once economically interconnected and politically dismembered, a world in which individual states linked by treaties, by shared customs, and by commerce were often at war and were always locked in a struggle for supremacy, whether military or economic.[38] A world, in short, much like our own. The logic of each state might be domestic peace in their expanding, often contested territories, but the outcome of their interaction could become quite the opposite internationally. This was the perennial tragedy of *economia civile,* the tradition of Enlightenment political economy practiced in the region in which this process had gone on for the longest, but that also, by contemporary standards, seemingly had stopped at the level of city-states and minor territorialities. "Italy," Verri noted late in life, lacked "a unifying center" of its own, a peninsular capital, and its only "common fatherland" remained the Roman Catholic Church.[39]

Perhaps the most interesting question, however, is not what went into such civil economics, but rather what it excluded, and what it *had* to exclude and even eradicate, an issue that relates the micro and macro dynamics of Schmoller's analysis and further helps elucidate the Academy of Fisticuffs' project, Enlightenment debates over commercial society, and the vexing role of crime—and particularly banditry—therein. To better contextualize the longer history of commercial sociability in the so-called age of mercantilism, in short, and indeed the politics of what eventually would be known as Enlightenment socialism, it is worthwhile turning to this idea of civil economics and, importantly, its threshold, its boundaries, and its emergence in light of that timeless agent of civil and economic discord: Cicero's "common enemy of all," the pirate, and more broadly, the bandit and outlaw, whose very

existence undermined civil society and what early modern Italians conceived of as the "viver Politico," the politicized or civic life.[40] *Achtung! Banditi!* indeed.

Misfit Justice

Somewhat curiously from a longer historical perspective, such "enemies of
mankind" and their aesthetic are today increasingly eulogized, whether
in the form of actor Johnny Depp or late celebrity chef Anthony Bourdain,
Wikileaks's Julian Assange, or the hacktivist collective Anonymous—and
more generally through an ever-increasing volume of academic publications, from Eric Hobsbawm's foundational work on "social bandits" through
Peter Leeson's libertarian buccaneers to Rodolph Durand and Jean Philippe
Verone's piratical organizations spearheading capitalism, the lattermost
plausibly inspired by Apple prophet Steve Jobs's famous slogan, "It's better
to be a pirate than to join the navy."[41] And who can forget the "objectivist"
novelist Ayn Rand's perhaps greatest literary creation, the umlauted and
oddly Swedish-sounding, Danish-derived Norwegian philosopher-pirate
Ragnar Danneskjöld, a Viking-capitalist with the "startling beauty of physical perfection" whose "smile" was like "the first green of spring on the
sculptured planes of an iceberg"? The curiously legitimate son of a Catholic
bishop of Protestant Norway, Ragnar eventually became a "pirate" and a
"bandit," joining John Galt's libertarian rebellion in *Atlas Shrugged* on a
mission to "destroy" the last memory of "Robin Hood," preying on humanitarian "relief vessels" carrying goods for the "Bureau of Global Relief"
and handing the resulting loot over to wealthy industrial leaders. Why?
Because Robin Hood, as Danneskjöld explained in words that have made
him an icon of the contemporary blogosphere, "was the man who robbed
the rich and gave to the poor. Well, I'm the man who robs the poor and
gives to the rich—or, to be exact, the man who robs the thieving poor and
gives back to the productive rich."[42]

These are merely particularly flamboyant expressions of a general piratical critique of government fielded across the political spectrum, increasingly so in recent years, from libertarians of the left and of the right.[43] Behold,
we are told, the rise of the "misfit economy," populated by "outsiders" uniquely
qualified for "disruptive innovation."[44] Whatever the complex political and

institutional causes of this motley movement, we live in a world that has
become remarkably enamored with the outlaw aesthetic, from the vigilante
to the villain, and more specifically with its creative and indeed productive
potential.[45] Compared to the great and widely emulated Italian *polizieschi*
movies of the 1970s and 1980s, for example, in which hideous crimes were
resolved by dedicated and often underdog police detectives representing the
state's judiciary branch, today's crime aesthetic frequently favors corrupt
and inept law enforcement officials, revenge fantasies, and wrongdoings ultimately avenged by extralegal vigilantes, often in the form of disillusioned
police officers taking matters into their own hands.[46] Needless to say, things
have not always been this way, and the long tradition of *economia civile* can
perhaps remind us of why.

Although for many historical sources bandits and pirates were essentially
interchangeable—"misfits" in today's parlance—others were careful to differentiate between these kinds of outlaws.[47] From one perspective that is
rather easy to adopt, pirates are simply bandits in boats. From a more nuanced
legal perspective, however, bandits and pirates are engaged in admittedly
analogous yet dissimilar activities: bandits tend to corrode the territorial
sovereignty of political communities, pirates assault the relations between
them. Banditry is a landlocked activity, by default occurring in a territory
claimed by one or more sources of authority the lawfulness of which they
challenge or, at the very least, momentarily disregard. Pirates often literally operate in a no-man's land, at sea, where they challenge not only territorial rights
but the existence of rights at all. Cicero defined "pirates" as "common enemies
of all" by virtue of their acting without "good faith" by threatening the chan-
nels of commerce—understood to be both trade and communication—and
thus of sociability itself, purposefully operating outside of and against the
"immense fellowship" of humanity and therefore outside of the parameters
of that most basic "obligation" that all human beings, even warring competitors, owed each other. Pirates were not simply foreigners to society, they
were antibodies of society and not owed anything, by anyone.[48] For practical purposes, however, piracy and banditry were often expressed in the
same breath in early modern Europe, and with good reason.

As long as there have been polities, said polities have contained members
who were unwilling to partake peaceably in them. From the Roman emperor
Tiberius, who dispatched four thousand troops to Sardinia to fight bandits

there, to Adolf Hitler, who rebranded partisans as bandits during World War II, the sovereigns of very different polities have historically come to violent terms with the problem of "banditry."[49] It is often argued that banditry resurges in periods of duress, and early modern Europe saw many kinds of duress—not merely material, in terms of subsistence anxieties and failed harvests, but also social, in terms of rapidly changing laws and norms, of veritable "regime changes" in contemporary parlance (though even Renaissance Italian chroniclers referred to the action of "mutare lo stato").[50] At a hitherto unknown speed, early modern rural communities—proverbial "traditional societies"—were not simply incorporated into ever larger and more *present* state organizations; they were simultaneously brought into connection with each other in often less than peaceful ways. The history of banditry is, from this perspective, also a counterhistory of the consolidation and increasingly institutionalized legitimacy of state power in early modern Europe, and an underappreciated aspect of its impact lies in its violent rebuttal of the very essence of commercial sociability as it began spreading outward from the Italian city-states of the Middle Ages. Modern proponents in the tradition of civil economics focus on the paradigm of "felicitá pubblica" (public happiness) so dear to the Academy of Fisticuffs, often emphasizing its medieval origins, and there can be no doubt that the problem of banditry's relation to trade, sociability, and "buon governo" (good government) in early modern political economy also benefits from being considered from such a deeper historical perspective.[51]

In effect, this problem was a veritable trope in late medieval and Renaissance political art in Italy, already present in the great Florentine painter Giotto di Bondone's monochromatic fresco depictions of the virtue of *Justice* and the vice of *Injustice* on the walls of the Scrovegni Chapel in Padua (ca. 1303–1305). The female figure of *Justice* is adorned with a crown, seated on a throne, and holds scales supporting, on her left, an angel about to smite a villain with a sword, and, on her right, an angel about to crown a sage. Her gaze is calm and directed straight at the viewer, a way for Giotto to communicate truthful honesty. Underneath her, Giotto depicted the joys of civil life under justice and good government in a two-dimensional bas-relief, including dancing, hunting, safe travel, even for women, and, crucially for our purposes, trade. The inscription below her feet has long faded, and the last line is now almost totally lost, but it begins with the word "mercator," or perhaps "mercatores," suggesting that the merchant, like the good knight

Giotto, *Justice,* ca. 1303–1305.

Giotto, *Injustice*, ca. 1303–1305.

mentioned in the preceding line, will rejoice at Justice's rule and be free to travel and trade, an activity understood to be positive given the larger moral economy of the fresco.

The parallel figure of *Injustice* on the opposite wall is more striking. An elderly, blind man in a ruined castle, with a judge's cap placed backward and long, demonic fingernails, holds a sword down by his side and seems caught on his throne, unable to move, held in place by a large, wildly growing forest that literally emerges from the wall itself, the pictorial triumph of the "selva oscura" or "dark forest" in which Dante opened his *Inferno,* and that eventually would find phonetic representation in the "boschi ombrosi," or "shadowy forests," of Monteverdi's *Orfeo.*[52] In the mock bas-relief underneath Giotto's Injustice, women are raped and killed, armed brigands haunt the roads and the woods, and trade and travel are impossible.[53] As the Victorian art historian John Ruskin read the seeming inactivity of *Injustice* itself, this "is, indeed, the depth of Injustice: not the harm you do, but that you permit to be done. . . . The baronial type exists still, I fear, in such manner, here and there, in spite of improving centuries." The agency of the fresco is, in this reading, human, in that civilization is a question of active legislation and governance, while trusting in nature and spontaneous events leads only to chaos. This was a truism Ruskin found reflected in the precarious and threatened nature of civil life as such, when he noted that "in Giotto's time woods were too many, and towns too few."[54]

Ruskin's analysis of the problem unwittingly echoed that of the elderly Pietro Verri, who had argued that "the oldest and most common art of despotism is to introduce a mutual distrust among men," for "like ideas, the sentiments of men cannot therefore develop and take full shape except through commerce and reciprocal communication." The "art of tyrants," he concluded, "is that of keeping men isolated like so many grains of sand, detached and loose, which remain very close to each other but do not form a mass and a whole."[55] Beccaria would repeatedly express the very same preoccupation, even casting it in explicitly sylvan terms in an early poem on commerce he penned in 1760. "Commerce," he rhymed, was the only force able to overcome the "forested passes [*selvosi gioghi*]" that "divided distant lands."[56]

A very similar aesthetic, and a very similar legal and political-economic argument, is evident already in the most picturesque and justly famous expressions in this "civic" tradition of the challenge posed by enemies of man-

kind to the nexus of states, markets, and sociability, namely Ambrogio Lorenzetti's fresco cycle in the Palazzo Pubblico of Siena, his 1338–1339 *Allegory
of Good and Bad Government.*[57] Doubtlessly inspired by Giotto, and one of the
most sophisticated and most commented upon expressions of political art in
world history, Lorenzetti's work defies singular explanations. But from our
present perspective, the adversarial relationship between banditry and civil
society in effect emerges as the very axis around which his fresco cycle turns.
Contemplating the work from left to right, as intended, one first encounters
the effects of *Bad Government in the Countryside,* with burning fields and villages, and bands of heavily armed bandits and brigands stalking the roads.
They are depicted as soldiers really, less of fortune than of anarchy. The scene
of utter devastation is only explained when one reaches the gate to *Bad Government in the City,* over which the harrowing undead figure of *Timor,* or Fear,
flies with a brandished black sword and a banner explaining, "Because each
seeks only his own good, in this city, Justice is subjected to Tyranny; where-
fore along this road nobody passes without fearing for his life, since there
are robberies outside and inside the city gates."[58]

One then enters the urban expression of *Bad Government,* in which houses
are falling down, only the arms dealer's shop remains open (brigands too,
after all, have their business needs), and people are attacked and defiled in
the streets with abandon by armed outlaws. Bad government is essentially
depicted through—and *characterized* by—the existence of bandits and brigands, by those not yet or no longer civilized in the Ciceronian sense, both
inside and outside the city walls. The very existence of these figures deso-
cialized territories by threatening trade and travel, commerce and communication, inciting civic vices of fear and selfishness. Continuing the eye's
march rightward across Lorenzetti's masterpiece, one sees the courts of *Bad
Government,* where the Devil has *Justice* bound at his feet, and *Good Government,* where *Justice* reigns supreme, before entering the vibrant and developing
(tall buildings are being constructed in the background) merchant metropolis achieved under *Good Government in the City.* The scene is characterized
by trade, education, and civic happiness, a quintessentially commercial
society in which, though the city itself is heavily fortified, no trace of violence can be found. The explanation can again be found outside the city
gates, this time in the shapely form of a female angel, named *Securitas,* in
one hand holding a gallows aloft with a hanged corpse dangling from it, in

Ambrogio Lorenzetti, Allegory and Consequences of Good and Bad Government (detail: the consequences of bad government in the countryside), ca. 1338–1339.

Ambrogio Lorenzetti, *Allegory and Consequences of Good and Bad Government* (detail: Fear), ca. 1338–1339.

Ambrogio Lorenzetti, *Allegory and Consequences of Good and Bad Government* (detail: the consequences of bad government in the city, and the court of bad government), ca. 1338–1339.

Ambrogio Lorenzetti, *Allegory and Consequences of Good and Bad Government* (detail: the court of good government), ca. 1338–1339.

Ambrogio Lorenzetti, *Allegory and Consequences of Good and Bad Government* (detail: the consequences of good government in the city), ca. 1338–1339.

the other holding a banner stating: "Without fear every man may travel freely and each may till and sow, so long as this commune shall maintain this lady Justice as sovereign, for she has stripped the wicked of all power."[59] Underneath her, merchants can be seen riding off to distant lands, and the surrounding landscape looks positively arcadian, with peaceful hamlets, hardworking farmers, and abundant harvests.

Across the plastered walls of the Palazzo Pubblico in Siena, Lorenzetti gracefully depicted one of the most enduring questions, and tensions, of political philosophy: that of the nature and consequences of *justice* in civil society. Proverbially speaking, what Lorenzetti offered was not "our way or the highway," for in theory the highway was precisely where the political leaders of Siena did not want their adversaries. The right dichotomy was our way or the gallows, a rather more finite destination, though in practice medieval Italian jurisprudence tended to be remarkably nonconfrontational, falling back on a politics of exile and bans to expel unwanted persons and factions.[60] *Justice* unbound contributed to extraordinary riches in the fresco, visualizing core features of the long-lasting Italian tradition of *economia civile* as it developed out of late medieval political humanism.

The female figure of unbound *Justice* is assisted by *Wisdom* in Lorenzetti's fresco, a heavenly figure suggesting the necessity of divine inspiration, and emanates two personal incarnations derived from late medieval readings of Aristotle also present in Giotto's earlier masterpiece: *Distributive Justice,* engaged in beheading (in this case a rather cheerful felon, it must be noted) and crowning citizens at her leisure, and *Commutative Justice* in charge of funding and arming the worthy. A rope in turn connects these two aspects of the "divine virtue" to *Concord,* who hands the rope on to a group of twenty-four representative male citizens of Siena. Order and concord were medieval dreams, and one should be careful about reading Lorenzetti's vision of Siena as anything more than a utopian reverie. Yet it projected an ideal of a remarkable longevity in the canon of Italian political philosophy, eventually interacting with the emergence of more succinctly economic thinking on the peninsula. And in spite of all the Thomistic influences on Lorenzetti's vision, the iconography of *Good Government* betrays a fundamental difference in its view of human nature. Quentin Skinner and others have argued that for Aquinas peace was simply the "absence of discord," a normal state of affairs from which one could deviate unless careful. War was, as such, accidental, and to be resisted. Whatever one's reading of Aquinas, Lorenzetti's imagery aligned with, and contributed to, a decidedly conflictual vector for Italian political economy that would come to profoundly influence thinking on these matters throughout the early modern period.[61]

Conflict and war, in this "civic" tradition, were endemic, spontaneous, sudden. Peace could be achieved and human relations socialized through

Ambrogio Lorenzetti, *Allegory and Consequences of Good and Bad Government* (detail: the consequences of good government in the countryside), ca. 1338–1339.

Ambrogio Lorenzetti, *Allegory and Consequences of Good and Bad Government* (detail: Security), ca. 1338–1339.

political means, but it was only a fragile exception to, and momentary victory over, the violent rule of nature. Alessandro Verri, himself a careful reader of Cicero, echoed these sentiments in *Il Caffè*:

> Social matters are characterized by that fast movement and that inclination to disorder and decay that they have always had to date and always will have, as their nature entails. Human passions always conflict with social institutions; I say if the latter are not strengthened and propped up, they will collapse under their continuous impetus. Just as in countries which fear the force of the sea or of rivers there are magistrates tasked with supervising the protection and repair of embankments, so it is necessary to protect and repair the laws, for the forces and interests that they must restrain are infinite and powerful.[62]

It was not order but disorder that was spontaneous, and inaction, as both Giotto and Lorenzetti depicted so clearly, lay at the core of injustice. *Peace*

was one of the central themes of both their fresco cycles, which in Lorenzetti's version took physical form at the very center of his oeuvre: a beautiful
woman holding an olive branch and reclining, pensively, on a massive suit
of armor. The parallel to the city under *Good Government* is striking. There
should be no need for fortifications and city walls, given there are no bandits
or armies on the other side. A deep knowledge that discord could—and by
necessity *would*—return, however, justified their continued presence, just as
Peace knew better than to discard her plate mail.[63] There was also a deeper
issue that remained unresolved in Lorenzetti's political vision, for though
"good government" in Siena seemingly had succeeded in socializing *people*
in the polity, and exterminating or exorcizing deviants from its hinterlands,
the problem of socializing *peoples* remained. However well a polity was regulated, it could still succumb to greater and more aggressive powers, as the
case would be when Siena herself fell to Florentine and Spanish troops in
1555.[64] This tension would haunt thinkers and statesmen in the small states
of Italy into the era of nineteenth-century national unification known as the
Risorgimento. Pietro Verri himself would ponder, and inspire his colleagues
to interrogate the meaning of, what, in early memoranda, he called "the rule
of good government," and in one of his last dialogues, written in the wake
of the French Revolution and Napoleon's invasion of Italy, the relationship
between "good government" and "bad government," "the common good,"
"social order," "justice," and how international conflicts and consequent warfare destroyed "humanity." That these all remained cardinal terms through
which to approach the overarching question of human sociability during the
Enlightenment testifies to the longevity of such a "civic" tradition of *buon governo* and *bene comune* in Italian thought, and to the Academy of Fisticuff's
deep conceptual hinterland.[65]

A similar vision of peace had, after all, been encapsulated in Sandro Botticelli's triumphant *Pallas and the Centaur* (ca. 1482), which depicts Pallas
Athena, also known to the ancient Greeks as *Athena Polias* or "Athena of the
City," goddess of wisdom and civilization, among other things, restraining
the beastly centaur. Subdued, even remorseful, man's animalistic side incarnated in the centaur looks to Athena for guidance, the background—replete
with fences demarcating and territorializing civil and civic life as well as merchant ships—reinforcing the impression that the mountainous wilderness
was being domesticated by an expanding civil sphere, humanity increasingly

managing, even landscaping, the material world.[66] Athena herself, dressed like the Spring of Botticelli's contemporary *Allegory of Spring,* holds the centaur's hair like a Judith might hold that of a beheaded Holofernes, but her complex visage is not without compassion, even pity, as she considers the wretched beast by her side.[67] "More than a physical place," as Wu Ming 4 has argued, "the forest is a concept," the "realm of the supernatural," a sphere "beyond civilization," apt not for "society" but for "wild men, bandits."[68]

This equation of forests with the wild, the asocial, and even antisocial, and specifically with banditry, would become so pervasive in early modern Lombardy that legislators described crime-ridden urban spaces as "forests" full of "homicides, wounds, and assassins."[69] Indeed, it would become something of a trope throughout Europe, harnessed effectively by the English lawyer and novelist Henry Fielding when, in 1751, he compared parts of London to "a vast Wood or Forest, in which a Thief may harbor with as great Security, as wild Beasts do in the Desarts [*sic*] of *Africa* or *Arabia*."[70] This complex and conflictual relationship between the natural and the civil, simultaneously symbolized and galvanized by the figure of the bandit, continued to inform art on the Italian peninsula well into the nineteenth century, most famously so in the period between Botticelli and Beccaria, in the form of the wild and outlaw-ridden landscapes of the celebrated Baroque painter and poet Salvator Rosa, one of the most favored artists of the European Grand Tour.[71] Just like the historical pirate, though, the contemporary bandit was eventually domesticated and redeemed. Rosa became so famous for his outlaw sceneries that two painters of the later Hudson River School in the United States, Thomas Cole and Thomas Moran, dedicated paintings to the theme of "Salvator Rosa Sketching the Banditi" between 1830 and 1860, ironically rendering them more as Elysian dreamscapes in the tradition of national romanticism, the precise opposite of what bandits had represented in early modern Italy.[72]

The metaphorical fight against untamed wilds was matched by centuries of widespread deforestation in early modern Italy—like elsewhere in Europe—controlling and civilizing the land by forcibly removing the Sherwoods of the world (trees and bandits alike).[73] Polities had worried about deforestation for centuries, Venice perhaps most acutely.[74] By the early years of the nineteenth century the tradeoff between the threat bandits posed to commerce and the economic potential of forests had become evident enough

Salvator Rosa, *Rocky Landscape with a Huntsman and Warriors*, ca. 1670.

Thomas Cole,
Salvator Rosa
Sketching the Banditti,
ca. 1832–1840.

that even the Brindisian naturalist and Vesuvius-scholar Teodoro Monticelli could lament the irony that deforestations did not "destroy, as is generally believed, the asylums of brigands, and of assassins, but in reality destroy the first source of the salubrity and wealth of the country, adding a new cause of desperate brigandage to those already known."[75] In Monticelli's eyes, banditry was an essentially economic phenomenon related to common poverty, a tradition of interpretation of which Cesare Beccaria had been one of the most eloquent exponents.

The Political Economy of Banditry

Italian polities waged wars on banditry—and each other—throughout the Renaissance and early modern periods. By the time Tommaso Garzoni penned his extraordinary *La piazza universale di tutte le professioni del mondo* (Universal marketplace of all the world's professions) (1587), "bandit" was a career option listed like any other, identified in a now well-established phraseology primarily in terms of the danger they posed to communication and commerce—to the arteries, in short, of the body politic. Just as "broken bridges" and "mud" impeded travel, "bandits" and "assassins" aborted interactions and the circulation of people and goods within and between countries.[76] In the reason-of-state tradition, the best-selling renegade Jesuit political philosopher Giovanni Botero, hailing from the Piedmontese town of Bene, would explain how the population of ancient Rome had exploded because it was able to offer security "at a time when the neighboring towns were oppressed by tyrants and the nearby lands were consequently full of bandits," thus rendering the connection between bad government and banditry explicit in theoretical terms not unlike those depicted visually by Giotto and Lorenzetti. For Botero too, banditry was at its core a threat to human commerce broadly conceived, and a ruler should fight it to "judiciously" maintain the infrastructure not merely of trade but of humanity, "for instance protecting the harbor with breakwaters, facilitating the loading and unloading of cargo, keeping the see free of pirates, making the rivers navigable, building suitable warehouses big enough to contain large stocks of merchandise, strengthening and repairing the roads, both over the plains and over the Mountains."[77]

The problem of banditry continued to be conceptualized in these terms into the eighteenth century, when a liminal figure like Ludovico Antonio Muratori, a baroque humanist librarian as well as an Enlightenment reformer long based in Milan and Modena, bemoaned that bandits threatened "the security of the roads," describing them as one of the greatest dangers to "public happiness" and the "glory of a government" alike.[78] An anonymous 1749 Venetian treatise, *Massime generali intorno al commerzio* (General maxims regarding commerce), plagiarized a little more than a decade later in Genoa, followed suit, presenting banditry as a symptom of economic decay and civil inertia, the violent manifestation of a vampiric worldview according to which people could "live on the shoulders of others."[79] In short, banditry remained the antithesis not only of medieval and early modern notions of "civic life," "common good," and "public happiness," but of the particular form of economic order and sociability forged in the city-states of the Italian peninsula and still influential in the Enlightenment. Far from being avatars of unfettered capitalism and commercial society, bandits were originally their very antithesis.

Banditry and brigandage were not merely an Italian preoccupation, of course, though Italian thinkers might have had a longer perspective on the phenomenon and their country hosted a relatively larger number of bandits than many others in Europe. Indeed, the role of banditry in eighteenth-century debates about political economy widely understood has long been neglected. The *abbé* de Saint Pierre noted, in his pathbreaking *Plan for Perpetual Peace in Europe,* the "bands of bandits" that from time to time arose to terrorize the Italian countryside, "rendering the roads and the canals unsafe, and the houses in the countryside dangerous to inhabit," strongly diminishing "the interior Commerce of the land." It is therefore noteworthy that among the primary benefits that he foresaw would result from a "permanent union" of the "system of European societies"—that is, from his plan for a perpetual peace—would be allowing countries to "promise that their merchants would no longer need to fear bandits on land, nor their ships pirates on the sea."[80] Similarly, Vattel had argued, in his *Law of Nations,* that the "utility of high-ways, bridges, canals, and, in a word, of all safe and commodious ways of communication, cannot be doubted," and that "one of the principal things that ought to employ the attention of the government with respect to the welfare of the public in general, and of trade in particular, must then relate to the high-ways, canals, &c. in which nothing ought to be neglected to render them safe and commodious."[81] As the English deist Matthew Tindall put it about a related type of outlaw, in words often attributed to the far better known writer Daniel Defoe, "the *pirate . . . destroyeth . . . all Government and all Order, by breaking all those Ties and Bonds that unite People in a Civil Society under any Government.*"[82]

Though evocative, these engagements were far less intense than that offered by Antonio Genovesi, who engaged with the problem at length in what was arguably the most influential work of political economy published in eighteenth-century Italy, and certainly one of the works that most profoundly influenced the Academy of Fisticuffs—his translation of the French edition of the Bristol merchant John Cary's *Essay on the State of England* (1695).[83] To Genovesi, perhaps the most crucial aspect of economic development lay in the promulgation of a "persuasion," a sentiment, animating economic life as such, based on the certainty that "fatica" (labor) paid off, that work and the output it created were rendered sacred in the form of private property. It was the very essence of commercial society itself, of a world order based on something recognizably capitalist in nature. Such a persuasion

> [only] emerged from the removal of all the motives for which the use and enjoyment of our goods are, or can be, impeded, and for which we fear for our property. Because if, by way of example, thieves and brigands are left to run with impunity in a nation . . . in this nation, I say, it being best for proprietors to remain in constant and cruel war to defend what is theirs, what industry, and what spirit of industry can ever prosper there?[84]

It is striking that the danger Genovesi saw for private property was not government interference or taxation, but bandits—an argumentational choice that makes further sense in a context in which private property is a civil rather than natural invention and right. Private property ultimately existed only because of the laws of civil society, and as such the act of taxation, again emanating from civil laws, was inherently lawful (however misguided it in effect could be). Banditry, of course, was an entirely different problem for private property as it took the form of an extralegal tax. For a commercial society to flourish, it had to unfold on a civil basis of legal security of property, grounded not in the absence of government but in its increasing capacity and territorial saturation. Only thus could individuals, connected to each other by solidifying avenues for commerce and communication, feel safe in pursuing their ventures. As mentioned earlier, Genovesi elsewhere equated this sentiment with the act of contemplating the world "with the eye of a merchant," the only attitude conducive to the production of an individual, and ultimately social "surplus," giving "movement and vigor" to internal as well as external trade.[85] This psychological foundation for commercial society was as powerful as it was fragile, and depended entirely on a sense of social trust and security; on individual and civic life—in short, on having been socialized. Genovesi returned to the challenge of maintaining trust and cohesion in a commercial society in the final essay he added to his three-volume edition of Cary, the *Ragionamento sulla fede pubblica* (Discourse on public trust).[86]

Activities such as banditry, Genovesi argued, were the greatest of all crimes. They were "crimes against public trust," acts able to "destroy the foundations of the mutual confidence in men, and of their security, which in civil nations are many, and varied." Bandits were, in short, enemies of sociability and of the "empire of civility," agents of anarchy and, through that, retrograde "savagery."[87] This was why, in Genovesi's opinion, "in all nations, even those, which only have a mere shadow of a Government, such crimes are ordinarily punished with death." For, echoing the moral message of Giotto and Lorenzetti's frescoes, were such crimes "allowed to happen, by necessity society will either dissolve or convert entirely into a band of brigands."[88] A polity could regress to savagery, for commercial society depended completely on the vigilant regulation and maintenance of civic trust; "the good faith, which is the spirit of Commerce," was contingent on the policing regulations to which "internal and external Commerce" were subject for the cause of the "common good." But Genovesi remained adamant that the only "great, stable, and internal foundation of true virtue" in the world remained "religion."[89]

Some of Genovesi's most careful readers had found themselves united in the Academy of Fisticuffs, and both Pietro Verri and Cesare Beccaria lauded the Neapolitan repeatedly and at length.[90] But though certainly building on Genovesi's work on the topic of sociability and commercial society in the tradition of "economia civile," Beccaria resolutely went beyond it. His epochal *On Crimes and Punishments* (1764) forced him to address the practice of banditry in a fashion that was both more nuanced and more immediate. For just as pirates and bandits were not the same, so bandits themselves came in many stripes and colors in early modern Italy. An exploration of their spectrum of appearances, and the shifting politics of their activities, can help contextualize Beccaria's unique take on the phenomenon and its role in the history of market socialization in early modern Northern Italy.

Political Bandits

Among history's many failed states, Montferrat was one of the happier, sharing many similarities—territorially as well as gastronomically—with Burgundy.[91] A truffled landscape historically wedged between the Republic of Genoa and the Duchies of Savoy and Milan, the area still known as Montferrat stretches from the Po River southward to the Apennine watershed between Piedmont and Liguria. A longtime Margravate of the Holy Roman Empire, it was briefly controlled by Spain during the years 1533–1536 before coming under the control of the Gonzaga of Mantua, from which it passed, in piecemeal fashion, to Savoy until its complete incorporation in 1708. Historically one of the wealthiest and, as its late eighteenth-century chronicler Giuseppe Antonio de Morani put it, "most fertile" areas of Italy, it remains one of the world's premier wine-producing regions and was an early exporter of high-value agricultural produce in the form of cured meats and cheeses.[92] Naturally, Montferrat was one of the more contested territories of early modern Italy, its political vicissitudes telling with regard to the longer history of the mechanisms elucidated by Schmoller.[93]

In particular, a forgotten Montferrine criminal trial against "bandits" who had been caught in Verolengo in 1569—nearly two and half centuries after Giotto's frescoes, and two hundred years before the publication of Beccaria's masterpiece—can shed useful light on the multifaceted role of banditry in the economic and political formation of early modern Italy, the emergence of international markets, and the larger question of socialization between people and, crucially, between peoples. The continuity of banditry as a concern represents a historical reality—bandits proliferated before "modernity"—but can also be seen as the inverse of a particularly Italian tradition of the civic good, from the Romans through the medieval *ben comune* to Enlightenment ideals of *economia civile*. In the historiography of modern Italy, "banditry" has largely come to be equated with armed resistance to the expanding central state following national unification, taking on anticapitalist and anti-statist aspects in Eric Hobsbawm's famous formulation of the "social bandit." This is particularly emphasized in treatments of traditionally ungovernable pastoral areas such as Sardinia.[94] The problem, of course, is that more Robin Hoods populate the literary than the historical record, and mainland forms of early modern banditry could take conceptually related yet distinct forms, speaking directly to the contemporary "civil" preoccupation with pacifying human interactions and the means of achieving it.[95]

The sleepy town of Verolengo, nested northeast of Turin near where the glacial Dora Baltea coming down through Aosta flows into the Po River, was once a thriving Roman settlement on the main road from Pavia to Turin and onward across the Alps to Gaul. In the early modern period it became an increasingly important, and disputed, commercial center with about a thousand inhabitants on the border between Mantuan Montferrat and Savoy, officially granted to Guglielmo Gonzaga of Mantua at the 1559 Peace of Cateau-Cambrésis ending the so-called "Last Italian War" between France and Spain.[96] Still, Verolengo seems to have remained rather somnolent until, on the evening of Saturday, 15 February 1569, shouting "bandits" stormed its fortress. Although they quickly were routed and hounded by Mantuan authorities, the deeper significance of the bandits' acts, and their role in the longer process of socialization with which we are dealing, is revealed by the surviving legal procedures against them.

Resistance had been growing across Montferrat since most of the region passed from the dying Paleologus dynasty—cadet branch to the former emperors of Constantinople—to the Gonzaga of Mantua in 1536, and in 1565 the longtime capital city of Casale Monferrato revolted yet again "to defend its ancient privileges" and, joining that esteemed tradition of righteous rebellion, to resist "arbitrary" taxation.[97] This local incident immediately came to affect the balance of powers between the larger states of Northern Italy and, through their roles in the larger system of Europe, the great imperial powers themselves. News of the revolt and its consequences reached even the ears of Philip II—who at the time was king of Spain, Portugal, and England, as well as Duke of Burgundy and Lord of the Seventeen Provinces of the Netherlands—and the Habsburg Holy Roman Emperor Maximillian II; neither of them wished to see regional conflicts in Italy ignite another continental war. The climate remained tense, however, and with

Guglielmo openly blaming Emanuele Filiberto of Savoy for instigating the sedition, it was thought that Spanish, French, and Savoy troops were all about to descend on Casale. Yet the great powers continued to favor diplomatic solutions, and Guglielmo Gonzaga was finally made to agree to Casale's terms to exchange ancient privileges for sole lordship over their land. Casale had to demolish its fort and disband its militia, and if the terms of the pact were ever broken, Gonzaga would have to pay the city 50,000 scudi and disobedient Casalese automatically would be deemed guilty of *lèse-majesté,* the treasonous crime of violating the majesty and authority of a ruler or a state.[98]

Therein lay the rub, for though the city of Casale was allowed to retain the "ancient privileges" of a medieval commune in terms of local decision-making capacities and economic administration, these ultimately proved ephemeral in light of the city's incorporation into the larger political sphere of the Gonzaga. A powerful current of Renaissance and early modern republican political philosophy, deeply influential also in the eighteenth century, equated liberty with the state of being subject to one's own laws, and freedom from arbitrary power.[99] Within this paradigm, the history of Montferrat presented an eloquent justification for this line of thought. For the very fact that disagreement with the Gonzaga was equated with the greatest political crime ever codified—the tremendous capital crime of *lèse-majesté*—in effect made the Casalese slaves to the shifting sentiments of an at-times arbitrary foreign ruler who, in the parlance of the day, had succeeded in "giving laws" to them. Having lost their fortress and their militia, and thus their capacity for civic protection—understood to be the communal defense of a civic ideal[100]—the polity of Montferrat simply ceased to be political as such. All their "ancient privileges" were ultimately trumped by the Gonzaga's overwhelming power of sovereignty. As happens so often in history, the principal area of contestation came to be questions of taxation. Many would simply not accept a new regime they considered *unjust,* and took up arms against their new sovereign.[101]

Equally infuriated, Emanuele Filiberto of Savoy threatened military action against Mantua and solemnly took the Casalese rebels and "bandits," now quite literally outlaws, under his wing.[102] During the next few years, rebels would strike at Casale and particularly its Gonzaghesque elements with surgical precision, engaging in both assaults and assassinations, even making an attempt on the life of Guglielmo Gonzaga himself. In retaliation, Guglielmo risked justified retribution by chasing Casalese rebels into Savoy territory, and by poisoning rebel leaders and plausible sympathizers, including Flaminio Paleologus, the last natural heir of the Dukes of Montferrat.[103] The remaining rebels, pushed into a corner by a war of attrition they did not have the resources to win, made a final, desperate gambit by occupying Verolengo, a strategic town from which, ideally under Savoyard protection, they could harass Gonzaga territories. Nearby Chivasso had been in Savoyard hands since 1435, and Verolengo itself had been a source of extreme contention at the 1559 Peace of Cateau-Cambrésis, making it a natural beachhead in Gonzaga lands. This was the complex context in which "bandits" stormed Verolengo that fateful winter's eve of 1569, proclaiming a "republic" that never would be. Upon hearing news that Gonzaga had directed three hundred troops to Verolengo, and with Emanuele Filiberto already having withdrawn his support for Casalese rebels involved in the endeavor the previous night, doubtlessly in the face of pressure from powers greater than himself, the "bandits" merely sacked the place before disbanding; a large number of them were soon arrested by Gonzaga's troops.[104]

As criminal proceedings began against the attackers of Verolengo, they were systematically described as "bandits" from Mantua and Montferrat who acted with the "help and succor of many foreigners and from other dominions," but it soon became clear that this had been no normal act of banditry. Not only had more than *one hundred* "bandits" stormed Verolengo, but they had charged "mano armata et bandiere spiegate a modo de soldati"—"armed and flying banners like soldiers." As the proceedings unfolded they were soon, in fact, branded "rebelli e banditi" by the court, and it was eventually revealed that their war cries had been more politically loaded than first suspected; witnesses soon attested that the bandits in question ostensibly had stormed the fortress "shouting Savoy, Savoy, Liberty, Liberty." We will probably never know whether they had meant that liberty lay with the Savoy or that the Savoy could help them reclaim their liberty, or whether they had shouted at all, but their explicit—if possibly imputed—aim of establishing a "republic," however chimerical, is suggestive. In the end the "criminals" were found guilty of having with "insegna spiegata" (banner flying) entered "Verolengo in the dominion of Montferrat shouting the name of another Prince and provoking the people to depart from their due obedience to their true supreme and natural ruler." In short, they were found guilty of "robbaria forza pubblica, rebellione et delicto di offesa maestà"—robbery, the crime called in Roman law *vis publica,* or violent acts against the integrity of public institutions—rebellion, and *lèse-majesté,* a perfect criminal cocktail for which it seems at least twenty-three Montferrine "rebels" were hanged and nineteen foreign "bandits" were sent to the galleys for life, their goods confiscated.[105]

There are endless ways in which the historiographical and archival classification of the "bandit" in this case becomes problematic. Against the stereotype of the rugged rural bandit dressing the part of an untamed creative misfit and outsider to social conventions, these "bandits" and "rebels" attacked Verolengo with all the trappings of an official army, "with weapons in hand and banners flying like soldiers." Symbolically, the difference was immense, and their cries for "liberty" were quite specific in their political content. This was not the vague longing for halcyon days of Hobsbawm's "revolutionary traditionalist" bandits, nor a piratical call for "creative anarchy," but a concrete equation of capitalized "Liberty" with the recent rule of the "Savoy."[106] Far from being "pre-political," in Hobsbawm's famous formulation, banditry was in this case a vehicle of territorial aggrandizement, closer, certainly, to covert military and mercenary operations than to freebooting in the classical sense.[107] The siege was manifestly not an act of resistance against "modernizing" processes, though the moniker "banditi" technically was quite correct, etymologically the past principle of "bandire" or "banish" (though their name also might have derived from their punishment having been "announced" by an official decree or "bando," or from the very fact that they acted against such a decree).[108] Bandits were literally outlaws, banished from the political sphere of law itself, and, in this meaning at least, correctly equated with "rebels," understood to mean people waging war on their own polity with the aim of changing it fundamentally, from the Latin *rebellare,* to "wage war against." A politicized bandit was by default a rebel, but the real question arises of whether all bandits, by virtue of their very acts, are not in a Ciceronian sense political precisely by virtue of their anticivic—and indeed antisocial, in that they resist the expansion of sociability—telos.[109]

The motley crew of Verolengo is striking in this context for several reasons. It was comprised of rebels banished from Casale, unwilling to accept the yoke of the Gonzaga and resorting to common acts of banditry, as well as sundry Savoy sympathizers, and they attacked, with the aim of conquering, a nearby town that also was in the process of negotiating its new civic identity at the exact border between competing and frequently hostile polities seeking, in a Schmollerian sense, to solidify their territorialities. They ultimately did not enjoy the support of the Savoy authorities, and were indeed expelled from their lands when they sought to retreat to nearby Chivasso after their plans unraveled, but consciously adopted the symbolic trappings of officialdom to combat political processes operating above their proverbial heads and to which they had remained powerless observers. In the end, in some ways these rebels *were* tragic "social bandits" of the Hobsbawmian type, precisely in their attempt to proclaim they were not bandits at all—not entirely unlike how many "bandits" in post-*Risorgimento* Southern Italy in effect were political rebels.[110] Their calls for a "republic" were a way of formulating, however vaguely, the need to be active participants in their own political lives. They might simply have been attempting to exchange one semi-absolutist ruler for another, but their choice nonetheless amounted to a lethal vote of civic identity.

But the line between "bandit" and "rebel" in Montferrat, and the ultimate futility of the vote at Verolengo—not only in terms of the conquest failing but in the larger sense that both competing polities ultimately would disappear anyway as civil spheres were consolidated—had in the final instance been decided not by local protagonists but by the distant sovereignties of Philip II and Maximilian II. There is, in the end, something vaguely Pirandellian about this band of bandits in search of historical actors willing to play them in the European theater of war.[111] Their numbers, after all, were considerable, given that Pizarro, under admittedly different circumstances, had conquered the whole Inca Empire a few decades earlier with a mere 160 men; but the point was that while both Emanuele Filiberto of Savoy and Guglielmo Gonzaga sought to give laws to Montferrat, they themselves had come to operate in a grander context in which even greater powers gave them laws in turn.[112] It was a notable chapter in the Schmollerian process of European unification, in which ever larger territories slowly and often painfully were integrated, pacified, and socialized—one is tempted to say disciplined or normalized—by increasingly centralized but still competing sovereignties. This process occurred unevenly, haphazardly, and not, as the case of Verolengo illustrates, without cost, both human and political, but the ultimate tragedy of solidifying state territorialities—with concomitant commercial socializations—which in Europe at times undermined the social coherence of the continent itself, would only increase in intensity. Verolengo was a late, if representative, convulsion of that first transition explored by Schmoller—the transition from Lilliputian states based on the territorial claims of medieval communes to the increasingly larger regional and infrastructural states of the Baroque.

Economic Bandits

The mechanisms of imperial competition and painful geographic consolidation elucidated by the events at Verolengo were by no means merely a late Renaissance phenomenon. They remained all too evident throughout the long eighteenth century, though inflected by changing circumstances and by the process of territorial amalgamation itself. The most intensely Machiavellian period of territorial flux in Italy was in effect over by the mid-eighteenth century, a period of brief and relative calm that would be overturned by the advent of the French Revolution. Under the aegides of Austrian, Spanish, and French powers, key regions in Northern Italy had consolidated, with varying degrees of geographic and political coherence and independence, in the wake of the War of Austrian Succession. Italy's relative decline simultaneously secured its integrity and safeguarded it from potentially explosive confrontations like that over Casale Monferrato. Yet the borderland politics of the Northern Italian hinterlands continued to dominate political and economic thinking throughout the age of reason, and banditry remained a constant source of exceptions and challenges to contemporary logics of centralized territoriality.[113]

During the harsh winter of 1725, for example, the citizenry of Valsesia, an Alpine valley on the border between Lombardy and Piedmont that had been under Savoy control since 1703, were finally allowed to carry firearms "by Measure of the Damages that said Valley suffers for bordering on diverse foreign states, exposed to Thieves, Vagabonds, and Bandits and infested and hurt by Wolves, Foxes, Bears, and other ferocious beasts." And it was particularly the "assassinations" committed there by "people from foreign States and jurisdictions" that caught the attention of central authorities. Where the state could not protect its citizens, citizens were given the right to protect

themselves, a long-established political practice in early modern Italy also theorized by the Swiss natural lawyer Vattel. "A traveler may," he argued, codifying widespread European legal norms, and "without hesitation," "kill the
robber who attacks him on the highway; because it would, at that moment,
be in vain for him to implore the protection of the laws and of the magistrate."[114]
Not surprisingly, alien bandits—agents not merely of foreign jurisdictions
but of ochlocracy—preyed upon the Valsesians where they were most vulnerable. They struck at night, and particularly during the long winter months
of increased darkness, and they struck marketplaces and the roads leading
to them, posing, as an official put it, *a grave danger to the people participating*
[*concorrono*] *in the markets.*" Not only that, but the bandits were well enough
informed to follow the scheduled market day throughout the valley, hitting
localities precisely on the days when they hosted merchants and traders.[115]
The bandits clearly were skilled entrepreneurs, in a Schumpeterian sense,
but if their inherently risky and "out-of-the-box" profit seeking represented a
proverbial rising tide, it was one that sank rather than lifted the other boats
in the valley. "Claiming," in the language of modern business, wealth they
had not helped "create," they were representatives of what Anton Blok has
called "violent peasant entrepreneurs."[116] Even the influential Irish financier
and political economist Richard Cantillon had theorized that "robbers"
were "undertakers" or "entrepreneurs" in the early eighteenth century precisely on the basis of their particular approach to capital, risk, and profit, but
the question remained, as the members of the Academy of Fisticuffs knew all
too well, how to properly balance individual and collective welfare.[117]

Like elsewhere in Europe, roads in northern Italy were fragile investments that were monitored, contested, and, of course, often taxed heavily,
and regulations for their use—such as a common prohibition on carrying
arms while traveling—were simultaneously socializing *and* sources of increased vulnerability to beasts and bandits of the Valsesian kind. Roads
were understood to be a means by which commerce and communication
could unify and crucially socialize territories, contributing to peace, economic development, and spatial sovereignty, but there was nothing automatic about this process. Roads have complex "territorial effects," not simply
connecting or demarcating spaces but indeed composing them.[118] And, contrary to certain ideological shibboleths, early modern roadbuilding and infrastructural maintenance—not to mention canal-building—were not simply

the achievement of enlightened self-interest.[119] Individuals lobbied for roads and for protection to peddle their wares where they found good prices, and governments sought to help them do so as a means of promoting welfare, tranquility, and territorial security alike. There would seem to be few areas of contemporary civil economy where private and public interests overlapped more synergetically than with regard to infrastructure, but where recent literature has explored tensions in the infrastructure state in terms of whether roads should be private or public, toll-driven or "free," it is easy to forget that lives were lost in early modern Europe over a very different kind of roadside liberty: namely, the freedom to trade and travel without being robbed or killed.[120]

The Norwegian-American economist Thorstein Veblen would, much later, employ terms such as "interstitial disturbance" and "sabotage" to describe acts of destructive rent-extraction at nodal points of capitalism. Banditry is perhaps the very oldest form of such behavior, and at times posed such threats to trade as to make regional systems of trade inoperative.[121] Entrepreneurial bandits, in short, resisted ongoing attempts to clarify, codify, and normalize what sorts of rent-seeking activities were deemed fruitful to society as a whole. If we think geographically about Steven L. Kaplan's differentiation between the "marketplace" and the "market principle" in early modern Europe, we can see that banditry in Valsesia was one of the gravest threats to the peaceful transition from one to the other, from the market understood to be a policed site of exchange to the market understood as a form of social organization, a mindset reflecting Genovesi's concept of seeing "the world with the eye of a merchant."[122] You might still be able to exchange goods on Tuesdays in the Valsesian township of Borgo d'Ale with bandits roaming the countryside, but the arteries connecting this to the rest of the economy—and importantly to the wider social fabric of the body politic and even other polities—were weakened, if not severed, by the very threat of lawlessness, not to mention actual attacks by brigands.[123]

When discussing such cases of "market emergence" today, Tarun Khanna and Krishna G. Palepu have offered a useful framework for identifying "institutional voids" or "lacunae" resulting from "the absence" of "market intermediaries," one of the most basic of which is the lack of "adequate physical infrastructure." The filling of such voids in the emergence of market societies is often far from painless, and sometimes involves dramatically changing preexisting conditions both real and symbolic, conditions for which, in Hobsbawm's vision of social banditry, some people might be willing to fight and die, whether in sixteenth-century Verolengo, eighteenth-century Lombardy, or twenty-first-century West Bengal.[124] But, as Adam Smith would argue, "as it is the power of exchanging that gives occasion to the division of labour, so the extent of this division must always be limited by the extent of that power, or, in other words, by the extent of the market."[125] What precisely Smith meant with this oft-quoted argument is of course debatable, for though he evidently did not merely intend the physical extent of a given marketplace when referring to "the market," he cannot realistically have alluded to twenty-first-century conceptions of a global self-regulating economy either. Perhaps he intended something in between—not unlike what the pugilists indicated with phrases such as "il mercato" and "l'economia"— referring to the actual territoriality of political economy. In his *Meditations on Political Economy*, Verri would similarly explain the spatial network of commercial society thus: "Cities are for a province what marketplaces are for a city. They are a gathering point, where sellers and buyers meet. The capital is in turn for cities what the latter are for provinces."[126] Trade could thus be seen as an economic as well as a sociological web of civic and territorial integration, to which political communities as such were obliquely situated. "Thicker" and more extensive markets, which at the time were both secured by, and, because of political fragmentation, potentially challenged by strengthening state structures, allowed for increased economies of scale and specialization.[127] But what did such market *places* look like at the time?

Markets as Places

Giovanni Michele Graneri was one of the greatest painters of so-called Bamboccio scenes in the eighteenth century, a tradition born from the popular paintings of the seventeenth-century Dutch painter Pieter van Laer, known as *Il Bamboccio,* and his hyperrealistic depiction of an Enlightenment market square might be illuminating in this regard. The baroque painter and art critic Giovanni Battista Passeri described the work of van Laer and his "imitators" as "unique in representing the plain truth, purely as it was," so that their "paintings seemed like an open window . . . without divergence or alteration."[128] Graneri's *Market in San Carlo Square* (1752) today hangs in the museum of Palazzo Madama in Turin, and depicts one of the central market squares of the old Savoy capital.[129] In the midst of crowds of gamblers, monks, inspectors, soldiers, priests, playing children, and public orators, market stalls offered everything from coal, firewood, textiles, and pottery through a wealth of meat and produce to cheese, bread, and grain. Surrounding the market are Turin's traditional porticoed streets lined with more permanent shops and cafés. Donkeys, cows, and horses have brought goods from afar, and people from all walks of life, from nobles to street urchins, have been drawn to the scene. Significantly, a minor brouhaha unfolds next to an armed official in the bottom right corner, underscoring the simultaneously carnivalesque and deeply regulated nature of early modern economic life—a melee of hands both visible and invisible.[130] In the background loom not only a regiment of Savoy troops but also the twin churches of Santa Cristina and San Carlo, powerful reminders that trade was embedded in a civic as well as spiritual world. Graneri's painting envisioned the market as a civic site, a locus of commerce, but it was far from exhaustive of its own meaning, extent, and importance for eighteenth-century life, or for that matter of Smith's definition.[131]

Although best known for more phantasmagoric canvases, the Genoese artist Alessandro Magnasco, also known as *Il Lissandrino,* at times turned to more Bambocciesque themes.[132] From an art-historical perspective it might be safe to assume that in his depiction of one of the most important markets in Milan in his painting *Mercato del Verziere,* Magnasco depicted the marketplace more liberally than Graneri did that of San Carlo in Turin, as evident not only from changes he made to the central column of the Cristo Redentore but also from the rather unlikely size of the centrally located cabbages, particularly in an era before genetically modified organisms (GMOs). Approaching Magnasco's painting as an idealized depiction of an eighteenth-century marketplace, however, nonetheless tells us much about how such sites were imagined around the time of the Academy of Fisticuffs. Located in today's Largo Augusto, the Verziere was the symbolic heart of Milan, or at the very least its stomach, and Magnasco made it nothing less than a simulacrum of society at large.[133] Like in Graneri's painting, the scene itself is framed by both religious and civic imageries, most obviously in the form of the Column of Verziere and the background churches, but of the two artists, Magnasco made the clearest statement regarding the role of state institutions. Not only is a miscreant hauled away in chains by a group of guards, but he is

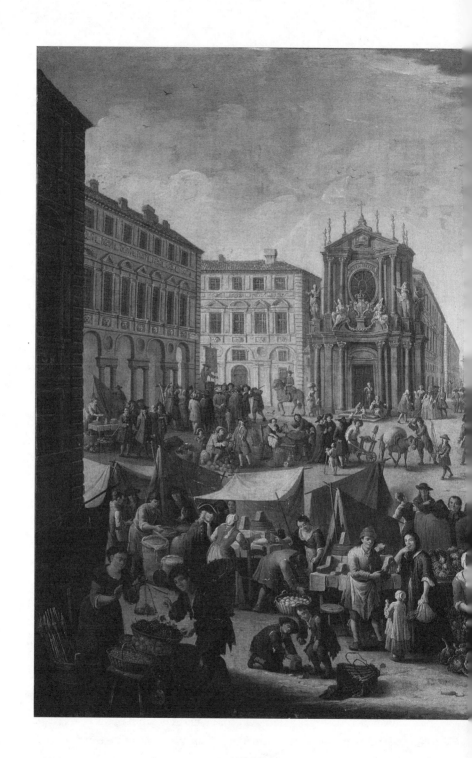

Giovanni Michele Graneri, *Market in Piazza San Carlo*, 1752.

Alessandro Magnasco, *The Verziere Market,* 1733.

being led to an imposing prison on the right-hand side of the painting. Noble
carriages mingle with beggars, entertainers amuse the crowds, and indoor
shops selling wine and textiles stand next to sundry stalls peddling everything from tableware and all sorts of fish and game to vast wheels of Par-
mesan and, of course, Brobdingnagian fruits and vegetables. And, in the background, like in so many coeval squares, figures can be seen mingling at a café.

The markets so realistically rendered by Graneri and Magnasco were
nodal points of an increasingly complex economic system of production and
exchange, which though preponderantly local drew on and connected Alpine
pastures and coastal free ports; the Po River and the faraway Indian Ocean;
local urban labor and transoceanic goods and resources, from coffee beans to
the South American metals used as currency throughout Europe.[134] Simultaneously, however, such markets emitted norms and legal practices through

the prism of policing and regulation in relation to time, space, and even spirit; passports were issued for the movement of grain and other goods in relation to such markets, and the rhythms of life were adapted to its clock; all the while states simultaneously facilitated and shackled economic interactions and the Church aimed to influence and even control commercial conduct.[135] The Smithian "extent of the market" depended on the undisturbed territoriality of economic life, on functioning roads and navigable seaways connecting ever more distant producers and consumers, and ultimately on the civilization of expanding territories in the sense of the spatial subjection of nature to the technological capacity and moral aims of one or more *civitates*. Far from capitalist champions of disruption and creative destruction, bandits and pirates were agents of entropy in this context, causing Valsesia and places like it to suffer a breakdown of commercial society and of civil economy, limiting not merely social territorial cohesion but also the extent of the market and therefore avenues for economic development.

The symbolic effects of rearming the citizenry and effectively deputizing them were, in this context, powerful, and in light of the ancient principle of political philosophy—and more specifically of social contract theory—according to which subjects owed sovereigns allegiance in exchange for physical protection, could only be conceptualized as a devolution, a resolute step backward on the accepted trajectory of civilization. As Beccaria, who wrote effusively about the right to bear arms generally, would write regarding the temptation to encourage bounty hunting in his *On Crimes and Punishments,* by empowering his citizens to take the law into their own hands a "sovereign" only "shows his weakness," for "those who have the power to defend themselves do not seek to buy it." Such measures were "the expedients of weak nations, whose laws are nothing but hasty repairs to a building in ruins that is crumbling on all sides," a sign that the polity was not "enlightened" and lacked "good faith and mutual trust"—that it lacked, in short, the basic building blocks of a civil economy, the "faith" and "trust" under threat by the so-called enemies of mankind.[136] The Valsesian case was a painful reminder not merely of the incongruence between states and markets but also of that between the ambitions of developing states and the very real limits to their technology and capacity for enforcement in the eighteenth century. For if it is easy to imagine an idealized process in which expanding states galvanized banditry to the point where they had to strengthen their territorial capacity, only to further expand and encourage banditry and so on, it was, to the extent that such a progression reflected a historical reality in which the state needed bandits and vice versa, as violent as it was slow, partial, and haphazard, not to mention deeply dependent on geographical factors. As Thomas W. Gallant has argued, "Bandits helped make states, and states made bandits."[137]

L'affare dei malviventi

Some of the greatest preoccupations of Northern Italian statesmen during the years in which Beccaria penned his celebrated work involved very similar problems regarding the relationship between banditry, commercial society, and state territoriality, and in precisely the Northern Apennine areas that later would host Lizzani's *Achtung! Banditi!*[138] The borders between French-backed Savoy and Habsburg Milan were, with some exceptions, reconsolidated in the wake of War of Austrian Succession in 1748, but this cannot be appreciated outside of a context in which major powers such as the French and Austrian Empires did not wish to risk continental warfare over contested townships on the Po Plain. The main problem of banditry in the region was facilitated, if not caused, by the small Republic of Genoa, whose diehard independence and mercenary approach to international allegiances made territorial disputes increasingly problematic at the time. Important passes through the Ligurian Alps, like Serravalle Scrivia, which in the past repeatedly had changed hands between Genoa, Savoy, and Milan, and furthermore had hosted numerous "feudal" domains of the Holy Roman Empire (which traditionally were not above supporting brigandage to undermine territorial sovereignties and safeguard their regional roles), were particularly contested for political as well as economic reasons, and entire borderland villages like Pozzolo became renowned as havens for smugglers, bandits, and "villains" in general—landlocked Tortugas at the core of the Old World.[139]

These outlaw enclaves were particularly damaging for regional and long-distance trade because the Apennines were a nodal point of commerce between the Tyrrhenian Sea and the Alps, connecting the Mediterranean to Northern Europe. Territorial integrity had been high on the list of diplomatic concerns for the Piedmontese ambassador to Genoa at the time, and Gabriele Verri, father of Beccaria's sometime mentor and nemesis Pietro Verri and a leading statesman who headed numerous territorial negotiations, considered the state's failure to neutralize this threat to be the most manifest sign of contemporary Milanese decline.[140] Just as the Gonzaga had once risked reprisals for tracking bandits out of their own jurisdiction, diplomatic scandals were frequently caused in eighteenth-century Italy when authorities arrested bandits across often remarkably porous, not to mention shifting, borders, whether Milanese, Genoese, or Savoyard, most famously when a special regiment of French troops kidnapped the great smuggler and bandit Louis Mandrin across the border in Savoy Rochefort in 1755 in order to bring him to justice and, eventually, to the wheel.[141]

The problem intensified markedly around the time of the Academy of Fisticuffs' writings in the early 1760s, however, and scores or perhaps literally hundreds of letters passed, sometimes daily, between Habsburg Plenipotentiary of Milan Count Firmian, Savoy Plenipotentiary of Turin Count de Viry, and Austrian State Chancellor Wenzel Anton von Kaunitz in Vienna regarding the issue of banditry, the dangers it posed, and the means of resolving it. The tax represented in terms of time and resources by what they came to call *l'affare dei malviventi* (the affair of the villains), was staggering.[142] "Bandits," the synonym for which no longer was "rebels" but "villains" or "malfeasants" in official documents, were "infected," outsiders to the body politic to be "extirpated," "destroyed," and "exterminated" to secure "public tranquility." The basic problem was simple. Writing to Firmian, Kaunitz underlined his commitment to pursue by "all means, both ordinary and extraordinary, as well as economic, the great object of ensuring the security and tranquility of the state."[143] By occupying the mountainous, liminal lands in the Apennines where Genoese Liguria, Lombardy, the old Montferrat, and Piedmont intersected, outlaws were able to safely harass the populations of Savoy and Milan, scuttling across the border to enjoy voluntary exile in Genoa whenever attempts were made to persecute them.[144] In Firmian's words, these attacks amounted to "scandalous atrocious incursions" challenging the sovereignty of their territories.[145] The obvious solution was suggested by the Count of Viry, who proposed a "Convention with the Republic of Genoa" to "remove" the "asylum of Genoese lands," which bandits "abuse to keep themselves safe and within reach of performing new crimes." The current situation rendered Savoy and Milan "dependent on the arbitrariness and caprice of the government of Genoa" to the point where it was "salutary" and "necessary" to do something.[146] In the political vocabulary of the day, Genoa's support for the bandits in the area posed a clear and present danger to the sovereignty and independence of its neighbors, not to mention regional trade and, by default, the territorial emergence of commercial societies there.

Both the Savoy and Milan governments deployed reinforcements to the borderlands, and experts were called in to provide the respective governments with "the desired enlightenment" on how to act.[147] Nothing less than a "cordon of troops" was laid across the mountains to "arrest, or at least keep away" the bandits "infesting the Societies" and "the peace of the Subjects."[148] Although the political scope of these bandits was superficially closer to their Valsese than their Casalese forerunners, terrorizing merchants and looting priestly abodes with equal exuberance, the consequences of their actions themselves remained profoundly political.[149] Bandits broke into houses with skeleton keys and by leveling walls; they bound people up by the dozens, including children and pregnant women, sometimes so roughly as to kill them; they maimed and they slew; and, according to reports, they stole everything from cash and gold through commercial merchandise to furniture, clocks, and lingerie. They could move in armed bands of more than twenty, wounding and killing soldiers they encountered. And to the great consternation also of the Genoese, they particularly haunted "merchants" along the "public roads," taking their funds, their goods, and, at times, their lives.[150]

The gravity of the situation is evident from contemporary descriptions of particular incidents, including one in July 1764 in which ten bandits occupying a bridge along one of the commercial arteries across the Northern Apennines opened fire on a contingent of sixteen grenadiers, the military elite of the Enlightenment. As the officials reported in parenthesis, this was "an evident sign that they [the bandits] believed themselves to be in a safe place."[151] Banditry, in short, was again usurping the territorial security of the solidifying states of Northwestern Italy. Military campaigns themselves were in the end deemed insufficient unless they were able to "cut the root of the evil," the "source of which" was "the free egress and security such people [bandits] enjoy in the Dominion of Genoa."[152] By the spring of 1764, Vienna had joined in pressuring Genoa to rethink its asylum policies in talks with Savoyard and Milanese officials, but the problem seemed merely to increase in intensity.[153]

A central aspect of diplomatic relations, and an important origin of practical international law, can be traced to early conventions to mutually expel wanted criminals and to collaborate in struggles with bandits, and progressively so during the early modern period through formalized standing extradition agreements.[154] But it was not the only way to think about the international ramifications of banditry at the time. As the reason-of-state theorist Scipione Ammirato wrote against the long tradition of Machiavellianism in political theory in his *Discorsi sopra Cornelio Tacito* (Discourses on Cornelius Tacitus) (1594), because of "reason of State, a Prince must favor the bandits of another Prince." Bandits, then, could be strategic weapons in international competition, and though they could undermine one's interests, the hope was that they would weaken neighbors more.[155] Mutual agreements to extradite bandits were keystones in the gradual construction of robust international institutions to facilitate trade, communication, and, ultimately, an expanding sphere of sociability. Diplomats knew that Lombardy and Savoy had enjoyed precisely such a treaty for more than a decade already, and the example of a comparable treaty between Lombardy and Genoa dating back to 1598 was dusted off for good measure, demonstrating the extent to which eighteenth-century statesmen themselves considered previous centuries relevant.[156] A similar pact was suggested again with Habsburg involvement in the form of a "Convention for the Reciprocal Delivery of Bandits and Malfeasants" between all the states of Northern Italy on 18 May 1765, a bold document codifying this limited but crucial sphere of international law.[157] Its main impetus and force cannot be reduced to facilitating rehabilitation and vengeance, or to apprehensions regarding territorial integrity, though both concerns played a part in the process. The pact was, strikingly, deemed necessary because of the dangers posed by banditry "to the public peace, to life, and not the least to the support of the subjects and the freedom of trade [*libertà del Commercio*], which equally benefits their interests"—in other words, were equally important to their welfare.[158] International penal law was here conceived of as a tool for creating, by projected civic and importantly *civil* force, a space in which trade could be "free" (though, needless to say, still taxed), with a remarkably economic vocabulary of "interests" and "benefits" to regulate the sorts of profit-seeking deemed acceptable—the sorts mirroring Verri's contemporary identification of the roots of "public happiness" in the alignment of "private and public interests."[159] The question of banditry was, as such, at the very forefront of debates over, and practices regarding, commercial society, the emergence of international law, and the solidification of global trade alike. As Vattel had argued in his *Law of Nations,* if an exile or banished man has been driven from his country for any crime, it does not belong to the nation in which he has taken refuge, to punish him for that fault committed in a foreign country. For nature does not give to men or to nations any right to inflict punishment, except for their own defense and safety; whence it follows, that we cannot punish any but those by whom we have been injured.[160]

But although *"the justice of each nation ought in general to be confined to the punishment of crimes committed in its own territories,"* Vattel concluded,

we ought to except from this rule those villains, who, by the nature and habitual frequency of their crimes, violate all public security, and declare themselves the enemies of the human race. Poisoners, assassins, and incendiaries by profession, may be exterminated wherever they are seized; for they attack and injure all nations, by trampling under foot the foundations of their common safety. Thus pirates are sent to the gibbet by the first into whose hands they fall. If the sovereign of the country where crimes of that nature have been committed, reclaims the perpetrators of them in order to bring them to punishment, they ought to be surrendered to him.[161]

Even Vattel, then, who repeatedly emphasized the politically territorial nature of crime and indeed state interest, made an exception for proverbial "enemies of mankind."[162] But this would prove to be just one of the many contexts in which, as Immanuel Kant later observed, Vattel was one of the numerous "sorry comforters" of his time, those whose "philosophically or diplomatically formulated codes do not and cannot have the slightest *legal* force, since states as such are not subject to a common external constraint."[163]

The problem with the proposed treaty to end banditry in the Apennines, and the reason it never got anywhere, resulted from the incommensurability of legal orders, the territorial tensions of the Schmollerian moment, and the absence of any truly effective intergovernmental organizations at the time. Different sovereign polities ranked the same crimes differently, and a uniform exchange of criminals, even if limited only to those guilty of crimes warranting capital punishment, would collapse different criminal taxonomies in inopportune ways. Genoa, for example, had suffered its own interstitial problems in recent years, and experienced a territorial fragmentation that both Savoy and Milan *de facto* supported. The ancient port city of San Remo, or Sanremo, on the Western Ligurian riviera—today best known for flowers and Italy's most famous music festival—had revolted against Genoese rule and declared allegiance with Savoy in 1753, mostly as a result of heavy duties and taxes levied on the territory at a time of economic turmoil following British naval bombardments in 1745. Although Genoa had ruthlessly reimposed its dominion over the city, numerous Sanremese rebels remained at large in Northern Italy.[164] Similarly, Genoa had lost control of the island of Corsica when, under the revolutionary Pasquale Paoli's influence, the island began its independent republican experience in 1755, a dramatic experiment—to which Lloyd personally contributed—which gained European fame for vaunting the first ever constitution based on "Enlightenment" principles.[165]

Initially Genoese envoys were positively inclined toward the suggested treaty, sharing many of the preoccupations of their neighbors. They, too, worried about the "infestation," how it might "perturb the public peace," and what "bandits" prowling along the main "public roads" would do to the "freedom of commerce," a phrase that in some documents was underlined for emphasis as "<u>libertà del Commercio</u>."[166] In a secret, numerically coded missive, Genoa's agent in Turin further noted the "benefits" that might result from "a state of perpetual friendship" between the states of Northern Italy.[167] Yet realpolitik remained resolutely in the way. Genoa, namely, had ulterior reasons to fear for what their envoys repeatedly would refer to as their "domestic affairs" and the "unbendable principles of domestic rights," protected by the "full, free, and independent Sovereignty of our city and district"—that is, the territorial claims of the Genoese Republic.[168] For while these negotiations were under way, Genoa's agent in Turin was hunting down Sanremese spies in the Piedmontese capital and even sending coded rumors that Savoy troops clandestinely might be headed to San Remo to support its rebels with the help of Habsburg "intelligence."[169] The *affare dei malviventi*, in short, seemed about to precipitate an all-out war over the tension between individual sovereignties and broader territorial socialization. All the states involved sought to "civilize" their territories, but the interplay between them rendered the process more contentious and more fragile both locally and globally.

A convention between Savoy, Milan, and Genoa securing the exchange of lawbreakers guilty of capital crimes would in the final instance exchange Genoese bandits for political exiles from Corsica and San Remo who lived outside of Liguria under the protection of the Holy Roman Emperor, but who in Genoa were guilty of *lèse-majesté*.[170] In fact, Genoa would not pardon the surviving Sanremese rebels until 1775.[171] Negotiations would continue for more than a year, but it was already evident by the late summer of 1764 that the *affare dei malviventi* would not be resolved diplomatically within the parameters allowed for by existing political realities. In an official dispatch the Genoese agent described a meeting with the Viennese ambassador to Turin, who told him that the inclusion of "the crime of rebellion" among those qualifying for reciprocal extradition had "set fire" to the entire project; but in a coded letter he could be more frank:

> In the above described discussion I had with the Viennese Minister regarding the reasons why the Negotiations over the Treaty collapsed, he added that he had been told that the King of Sardinia [that is, of Savoy] as "Vicario dell'Impero" could never have considered the men of San Remo to be rebels.[172]

The convention, therefore, failed after numerous "vain conferences," and a later Savoyard analyst put the blame for this squarely on Genoa's shoulders for not differentiating between simple banditry and political misdeeds of "Rebellion and *lèse-majesté*" within the category of capital crimes. But he accepted that the Genoese objections remained "well founded" in the still rigorously lupine world of international relations, a stance even Kaunitz came to adopt in private correspondence with Firmian in the summer of 1766.[173]

Legal scholars have traced the long and rich history of extraditions to the second millennium BCE, when a pattern first clearly emerged of sovereigns in the Middle East exchanging bandits as well as political and religious criminals—the ones who, given the technology of the time, were deemed most disruptive to authority—and generally agree that the extradition of nonpolitical crimes appeared and gradually was normalized only in the wake of the French Revolution.[174] What today is known as the "political offense exception," a clause in extradition treatises specifically exempting crimes of a political nature from extradition, was first codified in Belgium in 1833, an event that ostensibly overturned the millennial history of extraditions by shifting their purpose from safeguarding political and spiritual authority to enforcing domestic law.[175] The history of extradition treaties in early modern Italy suggests that the use of international diplomatic and legal measures to legalize domestic territories and thereby "provide for the public peace" preceded the French Revolution by decades, and that states on the Italian peninsula actively had already at midcentury sought to introduce a political offense clause to safeguard international trade and infrastructure.[176]

These treaties lie at the conceptual core of the tragedy of "economia civile," ever torn between the competing civilizing policies of territorial polities and the larger goals of peaceful international interaction. By its very nature, Genoa's sovereignty trumped measures that risked debilitating its authority, even if the Doge and Senate were all too aware of the advantages of peaceful international trade and collaboration in the region. With their interests in this sphere aligned, Savoy and Milan continued to sign criminal extradition treaties throughout the century, and all three states began committing greater resources to fighting bandits in their territories. Genoa not only increased the salaries of their police forces and appointed a "capitano contro banditi" (antibandit captain) in all their communal militias in these years, they also established rich bounties for the capture of such outlaws.[177] Even so, the problem of banditry in the Apennines would not be durably resolved until the wake of World War II, and would occur only within a radically different regional context in which the sovereignties involved in the *affare dei malviventi* (with the exception of distant Habsburg Vienna, itself undergoing a parallel process of realignment) had been absorbed into a larger national unit of authority encompassing the Italian peninsula. And, as Schmoller would have predicted, this national unit itself soon gave way to an even larger territorial form of sovereignty in the European Union, the growing pains of which will remain evident—and the future of which will remain uncertain—for years to come.

Beccaria's Bandits

In Beccaria's formulation of the social contract discussed in Chapter 2, individuals invoked sovereignty by investing it with a part of their natural liberty, in the process creating an authority in turn devoted to defending the liberties of its individual constituents and, ultimately, terrestrial justice, which the Milanese reformer equated explicitly with sociability itself.[178] Yet this partial sublimation of individual liberty into the greater liberty offered by subjection to their sovereign was not enough, for men were still not, and might never become, angels. So pessimistic was Beccaria's anthropology—which took criminal behavior to be inevitable in a rather Ciceronian fashion—that he resolutely believed crime, and thus the need for punishment, to be endemic. It is therefore all the more striking how Beccaria, who praised Antonio Genovesi on many other occasions, kept his distance from the ways in which the tradition of "economia civile" he represented had dealt with enemies of mankind, outsiders to its paradigm. True, Beccaria agreed with Genovesi, citizens had given up parts of their liberty to imbue a sovereign entity with the power to maintain justice and thus sociability, but they had crucially not given it power over life and death. As such, the "death penalty is not a *right*," he argued, but instead "the war of a nation against a citizen." As I have made clear, the only case in which Beccaria could accept an execution was in the hypothetical case in which someone "retains such connections and such power that he endangers the security of the nation even when deprived of his liberty, that is when his very existence can provoke a dangerous revolution in the established form of government."[179]

Needless to say, the Genoese bandits harassing trade routes across the Apennines into the Po Valley posed no such existential threat to society, whatever their crimes against commercial sociability and "free trade." And even though Beccaria favored "banishment" as a punishment for serious misdeeds, he again resisted traditional logics of retribution by suggesting— extraordinarily influentially, one might add in hindsight—that the property of outlaws should not be confiscated by the state because most such crimes were born from conditions of poverty in the first place, and confiscations, which hurt the plausibly innocent relatives of bandits, would merely serve to aggravate the cycle of destitution, crime, and injustice. According to Beccaria, the only way structurally to resolve the contemporary problem of banditry—and of crime more generally—was to ensure more sociable means of subsistence through popular enlightenment and, recalling his insistence on a state's right to interfere with private property in certain cases, a more equitable distribution of wealth, within and between nations.[180]

Beccaria's most explicit engagement with the "Affair of the Villains" in his *On Crimes and Punishments* may have appeared in a section titled "Asylums." "Within a country's borders," he explained in a passage that, when read in light of its long-neglected historical context, acquires new pertinence,

> there should be no place that is unregulated by laws. The power of the laws should follow every citizen like a shadow follows a body. Impunity and asylum differ only in degree, and just as the certainty of punishment makes more of an impression than its severity, asylums invite men to commit crimes more than punishments deter them. To multiply places of asylum is to create so many small sovereignties, for where laws are absent, new laws may take root that are opposed to the general laws and that thereby constitute a countervailing spirit to that of the whole body of society.[181]

By allowing criminals to disentangle themselves from civic space, asylums posed a lethal threat to the territorial rule of law, understood as a legal tapestry interweaving individuals to form "the whole body of society" in an environment simultaneously physical and conceptual. Even unraveling the edges of the social fabric, Beccaria insisted, risked the integrity of the whole cloth. With regard to the related question of "whether treaties between nations for the extradition of criminals are useful," however, he was less adamant. That is, at least until

> laws more suited to the needs of humanity, milder punishments, and an end to the dependence on arbitrariness and opinion have provided security for oppressed innocence and despised virtue; until tyranny has been isolated to the vast plains of Asia by that universal reason, which increasingly unites the interests of the throne and its subjects. Nonetheless, the notion that there is no patch of earth where true crimes are tolerated would be an extremely effective means of preventing them.[182]

Just as there existed an incongruity between states and markets, so there existed an incongruity between states and justice, to the point where the latter could be completely territorialized—and thus realized—only though the establishment of international treaties for the extradition of criminals. Ever the Fabian, though, Beccaria would not allow the lives of individuals to be put in jeopardy by exchanges between polities of unequal "development," here understood legally rather than, as in other places, economically. Given the context of ongoing disputes among Habsburg Milan, Savoy Piedmont, and the Republic of Genoa at the time, Beccaria's cryptic passage becomes an oblique critique of the Genoese persecution of Sanremese republican rebels (who certainly considered themselves virtuous innocents oppressed and despised by a tyrannical government), but also of the systemic dangers of the *de facto* asylum provided bandits in Liguria.

An early commentary Beccaria wrote on the fifth volume of Jean Le Rond D'Alembert's *Mélanges* also supports such readings of *On Crimes and Punishments*. "Experience," D'Alembert wrote, "has convinced me that this world is a sort of forest infested by brigands. History further assures me that it has always been so." To this Beccaria commented that these "reflections" were "in truth interesting," for D'Alembert "reads in history the crimes of men, and discover their evil; from this he learns to forgive his contemporaries' many defects which he sees deeply rooted in human nature, and which are *a necessary consequence of the situations in which men find themselves.*"[183] The task of Beccaria's legislator was to manipulate humanity and its environments, to civilize the dark forests of the world and of the mind, and to make illegalities both more difficult and more consequential, maintaining proportionality between crimes and punishments but simultaneously ensuring the "certainty" of the latter.[184] In the important chapter of *On Crimes and Punishments* entitled "Public Peace," he wrote:

> Lighting the streets at public expense; guards posted in the various quarters of the city; the plain and moral discourses of religion confined to the silence and sacred peace of temples protected by the public authority; public speeches in support of public and private interests delivered in the nation's assemblies, in parliaments, or wherever the majesty of the sovereign resides—these are all effective means of preventing a dangerous clustering of popular passions.[185]

Banditry and religious extremism, two striking priorities in Beccaria's scheme that say much of his context, were enemies of civil and civic life to be fought with the enlightenment of roads as well as of minds. The "certainty" of establishing such crimes of course required a notable capacity to monitor individual activity and enforce laws, which, at the time, often found itself diluted in line with the territorial expansion of early modern states. As he defined "internal police" in his lectures on political economy, it "covered all the rules that contribute to good order and to the facilitation of all the economic affairs of a state: cleanliness, security, and low prices [*buon mercato,* literally "good market"] are the principal objects of every civil police." As such, "the custody of public roads and vigilance on the borders" were key preoccupations of said "science," and "well-lit roads" were the vehicles for expanding the civic and economic sphere across dark territories—an ethos that appropriately found its apotheosis in the railway linkages of Italian national unification in the nineteenth century.[186] Building on a prevalent metaphor at the time, Beccaria further emphasized the importance of a truly capillary distribution of roads to connect the lands of a polity:

> The roads of states are like the canals in which fluids flow in living bodies; and as in these it is not enough that they are safe and free of any obstacles, but the minimal and invisible channels have to be open and easy for the animating liquid to flow, so must not only the roads that lead indefatigable travelers to the dominant cities in political bodies be solid and durable, but also those which serve the entire distribution of marketable goods in all the diverse parts of a province. Taking care only of the so-called main roads [*strade maestre*] while neglecting lateral roads, which are those that more than others serve to transport all things throughout the interior, is the greatest, but not therefore the least frequent political inconsistency.[187]

Beccaria would, in effect, frequently return to the problem of infrastructure in his lectures, to "difficult and scabrous roads," to "defective canals," to the need to "render transportation easier" by "enlarg[ing] and consolidate[ing] roads" and building "canals" in "all possible directions." These were "immortal works that render sovereigns conquerors of their own nation; conquests

consecrated by the thanks and prosperity of future generations, not cemented with the blood and laments of desolate provinces." Political
economy, in short, depended on the "conquest" of domestic territories, an
argument that stands at odds with the classic dichotomy between conquest
and commerce in the history of the discipline. Commerce in effect required
conquests, not only of nature but of people, such as bandits and Firmian's
malviventi, resisting the expansion of a civil sphere over the land. In a discarded draft of his lectures, Beccaria similarly wrote of how the human
condition itself, to escape the most primitive state of nature at the very beginning of civilization, required man "to arm himself and defend himself
against the assaults of ferocious beasts."[188] Political economy was, for Beccaria,
not an abstract discipline but instead deeply grounded in the actual physical
territory of a civic community, much like he developed his theory of commercial sociability in a context of acute warfare on bandits. The *affare dei
malviventi* was not a tangential preoccupation in Enlightenment Lombardy,
but of core relevance to the theory and practice of *economia civile.* As Verri
put it in his *Meditations on Political Economy,* "Guai se la fede pubblica s'oscuri!"
(Woe if public trust is obscured!).[189] "Industry," he argued, could be "animated"
by "bringing man closer to man," for

> the more man is isolated and distant from his similars, that closer is
> he to the savage state; on the contrary, the closer he is to the state of
> industry and of culture, the closer he is to a greater number of men;
> and every effort possible must be made to draw man to man, vil-
> lage to village, city to city. . . . Wherever there are taxes on internal
> transportation within the State, if the Legislator removes them he
> will effectively have drawn together the cities divided by the tax. . . .
> Wherever there are roads that are difficult for transportation or dan-
> gerous for security, if a good government [*buon governo*] levels them
> and makes them easy and safe, it will have drawn together all the
> lands and cities that communicate by way of those roads.[190]

Roads had the unique power to "multiply internal circulation" and therefore
"increase annual reproduction" or output. Infrastructure was a way to internal security, to economic development, and ultimately to power in international relations and, crucially, the territorial expansion of economic activity

and commercial society.[191] Roads and bridges were, Verri would reiterate as late as in the 1790s, the only way to connect *"the economy of the community"* to *"the economy of the provinces"* and finally to the *"general economy"* of a state.[192]

Spaces of Sociability

But neither was this somehow a Lombard phenomenon. Geographical size has been a thorn in the side of political theorists for millennia.[193] Indeed, similar mechanisms by which the territorialization of political economies characterizing the expansion of central state organizations into formerly "feudal" or simply unregulated regions generated local resistance, sometimes in the form of banditry, which in turn both necessitated increased centralized control and engendered a Manichaean language of animalistic savagery and sociable civilization, can be identified across cases as diverse as the Nile Delta at the time of the Roman Empire, Baroque Valencia, the thuggee in eighteenth- and nineteenth-century British India, the *rampoks* or armed robberies plaguing Dutch Batavia a century later, and, of course, the Sicilian Mafia.[194] And although some such cases took the form of Hobsbawm's "social banditry," most were far more opportunistic and haphazard in nature.[195] This was certainly the case in the early modern Apennines, and the pugilists' project to define a science of political economy and delineate forms of rent-seeking amenable to social relations must be read in its context.

Similarly, these mechanisms do not merely pose a historical problem, as evident from the experiences of contemporary states still very much involved in expanding their presences internally today, from Colombia to Indonesia, not to mention from the birth of entirely new categories of criminal activity in the wake of the most recent spatial, if digital and thus virtual, expansion of civil society.[196] For example, as Chris Poole (the elusive New York Internet entrepreneur and owner of the legendary hacktivist website *4chan*) explained in a rare interview, "manners are learned over a lifetime," and in the new online space it was "easier to fall down the wrong path" because there were so few restraints and such a short history of instilling and enforcing appropriate comportments. "I've never been in a fight in real life. It's a lot of effort and hassle. On the net you need 55 seconds and you make trouble. It's just so easy," Poole noted, expressing a general sentiment shared by, among others, Wikileaks' Julian Assange.[197] Indeed, as one particularly outspoken hacker recently put it, the Internet is a new "space" that, though contested by "police" and "draconian prosecutorial" forces, allows disparate groups "power in situations where we would otherwise be powerless."[198] In the eighteenth century, as today, the mechanism of state formation and its concomitant development of Ciceronian civil society demanded the tortuous legal socialization of individual activity across expanding territorial spaces, a process both galvanized and thwarted by the existence of competing loci of sovereignty.

Debora L. Spar has argued that certain commonalities characterize technological revolutions throughout history. Following some "innovation" breakthrough—whether the compass or the Internet—the new technology is subject to "commercialization," opening up a period of "creative anarchy" before market participants eventually realize the virtues of "rules" and regulation. Not surprisingly, her first chapter is devoted to piracy, that most flamboyant episode of "creative anarchy" following the "invention" of oceanic trade. "The advent of piracy," she contends, "was just a natural movement along the technological frontier . . . pirates simply took advantage of a classical gap between technology and law" until European "states" eventually stepped in to "rule the seas."[199] There is, of course, something to this interpretation, and, though the great early twentieth-century Belgian medievalist historian Henri Pirenne was discussing the ninth-century Viking embrace of trade, his statement that "piracy is the first stage of commerce" remains frequently quoted to this effect.[200] Already Montesquieu, after all, had opened his chapter "On the Commerce of the Greeks" in the *Spirit of the Laws* by noting, "The first Greeks were all pirates."[201]

There is, however, an important difference between the pirates described by Montesquieu and Pirenne—ancient communities that, originally having made their living on plundering others, eventually turned to trading with them—and those of twenty-first century pirate-lovers, who instead focus on individuals and small groups of largely metaphorical deviants preying along the frontiers of an already advanced states-system centuries, if not millennia, later. Indeed, a principal problem with these more enthusiastic acolytes of the "misfit economy," buzzing with the creative potential of transgression and creative destruction, is that they invariably take the secure existence of a commercialized society for granted as something to be safely disrupted and transformed. Yet it was only because of a long struggle by solidifying political communities to socialize pirates, bandits, and other agents of disruption that anything like "creative anarchy" could fruitfully exist. In light of our tumultuous histories, it seems clear that the slogan "disrupt or be disrupted" risks perverse consequences outside of contexts blessed with remarkable order and calm, institutionally as well as territorially.[202] In most of the world's polities, and certainly in those now known as "emerging markets," such conditions simply do not apply, perhaps the most foundational "institutional void" of all; crucibles of real banditry are hardly in need of metaphorical ones.[203] The theory of "creative destruction" of which "disruption" is a recent inflection itself of course predates the piratical vogue, famously elucidated by Schumpeter and by Friedrich Nietzsche before him. It might therefore be worthwhile remembering that Nietzsche's colleague and teacher in Basel, the art historian Jacob Burckhardt, warned that there existed "absolutely destructive forces under whose hoofs no grass grows."[204] For all his emphasis on reform, Beccaria was all too aware of the fact that not all disruption was creative.[205]

Enemies of All

Banditry and piracy are not, in the West, the problems they once were. But the ways in which our forebears dealt with them, and the language of enmity to the human race, linger on. American legal scholar John Yoo, the author of George W. Bush's infamous torture memos, has recently argued that even the Christian just-war tradition would consider "terrorists to be *hostis humani generis,* the enemy of all mankind, who [merit] virtually no protections under the [law]." On another occasion he mused that the status of "illegal enemy combatant" was not new at all: "What," after all, he asked, "were pirates?"[206] Intending no offense to Genovesi, he and Yoo (and even Lorenzetti) share a fundamental notion about the bandit, the pirate, the outlaw. Indeed, the still-thriving notion that banditry (or piracy, or terrorism) and a just civil-economic order are true opposites has long been part of the Western tradition. Given our infatuation with the symbolically piratical, however, we have come to find ourselves in the tragic situation in which real-life cases of contemporary piracy like that off the Horn of Africa are refused the moniker of "piracy," because, as leading business theorists have argued, simply "committing an illegal act at sea does not make one a pirate."[207] Having ennobled the symbolically piratical, we seem to have entirely lost touch with the reality of the crime, Somali pirates apparently being so bad they are expelled not merely from humanity but from human language as such.[208]

But another view has also persisted, one in which these polar opposites are not as far apart as we might believe or hope. We need only think of St. Augustine's justly famous remark in his early fifth-century *City of God:* "Remove justice and what are states but gangs of bandits on a large scale? And what are bandit gangs but kingdoms in miniature?"[209] It was in this tradition, albeit less profoundly, that the Milanese writer and revolutionary adventurer Count Giuseppe Gorani would complain that "the finances of Joseph II were nothing but brigandage."[210] Without justice, power could not be legitimate—instead it was an opening for a penumbral world in which sovereigns and bandits roamed the land with equal claim on moral authority. At the same time, without power, justice cannot be instituted. On the one hand, the bandit is the complete outsider, the threat to the commercial and civil order, the danger lurking at the edge of society. On the other, he is part of that order, the product of it, demanded by the economic and political ideas and practices at its core, and in many ways its mirror image.

For Beccaria, although the bandit is to be punished, reformed, or banished, he is not truly pushed outside humanity—indeed, he is imbued with inalienable rights by virtue of belonging to it, no matter his ostensible crimes. Rather than being the antithesis of sociability and commerce that we saw in Genovesi, or the antithesis of good government that we saw in the frescoes of Lorenzetti, Beccaria's bandit (or today's Somali pirate) is a product of society, a criminal but also a victim of poverty and social structures that themselves are *unjust* from the greater perspective of human sociability.[211] Unlike Genovesi, who thought banditry the worst of crimes against society and rightly deserving of death, in Beccaria we ironically see something very much like a true Christian reciprocity, though of a wholly secular sort, a dedication to sociability—and, as Chapter 5 will make clear, to "socialism" in the original meaning of the term—that makes the bandit an enemy of civil society (and, indeed, banishment is nothing else than civil death) but not an enemy of humanity. As such, Beccaria can ultimately be seen to represent a refinement, rather than a rejection, of these central tenets of "civil economics," and a theorist of a veritable political economy based on individual rights.[212]

Banditry was, in this sense, a neglected but important context for understanding not only the work of the Academy of Fisticuffs and Beccaria's *On*

Crimes and Punishments, but also contemporary socioeconomic dynamics and the tortuous relationship between solidifying states, long-distance trade, and the international sphere at the time. Bandits were important, if often ignored, protagonists of early marketization and the "mercantilist" period when our world's reigning economic structures first took shape, not merely practically but theoretically and conceptually. Whether explicitly political, as in Vero-lengo, or more privately rapacious, as in the Apennines, they were danger-ously rather than creatively disruptive symptoms at the bleeding edge of the Schmollerian moment, in which the competitively expanding economic, social, and political spheres of once-urban polities simultaneously facilitated and undermined the socialization of the world as such. And this was why any *just* project for perpetual peace, socializing the relations not merely between people but between peoples, had to begin with the basic rights of individuals rather than those of political authorities, whether communal, regional, or national. For until the world becomes just and, in Beccaria's terms, "socialized," the warning is that we might all be bandits.

CHAPTER FIVE

Enlightenment Socialisms

⸻ ➤●◄ ⸻

BANDITS WOULD CONTINUE TO THRIVE on the Italian peninsula in the years to come, becoming intrinsically intertwined with its very national identity both at home and abroad, and Beccaria's algebraic experiments to deter smugglers would have few immediate followers. His *On Crimes and Punishments,* however, hit Europe like a bombshell.[1] The short book had built on earlier arguments regarding penal reform, to the extent that Paul Friedland recently went as far as to claim that "none of Beccaria's ideas were original," but, as the Milanese reformer himself wrote, "it is not useless to repeat what others have written," particularly, one might add, if one does it with such verve.[2] No fewer than thirty-one Italian editions saw the light of day during the eighteenth century, and dozens of translations ensured that it would be the object of discussion from St. Petersburg through Stockholm, Paris, and London, to Philadelphia. Soon it became one of the most iconic books of the eighteenth century and of the "Enlightenment" as such.[3] Kaunitz noted with great pleasure that "if [Beccaria] has alarmed some Ecclesiastics with his well-known work *On Crimes and Punishments,* he has no less acquired great esteem among erudites at home and abroad."[4] As *The Monthly Review* of London put it in 1767, "it is really wonderful that a book written in vindication of the natural rights of mankind, should have been permitted to circulate through a country [Italy] enslaved by civil and ecclesiastical authority."[5] But there was plenty for defenders of the Old Regime to grab hold of, and it was hardly unexpected that the book rapidly was put on the Holy Office's *Index Librorum Prohibitorum* (Index of Prohibited Books).[6] And the French lawyer Pierre-François Muyart de Vouglans was representative of a widespread sentiment when, in a 1766 critical reply to Beccaria, he noted his "surprise" to find a work on criminal law to actually be "an apology for humanity, or rather a pleading in favor of that unhappy portion of mankind that is its scourge, dishonors it, and is sometimes even its destroyer."[7]

Yet one of the earliest critiques levied against Beccaria—and against the Fisticuffs more generally—was that *On Crimes and Punishments* was a "socialist" tract. There were, of course, obvious elements of the book that could invite such a charge in modern parlance, from its vocal critique of wealthy elites establishing legal codes that disproportionally burdened the lower classes to its radical, if tentative and enigmatic, challenge to the very institution of private property itself. The only problem is that the word "socialism" was largely a neologism with a distinct (and distinctly unlike our own) meaning at the time, so the historical charge of "socialism" does not directly relate to what seem like potentially "socialist" (in our sense) passages to modern readers of Beccaria's work.[8]

With something like their current meaning the "real entrance of this group of words into the European vocabulary," Arthur E. Bestor argued in a classic 1948 article on the linguistic history of socialism, came only with the Welsh industrialist and utopian Robert Owen's movement for social reform in the late 1820s and early 1830s, first in English, then in French, then in German.[9] Subsequent scholars have identified the first use of the term "socialist" in print in the November 1827 issue of the *London Co-Operative Magazine,* and the first use in manuscript form in a letter from the inventor and academic Edward Cowper to Robert Owen of November 2, 1822.[10] Though Bestor noted that "as early as 1803 the words *socialism, socialista,* and *socializzare* were used by an Italian writer," he observed in passing that they were used "in a sense almost diametrically opposed to the modern one." Furthermore, because "this usage was apparently without influence upon subsequent writers," it should "be considered a mere linguistic sport or mutation."[11] A number of questions thus arise: Why would someone criticize Beccaria and his coterie for being "socialists" in the mid-1760s? What did they in effect mean by it? And how, if at all, did Enlightenment socialism relate to its Romantic counterpart?

Derivatives of the Latin *socius*—"ally" or "partner"—such as "social" of course abounded in Europe at the time. The 1741 edition of the great *Vocabolario* of the *Accademia della Crusca,* or Academy of the Bran, or Chaff, a Florentine academy established in 1583 to defend the Italian language as derived from the Tuscan dialect, defined the varieties of sociability thus:

> SOCIABLE. *Adj. Social, Companionable.* Lat. *sociabilis.* Gr. κοινωνικός.
> *Varch. Ercol.* 31. Man is the most sociable, or companionable animal of all. *And below:* Many other animals which, if not civil etc. are at least sociable. *Gell. Let. 2. lez. 9.191.* Man, being a sociable animal that loves living with those of its own species, rejoices in the happiness of others.
>
> SOCIAL. *Adj. Who loves company.* Lat. *sociabilis, socialis.* Gr. κοινωνικός
> *Mor. S. Greg.* Obviously he who loathes patience soon abandons social life from impatience. *Buon. Fier. intr.* I. That I am a far more social person.[12]

That the Crusca drew on the examples of the sixth-century Pope Gregory the Great, the humanist Giovanni Battista Gelli, and the artistic polymath Michelangelo Buonarroti, best known for the ceiling of the Sistine Chapel, is telling with regard to the relative antiquity of the term and the sort of literature favored by the Academy. And Benedetto Varchi's *L'Hercolano,* one of the late Renaissance's premier dialogues on the Tuscan dialect written by a troubled historian of the Medici Grand Duchy, clearly established that sociability was a step on the ladder toward civility.[13]

This relationship between the social and the civil was also a leitmotif in the immense historiography on the *guerra sociale italica*—the Roman Social War or Allied War of 91–88 BCE, the great civil war through which, in the Roman historian Appian of Alexandria's phrase, "all the Italians became part of the Roman state."[14] Appian's equation of social and civil wars—society and the polity—would reverberate through the ages and throughout Europe in related terms like "social love," "social chain," "social laws," and finally "social contract," particularly following the publication of Jean-Jacques Rousseau's eponymous work. This contractarian current also emphasized the interrelationship between the social and the civil to the point of conceptual confusion—for example, Rousseau echoed Cicero in speaking of "the social state, where everything is under the authority of the laws," and at other times suggested that one led to the other.[15] Pietro Verri, for one, was clear that by "entering the society of men" one embarked on "the course of civil life."[16] But large parts of the early modern debate over sociability revolved around attempts by Protestant theorists of natural law, and particularly by Samuel von Pufendorf, to restrict natural law to the technologies of *socialitas* necessary to pacify human relations, encourage ever denser civil states, and "teach one how to conduct oneself to become a useful member of human society" without reference to a hypothetical afterlife.[17]

Looking back at earlier centuries, this was precisely the sort of relationship identified by the Franciscan lawyer and political economist Giacomo Giuliani of Padua, whose *Antisocialismo confutato* (Antisocialism refuted) (1803), to which I will return at length, marks one end point of this particular tradition of "socialism" that animated eighteenth-century debates on sociability. At his 1808 inaugural lecture on criminal law, Giuliani lamented the survival of grizzly forms of torture even in an age of "culture and societal civilizing [*sociale incivilmento*]."[18] Civilization depended on socialization, every step of the way from individuals, to people, and finally to peoples. As he later would put it, "the civilizing process is the effect of social perfectibility," and political economy was the key to its realization.[19] Ultimately these debates all revolved around attempts to delineate, improve, and expand a sphere of human activity ever more distant from the state of nature, cemented by various interpretations and depictions of sociability, at times even independent of nature or theology.

From its Latin roots, terminological variations on "sociability" had spread across the European vernaculars. The semantic drift from the original "social" to the neologistic "socialist" was in this context rather short, and occurred seemingly independently and without much consequence, for example, when an anonymous London pamphleteer of the early 1790s employed the word "socialist" as the antonym of a "savage":

> But these, we are told, are more enlightened days. Man, alas! in
> savage or in social life, is still the same selfish, restless, sanguinary

being; in savage life, his wants are fewer, and his power of doing mis-
chief more contracted; in social life his wants are insatiable, and
his means of devastation boundless. A very slender vocabulary en-
ables the savage to transact the business of life. Voluminous dictionaries enable the socialist to misinterpret the transactions of
his neighbour.[20]

The pamphleteer's point was to ridicule those who bewailed the horrors of
the French Revolution by underscoring "the depravity of human nature"
everywhere. In this instance the word "socialist" was ironically invented to
undermine itself. But these were rather loose semantic spasms around the
core problem of sociability, and what is striking about the earlier Germano-
Italian tradition is that it seems to have gelled, for a period of several decades,
into a coherent theoretical critique of "socialism," understood to mean
something quite specific and, seemingly, dangerous to the status quo of
early modern Europe.

Socialism Unmasked

Thanks to new digital technologies that have come to radically facilitate lexicographical archaeology in recent years, it seems likely that the first version
of the term "socialist" to ever appear in print did so in the form of the Latin
"socialistae" in the 1753 *Juris Naturae larva detracta compluribus libris sub titulo
Juris Naturae prodeuntibus ut Puffendorffianis, Heineccianis, Wolffianis etc. aliis,
quorum principia juris naturae falsa ostenduntur: ignorantiam quam catholicis af-
fingunt, in ipsis regnare proditur: cavillationes deteguntur; promissa splendida, ab
ipsis non servata exponuntur: pugnae et contradictiones eorum inter ipsos et secum
ipsis exhibentur; scopus illorum praecipuus, nimirum catholicae rei detrimentum
denudatur: nobilitas, juventus, politici periculi admonentur a P. Anselmo Desing,*
or, for short, Anselm Desing's *Natural Law Unmasked.*[21] A stout Catholic of
the Bavarian Benedictine Congregation, Desing (1699–1772) railed against the
impious writings of Protestant theorists of natural law in the tradition of Grotius and Pufendorf.[22] Though Desing did not bother to stop to explain his
neologisms, which probably already existed in the oral, and perhaps manuscript, culture of the Benedictine international, *socialistae* and *naturales
socialistae* were pejorative terms for those who believed that social life

Anselm Desing (1699–1772). Anonymous, *Anselm Desing*, ca. 1770.

on this earth was the ultimate end of politics and that something like civic
interests might prevail over spiritual considerations and the supremacy of
revelation.[23]

Whereas both Pufendorf and the German philosopher Christian Wolff
(1679–1754) had argued that religion was a society within the state, Desing
countered that it instead was the other way around, with "state and society"
being "states *within* the religious state." Worldly laws and politics remained
inescapably subject to the higher laws of religion.[24] Desing even included the
term *socialistae* in his work's analytical index, with the subfields "they exclude
the Gospel from natural law against their interest [*contra suum interesse exclu-
dunt a jure naturae evangelium*]" and, strikingly, "they differ little from Hobbesians
[*ab Hobbianis parum differunt*]." Socialists were, in the widest sense, irreligious secularists for Desing and the tradition he represented, and their
governing preoccupation with the preservation and expansion of society
addressed central concerns of contemporary political philosophy.[25]

Desing's dense work met with notable success, and, though unnoticed until
now, the terms *socialistae* and even *socialistarum,* "of socialists," reappeared

frequently in the work of the German Benedictine and Salzburg professor of philosophy Ulrich Huhndorff.[26] Desing was further praised, among others, by his friend the Benedictine Cardinal Angelo Maria Querini, former head librarian of the Vatican, and his concerns were mirrored by likeminded Catholics across Italy.[27] *Natural Law Unmasked* itself remained untranslated, but Desing's fame was great enough to warrant a 1769 Ferrarese edition, in Italian, of his *Opuscoli,* or *Pamphlets.* These Italian writings did not include the term "socialists," but they nonetheless eloquently summarized Desing's fundamental attack on modern natural law for having sought the "foundations of human society" in "vile, carnal" causes rather than by "raising" man's "gaze" toward the heavens. It seemed strange to Desing that everyone spoke of "the spirit of the laws" in wake of Montesquieu's magnum opus, yet conveniently forgot the semantic origins of the phrase: "If I am not mistaken, the spirit of the laws is something spiritual; divine is the Sovereign reason of that Supreme Being who arranges and regulates everything." There was a very real danger, Desing thought, that "reformers" would think *"reason alone"* could suffice as a tool for achieving worldly melioration.[28]

The fraught relationship between society and religion, state and church, was one of the most political expressions of this debate, and Italian translators also published Desing's *Le ricchezze del clero utili, e necessarie alla repubblica* (The wealth of the clergy useful and necessary to the Republic) in 1768, in which he quoted his *Natural Law Unmasked* explicitly to again champion the supremacy of religion in the world against those who, like the later Verri, argued that the Church was "a state within the state": "I have confuted this monstrous division of Pufendorf's in a book entitled *Larva detracta,* in which, for me it is demonstrated that . . . the Church is not *a state within Realms,* but that these are *states within the Church."*[29] Where Gustav von Schmoller would later identify early modern "natural law" as an intellectual movement to return some sense of community to mankind after the fall of Rome and the fragmentation of organized religion, Desing's argument against the "socialists" rested on a resolute rebuttal of its very premises.[30] There was no need for a new source of social cohesion for Desing, for that source had to remain the Catholic Church—which calls itself both "one" and "universal" (καθολική, *katholikē*), as in the Nicene creed—within whose sprawling halls human history unfolded.[31]

In fact, the same year that Beccaria clandestinely sent his *On Crimes and Punishment* to press in Livorno, the Dominican friar Bonifacio Finetti published *De principiis juris naturae et gentium adversus Hobbesium, Pufendorfium, Thomasium, Wolfium, et alios* (The principles of the law of nature and of nations against Hobbes, Pufendorf, Thomasius, Wolff, and others) in Venice. Known even in England as "the most astonishing linguist . . . that ever existed," Finetti was an academically inclined monk who "scarcely ever stirred from his cell" and received "all sorts of books and manuscripts" from "all the corners of the world." Yet he was, nonetheless, a man of his times, the vast library he collected including not only grammars, dictionaries, and Bibles for his research on the historical linguistics of Hebrew and other languages, but also numerous *"treatises of peace and commerce."*[32] Finetti is today best remembered for his vitriolic critiques of the Neapolitan historian and philosopher Giambattista Vico, whose conception of "Providence" he felt could have belonged to "a mere naturalist or fatalist." And, though a Dominican, Finetti was also an important agent for the dissemination of German Benedictine scholarship in Italy. He both quoted Desing positively and railed against the "socialistae" who, like Hobbes and Spinoza, had fallen "into the principle of utility" alone, which he wholeheartedly "condemned."[33] Finetti's passionate defense of Catholic dogma against the dangers of a secularized sociability and the imperatives of worldly "utility" was reprinted in 1777 and 1781, in Venice and Naples, and doubtlessly helped paint the backdrop against which Beccaria revolted and against which *On Crimes and Punishments* was received.

A mere year after Beccaria and Finetti published their books, Ferdinando Facchinei, a Benedictine then at the monastery of Val d'Astino, near Bergamo, in the territory of the Venetian Republic, raised the stakes of the debate. He was attuned to the vagaries of German scholarship, and harnessed Desing's and Finetti's vocabulary in the now infamous *Note ed osservazioni sul libro intitolato "Dei delitti e delle pene,"* or *Notes and Observations on the Book Entitled "On Crimes and Punishments,"* based on a set of manuscript annotations that only partially made their way into the published version.[34] The Tuscan jurist and philosopher Cosimo Amidei wrote to Beccaria that Facchinei "deserves to be punished with infamy, just as he already has been punished in the tribunal of reason," a statement that turned out to be remarkably prophetic.[35] History has not been kind to the "bizarre" Facchinei; one of his more inventive contemporary critics described him as having "a truly amphibious and hermaphroditic head," and it has been argued that he became "almost proverbial as a symbol of obtuse fanaticism."[36]

Yet Facchinei was hardly a throwback to some hypothetical Dark Ages.[37] He struggled against contemporary canons of censorship like many of his ostensibly more forward-looking contemporaries, claiming he "studied secretly" in the monastery to avoid being "stoned." Probably a "heretic and deist" in his youth, he was eventually jailed and perhaps tortured for his radical interests in the "never sufficiently praised Mr. Newton."[38] And he was no model Benedictine, at least considering his private correspondence: "A pox on whoever invented [religious] brothers! . . . If only I could speak!" he complained in the early 1750s.[39] A decade later, he still lamented the years spent "discussing *wine,* rice, and illnesses."[40] At times foul-mouthed and with a peculiar sense of humor, he considered himself "made to be, or live like, a Jesuit," one of the "Christian Philosophers," and the lengths to which he "joked" about being upset by his rebuttal by the order suggests he might have been quite upset after all.[41] Franco Venturi argued that Facchinei's youthful rebellion eventually turned into conservative cynicism, but it must be said that he continued to engage with rather mainstream "Enlightenment" topics in the 1760s, among other things teaching "experimental physics" and engaging with the perennial questions of public happiness and agricultural reform, praising not only Montesquieu and Jean le Rond d'Alembert, coeditor of the *Encyclopédie,* but also the Tuscan polymath Bartolomeo Intieri and his protégé Antonio Genovesi.[42] He waxed lyrical about reforms at the inauguration of a new Agricultural Society of Brescia in 1764, hailing examples offered by, and the emulation of, the "cultured and enlightened nations of Europe," including the Agricultural Society of Dublin, and, tellingly, the "valiant Marquis de Mirabeau," soon to be François Quesnay's right hand in the Physiocratic movement, and lamented those who mistakenly believed that "new and bad [*cattivo*]" were "synonymous."[43]

The Economic Hand of God

There is something tragic about Facchinei and the way in which he so eagerly wished to partake in the eighteenth-century movements for reform. As he wrote in private correspondence with the extraordinarily prolific Jesuit theologian and historian Antonio Zaccaria the year before Beccaria published *On Crimes and Punishments,* "I am only 36 years old; I am very healthy; I am filled with the desire to study, and to do good; and I could, and I will, write something useful to the public."[44] This was not far off from the sentiment of Pietro Verri: "Would that I could say something useful! Would that I could *do* it!"[45] What exactly the two imagined something *useful* to be, however, lay at the core of the tragedy soon to unfold, for Facchinei was adamant that the Fisticuffs had mistakenly put their faith in the *"bouleversant* liberty" of the "ultramontanes."[46] For all his commitment to, and interest in, the learning of his time, he could not let go of a higher mooring; without "the fear of God," he worried, society itself would collapse.[47] "Is it perhaps a sin to desire this Paradise here on earth? I remit, and adore Providence."[48]

And he seemed equally torn about the role of monasteries, wishing to prove that "religious communities" were "not only useful to the Catholic Religion spiritually, as one already argues against all the desperate fanatics, but also very useful *temporally,* against the author of the book=Affairs of France Poorly Understood," probably a reference to an anonymous, deeply antimonastic work by the French spy, and Casanova's friend, Ange Goudar.[49] Facchinei's faith in Providence was unshakable: "The religious economy is assisted by the economic hand of God [*mano economica di Dio*], which has taught the way to build many houses and religious hospitals to the benefit and ornament of the public."[50] Perhaps by "religious economy" Facchinei meant simply the domestic management of monastic life, or perhaps he meant something grander with regard to the larger household management of the Catholic Church or even creation itself. The current *Catechism of the Catholic Church* states:

> The Fathers of the Church distinguish between theology (*theologia*) and economy (*oikonomia*). "Theology" refers to the mystery of God's inmost life within the Blessed Trinity and "economy" to all the works by which God reveals himself and communicates his life. Through the *oikonomia* the *theologia* is revealed to us; but conversely, the *theologia* illuminates the whole *oikonomia*. God's works reveal who he is in himself; the mystery of his inmost being enlightens our understanding of all his works. So it is, analogously, among human persons. A person discloses himself in his actions, and the better we know a person, the better we understand his actions.[51]

As I have previously argued, however, by the eighteenth century the word "economia" had also come to signify something rather closer to our modern conception of "the economy" than certain scholars have suggested, particularly if one does not overly fetishize late twentieth-century ideals of disembeddedness and self-regulation, which, after all, have yet again been found wanting.[52] Indeed, the concept of an "Oeconomia Divina" had long circulated in Europe as a term signifying God's plan for mankind, but gained an even more explicit relevance for political economy in the mid-eighteenth century.[53] In Sweden, in particular, this idea of a providential economy was picked up by writers like Count Carl Gustaf Löwenhielm and, of course, Carl von Linné, better known as Linnaeus. From this perspective, the world was composed of three interacting levels of economic activity: the "great natural Economy or *Oeconomia Divina,*" the "general economy or *oeconomia publica,*" and finally "the particular economy or *oeconomia privata,*" and it was evident that God had a purposeful *plan* for the economic life in his creation.[54] In the exact same years, in Italy, Giuseppe Garampi—the collector, critic of Carli, and later cardinal—similarly argued that Providence arranged the "lands" of the world "with sovereign economy," and that God, as such, played the active role of administrator and "economist" of creation.[55] Facchinei, however, went farther than all of them when speaking of "the economy" as something that God affected with his "economic hand." In any case, his defense of Catholic economic administration was based on its ostensible success, explained by divine intervention through "the economic hand of God"—the creator's continuing and beneficial interference in economic administration.[56] There is even a hint of imperialism in his letter, suggesting, however opaquely, that the Church best manages the household not only of monastic life but also of creation itself, and therefore should be entrusted with the world's reins. And it is telling that, in one of his manuscript annotations to Beccaria's work that never made it into print, he bewailed that "now everyone speaks of Public Economy as if it were Religion," allowing political economy to trump theology as the framework of worldly administration.[57]

Scholars seem to have overlooked the fact that Facchinei had already confided in January 1763 that he was about to complete a "letter regarding the sum of pleasures and pains," in which he hoped to show that "it is only schmucks [*minchioni*] who don't find more pleasures than pains in this world as well [as in the next world]." The sudden appearance first of Verri's anonymous *Meditations on Happiness,* followed closely by Beccaria's similarly anonymous *On Crimes and Punishments,* therefore upset him deeply, perhaps also for careerist reasons.[58] These works, which appeared as if they were written by the same author, hiding behind a screen of anonymity, went not only against his understanding of his subject matter and of religion, but against his perception of authorship as well—it was (s)edition of the most cowardly sort. "I want to be a writer," Facchinei had written shortly before embarking on his critiques, "not masked, nor transformed, but as a gentleman."[59] Yet in spite of all his righteous erudition, there was something crude about Facchinei's literary manners, and something so violent about his critiques, which broke with the silent code of conduct in the eighteenth-century republic of letters, even with regard to inherently touchy subjects such as religion and human sociability. And one of the first reactions to his writing would, painfully for him, proclaim them "unworthy of a gentleman."[60]

Facchinei's fundamental problem with the Academy of Fisticuffs was the pugilists' failure to appreciate the "practical consequences of their actions," which by virtue of their naive sedition would lead to "certain ruin." Facchinei's *Notes and Observations,* Venturi concluded, were "a desperate and extreme defense of the traditional world."[61] Yet it was not that Facchinei disagreed with everything Beccaria had argued—far from it. He approved, for example, of the sentiment that luxury was a relative term and that the timely pursuit of it contributed to the welfare of a society, not to mention that "power" ultimately derived from "wealth."[62] The essential problem was that Beccaria, though his authorship remained unknown to Facchinei, "transcended, and was contrary to, Religion, and good sense," being a "false Christian" and "true Epicurean." *On Crimes and Punishments* was, as such, the "true daughter of *Rousseau's Social Contract.*"[63] Even worse, as Facchinei had put it in his earlier manuscript annotations, Beccaria was an "algebraist" with a downright "mechanistic spirit," driven by the most vulgar "libertinism."[64] In light of what we know of the Marquis's sentimental life, this was a particularly unhappy critique, though quite fitting for both Verri brothers.

Following Rousseau, Facchinei furthermore suggested, Beccaria had argued that "civil societies" historically had been "formed by the consensus of free and isolated men, joined together to secure their own lives, who for that purpose also formed some Laws, and elected various persons (*doubtlessly from their own ranks*) to be depositaries, and executors of said Laws," a theory that was "contrary to righteous reason, contrary to the Right of Sovereignty of all the states of our World, and contrary to the true religion." This, in short, was what the *"socialists"* argued, in Facchinei's eyes calling for worldwide secular and democratic revolution, but such imaginary societies had "never existed."[65] Indeed, he argued,

> there has never been on our Globe a perfect Society that originally was formed from the express and determined consent of Free men, as envisioned by our author [Beccaria], and I challenge all *Socialists,* and anyone else, to find me a single example in all the Histories, and all the Annals of the entire World, of a Society formed in that manner.[66]

Rather, it was evident from studying the history of the "origins of Republics, and of Empires, and regarding their enlargement, as well as their revolutions, and their decline, that the Law of the strongest has always prevailed," yet it was "because of such circumstances, and such combinations, that one sees (judging correctly) the work, and the contribution of an *invisible hand, yes, but a very powerful one."*[67]

The Thrasymachian definition of justice as "what is good for the stronger" here received divine approbation, suggesting Facchinei's reaction to the Fisticuffs was fueled by something far more specific than mere conservatism or mistrust of egalitarianism.[68] Faith in the providential order of the universe raged underneath the surface of his arguments like a subterranean current, only occasionally breaking the surface in an explicit reference to "the economic hand of God" or a "very powerful" if "invisible hand" guiding human affairs.[69] Encouraging agricultural productivity was one thing; challenging the very structures of worldly authority was something entirely different. Historians of economics have spilled much ink over invisible hands such as that invoked by Facchinei, most often with regard to Adam Smith's remarkably hermetic uses of the term. Although Smith employed the phrase both in an early essay on astronomy and, as we have seen, in his *Theory of Moral Sentiments,* it is his reliance on an "invisible hand" in *The Wealth of Nations* that has reverberated through later history of economics.[70] The passage in question, very seldom considered in its entirety, is worth quoting at length:

As every individual . . . endeavours as much as he can both to employ his capital in the support of domestic industry, and so to direct that industry that its produce may be of the greatest value; every individual necessarily labours to render the annual revenue of the society as great as he can. He generally, indeed, neither intends to promote the public interest, nor knows how much he is promoting it. By preferring the support of domestic to that of foreign industry, he intends only his own security; and by directing that industry in such a manner as its produce may be of the greatest value, he intends only his own gain, and he is in this, as in my other cases, led by an invisible hand to promote an end which was no part of his intention. Nor is it always the worse for the society that it was no part of it. By pursuing his own interest he frequently promotes that of the society more effectively than when he really intends to promote it. I have never known much good done by those who affected to trade for the public good. It is an affectation, indeed, not very common among merchants, and very few words need be employed in dissuading them from it.[71]

The unintended consequences of unregulated individual self-interest, "led as if by an invisible hand," did not immediately further cosmopolitan economic globalization in *The Wealth of Nations* at all; instead, it promoted the local economy and thus "society," as part of Smith's "natural progress of opulence."[72] Smith's "invisible hand," in other words, first leads individuals to invest in domestic rather than foreign industries, thus accomplishing by providential design what legislators throughout Europe for centuries sought to do through tariffs and prohibitions.

The degree to which an active divine agency was involved in Smith's scheme remains a matter of intense debate. To be clear, many argue that the logic of *The Wealth of Nations* depended on an essentially religious argument.[73] More than a century ago, however, Thorstein Veblen observed that Smith did not invoke a "meddling Providence" in his famous passage, instead relying on a "teleology," of a "quasi-spiritual" nature, dependent on "a comprehensive scheme of contrivances established from the beginning."[74] It was, in short, not that "God" kept interfering in the world through his "invisible hand," but rather that, given the nature of his creation, things just played out as if. Istvan Hont in many ways followed suit, arguing that Smith's theory of sociability, as he formulated it in his rejoinder to Pufendorf, was "crypto-theological," but added that he had employed the "invisible hand" metaphor "perhaps even sarcastically." Adam Smith had really meant to say that men acted "*as if* guided by an 'invisible hand'"; it was, again, not that Providence guided human affairs, just that human affairs happened to be providentially organized.[75] This notion that "God governs the world according to a benign plan," or "good engineering design," of which the "invisible hand" was a cardinal eighteenth-century expression, is, as Charles Taylor observed, "ancient, even pre-Christian."[76]

Contextualizing Smith's usage of the term in *The Wealth of Nations* to argue that citizens would prefer domestic to foreign industry even in the absence of tariffs, Emma Rothschild has similarly argued that the term was "a mildly ironic joke," arguing elsewhere that "it is clear that Smith did not have a providentialist or deist reason for his confidence; he did not believe that God had ordained a capitalist economy and that God was ensuring the outcomes would be satisfactory." Nonetheless he had "faith" in a general tendency of improvement in the world.[77] So divided is this literature on Smith that, after a lifetime of research, the late Warren Samuels recently concluded that the "continued use" of the term "invisible hand" "must at its base constitute an embarrassment."[78]

Facchinei's use of the term was closer to the mythical, "meddling" one of economics, to the way in which many eighteenth-century readers would have understood the phrase "invisible hand" on the basis of contemporary usage, and, perhaps, even to Smith's intended meaning.[79] And it serves to remind us that what is at stake in current debates over spontaneous order also loomed large in the eighteenth century. God's hand, sometimes invisible, sometimes not, was literally involved in managing the economy of creation, and challenging the providential order—challenging, in Facchinei's interpretation, the social and institutional status quo too far—was tantamount to sacrilege. As the Florentine writer and soon director of the Uffizi Gallery Giuseppe Pelli Bencivenni put it in his *Novelle letterarie,* parts of contemporary "economic science" sought to make it "geometrical," in emulation of "divine Providence" as a means of charting God's "order" and defending "Religion and Morality." Markets did not require regulation because, he assured his readers, "creation presupposes in the Creator the design of the conservation and good of the thing that is created."[80] God would simply not have created a market that was not perfect in the first place, and it is hardly surprising that acolytes of such theoretical trends in Italy happily transcended the civic and secular boundaries of Beccaria's science to fully embrace supernatural influences on political economy. The Tuscan parish priest Ferdinando Paoletti, for example, held "Sovereigns" to be "the terrestrial image of Eternal Providence," and Pelli himself argued "there are no better friends of Religion and of the Sovereigns than the *Economists*"—in other words, the French "sect" of Physiocracy most heavily invested in a politics of laissez-faire at the time.[81]

"The Wolf's Bite"

Many writers and thinkers agreed that regulatory reform was necessary; what divided them were the questions of what form it should take, how far it could be pushed, how far economic activities could safely be unleashed, how far popular enlightenment could be realized without resulting in revolution, and, quite bluntly, how far "liberty" could be pushed without devolving into anarchy.[82] Strikingly, given Beccaria's private fears, Facchinei noted that social contracts never could hold because "a soul, like those of Machiavelli or Galileo would never agree with the multitudes." Democratic sentiments could not square with the inherent inequality of people. So the truth remained that "men have never been without a master [*padrone*], never have they been independent," and the "first *paterfamilias* [*padre di famiglia*] was the first King, and the first magistrate, and the strongest of these, or the wisest has always been, so to speak, their Emperor."[83] All sovereignty ultimately derived from "the true system of the creation of man."[84] God had not intended power to be equally distributed; nobles, clergy, kings, and parents ruled for a reason, and the less people knew of the basis of law and order, the better. An enlightening program of public education regarding the laws, like that argued for by Beccaria, would ultimately merely "multiply crimes" as people became aware of what they were not supposed to do, ironically the very point the Academy of Fisticuffs had made in the forlorn case of the incestuous lesbians.[85] Kindred attempts at equalizing fortunes had historically failed, at times with unintended negative consequences. For, he reasoned, invoking an argument that in various inflections would become increasingly important in later centuries, had not "slaves" been treated far better than ostensibly free "domestic servants"?[86] Again, it is too easy to dismiss Facchinei's arguments as simply retrograde, because similar arguments continue to be made even to this day.[87]

The same could be said about the controversy over capital punishment. There was simply no doubt in Facchinei's mind that "society has the right to free itself of a villain in any way it deems most expedient."[88] Indeed, the death penalty lay at the very foundations of civilization. As he had put it in his first annotations to Beccaria, not only did "a Sovereign, or the State" have "reason to sacrifice anyone who wishes to wickedly resist its security," but even Beccaria's own concept of a social contract seemed to him to necessitate capital punishment. Without it, people would not

> obtain the ends for which they unite in society; because if society does not have such a right, the life of its members [soci] would be even less secure than they had been outside of society, that is when everyone lived in their original natural liberty. For if society leaves everyone the liberty to kill their own assailants, it would immediately become a funereal anarchy.[89]

Facchinei disagreed with practically all of Beccaria's assumptions regarding capital punishment, emphasizing that it was "not the certainty, but how great the harm" of punishment that best discouraged crime; what mattered was not knowing you would be caught, but knowing you might be broken on the wheel like a Torriggia or a Mandrin.[90] As Facchinei put it in his manuscript annotations, Beccaria engaged with "experimental metaphysics" when arguing that "the Wheel" did not "cause more fear than simple imprisonment."[91] Facchinei's first use of the word "socialists," in his annotations to Beccaria, occurred at the point where the latter rhetorically had asked, "Who has ever willingly given other men the authority to kill him?"[92] Facchinei's answer is worth quoting at length:

> It is everyone who reasonably wishes the greatest safety for their lives. But I also agree that man, given how rotten he is, is incapable of very much goodness, and from this one can deduce how impossible it is for men to wish to spontaneously form a stable society capable of securing the lives of those of whom it is composed. Society must either have the right to punish with the death penalty, which our Author [Beccaria] denies it; or men contradict themselves by

uniting in a society with the aim of better securing their lives, because a society that cannot punish the wicked with the death penalty cannot exist. There can be no security for life where there is no liberty to take it away from someone who is unworthy of living. Such is the human condition, and such is the *absurdity of the program of our modern socialists.*[93]

The crux of the matter remained whether there existed a human right to life, whether, by virtue of simply being born, an individual enjoyed an intrinsic right to not being deemed, in Facchinei's words, "unworthy of living" by anyone, whether society or the state. The related challenge was whether, given human nature, anything but death—and the terror of it—could discipline people into sociability. Could "socialists" really find a way for society to flourish without resorting to either sovereign or divine cruelty? Facchinei, for one, believed that the *"healthy terror"* of *"death"* was "the only *means to discourage* men from committing the crimes that destroy society," including, crucially, anything that undermined the institution of private property.[94] And there was also, as he put it in his published critique, the additional problem that killing was part of God's natural laws:

> I ask the most prejudiced Socialists: if a man, finding himself in his primitive natural state of liberty before having entered any Society, I ask does a free man have the right to kill another man who wishes in any way take his life? I am certain that all Socialists this time will respond yes.[95]

If people had a right to kill in any context whatsoever, which Facchinei argued even a "socialist" would agree they had under certain conditions, obviously capital punishment was based on, and justified by, natural law, not to mention divine will. The charge is telling, however, in that it extends well beyond the critique of a "socialist" as being an adherent of the theory of social contracts. Indeed, Facchinei employs the term to shed light on Beccaria's conjectural history of the state of nature, by default outside of the purview of social contracts. And it suggests, also in light of his worry about their democratic pretensions, that a "socialist" for Facchinei also was someone who cared about social issues and relations more broadly, and about what sorts of justice bound men even before the advent of the social contract and of society as such. Beccaria had, however, already admitted that murder was acceptable in cases of self-defense, and that in such instances it was the original aggressor who transgressed against natural law, not the defendant who had deployed lethal force. But this was hardly the only time Facchinei misinterpreted Beccaria.

Intriguingly though, for Facchinei a "socialist" was not someone who believed in the inherent, innate sociability of humankind but the very opposite. A socialist was someone who believed in socialization through the establishment and development of a secular and egalitarian social contract, which itself was an impossibility to him: "Because man is a social animal . . . naturally so proud and so driven to liberty and independence, it is inconceivable that he would spontaneously subject himself to and obey other men."[96] Facchinei was again misreading Beccaria, who repeatedly emphasized the hard-fought and far from spontaneous origins of society and man's harrowing "original sociability." But the intellectual baggage he brought to the discussion and the lenses through which he contemplated the larger debate go a long way toward explaining it. In a private letter, Facchinei had admitted: "I will certainly not hang around consulting Puffendorf [sic]; because I have never let my conscience depend on lawyers, nor casuists, but only on the Gospel, interpreted my way, which is that of the Pope, which to me is the most perfect plan, and system of Natural Laws."[97] Facchinei felt socialists were so misguided because they had read the wrong books and drawn the wrong lessons from history. It was, therefore, not without irony that Verri suggested Facchinei should read precisely some "Pufendorf" in his soon to be published reply.[98]

There was something inherently civilizing about "the Wolf's bite," Facchinei argued, with what might have been a subterranean reference to Hobbes and the ancient problem of lupine sacrality, and without such harshness and cruelty men would still have "lived in the forests, and the deserts, the way Bears and Lions live just like contemporary bandits."[99] Far from Beccaria and the other pugilists' faith in the gradual development of civilization and sensibilities, Facchinei underscored that "fear conserves realms," both internally and internationally.[100] In a note he wrote, "When has one ever found a nation without some occult enemy to fear?"[101] Cruelty and cowering were the keys to civility. Similarly, the spectacles of torture and public executions were necessary to maintain a state of fear within society, for though "torture is an evil, and a cruel evil, the evil and a cruelty are necessary to escape other greater evils and greater cruelties; it is a physical evil that results in much moral good and very great physical good."[102] In his eyes, torture and capital punishment were lesser evils compared to the collapse of society that they helped ward off. For the good of society, some people simply had, in terms identical to how Milanese legislators had approached the *affare dei malviventi* addressed in Chapter 4, to be "eradicated like bad weeds pernicious to the state."[103]

Yet the ultimate social glue—the real issue at stake in Facchinei's critique of "socialism"—was not worldly pain or social, economic, and political equality, but religion. Cloy jeremiads about inequality and injustice like Beccaria's did not convince Facchinei at all.[104] Indeed, reacting explicitly to the Marquis's monologue impersonating a desperate criminal, Facchinei noted that "had they been capable of understanding and making those arguments, they would never have become assassins." He willfully ignored the underlying thesis of On Crimes and Punishments regarding the ultimately social and economic causes of crime.[105] Instead, Facchinei maintained, "all that is not God, is evil, if one speaks of morals, and of virtue."[106] "The Social Contract is an impossible Chimera," he declared, but this did not mean he was opposed to natural law—far from it. What he supported, though, was *his* natural law, which was far better equipped to defend the Old Regime key institutions such as private property ("a natural right . . . *to some extent as necessary as life*") and the "holy Tribunal of the Inquisition."[107] Neither he, nor the "socialists," then, really believed in a thick form of natural sociability. What differed was their external mechanism for socialization: divine wrath and Providence or a social contract representing and enabling the gradual and egalitarian socialization of expanding civic communities.

In the end Facchinei held that On Crimes and Punishments, as a "socialist" tract, was erected on the fatal assumption that human society could be experienced, understood, and reformed on its own terms, a pathology of what he called "our very enlightened century."[108] "If our Politics is not a visible part of the true Religion," he thundered, "it will never be a good Politics, but a vague, broken Philosophy." Echoing Desing, one could simply not consider this world in isolation from the next, a mere "part" compared to the "whole" of "eternity."[109] As such, Beccaria's pamphlet contained nothing less than "the greatest and most seditious errors ever blasphemed to date against the sovereign rulers and against the Christian religion by the most impious heretics and by all the irreligious ancients and moderns."[110] It amounted to the vain ramblings of someone who deeply wished to be "thought the *Rousseau* of the Italians."[111]

Riposte

However ludicrous later historians have found Facchinei's arguments, Verri and Beccaria took them quite seriously. His attacks seemed all the more worrisome because of their place of publication: the most Serene Republic of Venice. Suspecting its anonymous author to be Venetian, local authorities there had banned *On Crimes and Punishments* on the grounds that it offered a veiled critique of one of the republic's most iconic institutions, the use of "secret accusations."[112] Beccaria, it seems, was paralyzed by the situation; he would "sigh and cry" in fear of reprisals.[113] Pietro Verri initially was more belligerent, coauthoring an anonymous *Risposta,* or *Reply,* to Facchinei with his brother Alessandro in mere days, and writing a lengthy sarcastic letter to Facchinei directly to let him know he thought him "ridiculous." But he also wrote cautious notes to his then-friend Gian Rinaldo Carli, noting that "anywhere that arsenic or an assassin can enter, the law of St. Mark must be respected."[114] And the pugilists had good reason to fear the wrath of Venice; at the time, *La Serenissima* frequently deployed extraterritorial assassins to dispatch its real and imagined enemies in the early modern equivalent of drone strikes.[115] The Verri brothers' defense of Beccaria, however, which by default also was a defense of the Academy of Fisticuffs itself, was almost entirely focused on the question of the ostensible irreligiosity of *On Crimes and Punishments,* a charge they rejected entirely by developing the book's distinction between crime and sin, which Verri himself perhaps had originated. Strikingly, though, they in many ways stepped back from *On Crimes and Punishments,* usurping Beccaria's voice to claim, in his authorial voice but clearly against his original convictions, that "I have said, and I repeat, that when the death penalty is useful and necessary, it is also just, and must be given."[116] As a publishing strategy, the Verri brothers' *Reply* might have been an effective and calculated dodge, but it ended up simultaneously painting Beccaria as a more than devout

Catholic, and weakened the core moral and reformist message of *On Crimes and Punishments*.

Beccaria himself responded only indirectly, including a new preface, "To the Reader," in future editions of his *On Crimes and Punishments* explaining his position. The laws that framed Old Regime Europe, it began, were "dregs of the most barbarous ages" that had to be reformed and brought into alignment with the present stage in the evolution of human societies: "The barbaric notions and the fierce ideas of our ancestral northern huntsman endure in the mind of the people, in customs and in the laws, which are always more than a century behind the actual enlightenment of a nation."[117] But in seeking to overthrow the legal rituals of his day, Beccaria now claimed that he did not mean to undermine authority in a radical way; his sentiments were far from Pyrrhonic. Instead he suggested, appealing to the contemporary vogue with what we now know as the public sphere, that his proposed reforms would "strengthen" "legitimate authority" because in a world where "opinion in men is more powerful than force," a ruler's "humanity" scaffolded sovereignty.[118] Men were governed by three "moral and political principles" leading *"toward happiness in this mortal life,"* and these were derived from "revelation, natural law, and the artificial conventions of society."[119] This was his crucial move in response to Facchinei, though it merely explicated the argumentative structure of the first edition:

> [Given that] the first two [principles], although divine and immutable, have been altered in a thousand ways in the depraved minds of men by false religions and arbitrary notions of vice and virtue, it seems necessary to examine, independent of any other consideration, that which arises from simple human conventions.[120]

Beccaria further related these three principles to "three distinct classes of vice and virtue: the religious, the natural, and the political," which "never ought to contradict each other." Yet their consequences differed, and it was of the "utmost importance" to maintain clear distinctions in debates about these issues. "It would be an error," he implicitly responded to Facchinei and other critics, "to charge someone speaking of social conventions and their consequences of holding principles that are contrary either to natural law or revelation, for he is not speaking about these matters." While "divine and natural justice" were "essentially immutable," "human justice or political justice" were entirely different things, "being," Beccaria paralleled Lloyd's manuscripts, "no more than a relation between an action and the variable condition of society." Criminal law was, in short, subject to an absolute division of labor that too often was transgressed. While it was up to "theologians" to decide on the "wickedness or goodness of an action," by "the same token" it was "the task of the scholar of public law to determine what is just and unjust in a political sense" in any given place at any given time, the same general contextual approach that the pugilists had argued for in the sphere of political economy.[121]

What this amounted to was a subtle yet genuinely inflammatory distinction between crime and sin—between politics and religion, the courts and the Confraternities of the Beheaded St. John the Baptist, this world and the next. Beccaria further elaborated, "The affairs of Heaven are ruled by laws altogether different from those that govern human affairs." So, for example, in a subsection devoted to "A Particular Type of Crime" that in the past had "covered Europe in blood" and "the smoke of human limbs," Beccaria resolutely banished spiritual delinquencies like witchcraft from the sphere of worldly legislation: "I am speaking only of the crimes that arise from human nature and from the social pact, and not of sins, whose punishments—even in this world—should be regulated by principles other than those of a limited philosophy."[122] This was perhaps where the Academy of Fisticuffs' secularizing project became most pointed, as Beccaria and his friends purposefully argued in favor of an utterly "disenchanted" political economy.[123]

Facchinei was relentless, however, and soon published a critique also of Pietro Verri's anonymous *Meditations on Happiness*, believing the book to be by the same pen, two "monstrous twins" by an anonymous author he now considered "truly the Rousseau of Italy."[124] This sparring between Facchinei and his hidden, hydra-like opponent produced less analysis than it did bile, on both sides of the equation, and variations of the word "socialist" did not appear again in their exchanges. Yet the word—and what it had begun to signify to contemporaries—remained at the very core of their polemic. Pietro Verri had even arrived at straightforwardly conflating "virtue" with "utility," and his definition of the social contract had been even more explicitly revolutionary than Beccaria's:[125]

Love of pleasure made men leave their primitive state of independence, and has gathered them in society. The social contract abolished ferocious muscular despotism, and with the industrious joining of many conspiring forces equilibrium was established among men. To do this it was indispensable to circumscribe man's use of natural liberty with certain artificial laws, which expropriate a part of liberty for the security of the rest. The end of the social contract is the welfare of every individual who concurs to form the society, which amounts to the public happiness, that is the greatest happiness possible divided as equally as possible.[126]

To Facchinei's sensitivities, there was something unnervingly boundless about the Fisticuffs' "socialist" vision for reform and the possibilities of improvement. Verri had, for example, written of how technological progress made contemporaries "more Enlightened" than their forerunners. "It seems," Facchinei ridiculed his opponent, that "he wished to write, that perhaps some day man will go so far as to be able to fly," to which the pugilists' Piedmontese ally and political economist Dalmazzo Francesco Vasco replied that, well, yes, why not?[127]

There is no doubt who proverbially won the argument, then or now. Indeed, as the years progressed, Verri's sketch, on the inside back cover of the page proofs for the Reply, became ever more prophetic. It shows an eighteenth-century male figure, in unmistakable clerical dress, weeping, perhaps after having read the book at hand. It cannot but be the young Father Facchinei, who, as Verri wrote to him, had deluded himself into "believing that he could persuade Italy that true Religion and true Dogma was hiding in the Cell of a Monk in Val d'Astino near Bergamo." His misstep in attacking the Academy of Fisticuffs, Verri continued, would haunt him forever: "The stain with which you have covered yourself in this encounter will never wash off."[128] And, in effect, Facchinei would never recover, bewailing late in life that he had been "hated and defamed," not to mention forced into "silence, slandered and oppressed," for his untimely Notes and Observations.[129]

It seems that neither Beccaria nor the Verri brothers would ever use the term "socialism" in print, but we know that they registered Facchinei's use

Probably Ferdinando Facchinei
(1725–1814). Marginalia by Pietro
Verri, ca. 1765.

of the term. In Alessandro Verri's preparatory notes for the *Reply,* for example, he wrote, as a suggestion for their point-by-point rebuttal, that

> p. 23 Where he [Facchinei] says *sect of Socialists.* One could also say of someone that they are part of the sect of impostors or slanderers.[130]

In the economy of the reply, it could in short have been a rhetorical strategy to counter a sect of socialists with a sect of slanderers, or an expression of the exhaustion of invective, but nowhere does the neologism seem to cause confusion. Having been acknowledged by neither Beccaria nor the Verri brothers in their direct reply to Facchinei, however, the term "socialist" would not play a major part in the vast literature to emerge out of *On Crimes and Punishments* until the nineteenth century, by which time the word had acquired its modern meaning and inspired reactions to different (yet related) aspects of the text. Particularly, "socialist" readings would highlight passages questioning the extent to which economic disparities could be tolerated, given the fundamental equation of justice and sociability—in other words, the degree of inequality societies actually could absorb—and, of course, his musings on the "terrible right" of property.[131] Before then, however, the Desingian signification *socialistae,* galvanized by Beccaria, would continue to make sporadic appearances in eighteenth-century Italy, and again in ways that can shed light on the crucial contemporary debate over society, equality, peace, and the necessity or not of regulation in worldly affairs.[132]

Et in Arcadia?

Appiano Buonafede (1716–1793), who was born Tito Benvenuto and adopted the name Agatopisto (from the Greek for "good faith," or "buona fede") Cromaziano upon joining the Academy of Arcadians in Rome, hailed from an old family that had hit hard times in the town of Comacchio, situated on a lagoon off the Adriatic in the easternmost wetlands of Emilia Romagna near Ferrara, then part of the sprawling Papal States. At the time, Comacchio was perhaps best known as the location of an acrimonious territorial dispute earlier in the century between the Holy See and the Dukes of Este, though Buonafede himself left at the age of eighteen to join the order of Benedictine Celestines.[133] Following philosophical studies in Bologna, he taught for several years in Naples, where he partook actively in the Newtonian furor that gripped its intellectual circles in the earlier part of the eighteenth century. Among his founding influences was no doubt Celestino Galiani, uncle of the better-known political economist Ferdinando Galiani, upon whose death Buonafede wrote a eulogy.[134] In Naples, Buonafede attended the final lectures of Giambattista Vico and defended Genovesi against charges of heresy. It was even believed that he had taught the young Ferdinando Galiani his notoriously gregarious style. But Buonafede was not merely an academic. He spent two years managing agricultural reforms in a monastery in Puglia before serving as an abbot in Bologna and eventually heading the Celestine Order from Rome.[135]

Buonafede might nonetheless best be remembered for his voluminous histories of philosophy and his very long, very public, and very ugly scholarly quarrel with Giuseppe Marco Antonio Baretti, in many ways the literary bad boy of the Italian Enlightenment.[136] After long peregrinations, the Piedmontese Baretti settled in London for most of his life, where he befriended the British lexicographer and man of letters Samuel Johnson and gained some celebrity for murdering a nighttime assailant with a silver dessert knife. No less a manly man than Thomas Carlyle was most impressed by this "rugged hard keen man" Baretti.[137] His *Frusta letteraria,* or *Literary Scourge,* had, Baretti

Giuseppe Marco Antonio Baretti
(1719–1789). Joshua Reynolds, *Portrait
of Joseph Baretti*, 1773.

admitted, "a terrible title," possibly in the sense of terrifying, and amounted
to "a pretty terrible thing," that immediately gave "a general alarm to all the
literati's [sic] of Italy."[138] It was a caustic, if sporadically witty journal dedicated to castigating the writers of its age, including both lovers of Arcadian
frivolities and recent works devoted to emulating foreign works of political
economy. Baretti was rather indiscriminate in his discrimination, and Buonafede and the Academy of Fisticuffs were—ironically, given their very
divergent standpoints in these debates—among the recipients of his most
scornful flagellations.[139] It was during Buonafede's polemic with Baretti that
he befriended Beccaria's nemesis Facchinei, who at the time considered "the
silly *Literary Scourge*" worthy of "infinite whippings, or rather worthy of kicks
in the a . . . [*calci in c . . .*]," and convinced him to republish and take credit
for his most famous reply to Baretti, the *Bue pedagogo,* or *Pedagogical Ox.*[140]
The enemies of one's enemies are not always one's friends.

But, in spite of their shared appreciation for the Neapolitan Enlightenment, as well as common opposition to suicide, there were important points
on which Buonafede and the pugilists could not see eye to eye.[141] The former's
son unwittingly touched upon it when he summarized Buonafede's lifelong
project as devoted to demonstrating "that the perfect Society was divinely

instituted, and revealed, opposed to the Society invented by man."[142] Not only was Buonafede critical of what he considered dangerously irreligious strains of eighteenth-century political and economic thought, but he was also decidedly skeptical with regard to foreign and non-Catholic influences on Italian debates.[143] Baretti, for one, had erred not only for attacking him but also for dragging the entire Italian branch of the Republic of Letters through the literary mud, and Buonafede consciously wrote against him "*da buon Italiano*" (as a good Italian).[144] Hence his lifelong praise for Genovesi and Vico, authors who, in his mind, "honor Italy" against the "vaunted boreal masters."[145]

His three-volume *Della restaurazione di ogni filosofia ne' secoli XVI, XVII e XVIII* (1785–1789), or the *Restoration of all Philosophies in the Sixteenth, Seventeenth, and Eighteenth Centuries,* was a detailed confutation of the path taken by political philosophy since the Protestant Reformation. At least in hindsight, Buonafede's main works can fruitfully be considered a seamless bulwark against the three evils of irreligion, imitation, and insomnia. The recurrent hobgoblin of his account was Thomas Hobbes, whose "system," though containing much that was "true and useful," pretty much singlehandedly had led modernity astray. And Buonafede's reasoning was, in this, heavily indebted both to Facchinei and to Anselm Desing, whom he praised at length. Hobbes had namely defined his natural law "poorly" in claiming "it aims solely at the *conservation of present life,*" since he excluded "the more solid sanction reserved in future immortality." Under the divine lens of infinity, man was instead "naturally needy of society," and the "absurd and repugnant system" of "political Hobbesianism" had changed "sovereigns" into "wolves and lions," confusing "sovereign power with the absolute, the arbitrary, the capricious, and the unlimited" in a way that betrayed its author's "violation of the unalienable human rights [understood very differently from Beccaria's] and the immobile laws of divinity."[146]

Buonafede had long lost patience with the supposed "novelty" of Hobbes's "bloody philosophy," for already in the "most remote antiquity" it had been argued that "*the natural state of man is war.*"[147] Divine revelation had, however, clarified that this was because of nurture, not nature. It was a corruption, man's fall from grace, not a reflection of his soul. One now lived in a world in which a Machiavellian insistence on "utility" had worsened the situation further, creating an existentially shortsighted moral landscape in which "everything that is beneficial is honest," precisely as Verri had argued mere years earlier.[148] Salvation, as such, lay in a renewed respect for "divine reason" as the source of "eternal and unchanging notions of the right and the honest." Somewhat ironically, given his struggles with emerging paradigms of utilitarianism, Buonafede suggested that his interpretation of things ultimately was more "useful" as well. For if the relationship between peoples mirrored that between people, the Hobbesian stance was simply intolerable. It was, he thought, much more "useful" for people to assume a natural state of peace in creation.[149]

But one could err in many ways in Buonafede's moral imagination, and if the Hobbesians risked irreligion by interpreting human nature too negatively, what he called "socialists" risked the same by interpreting it too positively. Hugo Grotius had admittedly gotten many things right. But basing his system on the idea that *sociability, or rather the custody of society, is the principle of every law of nature and of nations,*" he, too, was ultimately too irreligious for the stringent contours of Buonafede's philosophy. And Pufendorf, whose work was a "perpetual commentary on Grotius," had similarly ignored "the relationship to God, immortal souls, and the great and true happiness of future life." Modern natural law was obsessed with legislation, but it mistakenly ignored "the supreme legislator" on high, for only "God" could be "the foundation of every natural law and duty."[150] It is striking in these critiques how Buonafede built on Desing and Facchinei in referring to these authors as "socialist," going further in coining the term *socialismi,* "socialisms," to describe related theoretical arguments.[151] His denunciation of the English philosopher, Hobbes critic, and Bishop of Peterborough Richard Cumberland, in particular, is telling:

> Many other accusations already made against the systems of the *socialists* can be made against his [Cumberland's]: that although it is scattered with solemn and useful truths and is founded on the great principle of the *Greatest Love,* eighteen centuries have passed since the best of teachers [i.e., Jesus Christ] taught it without metaphysical burdens, and everybody understood him, and that it has been another forty centuries since the first men divulgated it without voluminous tomes, and posterity accepted it: and, finally, that it does not seem right to abandon the perspicuous and evident ideas of *love*

of God and of one's *neighbor* as old and plebeian in order to substitute
them with *nature, sociability,* the *highest benevolence, reasonable enti-
ties,* and at times even the *mechanical senses* and the *instincts.*[152]

Why, he asked, should one look for convoluted solutions to the question
of human sociability, when the truth was so simple? Hobbes had been
manifestly wrong in suggesting the natural state of man was one of "war,"
but the "socialists" had lost their way by seeking to prove the principle of
sociability—or at least the means of achieving it—without respect for Providence, by limiting the sphere of politics to this life of earthly existence. Although he never mentioned Henry Lloyd by name, the mechanistic understanding of man he had helped the Academy of Fisticuffs spearhead in Italy
haunted Buonafede's writings. Without externally imposed absolutes of
right and wrong, life became "an abyss" of "moral indifferentism" suitable
for a "Machiavelli."[153]

Buonafede, in short, considered the *"great principle of sociability"* to be of
crucial importance and agreed with many of the writers he castigated that
men were nasty, yet he disagreed with them vehemently over whether men
were so by divine inspiration, animal nature, or nurture.[154] It was theologically and, he thought, logically unsound to argue that the "natural state" of
man was war, at times seemingly because the idea was harder and sadder to
grapple with. Machiavelli's role in Buonafede's theoretical imagination is
therefore telling. On the one hand, Buonafede criticized the French historian and critic Abraham Nicolas Amelot de la Houssaye for attempting to
whitewash Machiavelli's intentions. On the other hand, he agreed with the
satirical Baroque reason-of-state critic Trajano Boccalini that Machiavelli
"does not teach men anything, except that which he learned from them."
Machiavelli was simultaneously corrupt and an honest observer of worldly
affairs. As Buonafede wrote in a poem on the Florentine secretary, "that
which he learned from the world, he taught to the world." Machiavelli as
such was the ideal messenger of man's fallen condition, concurrently bad
news and old news; "Machiavellism is a doctrine far older than Machiavelli,
and would rule the world, even if Machiavelli had never written anything."[155]
It was a situation from which man simply could not make it out alone. Buonafede therefore concluded his magnum opus with a warning to read the
works of Italian Catholics—and particularly Vico and Genovesi—as an

aegis against the "heterodox vortex" of modern ideas, and particularly against "the contradictions of the *socialisms* and of the *savageries*"—the divergent but equally dangerous myths, that is, of secular sociability and of the noble savage.[156] That Genovesi was one of the most efficient mediators of international ideas in eighteenth-century Italy, and that Verri himself once had claimed "all Italians" owed him "homage," completely escaped him.[157]

The meanings they attributed to the word "socialism" at times overlapped, but Buonafede's usage of the term differed from Facchinei's in key respects. Both saw "socialism" as a dangerously secular and even revolutionary affair, undermining existing hierarchies both temporal and spiritual. But where Buonafede differentiated between the ideals of a Pufendorf and of a Rousseau, one an avatar of "socialism," the other of "savagery," Facchinei had criticized both the Pufendorfian Beccaria and the savage Rousseau for being "socialists" on grounds of their shared interpretation of an original man-made social contract, no matter the different contents of the contracts they envisioned or, for that matter, their divergent religiosities. As in a Venn diagram of only partially overlapping identities, what remained at the core of Enlightenment "socialism" was a penchant for egalitarianism— in one instance auxiliarily bordering on communism through Beccaria's thought-experiment regarding a world without private property, and in the other a basically secular and economic interpretation of the process of socialization itself, of "commercial society," encapsulated in Pufendorf's definition of "the natural state" as one "opposed to life improved by human industry."[158] Paradoxically then, given the term's tumultuous later life, the charge of "socialism" originated as a pointed censure of secular commercial society and the burgeoning ideology that, soon enough, would come to be known as "capitalism."

CHAPTER SIX

The Threshold of Utopia

C ESARE BECCARIA NEVER RESPONDED to the "socialist" critique directly, but, even if the dreaded Venetian assassins failed to materialize, Ferdinando Facchinei's *Notes and Observations on the Book Entitled "On Crimes and Punishments"* nonetheless did their damage. Pietro Verri had hoped that the success of Beccaria's book could launch the Milanese Enlightenment, and thus him personally, to international fame, but his plan ultimately backfired, from the perspective of the Verri brothers, if not of Milan as such. Beccaria and Alessandro Verri did venture to Paris, where the encyclopedist André Morellet introduced them "to everyone" and they were soon feted by the city's *philosophes,* but their eventual misadventures there proved so divisive that their friendship, and their cultural and political project, never recovered.[1] Finally, the pugilists turned on each other, and with both Verri brothers actively beginning to undermine their former friend and protégé, the fisticuffs became ever more literal. Because Pietro decided to record his correspondence with Alessandro during the latter's journeys in a book for friends and posterity, even contemplating publishing the letters in book form, their rich epistolary offers unique insights on the dissolution of the Academy of Fisticuffs.[2]

The thick web of misinformation surrounding the fallout between Beccaria and the Verri brothers is hard to penetrate, but many factors contributed to making what Alessandro Verri could soon call "il tristissimo affare Beccaria," "the regrettable Beccaria affair."[3] Already in his very first letter to his brother, Alessandro began complaining about Beccaria's demeanor during their travels, while the latter wrote that "everything troubles me."[4] Beccaria had begun to "miss his family and above all his wife" before even leaving Lombardy, and soon descended into outright "melancholy." He was overcome by "feminine and childish imbecility," Alessandro wrote, wishing to return "home" to "his wife, his children," and "to cut such a bad figure that I cannot even imagine it."[5] Undoubtedly, Alessandro Verri and Cesare Beccaria made for poor traveling companions on a most basic, temperamental level. Beccaria looked like "a man on his way to the gallows" when he left his family, and, "if it had been up to him, he would not have done anything but visit bookshops" while abroad. He turned their apartment in Paris into a "coffeeshop" every morning, but, where Alessandro hungered for glory he did not receive, Beccaria "did not savor" all the attention lavished upon him.[6] The young Verri, on the other hand, wanted to truly experience Paris, and noted he would need "a thousand dicks [*mille cazzi*]" to keep up with "the libertinism of this country."[7] Indeed, he mused, "that blessed, independent libertinism may not have the sublime pleasures of tender and terrible love, but certainly it does not have its sadnesses, its anxieties."[8] Not having a wife or children, Alessandro Verri did not understand how Beccaria could "love" his family more than his friends, or for that matter his "open preference for his wife" over Pietro himself.[9] Putting family before fame, Pietro wrote, Beccaria, though "applauded by Europe," would nonetheless be "disrespected by his Milanese neighbor."[10]

As the hundreds of letters exchanged between the two Verri brothers make abundantly clear, these sentimental disagreements eventually grew to become a veritable obsession. Beccaria's dark mood and his adulatory reception by the *philosophes* D'Alembert, Diderot, d'Holbach, and others in Paris certainly aggravated the young Alessandro Verri, whose letters to Pietro grew increasingly vitriolic from wounded pride. "I must suffer him [for his dark moods] at home and see him put ahead of me outside," Alessandro wrote from Paris; and again, "Every time a presentation is needed eyes are primarily turned to Beccaria. In the present state of affairs I am really bored in society.

I am not at the forefront, I am timid, isolated, uncertain of the outcome of things; I speak little."[11] While Beccaria cut "a brilliant figure" in the Parisian salons, and was "celebrated and venerated," Alessandro whined to his brother of his "jealousy" and that "in his fortune [Beccaria] lacks a certain delicacy. He enjoys it and forgets his friend."[12] In private, we are told, Beccaria cried and worried for his wife and family; in public, he managed to charm the notoriously fickle *philosophes* of Paris, at least for awhile.

Not only did Beccaria prefer his family to his friends, but, content with his own fame, he did not sufficiently champion theirs. Even worse, the Verri brothers maintained that he actively had sought to usurp what glory was rightly theirs. This was the context in which Facchinei's attack, seemingly so easily deflected in print, in the end proved lethal for the Academy of Fisticuffs. It was bad enough that the success of Beccaria's *On Crimes and Punishments* overshadowed anything else that the group had done, but when the *philosophes* praised the *Reply* to Facchinei as well, which the Verris essentially had penned alone, Alessandro wrote to his brother, "he only once said . . . *I must confess that my friends helped me write it*."[13] This, Pietro replied, "was more powerful than any other anecdote" his brother had communicated, and marked the point of no return for the pugilists.[14] In the end, Beccaria returned to Milan after less than two months, far earlier than expected and against the express wishes of his wife and particularly of the Verri brothers, while Alessandro continued on to London and, eventually, Tuscany and Rome, where he finally chose to settle, even though he had joked he would go to "America" just to do the opposite of what Beccaria had done.[15] By the time the traveling companions went their separate ways, conditions were such that the young Verri wrote about Beccaria that he felt like "dargli dei pugni," that is like "punching him," or *actual* fisticuffs.[16] "Our society," Pietro Verri concluded, "is gone forever."[17]

Paolo Frisi, who was in Paris on his own accord while Beccaria and Alessandro Verri were there, and who somewhat cautiously sided with the Verri brothers in the ensuing conflict, suggested, in a letter he urged Pietro Verri to "burn," that Beccaria had "no organs for friendship" and "really came short, I don't think because of an evil heart but because of his temperament— that is, for always being at the center of his system." News of "the triumph of the book [*On Crimes and Punishments*] and of its author [Beccaria] in Paris" was, he assured Verri, "an illusion," for Beccaria had left the impression of being a "real madman," and the *"Philosophes . . .* have spoken more highly of the merits of your brother."[18] Morellet's *Memoirs* suggests a somewhat different story, though one in which Beccaria's visit equally had been "a sad experience of human weakness."[19] Having arrived consumed by "jealousy" over his "young" wife, Beccaria was "somber" and hardly spoke, unlike "his friend" Alessandro Verri, who had an "easy character" and "soon attracted the preference, care, and attention of society" in Paris. It was "this," Morellet recollected, that "finally turned the head of poor Beccaria" and made him decide to abort his stay in the French capital.[20] Whatever the case, the Verri brothers soon sought their revenge by convincing the world that Beccaria had merely supplied "the style and organization" to their own "material," even in the work that launched him and the Academy of Fisticuffs to fame: his *On Crimes and Punishments.*[21]

So far historians have tended to put the blame for the rupture on Beccaria's shoulders, plausibly because the voluminousness of the Verri correspondence weighs so heavily on the scales of historical analysis. Morellet's reminiscence that what ultimately sent Beccaria home was Alessandro's success adds a further layer of complexity to the story and to the quarreling personalities. That said, other factors were involved as well, particularly if one for a moment takes Beccaria's longing for his family seriously. It can hardly have helped, for example, that Beccaria's wife, Teresa, was involved in a lengthy relationship with his friend Bartolomeo Calderara, one that would leave her pregnant embarrassingly long before his return, or that one of her other lovers was Pietro and Alessandro Verri's younger brother Carlo, or that Beccaria's first child Giulia most probably was the fruit of Teresa's well-known affair with Pietro Verri himself. Tellingly, at the time when he orchestrated the rapprochement between Beccaria and his parents, Pietro Verri had been shocked by how long Teresa had been left "intact" by her husband. Now, however, he was the long-term escort, or *cicisbeo,* of Beccaria's much younger sister Maddalena, of whom Teresa for this reason was jealous. That Giulia in turn would give birth to the great writer Alessandro Manzoni in 1785 through an affair with Giovanni Verri, the younger brother of Pietro, Alessandro, and Carlo (making Pietro both uncle and grandfather to Alessandro Manzoni), may shed little light on Beccaria's issues at the time of his abortive journey to Paris, but it certainly explains important elements of Manzoni's own masterwork *I promessi sposi,* or *The Betrothed,* one of the truly canonical works of Italian literature. Indeed, it would be Pietro who, in light of Giulia's inopportune pregnancy, negotiated her marriage to Pietro Manzoni, an erudite nobleman from the Lombard city of Lecco. Beccaria was fully aware of being cuckolded all these years, and particularly pained by the public nature of Teresa and Maddalena's rivalry for the attentions of his former friend. Neither can it have escaped him entirely that, as Carlo Capra has demonstrated, Pietro Verri at one time or another had "more than friendly relations" with every single woman involved with the Academy of Fisticuffs, including even his own young aunt Antonia Barbiano di Belgioioso. Never mind that Verri later would rage against those "who, with the hypocritical appearance of friendship and good manners, seduced the wives of others and violated the trust of the bridal chamber."[22] Beccaria's jealousy was, in short, well grounded, and Michael O'Brien was right to warn us against cleanly separating affairs of "the heart" from those of "the head" in intellectual history.[23]

A few months after Beccaria's return to Milan, Pietro Verri worried that Beccaria's "gossip" of a wife might bring about a situation in which he would be "characterized as the author of domestic dissensions," and indeed we soon find him lamenting rumors that he had "simulated friendship" with Beccaria "only to fuck [*chiavare*] his wife." Verri's meek defense was that he had "showed

Giulia Beccaria (1762–1841) with her Son Alessandro Manzoni (1785–1873). [Andrea Appiani?], *Portrait of Giulia Beccaria and her Son Alessandro Manzoni as a Child*, ca. 1790.

proofs of friendship" toward Beccaria even after "terminating all correspondence with the nymph," but he showed little remorse, in his vast epistolary, for his numerous, often potentially compromising affairs.[24] Pietro Verri was about twice Teresa's age during their tryst, and the variety, and frequency, of his conquests testified to his continuing willingness to translate his rather radical moral philosophy into practical libertinism. The point here is not to moralize, but it remains that the intellectual life of the pugilists must have been influenced not merely by caffeine-based tropismatic mechanisms but also by the complex, competitive, and at times literally incestuous sexual relations of its members.[25] Animated and impulsive, their thoughts and actions soon exploded the imagined community they so alacritously had established.[26]

Sexual and literary rivalries invariably intermingled to poison their relationship, with Pietro Verri deeply upset that on his return to Milan Beccaria spent his time with his wife, rather than with him, and that he did not utter a syllable to suggest "that anyone in Paris knows I exist in this world." The crux of the matter soon made itself evident in the Verri brothers' correspondence. Wrote Pietro, *"Europe has declared that he is greater than me; my heart declares the very opposite."*[27] And it was Beccaria who was to blame, for, having usurped authorship of the *Reply* to Facchinei, he had proven himself "enemy of my glory, wishing me to be his satellite."[28] Unable to compete with Beccaria's fame abroad, the two brothers focused their jealousy on Milan, with Pietro assuring Alessandro in May 1767, "I do not believe that there is any young Milanese who presently enjoys as much esteem and favorable public opinion as you do; compared to you, Beccaria is a zero in the general estimation."[29] The two brothers subsequently doubted the reasons for Beccaria's wish to leave Paris early, at first refusing to believe that he returned home simply because he missed his wife. When Alessandro Verri spread calumnious rumors that "Beccaria was unable to service his wife more than twice a week at most" because he was "fat and big, like a castrato," Pietro Verri replied that "it seems impossible that a man who leaves a young wife intact for months and months is in love with her." What really, they said, had brought Beccaria home, admittedly somewhat at odds with his supposedly glorious reception in Paris, not to mention their own obsession with local recognition in Milan, was simply his "pusillanimous *milaneseria*," a local variety of "campanilismo," or Milanese provincialism, and also possibly an insult based on a whole set of stereotypes of the Milanese, including pettiness, gaudiness, and ostentation.[30] It is therefore interesting that Milanese high society seemed not to react as negatively to Beccaria's return as the brothers would have liked, and Alessandro himself wondered whether it could be "possible that the Milanese do not make any malicious reflections around our friend's return," adding that "I expect all kinds of them, and of the most bestial."[31]

More recently it has been suggested, based on Verri's character assassinations as well as the leniency toward homosexuals in On Crimes and Punishments, that Beccaria may have been gay or had homosexual experiences, but whatever his sexual inclinations and practices were, the intense emotional fallout from the group's rupture at the very least suggests the presence of intense homosocial bonds, sensitivities, and rivalry.[32] As Pietro Verri had written to his "brothers" Alessandro and Beccaria when they first left for Paris, "fuck [cazzo], I am almost a sodomite with the two of you."[33] Over time, of course, Beccaria became the proverbial third wheel of this relationship, and we find Alessandro writing to his brother Pietro that "you are my wife, and I am like those who cannot fu[ck] [chiav . . .] anyone but their wife."[34] From daily meetings before leaving for Paris, Beccaria and Verri began seeing each other weekly, then, eventually, only haphazardly or if forced to. Symbolic of their personal and intellectual breakup, upon his return from Paris Beccaria gradually began frequenting the Caffè dei Borsinari, at the opposite end of the Piazza del Duomo relative to the Caffè del Greco, which had hosted the Academy of Fisticuffs, and then, much to Verri's sarcastic delight, the Caffè Mazza, famous for its games rather than its cerebral debates.[35]

Whatever the complex causes of their falling out, a rapprochement between Verri and Beccaria only occurred in the wake of Teresa's slow and tragic death, from syphilis, tuberculosis, or both, in 1774.[36] Beccaria could not "resist without support," Verri wrote in the aftermath of Teresa's passing, adding that "six months will not pass before we see him remarried."[37] Indeed, Beccaria married Countess Anna Barbò so scandalously soon after Teresa's death that he was inclined to still wear black in mourning at his own wedding. Beccaria's second wife was a dear friend of Verri's late sister's daughter Maria Castiglioni, an orphan who had grown up in Pietro's household and whom Pietro had married in 1773, and their closeness brought the two former pugilists closer together again and helped normalize their relationship somewhat.[38] By that time, however, Verri felt Beccaria had become a mere shade of his former self, "more timid" than "any woman," and neither the carnal (for lack of a better word) nor the intellectual rival he once had been.[39]

A Second, Equal Book

In spite of their obsessive ire, the Verri brothers eventually sought to avoid making their polemic with Beccaria too public. Their reason for this reveals a great deal about their wounded prides and relative sense of their importance in the European Enlightenment. As discussed at length in their epistolary, they sincerely worried about making "another scene, like that between Hume and Rousseau," a reference to the perhaps strangest and certainly most famous public quarrel between intellectuals in eighteenth-century Europe. Having been offered asylum and support by Hume in Britain, Rousseau subsequently convinced himself that his host actually had been plotting his downfall all along, initiating a row that brought out the worst in both parties. That the members of the Academy of Fisticuffs compared themselves to luminaries like David Hume and Jean-Jacques Rousseau may have been quaint, bordering even on the delusional from a historiographical perspective, but it is telling with regard to how they conceived of their own and Milan's place at the time, not to mention what they believed was at stake in the *affare Beccaria*.[40] Pietro Verri even confronted Beccaria himself with the famous quarrel, and, not surprisingly, they disagreed on who the guilty party was, Verri siding with Rousseau and Beccaria with Hume.[41] And so, without making their attacks on Beccaria too explicit, the Verri brothers did what they could to harm his standing in the Italian republic of letters.

Principally this involved undermining Beccaria's authorship of *On Crimes and Punishments,* summarized in the caustic statement by the jurist and political economist Giovan Battista Freganeschi that "what good there is in it is not his," while "what there is of his is not good."[42] Extraordinarily, however, the Verri brothers themselves eventually went to some length looking for the textual sources of *On Crimes and Punishments,* in everything from Seneca to Pufendorf and Rousseau. Privately, in other words, they knew that, though they had provided an important impetus to *On Crimes and Punishments,* Beccaria himself had done more research than they liked to admit. And even they had to acknowledge that "the eloquence in it is Beccaria's."[43] Yet they maintained that he ultimately would have to write a *"second, equal book"* to prove his merit.[44] Beccaria himself had foreshadowed this when he first had sought to cut his time in Paris short. In response to Alessandro's warning that "public opinion" would ridicule him, Beccaria had replied that he "did not care about it, and that he would have written another work to shut everyone up," because "the most important thing is to live well."[45] Between 1764 and 1770, he therefore began planning two major works which he considered to be interrelated. One, which he eventually would publish to little acclaim in 1771, built on one of his articles in *Il Caffè* and was entitled *Ricerche intorno alla natura dello stile*, or *Studies Concerning the Nature of Style*.[46] It was a philosophical inquiry into the *belles lettres*—which he strikingly felt the need to justify for its hidden relation to his work on penal reform and political economy—that concluded with musings on the aesthetics of human sociability, the societal origins of justice, and mankind's progression from the "adolescence of all nations."[47] Now he argued that "morality, politics, fine arts, which are the sciences of the good, the useful, and the beautiful, are sciences that enjoy a greater proximity, or rather a broader identity of principles, than one might imagine: these sciences all derive from a single, primitive science, that is the science of man."[48]

A few decades later, European thinkers would similarly turn to the great problem of "social science," but Beccaria himself would never spell out these relations further. Perhaps he would have, had he been able to complete his other major project, which in many ways was the planned culmination of all his disparate interests, entitled *Il ripulimento delle nazioni*, or *The Refinement of Nations*. Originally referred to simply as a work on "legislation," which he apparently already had discussed with the *philosophes* of Paris and which his editor in Livorno had been expecting since the spring of 1765, the final title circulated among the literati of Europe by the summer of the following year.[49] It was intended as a sustained study of the history of human progress and civilization, for which Beccaria began amassing a specialized library of universal history, travel literature, and moral philosophy, ranging from Diodorus Siculus through Adam Smith's *Theory of Moral Sentiments* to the Tübingen naturalist Johann Georg Gmelin's *Voyage through Siberia*.[50] Yet Beccaria eventually abandoned the project, leaving only assorted manuscripts, in favor of university lectures and policy work. Between his lectures and his fragmentary writings, however, one can also sketch his unfulfilled vision of the history of human sociability, of the increasing power of commerce in the world, and, indeed, the means—however hard fought—of expanding them ever further, of socializing the relations not merely between *people* but between *peoples*.

Not surprisingly, Beccaria's numerous preparatory notes for *The Refinement of Nations* echoed his recurring preoccupations, such as the threat posed by too extreme degrees of economic "inequality," the need for jurisprudence to prevent the "disamalgamation of private and public interests," the necessary transformation of "customs" through different social "stages."[51] These ideas reappeared also in longer fragments he penned on the history of barbarism and on mores and customs, and particularly regarding the problem of *"too great an inequality of goods"* in society and how mankind slowly had progressed out of a past dominated by "the law of fear and slavery."[52] There was no doubt in Beccaria's mind that, building on the mechanistic moral philosophy nurtured in the Academy of Fisticuffs, human beings were "animals," deeply "material" in nature, who reacted to a complex web of pleasures and pains. Pleasure and pain, however, operated with different horizons of influence. "The immediate moving cause of actions is the flight from pain, the ultimate cause is the love of pleasure: the customs of a country are therefore determined more by the ills that grip it than by the good it enjoys or expects."[53] Pain, of course, as he had explored at length in *On Crimes and Punishments,* provided lessons, and civilization emerged through hardship. But now he began to reinterpret his conjectural narrative of social development in light of prescriptions drawn from his utilitarian moral philosophy. "Painful sentiments are necessary to men, and they are necessary to nations, a sad but evident necessity," he wrote, now seeming to agree with Facchinei's argument regarding the salutary consequences of the "wolf's bite," "but the minimum ills necessary to a nation must, as far as possible, be equally divided, much like the maximum happiness."[54] Much like he aimed for a certain egalitarianism of material welfare, Beccaria theorized that there should be a similar egalitarianism sensationalistically with regard to pleasures and pains. He concluded, though, that "the wisdom of nations is almost always the fruit of their past unhappiness."[55]

In one of the longer surviving fragments of *The Refinement of Nations,* entitled "Thoughts on the Barbarism and Culture of Nations and the Savage State of Man," Beccaria had suggested a conceptual matrix for analyzing nations at all stages of their historical development. On one axis he proposed a spectrum stretching from barbarism to culture, a measure of a nation's "ignorance of things that are useful to it" and the best "means" of achieving "individual happiness." The other axis stretched from savagery to sociability, gauging the degree of a nation's distance "from the greatest union that can exist between men, and from the greatest absolute happiness possible divided among the greatest possible number." A nation, Beccaria concluded, "can be savage and barbarian, it can be savage and nonbarbarian, it can be very barbarian and very sociable at the same time."[56] Like Rousseau, he identified the engine of social development in individual needs, but he rejected the notion that social developments could be somehow "unnatural," not to mention that the "progress" of civilization by necessity was an unhappy one.[57] "All man's sentiments, in any state he finds himself, are always natural," Beccaria underscored, doubtlessly drawing on the mechanistic physiology and moral philosophy he had helped develop in the Academy of Fisticuffs; as needs and sociability developed hand in hand, man's wants increased alongside his capacity to satisfy them. Socialized men changed over time, leading in turn to a "change" in the "nature of sociability itself," and its causes, as societies had expanded from the earliest villages to the states system of early modern Europe. "Sociability," in short, took different forms in tiny prehistoric villages and in the expanding commercial societies of contemporary Europe. An important corollary of this dynamism affected the character of legislation and political economy alike, which, far from being written in stone (literally, for some), had to be endlessly dynamic and adaptive to changing circumstances.[58] Indeed, justice depended on it:

> The moral philosopher sees the present advantages, the progress of
> the science of living happily, and finds them [to be the] effects of an-
> cient disorders, and dares to prophecy that today's evils are necessary
> movements and agitations, after which the peoples [of the world] will
> move back to a final, very remote state of equality and happiness.[59]

Again, juxtaposition with Rousseau can shed light on Beccaria's larger project. Rousseau had argued in The Social Contract that a hypothetical coastal country of "nothing but nearly inaccessible rocks" should "remain barbarous and fish-eaters," and that by so doing its people would "live the more tranquil for it, perhaps the better, and certainly the happier."[60] And even if one accepted the theorem that man was "naturally wicked," which, for the record, he did not, the polemical Genevan admitted that "some good might happen to come of the sciences at their hands; but it is perfectly certain that they will lead to far

more harm: Madmen should not be given weapons."[61] Beccaria instead
thought the greatest happiness was yet to come, and that it was only through
the arming of humanity—however madcap—with the arts and sciences
that it could be achieved. Where Rousseau's political project came to revolve
around damage control in the wake of civilization and the end of the halcyon state of nature, Beccaria's unwritten *Refinement of Nations* would have
carried a very different practical payload; it would have suggested legislation,
political economy, and in any case what critics called "socialism," as a means
of explaining and continuing the history of man's changing and expanding
socialization, to reclaim lasting "equality and happiness" in a civilized,
peaceful, and technological world.

Many of the preoccupations that had animated Beccaria's earliest writings would continue to inspire his more mature notes, including the dangers
of economic inequality in a polity and the "fatal" yet valuable nature of private property itself, but he would never spell out the full spectrum of his
ideas, nor the complex role he saw for private property in the history of human
progress. His continuing admonitions to his students, however, indicate that
his book would have taken Enlightenment debates far from where many of
his contemporaries in Scotland were, and that his ideal of commercial society
was based on very different foundations. "Property," he reminded his audience, "is the first-born daughter of society, not its mother."[62] But as fate would
have it, and much to the satisfaction of the Verri brothers, Beccaria's project
for *The Refinement of Nations* never reached fruition. Overcome by practical
duties, which plausibly also were a convenient excuse, Beccaria would instead
channel his reformist impulse into his university lectures and practical work
for the Habsburg administration. Schumpeter's previously mentioned verdict was that "Beccaria, almost certainly more richly endowed by nature,
gave to the public service of the Milanese 'state' what A[dam] Smith reserved for mankind."[63] There is much going for this. But his failure to live
up to the expectations set up by *On Crimes and Punishments* remained a personal as well as a professional tragedy, and rumor continued to have it that
he had not even authored *On Crimes and Punishments*.[64] As Morellet noted
forlornly in his *Memoirs*, once Beccaria "returned to Milan, he did little, and
his end did not reflect his debut."[65]

Yet just as Beccaria's concept of regulation and public policy was a "seamless web" encompassing all of human life from penal law to international
trade, so the various aspects of his life's work—both published and unpub-

lished, contemplative and active—were expressions of a central preoccupation with the enigma of human sociability—with the art, broadly speaking,
of managing the worldly affairs of mankind. As it happened, he "did" quite a
lot, only in ways that were easy for contemporaries—and historiography—to
overlook. Rousseau had been an uneasy guide for Beccaria's early writing,
but his *Social Contract* had concluded bluntly, with a frank admission of his
work's partial nature:

> After setting down the true principles of political right and trying
> to found the State on its basis, it would remain to buttress the State
> by its external relations; which would include the right of nations,
> commerce, the right of war and conquests, public right, leagues, ne-
> gotiations, treaties, etc. But all this forms a new object too vast for
> my short sight; I should always have fixed it nearer to myself.[66]

The Genevan would of course return explicitly to questions of international
relations of conquest and commerce in his *Considerations on the Government
of Poland* (1772), but by that time the vast gulf separating his project from
Beccaria's would be evident to all.[67] Though Beccaria never published a
second, equal work of theory, his efforts in the sphere of pedagogy and practice turned to the very same questions.

For, although his star was ascendant, Beccaria did not capitalize on his
success or build on his momentum. As "the defender, the protector of the
human species" and particularly of individual rights, increasingly became
the talk of the European world, and *On Crimes and Punishments* met with "universal applause," he consciously seemed to retreat from the proverbial lime-
light.[68] It was not that he lacked options. Thanking him for having "paved
the way for equality," Voltaire hoped Beccaria would visit, and Catherine the
Great herself even invited him to St. Petersburg to help write the new Russian legal code, potentially elevating him to the very highest echelons of intellectual fame.[69] But it was not to be. Beccaria began the paperwork needed
to undertake the long journey, but was still troubled by the consequences of
his sojourn in Paris, and so were his acquaintances at the very idea of him
embarking on another voyage. D'Alembert wrote to him, "It is said that
you think seriously about traveling to Russia; I do not know what your
reasons may be, but I beg you, my friend, to think again." Morellet was
even more blunt: "I do not understand."[70] Soon enough, the project fell
apart, the Verri brothers exulted in the news that Beccaria's voyage would

not happen, and correspondents noted that "the *gazettes* are silent regarding your voyage to St. Petersburg."[71] As part of the process of making his decision with regard to Catherine the Great's offer, Beccaria let it be known to Firmian and Kaunitz that he would have preferred an appointment at home, and, more than happy to help this Lombard national treasure enlighten his homeland, they soon found suitable employment for him teaching "Public Economy" in Milan. Catherine the Great, on her end, settled with the encyclopedist Denis Diderot.[72]

What's in a Name?

Habsburg influences in Milan might initially have ensured that Beccaria's chair was devoted to "Cameral Sciences, or Civil Economy," drawing also on a preponderantly Germanic tradition of academic state administration and political economy that embraced auxiliary disciplines such as mining and forestry. Forged in the horrors of the Thirty Years' War, cameralism originally emerged as an administrative practice for managing the small and medium-sized lands of Central and Northern Europe and maximizing their resources in a context of intense international competition. With time, however, it would become influential across Europe.[73] Carli, head of the Supreme Economic Council of the Duchy of Milan at the time of Beccaria's appointment, defined the aims of "The Cameral Science, or Civil Economy" in the spirit of the Fisticuffs as "researching, proportionally to the situation, quality, products, and customs of nations, the safest and easiest way of extending the greatest good possible over the greatest possible number of men." Although its name remained in flux, then, the discipline's purpose of universal material melioration, expressed in a mathematical language of proportionality and informed by a humanist contextual awareness, was clear. An undated manuscript note ostensibly in Beccaria's hand similarly defined "cameralism" as "that part of Legislation, and of Politics, that serves to increase the opulence of the subjects and of the state, and teaches the most proper and useful administration of the income of the Public and of the Sovereign."[74] In an official dispatch to the Duke of Modena, Maria Theresa of Austria described Beccaria's teaching as being devoted to "the theory of the cameral and economic objects of good Government," while Beccaria's Latin nomination diploma stated he was to teach "Oeconomia politica."[75] Yet in light of his actual lectures on "cameralism," Joseph von Sperges, secretary of the Italian Department in Vienna, suggested to Beccaria that he should reconsider the title of his endeavor:

> The sciences which you teach are not merely cameralist, though indirectly they are all beneficial to the public treasury; but they must no less serve to increase private fortunes, than bring advantage to communities, embracing, beyond the police [as in regulation and public policy] relative to the cultivation and conservations of the arts, also agriculture, commerce, the tilling of land, and so on . . . the denomination of science of public economy might perhaps suit the subject better.[76]

Cameralism, in von Sperges's understanding, was strictly limited to the economy of the polity, whereas Beccaria's lectures were devoted to the political economy in its entirety, a key to that nexus which he had called "the true relations between sovereigns and their subjects and among different nations" in *On Crimes and Punishments*.[77] Kaunitz himself, whose vast epistolary awareness of affairs in the Habsburg Empire and ability to make remarkably informed interventions were extraordinary, unproblematically equated "cameral sciences" with "the sciences of Finance, Commerce, etc." In a striking letter to Firmian of December 5, 1768, he wrote of the "subjects of Cameral and public economy," thus differentiating between the economy of the State as such and of its concomitant public, though the two—in effect, the public and the private spheres of the state—were intrinsically related, their study and promulgation institutionally and disciplinarily united. According to an official document, the subject matter of cameralism was rather an "art" than a "science," eminently "practical" in nature, and the instructor was to avoid "metaphysical abstractions," which Beccaria agreed were "useless." Ultimately Beccaria was to teach "the political science of the economy and of commerce," and the course of study was made obligatory for civil servants who wished to enter related fields.[78]

It is worth noting, however, that whatever one called the field of "political economy" at the time, understood as a holistic "science" of economic life, it increasingly came to be considered essential not only for bureaucrats and reformers, but also for, and by, business practitioners themselves. Paolo Greppi, for example, a young heir to a Milanese mercantile dynasty who was well acquainted with Beccaria's work, would travel to Madrid in 1777 hoping to learn there a different take on "Commerce," which was distinct from "commerce" and which he defined as a "subject of useful speculation" covering everything from bookkeeping to banking and domestic development in terms of theories of active and passive trades. He reported back to his father, however, only about the lack of theoretical and practical sophistication among Spanish businessmen and their inability to see beyond the "so tiny sphere" of their own distinct trades, precisely the sort of myopia Kaunitz, Carli, and Beccaria sought to vanquish through the Milanese chair in political economy.[79]

If the semantic confusion regarding what exactly to call the subject matter of Beccaria's teaching partly was a reflection of its novelty, nobody doubted its importance. Kaunitz was adamant that a university chair in these related disciplines was "one of the most important and useful to the country," probably meaning the Milanese State in Lombardy, given that the great cameralist, *Illuminati* leader, and Mozart patron Joseph von Sonnenfels already occupied such a chair in Vienna. Indeed, Kaunitz had hoped that the right candidate could be groomed for the job domestically, and that local Milanese could thus be given "room to develop their talents, and to be able to inspire in others maxims that were healthy and corresponding to the genius and spirit of this century in imitation of the most cultured nations."[80] Beccaria's decision not to go to Russia was, as such, a timely turn of events.

Curricular Emulation

From the outset, Beccaria's chair would emulate not only foreign institutions but also foreign curricula. Suggesting the work of Genovesi and Forbonnais as textbooks, Beccaria's old friend Carli, who was rising to ever higher levels in the Habsburg administration, furthermore followed the Neapolitans in highlighting the importance of widespread dissemination through teaching in the vernacular as well as the cardinal role of "history" for appreciating the vicissitudes of political economy.[81] Indeed, Genovesi's student Troiano Odazi, eventually his successor at the Neapolitan chair of political economy, would edit a 1768 Milanese edition of his mentor's *Lezioni di commercio ossia di economia civile* (Lectures on commerce, or rather of civil economics) and, tellingly, dedicate it to Carli himself, before befriending Beccaria in person.[82] As Beccaria put it in his own plan for the course, "the sterility of Latin" was to be abandoned to "make enlightenment more

common."[83] His broader curriculum was, tellingly at a time when Physiocracy supposedly conquered the hearts and minds of Europe, of a distinctly
Antiphysiocratic orientation. This, of course, did not mean that Beccaria
was somehow hostile to agriculture. Instead, he followed the well-worn
trope of emphasizing its importance for economic development, particularly higher-end refined products that foreigners had failed to emulate, such
as cheeses, cured meats, and of course wines.[84] Yet like the vast majority of
Italian political economists at the time, he was a vocal proponent of manufacturing, also for its empowering consequences for the agricultural sector,
a synergy he, again rather typically, associated with the "English" model.[85]

The same earlier best-sellers that had informed Verri's first ventures in political economy—and that still influenced his insistence on industrial development and the "construction of machines" late in life—now inspired Beccaria's
teaching, and he praised not only Colbert's industrial policies but also theoretical works by authors such as Ustáriz, Ulloa, Hume, and Genovesi.[86] Beccaria's
plan for his course drew heavily on Genovesi's influential meditation on the
English model, particularly in relation to the developmental importance of
manufacturing and the historical lessons of Italy's relative decline at the end of
the Renaissance. But his curriculum was also greatly indebted to an author with
whom Verri had engaged less, if at all—namely, the Paris-based Irish banker
Richard Cantillon, whose *Essay on the Nature of Trade in General* recently had
been translated in Venice.[87]

One of the most adventurous writers of the eighteenth century, Cantillon
made a fortune speculating under John Law's infamous scheme in the early
eighteenth century before penning one of the most sophisticated works of
economic theorizing of his age—most famously conceptualizing the role of
an "undertaker" or *entrepreneur* for the first time—and, finally, perhaps,
forging his own death in a murderous fire, replete with loyal witnesses and
an unrecognizable corpse, before escaping to the distant jungles of Dutch
Surinam. Whatever great mysteries remain regarding Cantillon's life, however, his *Essay* would circulate in manuscript form for decades, being plagiarized at great length in the British merchant and pamphleteer Malachy
Postlethwayte's 1751 publication *Universal Dictionary of Trade and Commerce* (itself a creative translation of French Inspector General of the Manufactures
Jacques Savary, whom Verri's father had encouraged him to read when he
first set out to study the subject) before finally being published in French

translation by the group surrounding Gournay in Paris and, from there, rapidly becoming a mainstay of Enlightenment political economy.[88] And it was a fitting work for Beccaria to draw upon.

To be clear, they did not agree on many fundamental questions. Cantillon, for example, insisted that "it is not easy to conceive how a Society of men can be formed" where "the Land belongs to no one in particular," while Beccaria had a far more cautious stance with regard to the primacy of private property in societal development (and particularly the question of which came first, property or society). That said, the majority of the *Essay* resonated profoundly with the preoccupations of the Academy of Fisticuffs, and Beccaria's in particular.[89] For one thing, Cantillon provided one of the most holistic analyses available at the time of the territorialization of commercial societies and the complex relations among individuals, rural villages, market towns, cities, capitals, and the international system. He furthermore emphasized the crucial role of infrastructure in shaping economic linkages across time and space; the centrality of risk-taking individual "entrepreneurs" in a society that was commercialized to the point where individuals became "consumers and customers one in regard to the other"; the importance of manufacturing and foreign trade; the danger of a "State" becoming "the dupe of another in Trade"; and the need for "regulation" to ensure that a polity exported industrial products and imported raw materials rather than the other way around.[90] Cantillon's brief *Essay*, in short, offered Beccaria a framework for theorizing about governmental interventions to encourage societal goals—based, needless to say much to his liking, on the foundations laid by the lives and times of individuals.[91]

Methodologically, Beccaria furthermore looked back to Genovesi's earlier chair in "Commerce and Mechanics" at the University in Naples by drawing, very much in line with Carli's proposal, on insights from fields of knowledge that today often are considered opposed in the imagination of economics—"history" and "physics."[92] Yet he eventually went far further than his Neapolitan colleague in both. Not only did his historical method play out in real archival research and an insistence on codifying "experience," but his choice to base political and economic investigations on the rigor and results of the natural sciences resulted even in algebraic formulations. The two pillars of his political economy both empowered and constrained each other, and so Beccaria was all too aware both of the difficulties of applying dogmas in different historical contexts, particularly foreign dogmas, and of the dangerous limitations to the "arithmetic precision" of his discipline. "Political arithmetic" was the means to "render useful and applicable the theories of the economic science," but it was entirely dependent on a deep, contextual understanding of the problem at hand.[93] Hence, and very much following cameralist creed, Beccaria stressed the "necessity and utmost importance of having an exact anatomy of all the minute fibers of the body politic."[94] Nature, which Beccaria liked to describe in a physical language of "forces and momentum," might tend toward "equilibria" on some high level of abstraction, but this was a remarkably fragile process that demanded perpetual adjustments and an awareness of "proportionality" in economic policy, no less than in crimes and punishments.[95]

Though Beccaria's lectures were predominantly earthly in orientation, there were moments when they addressed more empyrean matters. Like Facchinei, for example, Beccaria now also noted the role of Providence in shaping his subject matter, but with diametrically opposite results. Far from absolving mankind of control over their lives, Beccaria's invocation of Providence in his lectures served to prove that "what we call eventuality and fortune are subject to constant rules" fixed "by the eternal order and by the supreme providence of a regulating God."[96] It was a simultaneously empowering and terrifying thought. God might have set the cosmic clockwork of creation in motion, but it did not prescribe social order; humanity's successes, and failures, were its own. Similarly, Beccaria liked to rhetorically promote political economy as a science of "liberty," a term he never seems to have defined more explicitly, and as an exercise in "removing obstacles" to progress. As such, he argued that "restrictions must never be placed on liberty for the love of perfection, but only for the exigencies of necessity."[97] Yet, as his course made clear, said exigencies were never ending.

Forests and Trees

Beccaria may never have published his more mature thoughts, but it is evident from his university lectures, delivered for the first time in 1769, that he continued to elaborate on his earlier theories for several years, focusing his thoughts on the nature of legislation in society. More particularly, he deployed many of his earlier concepts and preoccupations, ranging from the

nature of the social contract to the challenges posed by the incongruity between states and markets, to shape his evolving theory of political economy.
Recasting his earlier praise of legislators, for example, he now called for "supreme directors," who with "arms and laws steer the internal operations of
society, defend it against external assaults, and excite movement and activity
in the quotidian indolence of men." The "multitude," the "people," had to "fur-
nish" these "directors" with the "means" to do so in the form of *"tributes,"*
or taxes. Just as men in the state of nature gave up a part of their liberty to
empower sovereignty with the capacity to safeguard them, so they gave up
a part of their material resources to similarly empower "directors" to structure, defend, and invigorate commercial societies. Human welfare in its entirety depended on successful *police*—public policy—a noble endeavor ever
at odds with "the limits of human capacity and the inexorable law of pain."[98]

The directors' role was simply to direct and channel the work of the polity's
citizens, for "the wealth of states only really emerges from the labor of individuals."[99] Not all labor was the same, however; some activities were more
conducive to economic development than others, and the role of directors
was therefore cardinal in perfecting development.[100] In an ideal world, Beccaria
was clear, "absolute liberty" should be the aim of political economy, or rather
what he referred to as the "nonsystem" of laissez-faire peddled by certain
economic theorists. In real life, however, there were endless geographical,
political, and economic complications to consider, not to mention humanity's
inherently criminal nature. "Partisans of liberty" stressed the "difficulty of
fixing limits of annual consumption," preferring dogmatic absolutes to the
dangers of purposeful action in the economy. Beccaria instead embraced the
challenge of vigilantly and relentlessly tailoring economic policies to endlessly changing conditions set out in his plan for the course. Legislators *could*
style the economic architectures of their polities, and some industries—
particularly high-value-added manufactures—deserved the "attention of
political economists," who ideally should "encourage" certain industries and
also "slow down ruinous commerce."[101] But to encourage industrial activities, he remained true to the Academy of Fisticuffs by preferring tariffs, premiums, and subsidies to outright prohibitions.[102] The real difficulty, however, lay not in successfully pursuing economic policies but instead in aligning
domestic economic needs with the ideals of international sociability.

Building on the world of *Il Caffè,* the language Beccaria adopted in his
lectures to describe the anarchic world of international trade was far from

peaceful. A variety of economic activities as wide as possible, he argued, would be a useful defense against the "reciprocal obstacles that nations impose on each other in the always spirited war of industry and of profit."[103] Legislation revolved around encouraging "the entire chain of economic affairs and actions of the state."[104] But these great chains of national affairs and activities were in turn intertwined through the inexorable incongruence between states and markets that characterized the early modern world. *"The political borders of a state are not always or almost never the same as its economic borders,"* Beccaria observed, and countries, *"however divided by sovereignty and mutually independent with respect to their political laws,"* were thus *"really a single nation strictly united by physical laws and dependent one on the other through their economic relations."*[105] What, precisely, did he have in mind?

Though Beccaria did not provide this specific example, he may well have thought of a case like that of the Alpine village of Juf, or the Swiss Cantons of Ticino and Grisons more generally—regions that, though politically separate from Northern Italy, had been intrinsically bound to it economically for centuries.[106] Though passes like Splügen, St. Bernard, and increasingly St. Gotthard became the corridors of choice for Northern European trade with Lombardy, a number of other passes allowed for smaller Alpine outposts to connect with the Northern Italian cities directly. The inhabitants of Juf, for example, in the Grisons, during the summers had traditionally raised cattle, which were taken for sale in Milan across the now-overgrown Septimer Pass (elevation 2,310 meters), on top of which a hostel remained open until 1778. Though an important aspect of their economic identity thus was Lombard, politically they were resolutely Swiss, and therefore large parts of their trade—which because of its location and trajectory was dastardly for state authorities to observe, regulate, and tax—risked being contraband by default.[107] These were living examples of the challenges posed by the fundamental incongruity between states and markets in early modern Europe, for "the division of nations" was, Beccaria emphasized, "factitious and not established by the nature of things."[108]

In this, Beccaria was partially at odds with his former mentor Pietro Verri. The latter's *Meditations on Political Economy* (1771), originally published by Aubert in Livorno, had quickly been republished with anonymous critical annotations by Pasquale in Venice, then the city's largest publisher.[109] It had, however, soon become clear that the author of the annotations was the old Fisticuffs member Carli, who also had written *The Stercoral Economy* discussed

in Chapter 3, and was now Beccaria's friend and Verri's superior as president
of the Supreme Council of the Economy. In line with his insistence on territorializing a state's economy, Verri had originally presented a maxim to
the effect that in order to ensure "internal circulation," one should "never
place taxes in such a way that they directly increase the costs of transportation from one place to another in the State."[110] Carli's lengthy reply to this
point reflected his principal critique of Verri—namely, that either "the speed
of his flight in such a vast and complicated Science has not permitted him, or
he disdained to turn his eyes to the variety of objects, and to the multitude of
perspectives, which reveal themselves to slower and more timid minds."[111]
With regard to the internal circulation of a state, the more timid Carli observed, a city might well be located near the borders of another state, which
meant transportation costs became a crucial factor in the economic territorialization of polities.

> It is usually admitted as an Axiom of good Political Economy that
> tariffs should be at the borders in order not to disturb internal cir-
> culation: but one should also distinguish between Political and
> Economic Borders. Political Borders are those which are set by the
> events of wars, by treaties of Peace, by the succession of Sovereigns;
> but Economic Borders depend on local situations of provinces more
> or less favorable toward Commerce, Agriculture, the Arts . . . which
> will vary as the relations between classes of Proprietors, Producers,
> the Industrious, etc. change.[112]

As a consequence of this, spatial considerations within a state had to inform
taxation practices to a greater extent than suggested by Verri. Large cities
near borders to other states, for example, could well have "Economic Borders" that diverged greatly from their "Political Borders," and real attempts
at territorializing the economy of a state had to take account of this.[113] Verri
replied to this critique in the so-called sixth edition of 1772, from which
Carli's annotations were absent, inserting the following paragraph in a later
section of the book devoted to "taxes on goods":

> Everyone will understand what a *border* is. Imagination sometimes
> creates words before the ideas for them exist, and *political* borders
> are distinguished from *economic* borders, much like between *arith-*

metic balances and *economic* balances, etc. It is easier for the human
mind to have borders than for commerce, the *economic* borders of
which are the entire globe, assuming it is free.[114]

The first part of the paragraph was a reply to Carli's annotation regarding
taxes and borders, the second probably a reply to his annotation regarding
how to best calculate the balance of a state's trade. This went back to a long-
standing disagreement between the two authors, where Carli suggested
Verri had compiled an "arithmetic balance" simply summing up the value of
what crossed Milan's borders rather than a real "Economic Balance, which
shows the amount of raw materials that have entered and exited [the country],
and the corresponding manufactures."[115] More than simply focusing on trade,
in other words, Carli insisted with the young Verri on the importance of *what*
was traded. Readers familiar with the various editions of the *Meditations*
would immediately have seen the purpose of Verri's cryptic insertion (to underline that it was Carli's intellect rather than trade that had limits), but when
divorced from Carli's original annotations, the result was rather hermetic.

It would be easy to dismiss these differences as driven purely by personal
animosities, but they actually reveal substantial epistemological divergence
at the foundations of their respective conceptions of contemporary political
economy.[116] In a manuscript reply to one anonymous critic who violently had
attacked the "abstract[ion] and general principles" of the *Meditations,* and its
author's "little experience with rural economy" and "abstraction from practice," Verri complained that, "in examining a book that contains nothing but
general theories, the examiner has no other horizon but that of the State of
Milan."[117] That was, of course, the critic's very point. Verri had long been
drawn to elegant abstractions, while the erudite Carli refused to let go of the
tree for the sake of describing the forest; or, rather, argued that a meaningful
description of a forest demanded a more careful survey of its individual trees
present. The anonymous critic observed, "If it then happens that in some
cases such subsidies can be beneficial; why then believe that, in general, they
can give little real utility?" Why posit as an axiom something that had so
many exceptions? What was the point, he asked, of echoing an argument
made eloquently and at length by Neapolitan political economists such as
Genovesi and Galiani, of composing "a Code of Legislation that ultimately
will serve either the Kingdom of the Moon, or imaginary spaces?"[118] Truth

be told it was not an entirely fair verdict, for Verri wrote at length of the need to differentiate policies depending on changing circumstances and on the need for tariffs and interventions, yet generally speaking his *Meditations* were closer to Lloyd's formalism than, for example, Beccaria's lectures were, though Verri was a lesser mathematician than both.[119]

That Beccaria ultimately would side with Carli in his lectures might seem surprising, given the distinctly idealist and, in terms of the current metaphor, sylvan nature of *On Crimes and Punishments,* and could well represent an intellectual shift explainable also in terms of his personal alienation from Verri. Equally, it might reflect his disenchantment with abstract theory in the wake of his abandonment of *The Refinement of Nations* and subsequent embrace of university work and practical policy. Whatever his motives, the granularity of Beccaria's lectures on political economy clearly fell closer to the ideas of Carli, to whom ironically he had first been introduced by Verri, and to the pragmatist tradition of Neapolitan political economy (deeply respected by Carli) than to those of his former mentor.[120] Galiani might, in effect, be one of the most important albeit neglected influences on these debates. Whereas Carli engaged favorably and at length with Galiani's extraordinarily influential work against the doctrinaire assumptions of Physiocracy, and Beccaria had met him in person, Verri felt the need in 1780 to "apologize" for not even "having read the works of the abbot Galiani."[121]

Peace and Political Economy

In the end, though, the ultimate aims of Beccaria, Carli, and Verri may not have differed all that much, even in the wake of their falling out. Although there was nothing permanent or providential about the commercial competition of the Westphalian states system, and though he was more attuned to, or focused on, its details than the Verri of the *Meditations,* Beccaria's work, too, aimed at its gradual overcoming, at the slow socialization of the international sphere through political economy and what, for lack of a better term, can be called economic globalization. It was a coherent, if piecemeal, vision, but it could be interpreted rather differently. As one of Verri's several anonymous critics observed, "present-day commerce is truly reduced to a state of revolution, and of declared war between one nation and the other, all intent on forcing the impossible, and transcending those terms that, they do not realize, that supreme Providence has set on each for their reciprocal subsistence."[122] The spread of commerce, and the competitive policies that by default followed as polities sought to survive and thrive in a world economy of delimited states and limitless markets, had, in short, driven legislators to hubris—they thought they could empower their polities indefinitely. As a consequence, commerce did not bring peoples *together,* it split them apart: "The more one wishes to bring man closer to man, and city closer to city, the more they will separate, and every Nation will be reduced to living on its own [*a far casa da se*]."[123] The anonymous critic—who echoed many of Facchinei's preoccupations with the dangers of human arrogance—provided no suggestions for how to overcome this perennial tragedy of political economy, but whatever their differences, the Verris, Carlis, and Beccarias of Europe (and there were many of them) were united in their faith in mankind's *capacity* to transcend limits and the strictures of supposed Providence.

Beccaria himself was all too aware of the possible dark side of commercial expansion and competition, but his theory that progress came through hardship might have provided him with a conceptual foil against disillusionment. His emphasis on the importance of considering details and variations in political economy was related to his deep awareness of how chains of interconnectivity all too easily could become shackles of enslavement between people and in international relations, and he consistently emphasized that a cardinal task of legislation lay in negotiating that "spirited war of industry and profit" to avoid becoming "dependent" on other nations.[124] Trade remained war by other means, and though he in no way envisioned international trade as necessarily peaceable or even mutually beneficial, he did see it as uniquely offering a means of neutering the most violent forms of competition. Commerce was not a fail-safe means of achieving peace, but it *could* be conducive to it.

And in line with his historicist approach to political economy, the past—and particularly the tempestuous past of the Italian city-states—served as Beccaria's road map in realizing this ideal, just as it had for Verri and Franci. For example, he lectured to his students that after abandoning conquest with the ruins of Rome, the Italian peninsula had "turned its restless activity toward the peaceful but no less domineering [*signoreggianti*] arts, and if not with such quick success and with such despotic influence, at least with greater and more placid and less dangerous security."[125] For Beccaria as for many of his contemporaries, there continued to be a risk that trade would become an alternative form of imperialism. Because of his theory that productivities differed between economic activities, and that some—particularly advanced manufactures—were more conducive to development than others, he remained quite adamant that *someone* always gained in any exchange, in relative if not absolute terms. In domestic trade, the balance of gains and losses were contained within the polity, but in international interactions, differential gains could quickly achieve systemic importance. The "profits of external commerce" could be "to the advantage of the citizenry at the expense of the noncitizenry, so that the sum of value increases for the members of the state, without the loss of any members of the same state."[126] So how could trade contribute to peace and the expansion of human sociability?

Although it was evident that "up to a certain point a nation can prosper at the expense of another," Beccaria suggested that "beyond a certain point our true prosperity produces the prosperity of others, given that man was not given an exclusive [right] to happiness or misery"; this was "a clear indication," he thought, that there existed "a secret communion of things" and that "nature intended" for a "brotherhood of humankind."[127] This was as close as he got to Smith's idea of "natural progress" or Facchinei's "economic hand of God"—to the idea, in short, that the process of sociability itself was driven by some expansive telos chiseled into the nature of things.[128] Yet given his failure to produce a more coherent account of this momentum in *The Refinement of Nations,* it remained an elusive ideal in his lectures. Adopting the traditional vocabulary of active and passive commerce, and of the balance of trade, Beccaria instead embraced the possibility that a fair and calibrated international exchange might pave the way for a gradual pacification of the world system.[129] Not all countries could harbor all manufactures, and the "introduction" of certain goods could be "useful to open a channel out for our things, and communications with other nations," thus gradually, incrementally, socializing relations ever more widely.[130] He adumbrated, in short, the possibility of a world order based on commercial rather than military competition, but one that, ironically, required the constant commitment of legislators to furthering their own nation's causes in international trade, not unlike how Hobbes initially had depicted his gladiators. And, much as Hobbes did, Beccaria, too, stopped short of theorizing an international social contract to unify the polities of the world.[131]

The crux of his retort to the "nonsystem" of meddling invisible hands lay in man's capacity to legislate his own and others' actions—to achieve intended consequences. This was greatly facilitated by Beccaria's understanding of human beings in rigorously materialist terms of biological machines involved in a perennial calculus of pleasures and pains, thus making them to a certain extent programmable actors in an environment woven into existence by laws.[132] Beccaria's call for widespread enlightenment in "this century of light and research" was grounded in very specific assumptions about human nature and the mechanisms of socialization.[133] Thus understood, regulation became nothing less than an existential concern. But it depended entirely on the deep knowledge and expertise of legislators and legislatees alike. Enlightenment thus was Beccaria's reply to the doctrine of the invisible hand in his lectures; it epitomized his faith in humanity and its capacity to improve itself in *this world;* it was a resolutely man-made project of expanding international commercial society dependent on political economy rather than theology or even military might, remaining determinedly "socialist" in the word's original signification.

Theory and Practice

Beccaria's tumultuous career allowed him—like Verri—a rare opportunity for a political economist of any era: the chance to practice what he wrote about, and what he preached.[134] And so he did, whether in terms of secularizing the polity or managing its economy, leaving his chair to a former colleague and friend in the Academy of Fisticuffs, Alfonso Longo, who better than anyone had approached the breach between Beccaria and the Verri brothers in an equitable manner.[135] It is therefore striking that, much to Verri's vexation, Longo would also choose as the textbook for his course Beccaria's friend Odazi's edition of Genovesi's lectures on *Civil Economics* over Verri's own *Meditations on Political Economy.*[136] However much Longo had praised Verri and Genovesi alike in his letters to Firmian, the choice of one over the other was not merely academic, but also inherently personal.[137] Genovesi himself had actually worried that the path outlined by Beccaria was "not the safest," and opposed him on a number of points, including the just valence of death penalties, but Longo's choice might ultimately speak to the importance of appreciating the human element—in the case of the Academy of Fisticuffs, one characterized by caffeinated homosocial rivalries—in intellectual history.[138]

Now that Beccaria was free from his academic duties, he could begin to devise applications of the "science" of regulation with which he had grappled for so long in theory, living out a precarious balancing act between theory and practice during his decades as an economic administrator and drawing inspiration from his earlier works. In a Herculean editorial effort by Rosalba Canetta, more than 6,500 of Beccaria's administrative notes, letters, and memoranda have now been published for the period 1771–1794.[139] These, which by no means represent the totality of his contributions and already suggest the limits of his alleged lethargy, range across an extraordinary array of issues, from providing state employment for astronomers and for accountants expert in "double-entry bookkeeping" through the question of whether to allow a hot-air balloon to fly over Milan, to provisions for foragers who had been poisoned by mushrooms and people who had eaten the meat of a cow that had died from rabies.[140]

The question of exactly how to engage with such materials of course remains historiographically vexing. Although archives retain a privileged position in the hierarchy of historical sources, their precise relation to the world of practice has frequently been challenged. As Andre Wakefield recently reminded us, the often tortuous relationship between theory and practice in early political economy must be interrogated far more carefully than it often is, and the question of why exactly one should trust such historical sources must be considered paramount.[141] Beccaria's memoranda were clearly composed with an audience in mind, though one rather different from that originally imagined by the Academy of Fisticuffs. On the one hand, he communicated with the Milanese state apparatus, its functionaries, employees, and literal policemen; on the other hand, he wrote for his colleagues in the upper echelons of the administration—some of whom, like Pietro Verri, were by now his sworn enemies—and for Firmian, Kaunitz, and the Viennese world they represented. In this context it is significant that Beccaria did not merely wish to ingratiate himself with authorities through his administrative writings, though that undoubtedly counted among his goals.

The exigencies of accountability to his peers and comprehensibility to his subordinates in many ways insulate these sources from the utopian world of contemporary "projectors," a term the pugilists anyway considered positively or negatively on a case-by-case basis.[142] It is true that coeval cameralists left archival traces of nonexistent fiscal chambers and unrealized and impossible plantations of tea on the Scandinavian tundra, but early modern memoranda can nonetheless help shed light on "how things," to quote Leopold von Ranke, "actually were."[143] More prosaically, the down-to-earth nature of Beccaria's work in the administration, and the cumulative, quotidian nature of his writings over such an extended period of time, similarly suggest that his intended reforms often were applied, and that, though he might have embellished on his successes to impress the powers that be, these sources nonetheless remain largely reliable witnesses to his translation of particular theoretical positions into practical policies at the time.[144] Indeed, far from the visionary projects of contemporaries that have so intrigued historiography, Beccaria's recurring preoccupations tended to revolve—as suggested by his tasks on the Supreme Council of the Economy and the Cameral Magistracy—around the health and integrity of people, food, and goods in Lombardy and abroad.[145] More abstract principles of course inflected his policies, not unlike they earlier had colored Lloyd's ballistic calculations. To highlight only one representative example, Beccaria would, for example, remain true to form by strikingly fusing spiritual and bodily concerns into a single sentence in the same subparagraph of an act relating to a Milanese correction facility, placing, without much ado, "spiritual assistance" in the same category as physical "illnesses," both worldly problems in need of state attention, regulation, and policing.[146] Political economy remained the science of secular human betterment.

Building a Market Society

Spiritual tribulations put aside, no sector of the economy remained more fragile in Beccaria's eyes, and more explosive for authority, than that of grain and other foodstuffs.[147] Many of his more cerebral acts and memoranda dealt explicitly with issues related to public provisioning, the "scope" of which was "uniting the attendance of markets" with "the security of public granaries"—uniting individual with communal well-being. In a long-gestated act that, among other things, led to the creation of a number of new market days throughout Lombardy (including on Mondays in the eastern town of Gorgonzola, which was already famous for its pungently delicious cheese), he came close to echoing his lectures. Probably with tacit reference to the Physiocrats, he noted how "in the opinion of many worthy men the best of all rationing systems was that of absolute liberty," and "nothing" was "easier to imagine and to propose." Yet "how many books and how many discussions" had resulted "from such a Project?" He might have had in mind Hobbes's warning not to be "deceived, by the specious name of Libertie," for the problem for Beccaria ultimately remained one of theory and practice. Historiographically speaking, to argue against liberty at the time was the equivalent of arguing against motherhood and apple pie, to be on the proverbial wrong side of history, yet Beccaria consistently refused to unthinkingly apply abstract dogmas to real economic problems. Greater economic liberty was clearly the long-term aim of his project, but it could not be achieved at once even if one ignored the human costs of such an experiment. Market socialization simply took too long for overnight measures to be sustainably effective. What policy demanded was an awareness of "actual circumstances" and the courage to act accordingly, though one should preferably avoid "continuous shifts" between "ease and difficulty of trade," as people then would "believe famine to be imminent."[148]

What united all of these disparate problems was the problem of public management for the common good, a daily and immensely time-consuming struggle to balance individual and public interests, to translate his theories for the establishment of commercial society into practice. This involved, building on his earlier work, the creation of a secure territorial political economy, necessitating institutional reforms including acts to render policies, weights, and measures regular throughout the state, but also sundry things such as the capture and killing of "ferocious beasts in the Milanese" countryside, tending to the "economy" of forests in the region, and setting up an "economic system" of nighttime illumination in Milan to reduce the "serious disorders of aggressions and robberies," particularly on "moonless" and "foggy" nights, in order to ensure "public tranquility and security."[149] Similarly, he was able to contribute directly to the fight against the *malviventi*—the bandits, brigands, smugglers, and other outlaws—that had offered such an important context for the Academy of Fisticuffs and his *On Crimes and Punishments* alike. He organized crime-fighting in the former fief of Retegno, which had become an "almost universal emporium" for thieves and bandits, was involved in the extradition of individual criminals, and eventually personally helped facilitate extradition treaties with the neighboring polities of Genoa, the Papal States, Parma, and the Kingdom of Sardinia, aiming for "perpetual" agreements whenever he could.[150]

In addition to his work to facilitate the territorial development and expansion of commercial society, however, Beccaria was also involved with, and often responsible for, more targeted policies to encourage work culture as well as specific economic activities in the Milanese state. These ranged from establishing workhouses to giving preference to Milanese over Piedmontese barge-rowers at river crossings and measures to counteract monopolies, mercantile collusions, and the hoarding of foodstuffs.[151] Often, however, he focused his attention on the development of domestic agriculture and manufactures, fine-tuning tariffs, taxes, and subsidies to promote the establishment of industries—and, strikingly, to introduce new "machines" for the textile industry—in Lombardy, or to give them preference in international trade.[152] Beccaria was very much a proponent of what economic historians have come to call proto-industrialization, but he was also at the forefront of industrialization proper.[153] Similarly, he worried greatly about the quality of manufactured exports and the "credit" enjoyed by Lombard products abroad.[154] If dynamic tariffs on the borders of Lombardy were a preferred instrument, however, he also devoted time and attention to specific local measures in line with his territorial conception of political economy, introducing, for example, manufactures in mountainous regions to offer poor families work during the winter months.[155] He directed small targeted premiums and subsidies to promising sectors, and warned that care had to be taken to avoid "alarming commerce" and "*deterring capitalists in the future from investing their money in trade.*" Instead, he worked to expand the "public credit and trust" on which "trade" depended.[156] Inversely, Beccaria worried, like so many Italian statesmen through the centuries, that skilled Lombard silk weavers might take their talents to England or America and foster emulation of Milanese goods abroad.[157] These measures of political economy were, needless to say, precisely those that, in his earlier lectures, he had argued would develop domestic commercial society and a just international order alike.

Throughout two decades of policy work, and across vastly different spheres, Beccaria emphasized the crucial importance of avoiding "dependence," for states as much as for individuals, on considering local conditions when formulating policy, and the importance of "experience" and historical examples as sources of authority in arguments about political economy.[158] Similarly, he warned of the need to think also of "the greater economy" in order for specialized measures to not "burden commerce."[159] The law was a powerful weapon, and reforms had to be carefully adjusted not to do more harm than good. "Mild remedies are slow, violent ones are dangerous," Beccaria echoed the trope of *nil repente*, voicing a clear preference for the former rather than the latter.[160] And much like in *On Crimes and Punishments*, he continued to insist on the need for the law to be "clear" and "equal" for everyone.[161] There was nothing revolutionary about the tenor of his proposals. He knew that "when it comes to abolishing an ancient law, to which people are accustomed, one can never consider enough the importance of avoiding decisions one might regret."[162] If anything, Beccaria's youthful passion was only further subdued, first by his break with the Verri brothers, then by his need—and willingness—to subject his work to Austrian dictates, something for which his former friends mocked him relentlessly. But if he followed orders and wished to avoid further personal problems, the ideas and interests of his youth doubtlessly continued to inform his work, even if in inflected form.[163]

Crime and Correction

Fittingly, a number of Beccaria's administrative acts revolved around prison reform, particularly as related to the new prison in Pizzighettone, near Cremona, and the ideas he first developed in the Academy of Fisticuffs again found practical realization through his work as a functionary. In a note on prison reforms in Milan, for example, he reiterated the importance of ensuring the "discipline of inmates" and, for reasons of justice as well as humanity, making sure that prisoners had "equal" experiences in different prisons throughout the state. And he continued to highlight the utility of "putting them to work."[164] In Pizzighettone, he was personally involved in making the "fate of convicts less harsh," including providing them with new "sheets, hay beds, and chains," and elsewhere he was involved in the minutiae of prison management down to the point of deciding on the wages of guards, ensuring the "equality" of carceral experiences, and even arranging for some prisoners to enjoy "a discreet liberty."[165] Strikingly, however, in some ways Beccaria now went even further in his treatment of these issues than he had in his *On Crimes and Punishments*. Philippe Audeagean has recently highlighted the fact that Beccaria never explicitly engaged with questions of rehabilitation in his early work, which focused on the preventive rather than the corrective nature of punishment.[166] In his practical work, however, Beccaria considered both aspects explicitly. With regard to a "correction house in Milan," for example, he now codified regulations to ensure the "discipline of those employed or detained there," but also to ensure that employees "use moderation with inmates"; he insisted that "order and discipline," on the one hand, and "mildness and moderation," on the other, would best serve the function of the correction facility.[167] And tellingly, given his earlier work, with regard to the instructions for ecclesiastical assistance to prisoners he insisted that the clergy provide not merely for the spiritual but also the civic salvation of inmates. They were, in short, to assist the state in turning prisoners into "good citizens," because

> experience has unfortunately proven that normally those who are brought to the House of Correction lack true principles not merely of piety, but also of social duties and that civic education that acts to contain every citizen within the limits of an honest man, the very reason their irregular behavior deserves correction.[168]

Crime remained a product of structural and social inequalities for Beccaria, but faced with the requirements of practical legislative reform, he eventually came to theorize and act upon the need for punishments not merely to deter future wrongdoings by others, but also to rehabilitate the punished— to amend the consequences of *injustice* in individual criminals—after the fact.

It was thus hardly fortuitous that Beccaria eventually was invited to contribute to the codification of a new Milanese Code on Crimes and Punishments.[169] He had helped clarify the difference between criminal acts and political crimes in practice, and would early on praise the Tuscan Legal Code of 1786, which many would argue he had influenced in the first place, for the stress it put on legal "uniformity" and for overcoming the "asperity" demanded by past, less sociable, less civilized eras. The crux of the matter, Beccaria believed, touching the very foundations of political theory, remained combining "due regard for the public peace and for civil liberty."[170]

We may never know who exactly penned the final report of the council [*giunta*] Beccaria led to revaluate the death penalty in 1792, but his ideas saturate the document.[171] The council was composed of Beccaria, his former student of political economy Francesco Gallarati-Scotti, and his lawyer-acolyte

Paolo Risi, both reformists who had taken *On Crimes and Punishments* to heart.[172] In a rich document, the three turned to "the highly important and much debated question of whether the death penalty should be numbered among punishments." Uniformly, they preferred "the surrogate punishment" of "more or less hard public labor, in proportion to the gravity of the crime itself." Indeed, all three signatories echoed Beccaria's *On Crimes and Punishments* by agreeing

> that capital punishment should only be given in the case of a positive necessity, and, in a peaceful state of a society and under the regular administration of justice, we have not been able to identify such a positive necessity except for the case of a criminal who, plotting to subvert the State, and even though imprisoned and zealously guarded, is still, because of his external or internal relations, in a situation able to disturb and endanger society again.[173]

And they "all arrived at the sentiment that, in the case of open seditions, riots, and assemblies of mobs, these can be momentarily repressed also with the execution of seditionists who offer resistance, as this is not a legal death penalty but the effect of a real intimation of war" in a situation in which society truly was threatened.[174] In this, they drew inspiration not merely from *On Crimes and Punishments,* but also, in a rather circuitous fashion, from the recent Austrian and Tuscan Legal Codes that the book had influenced, and particularly by Austrian's codification that capital punishment be acceptable only in cases of "imminent danger to the State, as in cases of sedition and riots."[175]

Rather than simply basing their arguments on humanitarian concerns, however, Beccaria's council highlighted the fact that the death penalty was "irreparable," a deeply problematic datum given the "inevitable imperfection of human evidence."[176] Most people would anyway prefer "death to a perpetual and wretched slavery," so forced labor could in many ways be considered a worse punishment than death.[177] And finally, there was the paradox, which Beccaria had addressed in *On Crimes and Punishments* and which later would be elaborated upon also by Albert Camus, that

> if it is important that people witness the power of the laws [through executions], then capital punishments cannot occur at very large intervals, which presupposes a high frequency of crimes; so in order

for this torture to be effective, it must not make the impression on men that it should, in other words it must be effective and ineffective at the same time.[178]

He may have criticized capital punishment for being unjust as well as useless, but one should not exaggerate the humanity of Beccaria's alternative. Forced labor was a terrible sentence in early modern Europe, and Richard Evans has suggested that more people might have died from the system of forced labor set up by Joseph II after he abolished the death penalty in 1788 than would have from actual executions, something surely not foreseen by Beccaria and his followers.[179]

The Powerful Hand of the Prince

The question of crimes and punishments, however, remained for Beccaria part of the larger question of managing and regulating the expansion of human sociability in a world increasingly characterized by commerce. And, throughout his careers as theorist and legislator, he would maintain that markets were human creations, and as such prey to human nature. In one of the very first proposals he vocalized in the Austrian administration, the aim of legislation was to "combine the liberty of the grain trade to the advantage of the nation with the cautions necessary for general sustenance." Although he hoped strongly that Milanese subjects would experience "the mildness of a freer and less regulated system," the "actual circumstances" demanded that provisioning remain a matter of statecraft as well as market forces—of what was known as reason of state.[180] It was an idea he held on to until the very end. Just as countries could "dominate" others through trade, so predatory participants in domestic markets—let alone bandits—could "give the law" and wrench destructive rents from their co-citizens at the expense of the common good. The only thing legislators could aim for was the "prosperous success" ensured by what in one case he described as that virtuous "half way between absolute liberty and constraints."[181]

So although Beccaria's ultimate goal remained the gradual liberalization ("not by leaps, but by degrees") of markets in harmony with the development of a given territory's culture, infrastructure, and sociability, precisely the way the Academy originally had theorized this process, he never envisioned "total liberty" as a condition unrelated to existing law and politics.[182] Again, juxtaposition with Smith is illuminating. From a rather different perspective, the Scotsman observed in his *Wealth of Nations* that "to expect, indeed, that the freedom of trade should ever be entirely restored in Great Britain, is as absurd as to expect that an Oceana or Utopia should ever be established in it."[183] Both Smith and Beccaria aimed for, and hoped for, an eventual, elusive, perhaps impossible system of free trade in the modern sense, but they disagreed over the history of this longer process of marketization. For Beccaria, there was no antediluvian world of free trade to which return, no "obvious and simple system of natural liberty" before the advent of regulation like that imagined by Smith, for expansive boundaries of sociability, and its territorialization, still emerging in the eighteenth century, would have been required for its existence.[184] Commercial societies took time and work to develop, and his project was for the establishment of, not some hypothetical return to, market relations.

The Marquis remained surprisingly true to the theoretical principles of the original Academy of Fisticuffs throughout his administrative career. When the political intendant in Bozzolo in Casalmaggiore, near Mantua, for example, applied for special provisions and local tariffs to "promote commerce and industry" there, Beccaria lauded the local "zeal" and encouraged "the most industrious" of Bozzolo's inhabitants to "promote the industry and commerce of their town [*paese*]." Yet he made it very clear that "one cannot and must not establish a tariff partial to Casal Maggiore," which would treat it differently from, and at the expense of, "the rest of Lombardy"—in other words, that one should not pursue policies that might undermine the territorialization of the state.[185]

In a lengthy report of the activities of his department in the spring of 1787, really a short treatise of political economy, Beccaria summarized that the essence of the discipline lay in "1. Rendering as difficult as possible the importation from abroad of all that we can reap and manufacture without detriment at home; 2. Rendering extremely easy the exportation of all that we reap and make, superfluous to our needs." The only problem lay in their "application." Crucially though, he counted financial and taxation issues, on the one hand, and transportation, roads, and canals, on the other, as the two main influences on commercial development.[186] Early on in his legislative days, he had often worried about grain provisions and the ability of Lombard infrastructure to ensure a steady and secure circulation of goods. In 1772, for example, Beccaria had warned against opening for freer trade to Casal Maggiore and "opening a way for smuggling by facilitating a market on the edge of the border, in a place that is not sufficiently safeguarded."[187] Later he would elaborate on the very real danger that transportation conditions in some places simply could not ensure grain supplies to all localities, a situation aggravated by what he saw as the monopolistic positions of local merchants, who preferred to hoard—or even export—their grain to keep local prices high.[188] Gradually, however, and very much aligned with official Austrian policy at the time, he encouraged opening trade beyond designated market days and places more widely.[189] In 1787, in a passage on "Fairs and Markets," Beccaria noted how such spaces of exchange historically had been established in "those times when commerce was preoccupied with excessive fears of contraband and famine, [and] it was thought that the public good required that determined spaces and times be prescribed" for trade. Similarly,

> fairs, which have a greater relationship with external trade, were authorized in those times and places in which almost every district, not to mention neighboring nations, had little or no communication between them, and the poor security of the disastrous roads, and forced feudal tributes, and the weight of taxes not calculated on the true principles of public economy rendered certain temporary and local exceptions necessary.[190]

A "completely opposite" situation, however, "had gradually arisen in this happy province, in which all the provisions of the Sovereign coincide to render transportation easy and safe." Through a number of reforms, "free trade" had been established "domestically," and this had "taken an extended and permanent course," with the paradoxical result that markets and fairs themselves "cannot flourish."[191] His career as a legislator, in short, spanned Lombardy's transition from a society in which there were markets to a market society, a "commercial society" in the parlance of the day, or what we today might refer to, without too great reservations, as a capitalist one. But it was not achieved overnight, and the creation of more or less effective territorial market relations in which individual merchants, entrepreneurs, and "capitalists" safely could pursue their economic endeavors was a purposeful project driven both from above and from below; even the eventual *absence* of regulation was, as such, a *post hoc* regulatory act and choice.[192]

The long time frame of Beccaria's involvement with practical political economy had allowed for precisely the gradual approach to legislation he favored, by way of which techniques could be tested in specified regions and then perfected for general use based on deep contextual knowledge of "local conditions."[193] And it was not without pride that he could note how cotton and linen manufactures finally had reached a "degree of consistency" two decades after the initial subventions to establish them.[194] Even though Beccaria never completed that "second, equal book" the Verri brothers had taunted him about, his contributions to the practical side of the Enlightenment should not be scoffed at.[195] Schumpeter's hunch, then, that Beccaria eventually "gave to the public service of the Milanese 'state' what A[dam] Smith reserved for mankind," is only strengthened by the evidence.[196] And it is worth noting that, throughout his diverse if interconnected careers, Beccaria would continue to put his faith and trust, not in Smith's cryptic "invisible hand" or Facchinei's meddling "economic hand of God," but in the symbolically potent phrase "the powerful hand of the Prince."[197]

Peace in Practice

In light of all of this, it is curious that Beccaria's life project has been derided as "utopian."[198] The ageless ideals of "the good life" as related to "the common good," of individual flourishing in a social world, found one of their most eloquent voices in his writings and lectures, but he had little patience for utopias. One of the recurring themes of *Il Caffè* and of his lectures and poetry works had been to warn against quixotic gambits for "perfection," and Beccaria's very choice of epigraph for *On Crimes and Punishments* could serve as an epitaph for the author himself:

> In all negociations of difficulty, a man may not look to sow and reap
> at once, but must prepare business, and so ripen it by degrees.
> —Francis Bacon, *Essays*, 47[199]

However revolutionary Beccaria's ideals might have been, he was ever the Fabian, whether in his work on the Council of Commerce in Austrian Lombardy or in his anonymous calls for action. Voltaire got the essence of this project right: "We are seeking to perfect everything in this century; so let us seek to perfect the laws on which our lives and fortunes depend."[200] But perfection took time, and Beccaria's calls for "Enlightenment" were as far from the trauma of revolution as could be imagined in eighteenth-century Europe. Revolutionary apprehensions were widespread even after the furor of the Seven Years' War, also among Beccaria's allies.[201] And as the Lucchese nobleman and amateur mathematician Giovan Stefano Conti wrote to the Ragusan astronomer Ruđer Josip Bošković, one of the founding members of the Academy of Fisticuffs and collaborator in *Il Caffè* then teaching at the University of Pavia, "It seems to me that all the Governments of all the States of Europe alongside France are in such a state that they should conserve the old rather than launch new endeavors. It seems to me that a great *bouleversement* in Europe must not be far away."[202] It is perhaps fitting that "socialism," a term invented to disparage plans, like Beccaria's, for gradual secular reformism, would with time come to signify revolutionary change—while "social science," originally, as will be clear in Chapter 7, a transcendental discipline of worldly regeneration, became an intellectual armory of the status quo.[203] History may be a "tool of skeptics," as Istvan Hont once wrote, but it is also a school of irony.[204]

Beccaria's temperament was not one at ease with shock therapies, and utopia for him was less a plan to be realized than a light to lead the way. As Franco Venturi's friend Alexander Gerschenkron would put it, "utopia" was a "trailblazer for reform."[205] Gregory Claeys has recently argued that, after Thomas More's *Utopia*, the term "utopia" would "more than anything else, come to mean a condition of institutionally supported, enhanced sociability and friendship, resting upon a broadly egalitarian foundation, but not necessarily communism."[206] By those standards, Beccaria's project to promote human sociability and economic development fits John Rawls's definition, in his Harvard lectures, of "political philosophy" as "realistically utopian," as a means of *"probing the limits of practicable political possibility."*[207] Earthly perfection might remain beyond man's grasp, but this did not exclude small steps toward it, what Immanuel Kant in his *Perpetual Peace* described as the "infinite process of gradual approximation."[208] In comparison, Plato had drawn a very different and no less influential conclusion in the history of political thought and action when, toward the end of book 9 of what eventually would become known as *The Republic*, he had Socrates tell Glaucon that his ideal republic "may perhaps be a pattern or model laid up in heaven somewhere, for anyone who chooses to see it—and seeing it, chooses to found a city within himself," but that it ultimately "makes no difference whether it exists anywhere, or ever will."[209] For the Fisticuffs, no less than for Kant and for Rawls, principles invited action.[210]

As it was, though, Beccaria never proposed a plan for "perpetual peace" as such, although his lectures, publications, and manuscript fragments point the way to an ideal of ever-expanding human sociability based on carefully attuned laws and economic policies aimed at neutralizing man's urge to dominate others, within polities and between them, by conquest as well as by commerce—to gradually socialize, in short, both people and peoples to achieve *justice* globally.[211] Between people the pivot was penal reform but also a heightened political attention to questions of inequality that galvanized criminal and antisocial behavior; between peoples it was attuning international trade so as to combat dangerous imbalances in the international system. In Beccaria's view, these measures were neither foolproof nor permanent, but they had the distinct advantage that they could be implemented. From this perspective, *On Crimes and Punishments* and his abandoned *Refinement of Nations* engaged with different aspects of the same basic problem of expanding human sociability in the world, something hinted at by the great *Risorgimento*-era historian Cesare Cantù when, in his study of Beccaria, he bewailed those "austere spirits" who "smile as mirthlessly at the abolition of the death penalty as they do at projects for perpetual peace."[212] It was a remarkably astute observation that cut to the very core of Beccaria's project and the nature of Enlightenment "socialism" alike. But the former was easier than the latter. As Verri would put it in wake of Beccaria's death, with the Napoleonic Wars lighting the skies of Europe, "The philosophers of the 18th century have struck down the errors of superstition, and without realizing it they have rendered more enlightened the power of sovereigns. If the century to come produces any philosophers, they will have to strike down the belief in arms."[213]

Plans for pacifying international relations have probably existed as long as there have been wars. Rousseau explained this in his comment to the Abbe Saint-Pierre's *Plan for Perpetual Peace* (1713), "the Greeks had their Amphictions [*sic*], the Etruscans their Lucumonies, the Latins their Feriae, the Gauls their Cities, and the last gasps of Greece became even more illustrious in the Achaean League."[214] Reaching for more permanent solutions than simple leagues and associations, the hermetic Renaissance magus Tommaso

Campanella proposed a plan for earthly pacification and salvation through the vehicle of an apocalyptic universal empire in his 1600–1601 work *Spanish Monarchy*.[215] And at the dawn of the eighteenth century, the Scottish parliamentarian Andrew Fletcher of Saltoun suggested a more radical restructuring of the international system through the dissolution of existing countries and the creation of an entirely new set of states of generally equivalent power.[216] Most participants in the debates over universal peace, however, favored more mundane solutions along the lines proposed by the French monk Émeric Crucé in 1623, who imagined that a permanent peace congress located in Venice, empowered to resolve international disputes and buttressed by a universal monetary union and standardized weights and measures, could ensure peace for "human society" in "perpetuity."[217] But while Kant, building on this august tradition, would theorize the socialization of man through radical institutional reform on a planetary scale, his young interlocutor Johann Gottlieb Fichte challenged this plan by arguing that no lasting peace could be possible while international trade continued to serve as a vehicle of power politics.[218]

This inherent tension in the architecture of perpetual peace projects had plagued many earlier contributors to these debates as well, for if the members of the Academy of Fisticuffs were right and relative wealth was a measure of comparative might, demilitarization was no guarantee against imperialism and, as Vattel ventriloquized a common phraseology, "a nation ought not to suffer foreigners to dictate laws to her, to interfere in her concerns, or deprive her of her natural advantages by any means."[219] Beccaria had already written explicitly about the relationship between wealth and power in his *On Crimes and Punishments,* and had expounded on this at length in his Milan lectures, at first glance arguing the exact opposite of Rousseau's conception of international trade as expounded in his then-unpublished "Judgment of the Plan for Perpetual Peace." There, Rousseau had noted

> The great advantages that should result for commerce from a general and perpetual peace, that they are very certain and incontestable in themselves, but that, being common to all, they will be real for no one, considering that such advantages are felt only by their differences, and that in order to increase one's relative power one must seek only exclusive goods.[220]

This was a variation of the *doux commerce* thesis according to which commerce softens manners, progresses civilization, and pacifies relations between people and peoples alike, though Rousseau had reversed the causation by suggesting that peace led to trade, and furthermore that peace would remove all commercial advantages insofar as they would be equally shared. Beccaria's political economy was far closer to the view transmitted in Rousseau's published "Abstract of Monsieur the Abbé de Saint-Pierre's Plan for Perpetual Peace" (1761), with which he certainly was familiar. It is true that, in this widely circulated work, Rousseau similarly presented "Commerce" as an antidote to power politics, harnessing the popular early modern imperialist idiom of "giving laws" to do so: "Commerce daily tends to put itself into equilibrium, depriving certain Powers of the exclusive advantage they used to draw from it, at the same time deprives them of one of the great means they used to have for laying down the law for the others."[221] A footnote Rousseau added to this vision of commerce as a pacifying force in international relations explained that, though "things have changed since I wrote this," the "principle will always be true" because it was "very easy to foresee that twenty years from now, England, with all its glory, will be ruined." Although it *seemed* that England indeed was establishing a world empire based on commerce, in effect giving the law through trade, unknown forces would with time put an end to its greatness, if for no other reason that all polities declined. Yet he clearly discerned, in the very same tract, that a sovereign inspired by "large economic views" would see that "the genuine conquests he makes over his neighbors are the more useful establishments he forms in his own States." *The* way to create relative inequalities of power between polities, then, was through competitive economic development.[222] This had been Beccaria's stance all along, that all goods as such were "exclusive" and conducive to changes in the relative positions of power between trading partners. So although he shared visions of universal socialization and perpetual peace, and though his renown as "the protector of humanity" eventually would outgrow him, the scope of his proposed reforms differed greatly.[223]

His senior Carli had already written to Paolo Frisi in 1762, before Demetrius began serving his coffee to the pugilists and before *On Crimes and Punishments,* that he feared what Beccaria's "fervid imagination" might do if channeled into "politics."[224] Beccaria's proposals would, however, remain conceptually rather than practically revolutionary, operating entirely within the existing, if convoluted, system of European states and their habitual modes of operation. While historiography has tended to highlight the "clash between jurisprudence and political economy" in his thought, such an opposition demands a very particular interpretation of both concepts.[225] Beccaria fought the *arcana iuris* tooth and claw, and was never tempted to defend laws as good by themselves, as somehow inherently just on the basis of technical legality, but his political economy nonetheless acted through the lowly levers of law and minute regulation. For Beccaria the path toward universal happiness—not to be confused with its actual realization—was paved, as society progressed, by the enlightenment ensured by incremental adjustments to the disciplinary structures shaping, and being shaped by, human behavior.

Only the gradual development of intelligent, adaptive laws, not sudden impositions or dramatic departures, could lead individuals to make ever more enlightened choices in the "felicific calculus" of pleasures and pains.[226] In the larger spectrum of cosmopolitan idealism, Beccaria's proclivities were far closer to Voltaire's than to Saint-Pierre's or Kant's. Peace could not, and should not, be realized through the establishment—oftentimes imagined to be despotic and steeped in blood, "violent and formidable to humanity" as Rousseau put it—of permanent institutions to safeguard it, nor, of course, by trust in Facchinei's "economic hand of God"; it could only be the gradual, the oh-so-gradual, outcome of reasoned knowledge, of gradually expanding socialization and toleration, and ultimately, of enlightenment itself.[227] In some ways Beccaria's very epistemology disavowed plans for anything "perpetual." The world, unbound from religious teleology, was in constant flux, and its politics by necessity relentlessly dynamic. No single solution could ever suffice, however noble its intentions or however successful it might prove at any given point in time. As the young nobleman Tancredi so quotably described this state of affairs to the Prince of Salina on the eve of the *Risorgimento* in Lampedusa's *The Leopard*, "If we want everything to stay the same, everything must change."[228]

What Beccaria ultimately proposed was an active political economy operating through continuous legal policing as the only means of pacifying, *within the limits of the possible,* competition between states. Given that wealth and power were positional goods, there could be no peaceful exit from international competition.[229] Other members of the Academy of Fisticuffs conceptualized this state of affairs differently. The pragmatic Sebastiano Franci, for example, wrote of the "bloodless war" of international economic competition, warning that it could simply serve as a preamble for veritable military conquests. Beccaria was more sanguine, but his political economy can in large part be read as an art for containing competition and keeping "the quiet war of industry" as "enlightened" and "humane" as possible.[230] Political and economic boundaries did not overlap in a world of states and markets, so there could be no organic shift from interdependence to autarky, but polities could, and should, seek to consciously develop a variety of economic sectors to secure a greater independence, in agricultural goods and, importantly if not principally, in manufactures. Only constantly shifting legal measures— tariffs, subsidies, prizes, and at times even prohibitions—could maneuver competing countries toward that ideal of "total liberty" among roughly equipoised polities engaged in a peaceful commerce of goods and culture. Peace in such a system demanded a continuous process of international emulation by which all participants sought to better their conditions, but such a solution would by necessity remain fragile so long as a basic incongruity between states and markets continued to structure international relations.[231]

Verri had gone one step further, imagining a world in which "all Nations agreed to abolish tariffs on goods." The "consequences" of such an experiment, it seemed clear to him, would be

> the same that result in a State, by removing taxes on its internal circulation. Nations would come closer together; contracts would multiply; industry generally and the annual reproduction would grow everywhere in Europe; men would enjoy greater comforts; but the power of States, that is the relation between one State and another, would remain the same.[232]

Global free trade, today more rigorously understood as the absence of tariffs rather than merely the freedom to exchange, might perhaps do to the international system what Beccaria had proven internal circulation could do to national economies—that is, unify them and strengthen bonds of sociability. And yet Verri harbored no doubts that this, for the moment, remained a daydream:

> As long as other States impose tariffs on goods, and work to prevent ours from being consumed within their borders, necessity demands that we, too, make the raw materials they receive from us more expensive, and comparatively when it comes to domestic consump-

tion we raise tariffs on foreign manufactures, so that ours have, as far as possible, preference.[233]

It was a glorious vision, but deeply contradictory. Since he first had begun to think about the subject, the core of Verri's political economy had revolved around the observation that different economic activities had different abilities to produce wealth, and that international economic imbalances could create unhealthy relations of dependence between nations. That was why he continued to justify the use of tariffs throughout his writings. Yet, in his more abstract work following the collapse of the Academy of Fisticuffs, he now argued that in an unregulated international environment, "the power of States, that is, the relation between one State and another, would remain the same." It was precisely the sort of theoretical leap that Carli and Beccaria criticized him for in the 1770s. Refusing to give up on the realism that informed his theories, Beccaria joined a number of other writers of the time to instead emphasize the need for trade to be made neutral—that is, limited to the exchange of activities with similar capacities for generating wealth. This, in essence, meant avoiding exchanges of manufactures for raw materials—such as those that characterized the European colonial system—in an attempt to avoid dangerous disequilibria of power between polities. As such, his project adumbrated the Italian founding father Giuseppe Mazzini's idea of achieving a greater union of humanity by moving from an "aggregate" to an "association" of polities through economic policies, much like Carli's nationalist writings did culturally.[234] In the limited and fragmentary form in which it survived, Beccaria's *Refinement of Nations* was not the most grandiose or visionary plan for perpetual peace, and certainly no match for his parallel project in *On Crimes and Punishments* to socialize individuals within states. Yet his work, theoretical and practical, very much helped delineate the world in which we still live. This was the cost, but also the benefit, of his bold choice to "stop," as Venturi put it, "on the threshold . . . of utopia."[235]

The End of an Era

Beccaria remained devoted to "civic" affairs until the end, and his final votes and memoranda are postdated two days after his death, at the age of fifty-six, on November 28, 1794.[236] The question of why exactly he refused to complete and publish his works on political economy or *The Refinement of Nations* remains vexing; supporters like Carli had been vocal in encouraging him to do so.[237] It has been argued that Beccaria became aware of the publication of Adam Smith's *Wealth of Nations* and realized he could not compete with its voluminous treatment of the subject, but there is little evidence for that.[238] Other, more direct causes would be his gangrenous conflict with Verri. Pathologically obsessed with his former protégé, Verri reacted with fury to the success and popularity of Beccaria's lectures, and wrote to his brother on October 10, 1770, "My vengeance against the professor of Public Economy will be to teach it to him." Seemingly as easy said as done, he promptly sat down at his desk and spent the next month frenetically writing, and publishing, his *Meditations*.[239] Given what we know of Beccaria's reactions to personal polemics, it is not surprising that he refused to take up the gauntlet and engage in yet another conflict, a task Carli after all had taken on with brio. Beccaria's vision of political economy had always been more pragmatic than Verri's—though at times also more methodologically sophisticated, which perhaps partly explains Verri's jealousy. Beccaria's embrace of policy might, from this perspective, have been the natural culmination of his pragmatism rather than simply a tragic surrender. Schumpeter, for one, looked back and still thought Beccaria in many ways beat no less a luminary than Adam Smith "hands down" as an economist.[240] Verri, however, felt vindicated by Beccaria's choice:

> You would not recognize him: he is a vulgar, very vulgar man, without a spark of energy or enthusiasm; flacid; lost in his ideas, oppressed by details, and a word never escapes him that awakens a beautiful, grand, or general idea. He does not even resemble the author of the book *On Crimes and Punishments*. I think the flower of youth and the continuous inspiration of our enthusiasm for him for a time obliged him to make an effort, such that, when speaking and writing, he rose on the tips of his toes and was excited by heroic sentiments, but his element really is mediocrity. He is only moved by fear . . . of the government, the court, the public.[241]

Beccaria's theoretical preferences and personality came together in this damning critique, which would echo for decades to come. With time, however, even Verri's hatred waned, perhaps because he had greater emotional woes on his plate. His brother Alessandro had never really returned to Milan, instead settling in Rome, but for decades they would cultivate one of the most expressive and thoughtful epistolaries in the eighteenth-century world. Following the death of their father Gabriele in 1782, however, quarrels over their inheritance brought decades of friendship to a brutal end in a matter of weeks, and soon enough Pietro was describing his brother in the same acrimonious terms he earlier had used to attack Beccaria. Their correspondence would only recover somewhat in 1792, adding yet another chapter of agonistic drama—so reflective of Verri's character—to the pugilists' longer history.[242] As part of the brothers' process of reconciliation, Pietro wrote to Alessandro describing Beccaria in somewhat more tempered terms in the late summer of 1793:

> if you met our old friend Beccaria you would not recognize him. . . .
> He almost fears every use of reason to be a cause of woe. The only
> bolt to which he resonates placidly is if you speak to him of the fine
> arts: Painting, Music, Poetry, Architecture; regarding the rest he is
> a crestfallen and pusillanimous slave, and it causes wonder and dis-
> gust in those who have made him become so. You know him, he is
> never mediocre. His system is not merely a skin, but penetrates to
> the marrow, and with his fatuous habitual smile those who bump
> into him [lo aborda] find it incredible that he is the vigorous and sub-
> lime author of On Crimes and Punishments.[243]

As Alessandro rightly observed, Beccaria's "celebrity is of a superior species. . . . I believe anyone who read only almanacs knows of that work [On Crimes and Punishments]."[244] The Verri brothers' negative verdicts of Beccaria's character throughout their immense epistolary, and their torn awareness of his undeniable fame, have weighed more heavily on historiography than Beccaria's endless memoranda, but it is worth noting that the two eventually made their peace with l'affare Beccaria. Pietro Verri had already begun missing the old days before Beccaria passed away, writing in 1793 that "the Academy of Fisticuffs was a passing phenomenon; it was sufficient to convince foreigners that Reason was deeply cultivated in Milan, but did not live long enough to widen its cultivation." In the end, it had only "lasted three years," but they would remain the most exhilarating of his life.[245] And with age, he grew ever closer to his Milanese homeland, gradually taking pride in what he used to be jealous of. Among the few glimpses of light he saw in his polity's recent history were the works of Paolo Frisi and Beccaria's *On Crimes and Punishments*. One could be "proud" of Milan, he wrote, for it was "the fatherland [*patria*] of Frisi, the fatherland of Beccaria."[246] If the Academy of Fisticuffs had been conceptualized as a vehicle for placing Milan on the intellectual map of Enlightenment Europe, it had doubtlessly been successful, if not in the way that Verri originally had intended. In the wake of the French Revolution, he went even further, urging his fellow Milanese to be "worthy contemporary citizens of the author of *On Crimes and Punishments*":[247]

> Where is the sepulchre of the immortal Beccaria? What monument of recognition have you erected, o Milanese, to that sublime genius, who from the universal darkness first dared to rise and indicate the great problem of social science, *the greatest possible happiness divided among the greatest number?* What act of recognition, o Milanese, have you erected to this great man, who has distinguished your Fatherland, and whose immortal *On Crimes and Punishments* is found translated in all the languages of Europe and located among the most sublime works of philosophy in all the libraries of the world?[248]

Only thus would the citizenry appreciate "the intimate connection that lies between the progress of reason and social happiness." And had not the first steps undertaken by France during its Revolution been to "honor *Rousseau* and *Voltaire?*" A "marble bust of *Cesare Beccaria*" seemed the least Milan could do to celebrate the newly erected Cisalpine Republic, born from the tumults of the Revolutionary Wars.[249] Even Alessandro would eventually learn to forgive Beccaria. Although he described Beccaria in bilious terms soon before his death in 1794, upset about "the lesson he had given [him] in Paris" in faraway 1766, he admitted to "his genius, and his knowledge," and that "even thinking about it bores me after 28 years."[250] Only in 1798, however, writing to his brother's widow regarding a visit from Beccaria's son Giulio, did he confirm that "the truly deep sorrows I suffered on the journey to Paris have been canceled with time, and now I do not remember anything but the merits of a great Man."[251] Perhaps, as Beccaria believed, wisdom eventually emerged through hardship, but his apotheosis in the Verri brothers' imagination was merely the first of numerous ironic twists as their works began their long histories.

Pietro Verri, continuing to write as death approached, was a thoughtful witness to, and participant in, the changes taking place as reform gave way to revolution in the late eighteenth century. Like many of his contemporaries, he came to adopt the term "social science" to describe his decades-long endeavor—not at all unlike what Beccaria called "the science of man"—that had begun with the Academy of Fisticuffs. Facchinei chastised them as being "socialist" for upholding and pursuing key aspects of this science, but events seemed ever more to vindicate the pugilists' vision.[252] Verri had no doubts, following an encounter with Napoleon Bonaparte in Milan, that the early modern process of territorial consolidation would continue and that, "in few years, Italy will be a single family."[253] And it is perhaps not surprising, in spite of his supposed hostility to "the Fatherland of Italians," that the news-letter *L'Ape delle cognizioni utili* (The bee of useful cognitions) published Car-li's dialogue for *Il Caffè* in 1835, attributing it to none other than Pietro Verri.[254] As the shock waves of the French Revolution spread through Europe, people had begun to search for the origins of the dramatic changes they were wit-nessing. The revolutionary *Termometro politico lombardo* (Lombard political thermometer) argued in its first issue that "the lights which always precede the aurora of liberty and of peace made it desired and loved. The mass of these lights," it noted, "had been greatly increased by the work of Beccaria, Longhi, Verri," thus suggesting an explicit connection between Enlightenment re-formism and revolution that would haunt historiography for centuries.[255] Verri himself was upset about the circulation of a "satire" in the summer of 1794 that identified a number of members of the Academy of Fisticuffs—including, of course, Verri and Beccaria—as Milanese Jacobins.[256]

Beccaria had begun his career as the most revolutionary of the two, only to gradually, for all the reasons mentioned, become a functionary of enlight-ened absolutism. Verri's trajectory was almost the opposite, as events and what he considered personal and professional failures late in life—in large part simply his wounded pride—led him to embrace even parts of the Terror as the means of securing revolutionary change.[257] He admitted to his brother at the time, though still maintaining the absolute sacredness of private prop-erty, that "even poor men are of our family, and have the same right that we have to happiness"—a right that was best safeguarded not by an enlightened despot but by a constitutionalism based on individual rights, as in the French and American models.[258] Verri's writings from the 1790s remained largely unknown until recent years, and his and Beccaria's names were intrinsically bound to the fortunes of the Academy of Fisticuffs thirty years earlier. Of the original group, only Alessandro Verri would live to see the dawn of the nineteenth century. Henry Lloyd had died in 1783, Beccaria in November 1794, Gian Rinaldo Carli in February 1795, and Pietro Verri, true to form, passed away during an administrative meeting on the evening of June 28, 1797. His death in many ways marked the end of the "Lombard Enlightenment," one of the most pioneering and intellectually dynamic moments in the history of eighteenth-century Europe.

Afterlives

The work of the Academy of Fisticuffs long outlived its members. As Verri and his companions knew well, "men die, and systems remain."[259] Ideas and legacies are, of course, not simply received; they are arrogated and inflected, often in unexpected places and by remarkably circuitous routes. Henry Lloyd probably had the most adventurous life of any member of the pugilists' network, and much the same can be said for his immediate afterlife. British spies stole his personal papers following his death near The Hague, and Catholic extremists exhumed his corpse soon afterward, mutilating it and dumping it in a ditch.[260] Verri fared better. His body was allowed to decompose naturally in a laconic marble tomb in the Sanctuary of Ornago, northeast of Milan, and his archives were neatly organized and safeguarded for posterity. But though he was honored by his homeland and became an iconic figure in the history of the Italian Enlightenment, he never achieved that international fame for which he had hoped in his youth, and which, I would argue, he deserved. A copy or two of the *Meditations* may have made their way into Adam Smith's library, inviting speculation as to possible "influences," but without any contemporary English translations, Verri remained a largely regional and continental European figure.[261] As Chapter 7 will show, Beccaria's afterlife was a different matter entirely, and even though his earthly remains were lost in a modest mass grave in a cemetery outside of the city gates, arguments still abound to the effect that he "changed Western civilization."[262] There is no doubt that he quickly became one of the most representative figures of the European Enlightenment, and that his galvanizing ideas eventually found fertile ground even in the seemingly least hospitable soil. For example, in his *On Crimes and Punishments* he had railed against the Confraternity of the Beheaded St. John the Baptist, but it was precisely in such circles that his ideas would have the most measurable impact, directly through legislative reform but also indirectly through the ways in which his works changed public opinion and inflected mores in the realm of crime and punishment. A case study might help illustrate just how.

The Opera Pia della Carità e della Morte, or Pious Work of Charity and Death, was founded in Casale Monferrato in 1784 "under the title of St. John the Beheaded to the Pious Assistance of Prisoners and Condemned by Justice in the City of Casale." It had about seventy members, drawn from "the three orders of Nobles, Citizens, and Businessmen, or Merchants."[263] Although dedicated to the "spiritual and temporal" welfare of incarcerated prisoners and those awaiting execution, their primary concern was with "the souls of the Executed," particularly during their dreadful final hours before execution. The congregation's minutes and regulations often revolved around the difficult "economy" of execution (such as procuring ladders, stretchers, and so on) and the problems of dealing with "Prisoners in humid, and fetid Prisons," the "horror" of providing succor to those about to be tortured and killed, and the hopes that their own "virtue" might be improved by contemplating "the miseries of others."[264]

> It cannot be denied that almost all the activities of our Religious Charity, or associated ones, cause horridness, and disgust in the squalor of the prisons, and the din of iron stocks and chains; among the plaintive gaggles of the lurid, ragged prisoners, and the frightening howls of the miserable condemned; by the atrocities of the gallows, the horror of the dead, and the coffin biers, and the stench of the sepulchers.[265]

Their guidelines drew inspiration principally from the Bible, but also from the classics of antiquity in emphasizing the importance of charity and moral fortitude. Intriguingly, however, they also condemned the harshness of prisons and punishments, the incongruity between the ostensible "humanity" and "enlightenment" of the century, on the one hand, and the "cruelty" of the law, on the other, as well as the "the anguish, the torture, the dampness, and the intemperance of ingeniously melancholy and tormentuous prisons." When, finally, the pious Casalese turned to the need for an "equilibrium between crimes and punishments," echoes of Beccaria became hard to ignore.[266] The source for their lament, however, was not the inflammatory *On Crimes and Punishments,* but instead Beccaria's former Pavia professor Giovanni Battista Roberti's *Annotazioni sopra la Umanità del secolo decimo ottavo* (Annotations regarding the humanity of the eighteenth century).[267] It was a remarkable, sarcastically entitled book, often published alongside a fictitious abolitionist exchange between an old Portuguese merchant and his younger, more ambitious British colleague, entitled *Lettera . . . sopra il trattamento de' negri* (Letter . . . on the treatment of negroes), which drew heavily on the work of Roberti's former student Beccaria. Although wide-ranging, and lambasting the contemporary treatment of prisoners, slaves, and human beings most broadly, Roberti also emphasized the degree to which "trade" had become "the idol of the wisest nations," yet had failed to live up to its historical promise to unite mankind.[268] In private correspondence, Roberti would write that "in the Marquis Beccaria I do not criticize anything except his rash [*temerario*] thought, which, as it is invisible cannot be punished by a judge, but still harms others," but, crucially, he accepted completely the distinction that *On Crimes and Punishments* had drawn "between sins and crimes."[269] Mere decades after the confrontation with Facchinei, in other words, many of Beccaria's principal arguments had seamlessly been incorporated into the Catholic mainstream, though sometimes referred to indirectly through less incendiary publications.

Times were changing, and the Casalese charity was founded during a period in which the economic affairs of such congregations came under increased strain. In the emulative spirit of the age, its functionaries sought to "align with the method practiced in various Cities" in order to act with "greater economy."[270] Even spiritual concerns, after all, had material needs. Already in 1762 the Confraternity of the Beheaded St. John the Baptist of the city of Bra, near Cuneo, had successfully petitioned for the right to set up a Monte di Pietà, or charitable pawnbroker, in order to improve their finances, but the late Enlightenment was not particularly hospitable to such confraternities in general.[271] The Milanese Confraternity was suppressed as early as 1784, and by 1799 the old Confraternity of the Beheaded St. John the Baptist of Turin had to come to terms with declining finances, caused by the "extraordinary number of prisoners" to assist, the "tangible reduction in alms," and the "alienation" of Church property following the Napoleonic invasion. Its headless plan was to hold a lottery, from which it would draw a 10 percent profit, each ticket adorned with the radiant severed head of St. John the Baptist.[272]

Soon, the fate that we saw befall Torriggia in Chapter 1 became a grizzly historical curiosity. By the mid-nineteenth century the viscerality of death had become entirely sanitized in the regulations of the diehard Confraternity of Casale Monferrato, its minutes more reminiscent of industrial account books than the mystical meditations with which they had begun. It was just one of countless corollaries of what Foucault described as a transformation of "the economy of punishment" that occurred in that period in Europe, also owing to the influence of the Academy of Fisticuffs, and particularly of Beccaria.[273] The Confraternity continued its work, however, adapting to the gradual decline of capital punishments and the ongoing improvement of prison conditions until faraway 1890, when, after a national Italian law—only dreamed of by Carli and Verri—finally abolished such "institutions having the goal of assisting prisoners." This forced the congregation to transform itself into a Patronato—a charitable institution helping those newly freed from prison find economic and social reintegration, fittingly a voluntary institution of "economia civile" aimed at addressing the social question of the day.[274] The Milanese Confraternity's long desacralized Church of San Giovanni decollato alle Case Rotte, on the other side of a square from the famous La Scala theater, was finally torn down in 1906, symbolically to make room for architect Luca Beltrami's new headquarters for the Banca Commerciale Italiana. With it went also the historical Caffè Martini, conceptual heir of Demetrio's Caffè del Greco as the principal hangout of intellectuals and revolutionaries during the 1848 revolutions.[275]

By then, however, the political and cultural chasm between the world that made the Academy of Fisticuffs and the world they made would be unbridgeable. The old world, with its ossified cruelties and intimate possibilities for reform, had vanished and its traces formed nothing but a dim idolon, a fading reverie.

CHAPTER SEVEN

Arches and Stones

B Y THE LATE EIGHTEENTH CENTURY, Anselm Desing's neologism "socialists" had achieved a relatively stable meaning in German debates to specifically designate followers of Pufendorf's school of natural law and commercial society. According to the Jena and later Halle lawyer and economist Gottlieb Hufeland (incidentally one of the first theorists of entrepreneurship), such people could "be called Socialists."[1] His colleague Johann Christoph Hoffbauer argued that Pufendorf "took the phrase: live sociably [*lebe gesellig*]" to be "the principle of Natural Law," and "his followers were therefore called Socialists [*Socialisten*]."[2] This tradition of interpretation, soon cemented in Germany, would find echoes in French and Italian debates well into the second half of the nineteenth century.[3] By then, of course, a wide array of "socialisms" were in circulation, and the term was beginning to gel in its eventually Romantic forms, spearheaded by Robert Owen in Britain and Charles Fourier in France. But it is appropriate that a final salvo of older Enlightenment understandings of socialism in the vernacular was fired in Italy.

In 1803 Giacomo Giuliani, who would soon be a professor of "Criminal and Procedural Law" at the University of Padua and later of "Political-Economic Sciences," published a volume entitled *Antisocialismo confutato*, or *Antisocialism Refuted,* in his hometown of Vicenza, which had recently been annexed again by the ever-shifting, ever-indefinable Austrian Empire.[4] Born in 1772, Giuliani was of a later generation than Beccaria, Verri, Lloyd, and their enemies, having come to age facing radically different circumstances in a world marked not by reform but by revolution. He was, furthermore, formerly a Franciscan—a member of the mendicant Order of Friars Minor, whose Basilica of Saint Anthony still dominates the Paduan urban and civil landscape. Like many of the protagonists of this story who have been almost entirely neglected by historiography, by the mid-nineteenth century Giuliani was already barely remembered as the author of works that, as one scholar put it rather uncharitably at the time, "nobody saves anymore from the dust and the termites."[5] Yet his life and work are still worth revisiting for the light they shed on the gradual transformation of the discourse of Enlightenment "socialism" and commercial society into that of "social science" and, eventually, into the socialisms and capitalisms of our own day. And though their endgames would differ, Giuliani, like Beccaria, began by interrogating the relationship between "criminal law" and the "philosophical history of man."[6]

The so-called Age of Revolutions, sparked by the 1776 American War of Independence and reaching its high point with the French Revolution of 1789, not to mention the torrent of revolutions continuing into the early nineteenth century in Latin America and the Caribbean, had resolutely changed the parameters of political possibility in the European world.[7] Napoleon's subsequent invasion of the Italian peninsula seemed to have dealt a mortal blow to Gian Rinaldo Carli's Petrarchan ideal of a unified Italy, as Dalmatia, Istria, and most of the Veneto was given to Austria in exchange for a cessation of hostilities against France at the 1797 Treaty of Campo Formio. Since then, Milanese revolutionaries saw the French puppet state of the Cisalpine Republic, based around the Po Valley, give way in 1802 to the explicit vassal state known as the Italian Republic, with Napoleon as its president. With his eventual assumption of the title of Emperor in 1804, the polity would change name yet again to the Kingdom of Italy, now with Napoleon instituted as king.[8] And, no less dramatically, the 1801 Concordat between Napoleon and Pope Pius VII had shifted the balance of power between secular and spiritual authority in Europe toward the former.[9] Throughout it all, the Academy of Fisticuffs' tradition of worldly political economy was continued in Milan by the utilitarian statistics of Melchiorre Gioia and others, but many certainties seemed to be up for grabs in a world of total war like that foreseen by the pugilists.[10]

Throughout these turmoils Beccaria's fame continued to grow exponentially, and well beyond the Italian peninsula. Though readers were aware of the fact that *On Crimes and Punishments* had not been written in splendid isolation, and that, indeed, "the whole was read, at different times, in a society of learned men in that city [of Milan], and was published at their desire," Beccaria rapidly transcended his origins in the Academy of Fisticuffs, just as Verri had feared he would.[11] Already in 1767, when the Piccadilly publisher and journalist John Almon publicized his English translation of Beccaria's *On Crimes and Punishments,* published with a translation of Voltaire's commentary, he could note:

> It is now about eighteen Months since the first Publication of this Work; in which Time it hath passed no less than six Editions in the original Language; the third of which was printed within six Months after its first Appearance. It has been translated into French; that translation hath also been several Times reprinted, and perhaps no Book on any Subject was ever received with more Avidity, more generally read, or more universally applauded.[12]

By 1798 Beccaria's apotheosis was complete, and an editorial by the anonymous "Philo-Italicus" in the London *Monthly Magazine* opened:

> I am not certainly informed whether the Italians have written the eulogium of the late Marquis Beccaria. Any particulars relating to the life of that illustrious character, whose name is already synonymous to those of philosophy and humanity, deserve to be transmitted to the remotest posterity, with all the instructive singularities that accompany the exertions of great minds.[13]

For "few books ever produced so memorable a revolution in the human mind, in government, and in courts of justice," as his *Crimes and Punishments,* and "Philo-Italicus" tellingly concluded with the observation that "it is no wonder if elevated characters, like his, are exposed more than others to the blasts of envy and detraction."[14] Old ideas gained new meanings, however, and for all of Beccaria's legislative Fabianism, his ideas were radically inflected during the Age of Revolutions, precisely what Carli once had worried might happen if his "fervid imagination" was allowed to influence "politics."[15] The work of the Academy of Fisticuffs had impacted Kaunitz and others in Vienna and, through the Habsburg administration, doubtlessly contributed to Maria Theresa's 1776 decree banning torture and limiting capital punishments as well as her son Joseph II's complete ban of 1784. Similarly, Beccaria had resolutely inspired Peter Leopold's new Tuscan legal code of 1786, famous for eliminating torture and abolishing the death penalty entirely.[16] Across the Atlantic, as John D. Bessler has shown, the Founding Fathers of the United States of America took *On Crimes and Punishments* to their collective breasts.[17] John Adams quoted Beccaria with "electrifying" effect during the Boston massacre trial of 1770, and Americans from President Thomas Jefferson to former Fox News host Glenn Beck have subsequently sought in Beccaria's writings support for, among other things, arguments against gun control.[18] David Lundberg and Henry F. May's classic study of colonial reading habits found Beccaria's *On Crimes and Punishments* in roughly a third of American libraries between 1700 and 1813, and in no less than 45 percent of libraries in the period 1791–1800. Similarly, Donald S. Lutz has showed that Beccaria was the sixth most cited "thinker" in the United States between 1760 and 1805.[19]

In France, his translator André Morellet was among those who quickly noted Beccaria's direct influence on the events of the French Revolution, and historians have since highlighted the perverse ways in which Beccaria's admittance that capital punishment might be acceptable in cases when the "security" of a polity was at stake helped fuel and give philosophical and juridical justification to massacres during the Terror.[20] And so, one of history's greatest opponents of capital punishment became, in this view, the architect of one of the most atrocious and arbitrary execution-regimes in recent centuries, in which tens of thousands of people were guillotined after mostly cursory hearings. But Beccaria's celebrity grew also as a political economist through the publication and various translations of his inaugural lecture on the subject, only to take off after the Milanese historian and politician Pietro Custodi included his lectures in his epochal fifty-volume collection of *Scrittori classici italiani di economia politica*, or *Classical Italian Writers of Political*

Economy, in 1804.[21] Soon he was found canonical enough as an economist even in early nineteenth-century Sweden to be ranked alongside celebrities such as Adam Smith, David Hume, François Quesnay, and Jean-Baptiste Say.[22] For better or for worse, then, Beccaria had become an obvious authority on legal, and to a lesser extent economic, matters throughout Europe and the Atlantic world by the time Giuliani put pen to paper.[23]

After Utopia

The immediate background for Giuliani's work, however, was rather the perceived excess than the success of the revolutionary era. In his own words, he wrote not only "in defense of civil society," but for the "security of society and the good of mankind" itself.[24] Against the barbarism of the time, he considered himself a champion of *"civilization,"* a term he liked to underline and which he in his university lectures toward the end of his life would define in the vastest of terms, "embracing diverse kinds of culture, that is the *mental,* the *moral,* the *political,* the *social,* the *economic,* and the *physical.*"[25] Recent events had shown that one could step backward as well as forward on the path of such civilization, and Giuliani's oeuvre revolved around the right tools for reversing the horrors of revolution and building a new and safer path for human progress.[26]

Antisocialism Refuted (the title of which one early reader found rather "obvious") was Giuliani's first major foray into the long-ongoing debates over human sociability.[27] In scribbles glued inside the binding of his personal copy of this rare volume, Piero Sraffa, whose thoughts on Lloyd and Verri were discussed in Chapter 3, noted precociously that Giuliani's book was "the first book to use the words 'socialismo' . . . and 'antisocialismo.' The book is an attack on Rousseau, 'the antisocialist,' i.e., individualist."[28] The question remains, of course, what Giuliani (or, for that matter, Sraffa) intended by the term "individualist," no less than by "socialism." There can be no doubt that Giuliani was deeply attuned to the debates over sociability that had animated eighteenth-century Italy, and particularly so with regard to the legal discussions that had resulted from Beccaria's *On Crimes and Punishments,* a work he frequently cited. At his 1808 inaugural lecture on criminal law, for example, Giuliani echoed Beccaria in lamenting the survival of grizzly forms of torture even in an age of "culture and social [or societal] civilizing [*sociale incivilimento*]."[29] And, like the pugnacious Milanese before him, the Franciscan maintained that "Criminal Jurisprudence" was "tightly bound up with" both "the destiny of civil society" and with "true national prosperity." Law, economics, and civil society, commerce and sociability, were all inexorably interwoven for this tradition of civic reform.[30] As he saw it, the progress of civilization depended on a concomitant socialization every step of the way from individuals to tribes, nations, states, and beyond. As he later would put it, "The civilizing process is the effect of social perfectibility," and law and political economy, he agreed with the Academy of Fisticuffs, were the keys to its realization.[31]

Yet Giuliani's use of the term "socialism" stood at a somewhat oblique angle to the cognates discussed in previous chapters. *Antisocialism Refuted* was essentially a reactionary defense of "the social machine," targeted against recent "malicious efforts" to "weaken the power of social and civil laws," as well as critical of "all the philosophical and political projects to render uncertain the fates of Thrones, of Republics, and of Civil Constitutions."[32] Giuliani thus saw himself as doing more than simply penning a straightforward restoration critique of revolutions, of which so many circulated at the time in Italy and in Europe generally.[33] The problem was not merely that anarchic, "antisocial" ideas undermined the monarchies of the Old Regime, but that they eroded civilization as such. They were, in short, the intellectual equivalent of the banditry that still plagued the Italian peninsula. And, as recognized by Sraffa, Giuliani's main opponent remained Rousseau, "the philosopher of the wilds, and of the forests," the "declared apologist of antisocialism."[34] Excessive schemes such as his, Giuliani warned, had sought to "render society odious with the most disadvantageous depictions, thus seeking to equip souls for independence" and "slowly planting the seeds of a furious revolution" in order to "return man to his natural state." This, however, was clearly "impossible to realize while he lived in society," thus setting the stage for a conflagration of civilizations. The Age of Revolutions, in short, had come about because "philosophical-political projects" such as Rousseau's had "seduced" people into believing that "society is in perfect opposition to real happiness," opening nothing less than "a tomb of horrors in civil society."[35] This, he argued, was "the effect of the political project of antisocialism," which he elsewhere also referred to as the "ruinous system of antisocialism."[36]

It should by now be clear that Giuliani's reading of the Genevan is deeply at odds with current historiographical consensus, but it was so commonplace at the time to associate Rousseau with precisely these kinds of plots that the question to ask seems to be why, precisely, his readers got him "wrong" for quite so many centuries.[37] Clearly, Giuliani did not read, or he chose to ignore, a footnote Rousseau included in his *Discourse on the Origins of Inequality* to preempt just such readings of his work: "What, then? Must Societies be destroyed, thine and mine annihilated, and men return to live in forests with the Bear? A conclusion in the style of my adversaries, which I would rather anticipate than leave them the shame of drawing it."[38] Rousseau's answer was resoundingly negative, but no matter. Giuliani resolutely maintained that one had to pick sides in the epic battle over social and economic equality instigated by Rousseau, because "civilized society and equality of fortunes are two incompatible ideas, like light and darkness." Where Beccaria had found ample room for nuanced if inconclusive reflections regarding the nature and limits of economic inequality in commercial society, Giuliani, writing in the aftermath of the French Revolution's reconfiguration of property and, indeed, campaigns of confiscation, instead echoed Facchinei in fear that "the impetuous Populace" again might "run to despoil the rich proprietors of their goods, driven by the ruinous doctrine of equality."[39]

The way out of current upheavals had to go through a better "analytical understanding of man," a goal that had obsessed everyone for the past centuries but had been engaged with in a "retrograde" manner.[40] Considering the likes of Grotius, Hobbes, Rousseau, Voltaire, Adam Ferguson, and "other thinkers," he refused to analyze their "extravagances," which would only lead him into "a tenebrous chaos."[41] Instead, he would set out to investigate

> whether man, considered in his intrinsic and extrinsic relations, is a naturally social being; if his state willed by nature is that of living in society, or in a state of segregation, of wandering and solitary life; if the development of his sentiments is repulsive to his natural being, and if the state of civilization is compatible with his original and primitive constitution.[42]

To return to the Erasmian dichotomy by which we began, were people inherently wolves, or were they sacred to one another? Giuliani's argument, against the "antisocialists" of the world who maintained that happiness lay in the isolation of the state of nature, was that "natural man is absolutely destined for social life" and, crucially, for "property."[43] Man's innate "perfectibility," his "fragility," his "faculty of thought," his wish to avoid "violence," and his penchant for "emulation" and "reciprocal communication" all suggested to Giuliani that the telos of humanity lay in gradual "aggregation" and "social life."[44] The "natural man," he maintained, was "also a social man," on his way to become what he called "socialized and civilized man." In his vision, there had simply never been a completely presocial state of nature.[45] He agreed with the "antisocialists" that human interactions *did* "transform" and "socialize" people, gradually rendering wolves sacred, but he did not see why this necessitated the assumption that all sociability as such was learned rather than innate.[46] Man might be programmed *for* society and yet, with time, be further socialized *by* it. In fact, such wider and deeper socialization was necessary, he admitted in a rare nod to Beccaria's more negative anthropology, given "man's inclination to be always ready to be ferocious when interest pushes him, and social power does not repress him, and punish him."[47] "Antisocialists" could not argue that man's search for security in society was a "social habit depending on institutions, and on the principles of civic education" rather than an innate instinct, as it was evident from all the "savages" in the "hidden places" of the planet that an embryonic form of familial and tribal socialization had to be inborn. On the basis of similar studies, it was demonstrably clear to him that no great happiness lay hidden and pristine in the dark corners and primeval wilderness of the world. Forests, he echoed an august Italian tradition, were to be fought.[48]

The real key to happiness was instead to spread the impulse of society and civilization ever onward, in a project the Eurocentrism of which he never questioned. In a remarkably prophetic passage, redolent of the rapid advances of the Industrial Revolution and marked by Sraffa in his personal copy, Giuliani contemplated what the future might hold in store: "America, which socializes itself, and civilizes itself," he mused, might "within a few years" lack none of Europe's "enlightenment, laws, institutions, magnificence, and brilliance."[49] Indeed, he foresaw a global territorial expansion of that social and economic network—in essence of "the market" discussed in previous chapters—he saw originating in Europe:

If the discovery of a small part of such a great Continent made in the memorable age of the advantageous Columbus brought the most prodigious and useful metamorphosis in the wealthy polities of a laughing Europe, which has felt its most advantageous influences, what happy revolution would not be brought about by the complete civilizing of that part of the New World? How many now divergent lines would not converge toward a common center? New branches of communication would open up; an entirely new order of interest would fix the calculating spirit of the politician, the public economist, and the merchant, and the entire great social machine would receive movement, power, and energy, running at a higher gear toward its enlargement. A thousand political and commercial relations would tie this new people to Europe, and to all the other known and inhabited parts of the World, and everyone would find distant resources for the civilizing of this entire continent.[50]

The whole world might, one day, be socialized and civilized through bonds of trade and communication anchored in the "sacredness of property," inviolable and, the Franciscan echoed Facchinei, instituted by Providence.[51] To underline the importance of this point, Giuliani saw "the existence of property and the introduction of the dominion over things" to be "one of the first truths" regarding "how to be sociable."[52] Yet he also repeated Roberti's claims that the method of Europe's commercialization so far largely had brought "chains" rather than welfare and "enlightenment" to the rest of the world, and that the rules of the game would have to change in this "so promising nineteenth century" to ensure worldwide prosperity.[53] There was much to improve in the world, Giuliani thought, but destructive revolutions, he agreed with the Academy of Fisticuffs, were not the answer; reforms were. Society should be cured, he maintained with what might be understood as Christian charity, not killed.[54] And, in light of the excesses of recent years, he returned to the purest form of enlightened despotism as the means of so doing:

The wise Philosopher must not propose the cause of humanity to the tribunal of the People, which is an incompetent judge to decide over the great affairs of societies. . . . He must call to the side of his enlightenment the Governments of the earth; when it comes to social and political reforms he must peacefully make the truth heard only by the ear of the Prince. O antisocialist philosophers, you must begin to diminish the immense ills of society by recalling your revolutionary writings.[55]

Far from cherishing the great eighteenth-century birth of a putative public sphere of reasoned political debate in Europe, Giuliani longed for the secretive world of reason of state and *arcana imperii* in the name of which Kaunitz had chastised Verri all those years earlier.[56] Only "society," which he considered synonymous with "civil society," could "guarantee the security of everyone" through centralized law enforcement in the state's hands, for the members of said society did not yet know their best interest.[57] Giuliani could argue, like a social contract theorist, that one of the great "advantages of the social state" was that "we peacefully can satisfy our needs, without fearing the violence that is frequented among the savages." But he did not think worldly happiness demanded political participation—far from it: progress would remain a social and economic rather than a politically expansive concept for Giuliani until the end.[58] Not surprisingly, the Franciscan was soon offered a series of positions by subsequent Napoleonic regimes.[59]

Socialist Economics

For Giuliani, "socialism" ultimately represented an awareness of the incredible complexity of the "chain" that bound societies together, and the ways of affecting its individual "links," but also a faith in its continuing progress; it was at the same time a political orientation and a field of knowledge regarding mankind, informed by man's innate sociability and sense of property.[60] Like the members of the Academy of Fisticuffs, he agreed entirely that "the more man is civilized, the further the sphere of his sentiments extends," thus necessitating shifting and intensifying policies as society expanded. Yet, in light of recent revolutions, Giuliani had no doubts that "whoever breaks public order, who violates the laws of society, and does not respect the political plan, offends nature itself."[61] Similarly, he distanced himself from Verri, Beccaria, and Desing's "socialists" by emphasizing the "sacred" rather than "political" nature of private property, conceived of as the foundation of all social order, and through his appeals to the power of Providence. But, for that, he was no

Facchinei. "Speak then, o philosophers," he intoned more moderately, "but write with maturity, without fanaticism, write without rendering yourselves dangerous to social unity, and all Princes will be grateful for your efforts, and second your votes in the justice of a cause, which decides the entire prosperity of a state."[62]

Giuliani continued to work in this tradition for decades, first as a professor of law, then, ultimately, of what had come to be known as pure "economics," though he continued to give lectures and offer courses on political philosophy until his death. Throughout, Giuliani's vision remained deeply historical, for, as he put it, "which branch of science is not enlightened by history?"[63] It was a difficult period for the Italian peninsula, which many considered at the apex of its historical decline vis-à-vis the rest of Europe—a land, as the French poet Alphonse Lamartine described it in the mid-1820s, where "everything is asleep."[64] Yet numerous scientific academies across Italy contributed to the development of political economy there, and Giuliani was among those who traveled between them and contributed actively to the project for regenerating Italy on the eve of the process of national unification known as the *Risorgimento*.[65] Of the many speeches he gave in the early 1800s, a large number focused on the sorts of question that had engrossed thinkers of the previous century, from the role of punishment in society to whether one should prefer domestic commerce to international trade. Giuliani never published a work devoted to the subject that, until recently, would have been called political economy, but whether by choice or appointment, it was clearly one of his chief professional preoccupations. The spirit of *Antisocialism Refuted* continued to permeate his later thinking, however, and no part of it more so than the ever-elusive question of human sociability on this earth and the means of its spatial expansion. He therefore maintained a soft spot for questions such as the role of navigation in history, which not only could say much about the "degree of civilization" in a society but also was its very vehicle, having "formed and forms the object of interest of the rushed politician, the cold economist, the avid merchant, and the ambitious conqueror." Not to mention that it brought one's mind to "history, that faithful deposit of the errors of peoples."[66]

Like David Hume and the Academy of Fisticuffs before him, Giuliani observed from the historical record that "trade" recently had "become a subject not merely private, but also of the economic vistas of legislative politics," giving rise to the need for political economy.[67] Like his Enlightenment predecessors, he continued to rely on an early modern language of "giving laws," "emulation," "jealousy of trade," and the "empire of industry" in his approach to the subject, just as he similarly equated "wealth" with "power."[68] And, when it came to the towering question of whether "external or internal trade was most important," he demonstrated a remarkable familiarity with the literature of previous centuries.[69] Surveying the writings of eighteenth-century political economists on the problem, he juxtaposed François Quesnay and Adam Smith, who put their faith in internal circulation, to earlier English writers of the late seventeenth century and, strikingly, "Verri and Beccaria" as those who instead preferred international trade as a vehicle for economic development.[70] From the perspective of the early nineteenth century, however, it seemed evident to Giuliani that time really *had* solved the problem for science: "History speaks for us; it narrates for us that the most industrious and wealthiest nations were those which enjoyed the most extended external commerce and which visited distant countries to trade with them."[71] The same argument had, needless to say, been made by most champions of external trade for centuries, but it became progressively ever easier to make and, in even clearer hindsight, it is hard to disagree with the verdict.

Reiterating a traditional sequence of such commercial societies from Corinth and Rhodes through Tyre and Carthage all the way to Venice, Portugal, Holland, and, of course, England, there could simply be no doubt in Giuliani's mind that success in international trade was one of the principal goals of political economy as well as one of its most evident signs of success.[72] He was most intrigued by the case of England, a country that was able to draw on distant raw materials from across its far-flung empire to fuel its "economic-industrial-commercial state," its "manufactures," and its "industrial system." But even England, by which he meant Great Britain, had relied on "enlightened policies" and a "reasoned plan to direct commercial interests" to ensure that its domestic economy was solid and not overly dependent on the "revolutions" of international trade.[73] In any case, the exact degree to which a government should encourage internal or external trade ultimately depended, as it had for Beccaria more than for Verri, on "the peculiar circumstances of a nation," for one could not proclaim "a general and theoretical maxim" on such matters without "the danger of its inapplicability or of grave inconveniences in the case of its application."[74]

Giuliani had a similarly hardheaded approach to most aspects of economics. In spite of Verri and Beccaria's quarrels over the precise definition of economic "liberty," for example, he happily lumped the two pugilists together in his lectures as "advocates of complete liberty" in domestic trade because both had argued for unified statewide (or "national") markets free from internal tariff barriers.[75] He himself insisted on dynamic yet "necessary restrictions" to ensure that "every branch of production must be *national,* that is directed to the *well-being* of the community, and combined with the economic *interest* not of the private *producer* but of the nation, and the system of its economy."[76] Similarly, and though the cases in which this was necessary were limited, there was no doubt in Giuliani's mind that the "*social* interest" could "demand" that "certain professions" be "subject to discipline," beginning with those involving "poison."[77] In the face of possible threats, the needs and desires of the social body resolutely trumped the rights of its individual members. Relatedly, he warned in his lectures that "entrepreneurs" and "*capitalists*" inevitably would amass the better part of wealth in a society, with possibly negative consequences as economic inequality gave way to other forms of inequity. And he often repeated that human industry should be freed and encouraged, yet only within the boundaries of "*sociability.*"[78] In spite of his earlier insistence on the "sacred" nature of private property, in short, he in the end believed, like Beccaria, in its ultimately necessary subjection to the demands of justice understood as sociability.

The solution to the dilemma lay in the virtues of good government, which, without arbitrary meddling, confiscations, and usurpations of property, could still successfully shape economies over time. "It conforms to economic Reason," he lectured, "that all the effort of the laws is directed, without offending the law" (that is, without resorting to arbitrariness) to "direct the functions of the national economy so that," among other things, "the number of the opulent are reduced to the *minimum possible,* say one in five-hundred to a thousand." Inversely, "the number of poor people must be reduced to a *minimum,* and they must be provided with *jobs* and assistance."[79] The goal of "economics," he riffed of the utilitarian mantras of the Academy of Fisticuffs, was to "produce goods with the *minimal* possible amount of effort and human *work,* with the *maximum* possible advantage and utility," particularly through reliance on the wonders of *"steam*-driven machines" as a means of improving the lot of the "community."[80] Not unlike near-contemporary prophets of "utopian socialism" so expertly explored by Gregory Claeys, including Owen in Britain and Fourier in France, Giuliani identified in recent industrial innovations an epochal power to change the fortunes of humanity as such—to gradually, peacefully empower society and sociability through the legal and economic harnessing of new technologies.[81]

With remarkably few exceptions, Italian political economists had admittedly been partial to manufacturing ever since textiles had enriched the peninsula in the late medieval period, and it has convincingly been argued that the vast silk industries of Northern Italy had qualified for the moniker "industrial" already in the seventeenth century.[82] The Academy of Fisticuffs had been no different, taking a clear stance against arguments (such as those of the Physiocrats) that disparaged the power of industry (understood as an economic activity and not merely as a personal character trait) to amass wealth and power for a polity.[83] In light of technological advances of the late eighteenth and early nineteenth centuries, however, Giuliani could take a step even further, envisioning a society that, for the first time, could transcend what scholars have come to call the organic economy.[84] The extraordinary increase in productivity made possible by coal-driven industrialization would inspire near-contemporaries to devise "socialist" schemes of communal property where everyone had their needs satisfied and, eventually, what came to be known as "communism," but Giuliani's own brand of "socialism" followed in the footsteps of the Academy of Fisticuffs. Far from arguing for state- or community-owned enterprises to harness this new technology and the material abundance it promised, he clarified that, with the exception of strategic industries and those with extremely high barriers to entry, "as a maxim we will observe that the state must not be a *manufacturer;* that it must not limit the industrial *liberty* of its citizens and keeping them from investing . . . their *capital.*"[85] Rather than rely on some simple binary relationship between socialism and individualism, planning and laissez-faire, Giuliani envisioned a process of gradual human perfectibility based on the development of a spatially ever-expanding industrial civilization founded on private property, commerce, communication, and universal respect for individual rights, the egalitarian and therefore sociable nature of which was maintained by lawful policy with regard to taxation and other means of "directing" an individualistic economy—by engagement, in short, with what eventually would be known as "fiscal sociology."[86] Throughout, and in spite of his spiritual and Napoleonic affinities, Giuliani was remarkable balanced, offering pros and cons for a wide array of economic arguments and, seemingly, always opting for an Aristotelian or, for that matter, Christian middle way.[87]

The theoretical argument—not to mention moral message—of his *Anti-socialism Refuted* was echoed verbatim in his Paduan lectures on "Political Sciences," which he delivered from the 1810s through the 1830s, adapting them to the rapidly changing circumstances.[88] Giuliani remained ever worried that "the exorbitant wealth of a few individuals" might "hurt the security of a government," and maintained, without great specificity, that "well-distributed wealth" was good for "both states and citizens."[89] During the 1830s he even began to mention economic "classes" in society, theorizing their conflicting "interests"—and the need for governments to "discipline" them, and relations between them, to ensure the endurance of sociability. Particularly, he was vexed by the ways by which technological progress and, as a necessary corollary, the spatial expansion of markets allowed for ever greater concentrations of private capital, and how this structurally changed the role and influence of what he called the class of the "wealthy" and "powerful" in polities.[90]

Though Giuliani was conscientious about his readings and the sources of his arguments, he seems to give no indication of familiarity with the Owenite and Saint-Simonian literature that, by this time, had already emerged in England and France, even when, in a short manuscript he wrote at the very end of his life, he began musing about different *"supreme purposes"* of societies, sketching a vision of *"a Society* not of *communion* and *commerce* but of *cooperative assistance* by all."[91] Giuliani's ideal of "civil economics," in short, was inflected by the central tenets of his Franciscan faith to the point that it neared current Catholic conceptions of the phrase as signifying the tertiary sector of an economy, a social order based neither on communism nor on entirely individualistic trade, but instead on voluntary and charitable economic relations—a usage that was related to but distinct from how the phrase was understood at the time of Beccaria, an author who nonetheless continued to influence Giuliani's thinking throughout his career, from the 1790s to the 1830s.[92] Similarly, Giuliani never ceased to rail against the "errors" of his nemesis, the "absurd" Rousseau.[93] And he maintained, with Beccaris, his youthful conviction that the progress of civilization depended wholeheartedly on the perfection of sociability, and that this demanded the careful cultivation of "capitalists" in a polity and a deep respect for what he liked to call the *"slow process* of human combinations."[94] However voluntaristic his economic ideals were, Giuliani's brand of "socialism" still required the nurture and regulation of "capitalists" to further the goals of earthly improvement and community. It had taken millennia for human civilization and sociability to progress to the point of coexisting polities, and who knew when a truly global community might be achieved, or, for that matter, what it might be capable of?

From Socialism to Social Science

The term "socialism" itself, however, eventually disappeared from Giuliani's vocabulary, substituted by a close and increasingly popular cognate. By the time of his university lectures, Giuliani, like the late Verri, had instead come to rely on different neologisms such as "social science" and "the science of society" to describe his endeavor to ensure the flourishing and coherence of an expanding commercial society. Although the phraseology of "social science" is habitually associated with the work of sociologists Émile Durkheim and Max Weber around the turn of the nineteenth century, it originally developed out of a very different Enlightenment context. Social science initially adopted not merely the concerns but also the analytical language of earlier political economy and, strikingly, of what some had called "socialism." As Michael Sonenscher has shown, the metadiscipline "social science" emerged in late eighteenth-century France out of timeless debates over the just relationship between morality and politics, which had been galvanized by revolutionary concerns with representative government, public finance, and the rights of man. Yet its precise meaning long remained elusive. The Parisian journal *L'Historien* noted in 1795, "We do not have a very clear idea of the difference between social science and political economy," but that one could perhaps "think of political economy as social science applied to administration and legislation of agriculture, manufacturing, trade, public works, navigation, taxation, or all the means required to make families subsist and nations prosper."[95] "Political economy," then, was not simply "a branch of the science of a statesman or legislator," as Smith had defined it, but instead a branch of that grander science of humanity itself, of sociability and worldly melioration.[96]

In Western thought, law had always been called the "civil science," so it is not surprising that a "scientia socialis," or "social science," might appear in the jurisprudential tradition, as when Jacobean jurist Sir Edward Coke called—or "aptly stileth," as Michael Hawke argued in his *Grounds of the Lawes of England* (1657)—the common law of England "a social (or sociable) and abundant science [*scientia socialis et copiosa*]: sociable, in that it agreeth with the principles and rules of other excellent sciences, divine and human."[97] As Stephen Gaukroger has observed, law, understood thusly, aimed to "uncover fundamental truths about the proper regulation of society, fundamental truths on par with those of moral philosophy, metaphysics, and natural philosophy."[98] This view pointed to the old sciences, but new ones were emerging. The earliest known occurrence of the phrase "social science" in an Enlightenment context was in the first edition of Abbé Emmanuel Sieyès's epochal 1789 pamphlet *Qu'est-ce que le tiers-état?* (What is the Third Estate?), which argued that the common people of France in effect constituted the whole of the French nation and which quickly came to enjoy currency at the time as a moral guide to the new world order and even a synonym for politics *tout court* in the wake of the French Revolution.[99] Social science was meant to overcome influential traditions of "jealous" political economy and imperial rivalry to pave the way for a brighter future for humankind as such, a larger project of which the Declaration of the Rights of Man and of the Citizen was a crucial product.[100] Yet, not unlike "socialism," social science was soon hijacked by the very national prejudices it sought to transcend. For a while, though, and in the eyes of many, it was precisely in the imperial maelstrom of the so-called Age of Revolutions that "social science" took shape, with its millenarian aim to establish an empire to end all others—an "empire," as many contemporaries began referring to it as with explicit references to Beccaria, "of humanity."[101]

The late Robert Wokler often emphasized the extent to which this "central science of modernity" reneged on the Enlightenment's values during the course of the nineteenth century, as it ceased to be a "science of legislation for the promotion of human happiness," built on a discourse of "rights" and aimed at "changing the world," to become instead a "modern social science" set on the preservation of the status quo.[102] This story thus far has been told largely in relation to French history and thinkers, but at the time it was equally valid for other parts of Europe, and particularly for the Italian peninsula. Following the Jacobin uprisings in Italy, for example, a paradox emerged from the very core of Italian political economy when some began to sense the discipline's inherent definitional contradictions as it had been pursued in early modern Europe. As noted by Verri, Beccaria, Roberti, and Giuliani, to mention only some among many, the laudable quest for human welfare and happiness had been derailed by narrower prejudices; and the very ruthlessness of international competition, on which the discipline relied and which it encouraged, by necessity seemed to undermine the well-being of humanity as such. The problem, in short, remained that of overcoming the world adumbrated by Hobbes, of socializing, in John Rawls's vocabulary, not merely *people* but *peoples*.[103] For many, "social science" held the promise of squaring the proverbial circle. And although they offered new insights on the basis of their changed circumstances and available technologies, this new generation of Italian "social scientists" actively drew on the rich intellectual tradition stretching back to the conceptualization of political economy as a science of public happiness derived from a general notion of social utility and individual rights spearheaded by the likes of Gaetano Filangieri in Naples and, before that, the Academy of Fisticuffs in Milan.[104] "The great problem of social science," Verri had channeled the pugilist's old motto in his 1796 eulogy of Beccaria, was to ensure *the greatest possible happiness divided among the greatest number.*"[105]

It was in this context that the Salernitan Jacobin revolutionary Matteo Angelo Galdi opened his extraordinary and entirely neglected *Dei rapporti politico-economici fra le nazioni libere*, or *Political-Economic Relationships between Free Nations* (1797–1798), by observing that "social science currently forms the study of all true friends of the liberty of nations," explaining that it aimed at nothing less than "overthrowing the monstrous edifice of tyranny and superstition, and restoring to man all the energy to which he by nature is susceptible, to accompany him on the great road that remains for him to reach the state of happiness." The new discipline of "social science" was born from "the great revolution" that finally would put "universal public rights and [the rights] of peoples" into practice, crucially by overcoming Europe's imperialist past and the "bloody wars" that had "immolated millions of men" over "some uninhabited reefs in the two Indies," to put an end to the "eternal state of war" and "reciprocal jealousy" tearing humanity apart. The first task of the new social science therefore lay in capitalizing on the "destruction" and "most violent crises" of the revolutionary period to provide a more solid foundation for the "great social dealings, that is the politico-economic relationships, of nations." Only this could pave the way for a grander form of "society"—to achieve "justice," "eternal peace," and "universal happiness" in the world.[106]

The brave new world violently brought about by the French Revolution and its global reverberations necessitated, in other words, a "social science" within a rigorous ethical framework in which projects for individual and national betterment did not come at the expense of humanity writ large. There was something undeniably millenarian about this movement, and as the nineteenth century progressed writers came to adopt a far more operational definition of the term "social science." Some called for "political economy" to "give way to social science," and others warned of confusing the two and reducing everything to a science of "happiness," but the secular trend from revolutionary idealism to disenchanted pragmatism was already evident.[107] By the time the journalist and economist Francesco Trinchera annotated the best-selling lectures of the Carraran-Genevan revolutionary politician and academic Pellegrino Rossi in 1843, "political economy" had indeed been absorbed into "social science," but the aim of the latter had become that of establishing the "relationships that exist between the duties imposed by the national economy, and the high mission of the State."[108] Not only did political economy, soon enough known as "economics," emerge as the preeminent social science, in the minds of many it had come to usurp it entirely.

As the Sicilian economist Placido de Luca observed in 1841, "the triumph of social science" lay in "reconciling" the principles of the "individual" and "society," yet only for the purposes of the "preservation and improvement of all the parts constituting the social body."[109] The problem, of course, lay in defining the precise boundaries of this body, which had quickly receded from Galdi's expansive vision of a species-wide global social body to the narrower confines of individual polities stuck in international competition that had characterized European history and, under the aegis of nationalism, would mar it so starkly in later centuries.[110] Political economy was first codified and institutionalized as a coherent field of discourse in relation to ongoing imperial rivalries in early modern Europe—and in the minds of some of its earliest proponents, "social science" emerged out of the perceived necessity to reconceptualize political economy to overcome international discord and socialize the relationships not only within polities but between them. Yet in some ways it ended up aggravating rivalries instead. For the way in which such "social science" was transformed, emulated, and institutionalized globally ultimately also followed the blackguard logic of empire, amounting to a resolute rejection of cosmopolitan idealism in favor of traditional realism. And through social science's power over the realm of individual agency, exemplified by Benjamin Franklin's moralizing and uniquely influential *Way to Wealth,* long considered an example of "social science," the agonistic politics of international competition expanded beyond the sphere of high policies to become embedded in the very habits of the quotidian.[111] It is a world that cannot fail to seem familiar to us, for it is our own, born from the ashes of Enlightenment social science.

This is, of course, not to say that the original, explicitly anti-imperial notion of "social science" died without a fight, and laments regarding the discipline's failure to live up to its moral promise of unifying humanity have reappeared over the centuries since, all the way to today.[112] Writing in 1834, the rural economist Giuseppe Romanazzi of Bari put this sentiment eloquently: "Once it had destroyed the edifice of the Middle Ages, social science resolved itself in simple doctrines of public economy, temporarily, we hope, even though this is an oscillation that can last for centuries, before one sees it settle, and extend itself into more natural and wider boundaries."[113] Odds are, we are in for a long wait. But whatever the future might hold, important aspects of "socialism" and "social science" in the long eighteenth century revolved around worldly peace and global sociability through commerce, not to mention secularism in its many formulations, and the relationship between the two was interrogated early on. Already in 1840, at the very origins of Romantic "socialism," the erudite social missionary James Napier Bailey wrote a short history of the term, noting that it "derived from the Latin *Socialis* or *Sociabilis,"* and that currently

> Socialism is the name of a system of opinions which has sprung into notice during the last thirty years, under the auspices, and principally through the exertions, of the celebrated and philanthropic Robert Owen. It is called Socialism because its disciples profess to

be animated by the purest principles of charity and good will to their fellow-men; and because it professes to embrace plans, which if adopted by society, would improve the condition of mankind, by lessening the amount of their physical sufferings giving time to their morals, and diffusing among them valuable knowledge. The system has been called also the "Science of Society." . . . Whatever the term employed to designate that system of opinions now called *Socialism,* would, however, be of small importance, were it not that sounds have often a great influence over ill-informed men, of whom, unfortunately, too many samples may be found amid the world's vast and teeming population.[114]

Elsewhere Bailey equated the socialist "Science of Society" straightforwardly with "Social Science," the millenarian discipline to manage the social relations of mankind.[115] Once Romantic socialism was well under way, then, the terms "socialism," "social science" and the "science of society" could all still be seen to signify similar ideas and assumptions regarding the possibility of socializing mankind and improving the conditions of its individual members. They represented a shifting, but in core ways coherent, tradition emerging out of Enlightenment debates over the political economy of commercial society, yet it cannot be ignored that the terms remain in a somewhat perverse position with respect to these concepts as presently understood. But how did a project of commercial society meant to nurture "capitalists" with the aim of furthering "sociability" give rise to the (apparently) diametrically opposed traditions of "capitalism" and "socialism"? To consciously court anachronism for the occasion: Were the members of the Academy of Fisticuffs somehow unwitting examples of what the young Karl Marx would have called "soldiers of Socialism" in the eighteenth century, paving the ground for what was to come?[116]

Gordian Genealogies

It would certainly be defensible to argue that it does not matter much either way; until recently these questions may even have been considered moot. After all, in the wake of the Soviet Empire's implosion, with pieces of concrete of dubious origins still being peddled across Europe as relics of the Berlin

Wall, the sociologist and political scientist Ralf Dahrendorf confidently stated that "socialism is dead."[117] For good or bad, though, ideas are hard to kill.[118] The family of political movements finding shelter under the capacious umbrella of "social democracy" never really disappeared, and had been incredibly influential nearly worldwide, but the "socialism" that eventually came to be equated with the Soviet Empire under Stalin has long demonized the concept in its entirety for large parts of the globe and of historiography—from Russian populist revolutionary Aleksandr Herzen's "eternal hope," socialism became, in Ayn Rand's memorable phrase, "a ragged skeleton rattling like a scarecrow in the wind over the whole world."[119] In American public life, where socialism lost the luster that it continued to enjoy in Europe and elsewhere, the term ceased to have much analytical meaning at all, largely becoming a byword for whatever it was that one did or did not like, often with reference to "justice" or "injustice," "liberty" or "slavery," the "literalist" or the "progressive." Nonetheless, the concept has enjoyed a remarkable resurgence in recent years, to the point where Werner Sombart's classic 1906 question "Why is there no socialism in the United States?" suddenly seems less poignant.[120]

The failure of democratic market societies to spontaneously emerge around the world, followed by the global economic crisis resulting from the unregulated securitization of collateralized debt obligations in 2008, the subsequent rediscovery of inequality as a political and economic challenge, and a renaissance of nationalism, populism, and totalitarianism in an increasingly multipolar world faced with the challenges of climate change, have again marked a return to ideological uncertainty.[121] At the same time, more than one billion people daily embrace a "hypercapitalist" "socialism with Chinese characteristics," as opaque as it has recently been successful.[122] However improbable this may have seemed a decade ago, scholars and pundits alike have turned *en masse* to the task of rethinking of political economy, and the terms "socialism" and "capitalism" both remain very much alive in world politics.[123] Yet these particular "isms"—nebulous and inchoate as they are—are more than a little reminiscent of St. Augustine's conception of time: "What, then, is time? I know well enough what it is, provided that nobody asks me; but if I am asked what it is and try to explain, I am baffled."[124]

Focusing on the checkered history of "socialism" in particular, the term has simply taken on so many meanings, often conflicting, over the past few centuries, that it has become difficult to discern what, if anything, really might have united, beyond pure semantics, the projects of Cesare Beccaria and Vladimir Lenin; Robert Owen's utopian commune of New Harmony, Indiana, and the Cambodian killing fields of the Khmers Rouges; Aleksandr Solzhenitsyn's *Gulag Archipelago* and Stieg Larsson's *The Girl with the Dragon Tattoo;* the Democratic People's Republic of Korea and the Scandinavian Model; 1760s Milan and 1960s Havana; 1810s New Lanark and 2010s Chongqing. The word "socialism" has been purposefully used to elucidate a remarkable spectrum of places, peoples, periods, and ideas, and it has carried some of the most positive and most negative connotations allowed for by human language. Though this certainly is not the place to survey nearly two centuries of scholarship and activism to chart the term's nearly endless polyvalence, some different, later perspectives on the shifting meaning of "socialism" may nonetheless help shed light on the term's meaning in older Enlightenment debates over commercial society, and on their consequences.[125] The point, to be clear, is manifestly not to claim the Academy of Fisticuffs for some more recent ideological project or another, but instead to adumbrate how different aspects of the group's project to further commercial society could resonate with now divergent—if not antithetical—traditions of economic and political thought, and what we might learn from the Gordian genealogies of socialism and capitalism.

In obvious ways, Beccaria was not a "socialist" by standards that had become widespread by the time of the 1848 revolutions. Turning to what many would consider the fountainhead of the concept as traditionally understood, and considering only the list of "measures" to be initially implemented in *The Communist Manifesto* (1848) as a litmus test, one would be hard-pressed to imagine the pugilists, or for that matter Giuliani, being card-carrying members of *that* particular branch of the "socialist" movement. They, too, were clearly vexed by how economic competition had become "a life and death question for all civilized nations" and by the degree to which "capital" was not merely a "personal" but a "social power," but it is noteworthy that even Beccaria would have vehemently resisted not only Marx and Engels's intended "abolition of property in land and application of all rents of land to public purposes" but also their call for the "confiscation of the property of all emigrants and rebels."[126] Without fetishizing it, Beccaria defended private property on both extremes of the spectrum, among landowners and rebels alike. As such, the Academy of Fisticuffs might well have fallen under Marx and Engels's rubric of earlier "Conservative, or Bourgeois, Socialism," which sought "all the advantages of modern social conditions without the struggles and dangers necessarily resulting therefrom," foolishly championing reform rather than revolution (though by virtue of their landed titles they could also have qualified for the even more misguided category of "Feudal Socialism").[127] To the degree that "socialism" is thus singularly identified with millenarian goals to abolish private property through communism—connecting a vast array of thinkers from the Zoroastrian prophet Mazdak to Plato, the Renaissance magus Tommaso Campanella, and of course Karl Marx—then eighteenth-century usages of the term were indeed a linguistic aberration.[128] Such a usage would jibe poorly even with the English novelist George Orwell's more modest claim, in his memoirs of the Spanish Civil War, *Homage to Catalonia,* that "Socialism, is the idea of equality; to the vast majority of people Socialism means a classless society, or it means nothing at all."[129]

Beyond these most basic expectations about the term, however, "socialisms" historically tended to harbor not merely economic ideals but also political, philosophical, and even emotive normative preferences. Looking back upon humanity's changing relationship to its material surroundings, for example, the Victorian Scotsman and Virgil scholar John William Mackail identified two distinct if dynamic aspects of "socialism" in human history; one was economic and focused on the communization of property, the other was moral and aimed at human "brotherhood," or unity.[130] Whatever Beccaria's juvenile musings questioning the necessity of private property, the author of *On Crimes and Punishment* might have been marshaled to this transhistorical tradition by virtue of the moral side of socialism in Mackail's scheme, but not the economic side. In fact, Beccaria had devoted most of his life to the achievement of one by virtue of the exact opposite of the other—human unity through regulated commercial sociability based on private property. Though both Beccaria and Giuliani frequently voiced concerns over economic inequality, they had not been willing to automatically equate an equality of worth with a complete equality of wealth.

Both *had* worried, though, about the role of power in a polity, and about how legal and economic inequalities could undermine sociability. This was one of the main reasons Facchinei had berated Beccaria for being a "socialist" in the first place. From this perspective, it may be worth considering the gaze of the twentieth-century Italian socialist Antonio Gramsci, best known for the *Quaderni del carcere* or *Prison Notebooks* he wrote—in prison rather than about prisons—between 1929 and 1935. In them, Gramsci noted that the then largely unknown Facchinei had precociously used the term "socialism" in his critique of Beccaria, long before the word was believed to have been invented; Gramsci asked rhetorically, without suggesting an answer, *"What did that word mean at the time?"*[131] To which one might pose a related question, *What did it mean to Gramsci?* In a short piece he had written in the wake of the Russian Revolution, Gramsci argued that far more than the *Risorgimento,* it was "socialism" that had produced a "social unity in Italy":

> [Socialism] meant that a peasant farmer from Puglia [in the South of Italy] and a worker from Biella [in the North] have come to speak the same language; that, in spite of the distance that separates them, they have come to express themselves in the same way when confronted by the same problem and to arrive at the same judgment of men and events. What other idea, in Italy, has ever achieved anything like this? Socialism has become the one ideal which unites the Italian people.[132]

Gramsci here transcended Carli's vision of a geographical and cultural Italy with a vision of an ideological Italy moored in a "socialism" of workers and peasant farmers vastly different from, if not diametrically opposite too, Beccaria's coffee-drinking, aristocratic faith in societal progress through secular political economy. "The Liberal Party," Gramsci continued, had, however, "shattered Italy" and "widened the gulf between north and south with its legislation on customs duties, creating a kind of industrial feudalism, which has broken Italy up into many different zones of opposing interests."[133] And this may be one area where core aspects of Enlightenment and Romantic socialism aligned, for both had engaged—Beccaria more precociously than Gramsci, with Giuliani occupying something of a middle ground in the wake of the Industrial Revolution—with the communicative power of commerce and, crucially, with the political and social consequences of the differential power of economic activities to create and appropriate wealth. No peace, they agreed, nor any sociability, however pugnacious, could subsist between *peoples* if some were allowed to control industry while others supplied raw materials, and in this Beccaria's project can be seen to reverberate in Gramsci's brand of socialism understood as producing "social unity" between heteronomous groups by secular economic means. Socialization, in short, required policy. It required effort.[134]

An even clearer connection can be drawn between Enlightenment preoccupations with inequality in commercial societies and the "social question" of the nineteenth century, even though, in this case, too, analogous terminologies can denote similarities but also differences.[135] For example, many of the most characteristic battle cries of Romantic "socialism"—including universal suffrage, a minimum wage, and prohibitions against child labor—would have been anathema to Beccaria and his ilk in their day. At the same time, entirely different languages could also be used to describe comparable things, and many of these "socialist" measures were soon normalized in large parts of the European world by other means and with other justifications.[136] Léon Say, grandson of the better-known economist Jean-Baptiste Say, saw "socialism" of this sort saturate the politics of *all* European states in the second half of the nineteenth century, exemplified in Prussia by the policies of Chancellor Otto von Bismarck, a redoubtable statesman seldom thought of in these terms any longer.[137] Perhaps the French historian and minister of labor and social welfare Albert Métin was right after all, in his 1901 *Le socialisme sans doctrines* (Socialism without doctrines), that effectively "socialist" policies like those he observed in antipodal Australia and New Zealand successfully could be realized—and of course had been historically—without any reference to the ideology of "socialism" as such.[138] What to some was socialism, to others was simply pragmatic politics to maintain a "capitalist" society.[139]

Indeed, continuing the cavalcade of anachronisms but on the other end of the traditional spectrum from socialism, there can be no doubt that a very large number of the "interventions" in favor of which Beccaria fought as a writer as well as during his decades of service in the Milanese administration form the backbone of what the German social scientist and political activist Ferdinand Lassalle, in a 1862 speech in Berlin, in a critical manner would call the "Nachtwächteridee" (night watchman idea) of the state—an idea that was soon embraced by many as the ideal of a "Nachtwächterstaat" (night watchman state) uniquely identified and even equated with a particularly pure manifestation of "capitalism."[140] This included, of course, not merely Beccaria's tireless judicial defense of individual rights and "freer" markets, but also his efforts to combat banditry and ensure the proper illumination of Milanese streets on dark nights. In this context, Facchinei had touched upon something profoundly important when, in his violent critique of *On Crimes and Punishments,* he argued that Beccaria had written "not for the good of the State, but solely for the good of society, and, indeed, he has sustained it to the detriment of the former, to the point of presuming that a private man has more rights than all of society put together or of those that represent it."[141] Facchinei's use of the term "society" here at first seems puzzling, but in the first instance he clearly intended the aggregate of private individuals in a polity, and in the second instance he intended that group as unified in a "state." His critique, in short, was that Beccaria had given individuals rights, qua human beings, that could not be challenged by the Leviathan state. Beccaria's "socialism," his very projects of socialization—such as fighting arbitrary punishments and highway bandits, and ultimately of creating a vibrant and expanding commercial society also through regulatory interventions—were all anchored in his ideal of inalienable individual rights not given *by* society but to be held *against* it.[142] In the final instance, his concepts of society and sociability reflected the needs, ambitions, utility, and happiness of individuals.

True, the Latin "socialistae" and its first vernacular renditions signified adherents to a general theory of human sociability derived from Pufendorfian visions of commercial society emanating from natural law. But equally importantly, it described a political framework—if not a sentiment—of caring first and foremost for human lives and of disentangling earthly political economy from the concerns of theology.[143] A clear fear fueling Facchinei's use of the term "socialist" had, after all, been that by putting such a strong emphasis on human betterment in *this* world, to the point of arguing for the equal worth of all individuals and challenging the very structures of society and its embedded inequalities, Beccaria preached an egalitarian and operational overturning of the status quo, the usurpation of "theology" by "political economy," and an impious revolt against "the economic hand of God."[144]

What Beccaria and his companions had suggested was, in other words, a deeply Protagorean political economy conceiving of worldly affairs—and most importantly betterment—as an aim in itself, the very core of the Enlightenment project as conceptualized by Franco Venturi and John Robertson. Concomitantly, Beccaria's proposed socialization of people as well as peoples became "socialist" in mitigating, if not abrogating, the role of power in human relationships, within and between polities. Far from being "almost diametrically opposed to the modern [meaning of the word]," as argued by some scholars, there were, then, deep if oblique resonances between Facchinei's charge of "socialism" and the term's reappearance (or inflection) in the nineteenth century, just as there were between eighteenth-century theories of commercial society and later notions of capitalism.[145]

The interwoven conceptual histories of capitalism and socialism in the nineteenth and twentieth centuries may be less surprising than one initially might assume. In 1907 Morris Hillquit, the founder of the Socialist Party of America, argued that his project to "transfer" the "ownership in the social tools of production—the land, factories, machinery, railroads, mines etc.— from the individual capitalists to the people" was "no more . . . utopian" than "the demands of the eighteenth century capitalist for the abolition of the privileges of birth were to his contemporaries," helping inaugurate a world in which "all babes are born alike, and all human beings enjoy the same rights and opportunities."[146] Similarly, and in the very same year, the founder of the British Labour Party, James Ramsay Macdonald, remarked, "Socialism is a tendency, not a revealed dogma, and therefore it is modified in its forms of expression from generation to generation. The goal remains the same, but the path twists and twines like every other human path." Though Macdonald's penchant was for communal control of economic resources, he maintained that this simply was a means, in his particular time, by which to achieve the ends of sociability—the only thing that could ensure the welfare and liberty of all individuals.[147] Both Hillquit and Macdonald, then, socialist leaders on respective sides of the Atlantic, saw their brands of socialism as clear continuations of eighteenth-century "capitalist" projects of emancipation like that embarked upon by Beccaria, completely unaware of the fact that, at the time, it had been derided precisely as "socialist." Something similar may, ultimately, have been what Hont had in mind when he referred

to eighteenth-century socialists as "market socialists"—as exponents of the
view that markets could be a means toward the end of sociability, rather
than, in the term's more famous twentieth-century signification in the wake
of the "socialist calculation debate," simply of state or communal control
over the means of production.[148] The Romantic emphasis on socialism as
complete economic egalitarianism was, in other words, simply one sharp-
ened facet of its richer eighteenth-century conception in relation to the existential question of the material conditions for human progress and sociability on this earth. Given the premises of the debate, one can appreciate
why someone might take the step toward actual communism, but it was a
step that ultimately was consciously considered and vehemently resisted by
the Academy of Fisticuffs and later Enlightenment "socialists" such as Giuliani (and, it must be said, by the numerical majority of nineteenth- and
twentieth-century "socialists" as well).

Praise and Blame in the History of Ideas

As is true of the works of most complex thinkers of the past, it is easy to see
how a number of aspects and elements of Beccaria's theories could be inflected
and aggrandized over time in the increasingly tempestuous history of ideologies. Just as his loophole allowing for capital punishments under extreme
circumstances in the end justified a revolutionary hecatomb, so his sentimental reference to "the terrible right" of property, and generally the pugilists' insistence that property was a political rather than natural or sacred
right, can conceivably have given way to arguments for the abolition of private property and in favor of public ownership of the means of production
through which socialism became communism in what used to be known as
the Second World. The Academy of Fisticuffs' emphasis on the need for
equality before the law could, in a massive act of extrapolation, similarly
lead to a truly classless society of absolute equals. Their detachment from
spiritual questions and emphasis on the need for politics to be secular may
eventually have crystallized in manifest *irreligion,* imperialistically so in the
Soviet League of the Militant Godless, though the Italian economist, engi-
neer, and sociologist Vilfredo Pareto had already observed that popular socialism had become a lay religion in its own right—or, as Gareth Stedman
Jones recently defined socialism, "a powerful and organized post-Christian

religion that, in the name of science, addressed itself to the oppressed."[149] And who knows, perhaps a seed of the pugilists' campaign in favor of manufacturing and the conquest of the uncivilized wilds—not to mention the art of Giotto, Lorenzetti, and Botticelli—eventually bloomed to pictorial representation in Albert Renger-Patzsch's *Eisen und Stahl* (Iron and Steel), a remarkable example of German 1930s new-objectivist photographic explorations of indus-

Albert Renger-Patzsch, *Iron and Steel*, 1931.

trial civilization in which nature and even humanity itself had disappeared almost entirely amid the colossal metalworks of modernity.[150]

It may well be tempting to recreate such vast temporal webs of influence and responsibility, praise and blame, but they ought to be taken with a grain of salt. Whatever affinities may be drawn across time and space, none of these outcomes were the pugilists' intention, nor, in some cases, were they even within their capacity to imagine. Quentin Skinner has rightly warned that "history" ever risks becoming "a pack of tricks we play on the dead."[151] The past seldom acquiesces to the moral demands of the moment, and is anyway indifferent to our indignation. Beccaria, or for that matter "The Enlightenment," was no more culpable for the Holocaust or Stalin's Gulags than Verri was for the Fascist barracks bearing his name in Italian Tripoli, which, after all, were named not after him but after the military captain and secret agent Pietro Verri (1868–1911).[152] Just as "socialism" by then had become a different "socialism" and "social science" a different "social science," so "Pietro Verri" had more than one signification. They were all related, though not the same, as intellectual influence is always a process of cumulative appropriation. The history of ideas must perforce be written in the sign of agency, not of inertia. Indeed, a no less plausible genealogy—also because it is repeatedly invoked— would bring us from Beccaria through Jeremy Bentham to modern utilitarianism and libertarian laissez-faire. That the pugilists' ideas can be extrapolated in such conflicting directions speaks eloquently to the protean nature of eighteenth-century political economy, the complexity, if not ambiguity of their thought, and the ease by which intellectual filiations can be created and, sometimes, forged. As Verri himself noted, "Men's ideas and beliefs change faster than languages do."[153] It is a testament to its intellectual richness that the Milanese Enlightenment remains a model for utilitarians, libertarians, and even the avant-garde of Catholic social economists to this day, all of whom find deep affinities with the ideas and terminologies that emerged from the Academy of Fisticuffs.[154]

This is not to say that such intellectual genealogies necessarily are false, only that they tell only parts of—and illuminate select aspects of—far more complex stories, with numerous possible outcomes. No less than with economic models, it is important, when we draw on their power, to be aware of the assumptions and abstractions on which they are based.[155] For although "socialism" eventually gained new meanings over the course of the nineteenth century, at times doubling down on certain aspects of its original

Postcard depicting the Pietro Verri Barracks in Tripoli, ca. 1933.

spectrum of signification to the point where its overall ideological orientation could be seen as entirely overturned, the word itself remains indebted to eighteenth-century concerns with commercial society and the economic policies necessitated by the incongruence between states and markets, with inequality, with peace, and with human perfectibility—a constellation of preoccupations that, at the same time, also contributed to the languages of "commercial society," "social science," and "capitalism." The full story of how "socialism" as the science of commercial sociability became something close to its own antonym as the bogeyman of "capitalism" remains to be told—though again the semantic drift itself might be less interesting than the vistas revealed along the journey. A view of the Academy of Fisticuffs should make it clear that, though related to both trajectories, they were their own thing, and worth engaging with on their own terms without the occluding intermediation of nineteenth-century ideologies.[156]

Indeed, the group's members were themselves eminently aware of the power of "words," which, as Pietro Verri noted, "are the arbiters of the universe. The words *ancient, modern, Guelph, Ghibelline, theory, practice,* and the like are the true magic words. It is true that these considerations do not elicit in us a very positive idea of the universal rationality of men."[157] The same, needless to say, is true of "socialism," which more than most words in the lexicon of political economy has justified Beccaria's rhetorical question "Do you not know that torrents of human blood have been spilt over words?"[158] Judging from the changing fortunes of both "socialism" and "capitalism" in recent decades, though, the time might be ripe to reconsider their origins, meanings, relations, and complex legacies. In relative terms, occurrences of the words "capitalism" and "socialism" in English texts published since 1750 digitized by Google peaked in the late 1970s, when "capitalism" briefly outperformed "socialism" before rapidly declining. In Italy, the peak occurred around the same time, though "socialism" still remained more popular, in relative terms, in Italian at the end of the last millennium than it at any time did in English. What this study should have made clear, however, is that although "big data" can elucidate long-term lexicographical trends, the actual words counted do not necessarily mean the same at the different places and times of their formulation. Sequential peaks and troughs in the popularities of both "socialism" and "capitalism" mapped the fortunes of concepts representing shifting spectra of meaning that, though related, ultimately were distinctive. As such, both terms invite repeated chronological interrogations to tease out their changing meanings, not unlike what David Armitage recently has done for the phrase "civil war," and the enmeshed ways in which their iterations relate over time.[159]

Marco Polo's Bridge

This study of the Academy of Fisticuffs and its enemies is not such an enterprise; instead, it has been a meditation on the original, complex moment in which the two concepts had not yet taken commonly recognizable forms, in which Milanese "civil economists" of the eighteenth century literally could be chastised as neologistic "socialists" in the process of making their "commercial society" safer for equally neologistic "capitalists." Few examples seem more apt to prove Mark Bevir's point that we must move beyond "a simplistic dichotomy between socialism and capitalism."[160] Neither category now seems particularly fruitful for understanding the issues most pressing to Beccaria—such as the question of human rights—or those most pressing in our current era, which is why the broader and emotionally more neutral eighteenth-century concepts of political economy and commercial society still might have something to offer the complex of concerns at hand, then and now. Perhaps, from this perspective, Minerva's owl has already taken flight.

The interdependent relationship between individual and society in the Fisticuffs' vision of political economy and commercial society—and in Enlightenment "socialism" more broadly—brings to mind the twentieth-century fabulist Italo Calvino's *Invisible Cities*, relating Marco Polo's wondrous tales to Kublai Khan. In one of their meetings,

> Marco Polo describes a bridge, stone by stone.
>
> "But which is the stone that supports the bridge?" Kublai Khan asks.
>
> "The bridge is not supported by one stone or another," Marco answers, "but by the line of the arch that they form."
>
> Kublai Khan remains silent, reflecting. Then he adds: "Why do you speak to me of the stones? It is only the arch that matters to me."
>
> Polo answers: "Without stones there is no arch."[161]

Beccaria was—often literally—in the business of building bridges, but his focus remained on the individual stones of their arches, a foundational tension that would inform all the major ideologies of subsequent centuries. It was a viewpoint not entirely unlike that adopted by the Irish playwright and flamboyant wit Oscar Wilde, when he poetically hoped that a "perfect harmony" of humanity might be brought about by "the new Individualism, for whose service Socialism, whether it wills it or not, is working."[162]

Whatever the hopes and aspirations of later "socialists," however, in their own time the members of the Academy of Fisticuffs had remained ever true to their realist origins. The group had emerged out of Pietro Verri's conflict with his family and harrowing experiences during the Seven Years' War, and turned to political economy as a means of making names for its members as well as reforming, and improving, the world. Together they made Milan one of the premier centers of the European Enlightenment, pioneering new ways of theorizing and furthering secular sociability both within polities, through radical juridical reforms, and between them, through active economic policies. They helped elevate the issue of the "rights of man" to new levels in European debates and politics alike, and were at the vanguard of secularization

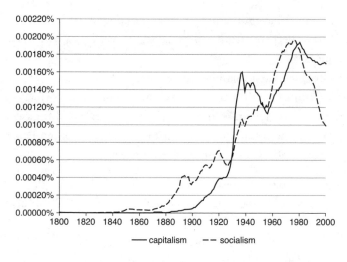

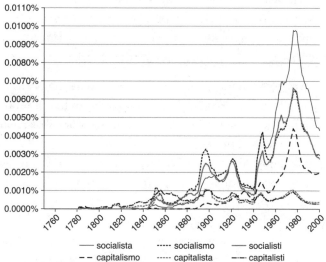

Google Ngram of the words "capitalism" and "socialism" in Italian
and English publications since 1750, and Google Ngram of variations of
"capitalism" and "socialism" in Italian publications, 1750–2000.

at the time, guilty as charged of Facchinei's claim that they wished to substitute
political economy for religion.[163] In dialogue with intellectual developments
throughout the continent, they even invented some of the most advanced
tools of economic analysis of their century, all the while remaining aware
enough of their limitations to not let them jeopardize practical work.

Their coffeepot society proved to be no less vulnerable to rivalries than their families had been, however, and the pugilists eventually turned on each other. It is tempting to ponder, in a counterfactual manner, what might have happened, and what they could have achieved, had their collaboration lasted a few years longer, not to mention if they could have maintained the sort of decades-long creative camaraderie that characterized central participants of the contemporary Scottish Enlightenment.[164] What if Beccaria's *On Crimes and Punishments* had shone a little less brightly on the Enlightenment sky, thus generating fewer jealousies and making the broader Milanese constellation more visible? Or if he had stayed in Paris longer and truly become Verri's envoy to the *philosophes*? Or if he had finished his second, equal book? Or, for that matter, if Verri had managed to keep his libertinism in check, or at least directed it elsewhere? It is difficult to ignore the fact that, for all their dedication to sociability, what ultimately spelled the end of the Academy of Fisticuffs was precisely their lack of it. And it is worth noting, from the perspective of intellectual history, that the rift between Verri and Beccaria was originally caused, not by conflicting ideas or economic interests, though some of these did emerge over time, but instead by conflicting sentiments. The age of reason was also one of passion.

The intensity of these desires and ambitions, however, may have been precisely what made the Academy of Fisticuffs such an extraordinary enterprise. And its members would anyway not have written what they did, or even been true to themselves, had they not also dedicated themselves to public administration, to regulating tariffs, building roads, and fighting bandits. They were, in the broadest sense, not merely remarkable prophets but also architects of commercial society. Long after the group imploded over questions of jealousy, pride, and particularly women, and the metaphorical doors of Demetrius's coffee shop had closed, the pugilists still kept its enlightening ideas alive, transmitting them to the next generation, even institutionalizing them. To this day they can still be discerned in media as disparate as placards advocating for human rights and mathematical economic models, and their work echoes in our daily struggles with crime and punishment, regulation and reform, justice and inequality, nationalism and cosmopolitanism, states and markets, the secular and the divine. Over the past centuries, overlapping aspects of their endeavors have been referred to under the rubrics of "socialism" as well as "capitalism," none of which might ultimately be satisfactory labels for what, in Enlightenment Italy, was called "civil economics" and then "social science," a vast secular project to gradually socialize and "improve" humanity through pugnacious relations of commerce and civilization. In this sense, the coffee brewed fresh by the Academy of Fisticuffs would still be drunk in the years and even the centuries to come. Like all the best coffee, it left its drinkers delighted and positively restless, if also quintessentially edgy.

Afterword

———⟶ ⊱•⊰ ⟵———

I N THE SUMMER OF 2015, 251 years after Beccaria published his *On Crimes and Punishments,* the city of Milan hosted an International Exposition, or what used to be known as a World's Fair. Inspired by a French institution of arranging national exhibitions, the "Great Exhibition of the Works of Industry of All Nations" held at the Crystal Palace in London in 1851 inaugurated an ongoing tradition of at least sixty-five similar Expos to date, including notably one in Paris in 1889, of which the Eiffel Tower is the most durable relic, and Chicago's "White City" of 1893.[1] At Milan's Expo, united by the theme "Feeding the Planet, Energy for Life" and stretching out over one million square meters, were pavilions for 145 of the world's 194 or so countries, from Afghanistan to Zimbabwe, joined by structures representing international organizations including the United Nations, civil society institutions such as the Andrea Bocelli Foundation and Oxfam, and companies ranging from the China Corporate Pavilion through the Expo's official soft drink Coca-Cola to McDonald's and Slow Food. Fittingly, the Expo even had an official "coffee partner": Illy. This literally global village, in which more than 20 million visitors could sample foods and marvel at wonders and ingenuities from almost everywhere on the planet, was very much like a realization of the wildest dreams of the Academy of Fisticuffs—the territorial simulacrum of a peaceful and secular worldwide commercial society. Churches had seemingly left the landscape, and, if anything, the whole fair was saturated by a postmodern form of environmental mysticism.[2]

The 2015 Expo in many ways did represent the culmination of Cesare Beccaria's project of political economy. In thematic and visual terms, a midway point between this commercial cosmopolitanism and Alessandro Magnasco's depiction of the eighteenth-century Verziere might well be another view of the very same market, this one painted in 1852 by the Brescian painter Angelo Inganni, who himself gained his name through international exhibitions. Strikingly, religion had been almost entirely sidelined in this Romantic visualization of the famous marketplace, the characteristic Verziere Column of Christ the Redeemer left conspicuously off center. Gone, too, were the guards, the prisons, and really any visible indication of state power at all. Consciously or not, Inganni depicted the gradual sublimation of the marketplace into the market principle, illustrating the transformation of a still-traditional society in which state and Church, or "Throne and Altar" as some would put it, largely had framed economic activity into a commercial society justified—and increasingly, though far from entirely, operated—in its own right. Recalling Desing's critique of Pufendorf and the debate over the just relation between states and the Church that was so central to the problem of Enlightenment socialism, Inganni's painting visually suggested that religion rested within commercial society rather than, as in Magnasco's, that commercial society rested within religion. Appropriately, given the Fisticuffs' role in these debates, the coffee shop, which previously had been relegated to the background in Magnasco's painting, was now promoted to the front right, anchoring the image's central axis of urban commerce and sociability.[3] I do not suggest anything inevitably teleological about this, but the pugilists had pointed in this precise direction, and coffee, from *Il Caffè* to Illy, presents a remarkable vantage point from which to assess the unfolding of this secular transformation.

Very much in the pugnacious spirit of the Academy of Fisticuffs, the Milan Expo also served as a powerful reminder of the conflicted architecture of the world economy that had been erected since the time of Beccaria, driven by a creative but also destructive incongruence between states and markets, countries and corporations, ideals and realities. Beyond the obvious paradoxes of Italy championing development in light of the country's

Angelo Inganni, *View of the Verziere*, 1852.

economic decline in the past decade, or of Ronald McDonald sharing the
stage with Slow Food's Carlo Petrini as ambassadors of healthy and sustain-
able subsistence in the world, the size of pavilions directly reflected the sums
countries and corporations were willing to pay for their rent, thus emphasizing the pressing fact that, though everyone came together as one world,
they did so from very different positions of power.[4] As George Orwell so eloquently put it in *Animal Farm,* "all animals are equal, but some animals are
more equal than others."[5] So far, it indeed seems clear that history has
proven the late Verri wrong and the late Beccaria right with regard to the
power politics of international trade; the "power" of countries continues to
reflect their degree of success in an ever more competitive global economy,
and states can progress as well as decline through trade.[6]

At the same time, the mechanisms described by Gustav Schmoller
continue to churn, as ever more people and ever greater territories are
brought into the expanding sphere of commercial sociability. The timeless,
mist-shrouded marshlands of Montferrat and the Po Plain—once a region
full of isolated villages and bandit crews—have now become an integrated

territory of both a unified Italy and an ever more closely bound yet still precarious European Union, not to mention a complex global network of mul-
tilateral organizations from the United Nations to the World Trade Organization. The region remains famous for the hams, cheeses, wines, and
(though daily to a lesser extent) manufactures that the Academy of Fisticuffs
promoted two and a half centuries ago, and one can still visit the weekly
market that Beccaria helped establish in Gorgonzola, now located in Viale
Kennedy, on Monday mornings. But as the Expo reminded us, Lombardy's
wines are now also decanted in Sydney; its truffles are auctioned off in
Tokyo; its boutique cars and sartorial luxuries are envied worldwide.[7] This is
the culmination of a long process of what eighteenth-century observers
called "commercial society," crucial aspects of which some chastised as "socialist" at the time, but which in hindsight we have come to call "capitalism."
Today these two terms occupy opposite ends of the economic spectrum as
habitually understood, even though they remain dastardly to define with
any conceptual precision. Yet at their cores the historical understanding of
socialism and our current concept of capitalism share a hope and a project
to unify disparate people and peoples through bonds of secular commercial
sociability rather than theology or, for that matter, war. As such, it is both
intriguing and hazardous to note that the word "socialization," conveying
something close to the original conception of "socialism" while simultaneously appealing to current notions of "capitalism," still continues to hold
currency at the utmost frontiers of the world economy.

Frontiers of Socialization

One of the smallest of the pavilions at the 2015 Milan Expo was that of East
Timor, the first new sovereign state of the twenty-first century and, for a long
time, precisely the sort of place that Beccaria and Giuliani had in mind when
bewailing the state of nature and the nature of European imperialism alike.
Having suffered centuries of Portuguese colonial neglect and decades of
Indonesian occupation, even genocide, the tropical half-island nation is, so far,
unique in world history for the way in which it was born. After a popular
referendum in 1999, in which its inhabitants resolutely voted for independence, the United Nations claimed sovereignty over the country for several
years while the basic building blocks of society and the polity were put in

place.[8] It was a striking example of how new territories still can be brought into the process elucidated by Schmoller, and of how a global community can socialize new participants. Whatever the problems of the country, and there are many, its rural areas are undergoing, on a time scale of months and years, transformations that Europe literally spent centuries on. And curiously, the official jargon for "educating" people in East Timor—for "introducing them to capitalism" along a broad axis stretching from convincing them of the benefits of a sovereign wealth fund for the country's oil revenues all the way to simply "making them produce for markets," or in other words for "bringing them on board" this newly minted "market society"—is "to *socialize*."[9] And intriguingly, the very same term "socialized" is similarly used to describe the way by which "capitalism" can be fostered in the ostensibly communist—albeit, again, far from in a pure and Platonic form—Democratic People's Republic of Korea, and its relations with surrounding countries "normalized" and "pacified."[10]

At the farthest frontiers of the contemporary world economy, then, people and peoples must still be "socialized" into "capitalism." It was essentially to this paradoxical nexus that East Timor's founding father and longtime guerilla fighter Xanana Gusmão pointed when, in a speech on economic reforms soon after independence, he stressed that "people's *interaction* must be encouraged." This was soon facilitated by state investments in infrastructure but also in mobile telecommunications, through which different "districts that were like islands" gradually became "a country" over the past two decades.[11] For, as the Bangladeshi entrepreneur and academic Iqbal Z. Quadir recently put it, explaining the vision behind his low-cost cellular company Grameenphone, "*communication facilitates specialization and exchange and thus commercial society*."[12] In twenty-first-century Bangladesh and East Timor, just as in eighteenth-century Lombardy, the obsessions of governance revolve around the problems of infrastructure and armed outlaws challenging the spatial reach of the state—with "enemies of society" who, alongside desperately poor roads and means of communication, hindered the "territorialization of the economy" and the "socialization" necessary to "create a new demographic dynamic"—but also with the science of commercializing a political community for the benefit of all, of what used to be known as "civil economics."[13] East Timor is in many ways the world's premier laboratory of state formation, uniquely and ironically made possible by the fact that large parts of the world had sought—however fleetingly—to transcend reason of state as such.[14] But it is worth noting that there are places in the world where the territorial-izing process of the Schmollerian moment has hardly started at all—such as the Central African Republic, the capital of which, Bangui, is at best a poorly governed city-state in a literal jungle of tribes, bandits, bloodied mineral re-sources, and unscrupulous foreign interests.[15] And even in an established "emerging market" like Nigeria, "bandits and robbers" are central preoccu-pations for entrepreneurs outside of—and crucially *between*—major cities.[16] Our "globalized" world still remains serrated by frontiers. They may increas-ingly be of an international rather than national character, but they have various kinds and degrees of solidity, and much depends on how, and whether, territories are incorporated into international flows of goods, people, and ideas.[17]

Over his decades of civil service Beccaria observed and celebrated how, through careful measures, Lombardy had been commercialized to the point at which market days were no longer needed because the reality of a market-place as a physical location had given way to the market as a cultural and territorial constant—which became possible because security had been established, political and importantly educational and cultural institutions introduced, infrastructure solidified, and processes of production and ex-change developed to the point where such minute regulations to make trade happen at specific times and places were no longer necessary and individual market participants truly could unleash their creative potentials. Through sustained and conscious effort, the market as a *place* had yielded to the market as a *principle* of social and territorial organization, as a way of life that Adam Smith—among many others—famously referred to as "commer-cial society." East Timor's capital of Dili may look like many other cities in developing economies (or, in today's parlance, "emerging markets," which is far more than a mere semantic difference), lined with shops and the occa-sional street seller, yet its countryside remains largely "unsocialized" in governmental terms, strikingly manifest in the numerous open, roofed con-crete marketplaces built around the country. The vast majority of these stand empty, melancholy testimonies to the distance separating the theory from the practice of commercialization. These markets might be used for shelter by people or animals but, even close to Dili, they remain far from the intended nodes in a growing territorial economy.

Open-air market near Dili, East Timor, 2016.

One can build markets physically, but without active buyers or sellers to use them, or goods to trade, they can never launch market societies as such. The experiences of eighteenth-century Lombardy, contemporary East Timor, and much in-between them uniformly suggest that the market principle is not, as is often assumed, the baseline human condition.[18] As the philosopher Charles Taylor and others have reminded us, the triumph of "market society" is very recent in the history of moral philosophy, and returning to Adam Smith and Cesare Beccaria is a means to study some of its earliest theorists.[19] Not only are markets historical developments; even our ways of thinking about them and engaging with them—the theories, the metaphors, the tacit assumptions, even the words—have their own histories, many of which we have forgotten.[20] The undeniable success of commercial societies has allowed us to disremember the arduous process by which they historically emerged and were solidified and, crucially, legitimized.[21] We have enshrined the ideal values of commercial society, realized only briefly and locally in human history, to an almost existential point where economics and other social sciences assumed human nature itself to be that of "homo economicus."[22] Unsurprisingly, however, on the basis of a considerable number of observations in small-scale communities worldwide, a team of scholars recently found no evidence of such a *homo economicus* "in any society studied" anywhere on the globe.[23] So-called capitalist values, in short, or what in the eighteenth century was known through variations of commercial sociability, have to be *learned*, just as Pufendorf and Beccaria had insisted.[24] This is by no means a new critique, and it resurfaces periodically in the history of political economy as a caveat regarding the validity of theoretical assumptions across time and space, and the dangers of taking the status quo for granted in matters of social science. Already in the early twentieth century Thorstein Veblen ridiculed the universal aspirations of many contemporary economists:

> A gang of Aleutian Islanders slushing about in the wrack and surf with rakes and magical incantations for the capture of shell-fish are held, in point of taxonomic reality, to be engaged in a feat of hedonistic equilibration in rent, wages, and interest. And that is all there is to it. Indeed, for economic theory of this kind, that is all there is to any economic situation.[25]

This deep-seated historical conflict between theory and practice would hardly have surprised Beccaria, who had learned all too well that commercial society was not the inexorable unfolding of an intrinsic teleology but an extraordinary achievement to be championed and safeguarded. Even in rural Lombardy, part of what for centuries had been one of the most commercialized territories in the world, it took decades of sustained work to build roads, drain swamps, banish bandits, and encourage economic activity before satellite villages of Milan could enjoy commercial relations as a quotidian experience, let alone embark on what we have come to hail as creative disruption. This was, perhaps, *the* central tenet of Enlightenment "socialism," which conceived of progress as a gradual, frail, and ultimately human-made accomplishment rather than simply the divinely willed telos of things.

Markets and Morals

The words by which we engage with these timeless phenomena may have changed and evolved, but the extent to which our debates remain vexed by many of the same existential concerns that animated Beccaria and Facchinei is striking. Foremost among these challenges remains, perhaps naturally, the issue of economic inequality, simultaneously the basic engine of commercial society and, at ever-elusive extremes, its nemesis.[26] Within and between states, we still navigate the relationship between "sufficiency" and "equality" in the world dominated by economic forces, and, as Samuel Moyn has recently reminded us, it remains that, from the standpoint of efficiency, "sufficiency may get along better with hierarchy than with equality."[27] Where Smith championed the ideal that relative inequality ultimately was irrelevant as long as everyone was better off in an absolute sense, Beccaria had warned that, given human nature, there were limits of inequity past which sociability itself might break down. Echoes of that great Enlightenment dispute still linger in—and even shape—our debates about human rights, global justice, and economic inequality. If centuries of engagement with the problem tell us anything, however, it is that few questions are more normative in nature, and that market societies, at different times and in different places, must perforce negotiate the complex politics of maintaining inequality within the shifting boundaries of what they ultimately deem efficient, legitimate, and, in Beccaria's terminology, *just*. In this, as in most matters of political economy, one size does not fit all.

But religion, too, still shapes not merely individual morals but macroeconomic debates to a far greater extent than we habitually acknowledge. Whether explicitly or not, postulates that Providence will ensure a better future, for example, naturally foster mindsets favoring nonintervention in markets as the chosen vehicle of progress.[28] And this link between religiosity and laissez-faire extends far beyond the fringes of the ivory tower. As the 2011 Baylor Religion Survey revealed, 22 percent of Americans think "the invisible hand of the market is really God at work."[29] To this day, Smith's uses of the phrase are quoted to justify precisely such a stance, which is ironic given that the *one* time he used it in *The Wealth of Nations* was to make a far more time-bound argument. For though his statement that businesspeople were "led by an invisible hand" to "preferring the support of domestic to that of foreign industry" may or may not have been factual in late eighteenth-century Scotland, it would certainly not have been so in most places at most times of world history, and, empirically speaking with regard to global capital flows, *manifestly* is not so today.[30] That said, the basic tension between human and divine agency in worldly melioration of course transcends the historical

vocabulary of economics as such. When, employing a very different conceptual language, the British-Nigerian writer Noo Saro-Wiwa recently lamented
the "link between living standards and the spiritual" in Nigerian popular
culture, and her futile attempts to convince her aunt that Europeans did not
"get wealthy because they *prayed*" but because they "took matters into their
own hands" and "realised they had control of their own destiny," she inad-
vertently echoed a central tension of the debate over Enlightenment socialism
that still resonates throughout the world.[31] Axel Honneth may not engage
with the eighteenth-century origins of the question, but his observation that
we now have come full circle in the struggle between "religion" and "socialism," to the extent that "religion is perceived as the ethical force of the
future, whereas socialism is regarded as a creature of the past," is all the more
striking in light of Facchinei's debate with Beccaria.[32] Much has been written
about the relationship between Church and State, but the relationship between Church and Market is—as Boyd Hilton so magisterially showed with
regard to the Evangelical foundations of laissez-faire in Victorian Britain—
no less deserving of interrogation, historically and in the present.[33]

The theory, or feeling, that progress is ensured by tacit or explicit divine
intervention may, of course, be *right*—though, in the absence of more osten-
tatious miracles, exceedingly difficult to prove—but it remains necessary,
today as in the eighteenth century, to emphasize that it embodies an approach to economic affairs that can only be deemed as supernatural in orientation. As the inimitable Harvard economist John Kenneth Galbraith put
it, it appeals to "the market" as a "semireligious totem."[34] The consequences
of such assumptions were succinctly put by Fritz Redlich, Joseph A.
Schumpeter's friend and "the major intellectual force" at the Harvard
Center for Research on Entrepreneurial History in the 1940s and 1950s:

> It goes without saying that if a man honestly believes in the harmony
> of the social universe, if he honestly believes that God will take care
> that public interest evolves from the prosecution of private interest,
> he must not only believe in *laissez-faire,* but also has no reason to feel
> social or national responsibility for his actions.[35]

Markets are deeply human institutions, and how we construe them says the
world about who we are, and who we are becoming. As for the age-old ques-

tions by which we began—of whether human nature is innately violent or sociable, to what extent it has been made sociable over time, and how—the jury remains out and, indeed, may never return.[36] Beccaria's vision of socialization stays poignant in this context because of its inherent historical realism and subsequently appealing practicality. For it is beyond doubt that true commercial sociability, which may be more fragile than we long have thought, remains one of the most fundamental "institutional voids" in many emerging markets to this day, and one of the most difficult hurdles to overcome in the quest for peaceful, worldwide economic integration *and* development.[37]

A Return to Political Economy

Similarly, a deeper history of the term "socialism" and, more recently, its ostensible inverse "capitalism" suggests the degree to which conceptual dogmatism is no longer—if ever it was—a particularly helpful guide to political economy, to economic development, or, indeed, to commercial society itself. Even at the height of the Cold War, after all, NATO governments were deeply involved in the sort of "interventionist" economic and social policies many would decry as "socialist," and, inversely, markets of course existed in the so-called Second World of socialist states, much like they today exist in the Democratic People's Republic of Korea.[38] And what is one to make of recent success stories such as Japan, South Korea, Taiwan, or Singapore, which remains a transit point for much travel to East Timor? The late Lee Kuan Yew, perhaps the closest the last century saw to an enlightened absolutist monarch, explained late in life that other Third World countries had failed to achieve what Singapore had because of their "interventionist economic policies" and because of their faith in "socialism and state enterprises," yet the Singaporean economic system is interventionist to a degree Jean-Baptiste Colbert—let alone Beccaria—hardly could have dreamed of, including everything from forced savings of more than 50 percent of income and vast targeted subsidies, ranging from public housing all the way to massive State Owned Enterprises (or, in Singaporean terms, Government-Linked Companies) such as Singapore Airlines and SingTel, not to mention that its chief Sovereign Wealth Fund Temasek remains one of the world's most strategic and opaque.[39] Explicitly drawing on the lessons of history, Yew pursued a checklist of Enlightenment principles, from faith in the "rule of law" through investments in "infrastructure" and "communications" to his gradualist reformist mantra *"make haste slowly"*—which no Beccaria, Galiani, or Necker could have put better—and a strategic agenda to move up the value-added ladder from heavy industries and chemicals through manufacturing to industries based on intellectual property.[40]

Yew may not have cried "Nil Repente!," but his mantra was itself directly derived from the Latin slogan *"Festina lente!,"* literally "make haste slowly!," attributed to Emperor Augustus by the first-century AD Roman historian Suetonius.[41] Strikingly, this had also been the motto of Grand Duke Cosimo I de' Medici of Tuscany, the architect of what very well may have been the first "developmental state" in world history, whose personal iconography visualized the sentiment through the image of a tortoise with a sail.[42] Making haste slowly and not doing anything sudden, Singapore has emerged as one of the world's wealthiest polities. The view over its bustling port and the endless vessels in the Straits of Malacca today dwarfs the vistas our ancestors would have had of the port cities of Genoa, Venice, Amsterdam, or London at the height of their power, but it does so, not only because Singapore has been a nodal point of global commerce for centuries, but also because de facto subsidies allow it to be the world's premier bunkering station.[43] At the same time, few who have visited would doubt that, in spite of its extraordinarily heavy-handed meddling with so-called market forces, the modern city-state is one of the most thoroughly commercialized and most successfully multi-ethnic societies the world has ever seen.

How to precisely label the polity therefore remains a matter of some contention. Scholars may dub Singapore a "hypercapitalist city-state," for example, but North Korean visitors still happily call it "a socialist country . . . just like my country!"[44] A Manichaean opposition between "protectionism" and "free trade," "socialism" and "capitalism," can, in short, tell us no more about contemporary Singapore than it can about eighteenth-century Lombardy, or, for that matter, about the history of individual rights. Both older and more recent history, then, from Beccaria's Milan to today's emerging markets, indicate that the more nuanced and capacious early modern languages and practices of "political economy" and "commercial society" still provide useful perspectives for understanding the complex and changing mechanisms of social welfare, marketization, and development in the world, historically as well as today.[45] As Daron Acemoglu suggested in a recent call to "forget" capitalism, "the notion of capitalism, by fixating on purely economic relations such as the ownership of capital and the means of production, misdirects our focus away from the *political economy*—and politics—of the economic arrangements a society has ended up with."[46]

In the same vein, an analytical benefit of the eighteenth-century idiom of "commercial society" is that the term forces us to consider its constituent parts, and demands that we interrogate the nature of their mutual dependence. Where "capitalism," as Acemoglu pointed out, lexicographically puts the emphasis on capital, and thus a distinct system or philosophy of productive investments, "commercial society" highlights the nature of a *societas* or "friendly association" as it relates to *commercium* or "trading" (*con* "together" and *merx* or *merces,* respectively "merchandize" or "pay"). Understood thus, the concept immediately reveals certain systemic strengths but also weaknesses and vulnerabilities, as even the grandest of global economies inevitably depends on the trust, credit, and "friendly" interactions of its individual participants. Literally and metaphorically, members have to proverbially buy into commercial society. Individuals are not teleologically bound to it, and it is worth remembering that periods of expanding commercial sociability and economic globalization have come and gone before.[47] To quote the Chicago economist Jacob Viner's explanation of the last time laissez-faire seriously fell out of favor: "No modern people will have zeal for the free market unless it operates in a setting of 'distributive justice' with which they are tolerably content"—that is, one that, to return to the pugilists' vocabulary, seems *just.*[48] Market sociability, let alone global economic sociability, takes effort and upkeep, and can wax as well as wane over time. As the East Timorese Nobel Peace Prize laureate José Ramos-Horta recently, and unwittingly, echoed the Ciceronian civic tradition portrayed by Lorenzetti and championed by Beccaria: "Peace and development requires continuing, diligent work . . . it doesn't happen just like that."[49]

The Empire of Humanity

The question with which Chapter 1 began, however, which originally made Beccaria's name and represented the very cornerstone of his broader project for sociability, was that of capital punishment. It is hard to exaggerate Beccaria's influence on subsequent debates over the practice, legality, and morality of executions in the centuries since the publication of his *On Crimes and Punishments,* and references to his name in the literature on the subject—historical as well as current—are nothing less than ubiquitous. From this perspective, Beccaria's *attualità*—his relevance and topicality—remains perennial and undisputed.[50] In all of history, few identities have been established between individual writers and their subjects that are more prevalent and robust than that between Beccaria and criminology, and with capital punishment most specifically.[51] Comparative figures might be Charles Darwin and evolution, or Casanova and libertinism, or, for that matter, Karl Marx and socialism; and Beccaria's subject remains no less passionately debated than theirs.

Although the causes of this are still disputed, there has nonetheless been a long and worldwide trend, in aggregate terms, toward the abolishment of the death penalty. Some studies go further, suggesting that—with the notably immense exceptions of the United States, Japan, and, of course, Singapore—capital punishment tends to decline with economic development and the strengthening of sociability and the state alike. At the time of Beccaria's writing, Torriggia would have been executed for murdering his wife in practically every polity on earth; today—*also* because of *On Crimes and Punishments,* though the argument exalting its sole importance in this process is far too easy to make—he would plausibly have risked capital punishment only in 37 out of 195 countries.[52] The related question of torture, too, remains at the forefront of our legal and ethical debates, and Beccaria's name and work continue to be invoked worldwide in the condemnation of it, though legal and paralegal forms of torture, not to mention torture as an investigative procedure and as a punishment, at times remain conflated even in the academic literature.[53] However unhappily for many intellectual historians, such conceptual confusion may, though, be true to his work, as Beccaria himself quickly transcended technical definitions of individual words and terms to simply become a "philosopher of humanity," a sentimental champion of the humane.[54] That said, both more- and less-recent history reminds us that, no less than globalization, such moments of resistance to torture and capital punishment in the name of human rights have come and gone before, demanding no less vigilance to protect and maintain.[55]

The reconstruction of Beccaria's efforts to secularize penal law and political economy as means of socializing humanity touches the very core of

Cover of Cesare Beccaria, *Dei delitti e delle pene* (Milan: Feltrinelli, 2014).

our present debates over the nature of individual rights, societies, and global order alike, representing one of the enduring and unresolved legacies of the Enlightenment in the modern world: that is, the question of our ability to coexist peacefully and to purposefully improve worldly conditions, domestically as well as internationally. Writing to the Ukrainian-born Harvard economist Alexander Gerschenkron, Franco Venturi once presented his "Einaudian edition" of Beccaria's works as "an attempt to say that the discussions of torture, persecution, [and] the death penalty still remain alive in the Europe (and Italy) of today."[56] My attempt has been to show the continuing

Flavio Costantini, *Cesare Beccaria*, 1987.

relevance also of Beccaria's economic writings, and more importantly of what the pugilists eventually called "social science" and "the science of man"—the larger project of establishing and expanding secular, human sociability to which their complete oeuvre contributed.

In Beccaria's day, the Seven Years' War galvanized debates over trade, peace, and the global expansion of sociability, but there have been many other moments when such questions have been brought to the fore in the wake of crises. More recently, toward the end of World War I, for example, in the wake of the collapse of our first grand period of globalization, theorists and statesmen began imagining a new world order to protect peace following the proverbial "War to End War."[57] It was in this spirit that Veblen, a self-professed heir of the Enlightenment quest for perpetual peace and critic of Karl Marx accused of "socialism," warned on New Year's Eve 1917 that the U.S. government would have to

take the public of this country and others into its confidence and give
them a few plain lessons in what the new duties of citizenship and
patriotism are likely to be under the new conditions [of world peace];
and more particularly to tell them how much of their ancient superstitions they will have to give up as the price of peace.[58]

As Veblen discerned, expanding spheres of sociability from individuals to
people and eventually to peoples necessitate changing norms and "superstitions," an insight that only became clearer after World War II, the most
destructive conflict in human history thus far.[59] In his 1945 dedication to Harvard Business School's dean, Walter B. Donham, who did more than anyone
to ensure the institution's early dedication to safeguarding the role of history
in political economy, Elton Mayo, who was then a professor of industrial research, presented his study of *The Social Problems of an Industrial Civilization*
as a reckoning with the shocks of the 1930s. These, Mayo warned, included
the return of "recurrent depressions," of "war and national self-assertion,"
and eventually of "a barbarian attack upon the foundations of civilization." It
was evident, he argued, that "society, here as elsewhere, was totally unpre-
pared for the events that followed the hateful year 1929." In offering a solution to the travails of the previous decades—economic crisis, populism, destructive nationalism, and the lure of authoritarianism—Mayo warned
against "extreme differences in the material standards of living" in a society,
as well as internal divisions "by group hostilities and hatreds." Under the
threat of "the atomic bomb" and the destruction of "civilization,"

> effective cooperation . . . is the problem we face in the middle pe-
> riod of the twentieth century. There is no "ism" that will help us to
> a solution; we must be content to return to patient, pedestrian work
> at the wholly neglected problem of the determinants of spontaneous
> participation.[60]

The Academy of Fisticuffs had been involved in the conceptually parallel
"pedestrian work" of building an ever-expanding "society" and dispelling
"superstitions" two and a half centuries earlier, and they too resist facile
"isms." As a project, this may make it rather more than less worthy of
engagement.

This is, of course, not to say that such schemes simply repeat themselves in the face of historical contingency, or that we can simply pick up where Beccaria or Mayo left off; our history must perforce remain torn between the perennial aspects of the human condition and the specificity—and contingency—of their expressions.[61] To appreciate their differences and similarities, we must consider the cumulative, sequential contexts in which related ideas and practice have been born and developed, as well as their temporal limits, variations, and echoes through the ages. Mark Twain may never actually have observed that "history does not repeat itself, it rhymes," but the general sentiment is no less trenchant because of it.[62] That said, Alessandro Verri himself advised against historical functionalism, observing that, though human experiences were connected across the ages, "history and erudite scholarship are an immense warehouse in which everyone can find the goods that serve their purpose."[63] Judicious work was therefore necessary for historical viewpoints to be useful, and Giuliani would similarly remind his students in Padua to "distinguish the *past* from the *present;* because not everything that was useful at one time can be so in subsequent ones, particularly if circumstances change a great deal."[64] Or as Friedrich Engels wrote in private correspondence with the economist—and Marx's Russian translator—Nikolai Frantsevich Danielson, "When we study the real economic relations in various countries and at various stages of civilisation, how singularly erroneous and deficient appear the rationalistic generalisations of the 18th century—good old Adam Smith who took the conditions of Edinburgh and the Lothians as the normal ones of the universe!"[65]

Such generalizations, we now know all too well, were neither a Smithian nor more generally an eighteenth-century appanage, and given the later history of Engels's own theories, his caveat is not without bittersweet irony. Yet it remains that a richer historical awareness cannot but help us think, and act, with greater clarity and perspective, and crucially so with regard to the universality of our theories and assumptions.[66] The history of Beccaria's "socialism," in particular, serves as a powerful reminder of the necessity of understanding the past on its own terms, all the while addressing fundamental questions with which we still struggle. So even if the semantic vicissitudes of socialism ultimately may seem of antiquarian interest, a mere "curiosity of intellectual history," they uniquely elucidate certain ideas and problems that continue to challenge us to this day—and principally the questions of what precisely we understand by, and hope to achieve through, individual rights, commercial society, human sociability, economic inequality, and improvement in a secular world of competing polities bound by international trade.[67] Even ideas we have chosen to decidedly reject, after all, contribute to shaping our collective worldviews, theories, and practices, often for far longer than one might be tempted to think, and therefore merit serious attention. John Maynard Keynes explained this phenomenon eloquently in a frequently quoted passage:

> Practical men, who believe themselves to be quite exempt from any intellectual influence, are usually the slaves of some defunct economist. Madmen in authority, who hear voices in the air, are distilling their frenzy from some academic scribbler of a few years back . . . soon or late, it is ideas, not vested interests, which are dangerous for good or evil.[68]

As Verri put it, "men die, and systems remain."[69]

In light of liberal capitalism's periodic crises of conscience and confidence—not to mention mounting challenges to its recent status as the world's sole "legitimate" ideology—a clearer awareness of its historical dynamics and inescapable social embeddedness can inspire both humility and resolve as we quest for our paths through time.[70] Perhaps most dangerously of all, we have convinced ourselves, on the basis of possibly fortuitous confluences in the historical experiences of the European world, that flourishing economies by necessity must be coterminous with representative politics and individual rights.[71] Yet "the Empire of Humanity" invoked with Beccaria's name, and the perpetual peace it promised, remains distant, evitable, a dream. The tensions between universal aspirations and localized needs, individuals and societies, states and markets, the ideal and the possible—tensions that eventually transformed the millenarian project of early social science into the narrow and pragmatic disciplinarity of our own times—show no signs of abating. Perhaps, though, the Academy of Fisticuffs will ultimately be proven right, and a global commercial society founded on justice and human dignity may yet be realized; but even to suggest that we may one day socialize *people* as well as *peoples* might be to court utopia.[72] Even so, this much is certain: it will not happen suddenly, it will not be easy, and we have many long days and long nights of work ahead of us.[73] Good thing we have coffee.

ARCHIVAL REFERENCES

Archives du Ministère des Affaires Étrangères, Paris, France
Archivio Baldasseroni Corsini, Florence, Italy
Archivio del Comune di Cremona, Cremona, Italy
Archivio di Stato di Genova, Genoa, Italy
Archivio di Stato di Milano, Milan, Italy
Archivio di Stato di Roma, Rome, Italy
Archivio di Stato di Torino, Turin, Italy
Archivio di Stato di Venezia, Venice, Italy
Archivio Storico Comunale di Casale Monferrato, Casale Monferrato, Italy
Archivio Verri, Fondazione Mattioli, housed at the Università di Milano under the
    tutelage of the Archivio Storico della Banca Intesa Sanpaolo, Milan, Italy
Archivo Histórico de la Casa de Loyola, Sanctuary of Loyola, Azpeitia, Spain
Baker Library, Harvard Business School, Boston
Biblioteca Ambrosiana, Milan, Italy
Biblioteca Antoniana, Padua, Italy
Biblioteca Civica Bertoliana, Vicenza, Italy
Biblioteca Civica Giovanni Canna, Casale Monferrato, Italy
Biblioteca Governativa di Lucca, Lucca, Italy
Biblioteca Nazionale Braidense, Milan, Italy
Biblioteca Nazionale Centrale di Firenze, Florence, Italy
Biblioteca Riccardiana, Florence, Italy
Boston Public Library, Boston

British Library, London
Chrysler Museum, Norfolk, VA
Civica Biblioteca Angelo Mai, Bergamo, Italy
Founder's Library, Fitzwilliam Museum, Cambridge, UK
Harvard Law School Library, Harvard University, Cambridge, MA
Harvard University Archives, Cambridge, MA
Houghton Library, Harvard University, Cambridge, MA
The Huntington Library, San Marino, CA
Kress Collection of Business and Economics, Baker Library, Harvard Business
    School, Boston
Museum of Fine Arts, Boston
Österreichische Nationalbibliothek, Vienna, Austria
Österreichisches Staatsarchiv, Vienna, Austria
Wren Library, Trinity College, University of Cambridge, Cambridge, UK

NOTES

Introduction

1. Ferdinando Facchinei, "Brevi note da porsi in pie' di pagina al libro dei Delitti e delle pene 1764," Archivio di Stato di Venezia, Venice, Italy, *Miscellanea di atti diversi manoscritti*, no. 71, fols. 15v and 16v. The charge did not appear in the later printed version of his critique, published as *Note ed osservazioni sul libro intitolato "Dei delitti e delle pene"* ([Venice]: n.p., 1765).

2. On Beccaria's importance, see, most succinctly, John D. Bessler, "The Economist and the Enlightenment: How Cesare Beccaria Changed Western Civilization," *European Journal of Law and Economics* 42, no. 2 (2016): 1–28.

3. Friedrich-Melchior Grimm, *Correspondance littéraire, philosophique et critique, adressé à un Souverain d'Allemagne, depuis 1753 jusqu'en 1769, par le Baron de Grimm et par Diderot*, 6 vols. (Paris: Longchamps et F. Buisson, 1812), 5:372–373; Alessandro Verri to Pietro Verri, 13 March 1767, in *Viaggio a Parigi e Londra (1766–1767): Carteggio di Pietro e Alessandro Verri*, ed. Gianmarco Gaspari (Milan: Adelphi, 1980), 353, 361.

4. Cesare Beccaria, *An Essay on Crimes and Punishments, Translated from the Italian; With a Commentary Attributed to Mons. De Voltaire, Translated from the French* (London: Almon, 1767), iv. On this edition, see Rosamaria Loretelli, "The First English Translation of Cesare Beccaria's *On Crimes and Punishments:* Uncovering the Editorial and Political Contexts," *Diciottesimo secolo* 2 (2017): 1–22.

5. What precisely the "Enlightenment" was remains an issue of great contention. For introductions and the surrounding historiographical debates, see, among others, James Schmidt, ed., *What Is Enlightenment? Eighteenth-Century Answers and Twentieth-Century Questions* (Berkeley: University of California Press, 1996); John Robertson, *The Case for the Enlightenment: Scotland and Naples, 1680–1760* (Cambridge: Cambridge University Press, 2005); Robertson's succinct yet profound *The Enlightenment: A Very Short Introduction* (Oxford: Oxford University Press, 2015); and Vincenzo Ferrone, *The Enlightenment: History of an Idea,* trans. Elisabetta Tarantino (Princeton, NJ: Princeton University Press, 2015). On the historiographical question of whether there was one or many Enlightenments, see, furthermore, Sophus A. Reinert, "In margine a un bilancio sui lumi europei," *Rivista storica italiana* 118, no. 3 (2006): 975–986. On caveats regarding the Enlightenment as the "myth of modernity," see Dan Edelstein, *The Enlightenment: A Genealogy* (Chicago: University of Chicago Press, 2010), 116–118.

6. On this debate, see, among many, many others, Istvan Hont, *Jealousy of Trade: International Competition and the Nation-State in Historical Perspective* (Cambridge, MA: Harvard University Press, 2005), 37–51, 159–184; Tim J. Hochstrasser, *Natural Law Theories in the Early Enlightenment* (Cambridge: Cambridge University Press, 2000), esp. 40–71; Eva Piirimäe and Alexander Schmidt, "Introduction: Between Morality and Anthropology—Sociability in Enlightenment Thought," *Journal of the History of European Ideas* 41, no. 5 (2014): 571–588; and John Robertson, "Sociability in Sacred Historical Perspective, 1650–1800," in *Markets, Morals, Politics: Jealousy of Trade and the History of Political Thought,* ed. Béla Kapossy, Isaac Nakhimovsky, Sophus A. Reinert, and Richard Whatmore (Cambridge, MA: Harvard University Press, 2018), 53–81.

7. Plautus, *Asinaria,* 495; Lucius Annaeus Seneca, *Epistulae morales ad Lucilium,* XCV, 33. In his *Adagia,* I.1.69 and I.1.70, Erasmus of Rotterdam reformulated these classical phrases and gave them the form by which they would become best known in early modern Europe: "homo homini deus [man is a god to man]" and "homo homini lupus [man is a wolf to man]." See William Barker, ed., *The Adages of Erasmus* (Toronto: University of Toronto Press, 2001), 37–41. This was further popularized by Thomas Hobbes, *On the Citizen* [*De Cive*], ed. Richard Tuck and Michael Silverthorne (Cambridge: Cambridge University Press, 1998), 3. On this, see also François Tricaud, "'Homo homini Deus,' 'Homo homini lupus': Recherche des deux formules de Hobbes," in *Hobbes-Forschungen,* ed. Reinhart Koselleck and Roman Schnur (Berlin: Duncker und Humblot, 1969), 61–70.

8. Hugo Grotius, *The Rights of War and Peace,* ed. Jean Barbeyrac and Richard Tuck, 3 vols. (Indianapolis: Liberty Fund, 2005), 1:79; Thomas Hobbes, *Leviathan,* ed. Richard Tuck (Cambridge: Cambridge University Press, 1996), 89.

9. For a meditation on this and other related questions in the context of eighteenth-century Switzerland, see Béla Kapossy, *Iselin contra Rousseau: Sociable Patriotism and the History of Mankind* (Basel: Schwabe, 2006). Relatedly, see the still-influential Albert O. Hirschman, *The Passions and the Interests: Political Arguments for Capitalism before Its Triumph* (Princeton, NJ: Princeton University Press, 1997); Hirschman, "Rival Views of Market Society," in *Rival Views of Market Society and Other Recent Essays* (New York: Viking, 1986), 105–141; and Jeremy Adelman's remarkable *Worldly Philosopher: The Odyssey of Albert O. Hirschman* (Princeton, NJ: Princeton University Press, 2013).

10. See, for example, "society, n.," Oxford English Dictionary Online, Oxford University Press, http://www.oed.com.ezp-prod1.hul.harvard.edu/view/Entry/183776?redirectedFrom=society. For a discussion of the term relevant to what follows, see Alessandro Verri, "Lo spirito di società," in *"Il Caffè," 1764–1766*, ed. Gianni Francioni and Sergio A. Romagnoli (Turin: Bollati Boringhieri, 1993), 396–402.

11. Hobbes, *On the Citizen*, 3–4, esp. 24. On the context of Hobbes's writing, see Blair Worden, *The English Civil Wars: 1640–1660* (London: Weidenfeld and Nicolson, 2009); on civil wars more broadly, see David Armitage, *Civil Wars: A History in Ideas* (New York: Alfred A. Knopf, 2017). On the ongoing process of state-formation at the time, see Charles Tilly, *Coercion, Capital, and European States, AD 990–1992* (Cambridge, MA: Harvard University Press, 1992).

12. John Rawls, *The Law of Peoples* (Cambridge, MA: Harvard University Press, 1999), 23.

13. Hobbes, *On the Citizen*, 231–232.

14. Hobbes, *Leviathan*, 90.

15. David Armitage, "Hobbes and the Foundations of Modern International Thought," in *The Foundations of Modern International Thought* (Cambridge: Cambridge University Press, 2013), 59–74, at 66–67. See also Noel Malcolm, "Hobbes' Theory of International Relations," in *Aspects of Hobbes* (Oxford: Oxford University Press, 2002), 432–456, at 434.

16. On the paucity of economic concerns in Hobbes, see Hont, *Jealousy of Trade*, 2.

17. On the enduring incongruity of states and markets, see Hont, *Jealousy of Trade*, 155. See also the essays in *The Economic Limits to Modern Politics*, ed. John Dunn (Cambridge: Cambridge University Press, 1992). Though inadequately studied, Joseph A. Schumpeter called this point a "commonplace"; see "The Lowell Lectures," in Schumpeter, *The Economics and Sociology of Capitalism*, ed. Richard Swedberg (Princeton, NJ: Princeton University Press, 1991), 339–400, at 386; see also Thorstein Veblen, "The Passing of National Frontiers [1918]," in Veblen, *Essays in Our Changing Order*, ed. Leon Ardzooni (New York: Viking, 1934), 383–390, esp. 387–389. For a recent statement of its centrality to contemporary concerns,

see Jürgen Kocka, *Capitalism: A Short History,* trans. Jeremiah Riemer (Princeton, NJ: Princeton University Press, 2016), 161; and for a surprising yet illuminating angle of analysis, see Hyun Ok Park, *The Capitalist Unconscious: From Korean Unification to Transnational Korea* (New York: Columbia University Press, 2015), esp. 5.

18. Quinn Slobodian, *Globalists: The End of Empire and the Birth of Neoliberalism* (Cambridge, MA: Harvard University Press, 2018), 10, discussing Carl Schmitt, *The Nomos of the Earth in the International Law of the Jus Publicum Europaeum,* trans. G. L. Ulmen (New York: Telos Press, 2003), 235. See, for a similar perspective, Paolo Prodi, *Settimo non rubare: Furto e mercato nella storia dell'Occidente* (Bologna: Il Mulino, 2009), 353–355.

19. See, for example, Pietro Verri, "Storia di Milano," in *Edizione nazionale delle opere di Pietro Verri,* ed. Carlo Capra et al., 8 vols. in 10 to date (Rome: Edizioni di storia e letteratura, 2003–2014) (hereafter cited as *ENOPV*), 4:69; and the Scotsman William Grant's commentary on François de Salignac de la Mothe de Fénelon in his "Essay II. Reflections on the Foregoing Sentiments," in *Two Essays on the Balance of Europe* (London: Darby, 1720), 27–58, at 40–41, for a context of which, see Iain McDaniel, *Adam Ferguson in the Scottish Enlightenment* (Cambridge, MA: Harvard University Press, 2013), 111–112. On the breakdown of polities, see Armitage, *Civil Wars.*

20. Immanuel Kant, "Perpetual Peace: A Philosophical Sketch," in Kant, *Political Writings,* ed. Hans Reiss, 2nd ed. (Cambridge: Cambridge University Press, 1991), 93–130. The literature on Kant's notion of perpetual peace and its legacy is ever-growing, but see, for an introduction, the essays in *Perpetual Peace: Essays on Kant's Cosmopolitan Ideal,* ed. James Bohman and Matthias Lutz-Bachmann (Cambridge, MA: MIT Press, 1997). For examples of the numerous similar projects that preceded Kant's, see Eşref Aksu, ed., *Early Notions of Global Governance: Selected Eighteenth-Century Proposals for "Perpetual Peace"* (Cardiff: University of Wales Press, 2008).

21. On the rise to prominence of economic concerns, see Sophus A. Reinert, "Rivalry: Greatness in Early Modern Political Economy," in *Mercantilism Reimagined: Political Economy in Early Modern Britain and Its Empire,* ed. Philip J. Stern and Carl Wennerlind (Oxford: Oxford University Press, 2013), 348–370.

22. In many ways this serves as a prelude to the more aggressive form of "globalization" currently preoccupying scholars—for examples of which see, among many others, Armand Mattelart, *Networking the World, 1794–2000,* trans. Liz Carey-Libbrecht and James A. Cohen (Minneapolis: University of Minnesota Press, 2000); Emily S. Rosenberg, ed., *A World Connecting, 1870–1945* (Cambridge, MA: Harvard University Press, 2012); and Jürgen Osterhammel, *The Transformation of the World: A Global History of the Nineteenth Century,* trans. Patrick Camiller (Princeton, NJ: Princeton University Press, 2014).

23. On the deeper history of natural law that set the stage for this moment, see Richard Tuck, *Natural Rights Theories: Their Origin and Development* (Cambridge: Cambridge University Press, 1982).

24. Jacob Viner, "The Economist in History," in Viner, *Essays on the Intellectual History of Economics*, ed. Douglas A. Irwin (Princeton, NJ: Princeton University Press, 1991), 226–247, at 227.

25. On the varied reception of the word, see, among others, Joshua Muravchik, *Heaven on Earth: The Rise and Fall of Socialism* (New York: Encounter Books, 2002); and John Nichols, *The S Word: A Short History of an American Tradition . . . Socialism* (London: Verso, 2011).

26. Mansour Shaki, "The Social Doctrine of Mazdak in Light of Middle Persian Evidence," *Archív Orientální* 46, no. 4 (1978): 289–306. For more recent "preludes" to socialism, see the still-relevant essays in *Preludi di socialismo nel XVII secolo*, ed. Giorgio Spini and Gaetano Cingari (Rome: Laterza, 1988).

27. On these movements, see, among others, Émile Durkheim, *Socialism and Saint-Simon*, ed. Alvin W. Gouldner (London: Routledge, 2009); Gregory Claeyes's magnificent *Machinery, Money and the Millennium: From Moral Economy to Socialism, 1815–1860* (Princeton, NJ: Princeton University Press, 1987); Jonathan Beecher, *Charles Fourier: The Visionary and His World* (Berkeley: University of California Press, 1990); Robert Wokler, "Ideology and the Origins of Social Science," in *The Cambridge History of Eighteenth-Century Political Thought*, ed. Mark Goldie and Robert Wokler (Cambridge: Cambridge University Press, 2006), 688–710; and Gareth Stedman Jones, "Millennium and Enlightenment: Robert Owen and the Second Coming of the Truth," in Kapossy, Nakhimovsky, Reinert, and Whatmore, *Markets, Morals, Politics*, 211–243.

28. Given the German and Italian context of this specific debate over "socialism," it fell outside the boundaries of the classic work by André Lichtenberger, *Le socialisme au XVIIIe siècle: Étude sur les idées socialistes dans les écrivains français du XVIIIe siècle avant la Révolution* (Paris: Félix Alcan, 1895). Broadly, on the conceptual origins of the terms "socialist" and "socialism," see the early chapters of Wolfgang Schilder, *Sozialismus*, in *Geschichtliche Grundbegriffe*, ed. Otto Brunner, Werner Bonze, and Reinhart Koselleck, 8 vols. (Stuttgart: Klett-Cotta, 1972–1997), 5:923–996. The classic treatments of the origins of "socialism" in Enlightenment Italy remain Franco Venturi, "Contributi ad un dizionario storico: 'Socialista' e 'socialismo' nell'Italia del Settecento," *Rivista storica italiana* 75 (1963): 129–140, truncated in Venturi, *Italy and the Enlightenment: Studies in a Cosmopolitan Century*, ed. Stuart Wolf, trans. Susan Corsi (London: Longman, 1972), 52–62, on which see Luciano Guerci, "Gli studi venturiani sull'Italia del '700: Dal *Vasco* agli *Illuministi italiani*," in *Il coraggio della ragione: Franco Venturi intellettuale e storico cosmopolita*, ed. Luciano Guerci and Giuseppe Ricuperati

(Turin: Fondazione Luigi Einaudi, 1998), 203–241, at 218–219; and Giorgio Spini, *Le origini del socialismo: Da utopia alla bandiera rossa* (Turin: Einaudi, 1992), 347–349, developed in Spini, "Sulle origini dei termini 'socialista' e 'socialismo,'" *Rivista storica italiana* 105 (1993): 679–697, republished in Spini, *Dalla preistoria del socialismo alla lotta per la libertá* (Milan: FrancoAngeli, 2002), 31–49.

29. Winston S. Churchill, *The Age of Revolutions* (New York: Dodd and Mead, 1957), 148–149. On this war, see, among others, Franz A. J. Szabo, *The Seven Years War in Europe, 1756–1763* (London: Routledge, 2007); and Daniel Baugh, *The Global Seven Years War, 1754–1763* (London: Routledge, 2011). On the transformative power of related expenses, see John Brewer, *The Sinews of Power: War, Money, and the English State, 1688–1783* (Cambridge, MA: Harvard University Press, 1988); and Hont, *Jealousy of Trade,* 340.

30. Hans Robert Jauss, "Literaturgeschichte als Provokation der Literaturwissenschaft," in *Literaturgeschichte als Provokation* (Frankfurt am Main: Suhrkamp, 1970), 144–207.

31. Hans Ulrich Gumbrecht, *Atmosphere, Mood, Stimmung: On a Hidden Potential of Literature* (Stanford, CA: Stanford University Press, 2012), 17. See, similarly, Hans Robert Jauss's "quereinschießendes Detail," in "Der Gebrauch der Fiktion in Formen der Anschauung und Darstellung der Geschichte," in *Formen der Geschichtsschreibung,* ed. Reinhart Koselleck, Heinrich Lutz, and Jörn Rüsen (Munich: Deutscher Taschenbuch Verlag, 1982), 415–451, at 450, citing Klaus Oettinger's discussion of "details" in relation to "sequences" and "general points of view" in his "Über Ein Beispiel, bei dem man Gedanken haben kann—Über die Zeitgeschictsschreibungen Johann Peter Hebels," *Der Deutschunterricht* 26, no. 6 (1974): 37–53, at 40–41. The term is further discussed in Ernst Hanisch, "Die linguistische Wende: Geschictswissenschaft und Literatur," in *Kulturgeschichte heute,* ed. Wolfgang Hardtwig and Hans Ulrich Wehler (Göttingen: Vandenhoeck und Ruprecht, 1996), 212–230, at 229; and in Marci Shore, *Caviar and Ashes: A Warsaw Generation's Life and Death in Marxism, 1918–1968* (New Haven, CT: Yale University Press, 2006), 6.

32. The historiography of capitalism is well established, but the "new history of capitalism" has in recent years emerged as a historiographical force to be reckoned with; for a flagship example of this, see Sven Beckert, *The Empire of Cotton: A Global History* (New York: Knopf, 2014). On the academic resurgence of the history of capitalism, see, among others, Jennifer Schuessler, "In History Departments, It's Up with Capitalism," *New York Times,* 6 April 2013; and the essays in *Capitalism: The Reemergence of a Historical Concept,* ed. Jürgen Kocka and Marcel van der Linden (London: Bloomsbury, 2016). For foundational, yet now often-neglected, milestones, see, among others, Werner Sombart, *Der moderne Kapitalismus: Historisch-systematische Darstellung des gesamteuropäischen*

Wirtschaftsleben von seinen Anfängen bis zur Gegenwart, 3 vols., 2nd ed. (Munich: Deutscher Taschenbuch Verlag, 1987); and Fernand Braudel, *Civilization and Capitalism, 15th–18th Century,* 3 vols., trans. Siân Reynolds (Berkeley: University of California Press, 1992).

33. It has been argued that "capitalism has always been a concept of difference," and in important ways the same was true of the terms "socialism" as well as "socialists" when they first were uttered; see the introduction in Kocka and van der Linden, *Capitalism,* at 2–3.

34. Hont, *Jealousy of Trade,* 45, 134, 159n–160n. On Hont, see Béla Kapossy, Isaac Nakhimovsky, Sophus A. Reinert, and Richard Whatmore, "Introduction," in Kapossy, Nakhimovsky, Reinert, and Whatmore, *Markets, Morals, Politics,* 1–22.

35. Some haziness may be required in the analysis of capitalism, and I agree with Michael Sonenscher's argument in *Work and Wages: Natural Law, Politics and the Eighteenth-Century French Trades,* with a new preface (Cambridge: Cambridge University Press, 2011 [1989]), 375, that "it is almost impossible to associate capitalism with a necessary configuration of production processes, products, markets, or legal and political institutions." As Frederic C. Lane long ago ventured, "as a social system . . . capitalism is a matter of degree: it is hard to find a society 100 percent capitalistic or 0 percent capitalistic"; see his "Meanings of Capitalism," in *Profits from Power: Readings in Protection Rent and Violence-Controlling Enterprises* (Albany: State University of New York Press, 1979), 66–71, at 70. Beyond questions of specific institutions and structures, however, much can be said for Thomas K. McCraw's broader definition of "the essence of capitalism" as "a psychological orientation toward the pursuit of future wealth and property"; see his introduction to *Creating Modern Capitalism: How Entrepreneurs, Companies, and Countries Triumphed in Three Industrial Revolutions,* ed. Thomas K. McCraw (Cambridge, MA: Harvard University Press, 1995), 1–18, at 4.

36. For examples of early uses of the term "capitalist," see Paul-Timoléon Delaforest, *Traité de l'usure et des intérets* (Cologne; Paris: Valat-la-Chapelle, 1769), 92; and, plausibly quite influentially, many works by Jacques Necker, including his *Réponse au Mémoire de M. l'abbé Morellet, sur la Compagnie des Indes . . .* (Paris: Imprimerie royale, 1769), 40; and, perhaps more famously, in Anne Robert Jacques Turgot's *Réflexions sur la formation et la distribution des richesses* (n.p.: n.p., 1788), esp. 72. Turgot's text was originally written in 1766 and first published in French in the *Ephémérides du citoyen* between 1769 and 1770. For the "public" focus of contemporary French usage, and examples of "capitalists" being understood as people who lend specifically to "states," see Michael Sonenscher, *Before the Deluge: Public Debt, Inequality, and the Intellectual Origins of the French Revolution* (Princeton, NJ: Princeton University Press, 2009), 2. Though Adam Smith himself never used the term "capitalist," it was introduced in editorial

annotations to his works already in the eighteenth century; see, for example, Adam Smith, *Fragment sur les colonies en general . . . traduit de l'Anglois* (Lausanne: Société typographique, 1778), 150n, a translation of his *Wealth of Nations*, bk. 4, chap. 7. Contrary to a common trope, however, the term had already made its way into the English language at the time in a translation of Charles Casauz, *Thoughts on the Mechanism of Societies* (London: Spilsbury, 1786), 61. The term circulated widely in the European world and received in-depth treatments in such diverse works as Johann Friedrich Kobe, *Der kluge Capitalist* (Nuremberg: G. F. Six, 1766), itself a translation of a 1761 Latin original, and José Maria de Uria Nafarrondo, *Aumento del comercio con seguridad de la conciencia* (Madrid: Ibarra, 1785), esp. 39. It was used—with its modern connotation—by the main protagonists of what is to follow, including Pietro Verri, "Discorsi [1781]," in *ENOPV*, 3:65–423, at 349; and Cesare Beccaria, "Attività del Dipartimento III nel 1786 [31 March 1787]," in *Edizione Nazionale delle Opere di Cesare Beccaria*, ed. Luigi Firpo and Gianni Francioni, 16 vols. in 17 (Milan: Mediobanca, 1984–2015) (hereafter cited as *ENOCB*), 10:223–267, at 242, 244. See also Beccaria's use of the term to describe an investor in a mine, in "Miniere di Valsassina [7 June 1779]," in *ENOCB*, 7:113–115, at 114. It is sometimes argued that the related term "capitalism" was invented "during the first global economy that clearly arose after 1848"; see, for example, Larry Neal's introduction to *The Cambridge History of Capitalism*, ed. Larry Neal and Jeffrey G. Williamson, 2 vols. (Cambridge: Cambridge University Press, 2014), 1:1–23, at 2. But it was used at least as early as the first decades of the nineteenth century; see, for example, its nonchalant appearance in Henry Marie Brackenridge, *Voyage to Buenos Ayres Performed in the Years 1817 and 1818, by the Order of the American Government* (London: Richard Phillips, 1820), 107.

37. On Marx, and how "the Marx constructed in the twentieth century bore only an incidental resemblance to the Marx who lived in the nineteenth," see Gareth Stedman Jones's magisterial *Karl Marx: Greatness and Illusion* (Cambridge, MA: Harvard University Press, 2016), 595. For illuminating takes on the rather different stories of Marx's legacies in Russia and China, see, among others, Stephen Kotkin, *Magnetic Mountain: Stalinism as Civilization* (Berkeley: University of California Press, 1995); and Ezra F. Vogel, *Deng Xiaoping and the Transformation of China* (Cambridge, MA: Harvard University Press, 2011). For the global consequences of these divergent trajectories, see Jeremy Friedman, *Shadow Cold War: The Sino-Soviet Competition for the Third World* (Chapel Hill: University of North Carolina Press, 2015).

38. On the long history of globalization and its historiography, see Sebastian Conrad, *What Is Global History?* (Princeton, NJ: Princeton University Press, 2016), with useful caveats at 210–214. On the problems in assuming that any spe-

cific definition of "socialism" somehow is transhistorically accurate, see Mark Bevir, *The Making of British Socialism* (Princeton, NJ: Princeton University Press, 2011), 13.

39. Reinhart Koselleck, *Futures Past: On the Semantics of Historical Time,* trans. Keith Tribe (New York: Columbia University Press, 2004); Stedman Jones, *Karl Marx*, 195.

40. On the group, see Franco Venturi, *Settecento riformatore,* 5 vols. in 7 (Turin: Einaudi, 1969–1990), 1:645–747; and the essays in Carlo Capra, *La felicità di tutti: Figuri e temi dell'Illuminismo Lombardo* (Rome: Aracne, 2017). On Bentham's verdict, see, among others, Aaron Thomas's preface in Cesare Beccaria, *On Crimes and Punishments and Other Writings,* ed. Aaron Thomas, trans. Aaron Thomas and Jeremy Parzen (Toronto: University of Toronto Press, 2008), xv–xxxii, at xv. For a biography of Beccaria, see Philippe Audegean, *Cesare Beccaria, filosofo europeo* (Rome: Carocci, 2014), which builds on Audegean's earlier French edition *La philosophie de Beccaria: Savoir punir, savoir écrire, savoir produire* (Paris: Vrin, 2010). On Pietro Verri, see Carlo Capra's magisterial *I progressi della ragione: Vita di Pietro Verri* (Bologna: Il Mulino, 2002); on the less-known Alessandro Verri, something of a dark horse who very much merits further studies, see Pierre Musitelli, *Le flambeau et les ombres: Alessandro verri, des Lumières à la Restauration* (Rome: École française de Rome, 2016).

41. For ease of reference I quote from Beccaria, *On Crimes and Punishments and Other Writings,* ed. Aaron Thomas, trans. Aaron Thomas and Jeremy Parzen (Toronto: University of Toronto Press, 2006). For the critical edition, see *ENOCB*, 1:215–368. On its historiography, see, among many others, Giuseppe Ricuperati, "Franco Venturi, Luigi Firpo e la riscoperta storiografica di Beccaria," in Vincenzo Ferrone and Giuseppe Ricuperati, *Il caso Beccaria: A 250 anni dalla pubblicazione del "Dei delitti e delle pene"* (Bologna: Il Mulino, 2016), 25–60.

42. To quote Franco Venturi, Beccaria's *On Crimes and Punishments* was "the most famous book of the Italian Enlightenment"; see Venturi, "Cesare Beccaria and Penal Reform," in his *Italy and the Enlightenment*, 154–164, at 154. On Beccaria's work being the most widely read treatise on penal reform, see among others Paul Friedland, *Seeing Justice Done: The Age of Spectacular Capital Punishment in France* (Oxford: Oxford University Press, 2012), 195.

43. See, among many, many others, Philip P. Purpura, *Criminal Justice: An Introduction* (Newton, MA: Butterworth-Heinemann, 1997), 265; and Study.com's online high school course "AP European History," chap. 9, lesson 17, by Christopher Sailus, "Cesare Beccaria: Theories, Impact and Jurisprudence," http://study .com/academy/lesson/cesare-beccaria-theories-impact-jurisprudence.html; Bessler, "The Economist and the Enlightenment."

44. Venturi, "Cesare Beccaria and Legal Reform," 155. On Beccaria's rich library, see Maria Francesca Turchetti, "Libri e 'nuove idee': Appunti sulla biblioteca illuministica di Cesare Beccaria," *Archivio storico Lombardo* 139 (2013): 183–236. On Venturi, see the essays in Guerci and Ricuperati, *Il coraggio della ragione;* and Adriano Viarengo, *Franco Venturi, politica e storia nel Novecento* (Rome: Carocci, 2014).

45. Beccaria, *On Crimes and Punishments,* 10–12. See also Madeleine van Bellen, "Die Begriffe *giustizia* bei Cesare Beccaria und den Brüdern Pietro und Alessandro Verri," in *Beiträge zur Begriffsgeschichte der italienischen Aufklärung im europäischen Kontext,* ed. Helmut C. Jacobs and Gisela Schlüter (Frankfurt am Main: Peter Lang, 2000), 151–164, esp. 153. The ur-source for Beccaria's argument might well be Samuel von Pufendorf, *On the Duty of Man and Citizen According to Natural Law,* ed. James Tully, trans. Michael Silverthorne (Cambridge: Cambridge University Press, 1991), 35–36: "All that necessarily and normally makes for sociality is understood to be prescribed by natural law. All that disturbs or violates sociality is understood as forbidden."

46. See, for this angle, Alberto Quadrio Curzio, "Cesare Beccaria e Pietro Verri: L'economia civile per il governo della 'cosa pubblica,'" in *Economisti ed economia: Per un'Italia europea: Paradigmi tra il XVIII e il XX secolo* (Bologna: Il Mulino, 2007), 43–56. For a recent manifesto of what this tradition has developed into, see Luigino Bruni and Stefano Zamagni, *L'economia civile* (Bologna: Il Mulino, 2015). For caveats, see, among others, Prodi, *Settimo non rubare,* 367–368.

47. For a particularly clear example of this, see Till Wahnbaeck, *Luxury and Public Happiness: Political Economy in the Italian Enlightenment* (Oxford: Oxford University Press, 2004), 156, 167, 184. On Beccaria and "Law and Economics," see also Bernard E. Harcourt, *The Illusion of Free Markets* (Cambridge, MA: Harvard University Press, 2011).

48. See, among others, Biancamaria Fontana, *Rethinking the Politics of Commercial Society: The Edinburgh Review 1802–1832* (Cambridge: Cambridge University Press, 1985), vii; *China and Historical Capitalism: Genealogies of Sinological Knowledge,* ed. Gregory Blue and Timothy Brook (Cambridge: Cambridge University Press, 1999), 1–9, at 4; Kocka, *Capitalism,* 11; and Patrick Murray, "On Studying Commercial Life (with Bibliographies)," in *Reflections on Commercial Life: An Anthology of Classic Texts from Plato to the Present,* ed. Patrick Murray (London: Routledge, 1997), 1–38, at 3–4. On the relationship between the two terms, see also Joseph A. Schumpeter, *Capitalism, Socialism and Democracy,* ed. Richard Swedberg (London: Routledge, 1994), 167; and Istvan Hont, *Politics in Commercial Society: Jean-Jacques Rousseau and Adam Smith,* ed. Béla Kapossy and Michael Sonenscher (Cambridge, MA: Harvard University Press, 2015), 6.

49. A sentiment, again, expressed clearly in Facchinei, "Brevi note," fols. 15v and 16v.

50. On the eighteenth-century emergence of social science, see Keith Michael Baker, "The Early History of the Term 'Social Science,'" *Annals of Science* 20 (1964): 211–226; Brian William Head, *Ideology and Social Science: Destutt de Tracy and French Liberalism* (Dordrecht: Martinus Nijhoff, 1985); Robert Wokler, "Ideology and the Origins of Social Science," in Goldie and Wokler, *Cambridge History of Eighteenth-Century Political Thought*, 688–709, esp. 691–693; Michael Sonenscher, "'The Moment of Social Science': The *Decade Philosophique* and Late Eighteenth-Century French Thought," *Modern Intellectual History* 6, no. 1 (2009): 121–146. See also the contributions to *Inventing Human Science: Eighteenth-Century Domains*, ed. Chrisopher Fox, Roy Porter, and Robert Wokler (Berkeley: University of California Press, 1995). It must be said that the Academy of Fisticuffs well may have drawn on the example of natural sciences to a greater extent than other contemporary acolytes of "social science," partially because they were less exposed to democratic experiences with "representative government" at the time; for a brilliant analysis of this, see Michael Sonenscher's introduction to Emmanuel Joseph Sieyès, *Political Writings*, ed. Michael Sonenscher (Indianapolis: Hackett, 2003), vii–lxiv, esp. xlvi.

51. For an unwittingly mirthful introduction to the genre, with suggested inflections for our "age of terrorism," see Jeff Herman and Deborah Herman, *Toasts for All Occasions*, rev. ed. (Franklin Lakes, NJ: New Page Press, 2004), esp. 130.

52. On the challenges of political economy and perpetual peace in early modern Europe, see the essays in *Commerce and Peace in the Enlightenment*, ed. Béla Kapossy, Isaac Nakhimovsky, and Richard Whatmore (Cambridge: Cambridge University Press, 2017). For a different but related history of "the beginning of secular social science freed from the theological encumbrances which had hampered its development in earlier centuries," see Peter Groenewegen, "Turgot, Beccaria and Smith," in *Eighteenth-Century Economics: Turgot, Beccaria and Smith and Their Contemporaries* (London: Routledge, 2002), 3–47, esp. 3, drawing on Stephen Leslie, *History of English Thought in the Eighteenth Century*, 2 vols. (New York: G. P. Putnam's Sons, 1876).

53. Richard Swedberg recently defined "hope" as "a wish for something to come true." See Swedberg, "A Sociological Approach to Hope in the Economy," in *The Economy of Hope*, ed. Hirokazu Miyazaki and Richard Swedberg (Philadelphia: University of Pennsylvania Press, 2017), 37–50, at 49. Seigo Hirowatari has added to this definition "by action"; see Yuji Genda, "Hope and Society in Japan," in Miyazaki and Swedberg, *The Economy of Hope*, 97–125, at 97–98. In the case of eighteenth-century Lombardy, and large parts of Enlightenment political economy, a fundamental tension was precisely whether something good would result from directed action or merely by letting be.

54. On this transition, see still Karl Polanyi, *The Great Transformation: The Political and Economic Origins of Our Time*, ed. Fred Block, intro. Joseph E. Stiglitz (Boston: Beacon Press, 2001), on which see Fred Block and Margaret R. Somers, *The Power of Market Fundamentalism: Karl Polanyi's Critique* (Cambridge, MA: Harvard University Press, 2014). On the simultaneously Promethean and dislocating consequences of this "market principle" for traditional societies, see Steven L. Kaplan, *Provisioning Paris: Merchants and Millers in the Grain and Flour Trade during the Eighteenth Century* (Ithaca, NY: Cornell University Press, 1984), esp. 25. For the argument that this shift occurred only in nineteenth-century America, see Michal Zakim and Gary J. Kornblith, "Introduction: An American Revolutionary Tradition," in *Capitalism Takes Command: The Social Transformation of Nineteenth-Century America*, ed. Michal Zakim and Gary J. Kornblith (Chicago: University of Chicago Press, 2012), 1–12, at 4. What follows is, in many ways, a prehistory of the better-understood transformations of the nineteenth century, on which see also Braudel, *Civilization and Capitalism*, 2:223–230. For a different, yet illuminating take on this process of marketization at the time, see Prodi, *Settimo non rubare*, 10–18. For a powerful argument for the periodic rises and declines of market economies through time, which conceptually would have appealed to the Academy of Fisticuffs given their cyclical view of economic affairs, see Bas van Bavel, *The Invisible Hand? How Market Economies Have Emerged and Declined since AD 500* (Oxford: Oxford University Press, 2016).

55. Paolo Malanima, *Economia preindustriale: Mille anni; dal IX al XVIII secolo* (Milan: Mondadori, 1997), 459–465; this is excellently paraphrased in Paola Lanaro, "Periferie senza centro: Reti fieristiche nello spazio geografico della terraferma veneta in età moderna," in *La pratica dello scambio: Sistemi di fiere, mercanti e città in Europa (1400–1700)*, ed. Paola Lanaro (Venice: Marsilio, 2003), 21–51, at 21.

56. See, for example, the view of statesman and political economist Anne Robert Jacques Turgot that, "far from being a proof of the flourishing state of commerce, [great fairs] can exist, on the contrary, only in states where commerce is embarrassed," in his entry "Foire," in *Encyclopédie . . .* , ed. Denis Diderot and Jean le Rond d'Alembert, 28 vols. (Paris: Briasson et al., 1751–1772), 7:39–41, at 41; for a critical discussion of which, see, among others, Anne Conchon, "Foires et marches en France au XCIIIe siècle: Definitions fiscales et économie du privilège," in *Fiere e mercati nella integrazione delle economie europee sec. XIII–XVIII*, ed. Simonetta Cavachiocchi (Florence: Le Monnier, 2001), 289–298; and Francesca Trivellato's excellent "La fiera del corallo (Livorno, XVII e XVIII secolo): Istituzioni e autoregolamento del mercato in età moderna," in Lanaro, *La pratica dello scambio*, 111–127, at 122–123. On the importance of fairs into the eighteenth century, see also Braudel, *Civilization and Capitalism*, 2:81.

57. Aldo Carera, "I mercati della tradizione," in *I mercati e le fiere della provincia di Milano tra XVIII e XX secolo,* ed. Maria Piera Bassi (Milan: Provincia di Milano, 1990), 17–61, at 28.

58. See, for example, Hazel Smith, *North Korea: Markets and Military Rule* (Cambridge: Cambridge University Press, 2015), 12–13; and Onwuka Njoku, *Economic History of Nigeria: 19th and 20th Centuries* (Enugu: Magnet Business Enterprises, 2001), 84. For Polanyi's continuing relevance for scholarship on marketization, see Benjamin Spies-Butcher, Joy Paton, and Damien Cahill, *Market Society: History, Theory, Practice* (Cambridge: Cambridge University Press, 2012), 4.

59. For which see, respectively, McDaniel, *Adam Ferguson,* and Hont, *Politics in Commercial Society.*

60. Adam Smith, *An Inquiry into the Nature and Causes of the Wealth of Nations,* ed. Edwin Cannan, 2 vols. (Chicago: University of Chicago Press, 1976), 1:26. For an earlier expression of this theory, see his 1762–1763 Glasgow lectures in Smith, *Lectures on Jurisprudence,* ed. Ronald E. Meek, D. D. Raphael, and P. G. Stein (Oxford: Oxford University Press, 1976), 14. On the four-stages theory, see Ronald L. Meek's still-relevant *Social Science and the Ignoble Savage* (Cambridge: Cambridge University Press, 1976); and, for the Scottish theory of commercial society and its origins, see Istvan Hont, "The Language of Sociability and Commerce: Samuel Pufendorf and the Theoretical Foundations of the 'Four Stages' Theory," in *Jealousy of Trade,* 159–184; Christopher J. Berry, *The Idea of Commercial Society in the Scottish Enlightenment* (Edinburgh: Edinburgh University Press, 2013); and Hont, *Politics in Commercial Society.*

61. The literature on Physiocracy is vast and ever-growing, but see Steven L. Kaplan, *Bread, Politics and Political Economy in the Reign of Louis XV,* 2nd ed. (London: Anthem, 2015); and Kaplan, *The Stakes of Regulation: Perspectives on "Bread, Politics and Political Economy" Forty Years Later* (London: Anthem, 2015); as well as Sonenscher, *Before the Deluge;* and Arnaud Orain and Philippe Steiner, "François Quesnay (1694–1774) and Physiocracy," in *Handbook on the History of Economic Analysis,* ed. Gilbert Faccarello and Heinz D. Kurz, 3 vols. (Cheltenham, UK: Edward Elgar, 2016), 1:28–39. On the growing resistance to Physiocracy in Europe, see the essays in *The Economic Turn: Recasting Political Economy in Eighteenth-Century Europe,* ed. Steven L. Kaplan and Sophus A. Reinert (London: Anthem, forthcoming). Keith Tribe may well be right, in his "The Word: Economy," in *The Economy of the Word: Language, History, and Economics* (Oxford: Oxford University Press, 2015), 21–88, at 51–52, that Physiocracy survived only as a "caricature" because critics focused so incessantly on certain aspects of their theories ("sterility" of manufacturing, etc.), but the degree to which Physiocrats themselves belabored this precise point suggests that the caricature originally took the form of a self-portrait.

62. François Quesnay, "Grains" [1757], in Quesnay, Œuvres économiques complètes et autres textes, ed. Christine Théré, Loïc Charles, and Jean-Claude Perrot, 2 vols. (Paris: INED, 2005), 1:161–212, at 208. On Smith's torn relationship with the Physiocrats, see Hont, Jealousy of Trade, 361–376.

63. For an early version of the phrase, see Thomas Carlyle, Chartism (Boston: C. C. Little and J. Brown, 1840), 58: "For, in one word, Cash Payment had not then grown to be the universal sole nexus of man to man." For Marx's famous engagement with the question, see his 1844 "Excerpts from James Mill's Elements of Political Economy," in Early Writings, ed. Lucio Colletti, trans. Rodney Livingstone and Gregor Benton (London: Penguin, 1992), 259–278, at 266. For an eminently readable meditation on the term, see Niall Ferguson, The Cash Nexus: Money and Power in the Modern World, 1700–2000 (New York: Basic Books, 2001).

64. Smith, Wealth of Nations, 1:433, drawing on David Hume, "On Commerce [1752]" and "Of Refinement in the Arts [1752]," both in Hume, Political Essays, ed. Knud Haakonssen (Cambridge: Cambridge University Press, 1994), 93–104, 105–114. On these issues, see also Hont, Politics in Commercial Society, 3. As Jerry Z. Muller succinctly put it, Smith's ideals were "intended to make men better, not just better off"; see Muller, The Mind and the Market: Capitalism in Western Thought (New York: Anchor Books, 2002), 52.

65. Smith's caveat regarding the division of labor involved the risk that working classes would, by endless repetition, become "as stupid and ignorant as it is possible for a human creature to become" (Wealth of Nations, 2:302–303), a vision taken to its logical extreme in Aldous Huxley, Brave New World (New York: Harper Millennial, 2006), esp. 222–223. For a rather fantastical yet profound take on the systemic dangers of overspecialization in commercial society, see also Max Brooks, World War Z: An Oral History of the Zombie War (London: Duckworth, 2013 [2006]), esp. 138–139.

66. Again, the classical work on this tradition of interpretation remains Hirschman, The Passions and the Interests; see also Norman Angell's earlier Europe's Optical Illusion (London: Simpkin, Marshall, Hamilton, Kent and Co., 1909). The literature on trade and peace is ever-growing, but for caveats see, among others, Katherine Barbieri, The Liberal Illusion: Does Trade Promote Peace? (Ann Arbor: University of Michigan Press, 2005); and, for a rather more optimistic take at the level of individuals, see Gordon Mathews, Ghetto at the Center of the World: Chungking Mansions, Hong Kong (Chicago: University of Chicago Press, 2011), 213.

67. On the empire of English, see Robert Phillipson's still-relevant Linguistic Imperialism (Oxford: Oxford University Press, 1992); on the increasing challenge of monoglottism in British graduate training in history, see Richard J. Evans, Cosmopolitan Islanders: British Historians and the European Continent (Cambridge: Cambridge University Press, 2009), 189–234. For the U.S. case, see Thomas Bender

et al., *The Education of Historians for the Twenty-First Century* (Urbana: University of Illinois Press, 2004), 57–58.

68. Erik S. Reinert, *How Rich Countries Got Rich . . . And Why Poor Countries Stay Poor* (London: Constable, 2007), 65–66.

69. Antonio Genovesi, *Storia del commercio della Gran Brettagna,* 3 vols. (Naples: Benedetto Gessari, 1757–1758), 1:111n; Benjamin Franklin, "Father Abraham's Speech [*The Way to Wealth*]," in *The Papers of Benjamin Franklin,* ed. Leonard W. Labaree et al., 41 vols. (New Haven, CT: Yale University Press, 1959–2014), 7:340–350, on which see Max Weber, *The Protestant Ethic and the Spirit of Capitalism and Other Writings,* ed. Peter Baehr and Gordon C. Wells (London: Penguin, 2002), and Sophus A. Reinert, "The *Way to Wealth* around the World: Benjamin Franklin and the Globalization of American Capitalism," *American Historical Review* 120, no. 1 (2015): 61–97.

70. The question of whether "capitalism" was an Italian, Dutch, or English "invention," and whether it was "Protestant" or "Catholic," has been the subject of a cottage industry over the past few centuries, but I maintain squarely the primacy of Italy. For lucid arguments along the same lines, from dramatically different places on the political spectrum, see Friedrich Engels, "Preface to the Italian Edition of 1893," in Karl Marx and Friedrich Engels, *The Communist Manifesto,* ed. Gareth Stedman Jones (London: Penguin, 2002), 215–217, at 216; Raymond de Roover, *The Rise and Fall of the Medici Bank, 1397–1494* (Cambridge, MA: Harvard University Press, 1963), 1; Richard A. Goldthwaite, *The Economy of Renaissance Florence* (Baltimore: Johns Hopkins University Press, 2009), 8: Sophus A. Reinert and Robert Fredona, "Merchants and the Origins of Capitalism," in *The Routledge Companion to Makers of Global Business,* ed. Teresa da Silva Lopes, Christina Lubinski, and Heidi Tworek (London: Routledge, forthcoming).

71. Ferrone, *The Enlightenment,* xi, building on Venturi, *Settecento riformatore,* 1:xiii; emphasis in original.

72. Sophus A. Reinert, "Lessons on the Decline and Fall of Great Powers: Conquest, Commerce, and Decline in Enlightenment Italy," *American Historical Review* 115, no. 5 (2010): 1395–1425.

73. For a not dissimilar perspective, see Duncan Bell, "What Is Liberalism?," in *Reordering the World: Essays on Liberalism and Empire* (Princeton, NJ: Princeton University Press, 2016), 62–90, at 90.

74. Laurence Sterne, *The Life and Opinions of Tristram Shandy, Gentleman* (London: Penguin, 2003), 64.

75. As such, it seeks to address the caveat in Sophus A. Reinert, *Translating Empire: Emulation and the Origins of Political Economy* (Cambridge, MA: Harvard University Press, 2011), 48.

76. Michael O'Brien, *Henry Adams and the Southern Question* (Athens: University of Georgia Press, 2007), esp. 151–152. See, similarly, Emma Rothschild, *Economic Sentiments: Adam Smith, Condorcet, and the Enlightenment* (Cambridge, MA: Harvard University Press, 2001); Rothschild, "Psychological Modernity in Historical Perspective," in *Rethinking the Development Experience: Essays Provoked by the Work of Albert O. Hirschman,* ed. Lloyd Rodwin and Donald A. Schön (Washington, DC: Brookings Institution and Lincoln Institute of Land Policy, 1994), 99–117; and, at more length, Rothschild, *The Inner Life of Empire: An Eighteenth-Century History* (Princeton, NJ: Princeton University Press, 2011); as well as, on "the sentimental basis of the emergence of ideas," Gregory Claeys, "Early Socialism as Intellectual History," *History of European Ideas* 40, no. 7 (2014): 893–904, at 901. This is, needless to say, far from a recent wish of historiography. Jacob Viner had already warned against intellectual history becoming "a lifeless, bloodless, anaemic academic discipline, one which isolates ideas from human minds and passions"; see Donald Winch, "Teaching: Jacob Viner," *American Scholar* 50, no. 4 (1981): 519–525, at 524.

77. Emma Rothschild, "Faith, Enlightenment, and Economics," in *Natural Law, Economics, and the Common Good: Perspectives from Natural Law,* ed. Samuel Gregg and Harold James (Exeter, UK: Imprint Academic, 2012), 17–23, at 22.

78. Anthony Gerald Hopkins, "Introduction: Globalization—An Agenda for Historians," in *Globalization in World History,* ed. Anthony Gerald Hopkins (London: Pimlico, 2002), 1–10, at 5; Charles S. Maier, *Leviathan 2.0: Inventing Modern Statehood* (Cambridge, MA: Harvard University Press, 2012), 8–11, originally published as chapter 1 in Rosenberg, *A World Connecting,* 29–282, and now supported by Maier's *Once within Borders: Territories of Power, Wealth, and Belonging since 1500* (Cambridge, MA: Harvard University Press, 2016). On where this ever-increasing connectivity might lead, see Parag Khanna, *Connectography: Mapping the Future of Global Civilization* (New York: Random House, 2016).

79. Hakim Bey [Peter Lamborn Wilson], *T. A. Z.: The Temporary Autonomous Zone* (Seattle: Pacific Publishing Studio, 2011 [1991]), 71.

80. Marx and Engels, *The Communist Manifesto,* 220–221.

81. Tarun Khanna and Krishna G. Palepu, *Winning in Emerging Markets: A Road Map for Strategy and Execution* (Boston: Harvard Business Press, 2010), 6.

82. Fernand Braudel, *The Mediterranean and the Mediterranean World in the Age of Philip II,* trans. Siân Reynolds, 1 vol. in 2 (Berkeley: University of California Press, 1995), 2:1238. On objectivity, see Peter Novick, *That Noble Dream: The "Objectivity Question" and the American Historical Profession* (Cambridge: Cambridge University Press, 1988).

83. Compare Wahnbaeck, *Luxury and Public Happiness,* 7.

84. Joseph A. Schumpeter, *A History of Economic Analysis,* ed. Elizabeth Boody Schumpeter (Oxford: Oxford University Press, 1954), 3. The historiographical resurgence of political economy was recently noted also by Nathan Perl-Rosenthal, "Comment: Generational Turns," *American Historical Review* 117, no. 3 (2012): 804–813, at 806n7. For a similar argument on how to approach the history of capitalism, see Sven Beckert, "The New History of Capitalism," in Kocka and van der Linden, *Capitalism,* 235–249, at 238–239.

85. David Hume, "Of Civil Liberty," in Hume, *Political Essays,* 51–57, at 52; Hont, *Jealousy of Trade,* 4–5. I have previously argued that this sentiment would require us to throw our historical net backward at least as early as medieval Italy; see my introduction to Antonio Serra, *A Short Treatise on the Wealth and Poverty of Nations (1613),* ed. Sophus A. Reinert (London: Anthem, 2011), 1–93, at 19. For a later, influential statement based on rather different ideological premises, see Karl Marx, "The German Ideology," in Marx, *Early Political Writings,* ed. Joseph O'Malley (Cambridge: Cambridge University Press, 1994), 119–181, at 160: "With manufacturing, relations of competition arose among the various nations, and the commercial struggle was carried out by means of wars, protective tariffs and prohibitions. . . . From this moment on, commerce had a political significance."

86. Franco Venturi, *Utopia e riforma nell'illuminismo* (Turin: Einaudi, 1970), 10. For a slightly altered English translation, see Venturi, *Utopia and Reform in the Enlightenment* (Cambridge: Cambridge University Press, 1971), 2.

87. See, however, James Schmidt, "Misunderstanding the Question 'What Is Enlightenment?' Venturi, Habermas, Foucault," *Journal of the History of European Ideas* 37 (2011): 43–52.

88. E.g., Robertson, *Case for the Enlightenment,* 371–376.

89. Venturi, *Settecento riformatore,* 1:xiv.

90. As Giles Constable has shown, by the eleventh and twelfth centuries the word *reformatio* had come to mean either "restoration and revival, in a backward-looking sense," or "rebirth and reformation, as a forward-looking change," not only on a "personal" level but also with regard "to institutions, including the church, the empire, and society as a whole." See Constable, *The Reformation of the Twelfth Century* (Cambridge: Cambridge University Press, 1998), 3. The literature on "improvement" is growing and will be discussed in later footnotes, but see, for representative examples, Richard Drayton, *Nature's Government: Science, Imperial Britain, and the "Improvement" of the World* (New Haven, CT: Yale University Press, 2000); and Paul Slack, *The Invention of Improvement: Information and Material Progress in Seventeenth-Century England* (Oxford: Oxford University Press, 2015).

91. On regulation as a fundamentally structuring enterprise, see Richard H. K. Vietor, *Contrived Competition: Regulation and Deregulation in America* (Cambridge, MA: Harvard University Press, 1994), 310. On the variegated theoretical history of economic development, see the essays in *Handbook of Alternative Theories of Economic Development*, ed. Erik S. Reinert, Jayati Ghosh, and Rainer Kattel (Cheltenham, UK: Edward Elgar, 2016).

92. Kaplan and Reinert, *The Economic Turn.*

93. Petrarch, *The Canzoniere or Rerum vulgarium fragmenta*, ed. Mark Musa (Bloomington: Indiana University Press, 1999), poem 146, 236–237.

94. Tim Rogan, *The Moral Economists: R. H. Tawney, Karl Polanyi, E. P. Thompson, and the Critique of Capitalism* (Princeton, NJ: Princeton University Press, 2018), 1.

95. Groenewegen, "Turgot, Beccaria and Smith," 3.

96. See, for a notable exception, Harcourt, *Illusion of Free Markets.*

97. See, for example, Carlo Antonio Vianello, *La giovinezza di Parini, Verri e Beccaria: Con scritti, documenti e ritratti inediti* (Milan: Baldini e Castoldi, 1933), 199; Groenewegen, "Turgot, Beccaria and Smith," 29, 36–37; and obliquely even Maier, *Once within Borders*, 118. For a measured reading of the "Physiocratic turn" in Lombardy, see Carlo Capra, *Gli italiani prima dell'Italia: Un lungo Settecento, dalla fine della Controriforma a Napoleone* (Rome: Carocci, 2014), esp. 178–181. On the importance of Antiphysiocracy, see the essays Kaplan and Reinert, *The Economic Turn;* and Arnaud Orain, "Figures of Mockery: The Cultural Disqualification of Physiocracy (1760–1790)," *European Journal of the History of Economic Thought* 22, no. 3 (2015): 389–419.

98. On Israel's project, see the numerous publications beginning with Jonathan Israel, *Radical Enlightenment: Philosophy and the Making of Modernity, 1650–1760* (Oxford: Oxford University Press, 2001). As a caveat, it is worth repeating John Robertson's point that "Enlightenment was not successfully articulated by radical irreligion"; see his *Case for the Enlightenment*, 377–378.

99. See, for a different reading, Wahnbaeck, *Luxury and Public Happiness*, 184–186.

100. Schumpeter, *A History of Economic Analysis*, 177. On Verri in particular through this lens, see Pier Luigi Porta and Roberto Scazzieri, "Pietro Verri's Political Economy: Commercial Society, Civil Society, and the Science of the Legislator," *History of Political Economy* 34, no. 1 (2002): 83–110, at 84. This tradition at least problematizes Michel Foucault's argument that "economic theory does not arise within the power apparatus" in his *The Punitive Society: Lectures at the Collège de France, 1972–1973*, ed. Bernard E. Harcourt, trans. Graham Burchell (Houndmills, UK: Palgrave Macmillan, 2015), 236.

101. Keith Tribe, "Sources, Arguments, and Prospect," in *The Economy of the Word*, 297–312, at 311.

102. Shore, *Caviar and Ashes*, 5.

103. Muhammad Ali, *Muhammad Ali Unfiltered: Rare, Iconic, and Officially Authorized Photos of the Greatest*, foreword by Lonnie Ali (New York: Simon & Schuster, 2016), 58.

1. Hard Knocks Café

1. On her world, see Michael Yonan, *Empress Maria Theresa and the Politics of Habsburg Imperial Art* (University Park: Pennsylvania State University Press, 2011).

2. For a similar argument regarding the quotidian in the historical record, see Steven L. Kaplan, *Provisioning Paris: Merchants and Millers in the Grain and Flour Trade during the Eighteenth Century* (Ithaca, NY: Cornell University Press, 1984), 8; and Edward Muir and Guido Ruggiero, "Introduction: The Crime of History," in *History from Crime*, ed. Muir and Ruggiero, trans. Corrada Biazzo Curry, Margaret A. Gallucci, and Mary M. Gallucci (Baltimore: Johns Hopkins University Press, 1994), vii–xviii, at vii.

3. Flyer promulgated by the Prefect Marquis Giuseppe Gerolamo Talenti Fiorenza and circulated by the Confraternity of the Beheaded St. John the Baptist, 4 June 1767, part of the Giancarlo Beltrame Collection and reproduced in Italo Mereu, *La pena di morte a Milano nel secolo di Beccaria* (Vicenza: Neri Pozza Editore, 1988), [85].

4. Mitchell B. Merback, *The Thief, the Cross and the Wheel: Pain and the Spectacle of Punishment in Medieval and Renaissance Europe* (Chicago: University of Chicago Press, 1999), 141. That is, it is an assessment that is hard to make without further empirical research of the sort upon which university ethics committees rightly frown. On the paradoxical role of ethics committees in the offshoring of human experiments, however, demonstrating the still-incomplete nature of global socialization, see Adriana Petryna, *When Experiments Travel: Clinical Trials and the Global Search for Human Subjects* (Princeton, NJ: Princeton University Press, 2009).

5. *Trewlicher Bericht eynes scrocklichen Kindermords beym Hexensabath*, Hamburg, 12 June 1607, the Lovecraftian horror of which is quoted in, among others, Merback, *The Thief, the Cross and the Wheel*, 160–161; Garrett G. Fagan, *The Lure of the Arena: Social Psychology and the Roman Games* (Cambridge: Cambridge University Press, 2011), 54–55; Steven Pinker, *The Better Angels of Our Nature: Why Violence Has Declined* (New York: Viking, 2011), 147; and Michael Kwass, *Contraband:*

Louis Mandrin and the Making of a Global Underground (Cambridge, MA: Harvard University Press, 2014), 245. The passage even appears on object labels in the sundry "Torture Museums" that have started appearing around Italy, including the Museo della Tortura, in Volterra, Italy.

6. Merback, *The Thief, the Cross and the Wheel,* 141.

7. Though much has been made of sadistic executioners in the literary imagination, most tended to simply do their job as well as possible, also out of fear of popular reprisals. See, among others, Joel F. Harrington, *The Faithful Executioner: Life and Death, Honor and Shame in the Turbulent Sixteenth Century* (New York: Farrar, Strauss and Giroux, 2013), esp. 47.

8. Biblioteca Ambrosiana, Milan, Italy (hereafter Ambrosiana), S.Q. + I.6, "Memoria per li confortatori di quell che possa farsi per superare la durezza in ridursi a morire christianamente e l'ostinazione ch'alcuna volta si trova nei condannati a morte," no date but eighteenth century, attached to Benvenuto da Milano, ed., *Sentenze Capitali,* 4 vols., n.d., vol. 1: *1471–1659,* 1–14, quotation at 13–14; emphasis added. This manuscript was brought to my attention by Mereu, *La pena di morte,* 27–37, which also discusses the specific Confraternity. On such confraternities generally, see Vincenzo Paglia, *La morte confortata: Riti della paura e mentalità religiosa a Roma nell'età moderna* (Rome: Edizioni di storia e letteratura, 1982); Adriano Prosperi, *Delitto e perdono: La pena di morte nell'orizzonte mentale dell'Europa Cristiana, XIV–XVIII secolo* (Turin: Einaudi, 2013), esp. 212–279; and the essays collected in Nicholas Terpestra, ed., *The Art of Executing Well: Rituals of Execution in Renaissance Italy* (Kirksville, MO: Truman State University Press, 2008), which includes the late fifteenth-century "Bologna *Comforter's Manual*" at 183–292. A similar manual for the Florentine context is in the Biblioteca Nazionale Centrale di Firenze, Florence, Italy (hereafter cited as BNCF), II.I.138. On the wide variety of such rituals across the continent, see Edward Muir, *Ritual in Early Modern Europe,* 2nd ed. (Cambridge: Cambridge University Press, 2005), 117. On the theatricality of executions—in France, but relevant for large parts of the continent—see John McManners, *Death and the Enlightenment: Changing Attitudes to Death in Eighteenth-Century France* (Oxford: Oxford University Press, 1985), 387.

9. Benvenuto Matteo, "Come facevasi giustizia nello Stato di Milano dall'anno 1471 al 1763," *Archivio storico Lombardo,* ser. 1, vol. 9, no. 3 (1882): 442–482, at 443.

10. Pierre Musitelli, "I manoscritti inediti di Alessandro Verri, Protettore dei carcerati (1763–1765)," *Line@editoriale,* no. 2 (2010): 21n14; Michel Foucault, *The Birth of Biopolitics: Lectures at the Collège de France, 1978–1979,* trans. Graham Burchell (Houndmills, UK: Palgrave Macmillan, 2008), 317.

11. Muir, *Ritual in Early Modern Europe,* 116.

12. Luigi Ficacci, ed., *Giovanni Battista Piranesi: The Complete Etchings*, 2 vols. (Cologne: Taschen, 2011), 1:118–143, on which see, among others, Marguerite Yourcenar, "The Dark Brain of Piranesi," in *The Dark Brain of Piranesi and Other Essays* (New York: Farrar, Straus, and Giroux, 1984), 237–259.

13. On contemporary prisons, and how they followed "the old principle of simple imprisonment in a secure, unpleasant place," see Norman Johnston, *Forms of Constraint: A History of Prison Architecture* (Urbana: University of Illinois Press, 2000), 28–66, quotation at 28.

14. For biblical stories of the platter, see Mark 6:24–25, Matthew 14:8. On the resulting iconographic tradition of *caput in disco*, see Soetkin Vanhauwaert, "A Chopped-Off Head on a Golden Plate: Jan Mostaert's *Head of Saint John the Baptist on a Plate Surrounded by Angels*," in *Death, Torture and the Broken Body in European Art, 1300–1650*, ed. John R. Decker and Mitzi Kirkland-Ives (Farnham, UK: Ashgate, 2015), 5–85. For a eucharistic analysis, see Eleonora Bairati, *Salomè: Immagini di un mito* (Nuoro: Ilisso, 1998), 116.

15. Serafino Biffi, *Sulle antiche carceri di Milano e del Ducato milanese, e sui sodalizj che vi assistevano i prigionieri ed i condannati a morte* (Milan: Bernardoni, 1884), 121–251.

16. Edward Palmer Thompson, *Whigs and Hunters: The Origin of the Black Act* (New York: Pantheon, 1975), 260; the conclusion was republished as "The Rule of Law" in *The Essential E. P. Thompson*, ed. Dorothy Thompson (New York: New Press, 2001), 432–442, quotation at 434. See also Daniel H. Cole, "'An Unqualified Human Good': E. P. Thompson and the Rule of Law," *Journal of Law and Society* 28, no. 2 (2001): 177–203.

17. Julius Clarus, *Sententiarum receptarum liber quintus* (Venice: Cornelio Arrivabene, 1587), 236r, § finalis, quaestio 99; Prosperus Farinacius, *Variae quaestiones et communes opiniones criminales* (Venice: Paganino de Paganini, 1589), 85v, quaestio 10. On them, see Ernst von Moeller's still-relevant *Julius Clarus aus Alessandria, der Kriminalist des 16. Jahrhunderts, der Rat Philipps II, 1525–1575* (Breslau: Schletter, 1911), esp. 228–232 for the publication history of the *Liber quintus*; Gian Paolo Massetto, *Saggi di storia del diritto penale Lombardo (Secc. XVI–XVIII)* (Milan: Edizioni universitarie di lettere economia diritto, 1994), esp. 11–227; Gian Paolo Massetto, *Un magistrate e una città nella Lombardia spagnola: Giulio Claro pretore a Cremona* (Milan: Giuffre, 1985), esp. 62; Niccolò Del Re, *Prospero Farinacci: Giureconsulto romano (1544–1618)* (Rome: Fondazione Marco Besso, 1999). For their continuing importance in Enlightenment Milan, see Pietro Verri, *Osservazioni sulla tortura* [drafted 1760], ed. Giulio Carnazzi (Milan: Rizzoli, 1988), 107–108, 142; and even Giacomo Giuliani, *Orazione inaugurale* (Padova: Penada, 1808), 20. See also Adriano Cavanna, "Giudici e leggi a Milano nell'età di Beccaria," in *Cesare Beccaria tra Milano e l'Europa*, ed. Sergio Romagnoli

and Gian Domenico Pisapia (Milan: Cariplo-Laterza, 1990), 168–195, at 171–172; Mario Alessandro Cattaneo, "Pietro Verri e la riforma penale," in *Pietro Verri e il suo tempo*, ed. Carlo Capra (Bologna: Cisalpino, 1999), 271–288; Carlo Capra, *I progressi della ragione: Vita di Pietro Verri* (Bologna: Il Mulino, 2002), esp. 202–203, 431–436.

18. Thomas Hobbes, *Leviathan*, ed. Noel Malcolm, 3 vols. (Oxford: Oxford University Press, 2012), 2:486 [162 in the original edition].

19. Montesquieu, *The Spirit of the Laws*, ed. Anne M. Cohler, Basia C. Miller, and Harold S. Stone (Cambridge: Cambridge University Press, 1989), 82.

20. Michel Foucault, *Discipline and Punish: The Birth of the Prison*, trans. Alan Sheridan (New York: Vintage, 1995), 49.

21. Pierre François des Vouglans, *Les loix criminelles de la France dans leur ordre naturel* (Paris: Merigot, 1780), 38, quoted differently and discussed in Richard Mowery Andrews, *Law, Magistracy, and Crime in Old Regime Paris, 1735–1789*, vol. 1: *The System of Criminal Justice* (Cambridge: Cambridge University Press, 1994), 300.

22. Paul Friedland, *Seeing Justice Done: The Age of Spectacular Capital Punishment in France* (Oxford: Oxford University Press, 2012), esp. 283–284. Building on the work of Foucault and Giorgio Agamben, Achille Mbembe defines this ultimate form of sovereignty as "necropower," or "the power and the capacity to dictate who may live and who must die"; see his "Necropower," *Public Culture* 15, no. 1 (2003): 11–40, at 11.

23. Edward Muir and Guido Ruggiero argue that "what societies label crime usually represents perceived ruptures or breaks in the ties that bind people together, the little deaths of social life," in their "Afterword: Crime and the Writing of History," in Muir and Ruggiero, *History from Crime*, 226–236, at 226.

24. The thriving historiography of discipline today rests largely on the foundational work of Foucault, *Discipline and Punish*, and the vast commentary it has engendered. See, for a reflection, Peter Spierenburg, "Punishment, Power and History: Foucault and Elias," in his *Violence and Punishment: Civilizing the Body through Time* (Cambridge: Polity Press, 2013), 75–91.

25. On this theme, see V. A. C. Gatrell, *The Hanging Tree: Execution and the English People, 1770–1868* (Oxford: Oxford University Press, 1994), 90–105; and Thomas W. Laqueur, "Crowds, Carnival and the State in English Executions, 1604–1868," in *The First Modern Society: Essays in English History in Honour of Lawrence Stone*, ed. A. L. Beier, David Cannadine, and James M. Rosenheim (Cambridge: Cambridge University Press, 1989), 305–355, at 339, drawing on Mikhail M. Bakhtin, *Rabelais and His World*, trans. H. Iswolsky (Cambridge, MA: Harvard University Press, 1968).

26. Laqueur, "Crowds, Carnival and the State," 340–341, drawing on René Girard, *Violence and the Sacred*, trans. Patrick Gregory (Baltimore: Johns Hopkins Uni-

versity Press, 1977), 297–299; and Friedrich Nietzsche, *On the Genealogy of Morality*, ed. Keith Ansell Pearson, trans. Carol Diethe, 2nd ed. (Cambridge: Cambridge University Press, 2006), 41. For further meditations on "sacrifice," see Hugo Reinert, "The Pertinence of Sacrifice: Some Notes on Larry the Luckiest Lamb," *borderlands* 6, no. 3 (2007), http://www.borderlands.net.au/vol6no3_2007/reinert_larry.htm.

27. The same wording was used in fliers issued by the noble equivalent—that is, the *Nobilissima congregatione di San Giovanni Decollato, alle Case Rotte*; see examples in Archivio di Stato di Milano, Milan, Italy (herafter cited as ASM), *Archivio generale del Fondo di religione, Milano—Confraternita S. Giovanni alle Case Rotte, no. 582*. My use of the term "carnivalesque" is here broader than that in Richard J. Evans, *Rituals of Retribution: Capital Punishment in Germany, 1600–1987* (Oxford: Oxford University Press, 1996), 880, where it denotes the relatively rare cases of crowds actually rebelling against executions. For an experimental application of social psychology to understand the myriad of emotions flooding crowds during executions and public displays of bodily trauma, see Fagan, *The Lure of the Arena*, 274–286, which draws also on the classic cultural history of executions, Gatrell, *The Hanging Tree*, particularly for the experiences of different social strata the latter discussed at 56–105 and 225–321. On the polyvalence of such spectacles, see also Friedland, *Seeing Justice Done*, esp. 259. For an exquisitely symbolic squaring of the circle of life and death, fornication and extermination, see Giacomo Casanova's memoir of the activities surrounding the execution of Robert-François Damies, who slowly was torn to shreds for his attempted assassination of Louis XV, in Casanova, *History of My Life*, 12 vols., trans. Willard R. Task (Baltimore: Johns Hopkins University Press, 1997), 5:56–59. Though Foucault discussed Damies's execution to great effect, in his *Discipline and Punish*, 3–6, he missed this particularly libidinous account of it, which well might have inspired the revolutionary friskiness of Wu Ming, *L'armata dei sonnambuli* (Turin: Einaudi, 2014), 15–17, 19–20.

28. Nietzsche, *Genealogy of Morality*, 41; emphasis in original. See, on this theme, Robert A. Schneider, "Rites de mort à Toulouse: Les exécutions publiques (1738–1780)," in *L'exécution capitale: Une mort donnée en spectacle XVIe–XXe*, ed. Régis Bertrand and Anne Carol (Aix-en-Provence: Publications de l'Université de Provence, 2003), 129–150, at 146, based on Schneider, *The Ceremonial City: Toulouse Observed, 1738–1780* (Princeton, NJ: Princeton University Press, 1995), 103.

29. Archivio di Stato di Roma, Rome, Italy, *Confraternita di S. Giovanni Decollato*, busta 10, "Libro del Proveditore della Venera[bile] Archi[confraternita] di S. Giovanni Decollato per le Giustizie, 21 gen. 1741–12 Febb. 1772," 271.

30. On Mandrin, see Kwass's wonderful *Contraband*. On the politics of "necroevasiveness," see Hugo Reinert, "The Corral and the Slaughterhouse: Knowledge, Tradition and the Modernization of Indigenous Reindeer Slaughtering Practices in the Norwegian Arctic," PhD diss., University of Cambridge, 2007, 160.

31. Norbert Elias, *The Civilizing Process: Sociogenetic and Psychogenetic Investigations* (Oxford: Blackwell, 2000), recently updated, simplified, and popularized by Pinker, *Better Angels*. For a similar argument regarding changing sensibilities in the face of suffering, see Lynn Hunt, *Inventing Human Rights: A History* (New York: W. W. Norton, 2007).

32. Pieter Spierenburg, *The Spectacle of Suffering: Executions and the Evolution of Repression; From a Preindustrial Metropolis to the European Experience* (Cambridge: Cambridge University Press, 1984), ix–x, 201–202. For a similar argument, see Paolo Prodi, *Una storia della giustizia* (Bologna: Il Mulino, 2000), 433. For the classic statement of statehood in such terms, see Max Weber, "The Profession and Vocation of Politics," in Weber, *Political Writings*, ed. Peter Lassman and Ronald Speirs, 309–369 (Cambridge: Cambridge University Press, 1994).

33. Harrington, *The Faithful Executioner*, 230, 263n6, builds explicitly on Elias and Spierenburg.

34. Spierenburg, *The Spectacle of Suffering*, 186, 192, 197–199.

35. Muir, *Ritual in Early Modern Europe*, 117; Emanuele Pagano, *"Questa turba infame a comun danno unita": Delinquenti, marginali, magistrati nel Mantovano asburgico (1750–1800)* (Milan: Franco Angeli, 2014), 85.

36. Adam Smith, *Lectures on Jurisprudence*, ed. Ronald E. Meek, D. D. Raphael, and P. G. Stein (Oxford: Oxford University Press, 1976), 129–130, 299. The historical dynamics of punishment in Smith seems understudied, but for a philosophical take, see Richard Stalley, "Adam Smith and the Theory of Punishment," *Journal of Scottish Philosophy* 10, no. 1 (2012): 69–89. On Smith's jurisprudence more broadly, see, among others, Knud Haakonssen, *The Science of a Legislator: The Natural Jurisprudence of David Hume and Adam Smith* (Cambridge: Cambridge University Press, 1981), 93–98; Ernest Metzger, "Adam Smith's Historical Jurisprudence and the 'Method of the Civilians,'" *Loyola Law Review* 56 (2010): 1–31; and Istvan Hont, "Adam Smith's History of Law and Government as Political Theory," in *Political Judgement: Essays for John Dunn*, ed. Richard Bourke and Raymond Geuss (Cambridge: Cambridge University Press, 2009), 131—171.

37. See, among others, Lionel Rothkrug, *Opposition to Louis XIV: The Political and Social Origins of the French Enlightenment* (Princeton, NJ: Princeton University Press, 1965), esp. 24; Jules Steinberg, *The Obsession of Thomas Hobbes: The English Civil War in Hobbes' Political Philosophy* (Oxford: Peter Lang, 1988).

38. "Libro di varie notizie e memorie della venerabile Compagnia di Santa Croce al Tempio," BNCF, II.I.138, contains a *libro dei giustiziati*, a list of 1,944 people executed in Florence beginning in 1343, the vast majority of them under the tumultuous republic and the early, precarious phase of the Medici principate. On these periods of Florentine history, see John M. Najemy, *A History of Florence, 1200–1575* (Hoboken, NJ: Wiley-Blackwell, 2008). On the confraternity, see Giovanni Battista Uccelli, *Della compagnia di S. Maria della croce al tempio* (Florence: Calasanziana, 1861). For the lower incidence of capital punishments in rural and "feudal" areas of Italy, see Stefano Calonaci, *Lo spirito del dominio: Giustizia e giurisdizioni feudali nell'Italia moderna (secoli XVI–XVIII)* (Rome: Carocci, 2018). On the role of executions in the principate, see John K. Brackett, *Criminal Justice and Crime in Late Renaissance Florence, 1537–1609* (Cambridge: Cambridge University Press, 1992), esp. 68. The term "feudal" was frequently used in eighteenth-century Italy, and continues to be used by historians of the period, to denote the complex reality of privileges, benefices, dues, and sometimes personal servitude that structured the trialogical relationship among lords (both secular and ecclesiastic), their lands, and those who worked them, usually in rural small-commodity production. For an example, see Pietro Verri, "Del sistema feudale," in *Edizione nazionale delle opere di Pietro Verri*, 8 vols. in 10 to date, ed. Carlo Capra et al. (Rome: Edizioni di storia e letteratura, 2003–2014) (hereafter cited as *ENOPV*), 4:348–353. A *locus classicus* of the Italian histriography of the phenomenon remains Anna Maria Rao, *L'"Amaro della feudalità": La devoluzione di Arnone e la quesitone feudale a Napoli alla fine del '700*, 2nd ed. (Naples: Luciano, 1997). The term "feudalism" has itself, of course, fallen under relentless attack in English-language academia in recent decades, for examples of which see Elizabeth E. R. Brown, "The Tyranny of a Construct: Feudalism and Historians of Medieval Europe," *American Historical Review* 79, no. 4 (1974): 1063–1088; and Susan Reynolds, *Fiefs and Vassals: The Medieval Evidence Reinterpreted* (Oxford: Oxford University Press, 1994). On the fact that it may nonetheless be "premature" to pronounce its death, see the editors' introduction to *Feudalism: New Landscapes of Debate*, ed. Sverre Bagge, Michael H. Gelting, and Thomas Lindkvist (Turnhout: Brepols, 2011), 1–15, at 13.

39. On the dangers of taking this argument too far, see Evans, *Rituals of Retribution*, 893.

40. I will return to this process of social, political, and economic transformation in Chapter 4, where I call it a veritable "Schmollerian Moment" in honor of its analyst Gustav von Schmoller, undisputed leader of the nineteenth-century German Historical School of Economics. But see generally Erik Grimmer-Solem, *The Rise of Historical Economics and Social Reform in Germany, 1864–1894* (Oxford: Oxford University Press, 2003).

41. On the origins of the phrase, see Quentin Skinner, *The Foundations of Modern Political Thought*, 2 vols. (Cambridge: Cambridge University Press, 1978), esp. 1:254; Aquinas, *Summa Theologica*, pt. IIa–IIae, quest. 96, art. 6; Jay S. Bybee, "Memorandum for Alberto R. Gonzales, Counsel to the President; Re: Standards of Conduct for Interrogation under 18 U.S.C. §§ 2340–2340A [1 August 2001]," in *The Torture Memos: Rationalizing the Unthinkable*, ed. David Cole (New York: New Press, 2009), 41–100, at 42. On Bybee and the "Bush Six," see Katherine Gallagher, "Universal Jurisdiction in Practice: Efforts to Hold Donald Rumsfeld and Other High-Level United States Officials Accountable for Torture," *Journal of International Criminal Justice* 7, no. 5 (2009): 1087–1116. See, more generally, the always interesting and sometimes infuriating work of Giorgio Agamben, particularly *Lo stato di eccezione* (Turin: Bollati Boringhieri, 2003).

42. Virgil, *Aeneid*, lines 22–23; Niccolò Machiavelli, *Il Principe*, I, in *Tutte le opere*, ed. Mario Martelli (Florence: Sansoni, 1971), 282, discussed in Robert Fredona, "*Liberate Diuturna Cura Italiam:* Hannibal in the Thought of Niccolò Machiavelli," in *Florence and Beyond: Culture, Society and Politics in Renaissance Italy, Essays in Honour of John M. Najemy*, ed. David S. Peterson with Daniel E Bornstein (Toronto: Toronto University Press, 2008), 419–434. On *Fortuna* in the thought of Machiavelli, see Hanna Fenichel Pitkin, *Fortune Is a Woman: Gender and Politics in the Thought of Niccolò Machiavelli; with a New Afterword* (Chicago: University of Chicago Press, 1999).

43. Charles Krauthammer, "The Truth about Torture," in *Torture: A Collection*, ed. Sanford Levinson (Oxford: Oxford University Press, 2004), 307–316, at 316; emphasis added.

44. Calculations based on the data collected in Mereu, *La pena di morte*, 44. Demographic context: Milan held about 124,000 inhabitants at the time. See Paul Bairoch, Jean Batou, and Pierre Chèvre, *La population des villes européennes de 800 à 1850* (Geneva: Droz, 1988), 45.

45. Cesare Beccaria, *On Crimes and Punishments and Other Writings*, ed. Aaron Thomas, trans. Aaron Thomas and Jeremy Parzen (Toronto: University of Toronto Press, 2008), 51, 53. On its being "notoriously misunderstood," see Piers Beirne, *Inventing Criminology: Essays on the Rise of "Homo Criminalis"* (Albany: State University of New York Press, 1993), 13. Although jurists remained interested in the Roman law distinction between *delictum* and *crimen*, "delitti" is traditionally and for our purposes can be comfortably translated as "crimes" in English, because Beccaria means violations of penal law more generally.

46. See William Barker, ed., *The Adages of Erasmus* (Toronto: University of Toronto Press, 2001), 37–41.

47. His monumental achievement remains his *History of My Life*.

48. Joseph A. Schumpeter, *A History of Economic Analysis*, ed. Elizabeth Boody Schumpeter (Oxford: Oxford University Press, 1954), 175. For a classic statement of Beccaria's influence on penal thought, see Evans, *Rituals of Retribution*, 127–133. On his impact, see also David Jacobson, "The Politics of Criminal Law Reform in Pre-Revolutionary France," PhD diss., Brown University, 1976, esp. 71, 83–89. For something of a counterargument downplaying Beccaria's influence on the movement to abandon torture in particular, see John H. Langbein, *Torture and the Law of Proof: Europe and England in the Ancien Régime* (Chicago: University of Chicago Press, 2006 [1976]), 65–69.

49. On these two projects, see Istvan Hont, *Politics in Commercial Society: Jean-Jacques Rousseau and Adam Smith,* ed. Béla Kapossy and Michael Sonenscher (Cambridge, MA: Harvard University Press, 2015), esp. 22–24. The literature on these two titans is staggering, but see particularly Michael Sonenscher, *Sans-Culottes: An Eighteenth-Century Emblem in the French Revolution* (Princeton, NJ: Princeton University Press, 2008); and Nicholas Phillipson, *Adam Smith: An Enlightened Life* (London: Penguin, 2010). For a different but similarly illuminating triangulation of authors, focused on their respective contributions to economics, see Peter Groenewegen, "Turgot, Beccaria and Smith," in *Eighteenth-Century Economics: Turgot, Beccaria and Smith and Their Contemporaries* (London: Routledge, 2002), 3–47, with excellent biographical comparisons on 6–20.

50. Jean-Jacques Rousseau, *The Confessions and Correspondence, Including the Letters to Malesherbes,* ed. C. Kelly, R. D. Masters, and P. Stillman, trans. C. Kelly (Hanover, NH: University Press of New England, 1995), 339–340.

51. Adam Smith, *The Theory of Moral Sentiments,* ed. D. D. Raphael and A. L. Macfie (Oxford: Oxford University Press, 1976), 342.

52. On Beccaria's fragmentary work, see Gianni Francioni's pathbreaking "Il fantasma del 'Ripulimento delle nazioni': Congetture su un'opera mancata di Cesare Beccaria," *Studi Settecenteschi* 5 (1984): 131–173.

53. See, for example, Verri, "Primi elementi per somministrare," in *ENOPV,* 6:665–666; Verri, "Storia dell'invasione de' francesi repubblicani nel milanese nel 1796," in *ENOPV,* 6:772–805, at 775.

54. See, for example, Pietro Verri, *Memorie,* ed. Enrica Agnesi (Modena: Mucchi Editore, 2001), 191–192, discussed also in Capra, *I progressi della ragione,* 65–74. The theme was clearly echoed in Alessandro Verri, "Della eccellenza, utilità e giustizia della flagellazione de' fanciulli: Ragionamento fra un Pedante ed un Ottentotto," in *"Il Caffè," 1764–1766,* ed. Gianni Francioni and Sergio A. Romagnoli (Turin: Bollati Boringhieri, 1993) (hereafter cited as *Il Caffè*), 453–460. For the original work so meticulously edited by Francioni and Romagnoli, see *Il Caffè ossia Brevi e Vari Discorsi distribuiti in Fogli Periodici,* 2 vols. (Brescia:

Giammaria Rizzardi, Galeazzi, 1765–1766). For such an argument taken perhaps too far, see Erik H. Erikson, *Young Man Luther: A Study in Psychoanalysis and History* (New York: W. W. Norton, 1993).

55. Cesare Beccaria to André Morellet, 26 January 1766, and Cesare Beccaria to Teresa Blasco Beccaria, 20 November 1766, both in *Edizione Nazionale delle Opere di Cesare Beccaria*, 16 vols. in 17, ed. Luigi Firpo and Gianni Francioni et al. (Milan: Mediobanca, 1984–2015) (hereafter cited as *ENOCB*), 4:219–228, 484. On Beccaria's first meeting with Verri, see Carlo Capra, "Beccaria e i Verri negli anni dei Pugni e del 'Caffè,'" in *Il caso Beccaria: A 250 anni dalla pubblicazione del "Dei delitti e delle pene,"* ed. Vincenzo Ferrone and Giuseppe Ricuperati (Bologna: Il Mulino, 2016), 87–110, at 87.

56. Capra, "Beccaria e i Verri," 88.

57. Cesare Beccaria, "Relazione di Beccaria" (late 1760), and the numerous missives included in Beccaria to Teresa Blasco, October 1760 to January 1761, in *ENOCB*, 4:25–27, 36–40.

58. See Cesare Beccaria to Giambattista Biffi, ca. 20 June 1763, in *ENOCB*, 4:77–79; Pietro Verri to Giuseppe Aubert, 26 October 1764, in Cesare Beccaria, *Dei delitti e delle pene,* ed. Franco Venturi (Turin: Einaudi, 1965), 117–118. On Teresa's pepperiness, see Marta Broneschi, *Quel che il cuore sapeva: Giulia Beccaria, i Verri, i Manzoni* (Milan: Mondadori, 2004), 19. On her bubbliness, see Roberto Bizzocchi, *A Lady's Man: The Cicisbei, Private Morals and National Identity in Italy* (Basingstoke, UK: Palgrave Macmillan, 2014), 194. On Beccaria as a Holmes or a Montalbano, see Elena Past, *Methods of Murder: Beccarian Introspection and Lombrosian Vivisection in Italian Crime Fiction* (Toronto: University of Toronto Press, 2012), 24. His lethargy was noted even by Leopold II in 1791. For his verdict, and those of his colleagues, see Carlo Capra's penetrating "Gli intellettuali e il potere: I casi di Beccaria e di Verri," in *L'età dei Lumi: Saggi sulla cultura Settecentesca,* ed. Antonio Santucci (Bologna: Il Mulino, 1998), 211–230, at 217.

59. For a voluminous file on the affair, see the documents in "Affare del Marchese Beccaria Padre e Figlio," ASM, *Autografi, no. 164: Uomini celebri: Cesare Beccaria.* Teresa was young, but it was certainly an acceptable age difference at the time. For a meditation on the boundaries of normality and transgression for such relations in the period, see Larry Wolff, *Paolina's Innocence: Child Abuse in Casanova's Venice* (Stanford: Stanford University Press, 2012). For the historical background for marriage patterns in Italy, see David Herlihy and Christiane Klapisch-Zuber's case of 1427 Florence, where the average woman was 18 and the average man 30 at the age of marriage, in *Tuscans and their Families* (New Haven, CT: Yale University Press, 1985), 210.

60. See one of the messages in Cesare Beccaria to Teresa Blasco, October 1760 to January 1761, in *ENOCB*, 4:37.

61. Broneschi, *Quel che il cuore sapeva*, 23.

62. Cesare Beccaria to Teresa Blasco, mid-January 1761 and 16 January 1761, in *ENOCB*, 4:30–33, 34–35.

63. This may be one of the most famous episodes in Beccaria's life, on which see, among others, Broneschi, *Quel che il cuore sapeva*, 11–12, 25–27; and Capra, *I progressi della ragione*, 182–183. Beccaria communicated the happy news to Giuseppe Firmian on 19 May 1762, in *ENOCB*, 4:56–58. On Verri's own experiences with house arrest, see Pietro Verri, "Pensieri miei pericolosi a dirsi [1783]," in *ENOPV*, 5:487–497, at 488.

64. Pietro Verri, "Alcune osservazioni che si credono discrete e meritevoli di attenzione [5 January 1776]," in *ENOPV*, 5:605–617, at 607.

65. See, for example, Cesare Beccaria to Giuseppe Firmian, 5 March 1762, in *ENOCB*, 4:54–55. For Verri's comment, see Broneschi, *Quel che il cuore sapeva*, 26.

66. On this fallout, see, among others, Gianni Francioni, "Note al testo," in *ENOCB*, 1:215–368, at 218–221. The most succinct nearly contemporary summary of the events, rigorously from Pietro Verri's perspective, remains his "Memorie sincere del modo col quale servii nel militare e dei miei primi progressi nel servigio politico (ca. 1764–1775)," in *ENOPV*, 5:145–148.

67. Giovanni Tessitore, *Cesare Beccaria: L'uomo e il mito; idealizzazione e realtà storica* (Milan: Franco Angeli, 2008), esp. 182. On Beccaria's extraordinary influence in Russia, in spite of his decision not to go, see, among many others, Inna Gorbatov, *Catherine the Great and the French Philosophers of the Enlightenment* (Bethesda, MD: Academia Press, 2006), esp. 29; and Ettore Gherbezza, *Dei delitti e delle pene nella traduzione di Michail M. Ščerbatov* (Florence: Firenze University Press, 2007).

68. Cesare Beccaria to Wenzel Anton von Kaunitz-Rittemberg [*sic*], 25 June 1765, in *ENOCB*, 4:100–101. On the Academy of Fisticuffs' influence on Kaunitz, see Franz A. J. Szabo, *Kaunitz and Enlightened Absolutism, 1753–1780* (Cambridge: Cambridge University Press, 1994), 34, 184. This was a normal way of seeking patronage and securing positions in the administration, and Beccaria's colleague Gian Rinaldo Carli would successfully do something similar the following month; see Gian Rinaldo Carli to Luigi Giusti, 13 July 1765, in Barbara Costa, "Gian Rinaldo Carli presidente del Supremo Consiglio di Economia Pubblica (1765–1771)," *Nuova rivista storica* 77, no. 2 (1992): 277–318, at 278; as well as Luigi Giusti to Gian Rinaldo Carli, 12 August 1765, Civica Biblioteca Angelo Mai, Bergamo, Italy, *Archivio Carli Rubbi*, fasc. I, 98, esp. 1r. Pietro Verri had already "courted" Kaunitz more physically in Vienna in 1759, for an example of which see Pietro Verri to Antonio Verri, 17 May 1759, in Pietro Verri, *Lettere inedite di Pietro Verri: 5 maggio 1759–1 dicembre 1760*, ed. Mario Zolezzi (Milan: Editrice vita e pensiero, 1965), 18–19. On such client-patronage relationships at the

time, see Anthony Molho's remarkable "Patronage and the State in Early Modern Italy," in *Klientelsysteme im Europa der Frühen Neuzeit,* ed. Antoni Mączak (Munich: R. Oldenbourg Verlag, 1988), 233–242.

69. Österreichische Nationalbibliothek, Vienna, Austria, Handschriftensammlung, ms. 15118, fols. 42–64, brought to my attention by Costa, "Gian Rinaldo Carli presidente," 280.

70. On his chair, see Angelo Mauri, "La cattedra di Cesare Beccaria," *Archivio storio italiano* 60 (1933): 199–262; Marco Bianchini, "Una difficile gestazione: Il contrastato inserimento dell'economia politica nelle università dell'Italia nordorientale (1769–1866)—Note per un'analisi comparativa," in *Le cattedre di economia politica in Italia: La diffusione di una disciplina "sospetta" (1750–1900),* ed. Massimo M. Augello et al. (Milan: Franco Angeli, 1988), 47–92, at 48–57; Wolfgang Rother, "The Beginning of Higher Education in Political Economy in Milan and Modena: Cesare Beccaria, Alfonso Longo, Agostino Paradisi," *History of Universities* 19, no. 1 (2004): 119–158; as well as the sundry manuscripts collected in "Atti e appunti relative a la nomina di Beccaria alla cattedra di Scienze camerali, con carteggio fra il conte Firmian, il principe di Kaunitz e Beccaria," Ambrosiana, Z 248–249 sup. On the Scuole Palatine, see Mario Scazzoso, "Le scuole palatine a Milano nell'età delle riforme," in *Economia, istituzioni, cultura in Lombardia nell'età di Maria Teresa,* ed. Aldo de Maddalena, Ettore Rotelli, and Gennaro Barbarisi, 3 vols. (Bologna: Il Mulino, 1992), 3:887–895. On the cameral sciences, or cameralism, see Keith Tribe, "Cameralism and the Sciences of the State," in *The Cambridge Companion to Eighteenth-Century Political Thought,* ed. Mark Goldie and Robert Wokler (Cambridge: Cambridge University Press, 2006), 525–546; Andre Wakefield, *The Disordered Police State: German Cameralism as Science and Practice* (Chicago: University of Chicago Press, 2008); Sophus A. Reinert, "Cameralism and Commercial Rivalry: Nationbuilding through Economic Autarky in Seckendorff's 1665 Additiones," *European Journal of Law and Economics* 19, no. 3 (2005): 271–286; Sophus A. Reinert, *Translating Empire: Emulation and the Origins of Political Economy* (Cambridge, MA: Harvard University Press, 2011), 233–238.

71. Carlo Giuseppe di Firmian to Cesare Beccaria, 1 November 1768, in *ENOCB,* 4:678–680, at 678–679n.

72. Carlo Capra, *La Lombardia austriaca nell'età delle riforme* (Turin: UTET, 1987), 365–366.

73. William Bradford to Luigi Castiglioni, 10 August 1786, praising Cesare Beccaria's work as a vehicle of "the empire of humanity," in Luigi Castiglioni, *Viaggio negli Stati Uniti,* 2 vols. (Milan: Marelli, 1790), 2:23–25.

74. See, among others, Dino Carpanetto and Giuseppe Ricuperati, *Italy in the Age of Reason, 1685–1789* (London: Longmans, 1987), 265; Norbert Jonard, "Cosmopolitismo e patriottismo nel 'Caffè,'" in Maddalena, Rotelli, and Barbarisi, *Eco-*

nomia, istituzioni, cultura, 2:65–95, at 95; see also, in the same volume, Giuseppe Rutto, "Riforme e patriottismi nell'Austria di Maria Teresa," 2:903–923.

75. The locus classicus of this tradition remains Albert O. Hirschman, *The Passions and the Interests: Political Arguments for Capitalism before Its Triumph* (Princeton, NJ: Princeton University Press, 1997). On eighteenth-century cosmopolitanism generally, see, from different perspectives, among others, Thomas J. Schlereth, *The Cosmopolitan Ideal in Enlightenment Thought* (Notre Dame, IN: University of Notre Dame Press, 1977); Sankar Muthu, "Conquest, Commerce, and Cosmopolitanism in Enlightenment Political Thought," in *Empire and Modern Political Thought,* ed. Sankar Muthu (Cambridge: Cambridge University Press, 2012), 199–231; and Luca Scuccimarra, *I confini del mondo: Storia del cosmopolitismo dall'antichità al Settecento* (Bologna: Il Mulino, 2006).

76. Pietro Verri, introduction to Pietro Secchi, "La coltivazione del tabacco," in *Il Caffè,* 55–56, at 55.

77. E.g., Giuseppe Visconti, "[Osservazioni meteorologiche fatte in Milano]," in *Il Caffè,* 78–82.

78. On the facilities of learned societies in Italy, see Eric Cochrane, *Tradition and Enlightenment in the Tuscan Academies, 1690–1800* (Chicago: University of Chicago Press, 1961); and, focused on an earlier period, Jane E. Evanson, Denis V. Reidy, and Lisa Sampson, eds., *The Italian Academies, 1525–1700: Networks of Culture, Innovation and Dissent* (London: Routledge, 2016). On essay contests, see Jeremy L. Caradonna, *The Enlightenment in Practice: Academic Prize Contests and Intellectual Culture in France, 1670–1794* (Ithaca, NY: Cornell University Press, 2012), esp. 118–142, which in many ways develops the work of Daniel Roche, *Le Siècle des Lumières en province: Académies et académiciens provinciaux, 1689–1789,* 2 vols. (Paris: Mouton, 1978). For the Kraken, see *Transactions of the Royal Society of Edinburgh* 2 (1790): 16. On the rise of economic societies more generally, see the essays in Koen Stapelbroek and Jani Marjanen, eds., *The Rise of Economic Societies in the Eighteenth Century* (Basingstoke, UK: Palgrave Macmillan, 2012).

79. On this painting, see Gianmarco Gaspari, "La cultura a Milano nell'età dei Lumi: Per una rivisitazione problematica," in *Le buone dottrine e le buone lettere: Brescia per il bicentenario della morte di Giuseppe Parini,* ed. Bartolo Martinelli, Carlo Annoni, and Giuseppe Langella (Milan: Vita e Pensiero, 2001), 3–19, esp. 5–7. For the journal volumes, see *Il Caffè.*

80. Markman Ellis, *The Coffee House: A Cultural History* (London: Weidenfeld and Nicolson, 2004), 205; Mark Pendergrast, *Uncommon Grounds: The History of Coffee and How It Transformed the World,* rev. ed. (New York: Basic Books, 2010), 8.

81. Gennaro Barbarisi, "Frisi e Verri: Storia di un'amicizia illuministica," in *Ideologia e scienza nell'opera di Paolo Frisi (1728–1784),* ed. Gennaro Barbarisi, 2 vols. (Milan: Franco Angeli, 1987), 2:353–379, at 354.

82. On the later administrative careers of the group's members, see Capra's brilliant "Gli intellettuali e il potere." On their failure to turn the nobility into a "class" according to the "determinist Marxism of the right wing of the third international," see Dylan Riley, "Privilege and Property: The Political Foundations of Failed Class Formation in Eighteenth-Century Austrian Lombardy," *Comparative Studies in Society and History* 45, no. 1 (2003): 190–213, at 210.

83. Verri, "Memorie sincere," 115–116; Pietro Verri to Gian Rinaldo Carli, 25 January 1765, and Pietro Verri to Gian Rinaldo Carli, 8 February 1765, both in Francesco De Stefano, "Cinque anni di sodalizio tra Pietro Verri e Gian Rinaldo Carli (1760–1765) con XXIV lettere inedite di Pietro Verri," *Atti e memorie della Società istriana di archeologia e storia patria* 45 (1933): 43–103, at 72–74, 74–78. For Verri's own 1761–1762 blueprint for a "literary academy" inspired by "emulation," see his "[Piano per un'accademia letteraria]," in *ENOPV*, 1:721–723. See also Franco Venturi, *Settecento riformatore*, 5 vols. in 7 (Turin: Einaudi, 1969–1990), 1:683. On Biffi in particular, see Franco Venturi, "Un amico di Beccaria e di Verri: Profilo di Giambattista Biffi," *Giornale storico della letteratura italiana* 134 (1957): 37–76. On Lambertenghi, see Carlo Capra, "Un intermediario tra Vienna e Milano: Luigi Lambertenghi e il suo carteggio con Pietro Verri," *Römische historische Mitteilungen* 31 (1989): 359–376. On Longo, see Stefano Caldirola, "Il lecchese Alfonso Longo riformatore lombardo," *Archivi di Lecco* 3, no. 4 (1980): 312–340; and Maria Francesca Turchetti, "Alfonso Longo e l'Accademia dei pugni (con quattro lettere inedite)," *Archivio storico lombardo* 140 (2014): 151–185. On the group more generally, see still Venturi, *Settecento riformatore*, 1:645–747; and particularly Carlo Capra, "L'Accademia dei pugni e la società lombarda," in *La felicità per tutti: Figure e time dell'illuminismo lombardo* (Rome: Aracne editore, 2017), 31–51, discussing also occasional visitors to the group on 38–39.

84. Capra, *I progressi della ragione*, 189. See also Pietro Verri's unpublished "[Al lettore]," in *Il Caffè*, 814. On the names of such societies, see also Cochrane, *Tradition and Enlightenment*. For Alessandro Verri's own ridicule of such names, see "Dei difetti della letteratura e di alcune loro cagioni," in *Il Caffè*, 539–560, at 549.

85. On what Verri read in particular, see Carlo Capra, "Pietro Verri e il 'genio della lettura,'" in *Per Marino Berengo: Studi degli allievi*, ed. Livio Antonielli, Carlo Capra, and Mario Infelise (Milan: Franco Angeli, 2000), 619–677. For a particularly evident echo of the *Persian Letters*, see Verri, "[Introduzione]," in *Il Caffè*, 11–14, at 13. On the the Academy of Fisticuffs' (and particularly Verri's) sharing of women as an example of contemporary aristocratic norms, see Capra, "L'Accademia dei pugni," 39–41, and below.

86. Pietro Verri to Giambattista Biffi, 29 September 1762, in Guido Sommi Picenardi, "Lettere inedite di Pietro Verri," *Rassegna nazionale*, 1 June 1912, 301–315, and 1 September 1912, 54–74, 307–308.

87. Cesare Beccaria to Giambattista Biffi, August 1762, in *ENOCB,* 4:62–63.

88. See particularly Teresa Amabile, "How to Kill Creativity," *Harvard Business Review,* September–October 1998, drawing also on her *Social Psychology of Creativity* (New York: Springer, 1983); on diversity, see Toby Marshall Egan, "Creativity in the Context of Team Diversity: Team Leader Perspectives," *Advances in Developing Human Resources* 7, no. 2 (2005): 207–225. On the challenges of cooperative and creative teamwork today, see Amy C. Edmondson, *Teaming: How Organizations Learn, Innovate, and Compete in the Knowledge Economy* (San Francisco: John Wiley, 2012).

89. Venturi, *Settecento riformatore,* 1:682–684. Beccaria, *On Crimes and Punishments,* 49, argued that republics needed "a despotic dictator with the courage of Sulla, and with as much genius for building as Sulla had for destroying." On Sulla, see Arthur Keaveney, *Sulla: The Last Republican* (London: Routledge, 2005). On Atticus, see still the sketch in Alice Hill Byrne, "Titus Pomponius Atticus: Chapters of a Biography," PhD diss., Bryn Mawr College, 1920.

90. For a different perspective on the relationship between consumption and sociability in eighteenth-century Italy, see Melissa T. Calaresu's wonderful "Making and Eating Ice Cream in Naples: Rethinking Consumption and Sociability in the Eighteenth Century," *Past and Present* 220, no. 1 (2013): 35–78. Generally, see also Brian Cowan, "Public Spaces, Knowledge, and Sociability," in *The Oxford Handbook of the History of Consumption,* ed. Frank Trentmann (Oxford: Oxford University Press, 2012), 251–266.

91. On the Longobards, see Stefano Gasparri, *Italia longobarda: Il regno, i Franchi, il papato,* 2nd ed. (Rome: Laterza, 2012). On the etymology of Lombard Street, see James Howell, *Londinopolis* (London: Streater, 1657), 82, which builds on John Stow's classic *A Survey of London* (London: Iohn Wolfe, 1598), 156–157. Florentines were added to this Lombard description by Robert Seymour's edition of Stow; see his *Survey of the Cities of London and Westminster,* 2 vols. (London: Read, 1733–1735), 1:415. See also, of course, Walter Bagehot's classic *Lombard Street: A Description of the Money Market* (New York: Scribner, Armstrong and Co., 1873). The global importance of Lloyd's Coffee House still awaits its storyteller.

92. On the territory through the lens of its landscape at the time, see Diane Harris's beautiful *The Nature of Authority: Villa Culture, Landscape, and Representation in Eighteenth-Century Lombardy* (University Park: Pennsylvania State University Press, 2003).

93. For the galvanizing consequences of Milanese imperialism in the Renaissance, see Hans Baron, *Crisis of the Early Italian Renaissance* (Princeton, NJ: Princeton University Press, 1966). Baron's basic premise, resonant at the time and places of his writing, was that the crisis offered by the existential

threat of an imminent Milanese invasion in 1402 stimulated intellectual life and focused debates on the question of how political communities could safeguard their liberty, virtue, and good life in historical time, leading to the reconsideration of classical tropes and modes of political theory and overturning Stoic models for scholarly detachments from civic affairs. The historiography on Baron's thesis is vast and often critical, but see John M. Najemy's review essay of Hans Baron, *In Search of Florentine Civic Humanism: Essays on the Transition from Medieval to Modern Thought*, 2 vols. (Princeton, NJ: Princeton University Press, 1988), in *Renaissance Quarterly* 45, no. 2 (1992): 340–350; and Najemy, "Baron's Machiavelli and Renaissance Republicanism," *American Historical Review* 101, no. 1 (1996): 119–129; James Hankins, ed., *Renaissance Civic Humanism: Reappraisals and Reflections* (Cambridge: Cambridge University Press, 2000); and, for its World War II context, Anthony Molho, "Hans Baron's Crisis," in Peterson with Bornstein, *Florence and Beyond*, 61–90. On Leonardo da Vinci's Milanese context, see Martin Kemp, *Leonardo*, rev. ed. (Oxford: Oxford University Press, 2011). On the longer histories of the Lombard League, including in the work of Pietro Verri, see Asker Pelgrom, "The Lombard League Traditions in Northern Italy," in *Statehood before and beyond Ethnicity: Minor States in Northern and Eastern Europe, 1600–2000*, ed. Linas Eriksonas and Leos Müller (Brussels: Peter Lang and Presses Interuniversitaires Européennes, 2005), 179–208, at 184.

94. Cesare Magni, *Il tramonto del feudo Lombardo* (Milan: Giuffrè, 1937); Marina Cavallera, "I confine e gli scambi tra domini sabaudi e Stato di Milano," in *Lo spazio sabaudo: Intersezioni, frontiere e confine in età moderna*, ed. Blythe Alice Raviola (Milan: Franco Angeli, 2007), 137–162, at 150–152. See also Jane Black's remarkable *Absolutism in Renaissance Milan: Plenitude of Power under the Visconti and the Sforza, 1329–1535* (Oxford: Oxford University Press, 2009).

95. See, on the theme, Girolamo Arnaldi, *Italy and Its Invaders*, trans. Antony Shugaar (Cambridge, MA: Harvard University Press, 2005); and the essays in Christine Shaw, ed., *Italy and the European Powers: The Impact of War, 1500–1530* (Leiden: Brill, 2006).

96. The historiography of early modern Milan rests squarely on the numerous works of Carlo Capra, but see particularly Carlo Capra and Domenico Sella, *Il Ducato di Milano dal 1535 al 1796* (Turin: UTET, 1984); and, for the earlier Spanish period, Stefano d'Amico, *Spanish Milan: A City within the Empire, 1525–1706* (Houndmills, UK: Palgrave Macmillan, 2012). On its relations with Austria, and really as the textbook on eighteenth-century Milan, see Capra, *La Lombardia austriaca*. On the Napoleonic period in particular, see Alain Pillepich, *Milan: Capitale napoléonienne, 1800–1814* (Paris: Lettrage, 2001).

97. Renato Pasta defined it a "coacervation" in *La battaglia politico-culturale degli illuministi lombardi* (Milan: Principato Editore, 1974), 8, quoted and discussed also in Jonard, "Cosmopolitismo," 65. See also, for context, J. H. Elliot, "A Europe of Composite Monarchies," in *Spain, Europe and the Wider World, 1500–1800* (New Haven, CT: Yale University Press, 2009), 3–24. On Italian ideas of Vienna in the eighteenth century, see Carmen Flaim, "'Un paese cotanto remoto e strano': Considerazioni italiane sulla cultura settecentesca viennese," in *Il Settecento tedesco in Italia: Gli italiani e l'immagine della cultura tedesca nel XVIII secolo,* ed. Giula Cantarutti, Stefano Ferrari, and Paola Maria Filippi (Bologna: Il Mulino, 2001), 217–256. On what "Austria" signified at the time, see Grete Klingenstein, "The Meanings of 'Austria' and 'Austrian' in the Eighteenth Century," in *Royal and Republican Sovereignty in Early Modern Europe: Essays in Memory of Ragnhild Hatton,* ed. Robert Oresko, G. C. Gibbs, and H. M. Scott (Cambridge: Cambridge University Press, 1997), 423–478. On Habsburg territorial policies generally, see Alfred J. Rieber, *The Struggle for the Eurasian Borderlands: From the Rise of Early Modern Empires to the End of the First World War* (Cambridge: Cambridge University Press, 2014), esp. 83–95.

98. On these territorial changes, their local as well as geopolitical consequences, and the importance of roads and passes in particular, see Renzo Mortarotti, *L'Ossola nell'età moderna: Dall'annessione al Piemonte al fascismo (1743–1922)* (Domodossola: Libreria Grossi, 1985), 97–111, 297, 519–524; Sergio Monferrini and Carlo Alessandro Pisoni, *Le Terre cedute del Lago Maggiore e Valli d'Ossola: Il Trattato di Worms e il passaggio dalla Lombardia al Piemonte* (Verbania: Alberti Libraio Editore, 2007), esp. 49–55, 75–81.

99. Franco Borlando, *Il problema delle communicazioni nel sec. XVIII nei sui rapport col Risorgimento Italiano* (Pavia: Treves-Treccani-Tumminelli, 1932), 78–81; Bruno Zanei, *L'opera di rinnovamento nella Lombardia austriaca durante il governo del Conte Carlo di Firmian* (Triest: Stabilimento tipografico Nazionale, 1948), 16, 80–84; Aldo Carera, "I mercati della tradizione," in *I mercati e le fiere della provincia di Milano tra XVIII e XX secolo,* ed. Maria Piera Bassi (Milan: Provincia di Milano, 1990), 17–61, at 43.

100. Alexander I. Grab, "Enlightened Despotism and State Building: The Case of Austrian Lombardy," *Austrian History Yearbook* 19, no. 1 (1984): 43–72, at 44–45. Contemporaries estimated the population to be around 125,000; see Giuseppe Visconti, "Della maniera di conservare robusta e lungamente la sanità di chi vive nel clima milanese," in *Il Caffè,* 498–532, at 516. This is not far from Bairoch, Batou, and Chèvre's previously mentioned estimate of 124,000, in *La population des villes européennes,* 45.

101. Domenico Sella, *Crisis and Continuity: The Economy of Spanish Lombardy in the Seventeenth Century* (Cambridge, MA: Harvard University Press, 1979), esp. 80–81,

124. On the theme of agriculture as a sort of manufacturing in Italy, focused on the nineteenth century, see Giuliana Biagioli and Rossano Pazzagli, eds., *Agricoltura come manifattura: Istruzione agraria, professionalizzazione e sviluppo agricolo nell'Ottocento* (Florence: Olschki, 2004). On the decline of Milanese manufactures, see Chapter 2 in this volume. On the limits of "feudalism" in this context, see also Mario Romani, *L'agricoltura in Lombardia dal periodo delle riforme al 1859* (Milan: Vita e pensiero, 1957), esp. 52.

102. Arthur Young, *Travels during the Years 1787, 1788, and 1789* (London: Richardson, 1794), 146.

103. Paolo Malanima, "A Declining Economy: Central and Northern Italy in the Sixteenth and Seventeenth Centuries," in *Spain in Italy: Politics, Society and Religion, 1500–1700*, ed. Thomas James Dandelet and John A. Marino (Leiden: Brill, 2007), 383–404, at 389.

104. Zanei, *L'opera di rinnovamento*, 89; Daniel M. Klang, *Tax Reform in Eighteenth Century Lombardy* (New York: Columbia University Press for East European Quarterly, 1977), 4–5; Romani, *L'agricoltura in Lombardia*, 19–21. On the relationship between urban elites and the countryside in early modern Lombardy, see also Cesare Mozzarelli, "L'antico regime in villa; Tre testi Milanesi: Bartolomeo Taegio, Federico Borromeo, Pietro Verri," in *L'antico regime in villa*, ed. Cesare Mozzarelli (Rome: Bulzoni, 2004), 9–47. On wealth distribution today, see Credit Suisse Research Institute, *Global Wealth Report 2015* (Zurich: Credit Suisse, 2015), 4.

105. Alexander I. Grab, "The Politics of Subsistence: Reforms in the Grain Trade and Bread Production in Austrian Lombardy in the Age of Enlightened Absolutism," PhD diss., University of California at Los Angeles, 1980, esp. 137–140; Grab, "Enlightened Absolutism and Commonlands Enclosure: The Case of Austrian Lombardy," *Agricultural History* 63, no. 1 (1989): 49–72, at 51; Riley, "Privilege and Property," 198; Romani, *L'agricoltura in Lombardia*, 13. For Verri's verdict, see his letter to Alessandro of 10 February 1768, in *CV*, 1:164.

106. Capra, *La Lombardia austriaca*, esp. 183; Carpanetto and Ricuperati, *Italy in the Age of Reason*, 223.

107. Szabo, *Kaunitz and Enlightened Absolutism*, 50. His personality was, seemingly, also attuned with those of Verri and Beccaria. Charles W. Ingrao described Kaunitz as "a prickly, sexually promiscuous hypochondriac" as well as a "committed proponent of Enlightenment ideas"; see Ingrao, *The Habsburg Monarchy, 1618–1815*, 2nd ed. (Cambridge: Cambridge University Press, 2000), 179. On the new "Italian Department" under Kaunitz, see Carlo Capra, "Luigi Giusti e il Dipartimento d'Italia a Vienna (1757–1766)," in Maddalena, Rotelli, and Barbarisi, *Economia, istituzioni, cultura*, 3:365–390. For one contemporary take on Kaunitz's role in the correspondence with this department, and the extent to

which he authored letters himself, see Pietro Verri, "Lettera riservata che spedii al Cavaliere Alessandro a Roma l'anno 1771 verso Dicembre," in *ENOPV*, 5:194–226, at 206–207. On these administrative changes in 1750s Milan, see also Cesare Mozzarelli, *Sovrano, società e amministrazione locale nella Lombardia Teresiana (1749–1758)* (Bologna: Il Mulino, 1982).

108. Elisabeth Garms Cornides, "La destinazione del conte Firmian a Milano: Analisi di una scelta," in Maddalena, Rotelli, and Barbarisi, *Economia, istituzioni, cultura*, 3:1015–1029, at 1020. On the opposition to "feudal fiscalism," see Capra, *Lombardia austriaca*, 304, discussed in Riley, "Privilege and Property," 199. On the reforms generally, see Ingrao, *The Habsburg Monarchy*, 178–197. On absolutist consolidations, see Istvan Hont, "The Permanent Crisis of a Divided Mankind: 'Nation-State' and 'Nationalism' in Historical Perspective," in *Jealousy of Trade: International Competition and the Nation-State in Historical Perspective* (Cambridge, MA: Harvard University Press, 2005), 447–528, at 456–463. For pertinent contemporary observations, see also Pietro Verri to Gian Rinaldo Carli, 12 January 1762, in De Stefano, "Cinque anni di sodalizio," 63.

109. Ingrao, *The Habsburg Monarchy*, 179, 181. On the longer political history of accounting, see Jacob Soll, *The Reckoning: Financial Accountability and the Rise and Fall of Nations* (New York: Basic Books, 2014).

110. On the history of these reforms, see Wilhelm Bleek, *Von der Kameralausbildung zum Juristenprivileg: Studium, Prüfung und Ausbildung der höheren Beamten des allgemeinen Verwaltungsdienstes in Deutschland im 18. und 19. Jahrhundert* (Berlin: Colloquium Verlag, 1972). On Lombardy as a "testing ground," see Ingrao, *The Habsburg Monarchy*, 185.

111. For a typical example of such meritocratic reforms in Bourbon Spain at the time, see María Victoria López-Cordón Cortezo, "The Merits of Good *Gobierno*: Culture and Politics in the Bourbon Court," in *The Spanish Enlightenment Revisited*, ed. Jesús Astigarraga (Oxford: Voltaire Foundation, 2015), 19–39, at 26. On meritocratic reforms and the challenges posed to them in the French context, see Sonenscher, *Sans-Culottes*, 281–361. For Piketty's argument, see his *Capital in the Twenty-First Century*, trans. Arthur Goldhammer (Cambridge, MA: Harvard University Press, 2014), 422. There is a large and ongoing debate over the longer history of the cultural emergence of modern capitalism, in which issues of "merit" of course appear, but see Joel Mokyr, *A Culture of Growth: The Origins of the Modern Economy* (Princeton, NJ: Princeton University Press, 2016), esp. 203; and Deirdre Nansen McCloskey, *Bourgeois Equality: How Ideas, not Capital or Institutions, Enriched the World* (Chicago: University of Chicago Press, 2015), esp. 641, on which see Barry R. Weingast, "Exposing the Neoclassical Fallacy: McCloskey on Ideas and the Great Enrichment," *Scandinavian Economic History Review* 64, no. 3 (2016): 189–201.

112. Sala del Trono, Ca'Rezzonico, Venice, Italy. On this fresco, see also William L. Barckham, "Tiepolo as a Painter of History and Mythology and as a Decorator," in *Giambattista Tiepolo, 1696–1770,* ed. Keith Christiansen (New York: Metropolitan Museum of Art, 1996), 105–186, at 181–185.

113. On the *Libro d'oro,* see, among others, Dorit Raines, "Cooptazione, aggregazione e presenza al Maggior Consiglio: Le casate del patriziato veneziano, 1297–1797," *Storia di Venezia* 1 (2003): 1–64.

114. On the Venetian ducat—an early gold standard—in relation to other coins and currencies, see, among others, Alan Stahl, "The Making of a Gold Standard: The Ducat and Its Offspring, 1284–2001," in *Money in the Pre-Industrial World: Bullion, Debasements and Coin Substitutes,* ed. John H. Munro (London: Routledge, 2012), 45–62, at 47. For the cost of coffee at the time, see Cesare Musatti, "Il conticino d'un caffettiere veneziano del Settecento," *Ateneo veneto* 32, no. 1 (1909): 125–129.

115. On his world, see Andrea Nante, Carlo Cavalli, and Susanna Pasquali, eds., *Clemente XIII Rezzonico: Un papa veneto nella Roma di metà Settecento* (Cinisello Balsamo: Silvana, 2008). It must be said that this fusion of commercial wealth and military virtue was nothing new in Venice, as is evident from the 1585–1595 ceilings by Tintoretto and Jacopo Palma il Giovane that adorn the Sala del Senato in the Ducal Palace, Venice, Italy, and their remarkable admixture of philosophers, naval power, mints, and Roman soldiers. Contrary to a frequently repeated argument in the historiography of political philosophy, the "virtue" and "nobility" of commerce was an ancient trope in Italy, for a discussion of which see Lauro Martines's groundbreaking *The Social World of the Florentine Humanists* (Princeton, NJ: Princeton University Press, 1963), 25–26; and Mark Jurdjevic, "Virtue, Commerce, and the Enduring Florentine Republican Moment: Re-Integrating Italy into the Atlantic Republican Debate," *Journal of the History of Ideas* 62, no 4 (2001): 721–743.

116. Capra, "Luigi Giusti," 385–386.

117. Venturi, *Settecento riformatore,* esp. 1:647. For an eloquent testimony to these Freudian conflicts, see Pietro Verri, "Pensieri miei pericolosi a dirsi [1783]," in *ENOPV,* 5:487–497. On the economic reforms of the time, see Carlo Capra, "Riforme finanziarie e mutamento istituzionale nello Stato di Milano: Gli anni sessanta del secolo XVIII," *Rivista storica italiana* 91, nos. 2–3 (1979): 313–368.

118. Verri, "Pensieri miei pericolosi a dirsi [1783]," in *ENOPV,* 5:487–497, at 487.

119. The most comprehensive account of Firmian's life remains the multivolume manuscript by Antonio Mazzetti, "Vita e reggimento del Conte Carlo di Firmian Ministro Plenipotenziario nella Lombardia sotto Maria Teresa e Giuseppe II," Biblioteca Comunale di Trento, Trento, Italy, BCT1 *(fondo miscellaneo), Antonio Mazzetti, 1356* (among other copies), on which see for a summary

Zanei, *L'opera di rinnovamento nella Lombardia austriaca*. On the Grand Tour and its many varieties, see Sophus A. Reinert, "Another Grand Tour: Cameralism and Antiphysiocracy in Baden, Tuscany, and Denmark-Norway," in *Physiocrats, Antiphysiocrats and Pfeiffer*, ed. Jürgen Backhaus (Berlin: Springer Verlag, 2011), 39–69.

120. See, for example, Firmian's letters to Lorenzo Mehus of 4 July 1744, 11 July 1744, 22 August 1744, 19 September 1744, and 31 September 1745, in BNCF, *Riccardiano 3494*, fols. 132r–133v, 134r–134v, 139r–142r, 145r–146r, 190r–192r. On Firmian's friends' reinterpretation of Machiavelli, see Mario Rosa, *Dispotismo e libertà nel Settecento: Interpretazioni "repubblicane" di Machiavelli* (Pisa: Edizioni della normale, 2005). On the importance of Pierre Bayle for the European Enlightenment, see Robertson, *Case for the Enlightenment*.

121. Firmian to Lorenzo Mehus, 19 August 1751 and 21 February 1751, BNCF, *Riccardiano 3497*, fols. 27r–29v, 32r–32v. The reference is to Niccolò Machiavelli, *Discorsi sopra la prima deca di Tito Livio*, ed. Francesco Bausi, 2 vols. (Rome: Salerno Editrice, 2001). On Machiavelli's correspondence, see John M. Najemy, *Between Friends: Discourses of Power and Desire in the Machiavelli-Vettori Letters of 1513–1515* (Princeton, NJ: Princeton University Press, 1994).

122. Bernardo Tanucci to Francesco Nefetti, 19 November 1754, in *Epistolario*, 20 vols. to date, ed. R. P. Coppini et al. (Rome: Istituto poligrafico e Zecca dello Stato, Libreria dello Stato; then Naples: Società napoletana di storia patria, 1980–2007), 3:187–188, at 188.

123. Firmian to Thomas Steavens, 16 August 1754 and 31 December 1754, British Library, London, *MS 34732*, fols. 77r–v, 883–889v. On Firmian from the perspective of intellectual history, see Pietro Verri's character assassination "Memoria sul Conte Carlo Firmian," in *ENOPV*, 6:296–302; and Elisabeth Garms-Cornides, "Riflessi dell'Illuminismo italiano nel riformismo asburgico: La formazione intellettuale del conte Carlo Firmian," in *L'Illuminismo italiano e l'Europa: Atti del convegno internazionale, Roma, 25–26 marzo, 1976*, ed. anon. (Rome: Accademia nazionale dei lincei, 1977), 75–96, esp. 80–81. For a recent historiographical survey, see Marcello Bonazza, "Dai 'buoni studi' al 'buon governo': La parabola di Carlo Firmian, plenipotenziario trentino a Milano," in *Trentini nell'Europa dei lumi: Firmian, Martini, Pilati, Barbacovi*, ed. Mauro Nequiro (Trento: Comune di Trento, 2002), 9–25. On Firmian's collection, see *Biblioteca Firmiana*, 5 vols. (Milan: Typis imperialis monasterii S. Ambrosii Majoris, 1783); and Stefano Ferrari, "Anatomia di una collezione d'arte: I dipinti e le sculture del conte Carlo Firmian," *Studi Trentini: Arte* 91, no. 1 (2012): 93–14; on its republican bent, see Klára Garas, "Les oeuvres de Gianbettino Cignaroli e de Pietro Rotari en Hongrie," *Bulletin du Musée hongrois de Beaux Arts* 39 (1972): 77–100, at 83, mentioning Firmian's purposeful commissioning of paintings with republican

themes. Garms-Cornides, "Riflessi dell'Illuminismo italiano," 82, connects this back to Firmian's earlier interest in a republican Machiavelli.

124. Borlando, *Il problema delle communicazioni*, 78–81; Zanei, *L'opera di rinnovamento*, 16, 79–84, 88, 91. For contemporary takes on the problem provided at Firmian's behest, see Luigi Lambertenghi, "Memoria sulle operazioni preliminari, che possono intraprendersi dalla Giunta governativa destinata a sopraintendere alla cura de' confini, delle acque e delle strade," Biblioteca Nazionale Braidense, Milan, Italy, Mss., AD.XV.20, no. 12; and Antonio Lecchi, *Considerazioni . . . intorno alle nuove arginature di Po ne' confine del Piacentino, e del Milanese* ([Milan?]: n.p., 1760).

125. The literature on "improvement" is, again, vast, but see, among others, Richard Drayton, *Nature's Government: Science, Imperial Britain, and the "Improvement" of the World* (New Haven, CT: Yale University Press, 2000); Robert Friedel, *A Culture of Improvement: Technology and the Western Millennium* (Cambridge, MA: MIT Press, 2010); and Paul Slack, *The Invention of Improvement: Information and Material Progress in Seventeenth-Century England* (Oxford: Oxford University Press, 2015). On the later stage of improvement and its global consequences, see Roland Wenzlhuemer, *Connecting the Nineteenth-Century World: The Telegraph and Globalization* (Cambridge: Cambridge University Press, 2013); and Emily S. Rosenberg, *A World Connecting, 1870–1945* (Cambridge, MA: Harvard University Press, 2012).

126. On Firmian and Winckelmann, see, among others, Stefano Ferrari, "Da Vienna a Milano: Genesi e reazioni alla prima traduzione della Storia delle Arti del Disegno di Winckelmann," in *Vie Lombarde e Venete: Circolazione e trasformazione dei saperi letterari nel Sette-Ottocento fra l'Italia settentrionale e l'Europa transalpina,* ed. Helmut Meter and Furio Brugnolo (Berlin: Walter de Gruyter, 2011), 259–272, esp. 264; Bonazza, "Dai 'buoni studi' al 'buon governo,'" 20. The literature on Winckelmann is boundless, but see, among others, Alex Potts, *Flesh and the Ideal: Winckelmann and the Origins of Art History* (New Haven, CT: Yale University Press, 2000). On Verri's conflicts with Firmian, see again his "Memoria sul Conte Carlo Firmian."

127. Pietro Verri, "[Maria Vittoria Ottoboni Boncompagni, già sposa Serbelloni. 1790]," in *ENOPV*, 5:567.

128. On his relationship with Barbara Corbelli at the time, see Broneschi, *Quel che il cuore sapeva*, 51–53. On Verri's "desperation," see Pietro Verri, "Pensieri miei pericolosi a dirsi [1783]," in *ENOPV*, 5:487–497, at 488, and, for the letter to his uncle, 488n8.

129. On these campaigns, see the critical account by Henry Lloyd in "The History of the Late War in Germany, Between the King of Prussia, and the Empress of Germany and Her Allies: Containing the Campaigns of 1758 and 1759," vol. 2

(1790), in *War, Society and Enlightenment: The Works of General Lloyd*, ed. Patrick Speelman (Leiden: Brill, 2005), 535–738, at 677–703, and 664–673 on Kunersdorf in particular. For a modern summary, see, among others, Christopher Clark, *Iron Kingdom: The Rise and Downfall of Prussia, 1600–1947* (London: Penguin, 2007), 203–204.

130. Carlo Antonio Vianello, *La giovinezza di Parini, Verri e Beccaria: Con scritti, documenti e ritratti inediti* (Milan: Baldini e Castoldi, 1933), 238–240; Capra, *I progressi*, esp. 144; Isidoro Bianchi, *Elogio storico di Pietro Verri* (Cremona: Manini, 1803), 88–90. See also Verri's "Al Padre Frisi sulla morte della Contessa Barbara D'Adda nata Marchesa Corbelli," in *ENOPV*, 1:202–206.

131. Verri, "Memorie sincere," 37–38. On this intriguing text, and the difficulties of dating it precisely, see Gennaro Barbarisi's introductory and concluding materials at 3–15, 153–156.

132. Verri, "Memorie sincere," 45; Ludovico Ariosto, *Orlando furioso*, ed. Lanfranco Caretti, intro. Italo Calvino, 2 vols. (Turin: Einaudi, 2005), canto IX, 73–79.

133. Ariosto, *Orlando furioso*, canto IX, 73–79, for a visual meditation on which see the film *Il mestiere delle armi*, dir. Ermanno Olmi (Rome: Cinemaundici, 2001).

134. The tradition of single combat itself predates the written record, but for an early depiction in the Bronze Age Near East, see Sinuhe's confrontation with the "peerless champion" from Retjenu in *The Tale of Sinuhe and Other Ancient Egyptian Poems, 1940–1640 BC*, ed. Richard B. Parkinson (Oxford: Oxford University Press, 1997), 32–34 (B 110–145). On the death of Achilles, see Ovid, *Metamorphoses*, trans. A. D. Melville, intro. E. J. Kenney (Oxford: Oxford University Press, 2009), 292. On this Homeric tradition, see Victor Davis Hanson, *The Western Way of War: Infantry Battle in Classical Greece* (Berkeley: University of California Press, 1996); and, for its repercussions in early modern Europe, see a most incisive discussion in J. G. A. Pocock, *Barbarism and Religion*, 6 vols. (Cambridge: Cambridge University Press, 1999–2015), 1:220–221.

135. Verri, "Memorie sincere," 46; Miguel de Cervantes Saavedra, *Don Quixote*, trans. John Rutherford (London: Penguin, 2003), 358, 982. On this passage, see Iván Jaksić, "Don Quijote's Encounter with Technology," *Cervantes: Bulletin of the Cervantes Society of America* 14, no. 1 (1994): 75–95, at 83.

136. François Rabelais, *Gargantua and Pantagruel*, ed. J. M. Cohen (London: Penguin, 1955), 194 and within for the carneval of bloody results of artillery.

137. David Hume, *The History of England*, 8 vols. (London: Cadell, 1790–1791), 2:432, discussed in Pocock, *Barbarism and Religion*, 2:248. The reason-of-state author Trajano Boccalini, too, privy to the dark side of the human soul, would call the arquebus a "hellish" and "diabolical engine," but hoped, in his assumed voice

of its original inventor, "that out of the horror of this so dreadfull Instrument, all men would be so terrified, as they would abominate the mystery of War." See Boccalini's *I ragguagli di Parnasso, or, Advertisements from Parnassus in Two Centuries: With the Politick Touch-stone* (London: Moseley and Heath, 1656), 92–93.

138. On what lay just across the horizon, see David A. Bell, *The First Total War: Napoleon's Europe and the Birth of Warfare as We Know It* (Boston: Houghton Mifflin, 2007).

139. On the powerful tradition of community-building citizen soldiers, see Barry Strauss, "Citizen-Soldier," *Parameters: US Army War College Quarterly* 33, no. 2 (2003): 66–77. On how the invention of the arquebus was a "centripetal force" in early modern history, creating "empires and nations," see Alfred W. Crosby, *Throwing Fire: Projectile Technology through History* (Cambridge: Cambridge University Press, 2002), 107–129. On war and patriotic sentiment in the eighteenth century, see, among others, Linda Colley, *Britons: Forging the Nation, 1707–1837*, rev. ed. (New Haven, CT: Yale University Press, 2009).

140. Verri, "Memorie sincere," 55, 94–99, seemingly drawing on Machiavelli, *Il principe,* chap. 15, p. 280.

141. Verri, "Memorie sincere," 59; emphasis added.

142. See again Smith, *Lectures on Jurisprudence,* 129–130, 299.

143. Verri, "Memorie sincere," 83–84.

144. Ibid., 97. Compare the tradition explored in J. G. A. Pocock, *The Machiavellian Moment: Florentine Political Thought and the Atlantic Republican Tradition*, with a new introduction by Richard Whatmore (Princeton, NJ: Princeton University Press, 2016 [1975]).

145. Verri, "Memorie sincere," 83. For a more recent example of this effect, see Chris Kyle with Jim DeFelice and Scott McEwen, *American Sniper: The Autobiography of the Most Lethal Sniper in U.S. History* (New York: HarperCollins, 2014), 163–164, 279, 341, and esp. 428–429: "I'm not the same guy as I was when I first went to war. No one is. . . . As a SEAL, you go to the Dark Side. You're immersed in it. Continually going to war, you gravitate to the blackest parts of existence. Your psyche builds up its defenses—that's why you laugh at gruesome things like heads being blown apart, and worse." On the similarities and differences of such experiences of warfare over time, see Alexander Rose, *Men of War: The American Soldier in Combat at Bunker Hill, Gettysburg, and Iwo Jima* (New York: Random House, 2016), 357–360.

146. Verri, "Meditazioni sulla economia politica," in *ENOPV*, vol. 2:2, at 480; Verri, "Primi elementi per somministrare," 660.

147. Verri, "Memorie sincere," 49–54, 63. See also Pietro Verri to Alessandro Verri, 15 September 1759, in *Lettere e scritti inediti di Pietro e di Alessandro Verri*, ed. Carlo Casati, 4 vols. (Milan: Galli, 1879–1881), 1:48–63; and, toward the very end of his

life, Pietro Verri to Alessandro Verri, 10 November 1795, in *ENOPV*, vol. 8, pt. 2:1023–1025, at 1024. On Lloyd, see Patrick Speelman, *Henry Lloyd and the Military Enlightenment in Eighteenth-Century Europe* (Westport, CT: Greenwood, 2002); and Franco Venturi, *Le vite incrociate di Henry Lloyd e Pietro Verri* (Turin: Editrice Tirrenia-Stampatori, 1977).

148. Verri, "Memorie sincere," 76–77; emphasis added.

149. Pietro Verri, "Promemoria contenente: Un progetto di perfezione [1763]," in *ENOPV*, 1:409–450, at 428; emphasis in original.

150. Steven L. Kaplan and Sophus A. Reinert, "The Economic Turn in Enlightenment Europe," and Kaplan and Reinert, "Political Economy and the Social," both in *The Economic Turn: Recasting Political Economy in Eighteenth-Century Europe*, ed. Kaplan and Reinert, 2 vols. (London: Anthem, forthcoming).

151. Voltaire, *"Bled ou Blé,"* in *Questions sur l'Encyclopédie*, ed. Nicholas Cronk and Christiane Mervaud, 7 vols. (Oxford: Voltaire Foundation, 2007–2013), 3:402–422, at 412–413. The passage is often quoted from later editions in which Voltaire's editors conflated the *Questions* with his *Dictionnaire philosophique*, and is something of a mainstay of the historiography of political economy. See, for example, Georges Weulersse's classic *Le Mouvement physiocratique en France (de 1756 à 1770)*, 2 vols. (Paris: Félix Alcan, 1910), 1:25; Catherine Larrere, *L'invention de l'économie au XVIIIe siècle: Du droit naturel à la physiocratie* (Paris: Presses Universitaires de France, 1992), 221; Paul Cheney, *Revolutionary Commerce: Globalization and the French Monarchy* (Cambridge, MA: Harvard University Press, 2010), 52; Anoush Fraser Terjanian, *Commerce and Its Discontents in Eighteenth-Century French Political Thought* (Cambridge: Cambridge University Press, 2013), 4n11; Benoît Malbranque, *Les économistes bretons et leur place dans le développement de l'économie politique (1750–1900)* (Paris: Institut Coppet, 2013), 73; Emma C. Spary, *Feeding France: New Sciences of Food, 1760–1815* (Cambridge: Cambridge University Press, 2014), 60.

152. Christine Théré, "Economic Publishing and Authors, 1566–1789," in *Studies in the History of French Political Economy: From Bodin to Walras*, ed. Gilbert Faccarello (London: Routledge, 1998), 1–56, at 15; see also Jean-Claude Perrot, "Nouveautés: L'économie politique et ses livres," in *Histoire de l'édition française*, ed. Roger Chartier and Henri-Jean Martin (Paris: Fayard, 1990), 298–326; and, for the comparison with novels, John Shovlin, *The Political Economy of Virtue: Luxury, Patriotism, and the Origins of the French Revolution* (Ithaca, NY: Cornell University Press, 2006), 4.

153. Reinert, *Translating Empire*, 46–47.

154. Reinert, "Another Grand Tour." For a striking further example of such "economic" travel, see Paolo Greppi to Antonio Greppi, 14 April 1777, in *Viaggio di quasi tutta l'Europa colle viste del commercio dell'istruzione e della salute: Lettere di*

Paolo e Giacomo Greppi al padre (1777–1781), ed. Stefano Levati and Giovanni Liva (Milan: Silvana Editore for the Archivio di Stato di Milano and the Camera di Commercio di Milano, 2006), 137–139.

155. On "economic milling," see Kaplan, *Provisioning Paris,* esp. 405–408; on the rise of agricultural societies, see the essays in Stapelbroek and Marjanen, *Rise of Economic Societies;* on the emergence of business news, see Andrew Pettegree, *The Invention of News: How the World Came to Know about Itself* (New Haven, CT: Yale University Press, 2014); generally, see Kaplan and Reinert, "The Economic Turn."

156. On the theme of accounting and accountability, see again Soll, *The Reckoning.* As Pietro Verri would summarize one of his constant preoccupations late in life, "the publication of accounts is an essential part of just government; mystery and obscurity are signs of robbery"; see his "Modo di terminar le dispute," in *ENOPV,* 6:840–844, at 841.

157. Cervantes, *Don Quixote,* 488; Pietro Verri, "Un ignorante agli scrittori del 'Caffè,'" in *Il Caffè,* 352–354, at 353; emphasis in original.

158. See, similarly, on humor and contemporary political economy, Sophus A. Reinert, "The Way to Wealth around the World: Benjamin Franklin and the Globalization of American Capitalism," *American Historical Review* 120, no. 1 (2015): 61–97, at 73–75.

159. Verri, "Memorie sincere," 89. On Lloyd inspiring Verri to turn to political economy, see Vianello, *La giovinezza di Parini,* 158.

160. Verri, "Memorie sincere," 89, echoed in Verri, "Lettera riservata," 210–211.

161. Verri, "Memorie sincere," 104, the argument continuing onto 105. True or not, it was widely held that a stultifying "Bartolism" had crept into Italian jurisprudence as early as the fifteenth century. For a brief overview of the phenomenon, see Francesco Calasso, "Bartolismo," in *Enciclopedia del diritto,* vol. 5 (Milan: Giuffrè, 1959), 71–74. The bibliography on Bartolus himself is staggering, but see Ennio Cortese, *Il diritto nella storia medievale,* vol. 2 (Rome: Il Cigno, 1995), 425–436, for a recent sketch.

162. Gabriele Verri to Pietro Verri, 13 September 1760, Archivio Verri, Fondazione Mattioli, housed at the Università di Milano under the tutelage of the Archivio Storico della Banca Intesa Sanpaolo, Milan, Italy (hereafter cited as Archivio Verri), 272.44, 1r. Parts of their correspondence are also reproduced in Stefano Baia Curioni, *Per sconfiggere l'oblio: Saggi e documenti sulla formazione intellettuale di Pietro Verri* (Milan: Franco Angeli, 1988), 105–212. It must be said that the idea of its being a "new science" was common at the time; see, for example, Wenzel Anton von Kaunitz-Rittberg to Cesare Beccaria, 1 December 1768, in *ENOPV,* 4:692–693, at 692.

163. Gabriele Verri to Pietro Verri 27 September 1760, Archivio Verri, 274.44, 1r.

164. Ibid.

165. See, for example, Till Wahnbaeck, *Luxury and Public Happiness: Political Economy in the Italian Enlightenment* (Oxford: Oxford University Press, 2004), 155, drawing on a long historiography.

166. Jacques Savary, *Le parfait Négociant* (Paris: Guignard, 1676), of which several folio editions existed by 1760. Savary's work was, famously, the inspiration for the equally celebrated Malachy Postlethwayt, *Universal Dictionary of Trade and Commerce* (London: A. Miller et al., 1757).

167. Girolamo Belloni, *Del commercio* (Rome: Palladio, 1750), on which see Sophus A. Reinert, "Girolamo Belloni," in *Enciclopedia italiana di scienze, lettere ed arti: Il contributo italiano alla storia del pensiero economico,* ed. Vera Negri Zamagni and Pier Luigi Porta (Rome: Istituto della enciclopedia italiana fondata da Giovanni Treccani, 2012), 271–274. On the editions of his work, see Erik S. Reinert, Kenneth Carpenter, Fernanda Reinert, and Sophus A. Reinert, "80 Economic Bestsellers before 1850: A Fresh Look at the History of Economic Thought," *The Other Canon Foundation and Tallinn University of Technology Working Papers in Technology Governance and Economic Dynamics,* paper no. 74 (2017), 54.

168. Verri, "Memorie sincere," 114–115.

169. Curioni, *Per sconfiggere l'oblio,* 69–70.

170. The first work Beccaria composed under the influence of the Fisticuffs had indeed been this rare pamphlet, published anonymously under the title *Del disordine e de' rimedij delle monete nello stato di Milano nel 1762* (Lucca: n.p., 1762), now available in *ENOCB,* vol. 3: *Scritti economici,* ed. Gianmarco Gaspari (Milan: Mediobanca, 2014), 15–52. For context, see *Sul disordine delle monete a Milano nel Settecento: Tre saggi di Cesare Beccaria e Pietro Verri,* ed. Alberto Quadrio Curzio and Robero Scazzieri (Milan: Electa, 1986); and Alberto Cova, "Pietro Verri e la riforma monetaria," in *Pietro Verri e il suo tempo,* ed. Carlo Capra (Bologna: Cisaplino, 1999), 763–788.

171. Beccaria, *Del disordine,* 20.

172. Ibid., 21, 22n–23n, 32, 36.

173. Ibid., 24, 31, 33. On the theme of Italian decline at the time, see again Sophus A. Reinert, "Lessons on the Decline and Fall of Great Powers: Conquest, Commerce, and Decline in Enlightenment Italy," *American Historical Review* 115, no. 5 (2010): 1395–1425.

174. On this episode, see Gianni Francioni's annotations to Pietro Verri, "Il Gran Zoroastro ossia astrologiche osservazioni su i veri principj della scienza monetaria in soccorso della 'Risposta ad un amico' [1762]," in *ENOPV,* 1:388–403; and Luigi Firpo, "Il primo saggio di Cesare Beccaria," *Rivista storica Italiana* 76 (1964): 671–706.

175. On secrecy and reason of state, see, among others, Peter S. Donaldson, *Machiavelli and the Mystery of State* (Cambridge: Cambridge University Press, 1992);

and John R. Snyder, *Dissimulation and the Culture of Secrecy in Early Modern Europe* (Berkeley: University of California Press, 2009). On the tradition of Tacitism, see Peter Burke, "Tacitism, Scepticism, and Reason of State," in *The Cambridge History of Political Thought, 1400–1700,* ed. J. H. Burns with Mark Goldie (Cambridge: Cambridge University Press, 1991), 479–498.

176. Kaunitz to Verri, 19 April 1764, in Casati, *Lettere e scritti,* 1:177–178. On these events, see the minute reconstruction in Capra, *I progressi della ragione,* 233–242. On the balances, see Daniela Parisi, "Gli studi economici del giovane Pietro Verri: I Bilanci del commercio," in *Pietro Verri e il suo tempo,* ed. Carlo Capra, 2 vols. (Bologna: Cisalpino, 1999), 789–811.

177. This was, as such, a chapter in the longer story of how secretive reason of state eventually gave way to public political economy, on which see Reinert, *Translating Empire,* esp. 69.

178. Pietro Verri, "Meditazioni sulla felicità," in *ENOPV,* 1:734–762, at 750–751. On the sentence about the "greatest happiness" being a *"slogan"* of the Academy of Fisticuffs, see Gianni Francioni's penetrating "Nota introduttiva," 676–697, at 685–687. On the broader history of the phrase, see also Robert Shackleton, "The Greatest Happiness of the Greatest Number: The History of Bentham's Phrase," *Studies on Voltaire and the Eighteenth Century* 90 (1972): 1461–1482. On sensationist philosophy at the time, often read through the influence of John Locke and Étienne Bonnot de Condillac, see John C. O'Neal, *The Authority of Experience: Sensationist Theory in the French Enlightenment* (University Park: Pennsylvania State University Press, 1996). In the Italian context, Condillac's experiences in Parma in the period from 1758 to 1767 would prove influential, on which see, among others, Luciano Guerci, *Condillac storico: Storia e politica nel Cours d'études pour l'instruction du Prince de Parme* (Milan: Ricciardi, 1978); Carminella Biondi, "Un philosophe alla corte di Parma: Étienne Bonnot de Condillac, precettore di don Ferdinando," in *Un Borbone tra Parma e l'Europa: Don Ferdinando e il suo tempo (1751–1802),* ed. Alba Mora (Reggio Emilia: Diabasis, 2005), 51–61; and Élisabeth Badinter, *L'Infant de Parme* (Paris: Fayard, 2008). For a popular account of the sensationist Enlightenment, see Carolyn Purnell, *The Sensational Past: How the Enlightenment Changed the Way We Use Our Senses* (New York: W. W. Norton, 2017).

179. Verri, "Meditazioni sulla felicità," 734–736. On the importance of this text as a point of both arrival and departure for Verri, see Francioni's "Nota introduttiva," 696.

180. Compare, among others, Timothy Mitchell, *Rule of Experts: Egypt, Techno-Politics, Modernity* (Berkeley: University of California Press, 2002), 81–82. Of course, eighteenth-century theorists did not envision "the economy" to be a disembedded and perfectly self-regulating market, but the question remains why on earth they should have done so in the first place. For a conceptual his-

tory of the evolution of the term "economy," see, from a purely English-language perspective, Ryan Walter, *A Critical History of the Economy: On the Birth of the National and International Economies* (London: Routledge, 2011); and, more broadly, Keith Tribe's magisterial "The Word: Economy," in *The Economy of the Word: Language: History, and Economics* (Oxford: Oxford University Press, 2015), 21–88. Tribe, however, apart from furtive references at 53n97, primarily deals with English, French, and German sources.

181. Suffice it to remember Giuseppe Visconti's suggestion, in his "Della maniera di conservare robusta e lungamente la sanità di chi vive nel clima milanese," in *Il Caffè*, 498–532, at 18, to "drink it mixed with milk or with egg yolk as much as you like."

182. Pietro della Valle, *Viaggi*, 4 vols. (Rome: Deversin, 1650–1663), 2:103. On della Valle, see, among others, Joan-Pau Rubiés, *Travel and Ethnology in the Renaissance: South India through European Eyes, 1250–1625* (Cambridge: Cambridge University Press, 2000), esp. 354–378.

183. Giovanni Domenico Civinini, *Della storia e natura del caffè* (Florence: Bernardo Paperini, 1731), 31.

184. Lotharius Vogemonte, *Trattato intorno allo stabililimento del commercio . . .* (Vienna: Lercher, 1709); Ferdinando Galiani, *Della moneta* (Naples: Raimondi, 1750), 244.

185. Antonio Genovesi, *Storia del commercio della Gran Brettagna*, 3 vols. (Naples: Benedetto Gessari, 1757–1758), 1:viii.

186. Alessandro Verri to Pietro Verri, 2 November 1766, in *Viaggio a Parigi e Londra (1766–1767): Carteggio di Pietro e Alessandro Verri*, ed. Gianmarco Gaspari (Milan: Adelphi, 1980), 60.

187. Verri, "Memorie sincere," 150; Verri, "Lettera riservata," 198, 203; Pietro Verri to Alessandro Verri, 2–3 November 1766, in *Viaggio a Parigi e Londra*, 67; see, similarly, anon., *Esame breve, e succinto dell'opera intitolata Meditazioni sulla economia pubblica* (Vercelli: Giuseppe Panialis, [1771?]), 66, for the phrase "Istoria dell'Economia." There was nothing unique about this usage, and phrases such as "economic affairs" abounded. For a nonspecialist example, speaking to a general audience, see Willem Bosman, *Viaggio in Guinea*, 3 vols., anonymous translation of the French translation of the original Dutch, ed. Giovanni and Carlo Mosca (Venice: Marcellino Piotto, [1754?]), 2:85. See also Sophus A. Reinert, "Authority and Expertise at the Origins of Macroeconomics," in *Antonio Serra and the Economics of Good Government*, ed. Rosario Patalano and Sophus A. Reinert (Basingstoke, UK: Palgrave Macmillan, 2016), 112–142. For arguments that the concept of "the economy" emerged in much later periods, see, among others, Michel Foucault, *Les mots et les choses: Une archéologie des sciences humaines* (Paris: Gallimard, 1966); Keith Tribe, *Land, Labour and Economic Discourse* (London: Routledge and Kegan Paul, 1978); Margaret Lynn Schabas, *The Natural*

Origins of Economics (Chicago: University of Chicago Press, 2005); Mitchell, *Rule of Experts,* 81–82, 298–303; Margaret Lynn Schabas, "Constructing 'The Economy,'" *Philosophy of the Social Sciences* 39, no. 1 (2009): 3–19.

188. Jules Michelet, "Advent of Coffee [1863]," reproduced in Roland Barthes, *Michelet,* trans. Richard Howard (Berkeley: University of California Press, 1992), 189–191. On Michelet, see Paule Petitier, *Jules Michelet: L'homme histoire* (Paris: Grasset et Fasquelle, 2006).

189. www.caffeflorian.com; Frederic C. Lane, *Venice: A Maritime Republic* (Baltimore: Johns Hopkins University Press, 1973), 433.

190. Jordan Goodman, "Excitantia: Or, How Enlightenment Europe Took to Soft Drugs," in *Consuming Habits: Global and Historical Perspectives on How Cultures Define Drugs,* 2nd. ed., ed. Jordan Goodman, Paul E. Lovejoy, and Andrew Sherratt (London: Routledge, 2007), 121–141; Woodruff D. Smith, "From Coffeehouse to Parlour: The Consumption of Coffee, Tea, and Sugar in North-Western Europe in the Seventeenth and Eighteenth Centuries," in Goodman, Lovejoy, and Sherrat, *Consuming Habits,* 142–157.

191. Quoted in Ellis, *The Coffee House,* 16–17. On this phenomenon, see Ralph S. Hattox, *Coffee and Coffeehouses: The Origins of a Social Beverage in the Medieval Near East* (Seattle: University of Washington Press, 1985). On such ports, see Karl Polanyi, "Ports of Trade in Early Societies," in *Primitive, Archaic and Modern Economies: Essays of Karl Polanyi* (Boston: Beacon Press, 1971), 238–260; and, for a deeper historical perspective and case study, Astrid Möller, *Naukratis: Trade in Archaic Greece* (Oxford: Oxford University Press, 2000).

192. Goodman, "Excitantia," 127, though this is an old argument. See, for example, "Old New York Coffee-Houses," *Harper's New Monthly Magazine,* March 1882, 481–499, at 482.

193. Pendergrast, *Uncommon Grounds,* 7, 15–16; Goodman, "Excitantia," 124–125.

194. As such, coffee was even more than "a microcosm of European relations with the rest of the world during a key historical period," as argued in Emma C. Spary, *Eating the Enlightenment: Food and the Sciences in Paris, 1670–1760* (Chicago: University of Chicago Press, 2012), 52; it literally changed the world itself. On how specialization in the production of different commodities, such as sugar and coffee, resulted in deeply different social and political structures, see Jeffry A. Frieden, *Global Capitalism: Its Fall and Rise in the Twentieth Century* (New York: W. W. Norton, 2007), 98–103. On the Columbian Exchange, see still Alfred W. Crosby Jr., *The Columbian Exchange: Biological and Cultural Consequences of 1492,* 30th anniv. ed. (Westport, CT: Praeger, 2003). On the related concept of the "Anthropocene," seen to begin in the late eighteenth century, see, among others, Paul J. Crutzen, "Geology of Mankind," *Nature* 415, no. 3 (January 2002): 23. For a broader framework for understanding human impact

on the environment in deeper history, see Patrick V. Kirch, "Archaeology and Global Change: The Holocene Record," *Annual Review of Environment and Resources* 30 (2005): 409–430.

195. On the domestication and spread of viniculture in ancient Greece and Rome, see Tim Unwin, *Wine and the Vine* (London: Routledge, 1991), 94–133; and Patrick E. McGovern, *Ancient Wine: The Search for the Origins of Viniculture* (Princeton, NJ: Princeton University Press, 2003), 14. On the Italian history of the tomato, see David Gentilcore, *Pomodoro! A History of the Tomato in Italy* (New York: Columbia University Press, 2010). For the important but less widely significant history of the potato there, see Gentilcore, *Italy and the Potato: A History, 1550–2000* (London: Continuum, 2012).

196. Daniel Lord Smail, *On Deep History and the Brain* (Berkeley: University of California Press, 2008), 154–155, 179–180; caffeine is not a typical autotropic mechanism on the same level as alcohol or opium, but it does "influence the body in other ways, typically by causing a cascading set of changes that ultimately generates higher levels of dopamine in synapses, albeit temporarily" (174–175). On the chemistry of coffee, see Bennet Alan Weinberg and Bonnie K. Bealer, *The World of Caffeine: The Science and Culture of the World's Most Popular Drug* (London: Routledge, 2002), 216–219. Somewhat ironically, historians of science have shown themselves rather less interested in the more strictly "scientific" aspects of coffee history. See, for example, Spary, *Eating the Enlightenment,* 91: "Coffee is an especially interesting historical subject, but neither because it belongs within a history of stimulants nor because its history provides us with an ancestry for modern-day coffee drinking. Instead, coffee illustrates the epistemological peculiarity of comestibles."

197. For a particularly harrowing example, see Norman Ohler, *Blitzed: Drugs in the Third Reich,* trans. Shaun Whiteside (Boston: Houghton Mifflin, 2017), esp. 105. Nonetheless, caveats born from the darker historiographical experiences of the twentieth century remain informative—see, for example, Marshall Sahlins, *The Use and Abuse of Biology: An Anthropological Critique of Sociobiology* (Ann Arbor: University of Michigan Press, 1976).

198. Yet books on the subject certainly can be satisfying. See particularly Tom Standage, *A History of the World in Six Glasses* (London: Atlantic Books, 2006); Steward Lee Allen, *The Devil's Cup: Coffee, the Driving Force in History* (Edinburgh: Canongate Books, 2000), 128–136.

199. For a balanced overview of numerous studies on the health consequences of caffeine intake, see Weinberg and Bealer, *The World of Caffeine,* 291–302, quotations at 299. The popular literature on the advantages and disadvantages of coffee remains divided between the halcyon Morton Satin, *Coffee Talk: The Stimulating Story of the World's Most Popular Brew* (Amherst, NY: Prometheus Books,

2011), and the more sober Antony Wild, *Black Gold: A Dark History of Coffee* (London: Harper Perennial, 2005), esp. 205. Wild recounts the cautionary tale of a famous NASA experiment with administering different hallucinogenics to household spiders and observing their resultant webs: "The chosen substances were caffeine, Benzedrine, marijuana, and chloral hydrate—the latter a sedative and hypnotic when used on humans. The result was bad news for caffeine consumers: the spider stoned on marijuana created a near-perfect web, save only for forgetting to finish it off; the speed-crazed one did little patches quite well with great gaps in between as if it kept getting distracted; the chloral hydrate head offered up a zonked-out *reduction ad absurdum* minimalist web; but the caffeine-crazed spider produced something that in no respect resembled the hub-and-spoke pattern of the conventional web. The conclusion was that spider's web-building capabilities were far more grievously impaired by caffeine than by the other psychoactive substances." Humans are, of course, not spiders, but see the frightening images in the unpaginated color insert.

200. Julian Offray de La Mettrie, "Machine Man," in La Mettrie, *Machine Man and Other Writings*, ed. Ann Thomson (Cambridge: Cambridge University Press, 1996), 1–39, quotation at 7. On eighteenth-century considerations of its consequences, particularly with regard to melancholy, see, for an eminently readable sensationist approach to the Enlightenment, Purnell, *The Sensational Past*, 56–57.

201. Francesco Merli, *Il buon uso del the, del caffè, del cioccolato* (Naples: Vincenzo Flauto, 1769), 32, 38, 43.

202. Verri, "Storia naturale del caffè," in *Il Caffè*, 14–17, quotation at 16.

203. Brian Cowan, *The Social Life of Coffee: The Emergence of the British Coffeehouse* (New Haven, CT: Yale University Press, 2005), 32, 54.

204. Merli, *Il buon uso*, 46.

205. Allen, *The Devil's Cup*, 26, 39.

206. John Cary, *An Essay on the State of England* (Bristol, England: W. Bonny, 1695), 154–155. On the social anxieties produced by the proliferation of coffeehouses, see Cowan, *The Social Life of Coffee*; for the case of Venice, see Wolff, *Paolina's Innocence*, 69–100.

207. Donald Quataert, *The Ottoman Empire, 1700–1922* (Cambridge: Cambridge University Press, 2000), 7. For the general sentiment, see Edward W. Said's still-relevant *Orientalism* (New York: Vintage Books, 1978), and the vast scholarship it has engendered.

208. Anon., "Caffés," in *Encyclopédie . . .* , ed. Denis Diderot and Jean le Rond d'Alembert, 28 vols. (Paris: Briasson, 1751–1772), 2:259.

209. For the case of Enlightened self-fashioning in Paris, see Spary, *Eating the Enlightenment*, 51.

210. Jürgen Habermas, *The Structural Transformation of the Public Sphere: An Inquiry into a Category of Bourgeois Society,* trans. Thomas Burger with Frederick Lawrence (Cambridge: Polity Press, 1991), 32–33. On the perpetual relevance of this theory for appreciating Enlightenment history, see James van Horn Melton, *The Rise of the Public in Enlightenment Europe* (Cambridge: Cambridge University Press, 2001). On the Starbucks-led end of the coffee shop as a locus of the public sphere, see Asaf Bar-Tura, "The Coffeehouse as a Public Sphere: Brewing Social Change," in *Coffee: Philosophy for Everyone, Grounds for Debate,* ed. Scott F. Parker and Michael W. Austin (Chichester, UK: John Wiley and Sons, 2011), 89–99. On coffee and the Enlightenment, see again Weinberg and Bealer, *The World of Caffeine,* 72–74; and Aytoun Ellis, *The Penny Universities: A History of the Coffee Houses* (London: Ballantyne, Hanson, and Co., 1956), 181–191. See also Peter Stallybass and Allon White, *The Politics and Poetics of Transgression* (London: Taylor and Francis, 1986), 94–95. For a useful rejoinder regarding the complex relationship between coffee culture and the public sphere, see the conclusion to Cowan, *The Social Life of Coffee.*

211. Smith, "From Coffeehouse to Parlour," 148–149; Dorinda Outram, *The Enlightenment,* 2nd ed. (Cambridge: Cambridge University Press, 2008), 13, 17; Elizabeth Horodowich, *Language and Statecraft in Early Modern Venice* (Cambridge: Cambridge University Press, 2008), 214.

212. G. B. Manuzzo to the Tribunale degli Inquisitori, 26 June 1757, in *Agenti segreti di Venezia, 1705–1797,* ed. Giovanni Comisso (Vicenza: N. Pozza, 1984), 83.

213. Voltaire, *The Coffee-House; or, Fair Fugitive* (London: J. Wilkie, 1760), 6; Woodruff D. Smith, *Consumption and the Making of Respectability, 1600–1800* (London: Routledge, 2002), 141. See also Allen, *The Devil's Cup,* 114–116; Ellis, *The Coffee House,* esp. 87.

214. Bruno Latour, *Science in Action: How to Follow Scientists and Engineers through Society* (Cambridge, MA: Harvard University Press, 1987). Latour's perspective was applied to coffeehouses by Larry Stewart in "Other Centres of Calculation, or, Where the Royal Society Didn't Count: Commerce, Coffee-Houses and Natural Philosophy in Early Modern London," *British Journal for the History of Science* 32, no. 2 (1999): 133–153.

215. Spary, *Eating the Enlightenment,* 98, though she in passing mentions that "as learned spaces, cafés were heterogenous, embracing belles-lettres, philosophie, geometry, political economy, and the natural sciences"—see 121 and, for coffeehouses as loci of financial innovation, 130–131.

216. Smith, "From Coffeehouse to Parlour," 148–149; on the story of how the Bank of New York was "projected" in the "Merchant's Coffee House" in the same city in 1784, see "Old New York Coffee-Houses," 497.

217. Ange Goudar [and Giacomo Casanova], *The Chinese Spy; or, Emissary from the Court of Pekin, Commissioned to examine into The Present State of Europe*, 6 vols. (London: S. Bladon, 1765), 4:1; emphasis added. See 4:186 on the genius of political economy, discussed in Reinert, *Translating Empire*, 13–14. On Casanova's involvement with the work, see his *History of My Life*, 10:287. On Goudar and his relationship to Casanova, see Jean-Claude Hauc, *Ange Goudar: Un aventurier des Lumières* (Paris: Champion, 2004).

218. Sebastiano Franci, "Dell'agricoltura; Dialogo: Afranio e Cresippo," in *Il Caffè*, 60–72, at 60.

219. Pietro Verri, "Introduzione," in *Il Caffè*, 11; emphasis in original.

220. On the international reception of *The Spectator*, though she does not mention the Academy of Fisticuffs, see Maria Lúcia Pallares-Burke, "*The Spectator*, or the Metamorphoses of the Periodical: A Study in Cultural Translation," in *Cultural Translation in Early Modern Europe*, ed. Peter Burke and R. Po-chia Hsia (Cambridge: Cambridge University Press, 2007), 142–159. On the relation of *The Spectator* to *Il Caffè*, see Luigi Ferrari, *Del "Caffè," periodico milanese del secolo xviii* (Pisa: Tipografia Successori Fratelli Nistri, 1899), 28–31. Members of the Academy of Fisticuff themselves wondered how their writings would be received in England among "the readers of *Schwist* and *Adisson*"; see Alessandro Verri to Pietro Verri, 15 December 1766, in *Viaggio a Parigi e Londra*, 148.

221. *The Spectator*, 8 vols. (London: S. Buckley and J. Tonson, 1712–1715), 1:4–7. On this widespread and polyvalent eighteenth-century trope of "improvement," see again, among others, Richard Drayton, *Nature's Government: Science, Imperial Britain, and the "Improvement" of the World* (New Haven, CT: Yale University Press, 2000); and Paul Slack, *The Invention of Improvement: Information and Material Progress in Seventeenth-Century England* (Oxford: Oxford University Press, 2015).

222. On the "Grecian in Devereux Court," which was founded by a Greek immigrant, catered to "the learned," and often made an appearance in *The Spectator* and *The Tatler*, see the lengthy annotation to *Addison's Spectator*, ed. George Washington Greene, 2 vols. (New York: Derby and Jackson, 1860), 1:6n. On how the model of *The Spectator* legitimized such cultural translations, see Pallares-Burke, "*The Spectator*," 158–159.

223. Alessandro Verri, "Ragionamento sulle leggi civili," in *Il Caffè*, 571–606, at 597.

224. Pietro Verri, "Introduzione" and "Storia naturale del caffè," in *Il Caffè*, 11–17. On the historical *Greco*, see Riccardo di Vincenzo, *Milano al Caffè: Tra Settecento e Novecento* (Milan: Hoepli, 2007), 22–25.

225. Verri, "Introduzione," 12. By this time this was, of course, a common trope across Europe; see, among others, Spary, *Eating the Enlightenment*, 108–110.

226. For a similar parallel between the Enlightenment Republic of Letters and the "60s Republic of Rock," see Michael J. Kramer, *The Republic of Rock: Music and Citizenship in the Sixties Counterculture* (Oxford: Oxford University Press, 2013), 9.

227. Verri, "Introduzione," 12. On this mythical dichotomy of taverns and coffee shops in the French context, see Thomas Brennan, *Public Drinking and Popular Culture in Eighteenth-Century Paris* (Princeton, NJ: Princeton University Press, 1988), 133.

228. Quoted in Emma Rothschild, *Economic Sentiments: Adam Smith, Condorcet, and the Enlightenment* (Cambridge, MA: Harvard University Press, 2001), 15.

229. Cesare Beccaria, "Frammento sugli odori," in *Il Caffè*, 39–47, at 42, on which see also Vittorio Marchis, "L'odore del 'Caffè,' ovvero, come colui che scherza spesso predice il futuro," in *Il giornalismo milanese dall'Illuminismo al Romanticismo*, ed. Pierre-Cécile Buffaria and Paolo Grossi (Paris: Istituto italiano di cultura, 2006), 157–164. On Beccaria's utilitarianism, see generally Gianni Francioni, "Beccaria filosofo utilitarista," in *Cesare Beccaria tra Milano e l'Europa*, ed. Sergio Romagnoli and Gian Domenico Pisapia (Milan: Cariplo-Laterza, 1990), 69–87. On Beccaria's egalitarianism being progressively expansive rather than simply majoritarian, see Albergo Burgio, "L'idea di eguaglianza tra diritto e politica nel *Dei delitti e delle pene*," in *Cesare Beccaria: La pratica dei lumi*, ed. Vincenzo Ferrona and Gianni Francioni (Florence: Oelschki, 2000), 79–98, at 83.

230. Verri, "Introduzione," 12. On the framework of the coffee shop, see also Helmut C. Jacobs, "Die Rahmenhandlung von *Il Caffè* im Spannungsfeld von inszenierter Mündlichkeit und Schriftlichkeit," in *Die Zeitschrift Il Caffè*, ed. Helmut C. Jacobs et al. (Frankfurt am Main: Peter Lang, 2003), 107–129.

231. Michelet, "Advent of Coffee [1863]," 189–191.

232. Quoted in Sergio Romagnoli, "'Il Caffè' tra Milano e l'Europa," in *Il Caffè*, xiii–lxxix, at xv.

233. Pietro Verri to Gian Rinaldo Carli, 9 March 1765, in De Stefano, "Cinque anni di sodalizio," 83.

234. Pietro Verri to Alessandro Verri and Cesare Beccaria [*"ai fratelli"*], 6 October [1766], in *Viaggio a Parigi e Londra*, 10.

235. Verri, "Introduzione," 12. It was clearly normal at the time to follow events one read about on maps, testified to also by Pietro Verri to Antonio Verri, 10 November 1759, in Pietro Verri, *Lettere inedite di Pietro Verri, 5 maggio 1759–1 dicembre 1760*, ed. Mario Zolezzi (Milan: Editrice vita e pensiero, 1965), 42–44, at 44.

236. Verri, "Meditazioni," 548; Capra, *I progressi della ragione*, 354.

237. "Al lettore," in *Il Caffè*, 5; emphasis added.

238. The classic treatment of this dichotomy remains Nannerl O. Keohane, *Philosophy and the State in France: The Renaissance to the Enlightenment* (Princeton, NJ: Princeton University Press, 1980), esp. 189–190.

239. See, among many, many others, E. J. Hundert, *The Enlightenment's Fable: Bernard Mandeville and the Discovery of Society* (Cambridge: Cambridge University Press, 1994), esp. 58–59; Hont, *Jealousy of Trade*, 37–51; and Hont, *Politics in Commercial Society*, esp. 39; Frederick Neuhouser, *Rousseau's Theodocy of Self-Love: Evil, Rationality, and the Drive for Recognition* (Oxford: Oxford University Press, 2008); Fonna Forman-Barzilai, *Adam Smith and the Circles of Sympathy: Cosmopolitanism and Moral Theory* (Cambridge: Cambridge University Press, 2010), 37–38.

240. Bernard Mandeville, *The Fable of the Bees*, ed. Frederick B. Kaye, 2 vols. (Oxford: Clarendon Press, 1924), 1:116, 369.

241. See, for example, Verri, "Considerazioni sul commercio dello stato di Milano [1763]," in *ENOPV*, vol. 2.2:107–345, at 173n; Verri, "Memorie sulla economia pubblica dello stato di Milano [1768]," in *ENOPV*, vol. 2.2:347–435, at 403.

242. Pietro Verri, "Meditazioni sulla economia politica," in *ENOPV*, vol. 2.2:391–676, at 438; emphasis added. On the importance of the politics of happiness for Verri's political economy, see also Pier Luigi Porta and Roberto Scazzieri, "Pietro Verri's Political Economy: Commercial Society, Civil Society, and the Science of the Legislator," *History of Political Economy* 34, no. 1 (2002): 83–110, esp. 101–102.

243. Charles L. Schultze, *The Public Use of Private Interest* (Washington, DC: Brookings Institution, 1977), developed in Thomas K. McCraw, *Prophets of Regulation* (Cambridge, MA: Harvard University Press, 1984), 308, and in Richard H. K. Vietor, *Contrived Competition: Regulation and Deregulation in America* (Cambridge, MA: Harvard University Press, 1994), 328.

244. Alfonso Longo, "Osservazioni su i fedecommessi," in *Il Caffè*, 115–132, quotation at 119.

245. For Hume and Smith on this, see Emma Rothschild, "Faith, Enlightenment, and Economics," in *Natural Law, Economics, and the Common Good: Perspectives from Natural Law*, ed. Samuel Gregg and Harold James (Exeter, UK: Imprint Academic, 2012), 17–23.

246. "Al lettore," in *Il Caffè*, 5.

247. Verri, "Introduzione," 11; the most interesting unpublished piece might be Alfonso Longo's "On the Natural Rights of Dogs"; see "Del diritto naturale dei cani," in *Il Caffè*, 824–836.

248. See, similarly, Capra, "L'Accademia dei pugni," 43.

249. Pietro Verri, "Sulla interpretazione delle leggi," in *Il Caffè*, 695–704, quotation at 700; emphasis in original.

250. Verri, "Introduzione," 13; emphasis added.

251. Emer de Vattel, *The Law of Nations*, ed. Béla Kapossy and Richard Whatmore (Indianapolis: Liberty Fund, 2008), 72 (Preliminaries, 11).

252. Compare Gianni Francioni, "Storia editoriale del 'Caffè,'" in *Il Caffè*, lxxxi–clxxvii, at lxxxiii, and Robert C. Allen, "The Great Divergence in European

Wages and Prices from the Middle Ages to the First World War," *Explorations in Economic History* 38 (2001): 411–447, at 416. This made *Il Caffè* rather expensive by contemporary standards of works in the broad category of political economy; for context, see Reinert, *Translating Empire*, 271–272.

253. For the cost of coffee at the time, see again Musatti, "Il conticino d'un caffettiere veneziano."

254. On Beccaria's salary, see, among others, Carlo Scognamiglio Pasini, *L'arte della ricchezza: Cesare Beccaria economista* (Milan: Mondadori, 2014), 140.

255. For "enlightening the multitude," see Pietro Verri, "Pensieri sullo spirito della letteratura d'Italia," in *Il Caffè*, 211–222, at 220. On the "people problem" in the Enlightenment, see Steven L. Kaplan, *The Stakes of Regulation: Perspectives on "Bread, Politics and Political Economy" Forty Years Later* (London: Anthem, 2015), esp. xviii n21.

256. For an example of "people" (*popolo*) and "simple masses" (*facile turba*), see Pietro Verri, "Le osservazioni degli influssi," in *Il Caffè*, 296–297, at 297; for "the multitude" (*moltitudine*), see Verri, "Gli studi utili," in *Il Caffè*, 311–318, at 312; and for "nonmanual citizen" (*cittadino non manuale*), see Cesare Beccaria, "De' fogli periodici," in *Il Caffè*, 411–419, at 415; emphasis added.

257. Beccaria, "De' fogli periodici," 418; Alessandro Verri, "Saggio di legislazione sul pedantesimo," in *Il Caffè*, 134–140, at 134.

258. Alessandro Verri, "Dell'ozio," in *Il Caffè*, 288–291, quotation at 290.

259. Alessandro Verri, "Commentariolo di un galantuomo di mal umore che ha ragione, sulla definizione: L'uomo è un animale ragionevole, in cui si vedrà di che si tratta," in *Il Caffè*, 624–653, at 649–650.

260. Alessandro Verri, "Di alcuni sistemi del pubblico diritto," in *Il Caffè*, 725–739, at 731–733.

261. Verri, "Commentariolo di un galantuomo," in *Il Caffè*, 624–653, at 646.

262. Alessandro Verri, "Pensieri scritti da un buon uomo per instruzione di un buon giovine," in *Il Caffè*, 189–198, at 191.

263. Pietro Secchi, "Anecdoto chinese," in *Il Caffè*, 333–338, at 337.

264. Longo, "Osservazioni," 115–132. On this theme in the Academy of Fisticuffs' work, see, among many others, Renato Pasta, "Beccaria 'philosophe': Alle origini del diritto penale come 'scienza sociale integrate,'" *Quaderni fiorentini per la storia del pensiero giuridico moderno* 44, no. 2 (2015): 897–909, at 903. On the "agricultural revolution" in Europe depending on precisely such a "transition from communalism characterized by collective rights and collective use of land to a new system characterized by the right of private property and individual freedom of action," see Alexander Grab, "Enlightened Absolutism and Commonlands Enclosure: The Case of Austrian Lombardy," *Agricultural History* 63, no. 1 (1989): 49–72, at 49, and the literature on which it draws. For Mon-

tesquieu's argument, see his *Spirit of the Laws,* esp. 157. It is, furthermore, worth noting that not all of the members of the Academy of Fisticuffs followed Longo to the point of arguing against hereditary nobility. See Capra, "L'Accademia dei pugni e la società lombarda," 44–45.

265. Longo, "Osservazioni," 117; emphasis added. For similar critiques of *fideicommissa,* or primogeniture laws, see Pietro Verri, "Dialogo fra un Mandarino chinese e un Sollecitatore," in *Il Caffè,* 460–463, at 462; and Alessandro Verri, "Ragionamento sulle leggi civili" and "Commentariolo di un galantuomo," both in *Il Caffè,* 571–606, at 592, and 624–653, at 650.

266. Pietro Verri, "Considerazioni sul lusso," in *Il Caffè,* 155–162, at 157–158.

267. Ibid., 158–159. On the Hebrew and Christian Jubilee years, see David Graeber, *Debt: The First 5,000 Years* (New York: Melville House, 2011), esp. 390. On the leveling impulses of the agrarian laws, see, of course, Cicero, *De legibus,* II.83, discussed in Eric Nelson, *The Hebrew Republic: Jewish Sources and the Transformation of European Political Thought* (Cambridge, MA: Harvard University Press, 2010), 61.

268. Verri, "Considerazioni sul lusso," 158–159.

269. For a long-term view of this cardinal challenge, with which we all very much still struggle, see Peter Garnsey, "Property and Its Limits: Historical Analysis," in *La Propriété et ses limites / Das Eigentum und seine Grenzen,* ed. Bénédict Winiger, Matthias Mahlmann, Sophie Clément, and Anne Kühler (Stuttgart: Franz Steiner, 2017), 13–38. For more recent meditations on the phenomenon of inequality in capitalist societies, see Thomas Piketty, *The Economics of Inequality,* trans. Arthur Goldhammer (Cambridge, MA: Harvard University Press, 2015); and Joseph E. Stiglitz, *Great Divide: Unequal Societies and What We Can Do about Them* (New York: W. W. Norton, 2016).

270. William Shakespeare, *As You Like It,* ed. Jack R. Crawford (New Haven, CT: Yale University Press, 1955), act 4, lines 128–129, p. 77.

271. Alessandro Verri, "Lo spirito di società," in *Il Caffè,* 396–402, at 402.

272. Alessandro Verri, "Digressioni sull'uomo amabile, sulla noia e sull'amor proprio," in *Il Caffè,* 677–685, at 682. See also, more generally, Verri, "Sullo spirito di società," and Verri, "La buona compagnia," both in *Il Caffè,* 396–402, 445–451. For a much later yet similar approach to the problem, see Elias, *The Civilizing Process,* esp. 367.

273. For a remarkable approach to this, see Lawrence E. Klein, *Shaftesbury and the Culture of Politeness: Moral Discourse and Cultural Politics in Early Eighteenth-Century England* (Cambridge: Cambridge University Press, 1994); as well as Hundert, *The Enlightenment's Fable,* esp. 120. For the Parisian example that so

influenced Italians, see Antoine Lilti, *Le Monde des salons: Sociabilité et mondanité à Paris au XVIIIe siècle* (Paris: Fayard, 2005), now translated as *The World of the Salons: Sociability and Worldliness in Eighteenth-Century Paris*, trans. Lydia G. Cochrane (Oxford: Oxford University Press, 2015).

274. Verri, "La buona compagnia," 447; emphasis in original.

275. On this, see Rebecca Messbarger, *The Century of Women: Representations of Women in Eighteenth-Century Italian Public Discourse* (Toronto: University of Toronto Press, 2002).

276. See, for a depressing gallery, Simona Feci and Laura Schettini, eds., *La violenza contro le donne nella storia: Contesti, linguaggi, politiche del diritto (secoli XV–XXI)* (Rome: Viella, 2017).

277. Verri, "Di alcuni sistemi del pubblico diritto," 735.

278. Compare Pietro Verri, "[Maria Vittoria Ottoboni Boncompagni, già sposa Serbelloni. 1790]," in *ENOPV*, 5:567, and "Lettere di Pietro e Maria," in *ENOPV*, 5:435–454.

279. Sebastiano Franci, "Difesa delle donne," in *Il Caffè*, 245–256.

280. Franci, "Difesa delle donne," 245. For a particularly succinct array of grievances, see the list of reasons not to marry in Giovanni Nevizzano, *Sylvae Nuptialis libri sex* (Lyon: Sub scuto Coloniensi, 1545).

281. Franci, "Difesa delle donne," 246.

282. Ibid., 247–248.

283. Ibid., 249.

284. Ibid., 250–252.

285. Ibid., 254. On the numerous sieges of Eger, see Kenneth M. Setton, *Venice, Austria, and the Turks in the Seventeenth Century* (Philadelphia: American Philosophical Society, 1991), 11. On the women of Eger, though with no reference to Franci's article, see Julia Papp, "Female Body—Male Body: The Valiant Hungarian Women of Eger and Szigetvár from the 16th Century in Historiography, Literature, and Art," *Cogent Arts & Humanities* 3 (2016): 1–17.

286. Franci, "Difesa delle donne," 255–256.

287. Messbarger, *The Century of Women*, esp. 102–103.

288. "Agli scrittori del *Caffè*," in *Il Caffè*, 704–705, at 704. On getting "jokes," see Robert Darnton, "Workers Revolt: The Great Cat Massacre of the Rue Saint-Séverin," in *The Great Cat Massacre and Other Episodes in French Cultural History* (New York: Basic Books, 1984), 75–106, at 78, drawing on Clifford Geertz, "Deep Play: Notes on the Balinese Cockfight," in *The Interpretation of Cultures* (New York: Basic Books, 1977), 412–453. See on this also Maria Lúcia Pallares-Burke, "Robert Darnton," in *The New History* (Cambridge: Polity Press, 2002), 158–183, esp. 159–160, 168.

289. Pietro Verri, "[Avvisi ai signori caffettieri]," in *Il Caffè*, 132–134; Alessandro Verri, "Saggio di legislazione sul pedantesimo," in *Il Caffè*, 134–140, at 139. Today, of course, we know better.

290. See, for example, Giuseppe Visconti, "Osservazioni meteorologiche fatte in Milano: Sul barometro," 78–82; Visconti, "Osservazioni meteorologiche fatte in Milano: Sul termometro; Su i venti," 96–104; Paolo Frisi, "Degl'influssi lunari," 291–296; Pietro Verri, "[Le osservazioni degli influssi . . .]," 296–297; Ruggero Boscovich, "Estratto del Trattato astronomico del signor de La Lande," 344–350; Paolo Frisi, "Saggio sul Galileo," 431–445; and Verri, "Commentario di un galantuomo," 624–653, all in *Il Caffè*.

291. See Pietro Verri's conclusion to Paolo Frisi, "Degl'influssi lunari," in *Il Caffè*, 291–297, at 296–297.

292. Alessandro Verri, "Commentariolo di un galantuomo di mal uomore che ha ragione," 629–630; emphasis added.

293. Pietro Verri, "Sulla fortuna," in *Il Caffè*, 606–615, at 606–607, 615. See also his "Alcuni pensieri sull'origine degli errori," in *Il Caffè*, 537–539, at 537.

294. Pietro Verri, "Il tempio dell'Ignoranza," in *Il Caffè*, 27–29. Against pedantic erudition, excluding scholarship, see also Alessandro Verri, "Saggio di legislazione sul pedantesimo," in *Il Caffè*, 134–140.

295. Letter signed "Filantropo," in *Il Caffè*, 29–30. See also the manuscript note added to Alessandro Verri, *Saggio sulla storia d'Italia*, Archivio Verri, 272–275, 487, discussed in Capra, *I progressi della ragione*, 180.

296. Alessandro Verri, "Rinunzia avanti notaio degli autori del presente foglio periodico al Vocabolario della Crusca," in *Il Caffè*, 47–50, at 48. On this topic, see Silvia Scotti Morgana, "Aspetti linguistici dei periodici milanesi dell'età teresiana," in Maddalena, Rotelli, and Barbarisi, *Economia, istituzioni, cultura*, 2:413–438.

297. Verri, "Rinunzia," 49–50; Sergio Romagnoli, "Il portafoglio ovvero i cani del *Caffè*," in *Studi di teoria e storia letteraria in onore di Pieter de Meijer*, ed. Dina Aristodemo, Costantino Maeder, and Ronald de Rooy (Florence: Franco Cesati, 1996), 177–183.

298. Franci, "Difesa delle donne," on which see Messbarger, *The Century of Women*.

299. Pietro Verri, introduction to Pietro Secchi, "La coltivazione del tabacco," in *Il Caffè*, 55–56. On patriotism and political economy in the eighteenth century, though focusing on France, see John Shovlin, *The Political Economy of Virtue*.

300. See, on this transition, again Reinert, *Translating Empire*, 69.

301. Habermas, *Structural Transformation*, 36–37. For Habermasian analyses of the Academy of Fisticuffs, see Edoardo Tortarolo, "*Opinione pubblica* und italienischen

Aufklärung—einige Lektürnotizen," in *Beiträge zur Begriffsgeschichte der italienischen Aufklärung im europäischen Kontext*, ed. Helmut C. Jacobs and Gisela Schlüter (Frankfurt am Main: Peter Lang, 2000), 133–145; Messbarger, *The Century of Women;* Sandro Landi, *Naissance de l'opinion publique dans l'Italie moderne: Sagesse du peuple et savoir de gouvernement de Machiavel aux Lumières* (Rennes: Presses Universitaires de Rennes, 2006), 165–168, 179–180; Raymond Abbrugiati, *Études sur Le Café (1764–1766): Un périodique des Lumières* (Aix-en-Provence: Publications de l'Université de Provence, 2006).

302. Venturi, *Utopia e riforma nell'Illuminismo* (Turin: Einaudi, 2001); and John Robertson, *The Case for the Enlightenment: Scotland and Naples, 1680–1760* (Cambridge: Cambridge University Press, 2005).

303. See similarly Reinert, *Translating Empire*, 287.

304. A foundational text in this tradition remains Stephen Greenblatt, *Renaissance Self-Fashioning: From More to Shakespeare* (Chicago: University of Chicago Press, 1980); but for recent examples see, among others, Ulinka Rublack, *Dressing Up: Cultural Identity in Renaissance Europe* (Oxford: Oxford University Press, 2010); Spary, *Eating the Enlightenment;* and Purnell, *Sensationalist Past*, esp. 66.

305. Spary, *Eating the Enlightenment*, 295.

306. Compare, again, Wahnbaeck, *Luxury and Public Happiness*, esp. 156.

2. Capital (and) Punishment

1. Pietro Verri, "Elementi del commercio," in *"Il Caffè," 1764–1766*, ed. Gianni Francioni and Sergio A. Romagnoli (Turin: Bollati Boringhieri, 1993) (hereafter cited as *Il Caffè*), 30–38; based on Verri, *Cose varie buone, mediocri, cattive del conte Pietro Verri fatti ne' tempi di sua gioventù, le quali con eroica clemenza ha transcritte di sua mano nell'anno 1763 ad uso soltanto proprio o degl'intimi amici suoi*, Archivio Verri, Fondazione Mattioli, housed at the Università di Milano under the tutelage of the Archivio Storico della Banca Intesa Sanpaolo, Milan, Italy (hereafter cited as Archivio Verri), 373.1, quote from fol. 187. See also Verri, *Meditazioni mie sul commercio fatte in Vienna 1760*, Archivio Verri, 374.8. See, on this, Verri, "Memorie sincere del modo col quale servii nel militare e dei miei primi progressi nel servigio politico (ca. 1764–1775)," in *Edizione nazionale delle opere di Pietro Verri*, 8 vols. in 10 to date, ed. Carlo Capra et al. (Rome: Edizioni di storia e letteratura, 2003–2014) (hereafter cited as *ENOPV*), 5:104–105, mentioning in particular "Forbonnais, Melon, Du Tot, Hume." For complications, see Pietro to Alessandro Verri, 24 January 1760 and 29 December 1760, both in *Lettere e scritti inediti di Pietro e di Alessandro Verri*, ed. Carlo Casati, 4 vols. (Milan: Galli, 1879–1881), 1:110–115, 134–138; Carlo Capra, *I progressi della ragione: Vita di Pietro*

Verri (Bologna: Il Mulino, 2002), 157 and 157n. The literature on Gournay's circle has grown exponentially in recent years, but see Michael Sonenscher, *Before the Deluge: Public Debt, Inequality, and the Intellectual Origins of the French Revolution* (Princeton, NJ: Princeton University Press, 2007), esp. 173–253; Sophus A. Reinert, *Translating Empire: Emulation and the Origins of Political Economy* (Cambridge, MA: Harvard University Press, 2011), 129–185; and the essays in *Le cercle de Vincent de Gournay: Savoirs économiques et pratiques administratives en France au milieu du XVIIIe siècle,* ed. Loïc Charles, Frédéric Lefebvre, and Christine Théré (Paris: INED, 2011).

2. Seizo Hotta, "European Sources of Pietro Verri's Economic Thought," in *Pietro Verri e il suo tempo,* ed. Carlo Capra, 2 vols. (Milan: Cisalpino, 1999), 2:709–726; Parisi, "Gli studi economici del giovane Pietro Verri: I bilanci del commercio," in Capra, *Pietro Verri ed il suo tempo,* 2:789–811; on this tradition generally see Reinert, *Translating Empire.*

3. Letter signed "Filantropo," in *Il Caffè,* 30.

4. On Forbonnais, see Michael Sonenscher, *Before the Deluge,* esp. 179–189. On his book-historical popularity at the time, see Erik S. Reinert, Kenneth Carpenter, Fernanda Reinert, and Sophus A. Reinert, "80 Economic Bestsellers before 1850: A Fresh Look at the History of Economic Thought," *The Other Canon Foundation and Tallinn University of Technology Working Papers in Technology Governance and Economic Dynamics,* paper no. 74 (2017), 57–69.

5. Verri was an ardent Antiphysiocrat throughout his life, *pace* statements to the contrary such as Carlo Antonio Vianello, *La giovinezza di Parini, Verri e Beccaria: Con scritti, documenti e ritratti inediti* (Milan: Baldini e Castoldi, 1933), 199. This was evident also to the Physiocrats. See, for example, the Swiss eclectic political economist Georg Ludwig Schmid d'Avenstein to Pietro Verri, dated only 1772, Archivio Verri, 274.39, 1r, who told him that "all of Paris" honored him on the basis of his *Meditations,* including even "the *Philosophes Economistes* [Physiocrats], in spite of your different sentiments and principles." On Schmid, who took the name d'Avenstein under curious circumstances, see Istvan Hont, "Correcting Europe's Political Economy: The Virtuous Eclecticism of Georg Ludwig Schmid," *History of European Ideas* 33, no. 4 (2007): 390–410.

6. On the role of French intermediary translations in the continent-wide dissemination of political economy, see Reinert, *Translating Empire,* 51–52. As is evident from his early writings, Verri relied heavily on the following: Forbonnais, *Elémens du commerce,* 2nd ed., 2 vols. (Leyden: Briasson, 1754); Bernardo de Ulloa, *Restablecimiento de las fabricas, y comercio español,* 2 vols. (Madrid: Antonio Marin, 1740), translated by Plumard de Dangeul as *Rétablissement des manufactures et du commerce d'Espagne,* 2 vols. (Amsterdam: Estienne, 1753); Jerónimo de Uztáriz, *Theórica y práctica de comercio y de marina,* 2nd ed. (Ma-

drid: Antonio Sanz, 1742), translated as *Théorie et pratique du commerce et de la marine* (Hamburg: Chrétien Herold, 1753); Charles King, *The British Merchant; or, Commerce Preserv'd*, 3 vols. (London: John Darby, 1721), translated by Forbonnais as *Le négotiant anglois, ou traduction libre du livre intitulé: The British Merchant*, 2 vols. (Paris: Estienne, 1753); John Cary's *Essay on the State of England* (Bristol: Bonny, 1695) in the dramatically altered edition of Antonio Genovesi, *Storia del commercio della Gran Bretagna*, 3 vols. (Naples: Gessari, 1757–1758); and David Hume's *Political Discourses* (Edinburgh: Fleming, 1752) from their French translation *Discours politiques*, 2 vols. (Amsterdam: Chez Michel Lambert, 1754), of which he transcribed passages in "Estratti da Hume," in *ENOPV*, vol. 2, pt. 1, 63–83. For references to his early sources, see his "Considerazioni sul commercio dello stato di Milano," in *ENOPV*, vol. 2, pt. 1, 107–345, at 111–112. On Verri's readings and library, see generally Carlo Capra, "Pietro Verri e il 'genio della lettura,'" in *Per Marino Berengo: Studi degli allievi*, ed. Livio Antonielli, Carlo Capra, and Mario Infelise (Milan: Franco Angeli, 2000), 619–677. See furthermore Hotta, "European Sources," 716; and Peter Groenewegen, "Reflections on Pietro Verri's Political Economy," in *Eighteenth-Century Economics: Turgot, Beccaria and Smith and Their Contemporaries* (London: Routledge, 2002), 270–281, at 271. On Cary's essay in translation, see Sophus A. Reinert, "Traduzione ed emulazione: La genealogia occulta della *Storia del Commercio*," in *Genovesi Economista*, ed. Bruno Jossa, Rosario Patalano, and Eugenio Zagari (Naples: Istituto italiano per gli studi filosofici, 2007), 155–192; and Reinert, *Translating Empire*. For Verri's praise, see "Sulla spensieratezza nella privata economia," in *Il Caffè*, 327. On Genovesi's influence on the Academy of Fisticuffs, see also Ruđer Josip Bošković to Giovanni Attilio Arnolfini, 26 November 1768, in *Carteggio di Giovanni Attilio Arnolfini*, ed. Gino Arrighi (Lucca: Azienda Grafica Lucchese, 1965), 35–36.

7. For a meditation on this, see Reinert, *Translating Empire*. On the best-selling status of the works Verri consulted, see, again, Reinert et al., "80 Economic Bestsellers before 1850."

8. On the history of this concept, see Andrea Maneschi, *Comparative Advantage in International Trade: A Historical Perspective* (Cheltenham, UK: Edward Elgar, 1998).

9. Verri, "Elementi del commercio," 37. This remains the theoretical core of a much maligned tradition of economics known as "mercantilism," on which see the essays collected in Philip J. Stern and Carl Wennerlind, eds., *Mercantilism Reimagined: Political Economy in Early Modern Britain and Its Empire* (Oxford: Oxford University Press, 2013). Core treatments remain Eli F. Heckscher, *Merkantilismen: Ett led i den ekonomiska politikens historia*, 2 vols. (Stockholm: P. A. Norstedt och Söners Förlag, 1931); Cosimo Perrota, *Produzione e lavoro*

produttivo nel mercantilismo e nell'illuminismo (Galatina: Congedo, 1988); and Lars Magnusson, *Mercantilism: The Shaping of an Economic Language* (London: Routledge, 1994). See also Sophus A. Reinert, "Rivalry: Greatness in Early Modern Political Economy," in Stern and Wennerlind, *Mercantilism Reimagined,* 348–370.

10. Verri, "Elementi del commercio," 30–32.

11. International Monetary Fund, *Balance of Payments and International Investment Position Manual,* 6th ed. (Washington, DC: International Monetary Fund, 2009); on the changes of which, see David Moss, *A Concise Guide to Macroeconomics: What Managers, Executives, and Students Need to Know,* 2nd ed. (Boston: Harvard Business School Press, 2014), 126–127. On Verri's theory of a balance of trade, see also Christine Lebeau, "Chiffres privés, chiffres politiques: L'inconcevable publication des Bilans de Pietro Verri (État de Milan, deuxième moitié du XVIIIe siècle)," in *L'information économique, XVIe–XIXe siècle,* ed. Dominique Margairaz and Philippe Minard (Paris: Comité pour l'Histoire économique et financière, 2008), 201–225.

12. Verri, "Elementi del commercio," 31; emphasis in original. The footnotes he added to the corresponding passages in Verri, "Meditazioni mie sul commercio fatte in Vienna. 1760," in *ENOPV,* vol. 2, pt. 1, 85–92, at 85–86n, indicate the sources were Forbonnais's *Elémens du commerce,*1:47, and Montesquieu, *The Spirit of the Laws,* ed. Anne M. Cohler, Basia C. Miller, and Harold S. Stone (Cambridge: Cambridge University Press, 1989), 352, respectively. The sentiment was, however, extremely widespread at the time. See Istvan Hont, *Jealousy of Trade: International Competition and the Nation-State in Historical Perspective* (Cambridge, MA: Harvard University Press, 2005); Reinert, *Translating Empire.* For an eerily accurate modern example of these dark mechanisms, see John Connell, "Nauru: The First Failed Pacific State?," *The Round Table: The Commonwealth Journal of International Affairs* 95, no. 383 (2006): 47–63.

13. Verri, "Elementi del commercio." On this tradition, see esp. J. G. A. Pocock, *The Machiavellian Moment: Florentine Political Thought and the Atlantic Republican Tradition* (Princeton, NJ: Princeton University Press, 2003); and Quentin Skinner, *Hobbes and Republican Liberty* (Cambridge: Cambridge University Press, 2008). For the alternative tradition to which Verri belonged, see Reinert, *Translating Empire,* 29.

14. Verri, "Elementi del commercio," 32–33. On Sparta in the eighteenth-century imagination, see Varad Mehta, "Sparta in the Enlightenment," PhD diss., Columbia University, 2009; on China, see Ashley Eva Millar, *A Singular Case: Debating China's Political Economy in the European Enlightenment* (Montreal: McGill–Queen's University Press, 2017).

15. Verri, "Elementi del commercio," 32.

16. For earlier English examples of this argument, with which Verri would have been familiar, see Reinert, *Translating Empire*, 118. The dilemma was put neatly by Joseph A. Schumpeter: "A protective duty may have no other effect than to increase the price of the protected commodity and, in consequence, its output; but it may also induce a complete reorganization of the protected industry which eventually results in an increase in output so great as to reduce price below its initial level." See his "Comments on a Plan for the Study of Entrepreneurship," in Schumpeter, *The Economics and Sociology of Capitalism*, ed. Richard Swedberg (Princeton, NJ: Princeton University Press, 1991), 406–428, at 411.

17. Verri, "Elementi del commercio," 32–33, 33–38, 38. For earlier Italian arguments along these lines, of which Verri certainly was aware, see Reinert, *Translating Empire*, 210–211.

18. Verri, "Elementi del commercio," 33–35, 36, drawing on Jean François Melon, *Essai politique sur le commerce*, 2nd ed. (n.p.: n.p., 1736), 1–11, 79–91, which was interpreted also in Genovesi, *Storia del commercio*, 1:lxxxv–lxxxvi, 35n–36n, 189n–190n, 212n–214n, 220n–221n, 367, 2:80n–81n. On these themes, see also Reinert, *Translating Empire*, 20, 211. On Law, see Antoin E. Murphy, *John Law: Economic Theorist and Policy-Maker* (Oxford: Oxford University Press, 1997).

19. Pietro Verri, "Proposizione per la riforma delle tariffe, ossia dato della mercanzia," in *ENOPV*, vol. 2, pt. 1, 735–749, at 745.

20. Verri echoed this argument for the economic power of pens in his "Lettera riservata che spedii al Cavaliere Alessandro a Roma l'anno 1771 verso Dicembre," in *ENOPV*, 5:194–226, at 210. On this passage by Verri being a "self-portrait," see Carlo Capra, *Gli Italiani prima dell'Italia: Un lungo Settecento, dalla fine della Controriforma a Napoleone* (Rome: Carocci, 2014), 181. For a similar near-contemporary Milanese case for economic legislators in similar terms, see Francesco Maria Carpani, "Discorso sopra la necessità di un Controllore, e dell'incumbenza del medesimo," Archivio di Stato di Milano, Milan, Italy (hereafter cited as ASM), *Atti di Governo 11, Commercio, Parte Antica, Cart. 3, P.G., 1740–1769*, 2r. On Carpani, see Carlo Capra, "Un precursore delle riforme: Francesco Maria Carpani (1705–1777)," in *L'Europa tra illuminismo e Restaurazione: Scritti in onore di Furio Diaz*, ed. Paolo Alatri (Rome: Bulzoni, 1993), 115–155; and Verri's own positive (at the time) later annotations in Carpani to Verri, 4 April 1753, Archivio Verri, 269.21, 2v. Antonio Genovesi had made very similar arguments with which Verri would have been familiar; see Genovesi, *Storia del commercio*, esp. 1:lxiii and 2:483. On early modern information management in relation to political economy, see Jacob Soll, *The Information Master: Jean-Baptiste Colbert's Secret State Intelligence System* (Ann Arbor: University of Michigan Press, 2009); for a study more focused on Italy, see Corey Tazzara, "Managing Free

Trade in Early Modern Europe: Institutions, Information, and the Free Port of Livorno," *Journal of Modern History* 86, no. 3 (2014): 493–529.

21. Verri, "Elementi del commercio," 33.

22. A sentiment shared by other writers for *Il Caffè*; see, for example, Pietro Secchi, "La coltivazione del tabacco," in *Il Caffè*, 56–58, at 57; and similarly Alessandro Verri, "Alcune riflessioni sulla opinione che il commercio deroghi alla nobiltà," in *Il Caffè* 256–274, 267.

23. The phrase "Nil Repente" was perhaps first made an emblem by Ferdinando Galiani in his violent critique of Physiocracy, *Dialogues sur le commerce des bleds* (Paris: n.p., 1770), 233, 257. On this theme, though not explicitly connecting it to an earlier tradition, see Gilbert Faccarello, "'Nil repente!': Galiani and Necker on Economic Reforms," *European Journal of the History of Political Economy* 1, no. 3 (1994): 519–550. For the longevity of the trope, see also H. G. Wells, *The New Machiavelli* (New York: Duffield and Co., 1910), 442.

24. Giambattista Vico, "De nostri temporis studiorum ratione," in Vico, *Opera latina*, ed. Giuseppe Ferrari, 2 vols. (Milan: Societas typographica classicorum Italiae scriptorum, 1835), 1:5–44, at 19; Vico, *On the Study Methods of Our Times*, trans. Elio Gianturco (Ithaca, NY: Cornell University Press, 1990), 32. On Galiani's familiarity with Vico, see, among others, Giorgio Tagliacozzo, "Economic Vichianism: Vico, Galiani, Croce—Economics, Economic Liberalism," in *Giambattista Vico: An International Symposium*, ed. Giorgio Tagliacozzo with Hayden V. White (Baltimore: Johns Hopkins University Press, 1969), 349–368; and Koen Stapelbroek, *Love, Self-Deceit and Money: Commerce and Morality in the Early Neapolitan Enlightenment* (Toronto: University of Toronto Press, 2008), esp. 128.

25. Hippocrates, *Aphorismi* II.51, for the above translation of which see "Aphorisms," in *Hippocrates*, vol. 4, trans. W. H. S. Jones (Cambridge, MA: Harvard University Press, 1931), 97–222, at 121. The received Latin translation (vulgata) of the Aphorisms, current long before Vico and still retained by Kühn in his well-known nineteenth-century edition, used the adverbial *repente* (or sometimes *de repente*) for the Greek *exapinēs* (equivalent to *exaiphnēs*, "suddenly"); see "Hippokratous aphorismoi," 706–768, with II.51 at 719, in *Medicorum graecorum opera quae exstant*, ed. Carolus Gottlob Kühn, vol. 23 (Leipzig: Cnobloch, 1837). Paraphrases of the Latin Hippocrates, such as *nihil repente*, were common; see, for example, Antonio Musa Brassavola, *In octo libros aphorismorum Hippocratis et Galeni commentaria* (Basel: Froben, 1541), 342–343; and, for a similar usage in the form of a maxim, Julius Caesar Scaliger, *In sex libros de causis plantarum Theophrasti* (Geneva: Crispin, 1561), 144 (commenting on Theophrastos, *Peri phutōn aitiōn*, II.19). On aphorisms and political economy, see Sophus A. Reinert, "The Way to Wealth around the World: Benjamin Franklin and the Globalization of American Capitalism," *American Historical Review* 120, no. 1 (2015): 61–97. It is, in

this context, striking that Galiani's perhaps favorite economic writer, the seventeenth-century Calabrian Antonio Serra, had based most of his political economy on precisely such a Hippocratic temporal analysis; see his *Breve trattato sulle cause che possono far abbondare li regni d'oro e d'argento, dove non sono miniere, con applicazione al regno di Napoli* (Naples: Lazzaro Scorrigio, 1613), 3; and Serra, *A Short Treatise on the Wealth and Poverty of Nations (1613)*, ed. Sophus A. Reinert, trans. Jonathan Hunt (London: Anthem, 2011), 111. For Galiani's verdict, see his *Della moneta*, 2nd ed. (Naples: Stamperia Simoniana, 1780), 409–410.

26. On Galiani as *"Machiavellino,"* see, among others, Reinert, *Translating Empire*, 213. This medical argument for prudence was still made by Genovesi; see his letter to Angelo Pavesi, 12 February 1765, in Genovesi, *Autobiografia e lettere*, ed. Gennaro Savarese (Milan: Feltrinelli, 1962), 264–265, perhaps also drawing on Serra.

27. See, for example, Niccolò Machiavelli, *Discorsi sopra la prima deca di Tito Livio*, ed. Francesco Bausi, 2 vols. (Rome: Salerno Editrice, 2001), 213–214; Machiavelli, "L'arte della guerra," and even *Il Principe*, in *Tutte le opere*, ed. Mario Martelli (Florence: Sansoni, 1971), 347–354 and 295–296, respectively. Machiavelli himself seemed to have a preference in *The Prince* for Fabius Maximus's nemesis Hannibal, on which see Robert Fredona, *"Liberate diuturna cura Italiam: Hannibal in the Thought of Niccolò Machiavelli,"* in *Florence and Beyond: Culture, Society and Politics in Renaissance Italy; Essays in Honour of John M. Najemy*, ed. David S. Peterson and Daniel E. Bornstein (Toronto: Centre for Reformation and Renaissance Studies, 2008), 419–434. For Machiavelli's preference for impetuousness in *The Prince* generally, see Gennaro Sasso, *Studi su Machiavelli* (Naples: Morano, 1967), 48–49. On Julius II, see Christine Shaw, *Julius II: The Warrior Pope* (Oxford: Blackwell, 1993).

28. See the frequently quoted letters by Philippe Joseph Létombe to Charles-François Delacroix, 30 May 1797, in *Correspondence of the French Ministers to the United States, 1791–1797*, ed. Frederick J. Turner, 2 vols. (Washington, DC: U.S. Government Printing Office, 1904), 2:1024–1025, and to Charles Maurice de Talleyrand-Périgord, 17 January 1798, in Archives du Ministère des Affaires Étrangères, Paris, France, *49 Correspondance Politique: États-Unis 145*, both quoted and discussed in Stanley Elkins and Eric McKitrick, *The Age of Federalism: The Early American Republic, 1788–1800* (Oxford: Oxford University Press, 1993), 567; and Jean Edward Smith, *John Marshall: Definer of a Nation* (New York: Henry Holt and Co., 1996), 226. On Jefferson and Machiavelli, see Paul A. Rahe, "Thomas Jefferson's Machiavellian Political Science," *Review of Politics* 57, no. 3 (1995): 449–481.

29. Verri, "Elementi del commercio," 33.

30. Genovesi, *Storia del commercio*, 1:viii, 160n; Reinert, *Translating Empire*, 203.

31. On the rather tortured history of this work, see still the introduction to Pietro Verri, *Considerazioni sul commercio dello stato di Milano*, ed. Carlo Antonio Vianello (Milan: Università L. Bocconi, 1939), v–xxi. On his plan for this work, see also Pietro Verri to Gian Rinaldo Carli, 3 September 1762, and Pietro Verri to Gian Rinaldo Carli, 27 June 1763, both in Francesco De Stefano, "Cinque anni di sodalizio tra Pietro Verri e Gian Rinaldo Carli (1760–1765) con XXIV lettere inedite di Pietro Verri," *Atti e memorie della Società istriana di archeologia e storia patria* 45 (1933): 43–103, at 64–65 and 68–70; as well as Verri, "Memorie sincere," 112–114, and the note he composed in Ornago on 12 July 1788, in *ENOPV*, 5:547–553, at 548. See also the text now edited in Pietro Verri, "Considerazioni sul commercio dello stato di Milano [1763]," in *ENOPV*, vol. 2, pt. 1, 107–345.

32. Verri, *Considerazioni*, 9.

33. For recent discussions on this theme of a dual decline, see Giorgio Ruffolo, *Quando l'Italia era una superpotenza: Il ferro di Roma e l'oro dei mercanti* (Turin: Einaudi, 2004); and Sophus A. Reinert, "Lessons on the Rise and Fall of Great Powers: Conquest, Commerce, and Decline in Enlightenment Italy," *American Historical Review* 115, no. 5 (2010): 1395–1425.

34. Verri, *Considerazioni*, 11, 16, 18, 21, 27; emphasis added. On the problem of polities ruled as provinces at the time, see John Robertson, *The Case for the Enlightenment: Scotland and Naples, 1680–1760* (Cambridge: Cambridge University Press, 2005), 147–200.

35. Verri, *Considerazioni*, 31. On Potosí, see, for a brief overview, Lewis Hanke's still-relevant *The Imperial City of Potosí: An Unwritten Chapter in the History of Spanish America* (The Hague: Martinus Nijhoff, 1956). Verri's argument here draws on an established tradition of political economy dating back to the Renaissance, for an influential exponent of which see Giovanni Botero, *Della ragion di stato* (Venice: I gioliti, 1589), 204: "E' tanta la forza dell'industria, che non è miniera d'argento, non d'oro nella nuova Spagna, ò nel Perù, che le debba esser pareggiata; e più vale il datio della mercatãtia di Milano al Re Cattolico, che le miniere di Potosì, ò di Salixco."

36. Verri, *Considerazioni*, 35–46.

37. For a later case of this mechanism, see Reka Juhász, "Temporary Protection and Technology Adoption: Evidence from the Napoleonic Blockade," *CEP Discussion Paper* No. 1322, 2014.

38. On Sinzendorf, see Árpád Győry von Nádudvar, "Sinzendorf, Philipp Ludwig," in *Allgemeine Deutsche Biografie* (Leipzig: Duncker und Humblot, 1934), 34:408–412.

39. Verri, *Considerazioni*, 65, 67; emphasis added.

40. On the political economy of this later moment, and its legacy, see, among others, Erik Grimmer-Solem, *The Rise of Historical Economics and Social Reform in*

Germany, 1864–1894 (Oxford: Oxford University Press, 2003); and Eugen Wendler, *Friedrich List im Zeitalter der Globalisierung: Eine Wiederentdeckung* (Wiesbaden: Springer Gabler, 2014).

41. Thomas H. Breen, *The Marketplace of Revolution: How Consumer Politics Shaped American Independence* (Oxford: Oxford University Press, 2004); Karl Gerth, *China Made: Consumer Culture and the Creation of the Nation* (Cambridge, MA: Harvard University Asia Center, 2004).

42. Verri made a very similar argument a year later in relation to the intersection of political and economic sovereignties; see his "Proposizione per la riforma delle tariffe," 736–737.

43. Verri, *Considerazioni*, 67–69, 70, 73–74.

44. Verri, "Considerazioni," in *ENOPV*, vol. 2, pt. 1, 203n1, suggests that a source for this sentiment, if not the analogy itself, was Emer de Vattel, *The Law of Nations*, ed. Béla Kapossy and Richard Whatmore [Indianapolis: Liberty Fund, 2008). See also Antonio Trampus, "The Circulation of Vattel's *Droit des gens* in Italy: The Doctrinal and Practical Model of Government," in *War, Trade and Neutrality: Europe and the Mediterranean in the Seventeenth and Eighteenth Centuries*, ed. Antonella Alimento (Milan: Franco Angeli, 2011), 217–232, 221. There were several similar statements in *Il Caffè*, but see Pietro Verri, "Considerazioni sul lusso," in *Il Caffè*, 155–162, at 159. For an earlier analogy of states and family, see François de Salignac de La Mothe Fénelon, *Telemachus, Son of Ulysses* [1699], ed. Patrick Riley (Cambridge: Cambridge University Press, 1994), 147.

45. Verri, *Considerazioni*, 79–80, 81, 84, 102, 121. On Bergamo's manufactures in the eighteenth century, see Walter Panciera, "Il lanificio bergamasco nel XVIII secolo: Lavoro, consumi e mercati," in *Storia economica e sociale di Bergamo: Il tempo della Serenissima*, ed. A. De Maddelena, M. A. Romani, and M. Cattini, vol. 3: *Un Seicento in controtendenza* (Bergamo: Fondazione storia di Bergamo, 2000), 99–131; and, for caveats and the comparative regional success of Lombard manufacturing, Luca Mocarelli, "Manufacturing Activity in Venetian Lombardy: Specialized Products and the Formation of a Regional Market," in *At the Centre of the Old World: Trade and Manufacturing in Venice and the Venetian Mainland, 1400–1800*, ed. Paola Lanaro (Toronto: Centre for Reformation and Renaissance Studies, 2006), 317–341, esp. 335 on the different sovereignties in Eastern and Western Lombardy. For a framework for analyzing such rural manufactures at the time, see the essays in Sheilagh C. Ogilvie and Markus Cerman, eds., *European Proto-Industrialization* (Cambridge: Cambridge University Press, 1996).

46. Pietro Verri to Gian Rinaldo Carli, 3 September 1762, in De Stefano, "Cinque anni di sodalizio," 64–65.

47. Verri, "Memorie sincere," 133; emphasis added. This political-economic transition from municipal to regional and on to national and ultimately international

economic societies through the instrument of the tariff was precisely what would lie behind Gustav von Schmoller's theory of "mercantilism" and interpretation of early modern European economic development; see Schmoller, *The Mercantile System and Its Historical Significance* (New York: Macmillan, 1897), 43–51.

48. Verri, *Considerazioni*, 124–125.

49. Ibid., 151, 157, 179. For a later eulogy of Colbert, see Pietro Verri to Alessandro Verri, 20 September 1768, in *Carteggio di Pietro e di Alessandro Verri dal 1766 al 1797*, ed. E. Greppi, F. Novati, A. Giulini, and G. Seregni, 12 vols. (Milan: Cogliati, then Milesi & Figli, then Giuffrè, 1910–1943) (hereafter cited as *CV*), 1:45–48. The literature on Colbert is immense, but see Soll, *The Information Master;* on Colbert's legacy in the eighteenth century, see Philippe Minard, *La fortune du colbertisme: État et industrie dans la France des Lumières* (Paris: Fayard, 1998).

50. Verri, *Considerazioni*, 197. Verri here engaged with one of the principal debates of eighteenth-century Europe. For similar statements by fellow members of the Accademia dei pugni, see, for example, Cesare Beccaria, "Elementi di economia pubblica," in *Edizione Nazionale delle Opere di Cesare Beccaria*, 16 vols. in 17, ed. Luigi Firpo and Gianni Francioni (Milan: Mediobanca, 1984–2015) (hereafter cited as *ENOCB*), 3:97–390, at 390 [4.IX.56], first published in 1804 as vols. 11 and 12 in *Scrittori classici italiani di economia politica*, ed. Pietro Custodi, 50 vols. (Milan: Destefanis, 1803–1816). See also Gian Rinaldo Carli to Girolamo Gravisi, 8 January 1765 and 6 February 1765, in Gian Rinaldo Carli, *Trecentosessantasei lettere di Gian Rinaldo Carli Capodistriano: Cavate dagli originali e annotate*, ed. Baccio Ziliotto (Trieste: Tipografia G. Caprin, 1914), 87–90, 95–96, as well as his more formal 1765 plan for the economic reform of Lombardy, in which he attacked the "fatally introduced opinion, that *commerce derogates from the Nobility*," Österreichische Nationalbibliothek, Vienna, Austria, Handschriftensammlung, ms. 15118, fols. 42–64. The fulcrum of the debate was Gabriel-François Coyer, *La noblesse commerçante* (London [but Paris]: Duchesne, 1756), which Alessandro Verri engaged with at length, and in often identical terms, in his "Alcune riflessioni sulla opinione," with similar results. The literature on this debate is vast; recent works include Jay M. Smith, *Nobility Reimagined: The Patriotic Nation in Eighteenth-Century France* (Ithaca, NY: Cornell University Press, 2005), esp. 114–118; John Shovlin, *The Political Economy of Virtue: Luxury, Patriotism, and the Origins of the French Revolution* (Ithaca, NY: Cornell University Press, 2006), 58–65; Shovlin, "Political Economy and the French Nobility, 1750–1789," in *The French Nobility in the Eighteenth Century: Reassessments and New Approaches*, ed. Jay M. Smith (University Park: Pennsylvania State University Press, 2012), 111–138; Paul Cheney, *Revolutionary Commerce: Globalization and the French Monarchy* (Cambridge, MA: Harvard University Press, 2010), esp. 68–69.

On the German echoes of this debate, see Ulrich Adam, *The Political Economy of J. H. G. Justi* (Bern: Peter Lang, 2006), 96–109, developed in Adam, "Justi and the Post-Montesquieu French Debate on Commercial Nobility in 1756," in *The Beginnings of Political Economy: Johann Heinrich Gottlob von Justi*, ed. Jürgen Backhaus (Berlin: Springer, 2009), 75–98. See also Reinert, *Translating Empire*, esp. 146–149, 168–169.

51. Verri, *Considerazioni*, 185.

52. For this Petrarchan ideal of *Italy*, see Petrarch, *The Canzoniere or Rerum vulgarium fragmenta*, ed. Mark Musa (Bloomington: Indiana University Press, 1999), poem 146, pp. 236–237, lines 12–14.

53. Verri, *Considerazioni*, 202. See also Pietro Verri, "Considerazioni sulla proposizione di restringere il lusso nello stato di Milano 1763," in *ENOPV*, vol. 2, pt. 1, 93–106, at 105–106. See similarly Luigi Lambertenghi, "Delle poste," in *Il Caffè*, 299–311, at 310.

54. Pietro Verri's conclusion to Sebastiano Franci, "Dell'agricoltura. Dialogo: Afranio e Cresippo," in *Il Caffè*, 60–73, at 73.

55. Franci, "Alcuni pensieri politici," in *Il Caffè*, 143–150.

56. Anna Paola Montanari, "Franci, Sebastiano," http://www.treccani.it/enciclopedia/sebastiano-franci_(Dizionario_Biografico)/.

57. Sebastiano Franci, "La guerra senza sangue," ed. Pietro Verri, Archivio Verri, 380.4; compare Franci, "Alcuni pensieri politici." For observations on the editorial history of this essay, see Gianni Francioni, "Storia editoriale del 'Caffè,'" in *Il Caffè*, lxxxi–cxlv, cxxxiii–cxxxiv, and the "apparato critico," in *Il Caffè*, 883–885. The passages below on Sebastiano Franci build on Sophus A. Reinert, "The Italian Tradition of Political Economy: Theories and Policies of Development in the Semi-Periphery of the Enlightenment," in *The Origins of Development Economics: How Schools of Economic Thought Have Addressed Development*, rev. ed., ed. Jomo K. Sundaram and Erik S. Reinert (London: Zed Books, 2006), 24–47.

58. Franci, "Alcuni pensieri politici," 143, 144.

59. Ibid., 144. See, for his take on this, Adam Smith, *An Inquiry into the Nature and Causes of the Wealth of Nations*, ed. Edwin Cannan, 2 vols. (Chicago: University of Chicago Press, 1976), 1:427.

60. Thomas Robert Malthus, in *An Essay on the Principle of Population* (London: Johnson, 1798), lent his name to an old mechanism in political economy, for an earlier description of which see Giovanni Botero, *Delle cause della grandezza delle città* (Rome: Martinelli, 1588), 74. On Malthus and Malthusianism, see Robert J. Mayhew, *Malthus: The Life and Legacies of an Untimely Prophet* (Cambridge, MA: Harvard University Press, 2014). For an example of how far the Malthusian-Darwinian argument can be taken, see Gregory Clark, *A Farewell to Alms: A*

Brief Economic History of the World (Princeton, NJ: Princeton University Press, 2007), esp. 19–40; and Oded Galor, *Unified Growth Theory* (Princeton, NJ: Princeton University Press, 2011), 232. For the continuing relevance of this trap in parts of the twenty-first-century world, see Andrey Korotayev et al., "A Trap at the Escape from the Trap? Demographic-Structural Factors of Political Instability in Modern Africa and West Asia," *Cliodynamics: The Journal of Theoretical and Mathematical History* 2 (2011): 276–303.

61. Of the four largest European cities in 1500, only Paris was not in Italy. See Jan de Vries, *European Urbanization, 1500–1800* (Cambridge, MA: Harvard University Press, 1984), 35. For examples of these arguments, see Giovanni Botero, *Della ragion di stato* (Rome: Vincenzio Pellagallo, 1590), 220; Serra, *Short Treatise,* 121. See also Reinert, *Translating Empire,* 203–204.

62. Franci, "Alcuni pensieri politici," 144.

63. Ibid., 147.

64. Ibid., 147–148.

65. Ibid., 148.

66. Ibid., 149. For a broad overview of such treaties at the time, see the essays in Antonella Alimento and Koen Stapelbroek, eds., *The Politics of Commercial Treaties in the Eighteenth Century: Balance of Power, Balance of Trade* (Cham: Palgrave Macmillan, 2017).

67. Ibid., 149–150; see similarly Pietro Verri, "Considerazioni sulla proposizione di restringere il lusso nello stato di Milano 1763," in *ENOPV,* vol. 1, pt. 2, 93–106, at 98. On the widespread influence of this vocabulary in contemporary Europe, see Reinert, *Translating Empire,* chap. 1.

68. Franci, "La guerra senza sangue," 1r.

69. Ibid., 4v.

70. Ibid., 4v, 5v, 6r–6v.

71. Ibid., 7r–7v.

72. Ibid., 8r. For a later and influential description of this nexus of war, trade, and politics, see Carl von Clausewitz's statement that "War is a clash between major interests, which is resolved by bloodshed—that is the only way in which it differs from other conflicts. Rather than comparing it to art we could more accurately compare it to commerce, which is also a conflict of human interests and activities and is still closer to politics, which in turn may be considered as a kind of commerce on a larger scale," in *On War,* ed. Michael Howard and Peter Paret (Princeton, NJ: Princeton University Press, 1989), 149, discussed in Sophus A. Reinert, "Wars and Empires," in *A Companion to Intellectual History,* ed. Richard Whatmore and Brian Young (Chichester: John Wiley & Sons, 2016), 402–416, at 408–409.

73. Pietro Verri to Gian Rinaldo Carli, 27 February 1765, in De Stefano, "Cinque anni di sodalizio," 79.

74. See Kaunitz to Verri, 19 April 1764, in Casati, *Lettere e scritti*, 1:177–178, also republished in Verri, *Considerazioni*, xiv–xvi.

75. Verri, "Al lettore," in *Il Caffè*, 5.

76. On this heuristically significant difference, see David Armitage, "Is There a Pre-History of Globalization?," in *Foundations of Modern International Thought* (Cambridge: Cambridge University Press, 2013), 33–45.

77. Cesare Beccaria, "De' fogli periodici," in *Il Caffè*, 411–419, 417.

78. For an array of different cosmopolitanisms at the time which, though focused on Germany, has relevance well beyond it, see Pauline Kleingeld, "Six Varieties of Cosmopolitanism in Late Eighteenth-Century Germany," *Journal of the History of Ideas* 60, no. 3 (1999): 505–524.

79. On the Mont Pèlerin Society, see the essays collected in *The Road to Mont Pèlerin: The Making of the Neoliberal Thought Collective*, ed. Philip Mirowski and Dieter Plehwe (Cambridge, MA: Harvard University Press, 2009). For a reading of the Academy of Fisticuffs pushing it in this direction, see Till Wahnbaeck, *Luxury and Public Happiness: Political Economy in the Italian Enlightenment* (Oxford: Oxford University Press, 2004).

80. Dino Carpanetto and Giuseppe Ricuperati, *Italy in the Age of Reason, 1685–1789* (London: Longmans, 1987), 265; Norbert Jonard, "Cosmopolitismo e patriottismo nel 'Caffè,'" in *Economia, istituzioni, cultura in Lombardia nell'età di Maria Teresa*, ed. Aldo de Maddalena, Ettore Rotelli, and Gennaro Barbarisi, 3 vols. (Bologna: Il Mulino, 1992), 2:65–95, at 95; see also, in the same volume, Giuseppe Rutto, "Riforme e patriottismi nell'Austria di Maria Teresa," 2:903–923.

81. Jonard, "Cosmopolitismo," 87; Luca Scuccimarra, *I confini del mondo: Storia del cosmopolitismo dall'Antichità al Settecento* (Bologna: Il Mulino, 2006), 383.

82. Hirschman himself was, needless to say, well aware of the limits of this "vision," for examples of which see, among others, Hirschman, *The Passions and the Interests: Political Arguments for Capitalism before Its Triumph* (Princeton, NJ: Princeton University Press, 1997), 117; and Hirschman, *National Power and the Structure of Foreign Trade* (Berkeley: University of California Press, 1945), on which see Jeremy Adelman, *Worldly Philosopher: The Odyssey of Albert O. Hirschman* (Princeton, NJ: Princeton University Press, 2013), 208–215.

83. Gian Rinaldo Carli, "La patria degli Italiani," in *Il Caffè*, 421–427. On Carli, see Luigi Bossi, *Elogio storico del conte commendatore Gian-Rinaldo Carli* (Venice: Carlo Palese, 1797). See, more recently, Antonio Trampus, "Gianrinaldo Carli at the Centre of the Milanese Enlightenment," *History of European Ideas* 32, no. 4 (2006): 456–476. For some examples of the older literature intent on finding in this article the roots of the Italian *Risorgimento* and nineteenth-century nationalism, see Francesco de Stefano, *G. R. Carli (1720–1795): Contributo alla storia delle*

origini del Risorgimento italiano (Modena: Società tipografica modenese, 1942); Baccio Ziliotto, *Gianrinaldo Carli da Capodistria e le origini del Risorgimento* (Trieste: Monciatti, 1953), esp. 20; Giovanni Gozzini, *Storia del giornalismo* (Milan: Mondadori, 2000), 65; and, more generally in the context of the rise of nationalism in Lombardy, though attributing the piece to Pietro Verri, Kent Roberts Greenfield, *Economics and Liberalism in the Risorgimento: A Study of Nationalism in Lombardy, 1814–1848* (Baltimore: Johns Hopkins Press, 1965), 173. On how close he was to Verri in the beginning, see Verri, "Memorie sincere," 105; and Gian Rinaldo Carli to Giuseppe Gravisi, 22 August 1765, in *Trecentosessantasei lettere,* 124–125. On Carli and the witchcraft debates, see Luciano Parinetto, *I lumi e le streghe: Una polemica italiana intorno al 1750* (Paderno Dugnano: Colibrì, 1998), esp. 143–168.

84. Carli, "La patria," 422.
85. Ibid., 423; Petrarch, *Canzoniere or Rerum vulgarium fragmenta,* poem 146, pp. 236–237, lines 12–14. On the history of a cultural "Italy," see Gene A. Brucker, "From *Campanilismo* to Nationhood: Forging an Italian Identity," in *Living on the Edge in Leonardo's Florence: Selected Essays* (Berkeley: University of California Press, 2005), 42–61; and Angelo Mazzocco, "Un'idea politica italiana in Petrarca?," in *Petrarca politico* (Rome: Istituto storico per il Medio Evo, 2006), 9–26. For a critique of the Petrarchan ideal of a culturally and literarily unified Italy, see Carlo Dionisotti, *Geografia e Storia della letteratura italiana* (Turin: Einaudi, 1999).
86. Carli, "La patria," 424–425.
87. Ibid., 427.
88. Gian Rinaldo Carli to Giuseppe Gravisi, 4 September 1765, in *Trecentosessantasei lettere,* 126–127.
89. See, for example, Francesco de Stefano, *Gian Rinaldo Carli (1720–1795): Contributo alla storia delle origini del Risorgimento italiano* (Modena: Società tipografica modenese, 1942); Baccio Zilicotto, *Gianrinaldo Carli da Capodistria e le origini del Risorgimento* (Trieste: Monciatti Editore, 1953); Hans Kohn, *The Idea of Nationalism: A Study of its Origins and Background* (New York: Macmillan, 1944), 504. On the *Risorgimento* as such, see the essays in Silvana Patriarca and Lucy Riall, eds., *The Risorgimento Revisited: Nationalism and Culture in Nineteenth-Century Italy* (Houndmills, UK: Palgrave Macmillan, 2012).
90. See, among many others, Koen Stapelbroek, "The Devaluation Controversy in Eighteenth-Century Italy," *History of Economic Ideas* 13, no. 2 (2005): 79–110, at 89, and Wahnbaeck, *Luxury and Public Happiness,* 146; but the antecedents go as far back as Vianello, *La giovinezza,* 199.
91. Pietro Verri to Gian Rinaldo Carli, 23 March 1765 and 27 March 1765, in De Stefano, "Cinque anni di sodalizio," 83–89, at 88; and Pietro Verri to Gian Rinaldo Carli, 17 April 1765, in Francesco Novati, *I manoscritti d'alcune biblioteche del Belgio e dell'Olanda* (Pisa: Tipografia del cav. F. Mariotti, 1896), 25–26. See also Pietro

Verri to Alessandro Verri, 13 November 1766, in *CV*, vol. 1, pt. 1, 54–65, at 59; as well as Emiliana Pasca Noether, *Seeds of Italian Nationalism, 1700–1815* (New York: Columbia University Press, 1951), 104–105, 186.

92. For a thoughtful approach to the problem, see Dominique Kirchner Reill, *Nationalists Who Feared the Nation: Adriatic Multi-Nationalism in Habsburg Dalmatia, Trieste, and Venice* (Stanford, CA: Stanford University Press, 2012).

93. Verri, "Memorie sincere," 18, 23, 27, 31, 34–35, 70, 80, 87, 121; Verri, "[Introduzione]," in *Il Caffè*, 11–14, at 13. His brother, too, happily wrote of "the country that today we call Italy" in his "Discorso sulla felicità de' Romani," in *Il Caffè*, 83–92, at 90.

94. Brian Porter, *When Nationalism Began to Hate: Imagining Modern Politics in Nineteenth-Century Poland* (Oxford: Oxford University Press, 2000), 212.

95. E.g., Verri, "Lettera riservata," 226.

96. Pietro Verri, note beginning "Per la fatica," in *ENOPV*, 5:503–504.

97. Pietro Verri, "Annotazioni di Pietro Verri all' 'Elogio' del Fabroni," in *Ideologia e scienza nell'opera di Paolo Frisi (1728–1784)*, ed. Gennaro Barbarisi, 2 vols. (Milan: Franco Angeli, 1987), 2:411–419, at 412–413.

98. Alessandro Verri to Gian Rinaldo Carli, 20 June 1767, in *CV*, vol. 1, pt. 2, 434–438, curiously misread as an attack on the concept of "*Italianità*" in Vianello, *La giovinezza*, 199. Closer studies of how the Verri brothers conceptualized different parts of the peninsula would be interesting. For their comparisons of Milan and Rome, see Francesco Bartolini, *Rivali d'Italia: Roma e Milano dal Settecento a oggi* (Rome: Laterza, 2006), 3–19.

99. Wenzel Anton von Kaunitz to Pietro Verri, 19 April 1764, Archivio Verri, 43, reproduced in Verri, "Memorie sincere," 130–131, and discussed in his "Lettera riservata," 196–197.

100. On the generally contested and negotiated nature of sovereignty at the time, see Lauren Benton, *A Search for Sovereignty: Law and Geography in European Empires, 1400–1900* (Cambridge: Cambridge University Press, 2010).

101. On the historical relation between nationalism, capitalism, and development, see, among others, Liah Greenfeld, *The Spirit of Capitalism: Nationalism and Economic Growth* (Cambridge, MA: Harvard University Press, 2001).

102. The analysis of world trade on which Verri based much of his work, in short, was Genovesi, *Storia del commercio . . .* , which itself was ultimately based on John Cary, *An Essay on the State of England* (Bristol, England: W. Bonny, 1695) rather than the now more famous Dudley North, *Discourses upon Trade* (London: Tho. Basset, 1691). On this, see also Sophus A. Reinert, "Blaming the Medici: Footnotes, Falsification, and the Fate of the 'English Model' in Eighteenth-Century Italy," *History of European Ideas* 32 (2006): 430–455; Reinert, *Translating Empire*, 231.

103. In April Carter, *The Political Theory of Global Citizenship* (London: Routledge, 2001), 36; Reinert, *Translating Empire*, 151–152.

104. On this, see Sankar Muthu, *Enlightenment against Empire* (Princeton, NJ: Princeton University Press, 2003), esp. 153–154.

105. See, relatedly, Pietro Verri's observation that "poverty is measured by the number of needs and the number of assistances that we need to receive from others in order to subsist," in Pietro Verri to the Supreme Council, 6 March 1766, fols. 2r–2v, Kress Collection of Business and Economics, Baker Library, Harvard Business School, Boston, *Pietro Verri Letters*.

106. Franci, "Alcuni pensieri politici," 146.

107. Robertson, *Case for the Enlightenment*, 371; on the importance of comparative emulation for political economy, see also Reinert, *Translating Empire*.

108. Pietro Verri, "Meditazioni sulla felicità," in *ENOPV*, 1:734–762, at 750, on which see Gianni Francioni's penetrating "Nota introduttiva," 677–697, at 686, for a stand-alone version of which see *Meditazioni sulla felicità*, ed. Gianni Francioni (Como: Ibis, 1996), 61, and Francioni's notes, 82. On this rather memorable phrase, soon picked up and lionized by Jeremy Bentham, see also Robert Shackleton, "The Greatest Happiness of the Greatest Number: The History of Bentham's Phrase," *Studies on Voltaire and the Eighteenth Century* 90 (1972): 1461–1482. On how early modern traders generally maintained their national identities and social networks, no matter how "cosmopolitan," see Margaret C. Jacob, *Strangers Nowhere in the World: The Rise of Cosmopolitanism in Early Modern Europe* (Philadelphia: University of Pennsylvania Press, 2006), 69.

109. I am here indebted to the concepts introduced by Benedict Anderson, *Imagined Communities: Reflections on the Origin and Spread of Nationalism*, new ed. (London: Verso, 2006).

110. Kwame Anthony Appiah, *Cosmopolitanism: Ethics in a World of Strangers* (New York: W. W. Norton, 2010), xvii; Appiah, "Cosmopolitan Patriots," *Critical Inquiry* 23, no. 3 (1997): 617–639, at 622. The Fisticuffs were, in short, not at all what Hakim Bey [Peter Lamborn Wilson] would call exponents of "rootless cosmopolitanism" or "psychic nomadism"—that is, "psychic travellers" with "shallow loyalties": Bey , *T. A. Z.: The Temporary Autonomous Zone* (Seattle: Pacific Publishing Studio, 2011 [1991]), 74. For a more grounded view of early modern cosmopolitanism, see Francesca Trivellato's notion of "communitarian cosmopolitanism" in her *The Familiarity of Strangers: The Sephardic Diaspora, Livorno, and Cross-Cultural Trade in the Early Modern Period* (New Haven, CT: Yale University Press, 2009), esp. 73.

111. On such arguments, see Eric Hobsbawm, *Nations and Nationalism since 1780: Programme, Myth, Reality* (Cambridge: Cambridge University Press, 1990), 25–31;

Keith Tribe, *"Die Vernunft des List:* National Economy and the Critique of Cosmopolitical Economy," in *Strategies of Economic Order: German Economic Discourse, 1750–1950* (Cambridge: Cambridge University Press, 1995), 32–65; Maurizio Viroli, *For Love of Country: An Essay on Patriotism and Nationalism* (Oxford: Oxford University Press, 1995), esp. 138. Other examples include Johann Gottlieb Fichte, *Addresses to the German Nation,* ed. Isaac Nakhimovsky, Bela Kapossy, and Keith Tribe (Indianapolis: Hackett, 2013), esp. 134; Stefano Recchia and Nadia Urbinati, eds., *A Cosmopolitanism of Nations: Giuseppe Mazzini's Writings on Democracy, Nation Building, and International Relations* (Princeton, NJ: Princeton University Press, 2009), 94–95, 125; and Jules Michelet, *Le peuple* (Brussels: Meline, 1846), 118. See, for a sketch of something similar, also Ghiṭa Ionescu, *The Political Thought of Saint-Simon* (Oxford: Oxford University Press, 1976).

112. In Anthony Grafton, "A Sketch Map of a Lost Continent: The Republic of Letters," in *Worlds Made by Words: Scholarship and Community in the Modern West* (Cambridge, MA: Harvard University Press, 2009), 9–34, at 9.

113. For an excellent study of this Republic of Letters, see Peter N. Miller, *Peiresc's Europe: Learning and Virtue in the Seventeenth Century* (New Haven, CT: Yale University Press, 2000).

114. Quoted and discussed in Edoardo Tortarolo, "'Opinione pubblica' e illuminismo italiano: Qualche appunto di lettura," in *Cesare Beccaria: La pratica dei lumi,* ed. Vincenzo Ferrone and Gianni Francioni (Florence: Olschki, 2000), 127–138, at 132.

115. See Pietro Verri's pseudo-letter of 2 August 1767, in his "Memorie sincere," *ENOPV,* 5:142–148, esp. 143.

116. Carlo Capra, "Riforme finanziarie e mutamento istituzionale nello Stato di Milano: Gli anni sessanta del secolo XVIII," *Rivista storica italiana* 91, nos. 2–3 (1979): 313–368.

117. Cesare Mozzarelli, "Il Magistrato Camerale della Lombardia Austriaca," *Römische historische Mitteilungen* 31 (1989): 377–396.

118. It is notable that current debates about cosmopolitanism continue to focus on "cultural" rather than political and economic concerns. A representative case is Appiah, "Cosmopolitan Patriots."

119. As clearly recognized also by contemporary Austrian authorities; see, for example, Joseph von Sperges to Pietro Verri, 16 November 1767, Archivio Verri, 274.48, 1r.

120. On the importance of a good tariff for Verri in these terms, see also his "Memorie sincere," 125, 133.

121. Pietro Verri, "Meditazioni sulla economia politica," in *ENOPV,* vol. 2, pt. 2, 391–570, 541–551, perhaps drawing on David Hume, "Of the Balance of Trade," in *Po-*

litical Essays, ed. Knud Haakonssen (Cambridge: Cambridge University Press, 1994), 136–149, at 148, though the argument was legion at the time. Compare Wahnbaeck, *Luxury and Public Happiness*, 177, and, more generally on Verri's supposed embrace of "free trade," the likes of Gene A. King Jr., "The Development of Free Trade in Europe," *2008 Free Market Forum*, Hillsdale College. Sebastiano Franci would, if anything, become even more set in his old ways. See his *La moneta oggetto istorico, civile, e politico. Parti due* (Milan: Giuseppe Galeazzi, 1769), 195, a revision of his 1757 manuscript "Pensieri politici, civili ed economici in forma di sistema per regolamento delle monete nello Stato di Milano," Biblioteca Nazionale Braidense, Milan, *AH.11.14*.

122. Pietro Verri, "Il tempio dell'Ignoranza," in *Il Caffè*, 27–29.

123. Kleingeld, "Six Varieties of Cosmopolitanism," 507–509, 518–521.

124. As Pietro Verri laconically opened the last volume of *Il Caffè*, published at the end of its last year of publication, "The small society of friends that has been writing these papers is disbanded"; see his "Al lettore," 407.

125. Verri, "Memorie sincere," 138; Verri, "Lettera riservata," 203. See also Vianello, *La giovinezza*, 201.

126. The numbers of memoranda Verri and Beccaria signed jointly are numerous, but see, for example, "All'annona," 27 April 1785, Reinert Collection.

127. Verri, "Memorie sincere," 138–139. On the necessity of reading these passages critically, see Vianello, *La giovinezza*, 179–181, and also 185, where he argues that Beccaria's book was better for not being composed under the "excessive weight of erudition."

128. See also Vianello, *La giovinezza*, 187. For a similar, if less democratic workshop-model of political economy at the time, see Loïc Charles and Christine Théré, "The Writing Workshop of François Quesnay and the Making of Physiocracy (1757–1764)," *History of Political Economy* 40, no. 1 (2008): 1–42.

129. Alessandro Verri, "Ragionamento sulle leggi civili," in *Il Caffè*, 571–606, at 580.

130. Pietro Verri, "La buona compagnia," in *Il Caffè*, 445–451, at 450.

131. See the numerous supplications in Archivio Verri, 481.2, and, on the topic, Pierre Musitelli, "I manoscritti inediti di Alessandro Verri, Protettore dei carcerati (1763–1765)," *Line@editoriale*, no. 2 (2010), esp. 3–4.

132. Anonymous copyist in the name of Alessandro Verri, "Supplica in difesa di Giovanni d'Auregard detenuto nelle carceri della Malastalla," Archivio Verri, 481.2, fols. 119–122, reproduced in Musitelli, "I manoscritti inediti," 12–13; emphasis added.

133. Ibid., fols. 123–124, reproduced in Musitelli, "I manoscritti inediti," 13–14. The specific crime in question has been little studied, but see, more broadly, Ju-

dith Brown, *Immodest Acts: The Life of a Lesbian Nun in Renaissance Italy* (Oxford: Oxford University Press, 1986), esp. 6.

134. Anonymous copyist in the name of Alessandro Verri, "Supplica in difesa di Anna Perina." The argument continues: "Giulio Claro [not Ilario] attests at § *Incestus* that such a crime at times would be punished with a pecuniary penalty only. On *L.Si quis viduam* [Dig. 48.28.5], incest together with rape is considered worthy of no greater penalty than deportation. And finally, the Senate of Granada, in the case of incest combined with adultery, with remission given by the husband with regard to the latter count, sentenced the Offender solely to exile and a pecuniary penalty, as Larrea testifies in his Decisioni Granatesi par. 1. Dis50. n. 21." This last reference is to the famous seventeenth-century Spanish jurist Johannes Baptista [Juan Bautista] Larrea's *Novae Decisiones Sacri Regii Senatus Granatensis* (Lugduni [Lyon]: Prost, 1623), on which see Paola Volpini, *Lo spazio politico del 'letrado': Juan Bautista Larrea magistrato e giurista nella monarchia di Filippo IV* (Bologna: Il Mulino, 2004). Interestingly, Montesquieu also relied on Dig. 48.28.5 to make a similar point in a chapter on "women's debaucheries" in his *Spirit of the Laws*, 108 and n33 [VII.13], plausibly inspiring the Academy of Fisticuffs' use of it.

135. In Biblioteca Ambrosiana, Milan, Italy, Becc. B. 202.

136. See, for example, Cesare Beccaria to Anonymous, 19 July 1763, and Beccaria to Morellet, 26 January 1766, in *ENOCB*, 4:80–81, 224. See also Verri, "Memorie sincere," 135–138. The title of *On Crimes and Punishments* might be a conscious reference to a common title in the history of jurisprudence. See, among others, the fellow Lombard Ludovico Sinistrari di Ameno, *De delictis, et poenis tractatus absolutissimus* (Venice: Hieronymum Albriccium, 1700).

137. See, on Verri's corrections, Gianni Francioni, "Notizia sul manoscritto della seconda redazione del *Dei delitti e delle pene* (con una appendice di inediti di Pietro Verri relative all'opera di Beccaria)," *Studi Settecenteschi* 1 (1985–1986): 229–296.

138. Pietro Verri to Alessandro Verri, 23 May 1767, in *Viaggio a Parigi e Londra (1766–1767): Carteggio di Pietro e Alessandro Verri*, ed. Gianmarco Gaspari (Milan: Adelphi, 1980), 433–438, at 435.

139. Cesare Beccaria to André Morellet, 26 January 1766, in *ENOCB*, 4:219–228, at 221. For Stendhal's verdict, see Bernard E. Harcourt, *The Illusion of Free Markets* (Cambridge, MA: Harvard University Press, 2011), 254n20. Machiavelli was wrongly accused of conspiracy, tortured, and briefly imprisoned by officials of the new Medici government of Florence in 1513, on which see John M. Najemy, *Between Friends: Discourses of Power and Desire in the Machiavelli-Vettori Letters, 1513–1515* (Princeton, NJ: Princeton University Press, 1993), 94. For Giannone's persecution for heterodox views and long imprisonment up to his death, see Robertson, *Case for the Enlightenment*, esp. 378. Galileo's fate was both more

pleasant and better known, but for a legal perspective, see the documents in Thomas F. Mayer, ed., *The Trial of Galileo, 1612–1633* (Toronto: University of Toronto Press, 2012). The classic essay on these matters remains Leo Strauss, *Persecution and the Art of Writing* (Chicago: University of Chicago Press, 1988), though the Academy of Fisticuffs seemed happier to leave problematic materials on the cutting-room floor than write them in between the proverbial lines.

140. "Al lettore," in *Il Caffè*, 5.

141. Cesare Beccaria, *On Crimes and Punishments and Other Writings*, ed. Aaron Thomas, trans. Aaron Thomas and Jeremy Parzen (Toronto: University of Toronto Press, 2008), 9; emphasis in original. On this phrase, see again Shackleton, "Greatest Happiness." Jean-Jacques Rousseau, "Of the Social Contract," in *The Social Contract and Other Later Political Writings*, ed. Victor Gourevitch (Cambridge: Cambridge University Press, 1997), 78, had opted for a rather different formulation: "If one inquires into precisely what the greatest good of all consists in, which ought to be the end of every system of legislation, one will find that it comes down to these two principal objects, *freedom* and *equality.*"

142. Beccaria, *On Crimes and Punishments*, 9–10.

143. Ibid., 10. Beccaria here summoned a vocabulary and phraseology employed by members of confraternities to assist prisoners and those condemned to death; see, for example, *Capitoli, ed ordini della nobilissima congregatione di San Gioanni Decollato, alle Case rotte, detta de'Bianchi, dell'eccelentissima città di Milano* (Milan: Heredi di Giovanni Battista Malatesta, 1654), 3. I consulted the copy in ASM, *Archivio generale del Fondo di religione, Milano—Confraternita S. Giovanni alle Case Rotte, no. 577*. On how "many" at the time "complain about the uncertainty of the law," see also Alessandro Verri, "Ragionamento sulle leggi civili," in *Il Caffè*, 571–606, at 571.

144. Ever since the publication of Jürgen Habermas's *The Structural Transformation of the Public Sphere: An Inquiry into a Category of Bourgeois Society*, trans. Thomas Burger and Frederick Lawrence (Cambridge: Polity Press, 1989 [1962]), the rise of "public opinion" and a "public sphere" in eighteenth-century Europe has remained one of the most debated questions in Enlightenment historiography. For key treatments, see Keith Michael Baker, "Public Opinion as Political Invention," in *Inventing the French Revolution: Essays on French Political Culture in the Eighteenth Century* (Cambridge: Cambridge University Press, 1990), 167–199; and James van Horn Melton, *The Rise of the Public in Enlightenment Europe* (Cambridge: Cambridge University Press, 2001). For the Italian context, see Tortarolo, "'Opinione pubblica,'"127–138, which focuses on the negative connotations of "opinion" for the members of the Academy of Fisticuffs on 128–130; and more recently Sandro Landi, "'Pubblico' e 'opinione pubblica': Osservazioni

su due luoghi comuni del lessico politico italiano del Settecento," *Cromohs* 13 (2008): 1–11, http://www.cromohs.unifi.it/13_2008/landi.html.

145. Beccaria, *On Crimes and Punishments,* 10.

146. Dugald Stewart, "Account of the Life and Writings of Adam Smith," *Transactions of the Royal Society of Edinburgh* 3 (1794): 55–137; emphasis in original, an independently published extract of which appeared, with no publisher, in 1794, in which the statement regarding conjectural history appeared on 34. More influentially the tract was included in Adam Smith, *Essays on Philosophical Subjects* (London: Cadell and Davies, 1795), vii–xcv, in which the statement appeared on xlii. For an earlier example of the phrase "conjectural history," see William Gostling, *A Walk in and about the City of Canterbury,* 2nd ed. (Canterbury, England: Simmons and Kirkby, 1777), 85–106. For Rousseau on "hypothetical history" and the "conjectural" approach, see his "Second Discourse," in Rousseau, *The Discourses and Other Early Political Writings,* ed. Victor Gourevitch (Cambridge: Cambridge University Press, 1997), 111–222, at 128, 159. On *Histoire Raisonnée,* see Phyllis K. Leffler's still-relevant "The 'Histoire Raisonnée,' 1620–1720: A Pre-Enlightenment Genre," *Journal of the History of Ideas* 37, no. 2 (1976): 219–240. On "conjectural history," see J. G. A. Pocock, *Barbarism and Religion,* 6 vols. (Cambridge: Cambridge University Press, 1999–2015), 2:310–318; on its earlier practice see Reinert, *Translating Empire,* esp. 81–84; on its later influence, see Frank Palmieri, *State of Nature, Stages of Society: Enlightenment Conjectural History and Modern Social Discourse* (New York: Columbia University Press, 2016). For a reasoned contemporary critique of "that sort of theory which has been pompously christened Conjectural History," see Henry Neuman's "Translator's Preface" to François Alexandre Frédéric de La Rochefoucauld-Liancourt, *Travels through the United States of North America,* trans. Henry Neuman, 2 vols. (London: Phillips, 1799), 1:iii–xiii, at vi–vii.

147. Genovesi, *Storia del commercio,* 1:19–20n; Reinert, *Translating Empire,* 216–217.

148. Beccaria, *On Crimes and Punishments,* 12. Although he would not have been familiar with it, Beccaria's analysis was deeply resonant with Rousseau's in his fragmentary "The State of War," in *The Social Contract,* 162–176, at 167, but also explicitly with Genovesi's translation of Cary, which he knew well.

149. Samuel von Pufendorf, *On the Duty of Man and Citizen,* ed. James Tully, trans. Michael Silverthorne (Cambridge: Cambridge University Press, 1991), 117; Jean-Jacques Rousseau, "Geneva Manuscript," in *The Social Contract,* 153–161, at 159: "Hobbes's error is therefore not to have established the state of war among men who are independent and have become sociable but to have assumed this state to be natural to the species, and to have given it as the cause

of the vices of which it is the effect." And, again, in his "The State of War," 163–164. See also Rousseau, "Last Reply," in *The Discourses*, 63–85, at 70n: "man is naturally good, as I believe"; and Rousseau, "Second Discourse," esp. 197. On the theme of the orangutan in the conjectural histories of the Enlightenment, see, among others, Carl Niekerk, "Man and Orangutan in Eighteenth-Century Thinking: Retracing the Early History of Dutch and German Anthropology," *Monatshefte* 96, no. 4 (2004): 477–502; Muthu, *Enlightenment against Empire*, 42–44, and more broadly, Richard Nash, *Wild Enlightenment: The Borders of Human Identity in the Eighteenth Century* (Charlottesville: University of Virginia Press, 2003).

150. Thomas Hobbes, *On the Citizen* [*De Cive*], ed. Richard Tuck and Michael Silverthorne (Cambridge: Cambridge University Press, 1998), 25; Samuel von Pufendorf, *Of the Law of Nature and Nations*, ed. Jean Barbeyrac, trans. Basil Kennett, 4th ed. (London: Carew, 1729), 625. On this point, see also Theodore Christov, *Before Anarchy: Hobbes and His Critics in Modern International Thought* (Cambridge: Cambridge University Press, 2015), 158.

151. Beccaria, *On Crimes and Punishments*, 10. For similarly worded statements, see, for example, Vattel, *The Law of Nations*, 67 [Preliminaries.1], 71 [Preliminaries.10], 133 [1.VIII.88], and 185 [1.XIII.158].

152. See also Frederick Rosen, "Utilitarianism and the Reform of the Criminal Law," in *The Cambridge Companion to Eighteenth-Century Political Thought*, ed. Mark Goldie and Robert Wokler (Cambridge: Cambridge University Press, 2006), 547–572, at 552. For an example of how this sovereignty could be revoked or "recalled," as it was during the French Revolution, see Verri, "Alcuni pensieri sulla rivoluzione accaduta in Francia," in *ENOPV*, 6:469–471, at 470.

153. James Madison, "Federalist No. 51," in *The Federalist Papers*, ed. Terence Ball (Cambridge: Cambridge University Press, 2003), 251–255, at 255. On Madison and Beccaria, see, among others, John D. Bessler, *Cruel and Unusual: The American Death Penalty and the Founders' Eighth Amendment* (Boston: Northeastern University Press, 2012), 340; and, for a much longer engagement, Bessler, *The Birth of American Law: An Italian Philosopher and the American Revolution* (Durham, NC: Carolina Academic Press, 2012), 205–209.

154. Beccaria, *On Crimes and Punishments*, 10. See also Thomas Hobbes, *Leviathan*, ed. Noel Malcolm, 3 vols. (Oxford: Oxford University Press, 2012), 2:254, who spoke of men "who naturally love Liberty, and Dominion overe others"; and Rousseau, "Of the Social Contract," 75, who similarly argued that "all peoples have a kind of centrifugal force by which they constantly act against one another and tend to enlarge themselves at their neighbors' expense, like Descartes's vortices." This was, not incidentally, one of the rare sentences underlined by John Adams in his personal copy; see his marginalia to Cesare Beccaria, *Dei delitti e delle pene*

(Harlem [but Paris], 1780) 130, Boston Public Library, Boston, John Adams Library, Adams225.10. On the inevitability of crime in Beccaria's moral universe, see, among others, Harcourt, *Illusion of Free Markets*, 64–65. As Elena Past recently argued, "the Beccarian line" of criminology "is not a sunny and optimistic one": see her *Methods of Murder: Beccarian Introspection and Lombrosian Vivisection in Italian Crime Fiction* (Toronto: University of Toronto Press, 2012), 14.

155. Beccaria, *On Crimes and Punishments*, 11.

156. Ibid., 7.

157. John Locke, *Two Treatises of Government*, ed. Peter Laslett (Cambridge: Cambridge University Press, 1988), 271, argued that even in the state of nature, "no one ought to harm another in his Life, Health, Liberty, or Possessions." On the fundamental role of divinity as a source of authority in Locke, see John Dunn, *The Political Thought of John Locke: An Historical Account of the Argument of the "Two Treatises of Government"* (Cambridge: Cambridge University Press, 1969), 127; for a discussion of which, see Istvan Hont, "Adam Smith's History of Law and Government as Political Theory," in *Political Judgment: Essays for John Dunn*, ed. Richard Bourke and Raymond Geuss (Cambridge: Cambridge University Press, 2009), 131–171, at 134, and 142 for the relationship between government and judicial power. On Beccaria's statement and his theory of the social contract more generally, see Francioni's footnotes to Beccaria, *Dei delitti e delle pene*, in *ENOCB*, 1:20n1, 26–27n1. Beccaria also expounded on his relationship to Hobbes in a now-lost letter, but see Cosimo Amidei to Cesare Beccaria, 21 April 1766 and 17 June 1766, both in *ENOCB*, 4:290–293, 324–325, as well as Antonio Rotondò's comment regarding this epistolary in Cosimo Amidei, *Opere*, ed. Antonio Rotondò (Turin: Giappichelli, 1980), 335–336. On Amidei and Beccaria, see Antonio Rotondò, introduction to Amidei, *Opere*, 7–147, at 59–83, now republished as "L'utopia giurisdizionalistica di Cosimo Amidei," in Rotondò, *Riforme e utopie nel pensiero politico toscano del Settecento*, ed. Miriam Michelini Rotondò (Florence: Olschki, 2008), 49–186, at 98–121.

158. Alessandro Verri, "Di alcuni sistemi del pubblico diritto," in *Il Caffè*, 725–739, at 737–738.

159. Beccaria, *On Crimes and Punishments*, 79; Pietro Verri, "Discorso sull'indole del piacere e del dolore," in *ENOPV*, 3:65–152, 123. William Stanley Jevons would famously go on to "treat Economy as a Calculus of Pleasure and Pain" in his *The Theory of Political Economy* (London: Macmillan, 1871), vii. On how the pugilists "anticipated Jevon's phrase," see Joseph A. Schumpeter, *A History of Economic Analysis*, ed. Elizabeth Boody Schumpeter (Oxford: Oxford University Press, 1954), 178.

160. Julian Offray de La Mettrie, "Machine Man," in La Mettrie, *Machine Man and Other Writings*, ed. Ann Thomson (Cambridge: Cambridge University Press, 1996), 1–39, at 23, 27.

161. Beccaria, *On Crimes and Punishments*, 18, 85, probably drawing on Rousseau, "Of the Social Contract," 72.

162. Beccaria, *On Crimes and Punishments*, 81; Friedrich Nietzsche, "Twilight of the Idols, or How to Philosophize with a Hammer," in Nietzsche, *The Anti-Christ, Ecce Homo, Twilight of the Idols: And Other Writings*, ed. Aaron Ridley and Judith Norman (Cambridge: Cambridge University Press, 2004), 153-229, at 157.

163. Beccaria, *On Crimes and Punishments*, 81. See, on this question, Eric Nelson, *The Hebrew Republic: Jewish Sources and the Transformation of European Political Thought* (Cambridge, MA: Harvard University Press, 2010).

164. Beccaria, *On Crimes and Punishments*, 12. See also Madeleine van Bellen, "Die Begriffe *giustizia* bei Cesare Beccaria und den Brüdern Pietro und Alessandro Verri," in *Beiträge zur Begriffsgeschichte der italienischen Aufklärung im europäischen Kontext*, ed. Helmut C. Jacobs and Gisela Schlüter (Frankfurt am Main: Peter Lang, 2000), 151-164, esp. 153. This was the ultimate justification for what Foucault called "the penal theory of criminal-social economy" in his *The °Punitive Society: Lectures at the Collège de France, 1972-1973*, ed. Bernard E. Harcourt, trans. Graham Burchell (Houndmills, UK: Palgrave Macmillan, 2015), 67.

165. Vattel, *The Law of Nations*, 296 [2.V.63]; Stephen C. Neff, *Justice among Nations: A History of International Law* (Cambridge, MA: Harvard University Press, 2014), 195.

166. Pufendorf, *On the Duty of Man and Citizen*, 35-36.

167. Rousseau, "Of the Social Contract," 66, but also 68 for his statement that "Laws are, properly speaking, nothing but the conditions of the civil association."

168. Needless to say, Beccaria would not have agreed with the basic premise of Rousseau's fragment "The State of War," 165: "Ask why morals are corrupted in proportion as minds are enlightened; unable to discover the cause, they will have the audacity to deny the fact."

169. Beccaria, *On Crimes and Punishments*, 59-60; anonymous copyist in the name of Alessandro Verri, "Supplica in difesa di Anna Perina," Archivio Verri, 481.2, fols. 123-124, reproduced in Musitelli, "I manoscritti inediti," 13-14.

170. Beccaria, *On Crimes and Punishments*, 17, 80.

171. Ibid., esp. 17-19, 26, 46, 50, 60-61, 86, 140, 153, 155-156. On Beccaria's influence on the Declaration, though with regard to a different article, see Jonathan Israel, *Revolutionary Ideas: An Intellectual History of the French Revolution from the Rights of Man to Robespierre* (Princeton, NJ: Princeton University Press, 2014), 356. In truth, Beccaria's arguments saturate most such declarations of the late eighteenth century. For the tragic involution of Beccaria's caveats, through which all deviation during the Terror could qualify someone as an enemy of mankind, see Dan Edelstein, *The Terror of Natural Right: Republicanism, the Cult of Nature, and the French Revolution* (Chicago: University of Chicago Press, 2009), 260. For

earlier examples of Beccaria's point, see Montesquieu, *The Spirit of the Laws*, 91–92; and Vattel, *The Law of Nations*, 192 [1.XIII.1171], noted also by Francioni in his notes to Beccaria, *Dei delitti e delle pene*, in *ENOCB*, 1:40n2. For Bentham's verdict, see his "Principles of Penal Law," in *The Works of Jeremy Bentham*, ed. John Bowring, 11 vols. (Edinburgh: William Tait, 1838–1843), 1:365–580, at 399, for a discussion of which see Hugh Dunthorne, "Beccaria and Britain," in *Crime, Protest and Police in Modern British Society: Essays in Memory of David J. V. Jones*, ed. David W. Howell and Kenneth O. Morgan (Cardiff: University of Wales Press, 1999), 73–96, at 87.

172. Beccaria, *On Crimes and Punishments*, 42. Rousseau, "Of the Social Contract," 116: "The Citizens being all equal by the social contract, all may prescribe what all ought to do, but no one has the right to require that another do what he himself does not do."

173. On this debate over commercial nobilities, see above and Chapter 3. The terminology of a "gothic" and "feudal" past to be overcome was contemporary in the eighteenth century; for examples, see Adam, *The Political Economy of J. H. G. Justi*, esp. 127.

174. See, with relation to women, Sebastiano Franci, "Difesa delle donne," in *Il Caffè*, 245–256, on which see Rebecca Messbarger, *The Century of Women: Representations of Women in Eighteenth-Century Italian Public Discourse* (Toronto: University of Toronto Press, 2002), 98–103.

175. Wenzel Anton von Kaunitz to Gian Rinaldo Carli, 9 January 1766, in "Il carteggio Carli-Kaunitz," ed. Umberto Marcelli, *Archivio storico italiano* 113 (1955): 388–407, at 391, also 552–581; 114 (1956): 118–135, 771–788.

176. Beccaria, *On Crimes and Punishments*, 18–20, 26, 42; emphasis in original. See, similarly, Hobbes, *Leviathan*, 476 [144].

177. Beccaria, *On Crimes and Punishments*, 13.

178. Ibid., 33.

179. Ibid., 33–34, reacting to the likes of Eliso Masini, *Sacro arsenale, ovvero Pratica dell'Uffizio della Santa Inquisizione* (Rome: San Michele, 1730), §6, 263. For context, see Giuliano Serges, "La tortura giudiziaria: Evoluzione e fortuna di uno strumento d'imperio," in *Momenti di storia della giustizia: Materiali di un seminario*, ed. Leonardo Pace et al. (Rome: Aracne, 2011), 213–320, esp. 275–291. See, more generally, Ariel Glucklich, *Sacred Pain: Hurting the Body for the Sake of the Soul* (Oxford: Oxford University Press, 2001).

180. Beccaria, *On Crimes and Punishments*, 34. For a similar argument, see more recently former deputy FBI director Oliver Ravel's observation that "People will even admit they killed their grandmother, just to stop the beatings": quoted in Christopher C. Joyner, "Terrorizing the Terrorists: An Essay on the Permissibility of Torture," in *The Theory and Practice of International Criminal Law: Essays*

in Honor of M. Cherif Bassiouni, ed. Leila Nadya Sadat and Michael P. Scharf (The Hague: Martinus Nijhoff, 2008), 227–252, at 244n64.

181. See, on this, still Piero Fiorelli, *La tortura giudiziaria nel diritto comune,* 2 vols. (Rome: Giuffré, 1953–1954); and, on Voltaire, Lisa Silverman, *Tortured Subjects: Pain, Truth, and the Body in Early Modern France* (Chicago: University of Chicago Press, 2001), 166–167.

182. Esther Cohen, *The Modulated Scream: Pain in Late Medieval Culture* (Chicago: University of Chicago Press, 2010), 257–260. On the symbolic polyvalence of pain in Medieval art and culture, see also Robert Mills, *Suspended Animation: Pain, Pleasure and Punishment in Medieval Culture* (London: Reaktion Books, 2005), 202. On the gradual overcoming of this mindset in French criminal law in the eighteenth century, see again Silverman, *Tortured Subjects.*

183. Gian Rinaldo Carli to Mazzucchelli, 8 September 1765, in Elio Apih, *Rinnovamento e illuminismo nel '700 italiano: La formazione culturale di Gian Rinaldo Carli* (Trieste: Deputazione di storia patria per la Venezia Giulia, 1973), 225; see similarly Pietro Verri to Alessandro Verri, 20 September 1780, in *CV,* 10:147–154, at 147. From Carli, this was anyway a mixed blessing. On the one hand, he considered Rousseau's *Social Contract* to be "the deadliest of all books" for its having "pushed the principles of an inexistent chimerical liberty beyond even Hobbes"; on the other hand, he praised Beccaria's work at length and approved of attempts to base political philosophy on a "precise analysis of human nature." According to Carli, Rousseau, "following Hobbes," had "made sovereigns and parents odious and subject to their children," utterly confusing "liberty with independence," and the "evil" that had resulted from his "seductive book" was "incredible." See Gian Rinaldo Carli to Girolamo Gravisi, 10 April 1776, and Gian Rinaldo Carli to Girolamo Gravisi, 21 August 1776, in *Trecentosessantasei lettere,* 181–182, 183–185. For a similar argument, see Paolo Frisi's diary of his meeting with Giacinto Sigismondo Gerdil in Turin in 1766, discussed in Vianello, *La giovinezza,* 184.

184. Rousseau, "Of the Social Contract," 64–65.

185. Ibid. On this issue, see also Paul Friedland, *Seeing Justice Done: The Age of Spectacular Capital Punishment in France* (Oxford: Oxford University Press, 2012), 202–205.

186. Beccaria, *Dei delitti e delle pene,* in *ENOCB,* 1:86; Beccaria, *On Crimes and Punishments,* 51.

187. Beccaria, *Dei delitti e delle pene,* in *ENOCB,* 1:86n3.

188. Rousseau, "Of the Social Contract," 60. This was plausibly part of what Isaiah Berlin once referred to as Rousseau's "state worship," in his introduction to Franco Venturi, *Roots of Revolution: A History of the Populist and Socialist Movements in Nineteenth Century Russia,* trans. Francis Haskell, intro. Isaiah Berlin (New York: Alfred A. Knopf, 1960), vii–xxx, at x. On Berlin's reading of Rous-

seau, see Christopher Brooke, "Isaiah Berlin and the Origins of the 'Totalitarian' Rousseau," in *Isaiah Berlin and the Enlightenment*, ed. Laurence Brockliss and Ritchie Robertson (Oxford: Oxford University Press, 2016), 89–98.

189. Beccaria, *On Crimes and Punishments*, 52; emphasis in original. He thus avoided the paradox Hobbes fell into when arguing both that members of the social covenant maintained a right to resist "Death, Wounds, and Imprisonment" and that *"Capitall"* punishment was one of "the Punishments set down in the Law" for "subjects"; see *Leviathan*, 214 and 486–488. Beccaria similarly disagreed with Pufendorf, *On the Duty of Man and Citizen*, 132–133.

190. Beccaria, *On Crimes and Punishments*, 55.

191. Ibid., esp. 13.

192. See again Verri, "Memorie sincere," 83; and for theoretical examples Beccaria would have been familiar with, see, among others, Montesquieu, *The Spirit of the Laws*, 84–85, and Vattel, *The Law of Nations*, 192 [I.XIII.171].

193. Beccaria, *On Crimes and Punishment*, 54, used most effectively by Albert Camus, "Reflections on the Guillotine," in Camus, *Resistance, Rebellion, and Death: Essays*, trans. Justin O'Brien (New York: Vintage, 1960), 173–234, at 194.

194. Beccaria, *On Crimes and Punishments*, 54–55.

195. Ibid., 54. On his fusion of humanitarianism and utilitarianism, see also Friedland, *Seeing Justice Done*, 205.

196. For examples of such frontispieces, see Beccaria, *Dei delitti e delle pene*, in ENOCB, 1:547, 562–563, 568–569, 577, 579, 584, 590, 608, 633, 652. On the image, see also Franco Venturi, "L'immagine della giustizia," *Rivista storica italiana* 76, no. 3 (1964): 707–719.

197. See the Livornese editions of 1821 and 1834, reproduced in Beccaria, *Dei delitti e delle pene*, in ENOCB, 1:633 and 652. On this theme, see again Venturi, "L'immagine della giustizia."

198. Immanuel Kant, *The Metaphysics of Morals*, ed. Mary J. Gregor (Cambridge: Cambridge University Press, 1996), 108; Rosen, "Utilitarianism," 556; Gisela Schlüter, "Kant lettore di Beccaria: Aspetti filologici del dibattito," in *Vie lombarde e venete: Circolazione e trasformazione dei saperi letterari nel Sette-Ottocento fra l'Italia settentrionale e l'Europa transalpina*, ed. Helmut Meter and Furio Brugnolo (Berlin: Walter de Gruyter, 2011), 249–257.

199. Kant, *The Metaphysics of Morals*, 59.

200. Beccaria, *On Crimes and Punishments*, 51.

201. Ibid., 41; emphasis in original.

202. Ibid., 55; emphasis in original.

203. Ibid., 43; emphasis added. On Physiocratic critiques of this statement in particular, see Harcourt, *Illusion of Free Markets*, 61. On the centrality of this idea to the Enlightenment itself, see Venturi, *Utopia e riforma nell'Illuminismo* (Turin:

Einaudi, 1970), 122. Rousseau offered a similar phraseology in his "Last Reply," 71 ("those dreadful words *thine* and *mine*") and similar emotive force in his classic attack on private property as what ended the "state of nature" in "Second Discourse," 144, 161, 167 ("in a word, so long as they applied themselves only to tasks a single individual could perform, and to arts that did not require the collaboration of several hands, they lived free, healthy, good, and happy"). For a modern use of the phrase, see Stefano Rodotà, *Il terribile diritto: Studi sulla proprietà privata e i beni comuni*, 3rd ed. (Bologna: Il Mulino, 2013).

204. See similarly Alfonso Longo, "Osservazioni su i fedecommessi," in *Il Caffè*, 115–132, at 117: "The inequality of humans, so loathsome to the poor, may well be the terrible though necessary outcome of civil society."

205. Despite further arguing that "in its theoretical form, modern socialism originally appears ostensibly as a more logical extension of the principles laid down by the great French philosophers of the eighteenth century," Engels did not elaborate further beyond token references to Morelly and Mably. See Friedrich Engels, *Socialism: Utopian and Scientific*, trans. Edward Aveling (New York: International Publishers, 2004), 31–33.

206. Hont, *Jealousy of Trade*, 440; Hont, *Politics in Commercial Society: Jean-Jacques Rousseau and Adam Smith*, ed. Béla Kapossy and Michael Sonenscher (Cambridge, MA: Harvard University Press, 2015), 70–71.

207. For brilliant meditations on the nature of property in the history of political thought, see Peter Garnsey, *Thinking about Property: From Antiquity to the Age of Revolution* (Cambridge: Cambridge University Press, 2007); and Garnsey, "Property and Its Limits: Historical Analysis," in *La Propriété et ses limites / Das Eigentum und seine Grenzen*, ed. Bénédict Winiger, Matthias Mahlmann, Sophie Clément, and Anne Kühler (Stuttgart: Franz Steiner, 2017), 13–38.

208. Aquinas, *Summa Theologica*, IIa–IIae, quest. 66, art. 7.

209. Hobbes, *Leviathan*, 208.

210. Rousseau, "Second Discourse," 172.

211. Smith, *Wealth of Nations*, 1:14, drawing on his "'Early Draft' of Part of the *Wealth of Nations*," in *Lectures on Jurisprudence*, ed. Ronald L. Meek, D. D. Raphael and P. G. Stein (Oxford: Clarendon Press, 1978), 562–581, at 563, and, as many have pointed out before me, probably inspired by works like Bernard Mandeville, *The Fable of the Bees*, ed. Frederick Benjamin Kaye, 2 vols. (Oxford: Oxford University Press, 1924), 1:26 and 26n, 169–181 [remark P]; Henry Martyn, *Considerations upon the East-India Trade* (London: Churchill, 1701), 72–73; and ultimately John Locke, "An Essay Concerning the True Original, Extent, and End of Civil Government," in *Two Treatises of Government*, 283–446, 314–315 (§41). On this "idiom," see Hont, *Jealousy of Trade*, 249 and 249n, 145, 389–443.

212. See, for this argument in context, Garnsey, *Thinking about Property*, 220.

213. Adam Smith, *The Theory of Moral Sentiments*, ed. Knud Haakonssen (Cambridge: Cambridge University Press, 1994), 184; emphasis added.

214. R. A. Markus, *Saeculum: History and Society in the Theology of Saint Augustine* (Cambridge: Cambridge University Press, 1970), viii.

215. Hont, *Jealousy of Trade*, 441.

216. Smith, *Lectures on Jurisprudence*, 9, discussed in Donald Winch, *Adam Smith's Politics: An Essay in Historiographic Revision* (Cambridge: Cambridge University Press, 1978), 51–52; and Hont, *Jealousy of Trade*, 417–419.

217. Smith, *Theory of Moral Sentiments*, 101.

218. Smith, *Wealth of Nations*, 2:42. On the numerous tasks of the state, see, among others, Andrew S. Skinner, "The Role of the State," in *A System of Social Science: Papers Relating to Adam Smith*, 2nd ed. (Oxford: Clarendon Press, 2004), 183–208.

219. Pierre-Joseph-André Roubaud, quoted and discussed at length in Steven L. Kaplan, *Raisonner sur les blés: Essais sur les Lumières économiques* (Paris: Fayard, 2017), 305–386.

220. David Hume, "Of Commerce," in *Political Essays*, ed. Knud Haakonssen (Cambridge: Cambridge University Press, 1994), 93–104, at 102.

221. David Hume, "Of Justice," in *Essays and Treatises on Several Subjects*, new ed., 2 vols. (London: Cadell et al., 1788), 2:215–234, at 220. For a similar argument, see the idea of "the circumstances of justice" in John Rawls, *A Theory of Justice* (Cambridge, MA: Harvard University Press, 1971), 126–130. On Hume's and Smith's different approaches, see again Hont, *Jealousy of Trade*, 413–419. On Hume's still rather stringent limits to state involvement, however, see Carl Wennerlind, "An Artificial Virtue and the Oil of Commerce: A Synthetic View of Hume's Theory of Money," in *David Hume's Political Economy*, ed. Carl Wennerlind and Margaret Schabas (London: Routledge, 2008), 105–126, at 106–108.

222. Beccaria, *Dei delitti e delle pene*, in *ENOCB*, 1:75 and 75n3.

223. Beccaria, *On Crimes and Punishments*, 71n.

224. See his piece in the *Éphémérides du citoyen* 3 (1769): 159–181, at 178; emphasis in original, discussed in Bernard Harcourt, *Illusion of the Free Market*, 61.

225. Pietro Verri, "Pensieri del conte Pietro Verri sullo stato politico del milanese nel 1790," part of "Idee politiche del conte Pietro Verri da non pubblicarsi 1790," in *ENOPV*, 6:390–425, at 409, all the while maintaining with Beccaria that it was a social invention; see, for example, his comments to article II of the French Declaration of the Rights of Man and of the Citizen in his "[Sulla *Dichiarazione dei diritti*]," in *ENOPV*, 6:611–627, at 613–615. See also Pietro Verri, "Examen du livre des délits et des peines [1767]," in *ENOPV*, 1:894–908, at 902–904.

226. Pietro to Alessandro Verri, 16 September 1767, in *CV*, vol. 1, pt. 2, 63, discussed in Carlo Capra, "Beccaria e i Verri negli anni dei Pugni e del 'Caffè,'" in *Il caso*

Beccaria: A 250 anni dalla pubblicazione del "Dei delitti e delle pene," ed. Vincenzo Ferrone and Giuseppe Ricuperati (Bologna: Il Mulino, 2016), 87–110, at 101 and similarly 108.

227. Verri, "Meditazioni," 423–424.

228. I have previously made this argument in Reinert, "Italian Tradition of Political Economy," 40–41. For a succinct later statement of this, see Pietro Verri, "Discorso recitato nella prima adunanza della società patriotica," in *ENOPV,* 3:557–580, at 576.

229. Both of these extremes of course have contemporary acolytes. For praise of Smith and the roadside beggar, see, among many others, Deirdre McCloskey, *Bourgeois Dignity: Why Economics Can't Explain the Modern World* (Chicago: University of Chicago Press, 2010), 347.

230. Beccaria, *On Crimes and Punishments,* 71.

231. Ludwig von Mises, *Socialism: An Economic and Sociologial Analysis,* trans. Jacques Kahane (Indianapolis: Liberty Fund, 1981 [1922]), 263–264. This was curiously pre-Hobbesian. *"Lupus agno lupus"*—"the wolf is a wolf to the lamb"— might be true, but it hardly makes for an enlightening aphorism of political philosophy.

232. Beccaria, *On Crimes and Punishments,* 71. On this, see also Gianni Francioni, *Gli illuministi e lo Stato: I modelli politici fra utopia e riforma* (Como: Ibis, 2012), 156–157. See, for a similar argument, Rousseau, "Second Discourse," 179: "The Right of property is only by convention and human institution."

233. Giovanni Gualberto de Soria, "Giudizio di celebre professore sopra il libro Dei delitti e delle pene," in Cesare Beccaria, *Dei delitti e delle pene,* ed. Franco Venturi (Turin: Einaudi, 1965), 198–205, at 199. On de Soria, see Luca Magnanima, *Elogio istorico e filosofico di Giovanni Alberto De Soria* (Livorno: Carlo Giorgi, 1777); Niccola Carranza, *Monsignor Gaspare Cerati provveditore dell'Università di Pisa nel Settecento delle riforme* (Pisa: Pacini, 1974), 277–280; Antonio Rotondò, "Il pensiero politico di Giovanni Gualberto De Soria," in *Studi storici sul Settecento europeo in onore di Franco Venturi,* ed. Raffaele Ajello et al. (Naples: Jovene, 1985), 987–1043, republished as "Utopia e riforma nel pensiero politico di Giovanni Gualberto De Soria," in Rotondò, *Riforme e utopie,* 187–240.

234. A similar point was made by Maria R. Di Simone, "Riflessioni sulle fonti e la fortuna di Cesare Beccaria," in *Cesare Beccaria: La pratica dei lumi,* ed. Vincenzo Ferrone and Gianni Francioni (Florence: Oelschki, 2000), 49–61, at 58. An inspiration might have been Rousseau, "The Social Contract," 81, who earlier had discussed "criminal laws, which at bottom are not so much a particular kind of law as the sanction for all the others."

235. Beccaria, *On Crimes and Punishments,* 9, 79; emphasis in original.

236. Ibid., 9–10, here echoing Verri, *Considerazioni*, 202. The importance of industrial warfare for Beccaria, and the role it played in trumping his rhetorical and theoretical flourishes in his political economy, was highlighted already by Gino Macchioro, *Teorie e riforme economiche finanziarie ed amministrative nella Lombardia del secolo XVIII* (Città di Castello: Tipografia dello stabilimento S. Lapi, 1904), 98–99.

237. See, again James Schmidt, ed., *What Is Enlightenment? Eighteenth-Century Answers and Twentieth-Century Questions* (Berkeley: University of California Press, 1996).

238. Beccaria, *On Crimes and Punishments*, 17.

239. Ibid., 67, perhaps engaging with Rousseau, "Of the Social Contract," 73–74, 84, 88, 96–97, and for a caveat, 104 and 104n, 111–112. Henry Lloyd, *An Essay on the Theory of Money* (London: n.p., 1771), 37, would translate this sentiment in more technically economic terms. On the problem of small states at the time, see Luciana Garibbo, *La neutralità della repubblica di Genova: Saggio sulla condizione dei piccolo stati nell'Europa del Settecento* (Milan: Giuffrè, 1972); Thomas Allison Kirk, *Genoa and the Sea: Policy and Power in the Early Modern Maritime Republic, 1559–1684* (Baltimore: Johns Hopkins University Press, 2005); Reinert, *Translating Empire*, esp. 238–245; Richard Whatmore, *Against War and Empire: Geneva, Britain and France in the Eighteenth Century* (New Haven, CT: Yale University Press, 2012).

240. Beccaria, *On Crimes and Punishments*, 35; emphasis added. This was, of course, a common trope at the time, for examples of which see Reinert, *Translating Empire*, and, for a particularly succinct summary, Vattel, *The Law of Nations*, 131 [I.VIII.85].

241. See similarly Harcourt, *Illusion of Free Markets*, esp. 21.

242. Beccaria, *On Crimes and Punishments*, 17. For Condorcet's work on this, see, for example, his *Essai sur l'application de l'analyse à la probabilité des décisions rendues à la plurailté des voix* (Paris: Imprimerie Royale, 1785). On Condorcet's debt to Beccaria, see, among others, David Williams, *Condorcet and Modernity* (Cambridge: Cambridge University Press, 2004), 15.

243. Carveth Read, *Logic, Deductive and Inductive* (London: Grant Richards, 1898), 272, a sentiment later attributed to, and employed by, Alfred Marshall, John Maynard Keynes, and Amartya Sen, among others. See, for example, Amartya Sen, "The Standard of Living: Lecture II, Lives and Capabilities," in Sen, *The Standard of Living*, ed. Geoffrey Hawthorne (Cambridge: Cambridge University Press, 1989), 20–38, 34; Robert Skidelsky, *Keynes: A Very Short Introduction* (Oxford: Oxford University Press, 2010), 168; and Geoffrey C. Harcourt with Catherine Watson, "Cambridge Economics," in Geoffrey C. Harcourt, *On Skidelsky's Keynes and Other Essays: Selected Essays of G. C. Harcourt* (Basingstoke, UK: Palgrave Macmillan, 2012), 319–326, at 325.

244. Rousseau, "Of the Social Contract," 66.

245. Beccaria, *On Crimes and Punishments*, 81.

246. Pietro Verri, "Gli studi utili" and "[Le riverenze]," in *Il Caffè*, 311–318, at 314, and 73–78, at 73. Descartes famously made "geometry" the very standard of rigor; see his "Meditationes de Prima Philosophia," in *Oeuvres de Descartes*, ed. Charles Adam and Paul Tannery, 13 vols. (Paris: Virn, 1964–1974), 7:69.

3. Cycloid Pudding

1. William S. Gilbert and Arthur Sullivan, "The Pirates of Penzance," in *The Complete Annotated Gilbert and Sullivan*, ed. Ian Bradley (Oxford: Oxford University Press, 1996), act 1, lines 452–459.

2. Carl von Clausewitz, *On War*, ed. Michael Howard and Peter Paret (Princeton, NJ: Princeton University Press, 1989), 457; Napoleon Bonaparte, *Notes inédites de l'Empereur Napoléon Ier sur les mémoires militaires du Général Lloyd*, ed. Ariste Ducaunnès-Duval (Bordeaux: Gounouilho, 1901); Beatrice Heuser, *Reading Clausewitz* (London: Pimlico, 2002), 193; Michael Howard, *Clausewitz: A Very Short Introduction* (Oxford: Oxford University Press, 2002), 24; and the more lenient Hugh Smith, *On Clausewitz: A Study of Military and Political Ideas* (Basingstoke, UK: Palgrave Macmillan, 2004), 57.

3. Bonaparte, *Notes inédites*, 8, 9, 11, 18. For an eminently readable account of the end of the Napoleonic Wars from the perspective of the British ship on which Napoleon finally surrendered, see David Cordingly, *The Billy Ruffian: The Bellerophon and the Downfall of Napoleon* (London: Bloomsbury, 2003), and see 304 for his reading-habits on St. Helena. On Napoleon's far richer readings of Adam Smith at the time, see Emma Rothschild, *Economic Sentiments: Adam Smith, Condorcet, and the Enlightenment* (Cambridge, MA: Harvard University Press, 2001), 1, 240, 247–251.

4. Abraham Rees, "Review of An Essay on the Theory of Money," *Monthly Review*, no. 46 (1772): 75–76; William Stanley Jevons, *Theory of Political Economy* (London: Macmillan, 1871), xlv–xvli. On Jevons's own precocious use of mathematics, see, among others, Nicolò de Vecchi, *Jevons: Il problema del calcolo logico in economia politica* (Milan: Etas Libri, 1976); and Margaret Schabas, *A World Ruled by Number: William Stanley Jevons and the Rise of Mathematical Economics* (Princeton, NJ: Princeton University Press, 1990).

5. There is, needless to say, nothing new about intellectual traditions downgrading the works upon whose shoulders they stand. See, among others, Anthony Grafton, "Introduction: The Humanists Reassessed," in *Defenders of the Text: The Tradition of Scholarship in an Age of Science, 1450–1800* (Cambridge, MA:

Harvard University Press, 1991), 1–22; Umberto Eco, *Serendipities: Language and Lunacy* (Orlando, FL: Harcourt Brace, 1998), 4–7; and—for the opposite technique of excessively praising one's forebears—Eco, "Foreword: Dicebat Bernardus Carnotensis," in Robert K. Merton, *On the Shoulders of Giants: The Post-Italianate Edition* (Chicago: University of Chicago Press, 1993), ix–xviii. Lloyd is absent in most histories of economic thought, but he appears briefly in Joseph A. Schumpeter, *A History of Economic Analysis* (Oxford: Oxford University Press, 1954), 315, 954, where his equations are already deemed "obsolete" in the context of his times, and, given Schumpeter's lack of familiarity with Lloyd's Milanese context, he is described as one of the "many isolated instances" of eighteenth-century mathematical economics. He is mentioned only briefly in Peter Groenewegen, "Reflections on Pietro Verri's Political Economy," in *Eighteenth-Century Economics: Turgot, Beccaria and Smith and Their Contemporaries* (London: Routledge, 2002), 270–281, at 270–271; and by the ceaselessly surprising Arthur Eli Monroe, *Monetary Theory before Adam Smith* (Cambridge, MA: Harvard University Press, 1923), 287–288, who was remarkably prescient in regard to the *Essay*'s intellectual debts to Antonio Genovesi, particularly given that he knew neither that Lloyd was the author of the essay he discussed nor that Genovesi's work had influenced Pietro Verri, and thus Lloyd.

6. Azar Gat, *The Origins of Military Thought: From The Enlightenment to Clausewitz* (Oxford: Oxford University Press, 1989), 67–78; and particularly Patrick Speelman, *Henry Lloyd and the Military Enlightenment in Eighteenth-Century Europe* (Westport, CT: Greenwood, 2002); and Speelman, "Editor's Preface," in *War, Society and Enlightenment: The Works of General Lloyd,* ed. Patrick Speelman (Leiden: Brill, 2005), xiii–xvi, at xii. This project was first begun by Franco Venturi, *Le vite incrociate di Henry Lloyd e Pietro Verri* (Turin: Tirrenia Stampatori, 1977); and Venturi, "Le avventure del generale Henry Lloyd," *Rivista storica italiana* 91, nos. 2–3 (1979): 369–433.

7. Lloyd was "the most intimate and confidential friend" of Richard Fitzwilliam, the 7th Viscount Fitzwilliam of Merrion, for which see Hannibal Evans Lloyd, *Memoir of General Lloyd, Author of the History of the Seven Years' War, etc. etc. by His Son, Hannibal Evans Lloyd* (London: Privately printed, 1842), 3. In 1861 Lloyd's granddaughter donated many of his papers to the Founder's Library, Fitzwilliam Museum, Cambridge, UK (hereafter cited as Fitzwilliam). The individual documents under the general classification *Henry Lloyd Papers* are not catalogued, and citations will therefore be labeled with the title or first line of the relevant fragment. Venturi's use of this material has been astutely commented on by Carlo Capra, *I progressi della ragione: Vita di Pietro Verri* (Bologna: Il Mulino, 2002), 149–150, n42. The best sources for Lloyd's early life are his son's privately circulated 1842 *Memoir of General Lloyd* and a letter by Lloyd's friend

John Drummond, "Mr. Drummond's Letter to the Editor," included in later editions of Henry Lloyd, *A Political and Military Rhapsody, on the Invasion and Defence of Great Britain and Ireland. By the Late General Lloyd to which is Annexed, a Short Account of the Author and a Supplement by the Editor,* 2nd ed. (London: Debret et al., 1792), xi–xix, as well as Germain-Hyacinthe de Romance de Mesmon's *Mémoires militaires et politiques du Géneral Lloyd* (Paris: 1801). I am grateful to Pedro de Brito for this last reference.

8. *Biographie universelle, ancienne et moderne, ou Histoire, par ordre alphabétique, de la vie publique et privée de tous les hommes . . .* , 85 vols. (Paris: Michaud, 1811–1862), 24:588, discussed in Venturi, "Le avventure," 431.

9. Basil Henry Liddell Hart, "Some Extracts from a Military Work of the 18th Century," *Journal of the Society for Army Historical Research* 12 (1933): 138–152, at 138. On Marlborough, see Winston S. Churchill, *Marlborough: His Life and Times,* 2 vols. (Chicago: University of Chicago Press, 2002). On the no less interesting Liddell Hart, see John J. Mearsheimer, *Liddell Hart and the Weight of History* (Ithaca, NY: Cornell University Press, 1988).

10. The following paragraph relies on Speelman, *Henry Lloyd,* 5–17.

11. See, among countless examples, Henry Lloyd, *An Essay on the English Constitution* (London: Printed for the author, 1770), 68.

12. On Ricardo Wall, see Diego Téllez Alarcia, *Absolutismo e ilustración en la España del siglo XVIII: El despotismo ilustrado de D. Ricardo Wall* (Madrid: Fundación Española de Historia Moderna, 2010).

13. Lloyd, *Memoir of General Lloyd,* 4. On Fontenoy, see Francis Henry Skrine, *Fontenoy and Great Britain's Share in the War of Austrian Succession, 1741–1748* (Edinburgh: W. Blackwood and Sons, 1907); Jean-Pierre Bois, *Fontenoy, 1745: Louis XV, arbiter de l'Europe* (Paris: Economica, 1996).

14. Pietro Verri to Alessandro Verri, 13 March 1769, in *Carteggio di Pietro e di Alessandro Verri dal 1766 al 1797,* ed. E. Greppi, F. Novati, A. Giulini, and G. Seregni, 12 vols. (Milan: Cogliati, then Milesi & Figli, then Giuffrè, 1910–1943) (hereafter cited as *CV*), 2:272.

15. Speelman, *Henry Lloyd;* Henry Lloyd, *An Essay on the English Constitution* (London: Printed for the author, 1770), 9.

16. Henry Lloyd, *Essay on the Artillery,* Fitzwilliam, *Henry Lloyd Papers,* 11; Pietro Verri to Alessandro Verri, 23 January 1768, in *CV,* vol. 1, pt. 2, 145; Henry Lloyd, *The History of the Late War in Germany Between the King of Prussia, and the Empress of Germany and her Allies* (London, 1767), preface.

17. Pietro Verri to Alessandro Verri, 13 September 1769, in *CV,* 3:54. This is evident from a plethora of letters, among which see Alessandro Verri to Pietro Verri, 11 January 1769, in *CV,* 2:127; Pietro Verri to Alessandro Verri, 13 March 1769, in *CV,* 2:272; Alessandro Verri to Pietro Verri, 31 March 1769, in *CV,* 2:302; and Pietro

Verri to Alessandro Verri, 13 September 1769, in *CV*, 3:54–56. Alessandro said "there is nothing to gain from such a character, capable of compromising a good friend in a hundred ways" in a letter to Pietro Verri, 20 September 1769, in *CV*, 3:73–74. The year before, Pietro had proclaimed "This [Lloyd] will be the last foreigner I bring into the [Milanese nobility's] houses" in a letter to Alessandro dated 28 March 1768, in *CV*, vol. 1, pt. 2, 294. On the difficulty of aligning Lloyd's different life-stories, see also Capra, *I progressi della ragione*, 148.

18. Lloyd, *History of the Late War*, preface.

19. For what is possibly his first usage of the term "line of operations," see Henry Lloyd, *A Rhapsody on the Present System of French Politics; on the Projected Invasion, and the Means to Defeat It* (London: W. Faden, 1770), 35, for a discussion of which see Speelman, *Henry Lloyd*, 114. On political arithmetic, see the preface to William Petty, *Political Arithmetick* (London: Robert Clavel, 1690), on which see Ted McCormick, *William Petty: The Ambitions of Political Arithmetick* (Oxford: Oxford University Press, 2009). On the comparative absence of mathematical principles in the moral philosophy of the Scottish Enlightenment, seen as nearly identical with "the Enlightenment" as such, see Christopher J. Berry, *The Idea of Commercial Society in the Scottish Enlightenment* (Edinburgh: Edinburgh University Press, 2013), 23.

20. Petty, *Political Arithmetick*. On the mathematical instruments of the Academy of Fisticuffs, see Paola Tubaro's wonderful "Un'esperienza peculiare del Settecento italiano: La 'scuola milanese' di economia matematica," *Studi settecenteschi* 20 (2000): 193–223, as well as Luigi Luini, "Scienze naturali e scienze sociali: Le chiose matematiche di Frisi a Verri e Lloyd," in *Alle origini del pensiero economico in Italia 2: Economia e istituzioni: Il paradigma lombardo tra i secoli XVIII e XIX*, ed. Alberto Quadrio Curzio (Bologna: Il Mulino, 1996), 127–145; Sophus A. Reinert, "'One Will Do with Political Economy . . . What the Scholastics Did with Philosophy': Henry Lloyd and the Mathematization of Economics," *History of Political Economy* 34, no. 4 (2007): 643–677; and briefer mentions in, among others, Marco Bianchini, *Alle origini della scienza economia: Felicità pubblica e matematica sociale negli economisti italiani del Settecento* (Parma: Studiorum, 1982); Reghinos D. Theocharis, *Early Developments in Mathematical Economics*, 2nd ed. (London: Macmillan, 1983); and Thomas Hutchison, *Before Adam Smith: The Emergence of Political Economy, 1662–1776* (Oxford: Blackwell, 1988).

21. Cesare Beccaria, "Tentativo analitico su i contrabbandi," in Gianni Francioni and Sergio A. Romagnoli, eds., *"Il Caffè," 1764–1766* (Turin: Bollati Boringhieri, 1993) (hereafter cited as *Il Caffè*), 173–175, at 173–174. On this essay see also Reinert, "'One Will Do with Political Economy"; Bernard E. Harcourt, *The Illusion of Free Markets* (Cambridge, MA: Harvard University Press, 2011), 64–65.

22. Michael Kwass, "The Global Underground: Smuggling, Rebellion, and the Origins of the French Revolution," in *The French Revolution in Global Perspective,* ed. Suzanne Desan, Lynn Hunt, and William Max Nelson (Ithaca, NY: Cornell University Press, 2013), 15–31. See, on the importance of contemporary smuggling, also Renaud Morieux, *The Channel: England, France and the Construction of a Maritime Border in the Eighteenth Century* (Cambridge: Cambridge University Press, 2016), 248–282.

23. Jean-Jacques Rousseau, in "Of the Social Contract," in Rousseau, *The Social Contract and Other Later Political Writings,* ed. Victor Gourevitch (Cambridge: Cambridge University Press, 1997), 39–152, at 85, similarly argued that "if in order to express myself in fewer words I momentarily borrow the language of geometry, I am nevertheless not unaware of the fact that geometric precision does not obtain in moral quantities." See also 105, and his famous 18 August 1756 letter to Voltaire, in Rousseau, *The Discourses and Other Early Political Writings,* ed. Victor Gourevitch (Cambridge: Cambridge University Press, 1997), 232–246, at 238.

24. Jonathan Swift, *Travels into Several Remote Nations of the World by Captain Lemuel Gulliver,* 2 vols. (London: Benjamin Motte, 1726), 2:5–7.

25. Ibid., 10–11, 13, 20, 22, 26: "Their Ideas are perpetually conversant in Lines and Figures. If they would, for example, praise the Beauty of a Woman, or any other Animal, they describe it by Rhombs, Circles, Parallelograms, Ellipses, and other geometrical Terms, or by Words of Art drawn from Musick, needless here to repeat."

26. Ibid., 26–27.

27. Ibid., 28–29; emphasis in original.

28. Franco Venturi, *Utopia e riforma nell'illuminismo* (Turin: Einaudi, 1970).

29. Beccaria, "Tentative analitico," 174.

30. Ibid., 174–175.

31. Ibid., 175. It is striking how similar the methodology is to Lloyd's in his *Essay on the Artillery,* 15v–16v.

32. Jean-Jacques Rousseau, "Discourse on the Sciences and Arts," in *Discourses,* 1–28, at 16.

33. Henry Lloyd, *Philosophical Essays on the Different Species of Governments,* p. 6, Fitzwilliam, *Henry Lloyd Papers.*

34. Henry Lloyd, *Continuation of the History of the Late War in Germany, Between the King of Prussia, and the Empress of Germany and her Allies . . .* (London: S. Hooper, 1781), 88. On this tradition, see Albert O. Hirschman, *The Passions and the Interests: Political Arguments for Capitalism before Its Triumph* (Princeton, NJ: Princeton University Press, 1997), 12–14.

35. Lloyd, *Essay on the English Constitution,* 13.

36. Lloyd, *Philosophical Essays*, 1–6.

37. The source of Lloyd's materialism was explicitly Claude-Adrien Helvétius, *De l'Esprit; or Essays on the Mind and its Several Faculties* (London, [1759]), esp. 3. Julian Offray de La Mettrie, in "Machine Man," in La Mettrie, *Machine Man and Other Writings*, ed. Ann Thomson (Cambridge: Cambridge University Press, 1996), 1–39, at 37–39, argued at times that man was a "clock," concluding "boldly that man is a machine and that there is in the whole universe only one diversely modified substance"; this may have inspired Helvétius, though Hobbes had already proposed a largely sensationist materialism in his 1651 *Leviathan*—see Thomas Hobbes, *Leviathan*, ed. Noel Malcolm, 3 vols. (Oxford: Oxford University Press, 2012), 2:4, 23—which Locke developed in his *Essay Concerning Human Understanding* (London: Basset, 1690 [but 1689]). See also the Christianized Epicurean current in the Enlightenment brought on by Pierre Gassendi's influential *Three Discourses of Happiness, Virtue, and Liberty* (London: Awnsham and John Churchill, 1699). For a brief history of this sensationist philosophy, see David Wootton, "Helvetius: From Radical Enlightenment to Revolution," *Political Theory* 28, no. 3 (2000): 307–336; and John C. O'Neal, *The Authority of Experience: Sensationist Theory in the French Enlightenment* (University Park: Pennsylvania State University Press, 1996).

38. Lloyd, *Philosophical Essays*, 5.

39. Ibid., 5, 7, 52, building on Hobbes, *Leviathan*, 3.

40. Henry Lloyd, *An Essay on the Theory of Money* (London: n.p., 1771), 37. Lloyd's statement formalized a very common theme of early modern political economy, exemplified above all by Petty's *Political Arithmetick,* preoccupied with the importance of population density for national development.

41. On this vogue, see Adelheid Voskuhl, *Androids in the Enlightenment: Mechanics, Artisans, and Cultures of the Self* (Chicago: University of Chicago Press, 2013).

42. On this process, see Eduard Jan Dijksterhuis, *The Mechanization of the World Picture* (Oxford: Oxford University Press, 1961); and Alfred W. Crosby, *The Measure of Reality: Quantification and Western Society, 1250–1600* (Cambridge: Cambridge University Press, 1997).

43. Lloyd, *Philosophical Essays*, 8–9, 10–13, 27, 36.

44. Ibid., 40.

45. See, on this "Radical Enlightenment," Jonathan Israel's controversial ongoing project: *Radical Enlightenment: Philosophy and the Making of Modernity, 1650–1750* (Oxford: Oxford University Press, 2001); Israel, *Enlightenment Contested: Philosophy, Modernity, and the Emancipation of Man, 1670–1752* (Oxford: Oxford University Press, 2006); Israel, *Democratic Enlightenment: Philosophy, Revolution, and Human Rights, 1750–1790* (Oxford: Oxford University Press, 2011). For a

different perspective, see Margaret C. Jacob, *The Radical Enlightenment: Panthe-ists, Freemasons and Republicans*, 2nd ed. (London: Cornerstone, 2006). For a historiographical overview, including essays by both Jacob and Israel, see Steffen Ducheyne, ed., *Reassessing the Radical Enlightenment* (London: Rout-ledge, 2017).

46. Lloyd, *Philosophical Essays*, 14–15, 54.

47. Ibid., 15, also Lloyd, *Continuation*, 90.

48. Lloyd, *Des Degrés des Sensibilité*, Fitzwilliam, *Henry Lloyd Papers;* see also Lloyd, *Continuation*, 81–82; Verri, "Meditazioni," esp. 395.

49. Lloyd, *Essay on the Theory of Money*, 45, echoing Alessandro Verri, "Ragion-amento sulle leggi civili," in *Il Caffè*, 571–606, at 599: "The more society and its culture grows, the more the matters of legislation grow." Bernard Mandeville, *The Fable of the Bees*, ed. Frederick Benjamin Kaye, 2 vols. (Oxford: Oxford Uni-versity Press, 1924), 1:369, on which see E. J. Hundert, *The Enlightenment's Fable: Bernard Mandeville and the Discovery of Society* (Cambridge: Cambridge Univer-sity Press, 1994); and Mikko Tolonen, *Mandeville and Hume: Anatomists of Civil Society* (Oxford: Voltaire Foundation, 2013).

50. Pietro Verri, *Meditazioni sulla felicità*, ed. Gianni Francioni (Como: Ibis, 1996), 61, on which see Gianni Francioni, "Note al testo," in *Edizione Nazionale delle Opere di Cesare Beccaria*, ed. Luigi Firpo and Gianni Francioni, 16 vols. in 17 (Milan: Mediobanca, 1984–2015), 1:215–368, at 75–89, esp. 82; and Robert Shackleton, "The Greatest Happiness of the Greatest Number: The History of Bentham's Phrase," *Studies on Voltaire and the Eighteenth Century* 90 (1972): 1461–1482.

51. Cesare Beccaria, *On Crimes and Punishments and Other Writings*, ed. Aaron Thomas, trans. Aaron Thomas and Jeremy Parzen (Toronto: University of To-ronto Press, 2008), 6.

52. Lloyd, *Essay on the English Constitution*, 15.

53. Jeremy Bentham to Voltaire, November 1776, in *The Correspondence of Jeremy Bentham*, vol. 1: *1752–76*, ed. Timothy L. S. Sprigge (London: Athlone Press, 1968), 367–368.

54. Jeremy Bentham to Samuel Bentham, in *The Correspondence of Jeremy Bentham*, vol. 4: *October 1788 to December 1793*, ed. Alexander Taylor Milne (London: Ath-lone Press, 1981), 202–204.

55. See also Lloyd's fragment beginning *L'homme est un animal . . .* , Fitzwilliam, *Henry Lloyd Papers*.

56. Lloyd, *Continuation*, 81, 95. See also La Mettrie, "Machine Man," 18, who simi-larly argued man was built to be "happy." It must also be noted that the only time Lloyd mentions Pierre Bayle, one of the most influential proponents of an Epicurean moral philosophy in the Enlightenment, he disagrees with him: "Bayle's Proposition to know whether a society of atheists could subsist appears

absurd, because mankind in general are but struck by objects so remote, but a great deal by those which act directly upon them"; see his *Philosophical Essays on the Different Species of Governments,* 21–22. For Lloyd, such existential questions may have been too removed from the concerns of daily life. On the importance of Bayle and his challenge at the time, see John Robertson, *The Case for the Enlightenment: Scotland and Naples, 1680–1760* (Cambridge: Cambridge University Press, 2005), 216–225.

57. Mark Hulliung, *The Autocritique of Enlightenment: Rousseau and the Philosophes* (Cambridge, MA: Harvard University Press, 1994), 116; Wootton, "Helvetius."

58. Lloyd, *Essay on the English Constitution,* 28; Lloyd, *Continuation,* 89.

59. Lloyd, *Essay on the English Constitution,* 4, building on Montesquieu; Lloyd, *Continuation,* 120.

60. Lloyd, *Essay on the English Constitution,* 5, 14; emphasis in original.

61. Pietro Verri, "Primi elementi per somministrare al popolo delle nozioni tendenti alla pubblica felicità," in *Edizione nazionale delle opere di Pietro Verri,* ed. Carlo Capra et al., 8 vols. in 10 to date (Rome: Edizioni di storia e letteratura, 2003–2014) (hereafter cited as *ENOPV*), 6:629–677, particularly 642, 665–666; emphasis in original. Isaiah Berlin, "Two Concepts of Liberty," in Berlin, *Liberty,* ed. Henry Hardy (Oxford: Oxford University Press, 2002), 166–217. On Enlightenment constitutionalism, see Vincenzo Ferrone, *The Politics of Enlightenment: Republicanism, Constitutionalism, and the Rights of Man in Gaetano Filangieri,* trans. Sophus A. Reinert (London: Anthem, 2012). On a less constitutional form of "political liberty" identified with direct participation in government that still was influential in early modern Europe, see Quentin Skinner, *Hobbes and Republican Liberty* (Cambridge: Cambridge University Press, 2008).

62. Gassendi, *Three Discourses,* 229–230.

63. Hannah Arendt, *On Violence* (New York: Harvest, 1969), 10–11.

64. Particularly in wake of J. G. A. Pocock's influential *The Machiavellian Moment: Florentine Political Thought and the Atlantic Republican Tradition* (Princeton, NJ: Princeton University Press, 1975), whose main argument regarding wealth and virtue was reiterated forcefully in Pocock, "Virtues, Rights, and Manners: A Model for Historians of Political Thought," in *Virtue, Commerce, and History: Essays on Political Thought and History, Chiefly in the Eighteenth Century* (Cambridge: Cambridge University Press, 1985), 37–50, at 48; and Pocock, *Barbarism and Religion,* 6 vols. (Cambridge: Cambridge University Press, 1999–2015), 2:265. On the trope, see also Istvan Hont, "Free Trade and the Economic Limits to National Politics: Neo-Machiavellian Political Economy Reconsidered," in *Jealousy of Trade: International Competition and the Nation-State in Historical Perspective* (Cambridge, MA: Harvard University Press, 2005), 187–266. On this tradition as part of a longer preoccupation with autonomy, see Michael

Sonenscher, "Liberty, Autonomy, and Republican Historiography: Civic Humanism in Context," in *Markets, Morals, Politics: Jealousy of Trade and the History of Political Thought*, ed. Béla Kapossy, Isaac Nakhimovsky, Sophus A. Reinert, and Richard Whatmore (Cambridge, MA: Harvard University Press, 2018), 161–210.

65. See, among others, Reinert, *Translating Empire*, esp. 23, 138; Steve Pincus, "Neither Machiavellian Moment nor Possessive Individualism: Commercial Society and the Defenders of the English Commonwealth," *American Historical Review* 103 (1998): 703–736; Mark Jurdjevic, "Virtue, Commerce, and the Enduring Florentine Republican Moment: Reintegrating Italy into the Atlantic Republican Debate," *Journal of the History of Ideas* 62, no. 4 (2001): 721–743; Fonna Forman-Barzilai, *Adam Smith and the Circles of Sympathy: Cosmopolitanism and Moral Theory* (Cambridge: Cambridge University Press, 2010), 199–201.

66. A tradition explored in Victor Davis Hanson, *The Western Way of War: Infantry Battle in Classical Greece* (Berkeley: University of California Press, 1996).

67. On the gendering of virtue, see Judith Brown, *Immodest Acts: The Life of a Lesbian Nun in Renaissance Italy* (Oxford; Oxford University Press, 1986), 205; and Hanna Fenichel Pitkin, *Fortune Is a Woman: Gender and Politics in the Thought of Niccolò Machiavelli* (Berkeley: University of California Press, 1984). On "manliness" in this tradition, see Harvey C. Mansfield, *Manliness* (New Haven, CT: Yale University Press, 2006). For the Academy of Fisticuffs' own take on it, see Sebastiano Franci, "Difesa delle donne," in *Il Caffè*, 245–256.

68. On such definitionally relativistic arguments, see the entry on "If by whiskey . . ." in William Safire, *Safire's Political Dictionary* (Oxford: Oxford University Press, 2008), 337.

69. On such Polybian "politics of time," see Pocock, *Barbarism and Religion*, vol. 3; Sophus A. Reinert, "Lessons on the Rise and Fall of Great Powers: Conquest, Commerce, and Decline in Enlightenment Italy," *American Historical Review* 115, no. 5 (2010): 1395–1425.

70. A conceptual package dating back to the world described in Victor Davis Hanson, *The Other Greeks: The Family Farm and the Agrarian Roots of Western Civilization* (Berkeley: University of California Press, 1999).

71. Mandeville, *Fable of the Bees*. The Epicurean current in Enlightenment moral philosophy that fueled the development of political economy, particularly in the Augustinian inflection given it by Port Royale thinkers and elaborated by Pierre Bayle and Mandeville, has been explored in depth by Hundert, *The Enlightenment's Fable*, and more recently and divergently by Pierre Force, *Self-Interest before Adam Smith: A Genealogy of Economic Science* (Cambridge: Cambridge University Press, 2003); and Robertson, *The Case for the Enlightenment*. On contemporary Stoicism, see Christopher Brooke, *Philosophic Pride: Stoicism*

and Political Thought from Lipsius to Rousseau (Princeton, NJ: Princeton University Press, 2012). On the limits of the dichotomy between Epicureanism and Stoicism as it relates to early modern European political economy, see Gilbert Faccarello, "A Tale of Two Traditions: Pierre Force's *Self-Interest before Adam Smith*," *European Journal of the History of Economic Thought* 13, no. 4 (2006): 701–712.

72. Sebastiano Franci, "Osservazione sulla questione se il commercio corrompa i costumi e la morale," in *Il Caffè*, 655–661.

73. Alessandro Verri, "Alcune idee sulla filosofia morale" and "Discorso sulla felicità de" Romani," both in *Il Caffè*, 685–695, at 686, and 83–92, at 88.

74. Adam Ferguson, *An Essay on the History of Civil Society*, ed. Fania Oz-Salzberger (Cambridge: Cambridge University Press, 1995), on which see Ian McDaniel, *Adam Ferguson in the Scottish Enlightenment: The Roman Past and Europe's Future* (Cambridge, MA: Harvard University Press, 2013).

75. Lloyd, *Continuation*, 85, 88; and similarly Ferguson, *Essay on the History of Civil Society*, 214.

76. The classic work on the intellectual fertility of misreading remains Carlo Ginzburg, *The Cheese and the Worms: The Cosmos of a Sixteenth-Century Miller*, trans. Anne C. Tedeschi (Baltimore: Johns Hopkins University Press, 1980). For theoretical approaches, see Umberto Eco, *Diario minimo* (Milan: Mondadori, 1963), and Harold Bloom, *The Anxiety of Influence: A Theory of Poetry* (New York: Oxford University Press, 1973).

77. Pietro Verri, "Meditazioni sulla economia politica (Livorno 1772)," in *ENOPV*, vol. 2, pt. 2, 341–570, at 485, 542–545.

78. Ibid., 459.

79. Ibid., 401–404; emphasis in original. On this, see also Capra, *I progressi della ragione*, 371.

80. Verri, "Meditazioni," 475; emphasis in original.

81. Ibid., 393, 405.

82. Ibid., 396–397; Adam Smith, *An Inquiry into the Nature and Causes of the Wealth of Nations*, ed. Edwin Cannan, 2 vols. (Chicago: University of Chicago Press, 1976), 1:26.

83. Verri, "Meditazioni," 400.

84. Ibid.

85. Ibid., 427–433, 556.

86. Ibid.

87. The Roman dictators have cast a long shadow over Western political thought, perhaps culminating in Carl Schmitt's *Die Diktatur* (Berlin: Duncker und Humblot, 1928), on which see, among so much recent scholarship, Kaius Tuori, "Schmitt and the Sovereignty of Roman Dictators: From the Actualisation of the Past to the Recycling of Symbols," *History of European Ideas* 41, no. 1 (2016): 95–106.

88. Verri, "Meditazioni," 556–558. Alessandro Verri considered this phrase worthy of "Tacitus"; see his "[Osservazioni di Alessandro Verri sul manoscritto delle *Meditazioni*; lettera del 21 novembre 1770]," in *ENOPV*, vol. 2, pt. 2, 573–584, at 584.

89. Verri, "Meditazioni," 557.

90. "Estratto del Giornale di Pisa," in Verri, *ENOPV*, vol. 2, pt. 2, 594–607, at 606.

91. In a letter of September 1796, Verri apparently wrote that his soul had always been republican; quoted in Carlo Capra, "'La mia anima è sempre stata repubblicana': Pietro Verri da patrizio a cittadino," in *Pietro Verri e il suo tempo*, ed. Carlo Capra (Bologna: Cisalpino, 1999), 519–540, at 533–534. For beneficial despotism see among other places Pietro to Alessandro Verri, 6 January 1781, in *CV*, 11:522, and even more strongly in Pietro to Alessandro Verri, 19 September 1795, in *ENOPV*, 8:982–984, at 982: "una nazione spossata e pervertita come la nostra sgraziata Patria, non può avere alcun bene se non sotto un saggio e benefico dispotismo." On the political thought of the late Verri, see Capra, "'La mia anima'"; and Bartolo Angliani, *La lumaca e il cittadino: Pietro Verri dal benefico dispotismo alla rivoluzione* (Rome: Aracne Editrice, 2012).

92. Pietro Verri, "Lettera del filosofo N.N. al Monarca N.N.," in *ENOPV*, 6:845–847. This is the argument of Capra, *I progressi della ragione*, 599.

93. Carli in [Pietro Verri], *Meditazioni sulla economia politica con annotazioni* (Venice: [Pasquale], 1771), 67.

94. Gian Rinaldo Carli to Wenzel Anton von Kaunitz Rittberg, 7 April 1770, in Francesco De Stefano, *G. R. Carli (1720–1795): Contributo alla storia delle origini del Risorgimento italiano* (Milan: Società tipografica modenese, 1942), 261–263, at 262, echoing Antonio Genovesi, *Storia del commercio della Gran Bretagna*, 3 vols. (Naples: Gessari, 1757–1758), 1:292–293n, on which see Sophus A. Reinert, *Translating Empire: Emulation and the Origins of Political Economy* (Cambridge, MA: Harvard University Press, 2011), 209.

95. Kaunitz to Carli, in De Stefano, *G. R. Carli*, 264–265.

96. Carli in [Verri], *Meditazioni sulla economia politica con annotazioni*, 36.

97. Verri, "Meditazioni," 394; emphasis in original.

98. It is worth mentioning that to dogmatic free traders of the mid-nineteenth century, Verri and Beccaria were both clearly "protectionists"; see Alberto Errera, "Una Nuova Pagina della vita di Cesare Beccaria: Capitolo III. L'economia politica a Milano nel secolo XVIII," *L'Economista d'Italia* 11, no. 2 (10 January 1878): 19–20.

99. Lloyd, *Essay on the Theory of Money*, iv–viii; Verri, "Meditazioni," 399–400.

100. John Locke, *Two Treatises of Government*, ed. Peter Laslett (Cambridge: Cambridge University Press, 1988), 292–293.

101. David Hume, *Political Essays*, ed. Knud Haakonssen (Cambridge: Cambridge University Press, 1994), 115–125; John Locke, *Some Considerations of the Consequences of the Lowering of Interest, and Raising the Value of Money* (London: Awnsham and Churchill, 1692), 6. On Hume's influence on the Academy of Fisticuffs, see still Marialuisa Baldi, *David Hume nel Settecento italiano: Filosofia ed economia* (Florence: La Nuova Italia, 1983), 39–44.

102. Pietro Verri to Alessandro Verri, 22 April 1781, in *CV*, 11:304. Correspondence from the previous year indicates that Pietro had partially abandoned the study of political economy by the time he reminisced: "I have not even read anything on *economia pubblica* for ten years now," he wrote his brother again on 15 January 1780, adding ,"What little I am capable of thinking on *economia pubblica*, I have thought," in *CV*, 11:13–14.

103. Piero Sraffa, "Notes on Pietro Verri, William [*sic*] F. Lloyd," Wren Library, Trinity College, University of Cambridge, Cambridge, UK, *Sraffa D1 / 10 (pre 1928)*, fol. 19. On Sraffa and his legacy, see Alessandro Roncaglia, *Sraffa: La biografia, l'opera, le scuole* (Bari: Laterza, 1999). On his inadequately studied "cafeteria group," see Sten Anderson, *Filosofen som inte ville tala: Ett personligt porträtt av Ludwig Wittgenstein* (Stockholm: Norstedts, 2012), 351–355. For a similar take on "pure economics," see Milton Friedman, "The Methodology of Positive Economics," in *Essays in Positive Economics* (Chicago: University of Chicago Press, 1953), 3–43, on which see the essays in Robert A. Cord and J. Daniel Hammond, eds., *Milton Friedman: Contributions to Economics and Public Policy* (Oxford: Oxford University Press, 2016).

104. Pietro Verri, "Assioma: Il denaro è la merce universale," in *ENOPV*, vol. 2, pt. 2, 235–245.

105. Sraffa, "Notes on Pietro Verri, William [*sic*] F. Lloyd," fol. 6. For his copy, see Giancarlo de Vivo, ed., *Catalogue of the Library of Piero Sraffa* (Milan: Fondazione Mattioli, and Turin: Fondazione Einaudi, 2014), 605–606, entry 6113.

106. In Pietro Verri, *Meditazioni sulla economia politica*, 6th ed., published with an appendix by Paolo Frisi, "Estratto del libro intitolato *An Essay on the Theory of Money*; London 1771 [by Henry Lloyd]" (Livorno: Nella Stamperia dell'Enciclopedia, 1772), 4, 237–238, also republished in *ENOPV*, vol. 2, pt. 2, 561–568.

107. Verri, "Meditazioni," 474; and similarly Alfonso Longo, "Osservazioni su i fedecommessi," in *Il Caffè*, 115–132, at 119. On "velocity" in today's parlance, see, for example, N. Gregory Mankiw, *Principles of Economics*, 6th ed. (Mason, OH: Cengage Learning, 2008), 650–652.

108. Lloyd, *Essay on the Theory of Money*, 27–31. Sraffa thought of equating Lloyd's theory of circulation with the modern concept of "velocity" in Sraffa, "Notes

on Pietro Verri, William [*sic*] F. Lloyd," fol. 8r. Lloyd's emphasis on circulation, like many other aspects of his political economy (including his affiliation with the House of Stuart), is remarkably reminiscent of the work of James Steuart. Not really being an author who neglects to mention his sources, however, it is striking that Steuart never seems to make an appearance in Lloyd's manuscripts. Although an exploration of their relationship, or even why one might be lacking, lies beyond the scope of the present argument, it may prove a fruitful field of inquiry in the future.

109. Lloyd, *Essay on the Theory of Money*, viii, 17–18; emphasis in original.

110. Ibid., 35; emphasis in original, plausibly drawing on Petty, *Political Arithmetick*, 65–69.

111. Verri, "Meditazioni," 493–495. For a more recent meditation on the strategies and predicaments of small industrial states, see Peter J. Katzenstein, *Small States in World Markets: Industrial Policy in Europe* (Ithaca, NY: Cornell University Press, 1985). For a thoughtful look at the larger question at the time of the Academy of Fisticuffs, see Richard Whatmore, *Against War and Empire: Geneva, Britain, and France in the Eighteenth Century* (New Haven, CT: Yale University Press, 2012).

112. See Ronald L. Meek's still-relevant *Social Science and the Ignoble Savage* (Cambridge: Cambridge University Press, 1976); Istvan Hont, "The Language of Sociability and Commerce: Samuel Pufendorf and the Theoretical Foundations of the 'Four Stages' Theory," in *Jealousy of Trade*, 159–184, at 160.

113. Lloyd, *Essay on the Theory of Money*, ii–iv.

114. Ibid., 136.

115. Verri, "Meditazioni," 400.

116. Locke, *Some Considerations of the Consequences*, 29.

117. Lloyd, *Essay on the Theory of Money*, 22–23.

118. It is worth noting that Alessandro Verri had suggested something similar in his "Discourse on the Happiness of the Romans," in *Il Caffè*, 83–92, 90: "After more than a century of massacres, under Augustus Rome found a peace spawned by the impotence to be free. It was a total lack of motion."

119. Lloyd, *Essay on the English Constitution*, 63–64.

120. Lloyd, *Essay on the Theory of Money*, 148; Lloyd, *Essay on the Constitution*, 71; Lloyd, *Political and Military Rhapsody*, 151; Verri, "Meditazioni," 422.

121. Rousseau, "Of the Social Contract," 84.

122. Lloyd, *Essay on the English Constitution*, 26–27; Verri, "Meditazioni," 423.

123. Lloyd, *Essay on the English Constitution*, 103.

124. Verri, "Meditazioni," 423–424, perhaps drawing on David Hume, "Of Commerce," in *Political Essays*, ed. Knud Haakonssen (Cambridge: Cambridge University Press, 1994), 93–104, at 102. On the Gini coefficient, see still Corrado Gini, *Variabilità e mutabilità* (Bologna: Tipografia Cuppini, 1912), on the original con-

text of which see Francesco Cassata, *Building the New Man: Racial Science and Genetics in Twentieth-Century Italy,* trans. Erin O'Loughlin (Budapest: Central European University Press, 2011), 31–42.

125. Lloyd, *Essay on the English Constitution,* 8–10, 17; Benjamin Franklin, "Explanatory Remarks on the Assembly's Resolves," 29 March 1764, in *The Papers of Benjamin Franklin,* ed. Leonard W. Labaree et al., 41 vols. (New Haven, CT: Yale University Press, 1959–2014), 11:134–144, at 143–144; Hobbes, *Leviathan,* 5; Harrington, *The Common-Wealth of Oceana* (London: Streater, 1656), 3, discussed in Matthew Wren, *Considerations on Harrington's Common-Wealth of Oceana* (London: Gellybrand, 1657), 12; Smith, *Wealth of Nations,* 1:35.

126. Lloyd, *Essay on the English Constitution,* 12.

127. Ibid., 24.

128. Verri, "Meditazioni," 426; emphasis in original.

129. Lloyd, *Essay on the English Constitution,* 38. The dictum was first formulated in Cicero, *Laws* III.iii.8. On the ambiguity of this idiom, see, among others, Michael Oakeshott, *The Politics of Faith and the Politics of Scepticism* (New Haven, CT: Yale University Press, 1996) (posthumously published, probably written in the 1950s), 39–42. The term is crucial for Quentin Skinner's conception of a Neo-Roman political tradition in early modern England, for which see, for example, his "Classical Liberty, Renaissance Translation, and the English Civil War," in *Visions of Politics,* 3 vols. (Cambridge: Cambridge University Press, 2002), 2:308–342. For other treatments of the term's ambiguity, from different perspectives, see Peter N. Miller, *Defining the Common Good: Empire, Religion and Philosophy in Eighteenth-Century Britain* (Cambridge: Cambridge University Press, 1993), esp. 39–40; and Hont, *Jealousy of Trade,* 128. For this kind of argument, see also David Hume, "Of Justice," in *Essays and Treatises on Several Subjects,* new ed., 2 vols. (London: Cadell et al., 1788), 2:215–234, at 220; Smith, *Wealth of Nations,* 2:42.

130. Lloyd, *Essay on the English Constitution,* 24.

131. Ibid., 43, 49–50, 67, 93.

132. Ibid., 75.

133. Ibid., 65; Beccaria, *On Crimes and Punishments,* 35.

134. Lloyd, *Essay on the English Constitution,* 65. On the centrality of capital punishment to English criminal law, see, among others, the classic *Albion's Fatal Tree: Crime and Society in Eighteenth Century England,* ed. Douglas Hay et al. (New York: Pantheon, 1976).

135. Lloyd, *Essay on the English Constitution,* 66.

136. Montesquieu, *The Spirit of the Laws,* ed. Anne M. Cohler, Basia C. Miller, and Harold S. Stone (Cambridge: Cambridge University Press, 1989), 403.

137. Lloyd, *Essay on the English Constitution,* 107n–108n; Lloyd, *Essay on the Theory of Money,* 81–86.

138. Anonymous review of "Meditazioni sulla economia politica; sesta edizione, accresciuta dall'autore, Livorno, Stamperia dell'Enciclopedia, 1772," *Nuovo giornale de' letterati d'Italia,*" May–June, 1773, 3:228–283, at 237.

139. Verri, *Meditazioni sulla economia politica,* 246, also in *ENOPV,* vol. 2, pt. 2, 565.

140. Frisi, "Estratto del libro," 237–253, also in *ENOPV,* vol. 2, pt. 2, 561–568.

141. Verri, *Meditazioni sulla economia politica,* 134; emphasis in original, also in *ENOPV,* vol. 2, pt. 2, 492n.

142. Tubaro, "Un'esperienza peculiare," 209. The only clear predecessor in the field of political economy would be Daniel Bernoulli's work on risk and marginal utility; see his "Specimen Theoriae Novae de Mensura Sortis," *Commentarii Academiae Scientiarum Imperialis Petropolitanae,* vol. 5 (1738): 175–192; for a translation of which, see "Exposition of a New Theory on the Measurement of Risk," trans. Louise Sommer, *Econometrica* 22, no. 1 (1954): 23–36. On this, see also David A. Moss, *When All Else Fails: Government as the Ultimate Risk Manager* (Cambridge, MA: Harvard University Press, 2002), 25–26.

143. Sraffa, "Notes on Pietro Verri, William [sic] F. Lloyd," fol. 7.

144. Lloyd, *Essay on the Theory of Money,* viii, 17–18. For an introduction to the later but related field of complexity economics, see W. Brian Arthur, *Complexity and the Economy* (Oxford: Oxford University Press, 2014); and, from a perspective of global comparative development that might have appealed to the Academy of Fisticuffs, see Ricardo Hausmann et al., *The Atlas of Economic Complexity: Mapping Paths to Prosperity* (Cambridge, MA: MIT Press, 2013).

145. Voltaire, *Letters Concerning the English Nation* (London: C. Davis, 1733), "Letter X on Trade," 69–72; emphasis in original.

146. See, among others on this, Verri, "Meditazioni" and Sebastiano Franci, "Alcuni pensieri," in *Il Caffè,* 143–150, at 144.

147. Lloyd, *Essay on the Theory of Money,* 25. The best analysis of this problem in early modern European political economy is found in the works of Steven L. Kaplan; see Kaplan, *Bread, Politics and Political Economy in the Reign of Louis XV,* 2nd ed. (London: Anthem, 2015). For Lloyd as for so many others, bread was clearly a matter of reason of state; see Lloyd, *Political and Military Rhapsody,* 10.

148. Lloyd, *Essay on the English Constitution,* 35. On the myths of Sully and Colbert at the time, see, among others, Franco Venturi, "Scottish Echoes in Eighteenth-Century Italy," in *Wealth and Virtue: The Shaping of Political Economy in the Scottish Enlightenment,* ed. Istvan Hont and Michael Ignatieff (Cambridge: Cambridge University Press, 1986), 345–362, at 358; Philippe Minard, *La fortune du colbertisme: État et industrie dans la France des Lumières* (Paris: Fayard, 1998); and Laurent Avezou, *Sully à travers l'histoire: Les avatars d'un mythe politique* (Paris: École des Chartes, 2001), with comparisons between the two running throughout.

149. Montesquieu, *Spirit of the Laws*, 356; David Hume, "Of the Jealousy of Trade," in Hume, *Political Essays*, 150–153, on which see, discussed in the grandest manner, Hont, *Jealousy of Trade*; and Hont, "The 'Rich Country–Poor Country' Debate Revisited: The Irish Origins and French Reception of the Hume Paradox," in *David Hume's Political Economy*, ed. Carl Wennerlind and Margaret Schabas (London: Routledge, 2008), 243–322; Reinert, *Translating Empire*, 221–222.

150. Lloyd, *Essay on the Theory of Money*, 89–90.

151. Petty, *Political Arithmetick*, 65–67.

152. Lloyd, *Essay on the English Constitution*, 30, 37–38, 77.

153. Lloyd, *Continuation*, 87; Lloyd, *Political and Military Rhapsody*, 22–23.

154. Lloyd, *Essai sur l'homme*, Fitzwilliam, *Henry Lloyd Papers*, 32.

155. In this sense, Lloyd's republicanism aligns with that of Machiavelli, whom he cites several times. Lloyd's knowledge of Machiavellian republicanism may have derived from more familiar sources, such as Pierre Bayle, Diderot's article in the *Encyclopédie*, or Rousseau's *Contrat Social*, all of whom redeemed Machiavelli as a republican in Lloyd's lifetime, on which see among others Maurizio Viroli, *Machiavelli* (Oxford: Oxford University Press, 1998), 115.

156. Montesquieu, *Spirit of the Laws*, 97; Lloyd, *Essay on the Theory of Money*, 76, 113; Lloyd, *Continuation*, 82; Lloyd, *Political and Military Rhapsody*, 25.

157. Lloyd, *Essay on the theory of Money*, 50; Hume, *Political Essays*, 111. It should be noted that Lloyd's explanation for the fall of Rome probably drew on a wide literature existing in the period, dating back at least to Montesquieu, *Reflections on the Causes of the Grandeur and Declension of the Romans* (London, 1734). Although he never cited the Baron von Bielfeld, who was a military political economist like himself, Lloyd's argument appears as one of the possible causes of "the decadence of nations" offered in his best-selling work; see Jacob Friedrich von Bielfeld, *Institutions politiques* (The Hague: Pierre Gosse Jr., 1760), 309–338. On the popularity of Bielfeld's opus among European publishers, see see Erik S. Reinert, Kenneth Carpenter, Fernanda Reinert, and Sophus A. Reinert, "80 Economic Bestsellers before 1850: A Fresh Look at the History of Economic Thought," *The Other Canon Foundation and Tallinn University of Technology Working Papers in Technology Governance and Economic Dynamics*, paper no. 74 (2017), 61–64.

158. Lloyd, *Essai philosophique sur les Gouvernements*, Fitzwilliam, *Henry Lloyd Papers*, 8; see also Venturi, *Le vite incrociate*, 38; Venturi, "Le avventure," 393–394.

159. He was remarkably coherent in expressing these thoughts; see Lloyd, *History of the Late War*, 88; Lloyd, *Essay on the English Constitution*, 102; Lloyd, *Continuation*, 89.

160. Montesquieu, *Spirit of the Laws*, 96, 100; Helvétius, *De l'Esprit*, 10; Pietro Verri, "Considerazioni sul lusso," in *Il Caffè*, 1:155–162, at 161.

161. Lloyd, *Essay on the Theory of Money*, 61.

162. Rousseau, "Of the Social Contract," 122.

163. Harrington, *Oceana*, 5; Wren, *Considerations*, 14–15, with explicit reference to Harvey's theory of circulation of blood at 9.

164. J. G. A. Pocock, "Cambridge Paradigms and Scotch Philosophers: A Study of the Relations between the Civic Humanist and the Civil Jurisprudential Interpretations of Eighteenth-Century Social Thought," in Hont and Ignatieff, *Wealth and Virtue*, 235–252, at 251.

165. The literature on early modern "science" is, needless to say, vast, but see, in this context, Vincenzo Ferrone, *Una scienza per l'uomo: Illuminismo e Rivoluzione scientifica nell'Europa del Settecento* (Turin: UTET, 2007); and Steven Shapin's classic *The Scientific Revolution* (Chicago: University of Chicago Press, 1998).

166. Montesquieu, *Spirit of the Laws*, 137; Verri, "Meditazioni," 491–492. On the difficulties of calculating such balances of power, see more recently Henry Kissinger, *World Order* (New York: Penguin, 2014), 371.

167. Lloyd, *Essay on the English Constitution*, 104; emphasis in original. Lloyd presented his analysis of *absolute force* as a contribution to a contemporary controversy: myriads of pamphlets portended the immediate rise or decline of England in relation to France; see ibid., 100–101, and Lloyd, *Essay on the Theory of Money*, 46–49; Speelman, *Henry Lloyd*, 76. Notable examples of this vast literature are the anonymous *A letter to a member of the honourable House of Commons, on the present important crisis of national affairs* (London: W. Morgan, 1762); William Knox, *The Present State of the Nation; Particularly with Respect to its Trade, Finances, &c &c.* (London: J. Almon, 1768); Thomas Mortimer, *The National Debt no National Grievance; Or the Real State of the Nation . . .* (London: J. Wilkie, 1768); Edmund Burke, *Observations on the Late State of the Nation* (London: J. Doodsley, 1769); all of which build on an earlier Williamite literature exemplified by the likes of Petty, *Political Arithmetick*, 64–86, and John Cary, *An Essay on the State of England* (Bristol, England: W. Bonny, 1695). The mercantilist and director of the English East India Company Matthew Decker, grandfather of Lloyd's friend Fitzwilliam, wrote one of the classic pamphlets on this argument; see Decker, *An Essay on the Causes of the Decline of the Foreign Trade; Consequently of the Value of the Lands of Britain, and of the Means to Restore Both* (London: George Faulkner, 1749).

168. On the power politics of war financing at the time, see still John Brewer, *The Sinews of Power: War, Money and the English State, 1688–1783* (Cambridge, MA: Harvard University Press, 1988).

169. Emer de Vattel, *The Law of Nations*, ed. Béla Kapossy and Richard Whatmore (Indianapolis: Liberty Fund, 2008), 198 [1.XIV.178].

170. Lloyd, *Essay on the Theory of Money*, 156.

171. Vattel, *The Law of Nations*, 202 [1.XIV.185].

172. Lloyd, *Essay on the Theory of Money*, 50; Lloyd, *Military and Political Rhapsody*, 21–25.

173. Helvétius, *De l'Esprit*, 15nH.

174. Though, it must be said, not all that different from modern "threat matrixes" dividing "power," equated with an army or navy, by "distance" from one's country; see, for example, Michael W. Doyle, *Ways of War and Peace: Realism, Liberalism, and Socialism* (New York: W. W. Norton, 1997), 184–186.

175. Deirdre N. McCloskey, *Knowledge and Persuasion in Economics* (Cambridge: Cambridge University Press, 1994), 163.

176. Montesquieu, *Persian Letters* (London: Penguin, 1993), 240, discussed in Tubaro, "Un'esperienza," 217.

177. E.g., William B. Provine, "Geneticists and the Biology of Race Crossing," *Science* 182, no. 4114 (1973): 790–796, at 796; Deirdre McCloskey, *The Rhetoric of Economics*, 2nd ed. (Madison: University of Wisconsin Press, 1998); McCloskey, *Knowledge and Persuasion in Economics*.

178. Henry Lloyd, *On Artillery*, Fitzwilliam, *Henry Lloyd Papers*, 3–4. See also, in a vein similar to Lloyd's dual interest in political economy and artillery, Judy L. Klein, *Statistical Visions in Time: A History of Time-Series Analysis, 1662–1938* (Cambridge: Cambridge University Press, 1997), for the "two-way" relationship between early modern statistics and ballistics.

179. J. G. A. Pocock, "The Varieties of Whiggism from Exclusion to Reform: A History of Ideology and Discourse," in *Virtue, Commerce, and History*, 215–310, 237.

180. Pietro Verri to Alessandro Verri, 13 September 1769, in *CV*, 3:56.

181. *Giornale de' letterati di Pisa*, vol. 4 (1771), 81–83; also "Estratto del Giornale di Pisa."

182. Verri, "Meditazioni," 504.

183. Lloyd, *Continuation*, vii–viii.

184. E.g., Rees, "Review."

185. [Gian-Rinaldo Carli], *Meditazioni sulla economia stercoraria ossia critica al libro intitolato Meditazioni sulla economia pubblica, 5 ottobre 1772*, Biblioteca Ambrosiana, Milan, Italy (hereafter cited as Ambrosiana), item 12 [18 in old classification system] of *X. 283 inf. Miscellanea*.

186. Pietro Verri immediately suspected Carli to be the author in his letter to Alessandro Verri, 5 December 1772, in *CV*, 5:224, while the latter proposed it might be their old nemesis Ferdinando Facchinei in his reply of 12 December 1772, in *CV*, 5:230–231. Indeed, Facchinei had criticized Beccaria's mathematical method of "lines," "numbers," and "equations" in his *Note ed osservazioni sul libro intitolato "Dei delitti e delle pene"* ([Venice]: n.p., 1765), 92. He was even clearer, calling Beccaria an "algebrist," in his unpublished "Brevi note da porsi in pie' di pagina al

libro dei Delitti e delle pene 1764," Archivio di Stato di Venezia, Venice, Italy, *Miscellanea di atti diversi manoscritti*, no. 71, fols. 12v, 16r. Louise d'Épinay, for one, wrote that Parisians guessed the author to be Ferdinando Galiani, in her letter to him of 26 December 1772, in Louise d'Épinay and Ferdinando Galiani, *Epistolario*, ed. Stefano Rapisarda (Palermo: Sellerio Editore, 1996), 600–602, at 601, plausibly inspired by Galiani's *Dialogues sur le commerce des blés* (Paris, 1770). For musings around the authorship, see also Salvatore Rotta, *L'illuminismo a Genova: Lettere di P. P. Celesia a F. Galiani*, 2 vols. (Florence: La Nuova Italia, 1974), 2:141–142. An old marginal annotation on the lower right-hand corner of 1r on the Ambrosiana copy of the manuscript suggests its author "probably" was "Gian-Rinaldo Carli."

187. Franco Venturi, *Settecento riformatore*, 5 vols. in 7 (Turin: Einaudi, 1969–1990), vol. 5, pt. 1, 568–569n247; and on the pamphlet more generally see 568–570; and Rotta, *L'Illuminismo a Genova*, 2:141–145.

188. [Carli], *Meditazioni sulla economia stercoraria*, 2r, 3v.

189. Pietro to Alessandro Verri, 5 December 1772, in *CV*, 5:224.

190. [Carli], *Meditazioni sulla economia stercoraria*, 2r, referencing Cicero, *De Senectute*, 54, in turn referencing Hesiod, *Work and Days*.

191. [Carli], *Meditazioni sulla economia stercoraria*, 3r; emphasis in original.

192. Ibid.

193. Ibid., 4r–4v. On the *Tableau*, see François Quesnay, *Tableau Économique*, ed. Marguerite Kuczynski and Ronald L. Meek (London: Macmillan, 1972).

194. On contemporary Sinophilia, and the Physiocrat Quesnay's fame as "the Confucius of Europe," see Ashley Eva Millar, *A Singular Case: Debating China's Political Economy in the European Enlightenment* (Montreal: McGill–Queen's University Press, 2017), 141–142.

195. [Carli], *Meditazioni sulla economia stercoraria*, 5r–5v; emphasis in original.

196. Anon., "Meditazioni sulla economia politica sesta edizione, accresciuta dall'autore, Livorno, Stamperia dell'Enciclopedia, 1772," *Nuovo giornale de' letterati d'Italia*," May–June 1773, 3:228–283, at 245.

197. Ignazio Radicati di Cocconato to Paolo Frisi, 7 March 1772, Ambrosiana, Mss. Y. 149 sup. F. 70v, discovered by Tubaro, "Un'esperienza," 215.

198. Jean le Rond d'Alembert, "Ecole, Philosophie de l," in *Encyclopédie . . .* , ed. Denis Diderot and Jean le Rond d'Alembert, 28 vols. (Paris: Briasson et al., 1751–1772), 5:303–304, at 304.

199. See, among others, Laurits Vilhelm Birch, "Moderne Scholastik: Eine kritische Darstellung der Böhm-Bawerkschen Theorie," *Weltwirtschaftliches Archiv* 24, no. 2 (1926): 198–227; Robert Heilbroner and William Milberg, *The Crisis of Vision in Modern Economic Thought* (Cambridge: Cambridge University Press, 1995), discussed in Uskali Mäki, "The Dismal Queen of the Social Sciences," in *Fact and Fiction in Economics: Models, Realism and Social Construction*, ed. Uskali Mäki

(Cambridge: Cambridge University Press, 2002), 3–32, at 5; Mark Blaug, "Ugly Currents in Modern Economics," in Mäki, *Fact and Fiction*, 35–56, at 36; Robert H. Nelson, "Scholasticism versus Pietism: The Battle for the Soul of Economics," *Econ Journal Watch* 1, no. 3 (2004): 473–497. On these debates, see further Erik S. Reinert, "Full Circle: Economics from Scholasticism through Innovation and Back into Mathematical Scholasticism," *Journal of Economic Studies* 27, nos. 4–5 (2000): 364–376; Wolfgang Drechsler, "On the Possibility of Quantitative-Mathematical Social Science, Chiefly Economics," *Journal of Economic Studies* 27, nos. 4–5 (2000): 246–259; Edward Fullbrook, ed., *The Crisis in Economics: The Post-Autistic Economics Movement—The First 600 Days* (London: Routledge, 2003). For a clear-headed evaluation, see Roger E. Backhouse, *The Puzzle of Modern Economics: Science or Ideology?* (Cambridge: Cambridge University Press, 2010).

200. Thomas Piketty, *Capital in the Twenty-First Century*, trans. Arthur Goldhammer (Cambridge, MA: Harvard University Press, 2014), 32.

201. Johann Jacob Meyen, *Wie kommt es, dass die Oekonomie bisher so wenig Vortheile der Physik und Mathematik gewonnen hat; und wie kann man diese Wissenschaften zum gemeinen Nutzen in die Oekonomie einführen, und von dieser Verbindung auf Grundsätze kommen, die in die Ausübung brauchbar sind?* (Berlin: Haude und Spener, 1770).

202. See anon., "Se vi sia ora qualche eccesso nell'uso, che vuol farsi del calcolo," in *Filosofia e cultura a Mantova nella seconda metà del Settecento: I manoscritti filosofici dell'Accademia Virgiliana*, ed. Marialuisa Baldi (Florence: La Nuova Italia, 1979), 151–196.

203. E. Roy Weintraub, *How Economics Became a Mathematical Science* (Durham, NC: Duke University Press, 2002); Geoffrey Hodgson, *How Economics Forgot History: The Problem of Historical Specificity in Social Science* (London: Routledge, 2001), 174; Philip Mirowski, *Machine Dreams: Economics Becomes a Cyborg Science* (Cambridge: Cambridge University Press, 2001), 9–10.

204. William Shakespeare, *The Tragedy of Othello, the Moor of Venice*, ed. Tucker Brooke and Lawrence Mason (New Haven, CT: Yale University Press, 1947), act 1, lines 19–26, p. 10.

205. "Old New York Coffee-Houses," *Harper's New Monthly Magazine*, March 1882, 481–499, at 490.

4. Achtung! Banditi!

1. *Achtung! Banditi!*, directed by Carlo Lizzani (Genoa: Cooperativa Spettatori Produttori Cinematografici, 1951), on which see Eligio Imarisio, ed., *Achtung! Banditi! Parole per film* (Recco: Le Mani, 2010).

2. See, for the early use of this expression, Michael Broers, *Napoleon's Other War: Bandits, Rebels and Their Pursuers in the Age of Revolutions* (Oxford: Peter Lang, 2010), 8; for its use in the context of Nazi Europe, see Philip W. Blood, *Hitler's Bandit Hunters: The SS and the Nazi Occupation of Europe* (Washington, DC: Potomac Books, 2006), xvi.

3. Max Weber, "The Profession and Vocation of Politics," in Weber, *Political Writings*, ed. Peter Lassman and Ronald Speirs (Cambridge: Cambridge University Press, 1994), 309–369, at 310–311; emphasis in original.

4. See the immense arc from Karl Polanyi, *The Great Transformation: The Political and Economic Origins of Our Time*, ed. Fred Block, intro. Joseph E. Stiglitz (Boston: Beacon Press, 2001), esp. 60, 66, 71; to Bernard E. Harcourt, *The Illusion of Free Markets: Punishment and the Myth of Natural Order* (Cambridge, MA: Harvard University Press, 2011), esp. 242; Bruce R. Scott, *Capitalism: Its Origins and Evolution as a System of Governance* (Heidelberg: Springer, 2011), 178–179; and Steven L. Kaplan, *The Stakes of Regulation: Perspectives on "Bread, Politics, and Political Economy" Forty Years Later* (London: Anthem, 2015).

5. Annabel S. Brett, *Changes of State: Nature and the Limits of the City in Early Modern Natural Law* (Princeton, NJ: Princeton University Press, 2011), 1, 3, 5

6. On the multiplicity of actors involved in early modern border-formation, see Tamar Herzog, *Frontiers of Possession: Spain and Portugal in Europe and the Americas* (Cambridge, MA: Harvard University Press, 2015), esp. 262; and, for an oceanic perspective, Renaud Morieux, *The Channel: England, France and the Construction of a Maritime Border in the Eighteenth Century* (Cambridge: Cambridge University Press, 2016), esp. 328. On the inherent fragility of such territorial legitimations, see Istvan Hont, *Jealousy of Trade: International Competition and the Nation-State in Historical Perspective* (Cambridge, MA: Harvard University Press, 2005), 451.

7. On Enlightenment banditry through the lens of smuggling, see Michael Kwass, *Contraband: Louis Mandrin and the Making of a Global Underground* (Cambridge, MA: Harvard University Press, 2014). On banditry and borders, see also Rosario Villari, "Conclusioni," in *Banditismi mediterranei: Secoli XVI–XVII*, ed. Francesco Manconi (Rome: Carocci, 2003), 413–415, at 415.

8. Henri Pirenne, *Economic and Social History of Medieval Europe* (New York: Harcourt, Brace, 1937), 216–217; Saskia Sassen, *Territory, Authority, Rights: From Medieval to Global Assemblages* (Princeton, NJ: Princeton University Press, 2006), 53, and 57 for a fleeting reference to the existence of pirates and robbers; Michael Mann, "The Autonomous Power of the State: Its Origins, Mechanisms and Results," *Archives européennes de sociologie* 25 (1984): 185–213; Mann, "Infrastructural Power Revisited," *Studies in Comparative International Development* 43, nos. 3–4 (2008): 355–365.

9. Bartolomeo Intieri to Antonio Cocchi, Napoli, 8 August 1752, Archivio Baldasseroni Corsini, Florence, Italy, 290/4, 1r. On Genovesi, see Sophus A. Reinert, *Translating Empire: Emulation and the Origins of Political Economy* (Cambridge, MA: Harvard University Press, 2011), 186–232. On the concept of *economia civile* in contemporary Italian and more widely Catholic economics, see, for a foundational statement, Stefano Zamagni and Luigino Bruni, *Economia civile: Efficienza, equità, felicità pubblica* (Bologna: Il Mulino, 2004).

10. The identification of this current with a refusal to accept the dichotomies of libertarianism and Marxism, and the antinomy "state-market," valuably paves the way for a more historical and indeed realist approach to political economy; see Stefano Zamagni interviewed by Nicola Curci, *Economia ed etica: La crisi e la sfida dell'economia civile* (Brescia: Editrice "La scuola," 2009), 72, 76.

11. For one particularly clear case of conceptual and terminological overlap, compare the various definitions of Beccaria's university chair in Wenzel Anton von Kaunitz-Rietberg to Karl Joseph von Firmian, 16 November 1767, in Barbara Costa, "'Un regolare sistema per la progressione degli studi': Il ruolo di Gian Rinaldo Carli nella riforma degli studi e della censura (1765–1775)," in *Con la ragione e col cuore: Studi dedicati a Carlo Capra*, ed. Stefano Levati and Marco Meriggi (Milan: Franco Angeli, 2008), 263–288, at 272; and Kaunitz-Rietberg to Firmian, 5 December 1768, in the voluminous Haus-, Hof- und Staatsarchiv, Österreichisches Staatsarchiv, Vienna, Austria, *Korrespondenz Lombardei 124*, 5r. Compare further to Gian Rinaldo Carli, "Piano per la cattedra di *Scienze Camerali* o sia di *Economia Civile*," 14 April 1768, Archivio di Stato di Milano, Milan, Italy (hereafter cited as ASM), *Autografi, no. 164, Uomini celebri: Cesare Beccaria*; and in Angelo Mauri, "La cattedra di Cesare Beccaria," *Archivio storico italiano* 60 (1933): 199–262, at 233–235; but see also Antonio Trampus, "Riforme politiche e 'pubblica felicità' negli scritti di Carli sul problema dell'educazione," *Quaderni Istriani: Contributi per la storia contemporanea della Venezia Giulia*, nos. 5–6 (1991–1992): 13–40, at 32–34. Not that there were not clearly articulated arguments that Beccaria's chair was in one thing rather than another; see the example of Giuseppe [Joseph von] Sperges to Cesare Beccaria, 27 March 1769, in *Edizione Nazionale delle Opere di Cesare Beccaria*, ed. Luigi Firpo and Gianni Francioni, 16 vols. in 17 (Milan: Mediobanca, 1984–2015) (hereafter cited as ENOCB), 5:47–48, suggesting Beccaria did not really teach "cameralism" at all; on which see Franz Pascher, "Freiherr Joseph von Sperges auf Palenz und Reisdorf," PhD diss., University of Vienna, 1965, e-dissertation with altered pagination (2009),109. The chair was simply called "The Chair of Economics" in Giambattista Vasco to [Firmian?], 9 May 1771, ASM, *Autografi, no. 164, Uomini celebri: Cesare Beccaria*, fol. 1r, a most curious letter essentially suggesting that Beccaria should be fired and

he himself given the chair. Alberto Errera, "Una nuova pagina della vita di Cesare Beccaria," *Memorie del Reale Istituto Lombardo di Scienze e Lettere* 12 (1876): 161–222, at 163, attributed the letter to "Tommaso Vasco," the assumed name of Giambattista Vasco once he joined the Dominican Order. This fits with the author's mention of having written a recent work on "Peasants," which may have been *La felicità pubblica considerata nei coltivatori di terre proprie* (Brescia: Rizzardi, 1769). On this Vasco, see Marrocco, *Giambattista Vasco* (Turin: Fondazione Luigi Einaudi, 1978).

12. See, for example, Pasquale Pasquino, "Theatrum Politicum: The Genealogy of Capital—Police and the State of Prosperity," in *The Foucault Effect: Studies in Governmentality; with Two Lectures by and an Interview with Michel Foucault,* ed. Graham Burchell, Colin Gordon, and Peter Miller (Chicago: University of Chicago Press, 1991), 105–118.

13. See, among many others, Joel S. Migdal, *Strong Societies and Weak States: State-Society Relations and State Capabilities in the Third World* (Princeton, NJ: Princeton University Press, 1988). As such, the fundamental question in James Scott, *Seeing Like a State: How Certain Schemes to Improve the Human Condition Have Failed* (New Haven, CT: Yale University Press, 1998)—"How does the state get a handle on the society?" (184)—is not always historically appropriate.

14. A point that is often easy to forget in light of Hegel's subsequent work; see Stuart Elden, *The Birth of Territory* (Chicago: University of Chicago Press, 2013), esp. 1.

15. Cicero, *De re publica,* 6.13.2 (here changing Cicero's expression, in the mouth of Scipio Africanus in the famous *Somnium Scipionis,* from the plural to singular); Thomas Hobbes, *Leviathan,* ed. Richard Tuck (Cambridge: Cambridge University Press, 1996), 9; Brett, *Changes of State,* 1.

16. John M. Najemy, "The Medieval Italian City and the 'Civilizing Process,'" in *Europa e Italia / Europe and Italy: Studi in onore di Giorgio Chittolini / Studies in Honour of Giorgio Chittolini,* ed. Paola Guglielmotti, Isabella Lazzarini, and Gian Maria Varanini (Florence: Firenze University Press, 2011), 355–369, meditating on Norbert Elias, *The Civilizing Process: Sociogenetic and Psychogenetic Investigations* (Oxford: Blackwell, 2000) (orig. German ed. 1939). Najemy's evidence also suggests the problems of investing the Protestant Reformation, or more particularly Calvinism, with as much transformative power as has been done in recent historiography; see, for example, Philip S. Gorski, *The Disciplinary Revolution: Calvinism and the Rise of the State in Early Modern Europe* (Chicago: University of Chicago Press, 2003). For caveats with regard to much literature on this "civilizing process," see Andre Wakefield, "Butterfield's Nightmare: The

History of Science as Disney History," *History and Technology* 30, no. 3 (2014): 232–251.

17. On the related Stoic tradition of political philosophy in early modern Europe, see Christopher Brooke, *Philosophic Pride: Stoicism and Political Thought from Lipsius to Rousseau* (Princeton, NJ: Princeton University Press, 2012).

18. On contemporary "territoriality," see Elden, *The Birth of Territory*, 322–330.

19. Playing on the term "cyberpunk," I have previously referred to the multiplicity of vectors of economic and political sovereignty in the early modern world with the moniker "baroquepunk"; see Sophus A. Reinert, "Rivalry: Greatness in Early Modern Political Economy," in *Mercantilism Reimagined: Political Economy in Early Modern Britain and Its Empire,* ed. Phil Stern and Carl Wennerlind (Oxford: Oxford University Press, 2014), 348–370. On the prevalence of such a vision also in late nineteenth-century imperialism in Africa, see Steven Press, *Rogue Empires: Contracts and Conmen in Europe's Scramble for Africa* (Cambridge, MA: Harvard University Press, 2017), esp. 250–251.

20. Scott, *Seeing Like a State,* esp. 2, 183.

21. "Ordini stabiliti dal sig. governatore don Ferrando Gonzaga l'anno 1549 da osservarsi nel fare la misura generale dello Stato di Milano," Archivio del Comune di Cremona, Cremona, Italy, *Misc. A, b. 146, cc. 124–125,* published in Ircas Nicola Jacopetti, *Il territorio agrario-forestale di Cremona nel catasto di Carlo V (1551–1561)* (Cremona: Annali della biblioteca statale e libreria civica di Cremona with the Camera di commercio industria artigianato e agricoltura, 1984), 192–194, quote from 192. On these themes in the respective traditions, see Antoine de Montchrestien, *Traicté de l'économie politique,* ed. Théodor Funk-Brentano (Paris: Plon, 1889), 34; quoted slightly differently and discussed in Pasquino, "Theatrum Politicum," 114; Alix Cooper, "'The Possibilities of the Land': The Inventory of 'Natural Riches' in the Early Modern German Territories," in *Oeconomies in the Age of Newton,* ed. Margaret Schabas and Neil DeMarchi (Durham, NC: Duke University Press, 2003), 129–153; and Ted McCormick, *William Petty and the Ambitions of Political Arithmetick* (Oxford: Oxford University Press, 2009).

22. Emer de Vattel, *The Law of Nations,* ed. Béla Kapossy and Richard Whatmore (Indianapolis: Liberty Fund, 2008), 91 [1.III.25].

23. On eighteenth-century changes, see, among others, Costanza Roggero Bardelli, "Fonti catastali sabaude: L'editto di Carlo Emanuele III per la Perequazione generale de' tribute del Piemonte (5 Maggio 1731)," in *La figura della città: I catasti storici in Italia,* ed. Angela Marino (Rome: Gangemi Editore, 1996), 49–59, at 51–55. On their emulation, see, for example, Christine Lebeau, "Exchanging Taxation Projects in Eighteenth-Century Europe: The Case of Italian Cadastres,"

in *Global Debates about Taxation,* ed. Holger Nehring and Florian Schui (Basingstoke, UK: Palgrave Macmillan, 2007), 21–35; Antonella Alimento, *Finanze e amministrazione: Un'inchiesta francese sui catasti nell'Italia del Settecento (1763–1764),* 2 vols. (Florence: Leo S. Olschki, 2008). On the longer history of cadastres, see, for example, Federick Mario Fales, ed., *Censimenti e catasti di epoca neo-assira* (Rome: Tipografia Don Bosco, 1973); Roger J. P. Kain and Elizabeth Baigent, *The Cadastral Map in the Service of the State: A History of Property Mapping* (Chicago: University of Chicago Press, 1992). The famous and precocious Florentine cadastre of 1427 was the centerpiece of David Herlihy and Christiane Klapisch-Zuber's groundbreaking *Tuscans and Their Families: A Study of the Florentine Catasto of 1427* (New Haven, CT: Yale University Press, 1985).

24. "Regio editto per la perequazione generale dei tributi nelle provincie del Piemonte [5 May 1731]," reproduced in Bardelli, "Fonti catastali sabaude," 49.

25. Michel Foucault, *The Punitive Society: Lectures at the Collège de France, 1972–1973,* ed. Bernard E. Harcourt, trans. Graham Burchell (Houndmills, UK: Palgrave Macmillan, 2015), 233.

26. Gustav von Schmoller, *The Mercantile System and Its Historical Significance* (New York: Macmillan, 1897), 43–51; this is an English translation of the first part of his multivolume *Studien über die wirtschaftliche Politik Friedrichs des Grossen,* or *Studies in the Economic Policy of Frederick the Great.* On Schmoller, see Vitantonio Gioia, *Gustav Schmoller: La scienza economica e la storia* (Lecce: Congedo, 1970); Birger P. Priddat, *Die andere Ökonomie: Eine neue Einschätzung von Gustav Schmollers Versuch einer "ethisch-historischen" Nationalökonomie im 19. Jahrhundert* (Marburg: Metropolis, 1995); Nicholas W. Balabkins, *Not by Theory Alone . . . : The Economics of Gustav von Schmoller and Its Legacy to America* (Berlin: Duncker und Humblot, 1988); and particularly Erik Grimmer-Solem's brilliant *The Rise of Historical Economics and Social Reform in Germany, 1864–1894* (Oxford: Oxford University Press, 2003). On mercantilism and its historiography, see again Lars Magnusson, *Mercantilism: The Shaping of an Economic Language* (London: Routledge, 1994); Stern and Wennerlind, *Mercantilism Reimagined.*

27. Schmoller, *The Mercantile System,* 8, 14, 30.

28. The formation of territorial states in Italy has been the subject of one of the most important historiographical transformations in the past fifty years. On this, see the pioneering work of Marino Berengo, "Il Cinquecento," in *La storiografia italiana negli ultimi vent'anni* (Milan: Marzorati, 1970), 485–518; and especially Giorgio Chittolini, *La formazione dello stato regionale e le istituzioni del contado* (Turin: Einaudi, 1979).

29. Schmoller, *The Mercantile System,* 48; emphasis in original.

30. Ibid., 48–50; emphasis in original.

31. On eighteenth-century economic nationalism and its legacy, see the epic footnote in Hont, *Jealousy of Trade*, 124n229, stretching onto 125. On the continuing import of this concept, see the essays in Eric Helleiner and Andreas Pickel, eds., *Economic Nationalism in a Globalizing World* (Ithaca, NY: Cornell University Press, 2005). See also Liah Greenfeld, *The Spirit of Capitalism: Nationalism and Economic Growth* (Cambridge, MA: Harvard University Press, 2001).

32. Schmoller, *The Mercantile System*, 50–51.

33. Ibid., 51, 64.

34. Ibid., 70–71. Although this narrative must be taken *cum grano salis*, it is striking that the character of international law transformed—qualitatively and quantitatively—precisely at the moment described by Schmoller. See, for sources, Wilhelm G. Grewe, ed., *Fontes historiae Iuris Gentium*, esp. vols. 1 (1380–1493) and 2 (1493–1815) (Berlin: De Gruyter, 1988–1995). Martin Kintzinger, "From the Late Middle Ages to the Peace of Westphalia," in *The Oxford Handbook of the History of International Law*, ed. Bardo Fassbender and Anne Peters (Oxford: Oxford University Press, 2012), 607–628, suggests the neat date of 1648 for the creation of international law as such, even though medieval Europeans sought to impose norms of conduct among polities and pan-European organizations.

35. Niccolò Macchiavelli, "Instructione ad Iuliano Lapo," in Macchiavelli, *Legazioni, commissarie, scritti di governo*, ed. Fredi Chiappelli with Jean-Jacques Marchand, 4 vols. (Bari: Laterza, 1971–1985), 3:32; emphasis added.

36. Eli F. Heckscher, *Merkantilismen: Ett led i den ekonomiska politikens historia*, 2 vols. (Stockholm: Norstedt, 1931); Karl Polanyi, *Great Transformation: The Political and Economic Origins of Our Time*, ed. Fred Block, foreword by Joseph E. Stiglitz (Boston: Beacon Press, 2001), esp. 66–73; Henri Pirenne, *Economic and Social History of Medieval Europe* (New York: Harcourt, Brace, 1937), 216–219; Fernand Braudel, *Afterthoughts on Material Civilization and Capitalism*, trans. Patricia M. Ranum (Baltimore: Johns Hopkins University Press, 1977), esp. 99–104. Scholars have noticed Schmoller's influence on these authors on different grounds. See, for the case of Heckscher, Lars Magnusson, "Eli Heckscher and His Mercantilism Today," in *Eli Heckscher, International Trade, and Economic History*, ed. Ronald Findlay et al. (Cambridge, MA: MIT Press, 2006), 231–246, at 236; for Polanyi, see Fred Block and Margaret R. Somers, *The Power of Market Fundamentalism: Karl Polanyi's Critique* (Cambridge, MA: Harvard University Press, 2014), 230–232; for Braudel, see Immanuel Wallerstein, "Fernand Braudel, Historian, 'homme de la conjoncture,'" in *Unthinking Social Science: The Limits of Nineteenth-Century Paradigms*, 2nd ed. (Philadelphia: Temple University Press, 2001), 187–201, at 188. See also Edwin F. Gay's meditation on

Schmoller and this "parallelism or interlocking of the two developments, economic or politic," in his 14 December 1921 letter to N. S. B. Gras, Huntington Library, San Marino, CA, *Edwin Francis Gay Papers, 1886–1973, GY 1035,* 1r. For a rather different yet illuminating discussion of the relationships between scale and political economy in the long history of our species, see Mary C. Stiner, Timothy Earle, Daniel Lord Smail, and Andrew Shryock, "Scale," in *Deep History: The Architecture of Past and Present,* ed. Andrew Shryock and Daniel Lord Smail (Cambridge, Berkeley: University of California Press, 2011), 242–272, at 259–260.

37. The literature on this process is by now, of course, varied, but for two seminal engagements with the problem, see Mark Greengrass, "Introduction: Conquest and Coalescence," in *Conquest and Coalescence: The Shaping of the State in Early Modern Europe,* ed. Mark Greengrass (London: Edward Arnold, 1991), 1–24; and Charles Tilly, *Coercion, Capital, and European States, AD 990–1992* (Oxford: Blackwell, 1992).

38. This is part of the "Enlightenment narrative" explored by J. G. A. Pocock, *Barbarism and Religion,* 6 vols. (Cambridge: Cambridge University Press, 1999–2015), for a lucid statement of which see 4:206.

39. Verri, "Pensieri politici sulla corte di Roma e sul governo veneto," in *Edizione nazionale delle opere di Pietro Verri,* ed. Carlo Capra et al., 8 vols. in 10 to date (Rome: Edizioni di storia e letteratura, 2003–2014) (hereafter cited as *ENOPV*), 6:472–485, at 477–479. On the broader history of city-states, for which Italy was so important, see Tom Scott, *The City-State in Europe, 1000–1600: Hinterland, Territory, Region* (Oxford: Oxford University Press, 2014), esp. 206–212 on their survival there.

40. Cicero, *De officiis,* III.29; "Del viver Politico, et Cristiano [9 April 1583]," in *Compendio di tutte le gride, et ordini publicati nella Città, et Stato di Milano* (Milan: Malatesti, 1609), 1, on which see Luigi Lacchè, *Latrocinium: Giustizia, scienza penale e repressione del banditismo in antico regime* (Milan: Giuffrè, 1988), 40.

41. See, among many, many examples, the Hollywood franchise *Pirates of the Caribbean* (Burbank, CA: Walt Disney Pictures, 2003–); Anthony Bourdain, *Kitchen Confidential: Adventures in the Culinary Underbelly* (London: Bloomsbury, 2000), the cultural impact of which influenced even the children's movie *Ratatouille,* directed by Brad Bird (Burbank, CA: Walt Disney Pictures, 2007), though its culinary advisor was the rather un-piraty Thomas Keller, whose Weberianly perfectionist approach to bureaucratic cooking is evident from his *The French Laundry Cookbook* (New York: Artisan Books, 1999) and the film *Chef's Story: Thomas Keller,* directed by Bruce Franchini (New York: Soho Culinary Productions, 2007); Micah Sifry, *Wikileaks and the Age of Transparency* (New Haven, CT: Yale University Press, 2011); Parmy Olson, *We Are Anonymous: Inside the Hacker*

World of LulzSec, Anonymous, and the Global Cyber Insurgency (New York: Little, Brown, 2012); Eric Hobsbawm, *Primitive Rebels: Studies in Archaic Forms of Social Movement in the Nineteenth and Twentieth Centuries* (New York: W. W. Norton, 1959); Peter T. Leeson, *The Invisible Hook: The Hidden Economics of Pirates* (Princeton, NJ: Princeton University Press, 2009); and Rodolphe Durand and Jean Philippe Verone, *The Pirate Organization: Lessons from the Fringe of Capitalism* (Boston: Harvard Business Review Press, 2013), which was perhaps inspired by Steve Jobs's influential maxim, quoted in, among other places, Walter Isaacson, *Steve Jobs* (New York: Simon and Schuster, 2013), 144. On Jobs as an archetype also of early modern Mediterranean pirates, see Nicholas Walton, *Genoa "La Superba": The Rise and Fall of a Merchant Pirate Superpower* (London: C. Hurst and Co., 2015), 81.

42. Ayn Rand, *Atlas Shrugged* (London: Penguin, 2007), 152, 192, 497, 500, 576. A simple search online testifies to Danneskjöld's continuing influence, but see also the likes of Walter E. Block and Peter Lothian Nelson, *Water Capitalism: The Case for Privatizing Oceans, Rivers, Lakes, and Aquifers* (Lanham, MD: Lexington Books, 2015), 129n3. On the contemporary obsession with physical perfection at the time, including the case of Rand, see Sophus A. Reinert, "The Economy of Fear: H. P. Lovecraft on Eugenics, Economics, and the Great Depression," *Horror Studies* 6, no. 2 (2015): 255–282.

43. The gamut is neatly represented by a conjoined reading of the more recent James C. Scott, *The Art of Not Being Governed: An Anarchist History of Upland Southeast Asia* (New Haven, CT: Yale University Press, 2009); and Terry L. Anderson and Peter J. Hill, *The Not So Wild, Wild West: Property Rights on the Frontier* (Stanford, CA: Stanford Economics and Finance, 2004).

44. Alexa Clay and Kyra Maya Phillips, *The Misfit Economy: Lessons in Creativity from Pirates, Hackers, Gangsters, and Other Informal Entrepreneurs* (New York: Simon and Schuster, 2015), drawing inspiration, like much of this literature, from Clayton M. Christensen's epochal *The Innovator's Dilemma: When New Technologies Cause Great Firms to Fail*, new ed. (Boston: Harvard Business Review Press, 2013).

45. For an incisive if irreverent take on the problem, see Chuck Klosterman, *I Wear the Black Hat: Grappling with Villains (Real and Imagined)* (New York: Scribner, 2013).

46. The examples are too many to cover, but compare, for example, *Banditi a Milano*, dir. Carlo Lizzani (Rome: Dino de Laurentiis Cinematografica, 1968), to *The Departed*, dir. Martin Scorsese (Burbank, CA: Warner Bros. et al., 2006). Fans of the genre understand that there is definitional slippage with the more famous *giallo* cinema. On these genres, see Roberto Curti, *Italia odia: Il cinema poliziesco italiano* (Turin: Lindau, 2006); Mikel J. Koven, *La Dolce Morte: Vernacular Cinema and the Italian Giallo Film* (Lanham, MD: Scarecrow Press, 2006).

See also Ulrike Kreger, *Genrespezifische Untersuchung des US-Slasher-Films im Vergleich zum italienischen "Giallo"* (Munich: Grin Verlag, 2009); and Andrea Pergolari's appropriately titled *La polizia s'incazza: Spie, assassini e sbirri nel cinema italiano* (Rome: Ultra, 2016). Admittedly, though it has a certain heuristic value, this argument can easily be taken too far, given the richness of recent cinema.

47. See, for example, Janice E. Thomson, *Mercenaries, Pirates, and Sovereigns* (Princeton, NJ: Princeton University Press, 1994), 156f19; Durand and Verone, *The Pirate Organization*, 13–14, 56.

48. Cicero, *De officiis*, III.107; I am here indebted to Daniel Heller-Roazen, *The Enemy of All: Piracy and the Law of Nations* (New York: Zone Books, 2009), 13–18; Harry D. Gould, *The Legacy of Punishment in International Law* (Houndmills, UK: Palgrave Macmillan, 2010), 84–89. Michel Foucault rightly pointed out the degree to which "criminals" generally were characterized as "social enemies" in the eighteenth century, but emphasized the way they attacked the "mechanisms of production" in his *The Punitive Society*, 33, 45–47, 253. For many of the authors surveyed here, the problem was more directly related to sociability and commerce, in the broader sense of trade as well as communication, which of course had subsequent consequences for productivity.

49. Christopher J. Fuhrmann, *Policing the Roman Empire: Soldiers, Administration, and Public Order* (Oxford: Oxford University Press, 2012), 156. On bandits in ancient Rome, see also Brent Shaw, "Bandits in the Roman Empire," *Past and Present* 105, no. 1 (1984): 3–52; Thomas Grünewald, *Räuber, Rebellen, Rivalen, Rächer: Studien zu Latrones im römischen Reich* (Stuttgart: Franz Steiner Verlag, 1999); Werner Riess, "The Roman Bandit (Latro) as Criminal and Outsider," in *The Oxford Handbook of Social Relations in the Roman World*, ed. Michael Peachin (Oxford: Oxford University Press, 2011), 693–714. On Nazi approaches to banditry, see Blood, *Hitler's Bandit Hunters*.

50. A culmination of this tension between change and armed resistance was recently explored by Broers, *Napoleon's Other War*. For the term *mutare lo stato*, see, among countless possibilities, Peter Godman's excellent *From Poliziano to Machiavelli: Florentine Humanism in the High Renaissance* (Princeton, NJ: Princeton University Press, 1998), 316.

51. On the medieval origins of Genovesi's "civil economics," see, among others, Zamagni and Bruni, *Economia civile*; Oreste Bazzichi, "Il modello socio-economico nel pensiero e nella predicazione di San Bernardino da Siena," in San Bernardino da Siena, *Antologia delle prediche volgari: Economia civile e cura pastorale nei sermoni di San Bernardino da Siena*, ed. Flavio Felice and Mattia Fochesato (Sienna: Edizioni Cantagalli, 2010), 205–226, at 222; Luigino Bruni and Stefano Zamagni, introduction to Antonio Genovesi, *Lezioni di economia civile*,

ed. Francesca Dal Degan (Milan: Vita e Pensiero, 2013), vii–xxii, x. More broadly, see also Joseph A. Schumpeter, *A History of Economic Analysis* (Oxford: Oxford University Press, 1954), 177. Even critics of their specific reading of the term "civile" reaffirm the medieval origins of the related paradigm; see Federico D'Onofrio, "On the Concept of 'Felicitas Publica' in Eighteenth-Century Political Economy," *Journal of the History of Economic Thought* 37, no. 3 (2015): 441–479, at 452.

52. Dante, *La divina commedia*, "Inferno," I.2.

53. On Giotto, see Francesca Flores d'Arcais, *Giotto*, trans. Raymond Rosenthal (New York: Abbeville Press, 2012). For different but enlightening interpretations, see Péter Bokody, "Justice, Love and Rape: Giotto's Allegories of Justice and Injustice in the Arena Chapel, Padua," in *The Iconology of Law and Order*, ed. Anna Kerchy et al. (Szeged: JATE Press, 2012), 55–66; and Judith N. Shklar, *The Faces of Injustice* (New Haven, CT: Yale University Press, 1990), 46–48. On the dichotomy between the city and the woods in Giotto's fresco, see also Martin Warnke, *Political Landscape: The Art History of Nature* (London: Reaktion Books, 1994), 43. For Dante's phrase, see *La divina commedia*, "Inferno," 1:1–2. See also Claudio Monteverdi, *Orfeo* (Venice: Amadino, 1609), act 2, 49. On the Scrovegni Chapel through the lens of usury, see Anne Derbes and Mark Sandona's beautiful *The Usurer's Heart: Giotto, Enrico Scrovegni, and the Arena Chapel in Padua* (University Park: Pennsylvania State University Press, 2008).

54. See, for his reading, John Ruskin, *Giotto and His Works in Padua: Being an Explanatory Notice of the Frescoes in the Arena Chapel* (London: George Allen, Sunnyside, Orpington, 1900), 188–190.

55. Verri, "Primi elementi per somministrare," in *ENOPV*, 4:631–632, 634–635.

56. Cesare Beccaria, "Della relazione che hanno l'osterie con il commercio," in *ENOCB*, 2:246–248, at 247.

57. On this fresco, and its immense literature, see Sophus A. Reinert, introduction to Antonio Serra, *A Short Treatise on the Wealth and Poverty of Nations (1613)*, trans. Jonathan Hunt (London: Anthem, 2011), 1–93, at 18–19. See, however, particularly Nicolai Rubinstein, "Political Ideas in Sienese Art: The Frescoes of Ambrogio Lorenzetti and Taddeo di Bartolo in the Palazzo Pubblico," *Journal of the Warburg and Courtauld Institutes* 21, nos. 3–4 (1958): 179–207; Quentin Skinner's "Ambrogio Lorenzetti and the Portrayal of Virtuous Government" and "Ambrogio Lorenzetti on the Power and Glory of Republics," both in *Visions of Politics*, 3 vols. (Cambridge: Cambridge University Press, 2002), 2:39–117. The similarity between the dancers in Giotto's *Justice* and those in Lorenzetti's *Good Government* has been noticed before; see, for example, Randolph Starn and Loren Partridge, *Arts of Power: Three Halls of State in Italy, 1300–1600* (Berkeley: University of California Press, 1992), 52.

58. For a transcription and translation, see Starn and Partridge, *Arts of Power*, 264.

59. Ibid., 266.

60. On the politics of exile and banditry, see, among others, Giuliano Milani, *L'Esclusione dal comune: Conflitti e bandi politici a Bologna e in altre città italiane tra 12. e 14. Secolo* (Rome: Istituto storico italiano per il Medio Evo, 2003); Christine Shaw, *The Politics of Exile in Renaissance Florence* (Cambridge: Cambridge University Press, 2000); Fabrizio Ricciardelli, *The Politics of Exclusion in Early Renaissance Florence* (Turnhout: Brepols, 2007), for a critique of which see John M. Najemy's review in the *English Historical Review* 124 (2009): 1474–1476. For the problem's classical origins, see Sara Forsdyke, *Exile, Ostracism, and Democracy: The Politics of Expulsion in Ancient Greece* (Princeton, NJ: Princeton University Press, 2005).

61. Skinner, "Ambrogio Lorenzetti," 68–69; developed also in John T. Hamilton, *Security: Politics, Humanity, and the Philology of Care* (Princeton, NJ: Princeton University Press, 2013), 158; both probably referencing Aquinas, *Summa theologiae*, IIa–IIae, quest. 29, art. 1. Although it does not affect Skinner's potent contrast between the Thomist view and the Roman or humanist "triumphal" view of peace, it is perhaps overly reductive to declare "the absence of discord" the Thomist definition of peace. After all, Aquinas says clearly that peace "includes concord but adds something [*includit concordiam et aliquid addit*]" and also notes that, although there can be no peace without concord, "peace does not exist everywhere that concord does [*non tamen ubicumque est concordia est pax*]."

62. Alessandro Verri, "Ragionamento sulle leggi civili," in *"Il Caffè," 1764–1766*, ed. Gianni Francioni and Sergio A. Romagnoli (Turin: Bollati Boringhieri, 1993) (hereafter cited as *Il Caffè*), 571–606, at 603.

63. Hamilton, *Security*, 158. For a similar analysis with reference to Immanuel Kant's *Perpetual Peace* and the problem of piracy, see also Heller-Roazen, *The Enemy of All*, 188–189.

64. John M. Najemy, *A History of Florence, 1200–1575* (London: Blackwell, 2006), 484.

65. Pietro Verri to the Supreme Council, 6 March 1766, fols. 1v and 3v, *Pietro Verri Letters*, Kress Collection of Business and Economics, Baker Library, Harvard Business School, Boston; Pietro Verri, "Primi elementi per somministrare al popolo delle nozioni tendenti alla pubblica felicità," in *ENOPV*, 6:629–677, esp. 631–635, 650, 655, 662, 664.

66. On the very early history of this process, see James C. Scott, *Against the Grain: A Deep History of the Earliest States* (New Haven, CT: Yale University Press, 2017), 68–92.

67. For this painting, see still E. H. Gombrich, "Botticellis's Mythologies: A Study in the Neoplatonic Symbolism of His Circle," *Journal of the Warburg and Courtauld Institutes* 8 (1945): 7–60, at 50–53.

68. Wu Ming 4 [Federico Guglielmi], *L'eroe imperfetto* (Milan: Bompiani, 2010), 68–69. The theme itself has found many expressions since the Renaissance, for a beautiful example of which see Frédéric Auguste Bartholdi, *Faunes et nymphes effrayes par un train ou Adieu la mythologie*, ca. 1870, Musée Bartholdi, Colmar, France.

69. Letizia Arcangeli, "'Come bosco et spelunca di latroni': Città e ordine pubblico a Parma e nello stato di Milano tra Quattrocento e Cinquecento," in Livio Antonielli, *Le polizie informali* (Soveria Mannelli: Rubbettino, 2010), 65–89, at 80.

70. Henry Fielding, *An Enquiry into the Causes of the Late Increase of Robbers*, 2nd ed. (London: Millar, 1751), 115–116.

71. Jonathan Scott, *Salvator Rosa: His Life and Times* (New Haven, CT: Yale University Press), 1996.

72. Thomas Cole, *Salvator Rosa Sketching the Banditi*, ca. 1832–1840, Museum of Fine Arts, Boston, 62.268, for the early history of which see Richard W. Wallace, "Salvator Rosa in America" (Wellesley, MA: Wellesley College Museum, 1979),118; Thomas Moran, *Salvator Rosa Sketching the Banditti [sic]*, 1860, Chrysler Museum, Norfolk, VA, 71.2127. On Moran, see Thurman Wilkins and William H. Goetzmann, *Thomas Moran: Artist of the Mountains*, 2nd ed. (Norman: University of Oklahoma Press, 1998). On Rosa's importance more broadly, see Malcolm Andrews, *Lansdcape and Western Art* (Oxford: Oxford University Press, 1999), 130–133.

73. On this locus classicus of outlawry and its modern incarnations, see Oren Barak and Chanan Cohen, "The 'Modern Sherwood Forest': Theoretical and Practical Challenges," in *Nonstate Actors in Intrastate Conflicts*, ed. Dan Miodownik and Oren Barak (Philadelphia: University of Pennsylvania Press, 2014), 12–33. On the similar case of France, see Kieko Matteson, *Forests in Revolutionary France: Conservation, Community, and Conflict, 1669–1848* (Cambridge: Cambridge University Press, 2015), 179–182.

74. On Venice and deforestation, see Karl Appuhn, *A Forest on the Sea: Environmental Expertise in Renaissance Venice* (Baltimore: Johns Hopkins University Press, 2009).

75. Teodoro Monticelli, *Memoria sulla economia delle acque*, 4th ed. (Naples: Stabilimento tipografico dell'Aquila, 1841 [1809]), 13, on which see Bruno Vecchio, *Il Bosco negli scrittori italiani del Settecento e dell'età napoleonica* (Turin: Einaudi, 1974), 224–227, and Giuseppe Foscari, *Teodoro Monticelli e l'economia delle acque nel Mezzogiorno moderno: Storiografia, scienze ambientali, ecologismo* (Salerno: Edisud, 2009). Earlier editions of Monticelli's work spoke of "malfeasants" instead; see, for example, Monticelli, *Sulla economia delle acque*, 3rd ed. (Naples: Torchi del Giornale costituzionale, 1820), 28.

76. Tomaso Garzoni, *La piazza universale di tutte le professioni de mondo* (Venice: Giovanni Battista Somasco, 1587), 447–448, 812–814.

77. Giovanni Botero, *On the Causes of the Greatness of Cities,* ed. Geoffrey Symcox (Toronto: University of Toronto Press, 2012), 31, 49–50. On Botero, see, among others, Robert Bireley, *The Counter-Reformation Prince: Anti-Machiavellianism or Catholic Statecraft in Early Modern Europe* (Chapel Hill: University of North Carolina Press, 1990), 45–71; and the essays in Artemio Enzo Baldini, *Botero e la "Ragion di stato"* (Florence: Leo S. Olschki, 1992).

78. Ludovico Antonio Muratori, *Della pubblica felicità oggetto de' buoni principi* (Lucca: n.p., 1749), 66, 127.

79. Anon., *Massime generali intorno al commerzio ed alle sue interne, ed esterne relazioni; o sia Principj universali, per ben coltivarlo per terra, e per mare: a linea di buon governo* (Venice: Albrizzi, 1749), 36–37, copied verbatim in Giuseppe Antonio Costantini, *Elementi di commerzio, o siano regole generali per coltivarlo, appoggiate alla ragione, alla pratica delle nazioni, ed alle autorità de' scrittori* (Genoa: Novelli, 1762), 40, published in a place and at a time when bandits were particularly harrowing.

80. Charles Irénée Castel de Saint-Pierre, *Projet pour rendre la paix perpetuelle en Europe,* 3 vols. (Utrecht: Schouten, 1713–1717), 1:265, 3:215–216.

81. Vattel, *Law of Nations,* 139–140 [1.IX.100–101]. He went on to praise the French examples of "numerous patrols" keeping bandits at bay, as well as for the Canal du Midi, on which see Chandra Mukerji, *Impossible Engineering: Technology and Territoriality on the Canal du Midi* (Princeton, NJ: Princeton University Press, 2009).

82. Matthew Tindall, "An Essay Concerning the Laws of Nations, and the Rights of Sovereigns," in *A Collection of State Tracts Publish'd during the Reign of King William III,* 3 vols. (London: n.p., 1705–1707), 2:462–475, at 471; emphasis added. This passage is frequently quoted but attributed to Daniel Defoe without further reference. For the perhaps earliest attribution to Defoe, see Anne Pérotin-Dumon, "The Pirate and the Emperor: Power and the Law on the Seas, 1450–1850," in *The Political Economy of Merchant Empires: State Power and World Trade 1350–1750,* ed. James D. Tracy (Cambridge: Cambridge University Press, 1991), 196–227, at 215.

83. Reinert, *Translating Empire,* 231.

84. Antonio Genovesi, *Storia del commercio della Gran Brettagna,* 3 vols. (Naples: Benedetto Gessari, 1757–1758), 2:16n.

85. Ibid., 1:11n.

86. Ibid., 3:473–505.

87. Genovesi, "Ragionamento sulla fede pubblica," in *Storia del commercio della Gran Brettagna,* 3:495. On the problem of trust in Genovesi, and for further references, see Reinert, *Translating Empire,* 226–227.

88. Genovesi, "Ragionamento sulla fede pubblica," 496.

89. Ibid., 498-499.

90. For only two examples in which the members of the Academy of Fisticuffs present Genovesi as the founder of political economy in Italy, see Beccaria, "Prolusione," in ENOCB, 3:95; and Verri, "Considerazioni," in ENOPV, 2:1,112.

91. Strangely, it does not make an appearance in recent works on the phenomenon, among which see Norman Davis, *Vanished Kingdoms: The Rise and Fall of States and Nations* (London: Allen Lane, 2011); and Daron Acemoglu and James Robinson, *Why Nations Fail: The Origins of Power, Prosperity, and Poverty* (New York: Crown, 2012).

92. Giuseppe Antonio de Morani, *Memorie istoriche della città e della chiesa di Casale Monferrato* [1800], Biblioteca Civica Giovanni Canna, Casale Monferrato, Italy, 091 73, 11.

93. On the historiography of frontiers in the area, see Giuseppe Ricuperati, "Frontiere e territori dello stato sabaudo come archetipi di una regione europea: Fra storia e storiografia," in *Lo spazio sabaudo: Intersezioni, frontiere e confine in età moderna*, ed. Blythe Alice Raviola (Milan: Franco Angeli, 2007), 31-55.

94. The literature on Sardinian banditry is considerable, but for a recent work see Alberto Ledda, *La civiltà fuorilegge: Storia del banditismo sardo* (Milan: Ugo Mursia, 2009). On the longer history of banditry in the Piedmontese highlands, see Tavo Burat [Gustavo Buratti], "Il tuchinaggio occitano e piemontese," in *Achtung Banditen: Contadini e montanari tra banditismo, ribellismo e resistenze dall'antichità ad oggi*, ed. anon. (Novara: Millennia, 2005), 18-32.

95. For bandits, see, among others Anton Bok, "The Peasant and the Brigand: Social Banditry Reconsidered," *Comparative Studies in Society and History* 14, no. 4 (1972): 494-503. On the relationship between literature and reality with regard to piracy, see Neil Rennie, *Treasure Neverland: Real and Imaginary Pirates* (Oxford: Oxford University Press, 2013). For a survey of early modern European banditry, noting the limitations of Hobsbawm's paradigm, see Julius R. Ruff, *Violence in Early Modern Europe, 1500–1800* (Cambridge: Cambridge University Press, 2001), 217–239. For a seemingly ideal case of social banditry of the self-consciously Robin Hoodesque variety, see, however, the case of the pirate John Ward, discussed in Peter Lamborn Wilson, *Pirate Utopias: Moorish Corsairs and European Renegadoes*, 2nd rev. ed. (Williamsburg, VA: Autonomedia, 2003), 57.

96. Felice De-Gioanni, *Verolengo: Cenni storici–coreografici* (Casale Monferrato: Stabilimento Arti Grafiche, 1932), 134–136, 156–157; on the town's earliest history, still an active battlefield of contemporary Italian politics preoccupied with Ligurian and Celtic influences, see Fabrizio Spegis, "Origini di Verolengo," *Quaderni verolenghesi* 5 (1997): 1–95; on the peace treaty and its intense focus on border disputes, see Joycelyn G. Russell, *Peacemaking in the Renaissance*

(Philadelphia: University of Pennsylvania Press, 1986), 133–223. For the contested case of Verolengo in particular, see Romolo Quazza, *Emanuele Filiberto di Savoia e Guglielmo Gonzaga (1559–1580)* (Mantova: Società Tipografica Modenese, 1929), 17. As to the economic fortunes of Verolengo, see De-Gioanni, *Verolengo,* 135.

97. On the Gonzaga and the Paleologus, see Stefano Davari, *Federico Gonzaga e la famiglia paleologa del Monferrato* (Genoa: Tip. Sordo-Muti, 1891). The first anti-Gonzaga rebellion in Casale arose, tellingly, as early as 1533 at the mere *prospect* of a transition; for this and for context, see Roberto Oresko and David Parrott, "The Sovereignty of Monferrato and the Citadel of Casale as European Problems of the Early Modern Period," in *Stefano Guazzo e Casale tra Cinque e Seicento,* ed. Daniela Ferrari (Rome: Bulzoni, 1997), 11–86, at 22. For an entertaining list of such tax revolts, see David F. Burg, *A World History of Tax Rebellions: Encyclopedia of Tax Rebels, Revolts, and Riots from Antiquity to the Present* (London: Routledge, 2003).

98. Blythe Alice Raviola, *Il Monferrato Gonzaghesco: Istituzioni ed élites in un microstato (1536–1708)* (Florence: Olschki, 2003), 56; Fabrizio Spegis, "'Giunti colà, si sciolsero e si sparpagliarono': Fuoriusciti casalesi tra Monferrato, Savoia e Francia (febbraio 1569)," *Bollettino storico vercellese,* A. 39, n. 2 (2010): 155–169, at 158–160. On the evocative crime of *lèse-majesté,* see Mario Sbriccoli, *Crimen laesae maiestatis: Il problema del reato politico alle soglie della scienza penalistica moderna* (Milan: Giuffrè, 1974).

99. Quentin Skinner, *Liberty before Liberalism* (Cambridge: Cambridge University Press, 1997); Skinner, *Hobbes and Republican Liberty* (Cambridge: Cambridge University Press, 2008).

100. For an examination of the complex role of the militia in Renaissance political and military life, see John M. Najemy, "'Occupare la tirannide': Machiavelli, the Militia, and Guicciardini's Accusation of Tyranny," in *Della tirannia: Machiavelli con Bartolo,* ed. Jérémy Barthas (Florence: Leo S. Olschki, 2007), 75–108. See also John Rigby Hale, "The End of Florentine Liberty: The Fortezza da Basso," in *Renaissance War Studies* (London: Hambledon, 1983), 31–62; and, for Casale in particular and for caveats regarding the actual efficiency of fortifications, see Oresko and Parrott, "The Sovereignty of Monferrato," esp. 25–27.

101. Raviola, *Il Monferrato Gonzaghesco,*56. On the question of sovereignty and rights at the time, see Kenneth Pennington, *The Prince and the Law, 1200–1600: Sovereignty and Rights in the Western Legal Tradition* (Berkeley: University of California Press, 1993).

102. Romolo Quazza, "Il Monferrato nei centosettanta anni di dominio gonzaghesco," *Convivium* 4 (1932): 383–391, at 385–386.

103. Spegis, "'Giunti colà, si sciolsero e si sparpagliarono,'" 163–166.

104. Quazza, *Emanuele Filiberto di Savoia e Guglielmo Gonzaga*, 17, 108–110; Spegis, "'Giunti colà, si sciolsero e si sparpagliarono,'" 167–169.

105. "Processo contro vari Banditi di Casale li quali avevano tentato di occupare la Fortezza di Verolengo, 1569," Archivio di Stato di Torino, Turin, Italy (hereafter cited as AST), *Monferrato, Materie Economiche ed altre*, Mazzo 10, *Criminale*, #3, 2r, 56v, 57v, 58r, 71r–73r. For context, and though they overlooked this document, see the summary of a contemporary chronicle in Vincenzo de Conti, *Notizie storiche sulla città di Casale e del Monferrato*, 11 vols. (Casale: Mantelli, then Casuccio, then Casuccio e Bagna, 1838–1842), 5:616–624; Spegis, "'Giunti colà, si sciolsero e si sparpagliarono.'" Needless to say, legal documents are not always perfect reflections of past events, and such overly convenient episodes clearly should be read with a grain of salt. See, on this problem, Natalie Zemon Davis, *Fiction in the Archives: Pardon Tales and Their Tellers in Sixteenth-Century France* (Stanford, CA: Stanford University Press, 1990). On these categories of Roman law, see Mario Sbriccoli's important article "Brigantaggio e ribellismi nella criminalistica dei secoli XVI–XVIII," in his *Storia del diritto penale e della giustizia: Scritti editi e inediti (1972–2007)*, 2 vols. (Milan: Giuffrè, 2009), 1:297–320.

106. For these ideal types, see Eric Hobsbawm, *Bandits* (New York: New Press, 2000), 31, 41; Debora L. Spar, *Pirates, Prophets and Pioneers: Business and Politics along the Technological Frontier* (London: Random House, 2001), published in the United States under the title *Ruling the Waves: Cycles of Discovery, Chaos, and Wealth from the Compass to the Internet* (New York: Harcourt, 2001).

107. Eric Hobsbawm, *Primitive Rebels: Studies in Archaic Forms of Social Movement in the 19th and 20th Centuries* (New York: W. W. Norton, 1959), esp. 6.

108. Desiderio Cavalca, *Il bando nella prassi e nella dottrina medievale* (Milan: Giuffrè, 1978). Because we are covering a large chronological territory, we must be careful to distinguish between the late medieval *bannitus pro maleficio*, who was subject to the criminal ban, usually after fleeing the jurisdiction of a judge, and who regularly appeared as the dangerous political exile (*fuoruscito* or *cacciato*) in medieval Italian chronicles, and the simple *latro* or *latrunculus*, the opportunistic "bandit" who indiscriminately made travel and trade dangerous. The ancient Romans knew very well the *latro*, but the medieval ban had Germanic roots. The clearest and most technically accurate discussion of the theory and practice of a medieval Italian ban is Anthony M. C. Mooney, "The Legal Ban in Florentine Statutory Law and the De bannitis of Nello da San Gimignano (1373–1430)," PhD diss., University of California at Los Angeles, 1976. See also, for real-world cases, the documents published in Peter Raymond Pazzaglini, *The Criminal Ban of the Sienese Commune, 1225–1310* (Milan: Giuffrè, 1979). I would suggest that the bandits in Verolengo must be seen as combining, though perhaps not technically, both types.

109. On the technical differences between bandits and rebels at the time generally, see Sbriccoli, *Crimen laesae maiestatis*, 117–148.

110. On the question of bandits and the *Risorgimento*, see, among others, Angelo Del Boca, *Italiani, brava gente? Un mito duro a morire* (Vicenza: Neri Pozza, 2005).

111. Luigi Pirandello, *Sei personaggi in cerca d'autore*, ed. Guido Davico Bonino (Turin: Einaudi, 2005 [1921]).

112. Kim MacQuarrie, *The Last Days of the Incas* (New York: Simon and Schuster, 2007), esp. 27.

113. On the territorial history of Lombardy in the period, see Roberto Mainardi, "Milano e la Lombardia alle soglie della 'modernità,'" in *Lombardia: Il territorio, l'ambiente, il paesaggio: L'età delle riforme*, ed. Carlo Pirovano (Milan: Electa, 1983), 7–36; for Piedmont, see Blythe Alice Raviola, "Sabaudian Spaces and Territories: Piedmont as a Composite State (Ecclesiastical Enclaves, Fiefs, Boundaries)," in *Sabaudian Studies: Political Culture, Dynasty, and Territory 1400–1700*, ed. Matthew Vester (Kirksville, MO: Truman State University Press, 2013), 278–297. On the tenuous territorial centralization of Savoy, see also Christopher Storrs's masterful *War, Diplomacy and the Rise of Savoy, 1690–1720* (Cambridge: Cambridge University Press, 1999).

114. On the tensions of armed citizenries in relation to banditry in late Renaissance Italy, see Arcangeli, "'Come bosco et spelunca di latroni,'" 78. On Valsesia, its geography, and its history between Lombardy and Piedmont, see Gian Paolo Garavaglia, "Un Confine 'fluido,' Sesia e Valsesia in età napoleonica," in *Alle frontiere della Lombardia: Politica, guerra e religione nell'età moderna*, ed. Claudio Donati (Milan: Franco Angeli, 2006), 227–256. For Vattel's argument, see his *Law of Nations*, 195 [I.XIII.176].

115. AST, *Paesi nuovo acquisto Valle di Sesia*, Mazzo 2, #22, "Memoriale a capi, riposte ad esso, supplica, esame, e lettere concernenti diverse dimande fatte da Regenti della Val Sesia," particularly the 1725 "Esame Sommario," 2v–5r; emphasis added. Such valleys had, of course, been victims of banditry since time immemorial; for a readable account from an earlier century, see Emilio Podestà, *I banditi di Valle Stura: Una cronaca del secolo XVI* (Ovada: Accademia Urbense, 1990). For an extended meditation on the problem of marauding beasts in early modern states, see, albeit for a different context, Jay M. Smith, *Monsters of the Gévaudan: The Making of a Beast* (Cambridge, MA: Harvard University Press, 2011), with references also to bandits on 17–18, 130, 347–348n99. On the timing of Savoy control, see Cristophe Gauchon, "Le cadaster d'un état Alpin: L'espace, les frontiers, les institutions," in *Cadastres et territoires / Catasti e territori: L'analyse des archives cadastrales pour l'interprétation du paysage et l'aménagement du territoire / L'analisi dei catasti storici per l'interpreta-*

zione del paesaggio e per il governo del territorio, ed. Andrea Longhi (Florence: Alinea editrice, 2008), 34–45, at 36.

116. Joseph A. Schumpeter, "The Creative Response in Economic History," in Schumpeter, *Essays on Entrepreneurs, Innovations, Business Cycles, and the Evolution of Capitalism,* ed. Richard V. Clemence and Richard Swedberg (New Brunswick, NJ: Transaction, 1989), 221–231, at 223; Anton Blok, *The Mafia of a Sicilian Village, 1860–1960: A Study of Violent Peasant Entrepreneurs,* foreword by Charles Tilly (Prospect Heights, IL: Waveland Press, 1974). On creating and claiming value, see, among others, Rakesh Khurana and Nitin Nohria, "It's Time to Make Management a True Profession," *Harvard Business Review,* October 2008, 70–77. Needless to say, this has been one of the core arguments of modern "socialist" traditions as well; see, for example, Gerald Allen Cohen, *Why Not Socialism?* (Princeton, NJ: Princeton University Press, 2009), 82, quoting Albert Einstein, "Why Socialism," *Monthly Review* 61, no. 1 (1949): 55–61, who in turn had drawn on Thorstein Veblen, *The Instinct of Workmanship and the State of the Industrial Arts* (New York: Macmillan, 1914), among others. On Veblen and predation, see Sidney Plotkin, "Thorstein Veblen and the Politics of Predatory Power," in *Thorstein Veblen: Economics for an Age of Crises,* ed. Erik S. Reinert and Francesca Lidia Viano (London: Anthem, 2012), 205–237.

117. Richard Cantillon, *Essay on the Nature of Trade in General,* ed. Anthony Brewer (Abingdon-on-Thames, UK: Routledge, 2001), 26.

118. Andrea Mubi Brighenti, "On Territorology: Towards a General Science of Territory," *Theory, Culture and Society* 27, no. 1 (2010): 52–72, 65–68; John Allen, "Topological Twists: Power's Shifting Geography," *Dialogues in Human Geography* 1, no. 3 (2011): 283–298.

119. Marco Battistoni, *Franchigie: Dazi, transiti e territori negli stati sabaudi del secolo XVIII* (Alessandria: Edizioni dell'orso, 2009), esp. 158. For a contemporary sovereign theorization of this principle, see Carlo Emmanuele III, *Regie Patentii d'approvazione dell'annesso Regolamento per la manutenzione, e riparazione delle Strade Reali, e pubbliche. in data de' 11. Settembre 1771* (Turin: Stamperia reale, 1771). On the importance of roads for trade, proto-industrialization, and economic development in the area, see, among others, Renzo Mortarotti, *L'Ossola nell'età moderna: Dall'annessione al Piemonte al fascismo (1743–1922)* (Domodossola: Libreria Grossi, 1985), 297. On Lombard roads as vehicles of trade and military territorialization, see Alessandra Dattero, "Percorrere il territorio nel Settecento: Militari asburgici in marcia tra Domini ereditari e Stati italiani," in Donati, *Alle frontiere della Lombardia,* 201–225, at 204. On the importance of roads for territorial unification, see Eugen Weber, *Peasants into Frenchmen: The Modernization of Rural France, 1870–1914* (Stanford, CA: Stanford University Press,

1976), 195–220. For the case of roads in relation to unification and socialization in eighteenth-century Italy, see Franco Borlando, *Il problema delle communicazioni nel sec. XVIII nei sui rapport col Risorgimento Italiano* (Pavia: Treves-Treccani-Tumminelli, 1932), 154. On the emergence of the infrastructure state and the extraordinary importance of public roads for territorial integration and economic development, see Jo Guldi, *Roads to Power: Britain Invents the Infrastructure State* (Cambridge, MA: Harvard University Press, 2012), esp. 194–197; throughout, Guldi strongly emphasizes the state-led nature of roadbuilding but engages with highwaymen only in passing, though see 174–177; for the New World, see John Lauritz Larson, *Internal Improvement: National Public Works and the Promise of Popular Government in the Early United States* (Chapel Hill: University of North Carolina Press, 2001), who, however, does not emphasize crime. For the case of canals, see also Mukerji, *Impossible Engineering;* for Lombardy in particular, see Andrea Castagna, *Il Naviglio di Paderno: Un'opera pubblica nella Lombardia del secondo Settecento* (Milan: Biblion, 2016), including 85–92 for their limits.

120. Economic works emphasizing the importance of infrastructure were, in effect, legion at the time; for an eloquent example, see Gregorio Pedro Pereira, *Dissertazione sopra la giusta valuta della moneta* (Faenza: Per Gioseffantonio Archi, [1757]), 97–98.

121. Thorstein Veblen, *The Theory of Business Enterprise* (New York: Charles Scribner's Sons, 1904), 31; Veblen, *The Engineers and the Price System* (New York: B. W. Huebsch, 1921), 1. For the current resurgence of interest in this aspect of Veblen's work, see the essays in Erik S. Reinert and Francesca Lidia Viano, eds., *Thorstein Veblen: Economics for an Age of Crises* (London: Anthem, 2012).

122. Steven L. Kaplan, *The Bakers of Paris and the Bread Question, 1700–1775* (Durham, NC: Duke University Press, 1996), 14–15; Kaplan, *The Stakes of Regulation,* chap. 1; Genovesi, *Storia del commercio della Gran Brettagna,* 1:11n.

123. AST, *Paesi nuovo acquisto Valle di Sesia,* Mazzo 2, #22, "Esame Sommario," 4v. Sven Beckert has rightly argued that "we need to pay more attention to the countryside" in the history of capitalism, in "The New History of Capitalism," in *Capitalism: The Reemergence of a Historical Concept,* ed. Jürgen Kocka and Marcel van der Linden (London: Bloomsbury, 2016), 235–249, at 242.

124. Tarun Khanna and Krishna G. Palepu, *Winning in Emerging Markets: A Road Map for Strategy and Execution* (Boston: Harvard Business Press, 2010), 14. For an example of what fills such voids, and the sometimes unhappy consequences of urban markets penetrating rural regions, see Rebecca Jean Emigh, *The Undevelopment of Capitalism: Sectors and Markets in Fifteenth-Century Tuscany* (Philadelphia: Temple University Press, 2009); and more broadly, Deepak Nayyar, "Globalization, History and Development: A Tale of Two Centuries," *Cambridge*

Journal of Economics 30, no. 1 (2006): 137–159, at 158. On "social bandits," see again Hobsbawm, *Bandits*. On the Singur Tata Nano controversy, see, among others, Laura Alfaro, Lakshmi Iyer, and Namrata Arora, "Tata Motors in Singur: Public Purpose and Private Property (B)," *Harvard Business School Case 709–029*, 2009 (rev. 2012). It is not without reason that Marcus Rediker recently summarized a lifetime of work on early modern pirates by equating the "meaning of the Jolly Roger, and perhaps of piracy altogether," with "the defiance of death itself," for which see his *Villains of All Nations: Atlantic Pirates in the Golden Age* (Boston: Beacon Press, 2004), 169.

125. Adam Smith, *An Inquiry into the Nature and Causes of the Wealth of Nations*, ed. Edwin Cannan, 2 vols. (Chicago: University of Chicago Press, 1976), 1:21.

126. Pietro Verri, "Meditazioni sulla economia politica (Livorno 1772)," in *ENOPV*, vol. 2, pt. 2, 341–570, at 495.

127. See, for example, Victoria N. Bateman, *Markets and Growth in Early Modern Europe* (London: Pickering and Chatto, 2012), 174, which builds on Paul Collier and Anthony J. Venables, "Trade and Economic Performance: Does Africa's Fragmentation Matter?," in *People, Politics, and Globalization: Annual World Bank Conference on Development Economics—Global, 2009*, ed. Justin Yifu Lin and Boris Pleskovic (Washington, DC: World Bank, 2010), 51–76, at 62, 67.

128. Giovanni Battista Passeri, *Vite de pittori, scultori ed architetti che anno lavarato in Roma morti dal 1641 fino al 1673* (Rome: Gregorio Settari, 1772), 55. On the movement, see Giuliano Briganti with Ludovica Trezzani and Laura Laureati, *The Bamboccianti: The Painters of Everyday Life in Seventeenth-Century Rome*, trans. Robert Erich Wolf (Rome: U. Bocci, 1983).

129. Giovanni Michele Graneri, *Mercato in piazza San Carlo*, 1752, Palazzo Madama, Turin, Italy, 540/D.

130. See, again, Kaplan, *The Stakes of Regulation*, esp. 50–60.

131. For a still-illuminating meditation on the nature of markets, and "what lies around the fair," see Luigi Einaudi, "Lectures on the Market," in Einaudi, *Selected Economic Essays*, ed. Luca Einaudi, Riccardo Faucci, and Roberto Marchionatti (Basingstoke, UK: Palgrave Macmillan, 2006), 39–65, at 57.

132. On Magnasco, see Marco Bona Castellotti and Fausta Franchini Guelfi, *Alessandro Magnasco (1667–1749)* (Milan: Mondadori Electa, 1996).

133. For a beautiful depiction of the market and its history, see Aldo Barilli et al., *Il ventre di Milano: Fisiologia della capitale morale* (Milan: Carlo Aliprandi, 1888), 102–115. On the theme of bellies and marketplaces, see, famously, Émile Zola, *La ventre de Paris* (Paris: Charpentier, 1873).

134. See, for example, Bruno Caizzi, *Industria, commercio e banca in Lombardia nel XVIII secolo* (Milan: Banca Commercial Italiana, 1968), 213–266; and Carlos Marichal, "The Spanish-American Silver Peso: Export Commodity and Global

Money of the Ancien Regime, 1550–1800," in *From Silver to Cocaine: Latin American Commodity Chains and the Building of the World Economy, 1500–2000,* ed. Steven Topik, Carlos Marichal, and Zephyr Frank (Durham, NC: Duke University Press, 2006), 25–52. For such a global approach to the origins of capitalism, see, among others, Sven Beckert, *The Empire of Cotton: A Global History* (New York: Alfred A. Knopf, 2014), esp. xxi. On the importance of free ports, see Corey Tazzara, *The Free Port of Livorno and the Transformation of the Mediterranean World, 1574–1790* (Oxford: Oxford University Press, 2017).

135. For a remarkable exposition of the granularity of Milanese markets at the time of Beccaria, see Aldo Carera, "I mercati della tradizione," in *I mercati e le fiere della provincia di Milano tra XVIII e XX secolo,* ed. Maria Piera Bassi (Milan: Provincia di Milano, 1990), 17–61, and see 33–34 for an example of the international hinterland of even peripheral markets.

136. Cesare Beccaria, *On Crimes and Punishments and Other Writings,* ed. Aaron Thomas, trans. Aaron Thomas and Jeremy Parzen (Toronto: University of Toronto Press, 2008), 72–73. On a similar, if far earlier, case, see Robert Fredona, "Baldus de Ubaldis on Conspiracy and *Laesa Maiestas* in Late Trecento Florence," in *The Politics of Law in Late Medieval and Renaissance Italy,* ed. Lawrin Armstrong and Julius Kirshner (Toronto: University of Toronto Press, 2011), 141–160.

137. For variations on this theme, see Thomas W. Gallant, "Brigandage, Piracy, Capitalism, and State-Formation: Transnational Crime from a Historical World-Systems Perspective," in *States and Illegal Practices,* ed. Josiah Heyman (Oxford: Berg, 1999), 25–61, at 25, 40–41, 50–52; Eric Tagliacozzo, *Secret Trades, Porous Borders: Smuggling and States along a Southeast Asian Frontier, 1865–1915* (New Haven, CT: Yale University Press, 2005), 369–370; Marcus Rediker, *Villains of All Nations: Atlantic Pirates in the Golden Age* (Boston: Beacon Press, 2004), 168–169.

138. The problem of banditry in liminal lands had, of course, been a trope of political philosophy; see, for example, Scipione Ammirato, *Discorsi sopra Cornelio Tacito* (Florence: Filippo Giunti, 1594), 140–148. On banditry in the period, see, among numerous others, Enzo Ciconte, *Banditi e briganti: Rivolta continua dal Cinquecento all'Ottocento* (Soveria Mannelli: Rubbettino, 2011), 23–61. In the case of nearby Savoy, this was perhaps most clearly evident in the case of Sardinia; see Maria Lepori, *Faide: Nobili e banditi nella Sardegna sabauda del Settecento* (Rome: Viella, 2010), 171–196. On the historical role of mountains (and specifically the Alps) as territories uniquely "offering resistence," see Enrico Camanni, *Alpi ribelli: Storie di montagna, resistenza e utopia* (Rome-Bari: Laterza, 2016).

139. On Liguria in this context, see the important microhistories by Osvaldo Raggio, *Faide e parentele: Lo stato genovese visto dalla Fontanabuona* (Turin: Einaudi, 1990), and Edoardo Grendi, *Il cervo e la repubblica: Il modello ligure di antico regime*

(Turin: Einaudi, 1993). On bandits specifically, see Gabriella Solavaggione, "Brigantaggio e contrabbando nella campagna lombarda del Settecento," *Nuova rivista storica* 1–2 (1970): 23–49, at 46–49; 3–4 (1970): 374–419; Battistoni, *Franchigie*, 182, 209–213, 229–240; Andrea Zanini, "Soldati corsi e famegli: La forza pubblica della Repubblica di Genova nel XVIII secolo," in *Corpi armati e ordine pubblico in Italia (CVI–XVX sec.),* ed. Livio Antonielli and Claudio Donati (Soveria Mannelli: Rubbettino, 2003), 141–180, emphasizing at 178 how feudal jurisdictions undermined territorial law-enforcement; Vittorio Tigrini, "Giurisdizione e transito nel Settecento: I feudi imperiali tra il Genovesato e la pianura Padana," in *Lungo le antiche strade: Vie d'acqua e di terra tra Stati, giurisdizioni e confine nella cartografia dell'età moderna,* ed. Marina Cavallera (Busto Arsizio: Nomos, 2007), 45–94, esp. 50; Andrea Zanini, "Feudi, feudatari ed economie nella montagna ligure," in *Libertà e dominio: Il sistema politico genovese: Le relazioni esterne e il controllo del territorio,* ed. Matthias Schnettger and Carlo Taviani (Rome: Viella, 2011), 305–316. On banditry and "feudal values," see Villari, "Conclusioni," 414. However, these problems themselves were ancient, occurring precisely at the intersection of Savoy, Milan, and Genoa; see, for mid-seventeenth-century occurrences, the many incidents collected in AST, *Incidenti con Genova,* Mazzo 1, fasc. 1. On pirate utopias, see the anarchist writer Wilson's *Pirate Utopias,* esp. 188–204; for the case of Tortuga, see Hakim Bey [Peter Lamborn Wilson], *T. A. Z.: The Temporary Autonomous Zone* (Seattle: Pacific Publishing Studio, 2011 [1991]), 83–84; for historiographical context, the essays in Peter Ludlow, ed., *Crypto Anarchy, Cyberstates, and Pirate Utopias* (Cambridge, MA: MIT Press, 2001). For a more historical analysis exploring also the dysfunctionality of such places, their role in early modern political economy, and the concentrated state action to get rid of them, see Niklas Frykman, "Pirates and Smugglers: Political Economy in the Red Atlantic," in Stern and Wennerlind, *Mercantilism Reimagined,* 218–238.

140. For the ambassador's orders, see AST, *Materie Politiche, Negotiazioni con Genova,* Mazzo 9, #2, "Istruzioni di S.Mta al Conte [Giuseppe Maria] Ferrero di Lauriano per la sua Commissione di Ministro presso La Repubblica di Genova," 30 January 1753, 3v–5r. For Verri on this, see Battistoni, *Franchigie,* 232.

141. See the numerous cases collected in those years in AST, *Incidenti con Genova,* Mazzo 5. On the illegal capture of Mandrin, see Kwass, *Contraband,* 204–216.

142. For the Milanese side of this correspondence, see particularly the collections in ASM, *AG 30, Potenze estere post. 1535, 44 Genova 1733–1801; AG 30, 210 Torino e Savoia 1761–1770; AG 28, Arresto e consegna di rei, convenzioni . . . (Genova), 1581–1799; AG 37 (Torino) 1761–1773,* particularly Kaunitz to Firmian, 24 September 1764, and Kaunitz to Firmian, 1 October 1764. For the rich and varied spectrum of humanity covered by this term—much of the emotive impact of which more

recently has been conveyed by the Trumpian phrase "bad hombres"—see Giacomo Todeschini, *Visibilmente crudeli: Malviventi, persone sospette e gente qualunque dal Medioevo all'età moderna* (Bologna: Il Mulino, 2007). On the territorial policing of the Milanese state at the time, see Livio Antonielli, "Polizie di città e polizie di campagna in antico regime: Il caso dello Stato di Milano a metà Settecento," in *Polizia, ordine pubblico e crimine tra città e campagna: Un confronto comparativo*, ed. Livio Antonielli (Soveria Manelli: Rubbettino, 2010), 17–48.

143. Note accompanying Kaunitz to Firmian, 15 April 1765, 1r, in ASM, *AG 28, Arresto e consegna di rei, convenzioni . . . (Genova), 1581–1799*. The use of such beastly, medical, and pathological metaphors for bandits was of course well-established; see, for two illustrious examples, the great reason-of-state theorist Ammirato, *Discorsi sopra Cornelio Tacito,*148; and Cosimo I to Pope Pius IV, 7 July 1563, Archivio di Stato di Firenze, *Medaceo 327,* fols. 173r–175r, esp. 174v.

144. ASM, *AG 28, Arresto e consegna di rei, convenzioni . . . (Genova), 1581–1799,* and particularly Firmian to Kaunitz of 4 August 1764, 1v–2r, Viry to Firmian, 8 May 1765, Viry to Firmian 18 May 1765, and Kaunitz to Firmian, 1 [5?] April 1765; AST, *Milano, Lettere diverse, 1751 in 1765,* Mazzo 12, #1, *Lettere dei Conti Cristiani, e di Firmian.* . . . See particularly the letters bound in a volume entitled *1754 Milano, 1754 . . . 1765,* and, for particularly purple prose, Viry to Firmian, 4 August 1764, 11 August 1764, 8 September 1764, 12 September 1764, 22 September 1764, 3 October 1764, 26 January 1765, 27 March 1765, and 18 May 1765, 53r–55r, 55v–56r, 59v–60r, 65v–67v, 74r–76v, 83r–84v, 86v–93v, and the unbound Firmian to Viry, 2 February 1765, 1r–1v. Needless to say, this is not to suggest that the Genoese themselves did not worry about domestic banditry. On their relentless war on the phenomenon, see, among others, Maria Desiderata Floris, "La repressione della criminalità organizzata nella Repubblica di Genova tra Cinque e Seicento: Aspetti e cronologia della prassi legislativa," in *Bande armate, banditi, banditismo e repressioni di giustizia negli stati europei di antico regime,* ed. Gherardo Ortalli (Rome: Jouvence, 1986), 87–106; and Zanini, "Soldati corsi e famegli."

145. AST, *Milano, Lettere diverse, 1751 in 1765,* Mazzo 12, #1, *Lettere dei Conti Cristiani, e di Firmian . . . ,* Firmian to Viry, 2 February 1765, 1r.

146. AST, *Milano, Lettere diverse, 1751 in 1765,* Mazzo 12, #1, *Lettere dei Conti Cristiani, e di Firmian . . . ,* volume entitled *1754 Milano, 1754 . . . 1765,* Viry to Firmian, 4 August 1764, 53v–56r.

147. AST, *Milano, Lettere diverse, 1751 in 1765,* Mazzo 12, #1, *Lettere dei Conti Cristiani, e di Firmian . . . ,* volume entitled *1754 Milano, 1754 . . . 1765,* Viry to Firmian, 3 October 1764, 67r–67v.

148. AST, *Materie Politiche, Negotiazioni con Genova,* Mazzo 9, *1753 al 1798,* no. 5, manuscript beginning "Alle rappresentanze," 1r.

149. AST, *Materie Politiche, Negotiazioni con Genova*, Mazzo 9, *1753 al 1798*, no. 5, manuscript beginning "Alle rappresentanze," 2r.

150. See the lengthy report on incidents dating back to 1762 submitted alongside the letter from Girolamo Gastaldi to the Doge and others, 25 January 1764, Archivio di Stato di Genova, Genoa, Italy (hereafter cited as ASG), *Archivio Segreto, 2505, Torino Anni 1764–1765*, Mazzo 18, esp. 2r–2v.

151. AST, *Materie Politiche, Negotiazioni con Genova*, Mazzo 9, *1753 al 1798*, no. 5, manuscript beginning "Alle rappresentanze," 2v.

152. AST, *Milano, Lettere diverse, 1751 in 1765*, Mazzo 12, #1, *Lettere dei Conti Cristiani, e di Firmian* . . . , volume entitled *1754 Milano, 1754 . . . 1765*, Viry to Firmian, 26 January 1765, 76r–76v.

153. AST, *Milano, Lettere diverse, 1751 in 1765*, Mazzo 12, #1, *Lettere dei Conti Cristiani, e di Firmian* . . . , volume entitled *1754 Milano, 1754 . . . 1765*, Viry to Firmian, 27 March 1765, 83r–84v.

154. On the Bronze Age origins of such conventions, see Stephen C. Neff, *Justice among Nations* (Cambridge, MA: Harvard University Press, 2014), 14; and for a diverse roster of such conventions in Italy, dating back to the mid-fifteenth century, ASM, Atti di Governo, 26, *Giustizia Punitiva, Parte Antica*.

155. Ammirato, *Discorsi sopra Cornelio Tacito*, 146, on which see also Lacchè, *Latrocinium*, 76, 78. This supports some of the broader arguments in Thomson, *Mercenaries, Pirates, and Sovereigns*, 149–152.

156. See the anonymous "Pro Memoria" dated 10 April 1764 enclosed with Gerolamo Gastaldi to the Doge and others, [29?] February 1764, 1v, as well as Gastaldi's own "Riflessioni sopra la minuta consegnata dal S. Conte Bogino," 1r, for the argument that times had changed too much to imitate such old models, both in ASG, *Archivio Segreto 2505, Torino Anni 1764–1765*, Mazzo 18. On such agreements in general, see Lacchè, *Latrocinium*, 73–80; and Emanuele Pagano, *"Questa turba infame a comun danno unita": Delinquenti, marginali, magistrati nel Mantovano asburgico (1750–1800)* (Milan: Franco Angeli, 2014), 98–101.

157. AST, *Milano, Lettere diverse, 1751 in 1765*, Mazzo 12, #1, *Lettere dei Conti Cristiani, e di Firmian* . . . , volume entitled *1754 Milano, 1754 . . . 1765*, Viry to Firmian, 18 May 1765, 86v–93v, esp. 91v. For one of endless examples, see AST, *Ducato di Monferrato*, Mazzo 17, #24, "Promessa del Marchese Guglielmo di Monferrato di far rimettere al Duca Carlo di Savoja li banditi, che si rifugieranno nei suoi stati pendente un anno" [4 September 1516]. Lombardy had recently signed such agreements not only with Piedmont but also with the Papal States and Venice; see, among other instances, *Convenzione per l'arresto dei Banditi, e Malviventi frà lo Stato Pontificio per una parte, e gli Stati della Lombardia Austriaca dipendente da S. M. R.I per l'altra*, Rome, 1 Jaunary 1755, renewing a 1750 agreement, again

renewed also in *Convenzione per l'arresto de banditi, e malviventi, frà lo Stato Pontificio e gli Stati della Lombardia Austriaca,* Rome, 1 January 1767.

158. AST, *Materie Politiche, Negotiazioni con Genova,* Mazzo 9, *1753 al 1798,* no. 5, manuscript beginning "Progetto di Convenzione colla Repubblica di Genova per gli Stati di Terraferma," 10 April 1764, IV. This language of banditry and "free trade" was already evident in Italy in the sixteenth century; see Lacchè, *Latrocinium,* 47.

159. On customs duties in the area, see again Battistoni, *Franchigie.* Pietro Verri said similar things over and over again, but see his "Meditazioni sulla economia politica," 438. This theme has been explored by, among others, Pier Luigi Porta and Roberto Scazzieri, "Pietro Verri's Political Economy: Commercial Society, Civil Society, and the Science of the Legislator," *History of Political Economy* 34, no. 1 (2002): 83–110. On the tradition of public happiness in particular, see Antonio Trampus, *Il diritto alla felicità: Storia di un'idea* (Rome-Bari: Laterza, 2008).

160. Vattel, *Law of Nations,* 227 [I.XIX.232].

161. Ibid., 227–228 [I.XIX.232–233]; emphasis added. The gaps in international criminal policing are filled by the so-called *aut dedere aut iudicare* principle—i.e., extradite or prosecute—with origins in the Renaissance Anglo-Italian jurist Alberico Gentili; see Thomas Erskine Holland, ed., *Alberici Gentilis De iure belli libri tres* (Oxford: Oxford University Press, 1877), chap. 21, "*De malefactis privatorum,*" esp. 96.

162. On Vattel, states, and international order, see Isaac Nakhimovsky, "Vattel's Theory of International Order: Commerce and the Balance of Power in the Law of Nations," *History of European Ideas* 33, no. 2 (2007): 157–173; and Nakhimovsky, "Carl Schmitt's Vattel and the 'Law of Nations' between Enlightenment and Revolution," *Grotiana* 31 (2010): 141–164.

163. Immanuel Kant, "Perpetual Peace: A Philosophical Sketch," in Kant, *Political Writings,* ed. Hans Reiss, 2nd ed. (Cambridge: Cambridge University Press, 1991), 103; emphasis in original.

164. See Nino Calvini, *La rivoluzione del 1753 a Sanremo,* 2 vols. (Bordighera: Istituto internazionale di studi liguri, 1953), esp. 1:13, 125–129; Sophie Caillieret, *L'affaire de San Remo, un episode méconnu des relations diplomatiques entre la France et la cour de Vienne (1753–1772),* Mémoire de maîtrise, Université d'Angers, Angers, 1999; Vittorio Tigrino, *Sudditi e confederati: Sanremo, Genova e una storia particolare del Settecento europeo* (Alessandria: Edizioni dell'Orso, 2009), 334–360. On Genoa's territorial state in international context, see the essays collected in Matthias Schnettger and Carlo Taviani, eds., *Libertà e dominio: Il sistema politico Genovese; Le relazioni esterne e il controllo del territorio* (Rome: Viella, 2011). On Genoa in the period, see generally Matthias Schnettger, *"Principe Sovrano" oder*

"Civitas Imperialis?" Die Republik Genua und das Alte Reich in der Früen Neuzeit (1556–1797) (Mainz am Rhein: Verlag Philipp von Zabern, 2006), esp. 363–412 on the San Remo affair. On San Remo and its festival today, see Leonardo Campus, *Non solo canzonette: L'Italia della ricostruzione e del miracolo attraverso il Festival di Sanremo* (Milan: Mondadori, 2015); and Fabio Melelli and Francesco Rondolini, *Il festival degli italiani: Sanremo raccontato dai suoi protagonisti* (Rome: Arcana, 2016).

165. On these issues, see Franco Venturi, *Settecento riformatore,* 5 vols. in 7 (Turin: Einaudi, 1969–1990), vol. 5, bk. 1, 3–222. On the importance of the Enlightenment influence on the Corsican revolt in the context of Venturi's lifelong antifascism, connecting his youthful writings on Paoli for *Giustizia e libertà,* see Giuseppe Ricuperati, *Un laboratorio cosmopolitico: Illuminismo e storia a Torino nel Novecento* (Naples: Edizioni scientifiche italiane, 2011), 160. On contemporary Genoese worries linking the revolts of San Remo and Corsica, see Tigrino, *Sudditi e confederati,* 339.

166. See, for example, the letter from the Doge, Governatori e Procuratori della Repubblica di Genova to Girolamo De Fornari, 23 June 1764, ASG, *Archivio Segreto, 2600, Vienna Anni 1763–1765,* Mazzo 83, 1r; "Progetto di Convenzione colla Repubblica di Genova per gli Stati di Terraferma," enclosed with Gastaldi to the Doge and others, 9 May 1764, 1v; and, for the roads, Gastaldi to the Doge and others, 13 June 1764 both in ASG, *Archivio Segreto 2505, Torino Anni 1764–1765,* Mazzo 18.

167. Coded missive from Gastaldi to the Doge and others, 21 March 1764, deciphered by an anonymous Genoese functionary, ASG, *Archivio Segreto 2505, Torino Anni 1764–1765,* Mazzo 18.

168. See, among others, the report in Girolamo Gastaldi to the Doge and others, [29?] February 1764, ASG, *Archivio Segreto, 2505, Torino Anni 1764–1765,* Mazzo 18, 2v; the Doge and others to Girolamo De Fornari, [9?] March 1767, ASG, *Archivio Segreto, 2600, Vienna 1766–1767,* Mazzo 83, 1r, 2r–2v. See also the lengthy letter of 18 June 1766.

169. Coded missive from Gastaldi to the Doge and others, 20 June 1764, ASG, *Archivio Segreto 2505, Torino Anni 1764–1765,* Mazzo 18.

170. AST, *Milano, Lettere diverse, 1751 in 1765,* Mazzo 12, #1, *Lettere dei Conti Cristiani, e di Firmian . . . ,* volume entitled *1754 Milano, 1754 . . . 1765,* Viry to Firmian, 18 May 1765, 86v–93v, esp. 91v–92r.

171. Calvini, *La rivoluzione del 1753 a Sanremo,* 2:151.

172. Coded missive from Gastaldi to the Doge and others, 13 August 1764, ASG, *Archivio Segreto 2505, Torino Anni 1764–1765,* Mazzo 18, 2r.

173. AST, *Materie Politiche, Negotiazioni con Genova,* Mazzo 9, *1753 al 1798, n. 5,* manuscript entitled "Ristretto delle intelligenze coerenti alla trattativa intrapresa nel

1764," 2 Settembre 1772, IV–4r, as well as Kaunitz to Firmian, 23 June 1766, in ASM, *AG 28, Arresto e consegna di rei, convenzioni . . . (Genova), 1581–1799*; emphasis perhaps added.

174. J. M. Munn-Rankin, "Diplomacy in Western Asia in the Early Second Millennium B.C.," *Iraq* 18, no. 1 (1956): 68–110, at 93.

175. James J. Kinneally III, "The Political Offence Exception: Is the United States–United Kingdom Supplementary Extradition Treaty the Beginning of the End?," *American University Journal of International Law and Policy* 2, no. 1 (1987): 203–227, at 206. For the deeper history of this institution, see Christine Van Den Wyngaert, *Political Offence Exception to Extradition: The Delicate Problem of Balancing the Rights of the Individual and the International Public Order* (Deventer: Kluwer, 1980).

176. See, among endless others, *Convenzione per l'arresto dei Banditi, e Malviventi frà lo Stato Pontificio per una parte, e gli Stati della Lombardia Austriaca dipendente da S. M. R.I per l'atra* ([Milan?]: n.p., [1755?]).

177. Zanini, "Soldati corsi e famegli," 146, 153.

178. Beccaria, *On Crimes and Punishments*, 10–12. See also Frederick Rosen, "Utilitarianism and the Reform of the Criminal Law," in *The Cambridge Companion to Eighteenth-Century Political Thought*, ed. Mark Goldie and Robert Wokler (Cambridge: Cambridge University Press, 2006), 547–572, at 552.

179. Beccaria, *On Crimes and Punishments*, 52; emphasis in original.

180. Ibid., 46–47, and 55. For a typical case of this form of punishment, see, for example, Enzo Ciconte, *Banditi e briganti: Rivolta continua dal Cinquecento all'Ottocento* (Soveria Mannelli: Rubbettino, 2011), 55–56. Beccaria's influential resistance to the practice is made emblematic even by legal historians in the tradition of Annamaria Monti, "Illegitimate Appropriation or Just Punishment? The Confiscation of Property in *Ancien Régime* Criminal Law and Doctrine," in *Property Rights and Their Violations: Expropriations and Confiscations, 16th–20th Centuries / La propriété violée: Expropriations et confiscations, XVIe–XXe siècles*, ed. Luigi Lorenzetti, Michela Barbot, and Luca Mocarelli (Bern: Peter Lang, 2012), 15–35, esp. 15.

181. Beccaria, *On Crimes and Punishments*, 72.

182. Ibid.

183. Cesare Beccaria, "Estratto del quinto tomo dei 'Mélanges' di D'Alembert," in *ENOCB*, 2:311–346, at 341; emphasis added; originally published in *Estratto della Letteratura europea* (1767): 2:142–159, 4:83–97; (1768): 1:113–126, extracting from and commenting on Jean Le Rond d'Alembert, *Mélanges de literature, d'histoire et de philosophie* (Amsterdam: Zacharie Châtelain et Fils, 1767 [but 1766]).

184. Beccaria, *On Crimes and Punishments*, 50.

185. Ibid., 25.

186. Cesare Beccaria, "Piano delle lezioni di pubblica economia che si danno nello spazio di due anni dal professore di questa scienza," in *ENOCB*, 3:67–77, at 74–75. On railways and nation-building in nineteenth-century Italy, see Albert Schram, *Railways and the Formation of the Italian State in the Nineteenth Century* (Cambridge: Cambridge University Press, 1997), and 152 for their economic and security consequences. On the polarizing effects of railroads in contemporary Germany, however, see Abigail Green, *Fatherlands: State-Building and Nationhood in Nineteenth-Century Germany,* rev. ed. (Cambridge: Cambridge University Press, 2004), 237.

187. Cesare Beccaria, "Elementi di economia pubblica," in *ENOCB*, 3:97–390, at 170–171 [2.I.9].

188. Cesare Beccaria, "Materiali preparatori e stesure rifiutate," in *ENOCB*, 3:593–599, at 595.

189. Verri, "Meditazioni sulla economia politica," 466.

190. Ibid., 506.

191. On the multiplying power of roads, see ibid., 506.

192. Pietro Verri, "Pensieri del conte Pietro Verri sullo stato politico del Milanese nel 1790," in *ENOCB*, 6:390–425, at 413–414; emphasis added.

193. See the vast conceptual arc from Jean-Jacques Rousseau, "Of the Social Contract," in Rousseau, *The Social Contract and Other Later Political Writings,* ed. Victor Gourevitch (Cambridge: Cambridge University Press, 1997), 39–152, at 74, to David Stasavage, *States of Credit: Size, Power, and the Development of European Polities* (Princeton, NJ: Princeton University Press, 2011), 158.

194. See, for example, Christopher J. Fuhrman, *Policing the Roman Empire: Soldiers, Administration, and Public Order* (Oxford: Oxford University Press, 2012), 155–156 and 156f32; Henry Kamen, "Public Authority and Popular Crime: Banditry in Valencia, 1660–1714," *Journal of European Economic History* 3 (1974): 654–687; Kim A. Wagner, *Thuggee: Banditry and the British in Early Nineteenth-Century India* (Houndmills, UK: Palgrave Macmillan, 2007), esp. 5; Margreet Van Till, *Banditry in West Java, 1869–1942,* trans. David McKay and Beverley Jackson (Singapore: National University of Singapore Press, 2011), esp. 107, 189–191; Anton Blok, *The Mafia of a Sicilian Village 1860–1960: A Study of Violent Peasant Entrepreneurs* (New York: Harper and Row, 1974), for useful perspectives on which see Filippo Sabetti, *Village Politics and the Mafia in Sicily* (Montreal: McGill–Queen's University Press, 2002). For a world-historical perspective on such "military entrepreneurship" emphasizing the role of land distribution, see Gallant, "Brigandage, Piracy," esp. 30.

195. For a selection of essays fruitfully charting the virtues and limitations of this perspective in the variegated case of Latin America, see Richard W. Slatta, ed., *Bandidos: The Varieties of Latin American Banditry* (Westport, CT: Greenwood Press, 1987).

196. E.g., Frank Safford and Marco Palacios, *Colombia: Fragmented Land, Divided Society* (Oxford: Oxford University Press, 2002), esp. ix; Elizabeth Pisani, *Indonesia Etc.: Exploring the Improbable Nation* (New York: Norton, 2014), 68.

197. Quoted in Olson, *We Are Anonymous*, 424. For a similar statement of criminality and spatial alienation online, see Julian Assange, *The Unauthorized Autobiography* (Edinburgh: Canongate Books, 2011), 76, for the appropriately complex authorship of which, see Andrew O'Hagan, "Ghosting," *London Review of Books*, 6 March 2014, 5–26; and for an explanation based on pure spatial anxieties, see Kevin Mitnick with William L. Simon, *Ghost in the Wires: My Adventures as the World's Most Wanted Hacker* (New York: Back Bay Books, 2011), 3. On this brave new world generally, see still the essays in Peter Ludlow, ed., *High Noon on the Electronic Frontier: Conceptual Issues in Cyberspace* (Cambridge, MA: MIT Press, 1996); and, with even clearer piratical resonances, Ludlow, *Crypto Anarchy*.

198. Jon Ronson, *So You've Been Publicly Shamed* (New York: Riverhead Books, 2015), 121–129. For a poignant meditation on "the definition of what constitutes a real space," see also Andrew Groen, *Empires of Eve: A History of the Great Wars of Eve Online* (n.p.: Andrew Groen, 2016), esp. 1.

199. Spar, *Ruling the Waves*, 26.

200. Henri Pirenne, *An Economic and Social History of Medieval Europe*, trans. I. E. Glegg (London: Kegan Paul, Trench, Trubner, 1936), 22; quoted in, among many others, Spar, *Ruling the Waves*, 23, and Geoffrey M. Hodgson, *How Economics Forgot History: The Problem of Historical Specificity in Social Science* (London: Routledge, 2001), 311, 135.

201. Montesquieu, *The Spirit of the Laws*, ed. Anne M. Cohler, Basia C. Miller, and Harold S. Stone (Cambridge: Cambridge University Press, 1989), 362.

202. For a lengthy meditation on this concept, see Josh Linkner, *The Road to Reinvention: How to Drive Disruption and Accelerate Transformation* (Hoboken, NJ: Wiley, 2014).

203. Khanna and Palepu, *Winning in Emerging Markets*.

204. Jacob Burckhardt, *Reflections on History* (London: Allen and Unwin, 1943), 214; for context, see also Lionel Gossman, *Basel in the Age of Burckhardt* (Chicago: University of Chicago Press, 2000), 344. On the history of creative destruction, see Erik S. Reinert and Hugo Reinert, "Creative Destruction in Economics: Nietzsche, Sombart, Schumpeter," in *Friedrich Nietzsche (1844–1900): Economy and Society*, ed. Jürgen G. Backhaus and Wolfgang Drechsler (Dordrecht: Springer, 2006), 55–85.

205. See also Jill Lepore's poignant "The Disruption Machine: What the Gospel of Innovation Gets Wrong," *New Yorker*, 23 June 2014, 30–36.

206. John Yoo, "Obama, Drones, and Thomas Aquinas," *Wall Street Journal*, 7 June 2012, quoted in Jane Mayer, *The Dark Side: The Inside Story of How the War*

on Terror Turned into a War on American Ideals (New York: Doubleday, 2008), 153. On the "torture memos," see David Cole, ed., *The Torture Memos: Rationalizing the Unthinkable* (New York: New Press, 2009).

207. Durand and Vergne, *The Pirate Organization*, 13–14, and again 56: "Somali bandits are not pirates." On Somali piracy in action, see Quy-Toan Do, *The Pirates of Somalia: Ending the Threat, Rebuilding a Nation* (Washington, DC: World Bank, 2013).

208. For a salutary reminder that Somali pirates encapsulate piracy as real rather than "self-referential," see Rennie, *Treasure Neverland,* 270. On the challenge of Somali piracy, see also Sophus A. Reinert and Alissa Davies, "Piracy in Somalia (A)" and "Piracy in Somalia (B)," *Harvard Business School Cases* 9-718-018 and 9-718-019 (Boston: Harvard Business School Publishing, 2017).

209. *City of God* 4.4.

210. Giuseppe Gorani, *Storia di Milano (1700–1796),* ed. Alcesti Tarchetti, foreword by Carlo Capra (Bari: Cariplo-Laterza, 1989), 231.

211. This was, in many ways, the approach of the Academy of Fisticuffs more broadly as well; see, for example, Alessandro Verri, "Dell'ozio," in *Il Caffè,* 288–291, at 290.

212. The literature on human rights is massive, but for the context of eighteenth-century Italy, see Vincenzo Ferrone, *The Politics of Enlightenment: Republicanism, Constitutionalism, and the Rights of Man in Gaetano Filangieri,* trans. Sophus A. Reinert (London: Anthem, 2012). Needless to say, Enlightenment Italy played an important role in the often-neglected prehistory of Samuel Moyn, *The Last Utopia: Human Rights in History* (Cambridge, MA: Harvard University Press, 2010). On the relationship between human rights and economic conditions, however, see now Samuel Moyn, *Not Enough: Human Rights in an Unequal World* (Cambridge, MA: Harvard University Press, 2018), with a reference to the origins of distributive justice during the Enlightenment at 17.

5. Enlightenment Socialisms

1. For context, see Attilio Brilli, *Un paese di romantici briganti: Gli italiani nell'immmaginario del Grand Tour* (Bologna: Il Mulino, 2003); Sophus A. Reinert, "'One Will Do with Political Economy . . . What the Scholastics Did with Philosophy': Henry Lloyd and the Mathematization of Economics," *History of Political Economy* 34, no. 4 (2007): 643–677.

2. Cesare Beccaria, *On Crimes and Punishments and Other Writings,* ed. Aaron Thomas, trans. Aaron Thomas and Jeremy Parzen (Toronto: University of Toronto Press, 2008), 25 (unless otherwise noted, all citations for *On Crimes and Punishments* in this chapter are to this edition); Paul Friedland, *Seeing Justice*

Done: The Age of Spectacular Capital Punishment in France (Oxford: Oxford University Press 2012), 205.

3. Luigi Firpo, "Le edizioni italiane del 'Dei delitti e delle pene,'" in *Edizione Nazionale delle Opere di Cesare Beccaria*, ed. Luigi Firpo and Gianni Francioni, 16 vols. in 17 (Milan: Mediobanca, 1984–2015) (hereafter cited as *ENOCB*), 1:535–699, at 537–623. On its international reception, see Venturi's survey in Cesare Beccaria, *Dei delitti e delle pene*, ed. Franco Venturi (Turin: Einaudi, 1965), 425–660.

4. Kaunitz to Firmian, 21 May 1767, Archivio di Stato di Milano, Milan, Italy, *Autografi, no. 164, Uomini celebri: Cesare Beccaria*, fol. 1r.

5. *The Monthly Review*, vol. 36 (London: Griffiths, 1767), 298–299, at 298.

6. On these events, see Girolamo Imbruglia, "Illuminismo e religione: Il *Dei delitti e delle pene* e la difesa dei Verri dinanzi alla censura inquisitoriale," *Studi Settecenteschi* 25–26 (2005–2006): 119–161; and Mario Pisani, *Cesare Beccaria e l'Index Librorum Prohibitorum* (Naples: Edizioni Scientifiche Italiane, 2013).

7. Pierre François des Vouglans, "Réfutation du traité des délits et peines [1766]," in Vouglans, *Les lois criminelles de la France dans leur ordre naturel* (Paris: Merigot et al., 1780), 811–831, at 811.

8. But for an argument connecting the eighteenth-century socialist critique of Beccaria to more recent forms of socialism, see Richard Bellamy's introduction to Cesare Beccaria, *On Crimes and Punishments and Other Writings*, trans. Richard Davies with Virginia Cox and Richard Bellamy (Cambridge: Cambridge University Press, 1995), ix–xxx, at xxiv.

9. Arthur E. Bestor, "The Evolution of the Socialist Vocabulary," *Journal of the History of Ideas* 9, no. 3 (1948): 259–302, at 277.

10. Jacques Gans, "L'Origine du mot 'socialiste' et ses emplois les plus anciens," *Revue d'histoire économique et sociale* 35 (1957): 79–83; G. de Bertier de Sauvigny, "Liberalism, Nationalism and Socialism: The Birth of Three Words," *Review of Politics* 32 (1970): 147–166, at 161–165; discussed in Gregory Claeys, "'Individualism,' 'Socialism,' and 'Social Science': Further Notes on a Process of Conceptual Formation, 1800–1850," *Journal of the History of Ideas*, 47, no. 1 (1986), 81–93, at 83n7.

11. Bestor, "Evolution of the Socialist Vocabulary," 277, referencing Giacomo Giuliani, *L'antisocialismo confutato: Opera filosofica* (Vicenza: Bartolommeo Paroni, 1803).

12. *Vocabolario degli Accademici della Crusca*, 5 vols. (Venice: Francesco Pitteri, 1741), 4:371–372. This was a private reprint of the fourth Florentine edition. On this remarkable collaborative enterprise, see, among others, Edgar Zilsel, *The Social Origins of Modern Science* (Dordrecht: Kluwer, 2003), 163. Although I have used more-recent editions, the references are, in order of appearance, to Benedetto Varchi, "L'Ercolano, ovvero Agli alberi, dialogo," in *Opere di Benedetto Varchi*, 2 vols. (Trieste: Lloyd Austriaca, 1858–1859), 2:7–183, at

25; Giovanni Battista Gelli, "Lettura seconda," in *Letture edite e inedite di Giovan Battista Gelli sopra la commedia di Dante*, ed. Carlo Negroni, 2 vols. (Florence: Fratelli Bocca, 1887), 1:285; St. Gregory the Great, *Morals on the Book of Job*, 3 vols. (Oxford: John Henry Parker, 1845), vol. 2, bk. 21, comment on Job 31:22, at 542; Michelangelo Buonarrotti, *La fiera: Commedia*, ed. Pietro Fanfani (Florence: Le Monnier, 1860), 13. I have corrected the translations where appropriate.

13. Varchi, "L'Ercolano," 25. Though not in quite such detail, the etymological origins of "socialism" were evident to the first self-professed "socialists" as well. See, for example, James Napier Bailey, *Preliminary Discourse on the Objects, Pleasures, and Advantages of the Science of Society* (Leeds: J. Hobson, 1840), 27.

14. E.g., Giovanni Botero, *Della ragion di stato* (Ferrara: Baldini, 1589), 255, all the way to Nicola Fortunato, *Discoverta dell'antico regno di Napoli col suo presente stato a pro della sovranità e de' suoi popoli* (Naples: Giuseppe Raimondi, [1766]), 56fA and beyond; Appian, *The Civil Wars*, trans. John Carter (London: Penguin, 1996), 1:53, 29.

15. Jean-Jacques Rousseau, "Of the Social Contract," in Rousseau, *The Social Contract and Other Later Political Writings*, ed. Victor Gourevitch (Cambridge: Cambridge University Press, 1997), 39–152, at 46.

16. Pietro Verri, "Badi: Novella indiana," in *"Il Caffè," 1764–1766*, ed. Gianni Francioni and Sergio A. Romagnoli (Turin: Bollati Boringhieri, 1993) (hereafter cited as *Il Caffè*), 532–537, at 532.

17. Samuel von Pufendorf, *On the Duty of Man and Citizen according to Natural Law*, ed. James Tully, trans. Michael Silverthorne (Cambridge: Cambridge University Press, 1991), 35, also 36–37, 117. See also Ian Hunter, *Rival Enlightenments: Civil and Metaphysical Philsophy in Early Modern Germany* (Cambridge: Cambridge University Press, 2001), 157–158, also 176–177 on Pufendorf's "programme for detranscendentalising moral philosophy" generally. For variations, see also Hunter, *The Secularization of the Confessional State: The Political Thought of Christian Thomasius* (Cambridge: Cambridge University Press, 2007), esp. 89–99.

18. Giacomo Giuliani, *Orazione inaugurale* (Padova: Penada, 1808), 33; Giuliani, *L'antisocialismo confutato*. On Giuliani, see Nazzarena Zanini, "Note bibliografiche sul giurista dell'Università di Padova Giacomo Giuliani (1772–1840) gia minore conventuale," *Il Santo* 33, nos. 1–2 (1993): 151–168.

19. Giacomo Giuliani, *"Scienze politiche,"* no date, early 1830s, Biblioteca Antoniana, Padua, Italy (hereafter cited as Antoniana), scafale 23, MS 772, vol. 2, 20r; Giuliani, *"[Lezioni] Della economia politica, 1828–1829,"* Antoniana, scafale 23, MS 774, 2v.

20. Anon., *Fact without Fallacy; or, constitutional principles contrasted with the ruinous effects of unconstitutional practices* (London: J. S. Jordan, [1793]), 41.

21. Anselm Desing, *Juris Naturae larva detracta* . . . (Munich: Gastl, 1753). Loosely translated, the title, with its evocatively Baroque staccato repetitions, reads: *Natural Law Unmasked: So many books under the title "Natural Law" have appeared, like the Puffendorfian, Heineccian, and Wolffian ones, etc., but their Natural Law principles are here exposed as false; the ignorance that they so fraudulently attribute to Catholics is shown to reign instead in them; their sophistries are revealed; their glittering promises are shown to be broken; their quarrels with each other and even with themselves are displayed; their main goal—without a doubt to harm Catholicism—is stripped bare; and a warning about these dangerous works is issued to nobles, youths, and statesmen.*

22. Leticia Cabrera, "Anselmo Desing o la rehabilitacion de la ciencia juridical en la ilustracion alemana," *Revista de Estudios Historico-Juridicos* 19 (1997): 169–186, at 172. On Desing and his life, see Ildefons Stegmann, *Anselm Desing, abt von Ensdorf, 1699–1772: Ein Beitrag zur Geschichte der Aufklärung in Bayern* (Munich: Kommissions-Verlag R. Oldenbourg, 1929); Hans Müller, *Ursprung und Geschichte des Wortes Sozialismus und seiner Verwandten* (Hannover: Verlag J. H. W. Dietz Nachf. GmbH, 1967), 30–35; Michael Printy, *Enlightenment and the Creation of German Catholicism* (Cambridge: Cambridge University Press, 2009), 117–118; Ulrich L. Lehner, *Enlightened Monks: The German Benedictines, 1740–1803* (Oxford: Oxford University Press, 2011), 171–174.

23. Giorgio Spini, *Dalla preistoria del socialismo alla lotta per la libertá* (Milan: FrancoAngeli, 2002), 34.

24. Desing, *Juris Naturae larva detracta*, 4–5.

25. Ibid., 236. For the Protestant equation of Pufendorf with Hobbes on ironically similar grounds at the time, see Richard Tuck, "The 'Modern' Theory of Natural Law," in *The Languages of Political Theory in Early-Modern Europe*, ed. Anthony Pagden (Cambridge: Cambridge University Press, 1987), 99–119, at 102–103. On how Pufendorf resurrected Hobbesian themes, see also Theodore Christov, *Before Anarchy: Hobbes and His Critics in Modern International Thought* (Cambridge: Cambridge University Press, 2015), 143–170. Although he never spelled this out, Istvan Hont wrote of how Pufendorf's "followers were described as the school of 'socialists' (or society-ists)"; see Hont, *Jealousy of Trade: International Competition and the Nation-State in Historical Perspective* (Cambridge, MA: Harvard University Press, 2005), 45.

26. Ulrich Huhndorff et al., *Ius naturae in suo principio cognoscendi expensum* . . . (Augsburg: Pingizer, 1755), 96, 107, 112, 121, 124. Very little is known of Huhndorff, but see Johan Friedrich von Schulte, *Die Geschichte der Quellen und Literatur des Canonischen Rechts von der Mitte des 16. Jahrhunderts bis zur Gegenwart* (Stuttgart: Enke, 1880), entry 139, pp. 192–193. See also Richard Bruch, *Ethik und Naturrecht im deutschen Katholizismus des 18. Jahrhunderts: Von der*

Tugendethik zur Pflichtethik (Tübingen: A. Francke Verlag, 1997), 94, and 256 for Huhndorff as part of a larger reaction against Pufendorfian theories of sociability.

27. Lehner, *Enlightened Monks*, 174; Johann Baptist Schneyer, *Die Rechtsphilosophie Anselm Desings O. S. B. (1699–1772)* (Kallmünz: Lassleben, 1932), 42–47; Herbert Schambeck, "Anselm Desings Kritik an der Vernunftsrechtslehre," in *Internationale Festschrift für Alfred Verdross: Zum 80. Geburtstag*, ed. René Marcic et al. (Munich: Wilhelm Fink Verlag, 1971), 449–478, at 458–459. On Desing's travels to Italy, including a visit to Querini in Brescia, see Klaus Kempf, "La visita del benedettino Anselm Desing alla biblioteca queriniana (12 agosto 1750)," in *Dalla libreria del vescovo alla biblioteca della città: 250 anni di tradizione della cultura a Brescia*, ed. Ennio Ferraglio and Daniele Montanari (Brescia: Grafo, 2001), 201–211. On Querini's German connections and visits to Benedictine monasteries, see also Mario Bendiscioli, "La Germania protestante tra ortodossia, pietismo, Aufklärung, nell'età e nella corrispondenza del cardinale Angelo Maria Querini," in *Cultura religione e politica nell'età di Angelo Maria Querini*, ed. Gino Benzoni and Maurizio Pegrari (Brescia: Morcelliana, 1982), 23–31, at 31.

28. Anselm Desing, *Opuscoli* (Ferrara: Giuseppe Rinaldi, 1769), esp. 90, 201, 259; emphasis in original, criticizing the reception of Montesquieu, *The Spirit of the Laws*, ed. Anne M. Cohler, Basia C. Miller, and Harold S. Stone (Cambridge: Cambridge University Press, 1989). On the Italian translations of Desing's work, see Franco Venturi, *Settecento riformatore*, 5 vols. in 7 (Turin: Einaudi, 1969–1990), 2:199–202.

29. Anselm Desing, *Le ricchezze del clero utili, e necessarie alla repubblica* (Ferrara: Gianantonio Coatti, 1768), 8. On the variations of this volume and their original context, see Printy, *Enlightenment and the Creation of German Catholicism*, 76–81. For Verri's later argument, see his "Pensieri politici sulla corte di Roma e sul governo veneto," in *Edizione nazionale delle opere di Pietro Verri*, ed. Carlo Capra et al., 8 vols. in 10 to date (Rome: Edizioni di storia e letteratura, 2003–2014) (hereafter cited as *ENOPV*), 6:472–485, at 472.

30. Gustav von Schmoller, *The Mercantile System and Its Historical Significance* (New York: Macmillan, 1897), 70–71.

31. The "worldwide unity of the Catholic Church" was essential to Augustine's "universal history," on which see Peter Brown, *Augustine of Hippo: A Biography* (Berkeley: University of California Press, 1967), 322–323, and has since remained so. For Patristic thought on the "marks" of the Church (one, holy, catholic, apostolic), see Angelo di Berardino, ed., *Ancient Christian Doctrine*, vol. 5: *We Believe in One Holy Catholic and Apostolic Church* (Downers Grove, IL: IVP Academic, 2010), esp. 54–87. On the continuing universalist impetus behind Catholic

historiography, see Eric W. Cochrane, "What Is Catholic Historiography?," *Catholic Historical Review* 61, no. 2 (1975): 169–190.

32. Giuseppe Marco Antonio Baretti, *An Account of the Manners and Customs of Italy; with Observations on the Mistakes of some Travellers, with Regard to that Country*, 2 vols. (London: T. Davies, 1768), 1:206–208; emphasis added; republished also in "Some Account of Father Finetti, a Dominican Friar; from *Baretti*'s account of the manners and customs of Italy," in the section "characters" of *The Annual Register, or a View of the History, Politics, and Literature, for the Year 1768*, 6th ed. (London: Woodfall, 1800), 37–40.

33. Bonifacio [Germano Federico] Finetti, *De principiis juris naturae et gentium adversum Hobbesium, Pufendorfium, Thomasium, Wolfium, et alios*, 2 vols. (Venice: Tommaso Bettinelli, 1764), 1:XVnA and 2:26. On Finetti, see the supplementary materials to his *Difesa dell'autorità della sacra scrittura contro G. B. Vico*, ed. Benedetto Croce (Bari: Laterza, 1936), esp. 89–91; and Venturi, *Settecento riformatore*, 2:251–252. On Finetti's polemic with Vico, see also Giuseppe Mazzotta, *The New Map of the World: The Poetic Philosophy of Giambattista Vico* (Princeton: Princeton University Press, 1999), 236; and Jonathan Israel, *Enlightenment Contested: Philosophy, Modernity, and the Emancipation of Man, 1670–1752* (Oxford: Oxford University Press, 2006), 532. On the connection between *honestum* and *utile* in Pufendorf and Grotius, see, among others, Tuck, "The 'Modern' Theory of Natural Law," 105. Strikingly, Desing, Huhndorff, and Finetti were discussed together for similar reasons in Richard Bruch, *Ethik und Naturrecht*, 258.

34. Ferdinando Facchinei, *Note ed osservazioni sul libro intitolato "Dei delitti e delle pene"* ([Venice]: n.p., 1765), based on Facchinei, "Brevi note da porsi in pie' di pagina al libro dei Delitti e delle pene 1764," Archivio di Stato di Venezia, Venice, Italy (hereafter cited as ASV), *Miscellanea di atti diversi manoscritti, no. 71*, first referenced briefly by Gianfranco Torcellan, "Cesare Beccaria a Venezia," in his *Settecento veneto e altri scritti storici* (Turin: G. Giappichelli, 1969), 203–234, at 215–216. Facchinei was very much attuned to developments in German scholarship; see, for example, his *Lettera intorno alla cagione fisica de' sogni* (Turin: Nella stamperia Mairesse, 1762). His engagement with Christian Wolff, in particular, was also noted by his contemporaries; see Giuseppe Baretti, *La frusta letteraria* (Milan: Società tipografica de' classici italiani, 1838), 246–253. On Facchinei, see Antonio Mambelli, "Il padre Ferdinando Facchinei: Poligrafo e polemista del Settecento," *Deputazione di storia patria per le province di Romagna* 8 (1956–1957): 221–246. On Facchinei's connection to the German publishing world, see Venturi, *Settecento riformatore*, 2:252. On the origins of the Vallembrosan Order, see Francesco Salvestrini, *Disciplina caritatis: Il monachesimo vallombrosano tra medioevo e prima età moderna* (Rome: Viella, 2008).

35. Cosimo Amidei to Beccaria, 21 April 1766, in *ENOCB*, 4:290–293, at 292.

36. [Gian Vincenzo Bolgeni], *L'accusatore convinto reo delle colpe falsamente apostate all'innocente* (Milan: Galeazzi, 1768), 37; Carlo Scognamiglio Pasini, *L'arte della ricchezza: Cesare Beccaria economista* (Milan: Mondadori, 2014), 100; Carlo Capra, "Beccaria e i Verri negli anni dei Pugni e del 'Caffè,'" in *Il caso Beccaria: A 250 anni dalla pubblicazione del "Dei delitti e delle pene,"* ed. Vincenzo Ferrone and Giuseppe Ricuperati (Bologna: Il Mulino, 2016), 87–110, at 99.

37. See, more generally on the Catholic Enlightenment in Italy, Ulrich L. Lehner, *The Catholic Enlightenment: The Forgotten History of a Global Movement* (Oxford: Oxford University Press, 2016), 41–46.

38. Ferdinando Facchinei to Giovanni Lami, 10 January 1750/1751 and 14 November 1762, Biblioteca Riccardiana, Florence, Italy (hereafter cited as Riccardiana), *Mss. Lami*, n. 3724, 2r–3v and 117v; Ferdinando Facchinei to Francesco Antonio Zaccaria, 11 April 1763, Archivo Histórico de la Casa de Loyola, Sanctuary of Loyola, Azpeitia, Spain (hereafter cited as AHCL), *Fondo Zaccaria*, b. 19, 1r. For the unpublished manuscript, see Ferdinando Facchinei, *Vita di Newton*, Biblioteca Nazionale Centrale di Firenze, Florence, Italy, I, I, 98 (D113), fols. 255–314. On this manuscript, see Richard Davies, "Newtoncini tra lumi e tenebre: Beccaria e Facchinei," in *Un fortunato libriccino: L'attualità di Cesare Beccaria*, ed. Richard Davies and Persio Tincani (Milan: Edizioni l'ornitorinco, 2014), 79–127, esp. 111.

39. Ferdinando Facchinei to Giovanni Lami, 20 September 1751 and 24 September 1751, Riccardiana, *Mss. Lami*, n. 3724, 94v–r and 98v.

40. Ferdinando Facchinei to Francesco Antonio Zaccaria, 17 January 1763, AHCL, *Fondo Zaccaria*, b. 19, 1v; emphasis in original.

41. Ferdinando Facchinei to Francesco Antonio Zaccaria, 11 April 1763, AHCL, *Fondo Zaccaria*, b. 19, 2r. See also Facchinei to Zaccaria, 17 April 1763, AHCL, *Fondo Zaccaria*, b. 19, 1r–1v.

42. See, for example, the list of his manuscripts in Mambelli, "Il padre Ferdinando Facchinei," 234–242; Franco Venturi, "Contributi ad un dizionario storico: 'Socialista' e 'socialismo' nell'Italia del Settecento," *Rivista storica italiana* 75 (1963): 129–140, at 130–131; for his teaching of "experimental physics," see also Facchinei to Zaccaria, 25 August 1763, AHCL, *Fondo Zaccaria*, b. 19, 1r.

43. Ferdinando Facchinei, "Discorso recitato nell'anno 1764 nella apertura d'una nuova Società d'agricoltura ch'era per istituirsi in Brescia," *La Minerva* 38 (May 1765): 230–235, at 234–235, on which see Michele Simonetto, *I lumi nelle campagne: Accademie e agricoltura nella Repubblica di Venezia, 1768–1797* (Treviso: Edizioni Fondazione Benetton and Edizioni Canova, 2001), 58–61, "enlightened nations of Europe" quoted on 60f212. On the Dublin society, see James Livesey, "A Kingdom of Cosmopolitan Improvers: The Dublin Society, 1731–1798," in *The Rise of Economic Societies in the Eighteenth Century: Patriotic Reform in Europe and*

North America, ed. Koen Stapelbroek and Jani Marjanen (Basingstoke, UK: Palgrave Macmillan, 2012), 52–72. On Mirabeau, and Physiocracy, see again, among others, John Shovlin, *The Political Economy of Virtue: Luxury, Patriotism, and the Origins of the French Revolution* (Ithaca, NY: Cornell University Press, 2006), 105–107; Paul Cheney, *Revolutionary Commerce: Globalization and the French Monarchy* (Cambridge, MA: Harvard University Press, 2010), 160–161.

44. Facchinei to Zaccaria, 24 November 1763, AHCL, *Fondo Zaccaria*, b. 19, 2r; emphasis in original.

45. Pietro Verri, *Meditazioni sulla economia politica* (Livorno: Stamperia della Enciclopedia, 1771), 4.

46. Facchinei to Zaccaria, addendum to letter of 17 April 1763, AHCL, *Fondo Zaccaria*, b. 19, 2v.

47. Ferdinando Facchinei, "Brevi note da porsi in pie" di pagina al libro dei Delitti e delle pene 1764," ASV, *Miscellanea di atti diversi manoscritti, no. 71*, esp. fol. 5r.

48. Facchinei to Zaccaria, 26 April 1763, AHCL, *Fondo Zaccaria*, b. 19, iv.

49. Facchinei to Zaccaria, addendum to letter of 17 April 1763, AHCL, *Fondo Zaccaria*, b. 19, 1v; emphasis in original, plausibly reacting to Ange Goudar, *Les Intérêts de la France mal entendus, dans les branches de l'agriculture, de la population, des finances, du commerce, de la marine, & de l'industrie. Par un citoyen*, 3 vols. (Amsterdam [but Avignon]: Jacques Coeur, 1756), 2:189–209; echoed in Facchinei, *Note ed osservazioni*, 79–85. On Goudar, see Jean-Claude Hauc, *Ange Goudar: Un aventurier des Lumières* (Paris: Honoré Champion, 2004). For similar debates over the role of Church wealth in society in German lands, including Desing, see Printy, *Enlightenment and the Creation of German Catholicism*, 72–81.

50. Facchinei to Zaccaria, addendum to letter of 17 April 1763, AHCL, *Fondo Zaccaria*, b. 19, 1v.

51. See *Catechism of the Catholic Church*, para. 236, http://www.vatican.va/archive/ccc_css/archive/catechism/p1s2c1p2.htm.

52. See, for another fitting example, how it was used in the Habsburg administration of Milan, in Gian Rinaldo Carli to Wenzel Anton von Kaunitz, 18 July 1766, in "Il carteggio Carli-Kaunitz," ed. Umberto Marcelli, *Archivio storico italiano* 93 (1955): 388–407, 552–581; 114 (1956): 118–135, 771–788; 93 (1955): 406–407.

53. See, for example, François Bonald, *Divina ecclesiae oeconomia* (Cologne: Crithius, 1611); and Pierre Poiret, *L'Économie divine*, 7 vols. (Amsterdam: Henry Wetstein, 1687).

54. It is sometimes said that the first occurrence of the phrase "oeconomia divina" in explicitly economic terms was in Carl Gustaf Löwenhielm, *Tal, om landtskötsel* (Stockholm: Lars Salvius, 1751), 9; but it had already been used the previous year in Linnaeus, *Oeconomia naturæ, eller Skaparens allvisa inrättning på vår jord, i agttagen vid de skapade tingens betraktande i de tre naturens riken, till deras*

fortplantning, vidmagthållande och undergång . . . (Stockholm: Kiesevetter, 1750), 47, and Linnaeus indeed used "oeconomia naturæ" and "oeconomia divina" synonymously. On this tradition, see Tore Frängsmyr, "Den gudomliga ekonomin: Religion och hushållning i 1700-talets Sverige," *Lychnos: Lärdomshistoriska samfundets årsbok* (1971–1972): 217–244; and Lars Magnusson, *Äran, korruptionen och den borgerliga ordningen: Essäer från svensk ekonomihistoria* (Stockholm: Atlantis, 2001), esp. 42.

55. Giuseppe Garampi, *Delle osservazioni sopra di un libro intitolato Dell' origine e del commercio della moneta e dell' instituzione delle zecche d'Italia: All' Haja MDCCLI; In quanto appartiene alla zecca pontificia e a Roma* (Rome: Stamperia di A. Rotilj, e F. Bacchelli, 1752), 33.

56. Facchinei to Zaccaria, addendum to letter of 17 April 1763, AHCL, *Fondo Zaccaria*, b. 19, 1v.

57. Facchinei, "Brevi note," fol. 16v.

58. Ferdinando Facchinei to Francesco Antonio Zaccaria, 17 January 1763, AHCL, *Fondo Zaccaria*, b. 19, 1v.

59. 3 November 1764, 2r. Facchinei, *Note ed osservazioni*, 188

60. [Bolgeni], *L'accusatore convinto reo,* quoted and embellished upon quite colorfully in Ciro Caversazzi, "Una lettera di Luigi Piccioni in difesa di un frate antibarettiano," *Bergomum* 14, no. 1 (1940):23–26, at 26.

61. Venturi, "Contributi ad un dizionario storico," 132.

62. Facchinei, *Note ed osservazioni*, 74.

63. Ibid., 4, 37, 41.

64. Facchinei, "Brevi note," fols. 73, 24v.

65. Facchinei, *Note ed osservazioni*, 7–9; emphasis added.

66. Ibid., 9; emphasis added.

67. Ibid.; emphasis added.

68. Plato, *The Republic*, 338c, ed. G. R. F. Ferrari, trans. Tom Griffith (Cambridge: Cambridge Univeresity Press, 2000), 15.

69. Facchinei to Zaccaria, addendum to letter of 17 April 1763, AHCL, *Fondo Zaccaria*, b. 19, 1v; Facchinei, *Note ed osservazioni*, 9.

70. Adam Smith, "The History of Astronomy," in Smith, *Essays on Philosophical Subjects*, ed. W. P. D. Wightman and J. C. Bryce (Oxford: Clarendon Press, 1980), 49–50; Smith, *The Theory of Moral Sentiments*, ed. D. D. Raphael and A. L. Macfie (Oxford: Clarendon Press, 1976), 184–185.

71. Adam Smith, *An Inquiry into the Nature and Causes of the Wealth of Nations*, ed. Edwin Cannan, 2 vols. (Chicago: University of Chicago Press, 1976), 1:477–478. For a representative reading of this passage, see Douglas A. Irwin, *Against the Tide: An Intellectual History of Free Trade* (Princeton: Princeton University Press, 1996), 77–78.

72. On the "cosmopolitical" critique of Smith, see Hont, *Jealousy of Trade*, 148–154; which draws also on Keith Tribe, *"Die Vernunft des List:* National Economy and the Critique of Cosmopolitical Economy," in *Strategies of Economic Order: German Economic Discourse 1750–1950* (Cambridge: Cambridge University Press, 1995), 32–65.

73. On the historiography of the phrase "invisible hand," see Peter Harrison, "Adam Smith and the History of the Invisible Hand," *Journal of the History of Ideas* 72, no. 1 (2011): 29–49; and, also considering its political impact, Bas van Bavel, *The Invisible Hand? How Market Economies Have Emerged and Declined since AD 500* (Oxford: Oxford University Press, 2016), esp. 4–5.

74. Thorstein Veblen, *The Theory of Business Enterprise* (New York: Scribner's Sons, 1904), 68–69; and Veblen, "The Preconceptions of Economic Science: II," in *The Place of Science in Modern Civilization and Other Essays* (New York: Huebsch, 1919), 114–147, esp. 114–117.

75. Hont, *Jealousy of Trade*, 39, 91, 113. Hont similarly argued that Smith "eschewed theology," in "Adam Smith's History of Law and Government," in *Political Judgment: Essays for John Dunn,* ed. Richard Bourke and Raymond Geuss (Cambridge: Cambridge University Press, 2009), 131–171, at 137.

76. Charles Taylor, *A Secular Age* (Cambridge, MA: Harvard University Press, 2007), 176–177.

77. Emma Rothschild, *Adam Smith, Condorcet, and the Enlightenment* (Cambridge, MA: Harvard University Press, 2001), 116–156; and Rothschild, "Faith, Enlightenment, and Economics," in *Natural Law, Economics, and the Common Good: Perspectives from Natural Law,* ed. Samuel Gregg and Harold James (Exeter, UK: Imprint Academic, 2012), 17–23, at 19. See similarly, for Smith's use of the "invisible hand" as consciously ironic, Alessandro Roncaglia, *Il mito della mano invisibile* (Bari: Laterza, 2005), 19. A recent study of the phraseology omitted national investments and international competition from Smith's account, making it seem as if the passage in question was simply about individual self-interest contributing to societal welfare; see Jonathan Sheehan and Dror Wahrman, *Invisible Hands: Self-Organization and the Eighteenth Century* (Chicago: University of Chicago Press, 2015), 267. The same is true of Harrison, "Adam Smith," 45–46.

78. Warren Samuels with Marianne F. Johnson and William H. Perry, *Erasing the Invisible Hand: Essays on an Elusive and Misused Concept in Economics* (Cambridge: Cambridge University Press, 2011), 290–291. The cultish appreciation of invisible hands in contemporary culture can indeed be embarrassing; see, for example, the parable of the capitalist "underpants gnomes" in "Gnomes," *South Park*, Season 2, Episode 17, Comedy Central, 16 December 1998, on which see Paul A. Cantor's brazenly panegyrical "Cartman Shrugged: The Invisible

Gnomes and the Invisible Hand in *South Park*," in *The Invisible Hand in Popular Culture: Liberty vs. Authority in American Film and TV* (Lexington: University Press of Kentucky, 2012), 189–212. Irony aside, Smith's "joke" itself had rather powerful, if unintended, consequences, for an account of which see, among others, Bruna Ingrao and Giorgio Israel, *La mano invisibile: L'equilibrio economico nella storia della scienza*, new ed. (Bari: Laterza 2006).

79. For a similar argument about Smith, see Harrison, "Adam Smith," 45, 49. See also Robert Wokler, "Rousseau's Reading of the Book of Genesis and the Theology of Commercial Society," *Modern Intellectual History* 3, no. 1 (2006): 85–94, now reprinted in Wokler, *Rousseau, the Age of Enlightenment, and Their Legacies*, ed. Bryan Garsten (Princeton, NJ: Princeton University Press, 2006), 113–120.

80. Giuseppe Pelli Bencivenni, "Lettera . . . di un nostro amico scritta al sig. N.N. sopra le scienze economiche," *Novelle letterarie* [Florence], vol. 5 (Florence: Allegrini, 1774), 292–294, 329–330, 342–345, 387–390. The review ran from no. 19, 13 May, to no. 24, 17 June, and was signed 2 April 1774. On their authorship, see Pompilio Pozzetti, "La vita letteraria di Giuseppe Bencivenni, già Pelli," *Giornale scientifico e letterario dell'Accademia italiana di scienze lettere ed arti*, vol. 2 (Pisa: Stamperia del giornale, 1810), 93–107, at 100–101. On Pelli's Physiocracy, see Mario Mirri, "Fisiocrazia e riforme: Il caso della Toscana e il ruolo di Ferdinando Paoletti," in *Governare il mondo: L'economia come linguaggio della politica nell'Europa del Settecento*, ed. Manuela Albertone (Milan: Fondazione Giangiacomo Feltrinelli, 2009), 323–441, at 364–368. On the Uffizi at the time, see Paula Findlen, "The 2012 Josephine Waters Bennett Lecture: The Eighteenth-Century Invention of the Renaissance: Lessons from the Uffizi," *Renaissance Quarterly* 66, no. 1 (2013): 1–34.

81. Ferdinando Paoletti, *I veri mezzi di render felici le società* (Florence: Stecchi and Pagani, 1772), [i]; Pelli, "Lettera . . . ," 387–390. On the influence of Physiocracy in Tuscany, and for further bibliography, see Mirri, "Fisiocrazia e riforme." On the sect's partial influence in Italy, see also Carlo Capra, *Gli italiani prima dell'Italia: Un lungo Settecento, dalla fine della Controriforma a Napoleone* (Rome: Carocci, 2014), 177–195.

82. On the tension between "liberty" and "liberticide" at the time, see Steven L. Kaplan, *The Stakes of Regulation: Perspectives on "Bread, Politics and Political Economy" Forty Years Later* (London: Anthem, 2016), 393.

83. Facchinei, *Note ed osservazioni*, 11–14.

84. Ibid., 14.

85. Ibid., 14, 19, 26; anonymous copyist in the name of Alessandro Verri, "Supplica in difesa di Anna Perina," Archivio Verri, Fondazione Mattioli, housed at the

Università di Milano under the tutelage of the Archivio Storico della Banca Intesa Sanpaolo, Milan, Italy (hereafter cited as Archivio Verri), 481.2, fols. 123–124, reproduced in Pierre Musitelli, "I manoscritti inediti di Alessandro Verri, Protettore dei carcerati (1763–1765)," *Line@editoriale*, no. 2 (2010): 1–29, at 13–14.

86. Facchinei, *Note ed osservazioni*, 29.

87. See recently *The Economist*'s retracted review of Edward Baptist, *The Half Has Never Been Told: Slavery and the Making of American Capitalism* (New York: Basic Books, 2014), still available through "Editor's Note: Our Withdrawn Review 'Blood Cotton,'" 4 September 2014, http://www.economist.com/news/books /21615864-how-slaves-built-american-capitalism-blood-cotton. See also the often hilarious hashtag *#EconomistBookReviews*.

88. Facchinei, *Note ed osservazioni*, 61.

89. Facchinei, "Brevi note," fols. 6v, 15r–15v.

90. Facchinei, *Note ed osservazioni*, 87, 99.

91. Facchinei, "Brevi note," fol. 12v.

92. Beccaria, *On Crimes and Punishments*, 51, 61, line 18 of the original 1764 edition, as correctly noted by Facchinei, "Brevi note," fols. 15r–15v.

93. Facchinei, "Brevi note," fols. 15r–15v; emphasis added.

94. Ibid., fols. 16r, 17v. See also Facchinei, *Note ed osservazioni*, 86–87, 125; emphasis in original.

95. Facchinei, *Note ed osservazioni*, 100; emphasis in original.

96. Ibid., 101.

97. Facchinei to Zaccaria, 25 August 1763, AHCL, *Fondo Zaccaria*, b. 19, 1r.

98. Pietro and Alessandro Verri, "Risposta alle Note ed Osservazioni sul libro *Dei delitti e delle pene* [1765]," in *ENOPV*, 1:801–857, 819.

99. Facchinei, *Note ed osservazioni*, 106.

100. Ibid., 164.

101. Facchinei, "Brevi note," fol. 9r.

102. Ibid., fols. 9r–9v.

103. Ibid., fol. 20r.

104. Facchinei, *Note ed osservazioni*, 111–112.

105. Facchinei, "Brevi note," fols. 17r–17v, reacting to Beccaria, *On Crimes and Punishments*, 55; emphasis in original.

106. Facchinei, "Brevi note," 5v.

107. Facchinei, *Note ed osservazioni*, 122–123, 148; emphasis added.

108. Facchinei, "Brevi note," fol. 12r.

109. Facchinei, *Note ed osservazioni*, 159–163.

110. Ibid., 187.

111. Ibid., 188; emphasis in original.

112. Facchinei in effect reacted at length to Beccaria's writings regarding secret accusations, and about Venice; see his "Brevi note," fols. 8v–9r; as well as his *Note ed osservazioni*, 51–58, 188. See, on this affair, Torcellan, "Cesare Beccaria a Venezia."

113. Alessandro to Pietro Verri, 4 March 1767, in *Viaggio a Parigi e Londra (1766–1767): Carteggio di Pietro e Alessandro Verri*, ed. Gianmarco Gaspari (Milan: Adelphi, 1980), 346; see also Cesare Beccaria to André Morellet, 26 January 1766, in *ENOCB*, 4:220.

114. [Pietro and Alessandro Verri], *Risposta ad uno scritto che s'intitola Note ed osservazioni sul libro Dei delitti e delle pene* (Lugano: Agnelli, 1765), based on a number of manuscripts in Archivio Verri, 378.4.1–8, parts of the "strapazzo" in 378.4.1 curiously in Beccaria's hand, 1r–2r. For the first full draft, see 378.4.2, entirely in Pietro Verri's hand. On the *Risposta*, see Gian Paolo Massetto, "Pietro e Alessandro Verri in aiuto di Cesare Beccaria," in *Pietro Verri e il suo tempo*, ed. Carlo Capra (Bologna: Cisalpino, 1999), 289–351; and Girolamo Imbruglia, "Illuminismo e religione: Il *Dei delitti e delle pene* e la difesa dei Verri dinanzi alla censura inquisitoriale," *Studi Settecenteschi* 25–26 (2005–2006): 119–161. Pietro Verri's letter to Ferdinando Facchinei was published with the date 30 March 1765 in *ENOPV*, 1:869–875, though that date only corresponds to that of his annotation on the back of the manuscript in Archivio Verri, 378.4.8, 2v. For his worries about Venetian assassins, see Pietro Verri to Gian Rinaldo Carli, 8 February 1765, in Francesco De Stefano, "Cinque anni di sodalizio tra Pietro Verri e Gian Rinaldo Carli (1760–1765) con XXIV lettere inedite di Pietro Verri," *Atti e memorie della Società istriana di archeologia e storia patria* 45 (1933): 43–103, at 78.

115. On Venice's bloodcurdling secret services, see Gaetano Cozzi, "Authority and the Law in Renaissance Venice," in John Rigby Hale, *Renaissance Venice* (London: Rowman and Littlefield, 1973), 293–334; and generally Paolo Preto, *I servizi segreti di Venezia: Spionaggio e controspionaggio ai tempi della Serenissima* (Milan: Il Saggiatore, 1994). For a remarkable historiographical experiment focused on early modern Venetian secret services, see Jonathan Walker, *Pistols! Treason! Murder! The Rise and Fall of a Master Spy* (Melbourne: Melbourne University Press, 2007).

116. Pietro and Alessandro Verri, "Risposta alle note," 852, and, similarly, on burning witches, 828.

117. Beccaria, *On Crimes and Punishments*, 59.

118. Beccaria, *On Crimes and Punishments*, 5.

119. Beccaria, *On Crimes and Punishments*, 6; emphasis added. There might well be echoes here of Rousseau, "Of the Social Contract," 41: "the social order . . . is therefore based on conventions."

120. Beccaria, *On Crimes and Punishments*, 6–7. On the politics of time and the relativity of vices and virtues, see also 18–19 and esp. 85.

121. Ibid.; Henry Lloyd, *Philosophical Essays on the Different Species of Governments*, Fitzwilliam, *Henry Lloyd Papers*, 40.

122. Beccaria, *On Crimes and Punishments*, 39, 77. On the question of crime and sin, and the different spheres represented by "revelation," "natural law," and "social pacts," see also the plausible originator of this idea, Pietro Verri, "Notizie preliminari indispensabili per criticare ragionevolmente gli scritti politici," in *ENOPV*, 1:858–860, which informed later editions of *On Crimes and Punishments;* as well as Pietro Verri, "[Contro il padre Almici in difesa di 'Dei delitti e delle pene,' 1765]," in *ENOPV*, 1:876–887.

123. Luciano Parinetto, *I lumi e le streghe: Una polemica italiana intorno al 1750* (Paderno Dugnano: Colibrì, 1998), 35–39. For a meditation on "disenchantment" and the possibility of controlling the world through "calculation" that helps shed light on the pugilists' project, see Max Weber, "Science as a Vocation," in Weber, *The Vocation Lectures*, ed. David S. Owen and Tracy B. Strong (Indianapolis: Hackett, 2004), 1–30, at 13.

124. Ferdinando Facchinei in Pietro Verri, *Meditazioni sulla felicità con note critiche* [Ferdinando Facchinei] *e risposta alle medesime d'un amico piemontese* [Francesco Dalmazzo Vasco] (Milan: Galeazzi, 1766), 2–4. It is worth noting, however, that even the Livornese publisher marketed the two volumes as having been written by the same anonymous author; see Cesare Beccaria to Giuseppe Aubert, 8–9 December 1764, in *ENOCB*, 4:83–86, esp. 84n2 for a discussion of the misunderstanding. On Aubert, see Adriana Lay, *Un editore illuminista: Giuseppe Aubert nel carteggio con Beccaria e Verri* (Turin: Accademia delle scienze, 1973).

125. Verri, *Meditazioni*, 79.

126. Ibid., 83–84.

127. Ibid., 54, 105, and Facchinei's note 17 at 49. For a modern edition of the reply, see Dalmazzo Francesco Vasco, "Meditazioni sulla felicità di Pietro Verri con note critiche di Ferdinando Facchinei e risposta alle medesime d'un amico piemontese (Dalmazzo Francesco Vasco) (1766)," in Vasco, *Opere*, ed. Silvia Rota Ghibaudi (Turin: Fondazione Luigi Einaudi, 1966), 51–105, at 77–78n17.

128. Drawing by Pietro Verri, on the inside back cover of the page proofs of *Risposta ad uno scritto che si intitola note, ed osservazioni sul libro Dei delitti, e delle pene, 1765*, Archivio Verri, 378.4.7; Pietro Verri to Ferdinando Facchinei, [30 March 1765?], Archivio Verri, 378.4.9, 2r.

129. Ferdinando Facchinei, *Miscellanea che può servir anche di aggiunta al Saggio di un nuovo metodo per insegnar gli elementi delle scienze a' fanciulli* (Bergamo: Dal cittadino Antoine, 1797), xiii.

130. Alessandro Verri [perhaps in another's hand?], "materiali preparatori," Archivio Verri, cart. 378.4.5, 1r.

131. See, for example, Giuseppe Giuliani, "Prefazione del traduttore," in Albert du Boys, *Dei principi della rivoluzione francese considerati come principi generatori del socialismo e del comunismo*, trans. Giuseppe Giuliani (Macerata: Alessandro Mancini, 1857), i–lxiv, at lix.

132. See, for example, Appiano Buonafede, *Della restaurazione di ogni filosofia ne' secoli XVI, XVII, e XVIII*, 3 vols. (Venice: Graziosi, 1785–1789), 3:52–57, and for his praise of Desing, see 150–151, 242.

133. On eighteenth-century Comacchio, see Antonio Samaritani, "Società e cultura a Comacchio nell'età del Buonafede," in *Appiano Buonafede (Comacchio 1716 / Roma 1793) un intellettuale cattolico tra l'Arcadia e i Lumi: Atti della Giornata di studi tenuta a Comacchio il 31 Ottobre 1987*, ed. anon., monograph, *Atti e memorie*, 4th ser., vol. 5 (Ferrara: A cura del Comune di Comacchio, 1988; but Ferrara: Stabilimento Artistico Tipografico Editoriale for the Deputazione Provinciale Ferrarese di Storia Patria, 1989), 13–41. On the reasons for Buonafede's leaving, see 23–24. On the dispute over Comacchio, see Luigi Bellini, *Comacchio nell'opera di L. Antonio Muratori* (Rome: Società Anonima Poligrafica Italiana, 1950), esp. 28–35. On Buonafede, see, among others, Amedeo Benati, "Appiano Buonafede Monaco Celestino: Appunti per una biografia religioso-culturale," in anon., *Appiano Buonafede*, 43–69. On the Arcadians, see Susan M. Dixon, *Between the Real and the Ideal: The Accademia degli Arcadi and Its Garden in Eighteenth-Century Rome* (Newark: University of Delaware Press, 2006), esp. 19–31.

134. On the remarkable figure of Celestino Galiani, see Vincenzo Ferrone, *Scienza Natura Religione: Mondo newtoniano e cultura italiana nel primo Settecento* (Naples: Jovene, 1982); Koen Stapelbroek, *Love, Self-Deceit and Money: Commerce and Morality in the Early Neapolitan Enlightenment* (Toronto: University of Toronto Press, 2008), 56–87.

135. Agatopisto Cromaziano Jr. [Antonio Buonafede], *Elogio storico, letterario di Agatopisto Cromaziano* (Ferrara: Rinaldi, 1794), 16–17, 20–21. On his Neapolitan years, see also Amedeo Benati, "Appiano Buonafede Monaco Celestino: Appunti per una biografia religioso-culturale," in anon., *Appiano Buonafede*, 47–48. For the eulogy of Galiani, see Appiano Buonafede, *De Caelestini Galiani Archiepiscopi Thessalonicensis vita commentarius* (Faenza: Benedetti, 1754); and later the entry in Buonafede, *Ritratti poetici, storici, e critici di vari moderni uomini* (Naples: Terres, 1775), 214–219. For his influence on Ferdinando Galiani, see Ferdinando Galiani, *Correspondance inédite de l'abbé Ferdinand Galiani, conseiller du roi de Naples, avec Mme d'Epinay, le baron d'Holbach, le baron de Grimm, et autres*

personnages célèbres du XVIIIe siècle, ed. Pierre Louis Ginguené and Francesco Salfi (Paris: Treuttel et Würtz, 1819), xl–xli; Saverio Mattei, *Galiani ed i sui tempi* (Naples: n.p., 1879), 10. Odds are this information came from Salfi, on whom see Luca Addante, *Patriottismo e libertà: L'Elogio di Antonio Serra di Francesco Salfi* (Cosenza: Luigi Pellegrini Editore, 2009); and the essays in Pasquale Alberto De Lisio, ed., *Francesco Saverio Salfi: Un Calabrese per l'Europa* (Naples: Società Editrice Napoletana, 1981). For contemporary criticisms regarding Buonafede's Dionysian, even "Boccaccian," lifestyle, and a not entirely convincing argument for their ostensibly airy foundations, see Benati, "Appiano Buonafede Monaco Celestino," 66–67.

136. On Buonafede's histories of philosophy, see Gregorio Piaia, "Letteratura e storia della filosofia in Appiano Buonafede," in anon., *Appiano Buonafede*, 85–122. On the obviously Germanic influences on his historiographical exercise, see also Mario Rosa, "Introduzione all'Aufklärung cattolica in Italia," in *Cattolicesimo e lumi nel Settecento italiano,* ed. Mario Rosa (Rome: Herder, 1981), 1–47, at 20–21. The model for Buonafede's most famous work was probably the revised edition of Johann Jacob Brucker, *Historia critica philosophiae a mundi incunabulis ad nostram usque aetatem deducta,* 6 vols. (Leipzig: Weidemann and Reich, 1766–1767), for an important reading of which see Tim J. Hochstrasser, *Natural Law Theories in the Early Enlightenment* (Cambridge: Cambridge University Press, 2000), 170–175.

137. Thomas Carlyle, *Two Notebooks of Thomas Carlyle,* ed. Charles Eliot Norton (New York: Grolier Club, 1893), 130–131. See also Norton's telling note: "Boswell has conferred immortality on Baretti, by the frequent mention of him in his *Life of Johnson,*" 131f. For Baretti's "honourable acquittal," see Thomas Davies to [James Granger], 21 October 1769, Houghton Library, Harvard University, Cambridge, MA (hereafter cited as Houghton), *bMS Hyde 10 (175) *2003JM-58/2004,* 1r. For a mature expression of Baretti's manly vitriol, see his savaging of his former friend Hester Lynch in *Invettive contro una Signora inglese (Hester Thrale Piozzi),* ed. Bartolo Anglani (Rome: Salerni Editrice, 2001). On this affair, see Marianna Dezio, *Hester Lynch Thrale Piozzi: A Taste for Eccentricity* (Newcastle upon Tyne, UK: Cambridge Scholars, 2010), esp. 26–34.

138. Giuseppe Marco Antonio Baretti to Giambattista Biffi, 24 December 1763, Houghton, *MS Hyde 66 (1),* 1r. This letter is, interestingly, written in English.

139. The Baretti-Buonafede polemic probably began with Baretti's critical review of Agatopisto Cromaziano [Appiano Buonafede], *Saggi di commedie filosofiche* (Faenza: Benedetti, 1754), in Baretti, *Frusta letteraria,* no. 18, 15 June 1764, 2:278–282; replied to in *Il bue pedagogo: Novelle menippee di Luciano da Firenzuola contro una certa Frusta pseudoepigrafa di Aristarco Scannabue* ([Lucca]: n.p., 1764). On the celebrated polemic that followed, see, among others, Gilberto Pizzamiglio,

"Appiano Buonafede e la polemica con il Baretti," in anon., *Appiano Buon-afede*, 71–84. Among the many writings to come out of this debate, a vitriolic twelve-page manuscript poem against Buonafede, plausibly by Baretti, seems to have gone unnoticed, bound with Giuseppe Marco Antonio Baretti, *La frusta letteraria di Aristarco Scannabue*, 2 vols. (Roveredo [Venice]: n.p., 1763–1764), Houghton, *HOU GEN *EC75.B2377.763f.* The book was bought by Charles Eliot Norton, who often traveled to Italy, in 1863, and bequeathed to Harvard on 9 April 1900. The poem's handwriting is remarkably similar to Baretti's own. On this debate, see generally Norbert Jonard, *Giuseppe Baretti (1719–1789): L'Homme et l'œuvre* (Clarmont: G. De Bussac, 1963), 252–267. For Baretti's critique of *Il Caffè*, see, among other instances, *Frusta letteraria*, no. 19, 1 July 1764, 300. On the polemic that followed, particularly with Pietro Verri, see Gianni Francioni, "Storia editoriale del 'Caffè,'" in *Il Caffè*, xcv–cix; and for a juxtaposition of the two journals, see Sergio Romagnoli, "Forme della recensione barettiana," in *Giuseppe Baretti: Un piemontese in Europa*, ed. Marco Cerruti and Paola Trivero (Alesandria: Edizioni dell'orso, 1993), 121–132. On Baretti's dislike of recent Italian political economy, and its emulation of ultramontane authors in particular, see Venturi, *Settecento riformatore*, 1:696n, largely on the basis of his violent review of Pietro Verri, *Bilancio del commercio dello stato di Milano* (n.p.: n.p., [1763]), in *Frusta letteraria*, no. 21, 1 August 1764, 328–330. Yet see Baretti's favorable review of Antonio Zanon's *Dell'agricoltura, dell'arti, e dell'commercio . . .*, 6 vols. (Venice: Modesto Fenzo, 1763–1766) in *Frusta letteraria*, covering at least no. 7, 1 January 1764, 93–101; no. 16, 15 May 1764, 237–244; and no. 23, 1 September 1764, 349–360. On the decidedly sparsely studied work of Zanon, an exquisite theorist and practitioner, see anon., *Elogio della società d'Agricoltura pratica di Udine al Signor Antonio Zanon* (Udine: Società d'Agricoltura pratica di Udine, [ca. 1770]); and Romano Molesti, *Il pensiero economico di Antonio Zanon* (Milan: Giuffrè, 1974).

140. Facchinei to Zaccaria, 8 February 1764, AHCL, *Fondo Zaccaria*, b. 19, 1r. The edition Facchinei helped publish was Appiano Buonafede, *Il bue pedagogo* (Venice: Colombani, 1765). On Facchinei being convinced to take credit for the entire work by Buonafede, see Giuseppe Marco Antonio Baretti to Giambattista Chiaramonti, 20 July 1766, in Giuseppe Marco Antonio Baretti, *Opere*, 4 vols. (Milan: Società tipografica de' classici italiani, 1838–1839), 4:163–165. [Buonafede], *Elogio storico*, 54–59, speaks of a "very witty and learned Vallumbrosan monk," who most probably was Facchinei. Baretti mentions, quite hatefully, Facchinei's involvement in his *Continuazione della Frusta letteraria del Signor Giuseppe Baretti Piemontese col nome immaginario di Aristarco Scannabue che contiene otto Discorsi in Risposta data al Bue pedagogico Opera del Padre Don Appiano Buonafede Abate Celestino, fra gli Arcadi Agatopisto Croma-*

ziano sotto nome di Don Luciano Firenzuola da Comacchio (Trento [Ancona?]: n.p. 1765), n. 31, 1 July 1765, 105.

141. Appiano Buonafede, *Istoria critica e filosofica del suicidio ragionato* (Venice: Dionisio Bassi, 1783), esp. 181.

142. [Buonafede], *Elogio storico*, 92.

143. His list of enemies, from Machiavelli to Helvetius, was long; see [Buonafede], *Elogio storico*, 38.

144. Buonafede, *Il bue pedagogo*, 5.

145. E.g., Appiano Buonafede, *Della restaurazione di ogni filosofia ne' secoli XVI, XVII, e XVIII*, 3 vols. (Venice: Graziosi, 1785–1789), 3:129, 249–257, 278. His son also remembered his father's particular love of Vico and Genovesi; see [Buonafede], *Elogio storico*, 87.

146. Buonafede, *Della restaurazione*, 3:52–57; for his praise of Desing, see 150–151, 242.

147. Appiano Buonafede, *Delle conquiste celebri: Esaminate col naturale diritto delle genti* (Lucca: Riccomini, 1763), 3, 24; emphasis in original.

148. Buonafede, *Delle conquiste*, 15–16, 32–33.

149. Ibid., 23, 38.

150. Buonafede, *Della restaurazione*, 3:65–66, 74, 88–89, 247, 249; emphasis in original.

151. Ibid., 111, 177, 256.

152. Ibid., 111–112; emphasis in original. He offers a vague reference to Cumberland, which plausibly could be to Richard Cumberland, *A Treatise of the Laws of Nature*, ed. Jon Parkin, trans. John Maxwell (Indianapolis: Liberty Fund, 2005), 196. On Jesus Christ, see Gerhard Lohfink, *Jesus von Nazareth: Was er wollte, wer er war* (Freiburg im Breisgau: Herder, 2011); and, for a rather pugnacious take on his teachings, Terry Eagleton, *Terry Eagleton Presents Jesus Christ: The Gospels* (London: Verso, 2007).

153. Buonafede, *Della restaurazione*, 3:148–149.

154. Ibid., 83.

155. Buonafede, *Ritratti*, 284–287; the reference is probably to Traiano Boccalini, *Ragguagli di Parnasso . . .* , 3 vols. (Amsterdam: Blaeu, 1669), 1:416. On Machiavelli and Amelot de la Houssaye, see Jacob Soll, *Publishing the Prince: History, Reading, and the Birth of Political Criticism* (Ann Arbor: University of Michigan Press, 2005). Rousseau had, of course, done something very similar; see "Of the Social Contract," 95: "While pretending to teach lessons to Kings, he taught great lessons to peoples. Machiavelli's *Prince* is the book of republicans." On Boccalini, see, among others, Harald Hendrix, *Traiano Boccalini fra erudizione e polemica: Ricerche sulla fortuna e bibliografia critica* (Florence: Leo S. Olschki, 1995).

156. Buonafede, *Della restaurazione,* 3:256–257; emphasis in original. On his forceful criticisms of Rousseau's "savageries," see 216–230.

157. Pietro Verri to Antonio Genovesi, undated fragment letter, Archivio Verri, *Cart. 276: Correspondenza di Pietro Verri a vari destinatori 1763–1795 [ex CAR 083.01-11] Fasc. 7. Antonio Genovesi—Milano [CAR 083.07].* Admittedly, he would later write to his brother that "Genovesi was neither clear, nor profound, nor did he have decisive principles"; see Pietro Verri to Alessandro Verri, 1 September 1779, in *Carteggio di Pietro e di Alessandro Verri dal 1766 al 1797,* ed. E. Greppi, F. Novati, A. Giulini, and G. Seregni, 12 vols. (Milan: Cogliati, then Milesi & Figli, then Giuffrè, 1910–1943), 11:362–365, at 365. On the importance of Genovesi as a mediator for foreign ideas, see Sophus A. Reinert, *Translating Empire: Emulation and the Origins of Political Economy* (Cambridge, MA: Harvard University Press, 2011), 230–232.

158. Pufendorf, *On the Duty of Man and Citizen,* 116.

6. The Threshold of Utopia

1. Alessandro Verri to Pietro Verri, 19 October 1766, in *Viaggio a Parigi e Londra (1766–1767): Carteggio di Pietro e Alessandro Verri,* ed. Gianmarco Gaspari (Milan: Adelphi, 1980), 24.

2. See, for example, Pietro Verri to Alessandro Verri, 4 October 1766 and 26 November 1766, in *Viaggio a Parigi e Londra,* 3 and 87 respectively.

3. Alessandro Verri to Pietro Verri, 13 March 1767, in *Carteggio di Pietro e di Alessandro Verri dal 1766 al 1797,* ed. E. Greppi, F. Novati, A. Giulini, and G. Seregni, 12 vols. (Milan: Cogliati, then Milesi & Figli, then Giuffrè, 1910–1943) (hereafter cited as *CV*), vol. 1, pt. 1, 297–307, 299; Alessandro Verri to Pietro Verri, 29 December 1766, quoted and discussed in Carlo Antonio Vianello, *La giovinezza di Parini, Verri e Beccaria: Con scritti, documenti e ritratti inediti* (Milan: Baldini e Castoldi, 1933), 182. See also, on the affair, Gianni Francioni, "A Parigi! A Parigi! Gli illuministi milanesi e la Francia," in *I viaggi dei filosofi,* ed. Maria Bettetini and Stefano Poggi (Milan: Raffaello Cortina, 2010), 113–133.

4. Alessandro Verri to Pietro Verri, 2 October 1766, and Cesare Beccaria to Pietro Verri, 2 October 1766, in *Viaggio a Parigi e Londra,* 3 and 441 respectively. On Novara as the place of Beccaria's original crisis, see also Cesare Beccaria's second letter to Pietro Verri of 2 October 1766 and Alessandro Verri to Pietro Verri, 2 November 1766, in *Viaggio a Parigi e Londra,* 441 and 53 respectively.

5. Alessando Verri to Pietro Verri, 19 October 1766, in *Viaggio a Parigi e Londra,* 22–27.

6. Alessandro Verri to Pietro Verri, 12 November 1766 and 18 November 1766, in *Viaggio a Parigi e Londra*, 77 and 104–105 respectively.

7. Alessando Verri to Pietro Verri, 19 October 1766, in *Viaggio a Parigi e Londra*, 28.

8. Alessandro Verri to Pietro Verri, 26 October 1766, in *Viaggio a Parigi e Londra*, 115.

9. Alessandro Verri to Pietro Verri, 15 January 1767, in *Viaggio a Parigi e Londra*, 241.

10. Alessandro Verri to Pietro Verri, 12 November 1766, and Pietro Verri to Alessandro Verri, 26–27 November 1766, in *Viaggio a Parigi e Londra*, 78 and 91 respectively.

11. Alessandro Verri to Pietro Verri, 25 October 1766, and Alessandro Verri to Pietro Verri, 2 November 1766, in *CV*, vol. 1, pt. 1, 33–37, 47–54. On the power of posture, see the long arc from Cicero, *De Finibus* V.35, to Amy Cuddy, *Presence: Bringing Your Boldest Self to Your Biggest Challenges* (Boston: Little, Brown, 2015), esp. 36–37.

12. Alessandro Verri to Pietro Verri, 25 October 1766, and Alessandro Verri to Pietro Verri, 2 November 1766, in *CV*, vol. 1, pt. 1, 33–37, 47–54. It is well known that Beccaria frequented the salon of Baron d'Holbach in particular; see, for example, Anthony Pagden, *The Enlightenment and Why It Still Matters* (New York: Random House, 2013), 123–124; but he also attended the salons of Mme Necker and Mme Geoffrin, where, from the perspective of political economy, he would have been more likely to run into Antiphysiocrats than Physiocrats; see Daniel Vaugelade, *Le salon physiocratique de La Rochefoucauld: Animé par la duchesse d'Enville (1716–1797)* (Paris: Publibook, 2001), 161; Bernard E. Harcourt, *The Illusion of Free Markets* (Cambridge, MA: Harvard University Press, 2011), 60; and particulary Steven L. Kaplan, *Raisonner sur les blés: Essais sur les lumières économiques* (Paris: Fayard, 2017), 186.

13. Alessandro Verri to Pietro Verri, 29 December 1766, in *Viaggio a Parigi e Londra*, 180–181; emphasis in original.

14. Pietro Verri to Alessandro Verri, 20 January 1767, in *Viaggio a Parigi e Londra*, 195. See also Pietro Verri to Paolo Frisi, 10 February 1767, in *Viaggio a Parigi e Londra*, 470.

15. Alessandro Verri to Pietro Verri, 18 November 1766, in *Viaggio a Parigi e Londra*, 95–97. See also, among others, Alessandro Verri to Pietro Verri, 19 October 1766, and Pietro Verri to Troiano Odazi, 13 November 1766, in *Viaggio a Parigi e Londra*, 20–29 and 454–455 respectively.

16. Alessandro Verri to Pietro Verri, 18 November 1766, in *Viaggio a Parigi e Londra*, 96.

17. Pietro Verri to Alessandro Verri, 7–10 January 1767, in *Viaggio a Parigi e Londra*, 153.

18. Paolo Frisi to Pietro Verri, 4 February 1767, in *Ideologia e scienza nell'opera di Paolo Frisi (1728–1784)*, ed. Gennaro Barbarisi, 2 vols. (Milan: Franco Angeli, 1988), 2:391–392.

19. André Morellet, *Mémoires inédits de l'abbé Morellet . . . sur le dix-huitième siècle et sur la Révolution*, 2nd rev. ed., 2 vols. (Paris: Ladvocat, 1822), 1:167–168.

20. Ibid., 1:168.

21. Pietro Verri to Paolo Frisi, 21 January 1767, in *Viaggio a Parigi e Londra*, 467–469; Pietro Verri to Alessandro Verri, 30 March 1767, in *CV*, vol. 1, pt. 1, 313–317, 314; Pietro Verri, "Memorie sincere del modo col quale servii nel militare e dei miei primi progressi nel servigio politico (ca. 1764–1775)," in *Edizione nazionale delle opere di Pietro Verri*, ed. Carlo Capra et al., 8 vols. in 10 to date (Rome: Edizioni di storia e letteratura, 2003–2014) (hereafter cited as *ENOPV*), 5:145–148, at 147. On this, see also Vianello, *La giovinezza*, 182.

22. Pietro Verri to Alessandro Verri, 21 February 1767, in *Viaggio a Parigi e Londra*, 301–309, at 302; Pietro Verri to Alessandro Verri, 30 March 1767, in *CV*, vol. 1, pt. 1, 313–317, at 314; Pietro Verri to Alessandro Verri, 3 April 1767, in *Viaggio a parigi e Londra*, 381–385, at 382; Pietro Verri to Alessandro Verri, 8 July 1767, in *CV*, vol. 1, pt. 1, 413; Pier Carlo Masini, *Manzoni* (Pisa: Biblioteca Franco Serantini, 1996), esp. 14–18, 25; Marta Boneschi, *Quel che il cuore sapeva: Giulia Beccaria, i Verri, i Manzoni* (Milan: Mondadori, 2004); Carlo Capra, *I progressi della ragione: Vita di Pietro Verri* (Bologna: Il Mulino, 2002), 187; and "L'Accademia dei pugni e la società lombarda," in Capra, *La felicità per tutti: Figure e temi dell'illuminismo lombardo* (Rome: Aracne editore, 2017), 31–51, at 39–41. See also Verri's telling description of the "cometary" Teresa Blasco Beccaria—"young, beautiful, and singularly lovely"—in his "Relazione d'una prodigiosa cometa osservata in Milano—1763," in Verri, *Milano in Europa*, ed. Mario Schettini (Milan: Cino del Duca, 1963), 73–78, at 75. On Beccaria and Manzoni, see furthermore Mario A. Cattaneo, *Carlo Goldoni e Alessandro Manzoni: Illuminismo e diritto penale* (Milan: Giuffrè, 1987); and the essays in Giorgio Panizza, ed., *Da Beccaria a Manzoni: La riflessione sulla giustizia a Milano; Un laboratorio europeo* (Cinisello Balsamo: Silvana Editore, 2015). For Verri's outrage at other people doing precisely what he did, see his "Memoria del Conte Pietro Verri in cui si espongono i motivi per i quali venne impiegato e poi dopo venti anni congedato," in *ENOPV*, 5:559–566, at 559. On these relations in light of the complex role of *cicisbei* at the time, see Roberto Bizzocchi, *A Lady's Man: The Cicisbei, Private Morals and National Identity in Italy* (Basingstoke, UK: Palgrave Macmillan, 2014), 195–202, 209–210. For Manzoni's masterwork, see Alessandro Manzoni, *I promessi sposi*, ed. Teresa Poggi Salani (Milan: Centro Nazionale Studi Manzoniani, 2013).

23. Michael O'Brien, *Henry Adams and the Southern Question* (Athens: University of Georgia Press, 2007), 151–152. Pietro Verri's very first letter to his "brothers"

once they lad left Milan for Paris, after all, went on at length about his visit to "the nymph," which, if Beccaria indeed suffered from jealousy, may have compounded his anxieties, see Pietro Verri to Alessandro Verri and Cesare Beccaria, 4 October 1766, in *Viaggio a Parigi e Londra*, 5.

24. Pietro Verri to Alessandro Verri, 19 February 1767 and 13–14 March 1767, both in *CV*, vol. 1, pt. 1, 217–225, at 220, and 286–290, at 286.

25. On sentimentality and intellectual history, see Gregory Claeys, "Early Socialism as Intellectual History," *History of European Ideas* 40, no. 7 (2014): 893–904, at 901.

26. It is hard not to agree with Carlo Capra, "Un intermediario tra Vienna e Milano: Luigi Lambertenghi e il suo carteggio con Pietro Verri," *Römische historische Mitteilungen* 31 (1989): 367, that "in Pietro Verri's judgments it is always difficult to distinguish objective evaluations of things from sentiments and personal resentments."

27. Pietro Verri to Alessandro Verri, 13–16 December 1766, in *CV*, vol. 1, pt. 1, 100–110, at 101, 109; emphasis added. See similarly Verri, "Memorie sincere," 147; and Pietro Verri to Paolo Frisi, 21 January 1767, in *Viaggio a Parigi e Londra*, 467–472, at 469.

28. Pietro Verri to Alessandro Verri, 2–3 February 1767, in *Viaggio a Parigi e Londra*, 226.

29. Pietro Verri to Alessandro Verri, 23 May 1767, in *Viaggio a Parigi e Londra*, 433–438, at 437, discussed in Edoardo Tortarolo, "'Opinione pubblica' e illuminismo italiano: Qualche appunto di lettura," in *Cesare Beccaria: La pratica dei lumi*, ed. Vincenzo Ferrone and Gianni Francioni (Florence: Olschki, 2000), 131.

30. Alessandro Verri to Pietro Verri, 13 March 1767, in *CV*, vol. 1, pt. 1, 297–307, at 299; Pietro Verri to Alessandro Verri, 3–4 April 1767, in *CV*, vol. 1, pt. 1, 320–324, at 321. Pietro Trifone, *Storia linguistica dell'Italia disunita* (Bologna: Il Mulino, 2010), 14. "Mileneseria" might well have been a neologism at the time; see Eugène Bouvy, *Le comte Pietro Verri (1728–1797): Ses idées et son temps* (Paris: Hachette, 1889), 24n. On "campanilismo," however, see Gene A. Brucker, "From Campanilismo to Nationhood: Forging an Italian Identity," in *Living on the Edge in Leonardo's Florence: Selected Essays* (Berkeley: University of California Press, 2005), 42–61. On the multiple meanings of, and context for, Verri's charge that Beccaria was a "castrato," see Martha Feldman, *The Castrato: Reflections on Nature and Kinds* (Berkeley: University of California Press, 2015). For an example of Beccaria being driven by *"mal di cuore,"* however, see Alessandro Verri to Pietro Verri, 29 December 1766, in *Viaggio a Parigi e Londra*, 183.

31. Alessandro Verri to Pietro Verri, 15 January 1767, in *Viaggio a Parigi e Londra*, 243.

32. Cesare Beccaria, *On Crimes and Punishments and Other Writings*, ed. Aaron Thomas, trans. Aaron Thomas and Jeremy Parzen (Toronto: University of Toronto Press, 2008), 62–65; Giovanni Tessitore, *Cesare Beccaria: L'uomo e il mito; idealizzazione e realtà storica* (Milan: Franco Angeli, 2008), 33–34, calls this a "sly conjecture." On such "homosociality" and variations of "erotic rivalry," see still Eve Kosofsky Sedgwick, *Between Men: English Literature and Male Homosocial Desire* (New York: Columbia University Press, 1985), esp. 162; and, for the perhaps deeper background of their feud, see Alan F. Dixson, *Primate Sexuality: Comparative Studies of Prosimians, Monkeys, Apes, and Humans*, 2nd ed. (Oxford: Oxford University Press, 2012), esp. 230–231.

33. Pietro Verri to Alessandro Verri and Cesare Beccaria [*"ai fratelli"*], 6 October [1766], in *Viaggio a Parigi e Londra*, 10.

34. Alessandro to Pietro Verri, 21 December 1766, in *Viaggio a Parigi e Londra*, 167.

35. Riccardo Di Vincenzo, *Milano al Caffè: Tra Settecento e Novecento* (Milan: Hoepli, 2007), 178–180. It has been argued that the Academy of Fisticuffs had a "satirical" approach to contemporary coffee culture; this seems hard to sustain in light of not only their writings but also their sentiments, but see Cornelia Klettke, "Der Kaffee als Droge der Aufklärer," in *Die Zeitschrift Il Caffè*, ed. Helmut C. Jacobs et al. (Frankfurt am Main: Peter Lang, 2003), 131–147.

36. Cesare Beccaria to anon., 4 January 1774, in *Edizione Nazionale delle Opere di Cesare Beccaria*, ed. Luigi Firpo and Gianni Francioni, 16 vols. in 17 (Milan: Mediobanca, 1984–2015) (hereafter cited as *ENOCB*), 5:429–431 and 429–430n; Pietro Verri to Cesare Beccaria, 16 June 1774, in *ENOCB*, 5:447–448 and 447n. See also Capra, *I progressi della ragione*, 396–397; Silvia Giacomoni, *Alessandro Manzoni: Quattro ritratti stravaganti* (Milan: Guanda, 2008), 50.

37. Quoted in Tessitore, *Cesare Beccaria*, 191.

38. For Verri's letter, and the issue of Beccaria's second marriage, see Tessitore, *Cesare Beccaria*, 191–194.

39. Pietro Verri to Alessandro Verri, 10 September 1774, in *CV*, 7:23, a famous letter on which see again Capra, *I progressi della ragione*, 397; Pietro Verri to Alessandro Verri, 17 May 1780, in *CV*, 11:69–72; and the many letters quoted in Tessitore, *Cesare Beccaria*, 193.

40. On Rousseau and Hume, see Alessandro Verri to Pietro Verri, 4 March 1767, in *CV*, vol. 1, pt. 1, 290–293, at 291. This is merely one of several letters regarding the affair in their correspondence. Interestingly, they tended to think the criticism of Rousseau was exaggerated; see, for example, Alessandro Verri to Pietro Verri, 19 October 1766, in *CV*, vol. 1, pt. 1, 19–27, at 26; Pietro Verri to Alessandro Verri, 24 January 1767, in *CV*, vol. 1, pt. 1, 171–174, at 172–173; and Pietro Verri to Paolo Frisi, 17 February 1767, in *Viaggio a Parigi e Londra*, 475–476. The infamous quarrel between Hume and Rousseau has recently seen a resurgence

of interest even in the popular literature; see David Edmonds and John Eidinow, *Rousseau's Dog: Two Great Thinkers at War in the Age of Enlightenment* (New York: Ecco, 2006); and, more eruditely, Robert Zaretsky and John T. Scott, *The Philosophers' Quarrel: Rousseau, Hume, and the Limits of Human Understanding* (New Haven, CT: Yale University Press, 2010). For an insightful contemporary take on the problem, see Adam Smith to David Hume, 6 July 1766, in *The Correspondence of Adam Smith*, ed. Ernest Campbell Mossner and Ian Simpson Ross (Indianapolis: Liberty Fund, 1987), 112–114.

41. Pietro Verri to Alessandro Verri, 24 January 1767, in *Viaggio a Parigi e Londra,* 201.

42. This was how the myth was channeled by Verri's close friend Giovan Battista Freganeschi's letter to Isidoro Bianchi, 18 January 1783, quoted and discussed in Vianello, *La giovinezza,* 181. See also, for an obvious example of Pietro Verri undermining Beccaria's authorial authority, his letter to Paolo Frisi, 21 January 1767, in *Viaggio a Parigi e Londra,* 467–469.

43. Pietro to Alessandro Verri, 2 August 1780, in *CV,* 11:110–111; and the extraordinary letter from Pietro Verri to Alessandro Verri, 20 September 1780, in *CV,* 11:147–154.

44. Alessandro Verri to Pietro Verri, 21 January 1769, in *CV,* 2:135; emphasis added.

45. Alessandro Verri to Pietro Verri, 9 October 1766, in *Viaggio a Parigi e Londra,* 55–56.

46. Cesare Beccaria, *Ricerche intorno alla natura dello stile,* in *ENOCB,* 2:63–206, building on Beccaria, "Frammento sullo stile," in *"Il Caffè," 1764–1766,* ed. Gianni Francioni and Sergio A. Romagnoli (Turin: Bollati Boringhieri, 1993) (hereafter cited as *Il Caffè*), 277–284. On this work and its relation to the rest of Beccaria's oeuvre, see Philippe Audegean's brilliant *Cesare Beccaria, filosofo europeo* (Rome: Carocci, 2014).

47. Beccaria, *Ricerche intorno alla natura dello stile,* 71–72, 206.

48. Ibid., 71.

49. Giuseppe Aubert to Cesare Beccaria, 8 March 1765, in *ENOCB,* 4:96–97, at 96; Daniel Fallenberg to Cesare Beccaria, 30 May 1766, in *ENOCB,* 4:313–314, at 313; Élie-Salomon-François Reverdil to Cesare Beccaria, 9 July 1766, in *ENOCB,* 4:329–331, at 330. On this unfinished masterwork, see again Gianni Francioni, "Il fantasma del 'Ripulimento delle nazioni': Congetture su un'opera mancata di Cesare Beccaria," *Studi Settecenteschi* 5 (1984): 131–173.

50. For a list of books amassed by Beccaria, see Francioni, "Il fantasma," 143–147; and more generally on his library, see Maria Francesca Turchetti, "'Libri e 'nuove idee': Appunti sulla biblioteca illuministica di Cesare Beccaria," *Archivio storico Lombardo* 139 (2013): 183–236. It is worth noting, as others have before, that Paul-Henri Thiry d'Holbach informed Beccaria of the imminent pub-

lication of Adam Ferguson's *Essay on the History of Civil Society* in a letter of 15 March 1767 (in *ENOCB*, 4:527–528), but that, not being able to read English, Beccaria would not have been able to consult it directly until its 1783 French translation. On this and on comparisons of Beccaria and Ferguson at the time, see Franco Venturi, "Scottish Echoes in Eighteenth-Century Italy," in *Wealth and Virtue: The Shaping of Political Economy in the Scottish Enlightenment*, ed. Istvan Hont and Michael Ignatieff (Cambridge: Cambridge University Press, 1983), 345–362, at 345–349; and Francioni, "Il fantasma," 150.

51. Cesare Beccaria, "Pensieri staccati," in *ENOCB*, 2:277–283, at 270, 282, 283 (thoughts 11, 21, and 32, respectively).

52. Cesare Beccaria, "Pensieri sopra la barbarie e coltura delle nazioni e su lo stato selvaggio dell'uomo," in *ENOCB*, 2:284–292, at 289, 291; emphasis added.

53. Cesare Beccaria, "Pensieri sopra le usanze e i costumi," in *ENOCB*, 2:293–304, at 301, recalling Beccaria, "Pensieri staccati," 283 [thought 31]: "La causa prossima delle azioni e la fuga del dolore, la causa finale e l'amor del piacere. Teorema generalissimo."

54. Cesare Beccaria, "Pensieri sopra le usanze e i costumi," 303, building on Beccaria, *On Crimes and Punishments*, 81–83; Ferdinando Facchinei, *Note ed osservazioni sul libro intitolato "Dei delitti e delle pene"* ([Venice]: n.p., 1765), 106.

55. Beccaria, "Pensieri sopra le usanze e i costumi," 304.

56. Cesare Beccaria, "Pensieri sopra la barbarie e coltura delle nazioni e su lo stato selvaggio dell'uomo," in *ENOCB*, 2:284–292, at 284.

57. The locus classicus in Beccaria's oeuvre on the historical role of needs is in his "Inaugural Lecture" in political economy, in Beccaria, *On Crimes and Punishments and Other Writings*, trans. Richard Davies with Virginia Cox and Richard Bellamy (Cambridge: Cambridge University Press, 1995), 129–140, at 133; but see also Beccaria, "Elementi di economia pubblica," in *ENOCB*, 3:97–390, at 104–105 [1.I.7], with rather Malthusian musings on 121–125 [1.III.31].

58. Beccaria, "Pensieri sopra la barbarie," 286–287. Needless to say, here he was merely formalizing a belief that was very widely held in early modern political economy, expounded even in "Observations by Jean-Jacques Rousseau of Geneva on an Answer Made to His Discourse," in Rousseau, *The Discourses and Other Early Political Writings*, ed. Victor Gourevitch (Cambridge: Cambridge University Press, 1997), 32–51, at 51. On this tradition more widely, see Sophus A. Reinert, "Rivalry: Greatness in Early Modern Political Economy," in *Mercantilism Reimagined: Political Economy in Early Modern Britain and Its Empire*, ed. Phil Stern and Carl Wennerlind (Oxford: Oxford University Press, 2014), 348–370, at 357–358.

59. Beccaria, "Pensieri sopra la barbarie," 286–287.

60. Rousseau, "Of the Social Contract," 79.

61. Rousseau, "Last Reply," in *The Discourses*, 63–85, at 69.

62. Beccaria, "Elementi di economia pubblica," 135–138 [1.II.38], 202 [2.IV.38], and esp. 237 [2.VI.70]. Other such connections between his earlier works and his manuscripts abound, but see, among others, his warning against intermediate bodies in the state, in Cesare Beccaria, "Pensieri staccato," in *ENOCB*, 2: 277–283, frag. 8, at 278, echoing *On Crimes and Punishments*, 42.

63. Joseph A. Schumpeter, *A History of Economic Analysis*, ed. Elizabeth Boody Schumpeter (Oxford: Oxford University Press, 1954), 180. On Smith and Beccaria, see furthermore Peter Groenewegen, "Turgot, Beccaria and Smith," in *Eighteenth-Century Economics: Turgot, Beccaria and Smith and Their Contemporaries* (London: Routledge, 2002), 3–47.

64. Alessandro Verri to Pietro Verri, 5 April 1780, in *CV*, 10:54–55.

65. Morellet, *Mémoires*, 1:168.

66. Rousseau, "Of the Social Contract," 152.

67. See, on Rousseau in this context, Graham Clure, "Rousseau, Diderot and the Spirit of Catherine the Great's Reforms," *History of European Ideas* 41, no. 7 (2015): 883–908.

68. Michelangelo Blasco to Cesare Beccaria, [late August–September, 1767], in *ENOCB*, 4:576–578, at 577; Giuseppe Visconti di Saliceto to Cesare Beccaria, 21 May 1768, in *ENOCB*, 4:628–629, at 628.

69. On Voltaire's invitation, see Barthélemy Chirol to Beccaria, 1 August, 1767, and Voltaire to Cesare Beccaria, 30 May 1768, in *ENOCB*, 4:560–561, 633–634. On Catherine the Great's invitation see, among others, Antonio Greppi to Cesare Beccaria, 31 March, 1767, in *ENOCB*, 4:529.

70. Jean-Baptiste Le Rond d'Alembert to Cesare Beccaria, 2 June 1767; this advice was also offered by Jean-René Loyseau to Cesare Beccaria, 9 January 1767, and by André Morellet to Cesare Beccaria, 14–15 March, 1767, all in *ENOCB*, 4:543–544, 492–496, and 522–525.

71. Otto Frederik Müller to Cesare Beccaria, 30 December 1767, in *ENOCB*, 4:607–609, at 608; Pietro to Alessandro Verri, 17 October 1767, in *CV*, vol. 1, pt. 2, 89–90.

72. See the correspondence in Archivio di Stato di Milano, Milan, Italy (hereafter cited as ASM), *Autografi, no. 164, Uomini celebri: Cesare Beccaria*. On the process, see again Tessitore, *Cesare Beccaria*, 182–188, and esp. the editorial footnote to letter 181 in *ENOCB*, 4:529n–531n.

73. Ernst Lluch, "Cameralism beyond the Germanic World: A Note on Tribe," *History of Economic Ideas* 5, no. 2 (1997): 85–99; Sophus A. Reinert, *Translating Empire: Emulation and the Origins of Political Economy* (Cambridge, MA: Harvard University Press, 2011), 233–238.

74. "Piano per la Catedra d'economia pubblica, o sia di Scienze Camerali," ASM, *Autografi, no. 164, Uomini celebri*, 1r.

75. In Angelo Mauri, "La cattedra di Cesare Beccaria," *Archivio storio italiano* 60 (1933): 199–262, at 258.

76. Giuseppe [Joseph von] Sperges to Cesare Beccaria, 27 March 1769, in *ENOCB*, 5:47–48. Franz Pascher, "Freiherr Joseph von Sperges auf Palenz und Reisdorf," PhD diss., University of Vienna, 1965 [e-dissertation with altered pagination, 2009], 109, suggests Sperges convinced Beccaria to rename his course. On Sperges, see furthermore Andreas A. DiPauli, "Der Freiherr Joseph von Sperges," *Neue Zeitschrift des Ferdinandeums für Tirol und Vorarlberg,* ser. 2, vol. 3 (1837): 1–57; Miriam J. Levy, *Governance and Grievance: Habsburg Policy and Italian Tyrol in the Eighteenth Century* (West Lafayette, IN: Purdue University Press, 1988), 36–39, 167; Reinhard Stauber, *Der Zentralstaat an seinen Grenzen: Administrative Integration, Herrschaftswechsel und politische Kultur im südlichen Alpenraum, 1750–1820* (Göttingen: Vandenhoeck und Ruprecht, 2001), 399–400. On the origins of the Italian department, see Carlo Capra, "Luigi Giusti e il Dipartimento d'Italia a Vienna (1757–1766)," in *Economia, istituzioni, cultura in Lombardia nell'età di Maria Teresa,* ed. Aldo de Maddalena, Ettore Rotelli, and Gennaro Barbarisi, 3 vols. (Bologna: Il Mulino, 1992), 3:365–390.

77. Beccaria, *On Crimes and Punishments*, 9. I have amended the translation slightly.

78. In Mauri, "La cattedra," 251–252; Beccaria, "Elementi di economia pubblica," 255–256 [3.-.-]; Barbara Costa, "'Un regolare sistema per la progressione degli studi': Il ruolo di Gian Rinaldo Carli nella riforma degli studi e della censura (1765–1775)," in *Con la ragione e col cuore: Studi dedicati a Carlo Capra,* ed. Stefano Levati and Marco Meriggi (Milan: Franco Angeli, 2008), 263–288, at 274.

79. See Paolo Greppi to Anotnio Greppi, 14 April 1777, in *Viaggio di quasi tutta l'Europa colle viste del commercio dell'istruzione e della salute: Lettere di Paolo e Giacomo Greppi al padre (1777–1781),* ed. Stefano Levati and Giovanni Liva (Milan: SilvanaEditore for the Archivio di Stato di Milano and the Camera di Commercio di Milano, 2006), 137–139. For his familiarity with Beccaria's *Dei delitti e delle pene,* see Paolo Greppi to Antonio Greppi, 3 November 1778, ASM, *Dono Greppi,* cart. 381.

80. Wenzel Anton von Kaunitz-Rietberg to Karl Joseph von Firmian, 16 November 1767, in Costa, "'Un regolare sistema,'" 272; Kaunitz-Rietberg to Firmian, 5 December 1768, in the voluminous Haus-, Hof- und Staatsarchiv, Österreichisches Staatsarchiv, Vienna, Austria, *Korrespondenz Lombardei 124,* 5r. On Sonnenfels, see Simon Karstens, *Lehrer—Schriftsteller—Staatsreformer: Die Karriere des Joseph von Sonnenfels (1733–1817)* (Vienna: Böhlau, 2011).

81. Gian Rinaldo Carli, "Piano per la cattedra di *Scienze Camerali* o sia di *Economia Civile,*" 14 April 1768, in ASM, *Autografi, no. 164, Uomini celebri;* and Mauri, "La cattedra," 233–235; and in *ENOCB,* 3:55–66; but see also Antonio Trampus,

"Riforme politiche e 'pubblica felicità' negli scritti di Carli sul problema dell'educazione," *Quaderni Istriani: Contributi per la storia contemporanea della Venezia Giulia,* nos. 5–6 (1991–1992): 13–40, at 32–34; Beccaria, "Inaugural Lecture," 139. Carli himself believed the teaching of the subject dated back to the age of Xenophon; see his "Per la Cattedra di Economia Pubblica di Milano," 12 June 1770, ASM, *Autografi, no. 164, Uomini celebri,* fol. 1r. On Carli's role in the establishment of Beccaria's chair, see Costa, "'Un regolare sistema,'" 272–275. On Carli's work on the Supreme Economic Council, see Barbara Costa, "Gian Rinaldo Carli president del Supremo Consiglio di Economia Pubblica (1765–1771)," *Nuova rivista storica* 77, no. 2 (1992): 277–318. On Forbonnais, see Michael Sonenscher, *Before the Deluge: Public Debt, Inequality, and the Intellectual Origins of the French Revolution* (Princeton, NJ: Princeton University Press, 2009), esp. 179–188.

82. Antonio Genovesi, *Lezioni di commercio ossia di economia civile,* ed. Troiano Odazi, 2 vols. (Milan: Agnelli, 1768), republished that same year with the imprint Bassano: Remondini. On Odazi, see still Giovanni Beltrani, "Don Troiano Odazi, la prima vittima del processo politico del 1794 in Napoli," *Archivio storico per le province napoletane* 21, no. 4 (1896): 853–887; and for his inaugural lecture, see Gabriele Cherubini, "Discorso di D. Troiano Odazi nella riapertura della cattedra di economia politica e commercio," *La rivista abruzzese di scienze e lettere* 5, no. 11 (1890): 485–500. More recently, see Franco Venturi, *Settecento riformatore,* 5 vols. in 7 (Turin: Einaudi, 1969–1990), vol. 5, pt. 2, 452; and particularly Giovanni Di Leonardo, *L'illuminista abruzzese Don Trojano Odazj: Dalle lezioni di Genovesi all'amicizia con Beccaria, dalla cattedra di economia alla cospirazione* (Mosciano: Media Edizioni, 2003).

83. Cesare Beccaria, "Piano d'istruzioni per la cattedra di scienze camerali o sia di economia civile," in Beccaria, *Opere,* ed. Sergio Romagnoli (Florence: Sansoni, 1958), 341–349, at 342.

84. Beccaria, "Elementi di economia pubblica," 244–245 [2.VI.79], 248–249 [2.VII.82]. It is worth remembering that, already at the time of the Great Fire of London in 1666, William Pen helped Samuel Pepys safeguard his papers, wine, and "parmazan" from the raging fires by burying them in the garden. See, on this, Deborah Valenze, *Milk: A Local and Global History* (New Haven, CT: Yale University Press, 2011), 100, but also 53–54. On the large-scale attempts to transplant Italian vines to Virginia at the time, see Thomas Pinney, *A History of Wine in America,* 2 vols. (Berkely: University of California Press, 2007), esp. 1:78–79.

85. Beccaria, "Elementi di economia pubblica," 261–263 [3.I.6].

86. Compare Cesare Beccaria, "Prolusione letta nell'apertura della nuova cattedra di scienze camerali," in *ENOCB,* 2:79–96, at 94–95, to Verri, "Considerazioni sul commercio dello stato di Milano," in *ENOPV,* vol. 2, pt. 1, 107–345, at 111–112. See

also Pietro Verri to anon., 26 October 1782, fol. 1r, *Pietro Verri Letters,* Kress Collection of Business and Economics, Baker Library, Harvard Business School, Boston (hereafter cited as Kress).

87. Beccaria, "Piano d'istruzioni," 345. Compare, for example, Beccaria's "Inaugural Lecture," 137–138, to the accounts discussed in Sophus A. Reinert, "Blaming the Medici: Footnotes, Falsification, and the Fate of the 'English Model' in Eighteenth-Century Italy," *History of European Ideas* 32 (2006): 430–455, esp. 442–443, as well as Reinert, "Lessons on the Decline and Fall of Great Powers: Conquest, Commerce, and Decline in Enlightenment Italy," *American Historical Review* 115, no. 5 (2010): 1395–1425. On Cantillon, see Antoin E. Murphy, *Richard Cantillon: Entrepreneur and Economist* (Oxford: Oxford University Press, 1987); for the translation, see Richard Cantillon, *Saggio sulla natura del commercio in generale,* ed. Giovanni Francesco Scottoni (Venice: Carlo Palese, 1767), though Beccaria seems to have relied on the French edition, *Essai sur la Nature du Commerce en Général* (London [but Paris]: Fletcher Gyles, 1755); see Venturi, *Settecento riformatore,* vol. 5, pt. 2, 450–451. Beccaria's reliance on Cantillon is widely accepted; for a comment, see Trampus, "Riforme politiche," 15.

88. Murphy, *Richard Cantillon,* 282–321.

89. Richard Cantillon, *Essay on the Nature of Trade in General,* ed. Anthony Brewer (Abingdon-on-Thames, UK: Routledge, 2001), 7.

90. Ibid., 7–11, 25, 95–99. The English "undertaker" and the French "entrepreneur" had two equivalents in the Italian language: the "impresaro" or "impresario," preferred by Verri and now most famous for its operatic usage, and Cantillon's Italian translator's choice of imprenditore, for which Italian dictionaries offered the English translation "enterpriser" and which had a long history in the Italian language. A French-Italian dictionary, in turn, suggested for the term "entrepreneur" either "imprenditore, appaltatore, capo mastro di qualche fabbrica." See Cantillon, *Saggio,* 67; Giacomo Pergamini, *Il memoriale della lingua Italiana* (Venice: Cagnolini, 1688), 97; Ferdinando Altieri, *Dizionario Italiano ed Inglese,* 2 vols. (London: Innys, 1727), vol. 2, unpaginated entry for "imprenditore"; Annibale Antonini, *Dizionario italiano, latino e francese,* 2 vols. (Lyon: Duplain, 1770), 2:271.

91. On the importance of the "entrepreneur" for Beccaria, see still Daniel M. Klang, "Cesare Beccaria, Pietro Verri e l'idea dell'imprenditore nell'illuminismo milanese," in *Cesare Beccaria tra Milano e l'Europa,* ed. Sergio Romagnoli and Gian Domenico Pisapaia (Milan: Cariplo-Laterza, 1990), 371–406.

92. On Genovesi's chair, and further readings, see Reinert, *Translating Empire,* esp. 194–195. On its similar justification, see Bartolomeo Intieri to Antonio Cocchi, 18 June 1754, Archivio Baldasseroni Corsini, Florence, Italy (hereafter cited as ABC), 215/4, 1v. On Intieri's ideal that "physics is the foundation of the economy

of politics [*dell'economica della Politica*]," see Bartolomeo Intieri to Antonio Cocchi, Napoli 8 August 1752, ABC, 290/4, 1r. On the relationship between history and economics today, see, among others, Geoffrey M. Hodgson, *How Economics Forgot History: The Problem of Historical Specificity in Social Science* (London: Routledge, 2001).

93. Beccaria, "Elementi di economia pubblica," 117–118 [1.II.26], 130–132 [1.III.34], 144–146 [1.III.44]. Beccaria's interest in "physics" and "history" was mirrored also in his dual praise of Isaac Newton and David Hume; See 281–284 [3.II.26].

94. Beccaria, "Elementi di economia pubblica," 117–118 [1.II.26] and again 192 [2.III.29]. On the importance of this trope in cameralism, see Reinert, *Translating Empire*, 234–245, 249; Alix Cooper, *Inventing the Indigenous: Local Knowledge and Natural History in Early Modern Europe* (Cambridge: Cambridge University Press, 2007).

95. See, among other places, Beccaria, "Elementi di economia pubblica," 119–121 [1.II.28], 143 [1.III.42], 200–201 [2.IV.35], 238–239 [2.VI.72], 255–256 [3.-.-].

96. Ibid., 146 [1.III.45].

97. Ibid., 118 [1.II.27].

98. Ibid., 100–101 [1.I.3–4], 108 [1.I.12], and 110 [1.I.18]; Beccaria, *On Crimes and Punishments,* 10. On these early efforts to keep Beccaria in Milan, see Sperges to Kaunitz, 9 May 1767, esp. fol. 2r, as well as 2 June 1767, and Kaunitz to Sperges, 3 July 1767, fol. 1r–1v, in which Kaunitz made it clear that he approved of Beccaria's application to leave Milan and favored his short journey to Russia for the sake of rendering "more famous the name of a subject of Her Majesty . . . in countries so far from Italy." See also Firmian to Kaunitz, 14 April 1767, and Kaunitz's replies of 27 April and 21 May 1767, in which he expressed the wish to see Beccaria remain in Milan and local "philosophical" talent cultivated rather than lost to "foreigners." On Beccaria's decision ultimately not to go to Russia and to instead be "useful" in Milan, see Sperges to Kaunitz, 10 January 1769. All in ASM, *Autografi, no. 164, Uomini celebri.*

99. Beccaria, "Elementi di economia pubblica," 362–363 [4.V.35].

100. Beccaria here drew on a traditional Italian economic historiography dating back to the Middle Ages, on which see Sophus A. Reinert, "Rivalry: Greatness in Early Modern Political Economy," in *Mercantilism Reimagined: Political Economy in Early Modern Britain and Its Empire,* ed. Philip J. Stern and Carl Wennerlind (Oxford: Oxford University Press, 2013), 348–370.

101. Beccaria, "Elementi di economia pubblica," 192–193 [2.IV.30], 200–201 [2.IV.35], 206–209 [2.V.42], 214–216 [2.V.46], 253–254 [2.VIII.89], 271–273 [3.II.18], 279–281 [3.II.25], 347–350 [4.IV.28].

102. Ibid., esp. 221–228 [2.V.52–59], 249–250 [2.VII.83], 273–279 [3.II.20–24].

103. Ibid., 264–265 [3.II.9], 350–352 [4.IV.30].

104. Ibid., 287–290 [3.III.28]. On the importance of complexity for economic development, see W. Brian Arthur, *Complexity and the Economy* (Oxford: Oxford University Press, 2014); for a worldwide assessment, see Ricardo Hausmann and César Hidalgo, *The Atlas of Economic Complexity: Mapping Paths to Prosperity* (Cambridge, MA: MIT Press, 2014).

105. Beccaria, "Elementi di economia pubblica," 109 [1.I.16]; emphasis added. He had already argued the same in one of his very earliest publications, "Del disordine e de' rimedi delle monete nello stato di Milano nel 1762," in *ENOCB*, 3:15–52, at 24.

106. On the culturally and economically Lombard yet politically "robustly Swiss" Ticino, for example, see Adriano Cavanna, Giulio Vismara, and Paola Vismara, *Ticino medievale: Storia di una terra lombarda* (Locarno: Dadò, 1990), 121.

107. The literature on Alpine smuggling is vast, but see, for different centuries, among others, Massimo Mandelli and Diego Zoia, *La carga: Contrabbando in Valtellina e Valchiavenna* (Sondrio: L'officina del libro, 1998); and the backward-looking parts of Marco Polli, *Zollpolitik und illegaler Handel: Schmuggel im Tessin 1868–1894: Soziale, wirtschaftliche und zwischenstaatliche Aspekte* (Zurich: Chronos, 1989), discussing the bandits from Chapter 4 of this volume at 33–36; for a general overview, see Anne Montenach, "Pouvoir, territoire et économie de la frontiére: Jalons pour une histoire de la contrebande dans les Alpes à l''époque moderne," in *Oeconomia Alpium I: Wirtschaftsgeschichte des Alpenraums in vorindustrieller Zeit: Forschungsaufriss, -Konzepte und –Perspektiven,* ed. Markus A. Denzel et al. (Berlin: De Gruyter, 2017), 233–248. On Swiss bovine exports to Lombardy at the time, see Gianpiero Fumi, "L'esportazione di bestiame dalla Svizzera e l'allevamento bovino in Lombardia (secoli XVIII–XIX)," in *Regioni alpine e sviluppo economico; Dualismi e processi d'integrazione (sec. XVIII–XIX),* ed. Fausto Piola Caselli (Milan: Franco Angeli, 2003), 153–188, at 156. On the Septimer Pass hospice, see Walter Woodburn Hyde, "The Alpine Passes in Nature and History," *Scientific Monthly* 45, no. 4 (1937): 317–330, at 325–326.

108. Beccaria, "Elementi di economia pubblica," 113–115 [1.II.23].

109. [Pietro Verri], *Meditazioni sulla economia politica con annotazioni* (Venice: [Pasquale], 1771).

110. Ibid., 201.

111. Ibid., 250.

112. Carli's annotations in ibid., 207.

113. Carli's annotations in ibid., 207–209.

114. Pietro Verri, "Meditazioni sulla economia politica (Livorno 1772)," in *ENOPV,* vol. 2, pt. 2, 341–570, at 528, 528n–530n, 544, though the editorial apparatus makes the exchange hard to follow.

115. Carli's annotations in [Verri], *Meditazioni sulla economia politica con annotazioni,* 138–139, reflected also in his "Breve ragionamento sopra i bilanci

economici delle nazioni," in Carli, *Delle opere del Signor Commendatore Gianrinaldo Conte Carli*, 19 vols. (Milan: Imperial Monistero di s. Ambrogio Maggiore, 1784–1787), 1:49–97, at 82. The different typologies were ostensibly represented by Pietro Verri's "Bilancio generale del commercio dello Stato di Milano [per il 1762]," in *ENOPV*, vol. 2, pt. 1, 541–610; and Gianrinaldo Carli, "Compendiosa relazione del commercio dello Stato di Milano, col confronto della attività, e passività di esso, apparente nei generali bilanci degli anni 1762, e 1766 umilissimamente rassegnate alla S. C. M. dal Presidente Gian Rinaldo Carli col permesso della medesima M.S.," in Carli, *Saggi inediti di Gian Rinaldo Carli sull'economia pubblica dello stato di Milano,* ed. Carlo Antonio Vianello (Florence: Olschki, 1938), 143–162. On this and other quarrels between Carli and Verri, though without specific reference to these passages, see Barbara Costa, "'Disciplina ragionata' e 'libertà indefinita' nei rapporti fra Gian Rinaldo Carli e Pietro Verri," in *Gianrinaldo Carli nella cultura europea del suo tempo*, ed. Antonio Trampus (Triest: Deputazione di Storia Patria per la Venezia Giulia), monograph, *Quaderni giuliani di storia* 25, no. 1 (2004): 2004, 15–36, esp. 28–29 on balances.

116. On this question in general, see ibid., 33; and Capra, *I progressi della ragione*, 367–368.

117. Pietro Verri, "[Un'altra risposta all'*Esame breve e succinto* . . .]," in *ENOPV*, vol. 2, pt. 2, 610–616, at 614, replying to anon., *Esame breve, e succinto dell'opera intitolata Meditazioni sulla economia pubblica* (Vercelli: Giuseppe Panialis, [1771?]), 23, 75, 134–135, on which see Venturi, *Settecento riformatore*, vol. 5, pt. 1, 533–538; and Capra, *I progressi della ragione*, 360–362. Whoever the author was, and in spite of Verri's defense, he or she was remarkably well versed not merely with actual agricultural and commercial practice around Europe but also with the classics from Plato through Tacitus to Thomas More, and even the history of political economy itself, including Gresham, Sully, Colbert, Charles Davenant, John Cary, Bielfeld, Giovanni Francesco Pagnini, Rousseau, and the "Abate di S. Pietro"; see *Esame breve*, 37, 47, 69, 76, 90, 109, 113, 117, 126–128.

118. Anon., *Esame breve*, 37–38. The relocation of dogmatic theories of laissez-faire to distant planets happens occasionally in the history of economics. See, for example, Antonio Genovesi, *Storia del commercio della Gran Brettagna scritta da John Cary* . . . , 3 vols. (Naples: Casari, 1757–1758), 1:292–293n; and William Cunningham, *The Rise and Decline of the Free Trade Movement* (London: C. J. Clay and Sons and Cambridge University Press Warehouse, 1904), 2–4.

119. See, for just some examples of Verri's contextual approach to legislation, Pietro Verri, "Dialogo fra l'imperatore Giuseppe Secondo e un filosofo," in *ENOPV*, 6:444–453, at 452. See similarly his 1796 "[Giudizi di Pietro Verri sulle dissertazioni presentate al celebre concorso 'Quale dei governi liberi meglio con-

venga alla felicità dell'Italia']," in *ENOVP*, 6:837–839, particularly his verdict for #14: "Propone per modello la Svizzera: di nessuna utilità," at 838.

120. This theoretical affinity between Beccaria and Galiani was noted but not explored by Ulisse Gobbi, *La concorrenza estera e gli antichi economisti italiani* (Milan: Ulrico Hoepli, 1884), 173. On Verri's introduction of Beccaria to Carli, see Pietro Verri to Gian Rinaldo Carli, 3 September 1762 [but 1761], in Francesco De Stefano, "Cinque anni di sodalizio tra Pietro Verri e Gian Rinaldo Carli (1760–1765) con XXIV lettere inedite di Pietro Verri," *Atti e memorie della Società istriana di archeologia e storia patria* 45 (1933): 43–103, at 66. On Carli's debt to Galiani, see his "Del libero commercio de' grani," in *Delle opere*, 1:100–148, esp. 108–109, 117–119, building on Ferdinando Galiani, *Dialogues sur le commerce des bleds* (London [but Paris]: n.p., 1770), 11–12, 118, 122, and perhaps answering Galiani's trenchant call for empirical rather than mathematically abstract observations on 135–138, 270–273.

121. Pietro to Alessandro Verri, 15 January 1780, in *CV*, 11:13–14. On this letter and its context, see Bartolo Anglani, *"Il dissotto delle carte": Sociabilità, sentimenti e politica tra i Verri e Beccaria* (Milan; Franco Angeli, 2004), 303. On Beccaria's meetings with Galiani in Paris, see Alessandro to Pietro Verri, 15 January 1767, in *Viaggio a Parigi e a Londra*, 244–245. For Carli's engagement, see his "Del libero commercio de' grani," esp. 108–109 and 117–119.

122. Anon., *Esame breve*, 141–142.

123. Ibid.

124. Beccaria, "Elementi di economia pubblica," 236 [2.VI.69]. Yet Beccaria never flirted with radical alternatives to a social order based, on some level, on an interdependent division of labor the way Rousseau did on multiple occasions, among others in his "Preface to *Narcissus*" and "Second Discourse," in *The Discourses*, 92–106, at 100, and 111–222, at 159.

125. Beccaria, "Elementi di economia pubblica," 241 [2.VI.75].

126. Ibid., 342–344 [4.IV.24].

127. Ibid., 198–200 [2.IV.34]. This might well be a veiled reference to David Hume's essay "Of the Jealousy of Trade," in Hume, *Political Essays*, ed. Knud Haakonssen (Cambridge: Cambridge University Press, 1994), 150–153.

128. Adam Smith, *An Inquiry into the Nature and Causes of the Wealth of Nations*, ed. Edwin Cannan, 2 vols. (Chicago: University of Chicago Press, 1976), 1:477–478; Facchinei to Zaccaria, addendum to letter of 17 April 1763, Archivo Histórico de la Casa de Loyola, Sanctuary of Loyola, Azpeitia, Spain (hereafter cited as AHCL), *Fondo Zaccaria*, b. 19, 1v.

129. Beccaria, "Elementi di economia pubblica," 242–244 [2.VI.78], 345–347 [4.IV.28].

130. Ibid., 258–260 [3.I.3].

131. Thomas Hobbes, *Leviathan,* ed. Noel Malcolm, 3 vols. (Oxford: Oxford University Press, 2012), 2:90.

132. Beccaria, "Sulla materia," in *ENOCB,* 2:308–309. On this nexus, see Max Weber, "Science as a Vocation," in Weber, *The Vocation Lectures,* ed. David S. Owen and Tracy B. Strong (Indianapolis: Hackett, 2004), 1–30, at 13.

133. Beccaria, "Elementi di economia pubblica," 156 [1.III.34], 187 [2.III.24].

134. For an overview of Beccaria's administrative career, see Carlo Capra, "Cesare Beccaria funzionario e l'evoluzione delle sue idee," in *La felicità per tutti: Figure e temi dell'illuminismo lombardo* (Rome: Aracne editore, 2017), 95–113, esp. 97–98. For a more focused study of his influence on the silk industries in Como, see Fabrizio Cartocci, *Cesare Beccaria e l'industria serica comasca* (Como: Alessandro Dominioni Editore, 2014).

135. On the transition of Beccaria's chair, see Carlo Antonio Vianello, "L'abate Longo successore del Beccaria nella cattedra di economia pubblica," *Archivio storico lombardo* 63 (1937): 513–527, esp. 513 and the discussion of Longo's curriculum on 517–519. Vianello was, however, mistaken in attributing the set of lecture notes in Ambrosiana, *cod. D 98,* to a student of Longo. The notes were by a student of Agostino Paradisi at the chair of political economy in Modena, on which see Sophus A. Reinert, "Lessons on the Rise and Fall of Great Powers: Conquest, Commerce, and Decline in Enlightenment Italy," *American Historical Review* 115, no. 5 (2010): 1395–1425. Although at times critical of the Physiocrats, Longo would correspond with Victor de Riqueti, Marquis de Mirabeau (for Mirabeau's letters to Longo, see the collection in the Musée Louis Arbaud, Aix-en-Provence, France, *Correspondance du marquis de Mirabeau,* regg. 19–22) and publish, with annotations, Mirabeau's *Les devoirs,* ed. Alfonso Longo (Milan: Monastero imperiale di S. Ambrogio, 1780), on which see Liana Vardi, *The Physiocrats and the World of the Enlightenment* (Cambridge: Cambridge University Press, 2012), 176–177.

136. For Longo's suggested reading list, notably cool in its discussion of the Physiocrats, see Alfonso Longo to Karl Joseph von Firmian, 6 July 1773, ASM, *Studii, parte antica, 306.* For divergent interpretations of this document, and particularly with regards to the role allotted to Pietro Verri's *Meditazioni sulla economia politica* (Livorno: nella stamperia dell'Enciclopedia [Aubert], 1771), see Marco Bianchini, "Una difficile gestazione," 58–60; Massimo M. Augello and Marco E. L. Guidi, "Trattati e manuali di economia in Italia: Uno studio comparative dell'economia politica nel XVIII e XIX secolo," in *Liber Amicorum per Umberto Bertini: L'uomo, lo studioso, il professore,* ed. Fabio Fortuna (Milan: Franco Angeli, 2012), 42–66, at 53; and Capra, *I progressi della ragione,* 398, building on the decidedly upset letter by Pietro Verri to Luigi Lambertenghi, 18 January 1774, Archivio Verri, Fondazione Mattioli, housed at the Università di Milano under

the tutelage of the Archivio Storico della Banca Intesa Sanpaolo, Milan, Italy (hereafter cited as Archivio Verri), 277, reacting to Longo's ostensible preference for Antonio Genovesi, *Lezioni di commercio o sia d'economia civile*, ed. Maria Luisa Pesante (Naples: Istituto italiano per gli studi filosofici, 2005). One can assume that Longo knew this work through its 1768 Milanese edition by Troiano Odazi published by Agnelli and dedicated to Gian Rinaldo Carli. On the various editions of Genovesi's *Lezioni*, see Perna's rich apparatus to Genovesi, *Lezioni di commercio*, 893–903 and, for the Milanese edition in particular, 913–916; as well as Maria Luisia Perna, "L'edizione delle Lezioni di commercio di Antonio Genovesi," in *Genovesi economista*, ed. Bruno Jossa, Rosario Patalano, and Eugenio Zagari (Naples: Istituto italiano per gli studi filosofici, 2007), 59–66, at 63.

137. For his high praise of both Genovesi and Verri, see again Alfonso Longo to Karl Joseph von Firmian, 6 July 1773, ASM, *Studii, parte antica*, 306.

138. Antonio Genovesi to Antonio Cantelli, 30 April 1765, in Antonio Genovesi, *Scritti*, ed. Franco Venturi (Turin: Einaudi, 1977), 266–267. More generally on Genovesi's critiques of Beccaria, see Maria Luisa Perna's annotations to Genovesi, *Lezioni di commercio*, 463–464n8.

139. *ENOCB*, vols. 6–16. These documents, not to mention Verri's equivalents, render puzzling Matthew S. Anderson's statement that "the Verri brothers and Beccaria, the leading figures in the Milanese Enlightenment, had little interest in either agriculture or industry and knew little about them"; see Anderson, "The Italian Reformers," in *Enlightened Absolutism: Reform and Reformers in Later Eighteenth-Century Europe*, ed. Hamish M. Scott (Ann Arbor: University of Michigan Press, 1990), 55–74, at 69.

140. See the following by Cesare Beccaria, all in *ENOCB*: "Domanda d'impiego [7 January 1776]," 6:671; "Domanda d'impiego [26 January 1776]," 6:674; "Astronomi di Brera [24 June 1788]," 10:404; "Pallone aerostatico a Milano [3 January 1791]," 13:17; "Idrofobia a Melzo [8 August 1791]," 13:342. For another case of canine rabies, "Quarantena nei porti Veneziani: Rabbia canina a Magenta [8 July 1793]," 15:406; "Morte per funghi a Milano [4 October 1790]," 7:566; but see also "Funghi velenosi a Pavia [18 November 1793]," 15:667, and "Funghi velenosi a Pavia [2 December 1793]," 15:722, as well as "Funghi velenosi a Pavia [28 April 1794]," 16:338.

141. Andre Wakefield, *The Disordered Police State: German Cameralism as Science and Practice* (Chicago: University of Chicago Press, 2009), esp. 90–91, reacting to a historiographical paradigm exemplified by Marc Raeff, *The Well-Ordered Police State: Social and Institutional Change through Law in the Germanies and Russia, 1600–1800* (New Haven, CT: Yale University Press, 1983).

142. See, for example, Pietro Secchi, "Contradizioni morali," in *Il Caffè*, 464–471, at 466.

143. For good examples of such unlikely projects, see, among others, Lisbet Ko-
erner, *Linnaeus: Nature and Nation* (Cambridge, MA: Harvard University Press,
1999), 149–152; Wakefield, *The Disordered Police State*, 134–144. On Ranke and his
famous slogan, see Peter Novick, *That Noble Dream: The "Objectivity Question"
and the American Historical Profession* (Cambridge: Cambridge University Press,
1988). For the Accademia's own awareness of the problem, see Sebastiano
Franci, "Dell'agricoltura. Dialogo: Afranio e Cresippo," in *Il Caffè*, 60–73, at 70.

144. Indeed, already in the mid-nineteenth century it was argued that "whoever
wishes to write the history of Lombardy's political economy and industry will
have to treasure the papers in the Milanese archive with regard to what Beccaria did as councellor and cameral magistrate"; see Alberto Errera, "Una
Nuova Pagina della vita di Cesare Beccaria: Capitolo II. Beccaria Impiegato,"
L'Economista d'Italia ii, no. 2, 10 January 1878, 19.

145. Cesare Beccaria, "Vendita di bovini infetti [6 April 1789]," in *ENOCB*, ii:264. On
his tasks, and the extra ones he took on, see Capra, "Cesare Beccaria
funzionario," 96.

146. Cesare Beccaria, "Casa di correzione di Milano, minute di lettera, 31 October 1791," in *ENOCB*, 13:596–598, at 597.

147. This was, needless to say, true almost everywhere; see Steven L. Kaplan, *The
Stakes of Regulation: Perspectives on "Bread, Politics, and Political Economy" Forty
Years Later* (London: Anthem, 2015), esp. 12.

148. Cesare Beccaria, "Istituzione di nuovi mercati [consulta e verbale di ri-
unione]," 16 July 1779, in *ENOCB*, 7:121–137, at 125–127. For the Hobbes quote, see
Leviathan, 149. On the simultaneous danger of applying the "minute regula-
tory cares of the economy of a private family" to an entire trade, however, as
well as the fear of famine, see also Beccaria's "Nuovo Piano annonario," 28
April 1781, in *ENOCB*, 7:56–483, at 459–460, 466, 468. On the *opinion* of famine in
the eighteenth century, see Steven L. Kaplan, *The Famine-Plot Persuasion in
Eighteenth-Century France* (Philadelphia: American Philosophical Society, 1982).
For a map of the new markets established by the 1779 reform, see Giovanna
Tonelli, "Luoghi e momenti di mercato nelle testimonianze d'archivio
(XVIII–XIX secolo)," in *I mercati e le fiere della provincia di Milano tra XVIII e XX
secolo*, ed. Maria Piera Bassi (Milan: Provincia di Milano, 1990), 63–128, at 67. On
the criticisms Beccaria faced at the time for his slow work on the project, and
other matters, see Capra, "Cesare Beccaria funzionario," 99–100.

149. Cesare Beccaria, "Attività del Dipartimento III nel 1786 [31 March 1787]," in
ENOCB, 9:223–267, at 247; Beccaria, "Bestie feroci nel Milanese [27 August 1792],"
in *ENOCB*, 14:429–432; Beccaria, "Bestia feroce a Bovisio [1 September 1794]," in
ENOCB, 16:699–703; Beccaria, "Regolamento dei boschi [1775]," in *ENOCB*, 6:656–
670, at 656; Beccaria, "Illuminazione di Milano: Medico Baronio. Polizia a Pavia."

Protocolli delle Preture lombarde [4 January 1790]," in *ENOCB*, 10:26–28, at 26–27.

150. See, among others, the following by Cesare Beccaria: "Sicurezza a Retegno [15 November 1790]," in *ENOCB*, 12:620–623, at 621; "Lotteria di Milano: Estradizione di un malvivente [28 February 1791]," in *ENOCB*, 13:59; and, among his numerous reports titled "Convenzione per l'estradizione dei malviventi," in *ENOCB*: [29 March 1790] at 12:218; [28 March 1791] at 13:72–74; [3 May 1790] at 12:264; [6 September 1790] at 12:508, 509; [13 September 1790] at 12:514; [4 June 1792] at 14:251.

151. Cesare Beccaria, "Trasporto dei grani da Sesto Calende a Laveno [3 and 17 March 1773]," in *ENOCB*, 6:138; Beccaria, "Libera panizzazione a Como [26 February 1787]," in *ENOCB*, 9:140; Beccaria, "Disciplina degli operai [12 March 1787]," in *ENOCB*, 9:177–180; Beccaria, "Disciplina degli operai [11 October 1790]," in *ENOCB*, 12:579.

152. See, for example, Cesare Beccaria, "Sequestri di vettovaglie e tasse sulle merci a Cremona. Scuola veterinaria di Milano: Manifatture tessili [12 March 1787]," in *ENOCB*, 9:183–184, at 184; Beccaria, "Dazio sui tessuti esteri: Macchinari per le manifatture di cotone," in *ENOCB*, 11:451–452.

153. On this debate and its relevance to Northern Italy, see still Carlo Marco Belfanti, "The Proto-Industrial Heritage: Forms of Rural Proto-Industry in Northern Italy in the Eighteenth and Nineteenth Centuries," in *European Proto-Industrialization*, ed. Sheilah C. Ogilvie and Markus Cerman (Cambridge: Cambridge University Press, 1996), 155–170.

154. Cesare Beccaria, "Tessitura della seta a Como [24 August 1789]," in *ENOCB*, 11:550–554, at 553.

155. Cesare Beccaria, "Provvedimenti per le famiglie povere [11 May 1789]," in *ENOCB*, 11:312.

156. Cesare Beccaria, "Attività del Dipartimento III nel 1786 [31 March 1787]," in *ENOCB*, vol. IX, 223–267, at 242, 244; emphasis added.

157. Cesare Beccaria, "Emigrazione di tessitori [30 June 1789]," in *ENOCB*, 11:432. On the widespread idea at the time that Italy's economic decline in the late Renaissance similarly had been caused by the subcontracting of Medici woolens to England, see Sophus A. Reinert, Blaming the Medici: Footnotes, Falsification, and the Fate of the English Model in Eighteenth-Century Italy," *Journal of the History of European Ideas* 32, no. 4 (2006): 430–455.

158. See the following by Cesare Beccaria, all in *ENOCB*: "Miniere Lombarde [6 July 1773]," 6:257–264, at 257; "Pesa dei fieni [20 June 1775]," 6:619–623; "Rapporti commerciali con gli Svizzeri [10 May 1784]," 8:44–62, at 49; "Riflessioni intorno al Piano delle leggi cambiali [1771?]," 6:70–83, at 70; and "Visita al distretto di Viadana [26 February 1787]," 9:154–155, at 155.

159. Cesare Beccaria, "Camera mercantile di Mantova [12 February 1787]," in *ENOCB*, 9:116.

160. Cesare Beccaria, "Brevi riflessioni che si subordinano dal relatore per le superiori determinazioni," in "Disciplina degli operai [12 March 1787]," in *ENOCB*, 9:171–180, at 172.

161. Cesare Beccaria, "Riflessioni intorno al Puano delle leggi cambiali [1771?]" in *ENOCB*, 6:70–83, at 71; Beccaria, "Puano della caccia [19 January 1789]," in *ENOCB*, 11:36–86, at 38.

162. Cesare Beccaria, "Meta della legna a Milano [5 February 1787], in *ENOCB*, 9:92–93, at 93. See similarly Beccaria, "Attività del Dipartimento III nel 1786 [31 March 1787]," in *ENOCB*, 9:223–267, at 250.

163. Capra, "Cesare Beccaria funzionario," 100–102.

164. Cesare Beccaria, "Casa di correzione di Milano [26 September 1791]," 488–491, at 489–490.

165. Cesare Beccaria, "Estastolo di Pizzighettone [10 October 1791]," in *ENOCB*, 13:562–564, at 562, 564; Beccaria, "Casa di correzione di Milano [31 October 1791]," in *ENOCB*, 13:596–601, at 597.

166. Philippe Audegean, "Correggere e punire: Beccaria e la funzione rieducativa delle pene," in *Il caso Beccaria: A 250 anni dalla pubblicazione del "Dei delitti e delle pene,"* ed. Vincenzo Ferrone and Giuseppe Ricuperati (Bologna: Il Mulino, 2016), 61–86.

167. Cesare Beccaria, "Casa di correzione di Milano: Revisione delle gazzette [26 July 1790]," in *ENOCB*, 12:407–417, at 409–410, 412.

168. "Casa di correzione di Milano: Revisione delle gazzette [26 July 1790]," in *ENOCB*, 12:412.

169. Cesare Beccaria, "Codice generale sui delitti e sulle pene [13 October 1788]," in *ENOCB*, 10:668.

170. Cesare Beccaria, "Delitti politici e delitti criminali: Pretore d'Inverigo. Processo Oriani. Sepolture a Pavia. Attività delle Preture [24 May 1790]," in *ENOCB*, 12:303–305, at 303; Beccaria, "Nuovo Codice penale [12 July 1790]," in *ENOCB*, 12:373–377, at 374–375.

171. Cesare Beccaria, Francesco Gallarati-Scotti, and Paolo Risi, "Voto degli infrascritti individui della giunta delegata per la riforma del sistema criminale nella Lombardia austriaca risguardanete la pena di morte [24 January 1792]," in *ENOCB*, 16:965–972.

172. See, among others, Nicola Raponi, "Un discepolo e amico del Beccaria: Francesco Gallarati Scotti," *Rivista di Storia del diritto italiano* 36 (1963): 128–170; and the deeply Beccarian work, Paolo Risi, *Animadversiones ad criminalem iurisprudentiam pertinentes* (Milan: Joseph Galeatius, 1766), on which see Stefano Solimano, "Paolo Risi e il processo penale (1766)," *Studi di storia del diritto 3* (2001): 419–501.

173. Beccaria, Gallarati-Scotti, and Risi, "Voto," 966, echoing Beccaria, *On Crimes and Punishments*, 52, almost verbatim.

174. Ibid., 966, again echoing Beccaria, *On Crimes and Punishments*, 52, "the death penalty is not a *right*, but the war of a nation against a citizen." Emphasis in original.

175. Ibid., 967; *Codice generale sopra i delitti e le pene* (Roveredo: Marchesani, 1787), 18.

176. Beccaria, Gallarati-Scotti, and Risi, "Voto," 968, 970.

177. Ibid., 968. These sentiments would, notably, be vocalized also by jaded Parisians during the Terror, for which see Paul Friedland, *Seeing Justice Done: The Age of Spectacular Punishment in France* (Oxford: Oxford University Press, 2012), 258.

178. Beccaria, Gallarati-Scotti, and Risi, "Voto," 970, building on Beccaria, *On Crimes and Punishments*, 54. For Camus's use, see his "Reflections on the Guillotine," in Camus, *Resistance, Rebellion, and Death: Essays*, trans. Justin O'Brien (New York: Vintage, 1960), 173–234, at 194.

179. Richard J. Evans, *Rituals of Retribution: Capital Punishment in Germany, 1600–1987* (Oxford: Oxford University Press, 1996), 133.

180. Cesare Beccaria, "Piano d'Annona [bozza di consulta]," 23 December 1771, in *ENOCB*, vol. 16, pt. 2, 978–983, at 979.

181. Cesare Beccaria, "Sistema annonario della Lombardia Austriaca [Consulta e minuta di relazione]," 16 January 1793, in *ENOCB*, 15:26–33, at 29, 32.

182. Beccaria, "Istituzione di nuovi mercati [consulta e verbale di riunione]," 16 July 1779, in *ENOCB*, 7:125–127.

183. Smith, *Wealth of Nations*, 1:493.

184. For Smith's argument, see ibid., 2:208, on which see Istvan Hont, "Commercial Society and Political Theory in the Eighteenth Century: The Problem of Authority in David Hume and Adam Smith," in *Main Trends in Cultural History: Ten Essays*, ed. Willem Melching and Wyger Velema (Amsterdam: Rodopi, 1994), 54–94, at 80.

185. Cesare Beccaria, "Promozione delle attività economiche a Casalmaggiore [27 December 1786]," in *ENOCB*, 7:970. See similarly his "Attività del Dipartimento III nel 1786 [31 March 1787]," in *ENOCB*, 9:223–267, at 230; and, for one of many earlier pugilistic arguments in favor of "the uniformity of systems" in political economy, Pietro Verri to the Supreme Council, 6 March 1766, fol. 4r, *Pietro Verri Letters*, Kress.

186. Beccaria, "Attività del Dipartimento III nel 1786 [31 March 1787]," in *ENOCB*, 9:223–267, at 224–225. These sentiments were similarly echoed in Beccaria, "Tariffa daziaria [6 October 1788]," in *ENOCB*, 10:661–662.

187. Cesare Beccaria, "Mercato di Casalmaggiore [23 July 1772]," in *ENOCB*, 6:139.

188. Cesare Beccaria, "Aumento del prezzo dei grani nel Lodigiano [2 March 1773]," in *ENOCB*, 6:214–215.

189. Cesare Beccaria, "Istituzione di nuovi mercati [8 and 17 July 1776]," in *ENOCB*, 6:694–699, at 697. For the policy context, see, among others, Aldo Carera, "I mercati della tradizione," in *I mercati e le fiere della provincia di Milano tra XVIII e XX secolo*, ed. Maria Piera Bassi (Milan: Provincia di Milano, 1990), 17–61, 53–56.

190. Cesare Beccaria, "Attività del Dipartimento III nel 1786 [31 March 1787]," in *ENOCB*, 9:223–267, at 250.

191. Ibid. Here he may have echoed the previously mentioned Anne Robert Jacques Turgot's entry for "Foire," in *Encyclopédie . . .* , ed. Denis Diderot and Jean le Rond d'Alembert, 28 vols. (Paris: Briasson et al., 1751–1772), 7:39–41, at 41.

192. See on this also Harcourt, *Illusion of Free Markets*, 25, 62.

193. Cesare Beccaria, "Attività del Dipartimento III nel 1786 [31 March 1787]," in *ENOCB*, 9:223–267, at 244, 266.

194. See the deceptively labeled Cesare Beccaria, "Casa di correzione di Milano [10 June 1794]," in *ENOCB*, 16:469–472, at 469.

195. Alessandro Verri to Pietro Verri, 21 January 1769, in *CV*, 2:135.

196. Schumpeter, *History of Economic Analysis*, 175.

197. Cesare Beccaria, "Attività del Dipartimento III nel 1786 [31 March 1787]," in *ENOCB*, 9:223–267, at 233. Compare Facchinei to Zaccaria, addendum to letter of 17 April 1763, AHCL, *Fondo Zaccaria*, b. 19, 1v.

198. E.g., Pierre Rosanvallon, *The Demands of Liberty: Civil Society in France since the Revolution*, trans. Arthur Goldhammer (Cambridge, MA: Harvard University Press, 2007), 6.

199. Beccaria, *On Crimes and Punishments*, 4, quoting Francis Bacon, "Of Negotiating," in Bacon, *The Essays*, ed. John Pitcher (London: Penguin, 1986), 103–104, at 104. See, similarly, Beccaria, "Il piacere dell'immaginazione," in *Il Caffè*, 476–480, at 480; and Pietro Verri, "Sulla interpretazione delle leggi," in *Il Caffè*, 695–704, at 696–697.

200. Voltaire, "Commentary on the Book on Crimes and Punishments," in Voltaire, *Political Writings*, ed. David Williams (Cambridge: Cambridge University Press, 1994), 244–279, at 279.

201. See, among others, Reinert, *Translating Empire*, esp. 132; Reinert, "Lessons on the Rise and Fall"; Sonenscher, *Before the Deluge;* Gian Rinaldo Carli to Giuseppe Gravisi, 15 August 1765, in Gian Rinaldo Carli, *Trecentosessantasei lettere di Gian Rinaldo Carli Capodistriano: Cavate dagli originali e annotate*, ed. Baccio Ziliotto (Trieste: Tipografia G. Caprin, 1914), 123–124; Giuseppe Visconti, "[Osservazioni meteorologiche fatte in Milano]," in *Il Caffè*, 78–82, at 79, even speaks of his age as one of "universal physical revolution"; see similarly Alessandro Verri, "Discorso sulla felicità de' Romani," in *Il Caffè*, 91.

202. Giovan Stefano Conti to Ruđer Josip Bošković, 13 September 1769, in *Giovan Stefano Conti: Lettere a Ruggiero Giuseppe Boscovich*, ed. Edoardo Proverbio, 2 vols.

NOTES TO PAGES 337–338

(Rome: Accademia nazionale delle scienze, 1996–1998), 1:231–233, at 232. On Conti, see Tommaso Trenta, "Origini, Progressi, e vicende dell'Accademia degli Oscuri," Biblioteca Governativa di Lucca, Lucca, Italy, *MS 557*, 381–405.

203. On the case of social science, see Robert Wokler, "Ideology and the Origins of Social Science," in *The Cambridge History of Eighteenth-Century Political Thought*, ed. Mark Goldie and Robert Wokler (Cambridge: Cambridge University Press, 2006), 688–710, at 707–709. For earlier statements of unease with this transition of social science, see Giuseppe Romanazzi, *Note e considerazioni sull'affrancazione de' canoni e sul libero coltivamento del tavoliere di Puglia* (Naples: Tramater, 1834), 104; John Hobson, quoted and discussed in Gregory Claeys, *Imperial Sceptics: British Critics of Empire, 1850–1920* (Cambridge: Cambridge University Press, 2010), 272; Mark Mazower, *Governing the World: The History of an Idea* (London: Penguin, 2012), 95–100, 292.

204. Istvan Hont, *Jealousy of Trade: International Competition and the Nation-State in Historical Perspective* (Cambridge, MA: Harvard University Press, 2005), 156.

205. Alexander Gerschenkron to Franco Venturi, 14 June 1969, Harvard University Archives, Cambridge, MA, HUG (FP) 45.10, Alexander Gerschenkron, General Correspondence (1948–1949–1975), Box 20 of 21, T (1966) to W (1956–1957), 2r.

206. Gregory Claeys, "News from Somewhere: Enhanced Sociability and the Composite Definition of Utopia and Dystopia," *History* 98, no. 330 (2013): 145–173, at 154.

207. John Rawls, *Lectures on the History of Political Philosophy*, ed. Samuel Freeman (Cambridge, MA: Harvard University Press, 2007), 10–11; emphasis in original. On Rawls's application of this ideal to international relations, see his *The Law of Peoples* (Cambridge, MA: Harvard University Press, 1999), 4–6, 127–128. Beccaria's project was to approach the problem from a different direction, an expression of what Ralph Dahrendorf called "effective hope" and Richard Swedberg defines as "realistic" rather than "utopian hope"; see Dahrendorf's *Inequality, Hope, and Progress* (Liverpool: Liverpool University Press, 1976), discussed and built on in Richard Swedberg, "A Sociological Approach to Hope in the Economy," in *The Economy of Hope*, ed. Hirokazu Miyazaki and Richard Swedberg (Philadelphia: University of Pennsylvania Press, 2017), 37–50, at 40.

208. Immanuel Kant, "Perpetual Peace: A Philosophical Sketch," in Kant, *Political Writings*, ed. Hans Reiss, 2nd ed. (Cambridge: Cambridge University Press, 1991), 130.

209. *The Republic*, ed. G. R. F. Ferrari, trans. Tom Griffith (Cambridge: Cambridge University Press, 2000), 592b, p. 312. On its history, see, among many others, Eric Nelson, *The Greek Tradition in Republican Thought* (Cambridge: Cambridge University Press, 2004).

210. See the succinct statement in Rawls, *The Law of Peoples*, 128.

211. For a similar, later project, see Thomas Hopkins, "The Limits of 'Cosmopolitical Economy': Smith, List, and the Paradox of Peace through Trade," in *Paradoxes of Peace in Nineteenth Century Europe*, ed. Thomas Hippler and Miloš Vec (Oxford: Oxford University Press, 2015), 77–91, at 91.

212. Cesare Cantù, *Beccaria e il diritto penale* (Florence: Barbèra, 1862), 311. On this work, see, among others, Cesare Mozzarelli, "Riforme istituzionali e mutamenti sociali nella Lombardia dell'ultimo Settecento," in Romagnoli and Pisapia, *Cesare Beccaria tra Milano e l'Europa*, 479–494, at 481–482.

213. Verri, "Sulle sepolture," in *ENOPV*, 6:343.

214. Jean-Jacques Rousseau, "Abstract of Monsieur the Abbé de Saint-Pierre's Plan for Perpetual Peace," in *The Plan for Perpetual Peace, On the Government of Poland, and Other Writings on History and Politics,* trans. Christopher Kelly and Judith Bush, ed. Christopher Kelly (Lebanon, NH: University Press of New England for Dartmouth College Press, 2005), 27–49, 29. For context, see Silvia Maria Pizzetti, "La costruzione della pace e di una società internazionale nell'Europa moderna fra *jus gentium* e cosmopolitismo (secoli XVII–XVIII)," in Levati and Meriggi, *Con la ragione e col cuore*, 209–241; Céline Spector, "Le Projet de paix perpétuelle: De Saint-Pierre à Rousseau," in *Principes du droit de la guerre: Ecrits sur le Projet de Paix Perpétuelle de l'Abbé de Saint-Pierre,* ed. Blaise Bachofen and Céline Spector (Paris; Vrin, 2008), 229–294.

215. On the complex philology of *The Spanish Monarchy*, see John M. Headley, *Tommaso Campanella and the Transformation of the World* (Princeton, NJ: Princeton University Press, 1997), 204–212; on its political economy, see also Sophus A. Reinert, introduction to Antonio Serra, *A Short Treatise on the Wealth and Poverty of Nations (1613)*, trans. Jonathan Hunt (London: Anthem, 2011), 1–93, at 65n222.

216. Andrew Fletcher, "An Account of a Conversation concerning a Right Regulation of Governments for the Common Good of Mankind," in Fletcher, *Political Works,* ed. John Robertson (Cambridge: Cambridge University Press, 1997), 175–215, at 203. On this plan, see also Shigemi Muramatsu, "Andrew Fletcher's Criticism of Commercial Civilization and His Plan for European Federal Union," in *The Rise of Political Economy in the Scottish Enlightenment*, eds. Tatsuya Sakamoto and Hideo Tanaka (London: Routledge, 2003), 8–21.

217. Émeric Crucé, *Le novveav Cynée*, ed. Thomas Willing Balch (Philadephia: Allen, Lane, and Scott, 1909), 84, 100–104, 190, 320. See, on this tradition, Hont, *Jealousy of Trade,* 258–266, and esp. 262n182; and, for a different rogues gallery, Marco Geuna, "Le relazioni fra gli Stati e il problema della guerra: Alcuni modelli teorici da Vitoria a Hume," in *La pace a le guerre: Guerra giusta e filosofie della pace,* ed. Annamaria Loche (Cagliari: CUEC, 2005), 45–130.

218. Kant, "Perpetual Peace," on which see, among others, Massimo Mori, *La pace e la ragione: Kant e le relazioni internazionali: Diritto, politica, storia* (Bologna: Il Mulino, 2008); and, for the far-from-peaceful historiographical battle over it in the English language, Eric S. Easley, *The War over Perpetual Peace: An Exploration into the History of a Foundational International Relations Text* (London: Palgrave Macmillan, 2004); Johann Gottlieb von Fichte, *The Closed Commercial State*, ed. Anthony Curtis Adler (Albany: State University of New York Press, 2012), on which see Isaac Nakhimovsky, *The Closed Commercial State: Perpetual Peace and Commercial Society from Rousseau to Fichte* (Princeton, NJ: Princeton University Press, 2011). On international trade as a means of "giving laws" and thus "conquering" other polities by nonmilitary means, see Reinert, *Translating Empire*, esp. 26–29.

219. Emer de Vattel, *The Law of Nations*, ed. Béla Kapossy and Richard Whatmore (Indianapolis: Liberty Fund, 2008), 173 [1.XII.147].

220. Jean-Jacques Rousseau, "Judgment of the Plan for Perpetual Peace," in Rousseau, *The Plan for Perpetual Peace, On the Government of Poland, and Other Writings on History and Politics*, trans. Christopher Kelly and Judith Bush, ed. Christopher Kelly (Hanover, NH: Dartmouth College Press, 2005), 53–60, 56.

221. Jean-Jacques Rousseau, "Abstract of Monsieur the Abbé de Saint-Pierre's Plan," 35. On this passage in the wider context of the idiom of "giving laws," see also Reinert, *Translating Empire*, 17.

222. Rousseau, "Abstract of Monsieur the Abbé de Saint-Pierre's Plan," 35n, 43.

223. On the historiographical trope of Beccaria being an embodiment of Amnesty International *avant la lettre*, see Giovanni Tessitore, *Cesare Beccaria: L'uomo e il mito; idealizzazione e realtà storica* (Milan: Franco Angeli, 2008).

224. Gian Rinaldo Carli to Paolo Frisi, 30 August 1762, in Cesare Beccaria, *Scritti e lettere inedite*, ed. Eugenio Landry (Milan: Hoepli, 1910), 257–259.

225. The fountainhead of this tradition might have been Daniel M. Klang, "Cesare Beccaria and the Clash between Jurisprudence and Political Economy in Eighteenth-Century Lombardy," *Canadian Journal of History* 23, no. 3 (1988): 305–336.

226. To use a term inspired by the algorithm proposed in Jeremy Bentham, *An Introduction to the Principles of Morals and Legislation* (London: Payne, 1789), esp. chap. 4.

227. Compare Voltaire, *De la paix perpétuelle* (Geneva: n.p., 1769) (translated, with extensive annotations, only after Beccaria's death as Voltaire, *Della pace perpetua* [Milan: Raffaele Netti, 1797–1798] with Kant, "Perpetual Peace." For Rousseu's memorable phrase, see his "Judgment of the Plan for Perpetual Peace," 60. For the "economic hand of God," see again Facchinei to Zaccaria, addendum to letter of 17 April 1763, AHCL, *Fondo Zaccaria*, b. 19, IV.

228. Giuseppe Tomasi di Lampedusa, *Il gattopardo* (Milan: Feltrinelli, 2005 [1958]), 32.

229. Reinert, *Translating Empire,* esp. 26–27; Reinert, "Rivalry," 362.

230. Sebastiano Franci, "La guerra senza sangue," ed. Pietro Verri, Archivio Verri, 380.4; and Sebastiano Franci, "Alcuni pensieri politici," in *Il Caffè,* 143–150, on which see Reinert, *Translating Empire,* 15–16; Beccaria, *On Crimes and Punishments,* 9–10.

231. For perspectives on this challenge, see Hont, *Jealousy of Trade,* 111–156; Reinert, *Translating Empire,* esp. 40; Béla Kapossy, Isaac Nakhimovsky, and Richard Whatmore, "Introduction: Power, Prosperity, and Peace in Enlightenment Thought," in *Commerce and Peace in the Enlightenment,* ed. Kapossy, Nakhimovsky, and Whatmore (Cambridge: Cambridge University Press, 2017), 1–19, at 6.

232. Verri, "Meditazioni," 544.

233. Ibid.

234. Stefano Recchia and Nadia Urbinati, eds., *A Cosmopolitanism of Nations: Giuseppe Mazzini's Writings on Democracy, Nation Building, and International Relations* (Princeton, NJ: Princeton University Press, 2009), 94–95, 125, inspired, perhaps, by Rousseau, "Of the Social Contract," 48; Reinert, "Rivalry," 360. For a similar argument, see Giuliano Gaeta, *Coscienza nazionale e sopranazionale in Gian Rinaldo Carli* (Triest: Edizioni "Italo Svevo," 1976), 26.

235. Franco Venturi, *Utopia e riforma nell'illuminismo* (Turin: Einaudi, 1970), 126. See also Renato Pasta, "Attualità di un 'Moralista': Cesare Beccaria e il diritto penale," in *La buona giustizia: In margine a Dei delitti e delle pene di Cesare Beccaria,* ed. Paolo Brembilla et al. (Florence: Feeria, 2016), 41–63, at 62.

236. E.g., Cesare Beccaria, "Macellai a Milano [10 June 1794]," in *ENOCB,* 16:455–456; and see, for the postdated memoranda, *ENOCB,* 16:960.

237. Carli, "Per la Cattedra di Economia Pubblica di Milano," fol. 2r.

238. Carlo Scognamiglio Pasini, *L'arte della ricchezza: Cesare Beccaria economista* (Milan: Mondadori, 2014), 174.

239. Pietro to Alessandro Verri, 10 October 1770, in *CV,* 4:18. For a number of lists of attendees to Beccaria's lectures, see "Cataloghi degli Auditori delle Lezioni di Pubblica Economia," ASM, *Autografi, no. 164, Uomini celebri.*

240. Schumpeter, *History of Economic Analysis,* 180–181.

241. Pietro to Alessandro Verri, 21 July 1773, in *CV,* 6:94.

242. For examples, see Capra, *I progressi della ragione,* esp. 490; as well as Gaia Guidolin, "Analisi linguistica del carteggio di Pietro e Alessandro Verri (1766–1797)," PhD diss., University of Padua, 2011, 5–6. For Verri's own take, see also his "Memorie sulle dissensioni e divisioni della famiglia Verri dopo la morte del Conte Gabriele Verri seguita nel 1782: Scritte l'anno 1788 dal Conte Pietro Verri," in *ENOPV,* 5:515–546.

243. Pietro to Alessandro Verri, 24 August 1793, in *ENOPV*, 3:453–456, at 453.

244. Alessandro to Pietro Verri, 12 July 1780, in *CV*, 11:106.

245. Pietro to Alessandro Verri, 24 August 1793, in *ENOPV*, 3:453–456, at 454.

246. Verri, "[Sulle sepolture, sulla società milanese, sulla milizia]," in *ENOPV*, 6:335–344, at 338–339.

247. Verri, "Pensieri del Conte Pietro Verri sullo stato politico," 424.

248. Verri, "Mozione del cittadino Verri municipalista alla municipalità di Milano," in *ENOPV*, 6:816–819, at 816; emphasis in original.

249. Ibid., 816, 818–819; emphasis in original. The phrase gave the name to Capra's splendid biography of Verri, *I progressi della ragione*.

250. Alessandro to Pietro Verri, 13 Aril 1794, in *ENOPV*, 8:678–680, at 678.

251. Alessandro Verri to Vincenza, 12 May 1798, in *ENOPV*, 8:678n2.

252. Verri, "Primi elementi per somministrare," 665–666; Verri, "Storia dell'invasione de' francesi repubblicani nel milanese nel 1796," in *ENOPV*, 6:772–805, at 775.

253. Pietro to Alessandro Verri, 6 May 1797, in *ENOPV*, 8:1323–1325, at 1325.

254. *L'Ape delle cognizioni utili* (Capolago: A spese degli editori, year III, 1835, May), 145–147, continued in July, 196–198. See, on this, though he did not notice the mistaken attribution, Kent Robert Greenfield, *Economics and Liberalism in the Risorgimento: A Study of Nationalism in Lombardy, 1813–1848* (Baltimore: Johns Hopkins University Press, 1965), 173. On Verri's political economy as a bridge from "Illuminismo" to "Risorgimento" in Italy, see John Robertson, "Pietro Verri between Enlightenment and Risorgimento," *Journal of Modern Italian Studies* 17, no. 5 (2012): 527–531, at 530.

255. Quoted in Capra, *I progressi della ragione*, 584. For the actual journal, see Vittorio Criscuolo, ed., *Termometro politico della Lombardia*, 4 vols. (Rome: Istituto storico italiano per l'età moderna e contemporanea, 1989–1996).

256. Pietro to Alessandro Verri, 18 June 1794, in *ENOPV*, 8:760–763, at 760–761. Carli also reacted to the excesses of the French Revolution with revulsion; see Gian Rinaldo Carli to Saverio Bettinelli, 22 April 1793, in Giovanni Catalani, ed., *La lumaca, la gallina e i figli del diavolo: Lettere di Gianrinaldo Carli a Saverio Bettinelli* (Verona: Edizioni QuiEdit, 2009), 31–33.

257. Capra, "Cesare Beccaria funzionario," 113; Capra, "Pietro Verri e la Rivoluzione francese," in *La felicità di tutti: Figuri e temi dell'Illuminismo Lombardo* (Rome: Aracne, 2017), 309–325, 320.

258. Pietro to Alessandro Verri, 8 December 1792, in *ENOPV*, vol. 8, pt. 1, 196, and for his constitutionalism Carlo Capra, "La felicità di tutti: Filangieri e l'ultimo Verri," in *La felicità di tutti*, 271–290, at 288. On the great queston of Enlightenment constitutionalism in Italy, in general and with reference to Verri, see, among others, Antonio Trampus, *Storia del costituzionalismo italiano nell'età dei*

lumi (Bari: Laterza, 2009), 233–239; and Vincenzo Ferrone, *The Politics of Enlightenment: Constitutionalism, Republicanism, and the Rights of Man in Gaetano Filangieri,* trans. Sophus A. Reinert (London: Anthem, 2014), esp. 4. On Verri's defense of private property until the end, see Verri, "Primi elementi per somministrare," in *ENOPV,* 6:631–632, 634–635; and also Capra, "Verri e la Rivoluzione francese," 318.

259. Verri, "Meditazioni," 556–558.

260. Patrick Speelman, *Henry Lloyd and the Military Enlightenment in Eighteenth-Century Europe* (Westport, CT: Greenwood Press, 2002), 117.

261. Hiroshi Mizuta, *Adam Smith's Library: A Supplement to Bonar's Catalogue with a Check-List of the Whole Library* (Cambridge: Cambridge University Press, 1967), xiii, 149; Capra, *I progressi della ragione,* 382. On the editions and translations of Verri's *Meditazioni,* see Peter Groenewegen, "Pietro Verri's Mature Political Economy of the *Meditazioni:* A Case Study in the Highly Developed International Transmission Mechanism of Ideas in Pre-Revolutionary Europe," in *Political Economy and National Realities,* ed. Manuela Albertone and Alberto Masoero (Turin: Fondazione Luigi Einaudi, 1994), 107–125.

262. Tessitore, *Cesare Beccaria,* 207; John D. Bessler, "The Economist and the Enlightenment: How Cesare Beccaria Changed Western Civilization," *European Journal of Law and Economics* 42, no. 2 (2016): 1–28.

263. Anon., *Regole e capitoli per l'opera pia della carità, e della morte eretta sotto il titolo di S. Gio. Decollato alla pietosa assistenza de' carcerati, e condannati dalla giustizia nella città di Casale* (Vercelli: Giuseppe Panialis, 1785), 15, 70. There of course existed a long tradition of such rulebooks, for a regionally influential example of which see *Capitoli, ed ordini della nobilissima congregazione di San Gioanni Decollato, alle Case rotte, detta de' Bianchi, dell'inclita città di Milano* (Milan: Heredi di Giovanni Battista Malatesta, 1654).

264. Archivio Storico Comunale di Casale Monferrato, Casale Monferrato, Italy (hereafter cited as ASCCM), *Società di Patronato pei liberati dal Carcere* (1784–1965). These fifteen linear meters of materials are yet to be organized and catalogued, and I am grateful to Luigi Mantovani for invaluable assistance in navigating them. I name documents by their titles or opening lines. "Registro di convocati del Consiglio particolare dell'Opera Pia della Carità e della Morte incominciato il 28 Marzo 1785 e terminato il 6.1.1885," entry for 21 April 1785, 5r–5v. See also 6v for the reference to the "anime dei Giustiziati." See also anon., *Regole e capitoli,* 5, 52.

265. Anon., *Regole e capitoli,* 4.

266. Ibid., 9–13, esp. 11. For the venerable nature of such descriptions themselves, however, see, for example, ASM, *Capitoli, ed ordini della nobilissima congregazione di San Gioanni Decollato,* 3.

267. Giambattista Roberti, *Annotazioni sopra la umanitá del secolo decimo ottavo* (Turin: Briolo, 1781), 9. On Roberti, see Giovanni Battista Sandonà, *Ragione e carità: Per un ritratto di Giambattista Roberti* (Venice: Istituto Veneto di Scienze, Lettere ed Arti, 2002), esp. 236–276 on *La umanità*. Roberti had taught Pietro Verri as well, and see Verri's "Al suo Padre Roberti stimatissimo Verri il poeta giovane, midonte detto fra I pastor d'Arcadia [1749]," in *ENOPV*, 1:21–26, and their most friendly 1771 correspondence in Archivio Verri, 274.35, particularly the letter in which Roberti discusses his "Discorso Cristiano con un Dialogo Filosofico sopra il lusso," in *Del lusso discorso cristiano con un dialogo filosofico*, 2 vols. (Bassano: Remondini, 1772), 17 September 1771, 1v–2r.

268. As Giovanni Battista Giovio summarized the work in his "Elogio del Conte AB: Giambattista Roberti," in Roberti, *Opere*, 2nd ed., ed. Tiberio Roberti, 15 vols. (Bassano: Remondini, 1797), 12:263–364, at 340: "This word *Humanity* is in everyone's mouth, on all pens, and it blends with trade and navigation."

269. Giambattista Roberti to Giovanni Battista Giovio, 24 November 1784, in Roberti, *Opere*, 158–160, at 159. He repeated this acceptance of Beccaria's differentiation between crime and sin in *Opere*, vol. 7: *De dubbi, e de' presidi*, 240–242.

270. ASCCM, *Società di Patronato pei liberati dal Carcere* (1784–1965), "Registro di convocati del Consiglio particolare dell'Opera Pia della Caritá e della Morte incominciato il 28 Marzo 1785 e terminato il 6.1.1885," entry for 26 May 1785, 9v, entry 4.

271. Archivio di Stato di Torino, Turin, Italy (hereafter AST), *Luoghi pii di qua da'Monti, Mazzo 7 d'addizione, Bra, Confraternita di S. Gio decollato,* "Supplica della Confraternita di S. Gioanni decollato eretta nella Citata di Bra, per ottenere la permissione di eriggere un Monte di Pietá in detta Città perpetuamente unito a detta loro Confraternita; e l'Approvazione dei Capi ivi uniti di stabilimento, e regole di esso Monte [3 February 1762?]," 2 [1v].

272. Serafino Biffi, *Sulle antiche carceri di Milano e suoi sodalizi che vi assistevano i prigioneri ed i condannati a morte* (Milan: Bernardoni, 1864), 95–119; AST, *Materie economiche Gabella de' Giuochi, e Lotterie, Mazzo 2 di 2a addizione, no. 21,* "Supplica de Venerando Oratorio di S. Gio Battista Decollato della Misericordia per ottenere il permesso di fare eseguire il quivi unito Piano di Lotteria," 1r–3v. The historiography of lotteries has exploded in recent years, but see recently, with a focus on nearby Genoa, Giovanni Assereto, *Un giuoco così utile ai pubblici introito: Il lotto di Genova dal XVI and XVIII secolo* (Treviso / Rome: Fondazione Benetton Studi Ricerche / Viella, 2013).

273. See, for example, anon., *Epilogo delle regole e capitoli per l'opera pia della Caritá e Morte Sanzionati con Regie Patenti del 23 Novembre 1784 e loro variazioni regolarmente consentite dalla Congregazione nella sua seduta del. 1 Dicembre 1833 e nell'altra del 24 Maggio 1857* (Casale: Dalla Tipografia e Libreria di G. Nani, 1858), 15–16; Michel

Foucault, *Discipline and Punish: The Birth of the Prison*, trans. Alan Sheridan (New York: Vintage, 1995), 7, 112, 122.

274. ASCCM, *Società di Patronato pei liberati dal Carcere (1784–1965)*, "Registro dei Verbali della Congregazione Generale dei Soci-Confratelli della Opera Pia della Carità e Morte in Casale Monferrato dal 19 Marzo 1785 al 5.9.1909," entry for 29 November 1891, entry 9, and entry for 26 June 1892, entry 5.

275. Attilia Lanza, *Milano e i suoi palazzi: Porta Vercellina, Comasina e Nuova* (Milan: Libreria Meravigli Editrice, 1993), 138–139.

7. Arches and Stones

1. Gottlieb Hufeland, *Lehrsätze des Naturrechts und der damit verbundenen Wissenschaften* (Jena: Cuno's Erben, 1790), 16.

2. Johann Christoph Hoffbauer, *Naturrecht aus dem Begriffe des Rechts entwickelt* (Halle: Hemmerde und Schwetschke, 1793), 329 and 329n2.

3. See, for example, Hugo Grotius, *Le droit de la guerre et de la paix*, trans. and ed. Paul Pradier-Fodéré, 3 vols. (Paris: Guillaumin, 1867), 1:63n, "De la nom de *socialiste* qu'on a donné à cette école, dans laquelle se rangent Puffendorf, Cocceius et Burlamaqui." On these traditions, see Hans Müller, *Ursprung und Geschichte des Wortes Sozialismus und seiner Verwandten* (Hannover: Verlag J. H. W. Dietz Nachf. GmbH, 1967), 34; and Giorgio Spini, "Sulle origini dei termini 'socialista' e 'socialismo,'" in *Dalla preistoria del socialismo alla lotta per la libertà* (Milan: Franco Angeli, 2002), 31–49, at 42–43.

4. Sebastiano Rumor, *Gli scrittori vicentini dei secoli decimottavo e decimonono*, 3 vols. (Venice: Tipografia Emiliana, 1905–1908), 2:56.

5. Ruggiero Bonghi, *La vita e i tempi di Valentino Pasini* (Florence: Barbèra, 1867), 6. On Giuliani, see Nazzarena Zanini, "Note bibliografiche sul giurista dell'Università di Padova Giacomo Giuliani (1772–1840) gia minore conventuale," *Il Santo* 33, nos. 1–2 (1993): 151–168; Ferdinando Cavalli, "La scienza politica in Italia," *Memorie del Reale Istituto Veneto di scienze, lettere ed arti* 21 (1879): 39–127, 227–290, 577–649, 577–580; and particularly Ignazio Savi, *In occasione delle faustissime nozze dei signori Stefano Crovato e Maria Raugna-Scaramuzza* ([Vicenza: Gaetano Longo], [1876]), an exceedingly rare pamphlet kept in the Biblitoeca Civica Bertoliana, Vicenza, Italy, classification number VIA0146919.

6. Savi, *In occasione delle faustissime nozze*, 5–6.

7. See, among others, R. R. Palmer, *The Age of Democratic Revolution: A Political History of Europe and America, 1760–1800*, updated ed. (Princeton, NJ: Princeton University Press, 2014); David Armitage and Sanjay Subrahmanyam, eds., *The Age of Revolutions in Global Context, c. 1760–1840* (Basingstoke, UK: Palgrave Mac-

millan, 2010); and Janet Polasky, *Revolutions without Borders: The Call to Liberty in the Atlantic World* (New Haven, CT: Yale University Press, 2015).

8. On this, and the Cisalpine Republic, see R. R. Palmer, *The Age of Democratic Revolution*, intro. David Armitage (Princeton, NJ: Princeton University Press, 2014 [1959]), 603–613; David Avrom Bell, *The First Total War: Napoleon's Europe and the Birth of Warfare as We Know It* (New York: Houghton Mifflin, 2007), 194.

9. Nigel Aston, *Christianity and Revolutionary Europe, c. 1750–1830* (Cambridge: Cambridge University Press, 2002), esp. 256–257. On Rome at the time, see also Susan Vandiver Nicassio, *Imperial City: Rome under Napoleon* (Chicago: University of Chicago Press, 2005).

10. On Gioia, at the time spelled Gioja, see Roberto Romani, *National Character and Public Spirit in Britain and France, 1750–1914* (Cambridge: Cambridge University Press, 2002), 93–99, though Romani does not emphasize the pre-Benthamite Milanese influence on Giuliani's writings, evident from the endless references to the works of Beccaria and Verri in, for example, Gioia, *Nuovo prospetto delle scienze economiche*, 6 vols. (Milan: Pirotta, 1815–1817). On Napoleon's transformation of warfare, see Bell, *The First Total War*; and Jean-Yves Guiomar, *L'invention de la guerre totale: XVIIIe–XXe siècles* (Paris: Le Félin, 2004).

11. *The Monthly Review*, vol. 36 (London: Griffiths, 1767), 298–299, at 298.

12. Cesare Beccaria, *An Essay on Crimes and Punishments, Translated from the Italian; with a Commentary Attributed to Mons. De Voltaire, Translated from the French* (London: Almon, 1767), iv. On this edition, see again Rosamaria Loretelli, "The First English Translation of Cesare Beccaria's *On Crimes and Punishments*: Uncovering the Editorial and Political Contexts," *Diciottesimo secolo* 2 (2017): 1–22. See also *A List of Books and Pamphlets printed for J. Almon, Bookseller and Stationer, opposite Burlington-House, in Piccadilly* ([London?], 1767?), 3. At a price of 4s 6d, Beccaria's *On Crimes and Punishment* came at more than twice the highest cost of a copy of a best-selling work of political economy like John Cary's *Essay on the State of England* in eighteenth-century England (enough to cover getting "dead drunk" on gin for a month), suggesting also that it appealed to a more selective audience. See Sophus A. Reinert, *Translating Empire: Emulation and the Origins of Political Economy* (Cambridge, MA: Harvard University Press, 2011), 125–126. For contemporary costs, see Kristin Olsen, *Daily Life in Eighteenth-Century London* (Westport, CT: Greenwood Press, 1999), 198–201. On the intriguing figure of Almon, see, among others, James Raven, *The Business of Books: Booksellers and the English Book Trade, 1450–1850* (New Haven, CT: Yale University Press, 2007), 209–214.

13. Philo-Italicus, "Account of the Late Marquis Beccaria," *Monthly Magazine, and British Register*, October 1798 (London: R. Phillips,1798), 4:260, republished without author in *The Scots Magazine*, March 1799 (Edinburgh: Chapman and Co., 1799), 61:151–152.

14. Philo-Italicus, "Account of the Late Marquis Beccaria," 260.

15. Gian Rinaldo Carli to Paolo Frisi, 30 August 1762, in Cesare Beccaria, *Scritti e lettere inedite*, ed. Eugenio Landry (Milan: Hoepli, 1910), 257–259.

16. See, among others, Franz A. J. Szabo, *Kaunitz and Enlightened Absolutism, 1753–1780* (Cambridge: Cambridge University Press, 1994), esp. 34, 184; Giovanni Tessitore, *Cesare Beccaria: L'uomo e il mito; idealizzazione e realtà storica* (Milan: Franco Angeli, 2008), esp. 127; John D. Bessler, *Cruel and Unusual: The American Death Penalty and the Founders' Eighth Amendment* (Lebanon, NH: Northeastern University Press, 2012), 46; R. S. Agin, "The Debate on Judicial Torture in Austrian Lombardy," *Studies in Eighteenth-Century Culture* 46 (2017): 95–106, at 102–104, which also offers an excellent corrective to the argument that the influence of *philosophes* on the abolition of torture is a "fairy tale" in John Langbein, *Torture and the Law of Proof: Europe and England in the Ancien Régime* (Chicago: University of Chicago Press, 1977), 10. Torture may slowly have been waning because of "changes in legal proof" at the time, but the abolition nonetheless depended on individual legislators acting on the basis of certain ideas and sentiments.

17. John D. Bessler, *The Birth of American Law: An Italian Philosopher and the American Revolution* (Durham, NC: Carolina Academic Press, 2014).

18. For examples of Beccaria's influence in the United States, also in popular sources, see David McCullough, *John Adams* (New York: Simon and Schuster, 2001), 67; Bernard E. Harcourt, *The Illusion of Free Markets* (Cambridge, MA: Harvard University Press, 2011), 56; 50; Stuart Banner, *The Death Penalty: An American History* (Cambridge, MA: Harvard University Press, 2002), esp. 91–97; Bessler, *Cruel and Unusual*, 50; Glenn Beck, *Arguing with Idiots: How to Stop Small Minds and Big Government* (New York: Simon and Schuster, 2009), 44. For a discussion of usages such as Beck's, see Saul Cornell, *A Well-Regulated Militia: The Founding Fathers and the Origins of Gun Control in America* (Oxford: Oxford University Press, 2006), 224n19. See also even more popular accounts, such as John Hostettler, *Twenty Famous Lawyers* (Hook, UK: Waterside Press, 2013), 75. Beccaria's writings on gun control were highlighted by Thomas Jefferson in his commonplace book, and line up not only with the Second Amendment of the U.S. Constitution but also with the standard tropes of National Rifle Association rhetoric. Even if we acknowledge the extraordinary difference between the weaponries of the eighteenth and twenty-first centuries, there is little conceptual distance between Beccaria's statement that "the laws that forbid one to bear arms . . . disarm only those who are neither inclined nor determined to commit crimes," in *On Crimes and Punishments*, 78, and the bumper-sticker logic "If you outlaw guns, only outlaws will have guns."

19. David Lundberg and Henry F. May, "The Enlightened Reader in America," *American Quarterly* 28, no. 2 (1976): 262–292, at 285; Donald S. Lutz, "The Relative Influence of European Writers on Late Eighteenth-Century American Political Thought," *American Political Science Review* 78, no. 1 (1984): 189–197, at 194.

20. André Morellet, *Mémoirs de l'abbé Morellet*, 2 vols. (Paris: De Ladvocat, 1821), 1:160; Timothy Tackett, *The Coming of the Terror in the French Revolution* (Cambridge, MA: Harvard University Press, 2015), 35. See similarly Richard J. Evans, *Rituals of Retribution: Capital Punishment in Germany, 1600–1987* (Oxford: Oxford University Press, 1996), 129–130.

21. See Pietro Custodi, ed., *Scrittori classici italiani di economia politica*, 50 vols. (Milan: De Stefanis, 1802–1816), vols. 10–11, both published in 1804. On Custodi, see Daniele Rota, *Pietro Custodi: La figura e l'opera* (Annone di Brianza: Cattaneo Editore, 1991). For Beccaria's inaugural lecture, see his *Prolusione letta dal regio professore nelle Scuole Palatine Marchese Cesare Beccaria Bonesana nell'apertura della nuova Cattedra di Scienze Camerali* (Florence: Allegrini, 1769), translated as *A Discourse on Public Economy and Commerce* (London: Dudsley and Murray, 1769); and "Discours prononcé le neuf Janvier 1769, par M. Le Marquis César Beccaria Bonesana à l'ouverture de la nouvelle Chaire d'"Économie Politique, fondée par S.M. l'Impératrice dans les Écoles Palatines de Milan," *Éphémérides du citoyen* 4 (1769): 53–152.

22. Adam Smith, *Politisk undersökning om lagar, som hindra och tvinga införseln af sådana utländska varor, som kunna alstras eller tillverkas inom landet* [a translation of bk. 4 of *The Wealth of Nations*], trans. Erik Erl. Bodell (Gothenburg: S. Norberg, 1804), 8. The rest of Bodell's list, including the likes of Pedro Rodriguez de Campomanes, brings to mind Quentin Skinner's argument about the surprising dynamics of canonicity; see Skinner, *Liberty before Liberalism* (Cambridge: Cambridge University Press, 1997), 111. For a similar Swedish list including Beccaria, more focused on the theory of international trade, see Count Claes Carl Henrik Posse, *Betraktelser öfver åtskilliga ämnen uti stats-hushållningen, med afseende på Sverige* (Stockholm: Tryckte hos C. Deleen, 1823), 4n.

23. See, for only two of legions of examples, John McArthur, *Principles and Practice of Naval and Military Courts Martial*, 2 vols. (London: Butterworth et al., 1805), esp. 2:3–4; Nathan Dane, *A General Abridgment and Digest of American Law*, 8 vols. (Boston: Cummings, Hilliard, et al., 1823), esp. 629–630.

24. Giacomo Giuliani, *L'antisocialismo confutato: Opera filosofica* (Vicenza: Bartolommeo Paroni, 1803), vii, 7.

25. Giacomo Giuliani, "Delle Scienze Politiche: Polizia, 1833," Biblioteca Antoniana, Padua, Italy (hereafter cited as Antoniana), scafale 23, Codice 776, fasc. 3, 17v; emphasis in original.

26. Giacomo Giuliani, *Orazione inaugurale dell'abate Giacomo Giuliani P. Professore di diritto e procedura criminale recitata nella grand' aula della R. università di Padova il giorno 29 maggio 1808* (Padova: Penada, 1808), 33; Giuliani, *L'antisocialismo confutato*.

27. Cavalli, "La scienza politica," 578.

28. Giuliani, *L'antisocialismo confutato*, Sraffa 659, Wren Library, Trinity College, University of Cambridge, Cambridge, UK, on which see also Giancarlo de Vivo, ed., *Catalogue of the Library of Piero Sraffa* (Milan: Fondazione Mattioli, and Turin: Fondazione Einaudi, 2014), 198, entry 2015.

29. Giuliani, *Orazione inaugurale*, 33; Giuliani, *L'antisocialismo confutato*.

30. Giuliani, *Orazione inaugurale*, 1, 33–37.

31. Giacomo Giuliani, "*Scienze politiche*," no date, early 1830s, Antoniana, scafale 23, MS 772, vol. 2, 20r; Giuliani, "[*Lezioni*] *Della economia politica*, 1828–1829," Antoniana, scafale 23, MS 774, 2v.

32. Giuliani, *L'antisocialismo confutato*, 1–2.

33. The most famous Italian example might be Vincenzo Cuoco, *Historical Essay on the Neapolitan Revolution of 1799*, trans. David Gibbons, ed. and intro. Bruce Haddock and Filippo Sabetti (Toronto: University of Toronto Press, 2014). On Cuoco, see, among others, Fulvio Tessitore, *Filosofia: Storia e politica in Vincenzo Cuoco* (Lungro di Cosenza: Marco Editore, 2002).

34. Giuliani, *L'antisocialismo confutato*, 37, 47, 73.

35. Ibid., 2–3.

36. Ibid., 4–5.

37. For key reinterpretations of Rousseau, see, among others, Michael Sonenscher, *Sans-Culottes: An Eighteenth-Century Emblem in the French Revolution* (Princeton, NJ: Princeton University Press, 2008); Istvan Hont, *Politics in Commercial Society: Jean-Jacques Rousseau and Adam Smith*, ed. Béla Kapossy and Michael Sonenscher (Cambridge, MA: Harvard University Press, 2015); Graham Clure, "Rousseau, Diderot and the Spirit of Catherine the Great's Reforms," *History of European Ideas* 41, no. 7 (2015): 883–908.

38. Jean-Jacques Rousseau, "Discourse on the Sciences and Arts," in Rousseau, *The Discourses and Other Early Political Writings*, ed. Victor Gourevitch (Cambridge: Cambridge University Press, 1997), 203.

39. Giuliani, *L'antisocialismo confutato*, 111–120. On the fascinating and multifaceted question of property during the French Revolution, see Hannah Callaway, "Revolutionizing Property: The Confiscation of Émigré Wealth in Paris and the Problem of Property in the French Revolution," PhD diss., Harvard University, 2015, esp. 211–216; and Rafe Blaufarb, *The Great Demarcation: The French Revolution and the Invention of Modern Property* (Oxford: Oxford University Press, 2016).

40. Giuliani, *L'antisocialismo confutato,* 9–10.

41. Ibid.

42. Ibid., 10–11.

43. Ibid., esp. 10–11, 86, 171.

44. Ibid., 11–16.

45. Ibid., 17, 80.

46. Ibid., 17–19.

47. Ibid., 28.

48. Ibid., 30.

49. Ibid., 40.

50. Ibid., 41–42.

51. For his arguments regarding the sacredness of private property, see, for example, ibid., 27.

52. Ibid., 171–172.

53. Ibid., 42.

54. Ibid., 51–52, 56.

55. Ibid., 56.

56. On the public sphere, see, of course, Jürgen Habermas, *The Structural Transformation of the Public Sphere: An Inquiry into a Category of Bourgeois Society,* trans. Thomas Burger and Frederick Lawrence (Cambridge: Polity Press, 1989). On its emergence in early modern Europe, see James Van Horn Melton, *The Rise of the Public Sphere in Enlightenment Europe* (Cambridge: Cambridge University Press, 2001). On the tension between the public and the secret in this context, see Jacob Soll, *The Information Master: Jean-Baptiste Colbert's Secret State Intelligence System* (Ann Arbor: University of Michigan Press, 2009); and Reinert, *Translating Empire.* On Kaunitz and Verri, see again Carlo Capra, *I progressi della ragione: Vita di Pietro Verri* (Bologna: Il Mulino, 2002), 238.

57. Giuliani, *L'antisocialismo confutato,* 52, 68–69.

58. Ibid., 49–50. ·

59. On the remarkable history of Franciscan economic analysis, see Giacomo Todeschini, *Ricchezza Francescana: Dalla povertà volontaria alla società di mercato* (Bologna: Il Mulino, 2004).

60. Giuliani, *L'antisocialismo confutato,* 186–187.

61. Ibid., 70, 77.

62. Ibid., 83.

63. Giacomo Giuliani, "Trattato di Giurisprudenza Criminale [no date]," Antoniana, Scafale 36, Codice 553, 1:18v.

64. Quoted and discussed in Silvana Patriarca, *Italian Vices: Nation and Character from the Risorgimento to the Republic* (Cambridge: Cambridge University Press, 2010), 22–23.

65. See, on such associations and the development of political economy at the time, the essays in Massimo M. Augello and Marco E. L. Guidi, eds., *Associazionismo economico e diffusione dell'economia politica nell'Italia dell'ottocento,* 2 vols. (Milan: Franco Angeli, 2000), vol. 1. For an overview of Italian economics in the period, see Riccardo Faucci, *L'economia politica in Italia: Dal Cinquecento ai nostri giorni* (Turin: UTET, 2000), 127–183.

66. Giacomo Giuliani, "Considerazioni sulle cagioni, che influiscono a formare un popolo navigatore, ed a distinguersi nella Marina; Memoria letta alla Accademia nel giorno 19 Settembre 1816," Antoniana, Scafale 23, Codice 690, 136r–145v, 136r, 138r, 141v.

67. Ibid., 140r–140v. On this larger moment, see also Istvan Hont, *Jealousy of Trade: International Competition and the Nation-State in Historical Perspective* (Cambridge, MA: Harvard University Press, 2005), 4; and, for its earlier origins in Italy, Sophus A. Reinert, introduction to Antonio Serra, *A Short Treatise on the Wealth and Poverty of Nations (1613),* trans. Jonathan Hunt (London: Anthem, 2011), 1–93, at 19; and, more at length, Sophus A. Reinert, "Rivalry: Greatness in Early Modern Political Economy," in *Mercantilism Reimagined: Political Economy in Early Modern Britain and Its Empire,* ed. Philip J. Stern and Carl Wennerlind (Oxford: Oxford University Press, 2013), 348–370.

68. Giuliani, "Considerazioni sulle cagioni," 144v–145v; Giuliani, "Economia Pubblica, 1813," Antoniana, Scafale 23, Codice 654, 135r; Giuliani, "Sulla preferenza del Commercio estero; Memoria letta il 5 Maggio 1825," Antoniana, Scafale 23, Codice 690, fols. 154r–163v, at 154r. On these themes, see Hont, *Jealousy of Trade,* 5–8, 115–124; Reinert, *Translating Empire,* esp. 1.

69. Giuliani, "Sulla preferenza del Commercio," 154r.

70. Ibid., 154r–154v.

71. Ibid., 156v.

72. Ibid., 157v–158v. On this trope, see Reinert, *Translating Empire,* 83.

73. Giuliani, "Sulla preferenza del Commercio," 158–162r.

74. Ibid., 162v–163r.

75. Giacomo Giuliani, "Scienze Economiche, 1828–1829, vol. III of III," Antoniana, Scafale 23, Codice 774, [1r].

76. Ibid., 2v; emphasis in original.

77. Ibid., 3r–3v; emphasis in original.

78. Giacomo Giuliani, *Economia, 1820–1821,* Antoniana, Scafale 23, Codice 772, pamphlet 3, 3v–4r; Giuliani, "Della Economia Politica e delle Finanze, Corpo di Lezioni complete 1833," Antoniana, Scafale 23, Codice 774, 7; emphasis in original.

79. Giacomo Giuliani, "Della Economia Politica e delle Finanze," 5, 7, 24; emphasis in original.

80. Ibid., 25–28; emphasis in original.

81. On the nexus of technological change and utopian socialism, see still Gregory Claeys, *Machinery, Money and the Millennium: From Moral Economy to Socialism, 1815–1860* (Princeton, NJ: Princeton University Press, 1987).

82. On the importance of manufactures in Italian political economy, see Sophus A. Reinert, "The Italian Tradition of Political Economy: Theories and Policies of Development in the Semi-Periphery of the Enlightenment," in *The Origins of Development Economics: How Schools of Economic Thought Have Addressed Development,* ed. Jomo K. Sundaram and Erik S. Reinert (London: Zed Books, 2006), 24–47. On the appropriateness of employing the word "industrial" to describe manufacturing activities before the "Industrial Revolution," see Carlo Poni, *La seta in Italia: Una grande industria prima della rivoluzione industriale* (Bologna: Il Mulino, 2009), 61–62.

83. On the differences and relationships between these two ideas of "industry," see Sophus A. Reinert, "The Way to Wealth Around the World: Benjamin Franklin and the Globalization of American Capitalism," *American Historical Review* 120, no. 1 (2015): 61–97; but particularly Jan de Vries, *The Industrious Revolution: Consumer Behavior and the Household Economy, 1650 to the Present* (Cambridge: Cambridge University Press, 2008).

84. On this shift in the source of energy from organic to inorganic in the context of the Industrial Revolution, see E. A. Wrigley, *Energy and the English Industrial Revolution* (Cambridge: Cambridge University Press, 2010).

85. Giuliani, "Della Economia Politica e delle Finanze," 45; emphasis in original.

86. Jürgen Backhaus, "Fiscal Sociology: What For?," *American Journal of Economics and Sociology* 61, no. 1 (2002): 55–77, at 55–58.

87. Giuliani, "Della Economia Politica e delle Finanze," 45–56.

88. Giacomo Giuliani, "Corso di scienze politiche dell'anno 1817–1818," Antoniana, Scafale 36, MS 772, fasc. I, 5r–5v; Giuliani, "Scienze Politiche, 1835–36," Antoniana, Scafale 36, MS 772, fasc. I, 8v.

89. Giuliani, "Scienze Politiche, 1835–36," fasc. 2, 2v. See similarly, and at length, Giuliani, "Della Economia, 1836–1837 [1840–1841]," Antoniana Scafale 36, MS 772, 25v.

90. Giualiani, "Della scienze delle leggi positive, 1833 [different manuscript]," Scafale 36, Codice 777, 19v–20r. For a more recent analysis of this precise mechanism, see Robert H. Frank and Philip J. Cook, *The Winner-Take-All Society: Why the Few at the Top Get So Much More than the Rest of Us* (London: Penguin, 1995), esp. 2.

91. Giacomo Giuliani, "Introduzione alle Scienze Politiche ossia Della Politica in genere, 1840," Antoniana, Scafale 36, MS 772, 3r; emphasis in original.

92. Giacomo Giuliani, "Delle Scienze Politiche: Polizia, 1833," Antoniana, Scafale 36, Codice 776, fasc. 4, [5r]; Giuliani, "Della Scienza delle leggi positive, 1833," Antoniana, Scafale 36, Codice 777, 7r. See, for this Christian conception, among others Luigino Bruni and Stefano Zamagni, *Economia civile: Efficienza, equità, felicità pubblica* (Bologna: Il Mulino, 2004).

93. Giacomo Giuliani, "Della Scienza delle leggi positive, 1830," Antoniana, Scafale 36, Codice 777, fasc. 1, 10v–11r.

94. Giuliani, "Scienze Politiche," Antoniana, Scafale 36, Codice 772, vol. 2, fasc. 2, 20r; Giuliani, "Corso di scienze politiche dell'anno 1817–1818," fasc. 1, 5r; emphasis in original.

95. Michael Sonenscher, "'The Moment of Social Science': The *Decade Philosophique* and Late Eighteenth-Century French Thought,' *Modern Intellectual History* 6, no. 1 (2009): 121–146, at 129–131.

96. Adam Smith, *An Inquiry into the Nature and Causes of the Wealth of Nations*, ed. Edwin Cannan, new pref. by George J. Stigler (Chicago: University of Chicago Press, 1976), 449. Key interpretative texts regarding Smith's definition remain Donald Winch, *Adam Smith's Politics: An Essay in Historiographic Revision* (Cambridge: Cambridge University Press, 1978); Knud Haakonssen, *The Science of a Legislator: The Natural Jurisprudence of David Hume and Adam Smith* (Cambridge: Cambridge University Press, 1981).

97. Sir Edward Coke, 7 *Reports* 28a, in *The Selected Writings of Sir Edward Coke*, ed. Steve Sheppard, 3 vols. (Indianapolis: Liberty Fund, 2003), 1:231–232; Michael Hawke, *Grounds of the Lawes of England* (London: Twyford, 1657), 2.

98. Stephen Gaukroger, *Francis Bacon and the Transformation of Early-Modern Philosophy* (Cambridge: Cambridge University Press, 2001), 63.

99. Emmanuel Sieyès, "What Is the Third Estate?," in Sieyès, *Political Writings,* ed. Michael Sonenscher (Indianapolis: Hackett, 2003), 92–162, at 115; Robert Wokler, "The Enlightenment and the French Revolutionary Birth Pangs of Modernity," in *The Rise of the Social Sciences and the Formation of Modernity: Conceptual Change in Context, 1750–1850*, ed. Johan Heilbron, Lars Magnusson, and Björn Wittrock (Dordrecht: Kluwer, 1998), 35–76, at 43–47; Cheryl B. Welch, "Social Science from the French Revolution to Positivism," in *The Cambridge History of Nineteenth-Century Political Thought*, ed. Gareth Stedman Jones and Gregory Claeys (Cambridge: Cambridge University Press, 2011), 171–199, at 171. On the origins of "social science," see further Keith Michael Baker, "The Early History of the Term 'Social Science,'" *Annals of Science* 20 (1964): 211–226; Brian William Head, *Ideology and Social Science: Destutt de Tracy and French Liberalism* (Dordrecht: Martinus Nijhoff, 1985); Robert Wokler, "Ideology and the Origins of Social Science," in *The Cambridge History of Eighteenth-Century Political Thought,*

ed. Mark Goldie and Robert Wokler (Cambridge: Cambridge University Press, 2006), 688–709, esp. 691–693.

100. On which see Lynn Hunt, *Inventing Human Rights: A History* (New York: Norton, 2007); and, for caveats, Samuel Moyn, *Human Rights and the Uses of History* (London: Verso, 2014). On early modern economic jealousy, see Hont, *Jealousy of Trade*, 340.

101. This vocabulary of imperial humanity was widespread, particularly with regard to penal reforms, imperial economic injustices, and emerging abolitionist sentiments; for examples see John Coakley Lettsom, "On the Howardian Fund and Prison Charities," *The Gentlemen's Magazine*, vol. 57 (London: John Nichols, 1757), 464; Benjamin Franklin, "The Colonist's Advocate: VII," in *The Papers of Benjamin Franklin*, ed. Leonard W. Labaree et al., 41 vols. (New Haven, CT: Yale University Press, 1959–2014), 17:52–55, at 53; William Bradford to Luigi Castiglioni, 10 August 1786, praising Cesare Beccaria's work as a vehicle of "the empire of humanity," in Luigi Castiglioni, *Viaggio negli Stati Uniti*, 2 vols. (Milan: Marelli, 1790), 2:23–25; Jullien to Benjamin Franklin, 13 February 1779, in *Papers*, 28:533–534; Benjamin Rush to John Coakley Lettsom, 18 May 1787, in *Letters of Benjamin Rush* (Philadelphia: American Philosophical Society, 1951), 417; Thomas Clarkson, *The History of the Rise, Progress, and Accomplishment of the Abolition of Slave-Trade by the British Parliament*, 2 vols. (London: Longman, Hurst, Rees, and Orme, 1808), 1:545, establishing an idiom influential well into the nineteenth century—see, for example, [Lucius A. Hine?], "Our Coloured Population: A Negro State," *Quarterly Journal and Review* [Cincinnati] 1, no. 3 (1846): 193–204, at 199.

102. Wokler, "Ideology and the Origins of Social Science," 707–709.

103. Thomas Hobbes, *On the Citizen* [*De Cive*], ed. Richard Tuck and Michael Silverthorne (Cambridge: Cambridge University Press, 1998), 3–4; John Rawls, *The Law of Peoples* (Cambridge, MA: Harvard University Press, 1999), 23.

104. On this tradition see, among others, Vincenzo Ferrone, *La società giusta ed equa: Repubblicanesimo e diritti dell'uomo in Gaetano Filangieri* (Rome: Laterza, 2003); Antonio Trampus, *Il diritto alla felicità: Storia di un'idea* (Rome: Laterza, 2008); Sophus A. Reinert, "Political Economy and the Rights of Man," in Vincenzo Ferrone, *The Politics of Enlightenment: Constitutionalism, Republicanism, and the Rights of Man in Gaetano Filangieri*, trans. Sophus A. Reinert (London: Anthem, 2012), vii–ix. For the mutually extremely appreciative correspondence between Verri and Filangieri, see Verri to Filangieri, 26 August 1780, and Filangieri to Verri, 19 September 1780, both in Archivio Verri, Fondazione Mattioli, housed at the Università di Milano under the tutelage of the Archivio Storico della Banca Intesa Sanpaolo, Milan, Italy, 270.21.

105. Verri, "Mozione del cittadino Verri municipalista alla municipalità di Milano," in *Edizione nazionale delle opere di Pietro Verri,* ed. Carlo Capra et al., 8 vols. in 10 to date (Rome: Edizioni di storia e letteratura, 2003–2014), 6:816–819, at 816; emphasis in original.

106. Matteo Angelo Galdi, *Dei rapporti politico-economici fra le nazioni libere* (Milan: Presso Pirotta e Maspero stampatori-librai, year 6 [1797 or 1798]), unpaginated "avviso ai lettori" and 3–8, 12; on Galdi, see Maria Rosa Strollo, *L'istruzione a Napoli nel "decennio francese": Il contributo di Matteo Angelo Galdi* (Naples: Liguori, 2003).

107. Nicola Giuseppe Corvaia, *La bancocrazia,* 2 vols. (Milan: A. Ubicini, 1840), 1:253; Fabio Invrea, *Discorsi sulla pubblica ricchezza ossia sopra di quanto la costituisce sulla di lei origine, aumento, e ripartizione* (Genoa: Ferrando, 1846), 100–101, misquoting Karl Heinrich Rau, *Lehrbuch der politischen Oekonomie,* 3rd ed., 3 vols. in 5 (Heidelberg: C. F. Winter, 1837–1851), 1:47. To make his point, Rau had warned of turning political economy into "Staatswissenschaft," not "scienza sociale." Curiously, the first known reference to "social science" in the English language is in William Thompson's 1824 *Inquiry into the Principles of the Distribution of Wealth Most Conducive to Human Happiness* (London: Longman et al. 1824), viii–ix, which essentially equated it with "the art of social happiness." On this see Wokler, "Ideology and the Origins of Social Science," 702.

108. Francesco Trinchera in Pellegrino Rossi, *Corso di economia politica, prima versione italiana con note di Francesco Trinchera arricchita dalla giunta della storia dell'economia di Ch. H. Rau e da due articoli del cav. Luigi Blanch,* 2 vols. (Naples: Dallo stabilimento del Guttemberg, 1843), 2:263. On Rossi, see the essays in Michele Finelli, ed., *Pellegrino Rossi: Giurista, economista e uomo politico (1787–1848)* (Soveria Mannelli: Rubbettino, 2011). On the editions of his work, see Erik S. Reinert, Kenneth Carpenter, Fernanda Reinert, and Sophus A. Reinert, "80 Economic Bestsellers before 1850: A Fresh Look at the History of Economic Thought," *The Other Canon Foundation and Tallinn University of Technology Working Papers in Technology Governance and Economic Dynamics,* paper no. 74 (2017), 91–92.

109. Placido de Luca, *Dell'utile o svantaggio che producono all'industria i privilegi: Memoria estemporanea pel concorso alla cattedra di economia e commercio nella R. Università degli studii di Catania,* 2nd ed. (Naples: Matteo Vara, 1841), 5–6.

110. The literature on this is, needless to say, immense, but for crucial perspectives and further references, see Eric Hobsbawm, *Nations and Nationalism since 1780: Programme, Myth, Reality,* 2nd ed. (Cambridge: Cambridge University Press, 1992); and Hont, *Jealousy of Trade,* 447–528.

111. Benjamin Franklin, "Father Abraham's Speech" ["The Way to Wealth"], in *Papers*, 7:340–350, on which see Reinert, "The Way to Wealth." For an example of its being called "social science," see Ambroise Clément, *Essai sur la science sociale: Économie politique—morale éxperimentale—politique théorique*, 2 vols. (Paris: Guillaumin, 1867), 1:65.

112. See, for variations, John Hobson, quoted and discussed in Gregory Claeys, *Imperial Sceptics: British Critics of Empire, 1850–1920* (Cambridge: Cambridge University Press, 2010), 272; and Wokler, "Ideology and the Origins of Social Science," 707–709. For the role played by "social science" at different times in the nineteenth and twentieth centuries, see Mark Mazower, *Governing the World: The History of an Idea* (London: Penguin, 2012), 95–100, 292.

113. Giuseppe Romanazzi, *Note e considerazioni sull'affrancazione de' canoni e sul libero coltivamento del tavoliere di Puglia* (Naples: Tramater, 1834), 104. See similarly John Hobson, quoted and discussed in Gregory Claeys, *Imperial Sceptics: British Critics of Empire, 1850–1920* (Cambridge: Cambridge University Press, 2010), 272; and Wokler, "Ideology and the Origins of Social Science," 707–709.

114. James Napier Bailey, *Preliminary Discourse on the Objects, Pleasures, and Advantages of the Science of Society* (Leeds, UK: Hobson, 1840), 27. On Bailey, see Gregory Claeys, *Citizens and Saints: Politics and Anti-Politics in Early British Socialism* (Cambridge: Cambridge University Press, 1989), 234–235.

115. Bailey, *Preliminary Discourse*, 5.

116. Karl Marx, "Critical Marginal Notes on the Article 'The King of Prussia and Social Reform: By a Prussian' (1844)," in Marx, *Early Political Writings*, ed. Joseph O'Malley (Cambridge: Cambridge University Press, 1994), 97–114, 112.

117. Ralf Dahrendorf, *Reflections on the Revolutions in Europe* (New York: Random House, 1990), 38. On the symbolism of this moment, see Mark Bevir, *The Making of British Socialism* (Princeton, NJ: Princeton University Press, 2011), 2.

118. Not surprisingly, many economists and cultural critics alike tap into the rampant popularity of the undead in popular culture to explain the survival—and reanimation—of theories for which the bell ostensibly long ago tolled; see, for example, John Quiggin, *Zombie Economics: How Dead Ideas Still Walk among Us* (Princeton, NJ: Princeton University Press, 2010), 1.

119. Alexandr Herzen, *From the Other Shore*, trans. Moura Budberg (London: Weidenfeld and Nicholson, 1956), 89; Ayn Rand, "The Monument Builders," in *The Virtue of Selfishness: A New Concept of Egoism* (New York: Signet, 1964), 100–107, at 100. On Stalin's brand of socialism, see Stephen Kotkin, *Stalin*, vol. 1: *Paradoxes of Power, 1878–1928* (New York: Penguin, 2014). On Herzen from the perspective of a careful reader of Beccaria, see Franco Venturi, *Roots of Revolution: A History of the Populist and Socialist Movements in Nineteenth*

Century Russia, trans. Francis Haskell, intro. Isaiah Berlin (New York: Alfred A. Knopf, 1960), 1–35.

120. Hårold Meyerson, "Why Are There Suddenly Millions of Socialists in the United States?," *The Guardian* (London), 29 February 2016, which fruitfully can be read alongside Werner Sombart, *Warum gibt er in den Vereinigten Staaten keinen Sozialismus?* (Tübingen: Mohr [Siebeck], 1906).

121. The respected Ghanaian businessman Ken Ofori-Atta, formerly of Morgan Stanley and Salomon Brothers, described these still-ongoing economic turmoils as "the financial markets' equivalent of the fall of the Berlin Wall," and there certainly are similarities between the two events. See Ken Ofori-Atta, "The Impact of the Global Financial Crisis on Business in Ghana," in *Leadership, Entrepreneurship, and Values: Selected Speeches, Statements and Writings* (Accra: Frangipani, 2009), 203–209, at 204. The historiography on the past decade has exploded, but for notable treatments of aspects of this epochal change, see Asle Toje, *Jernburet: Liberalismens Krise* (Oslo: Dreyer, 2014); John B. Judis, *The Populist Explosion: How the Great Recession Transformed American and European Politics* (New York: Columbia Global Reports, 2016); Pankaj Mishra, *Age of Anger: A History of the Present* (New York: Farrar, Straus and Giroux, 2017).

122. On whether it should be called "socialism with Chinese characteristics" or "capitalism with Chinese characteristics," see Yasheng Huang, *Capitalism with Chinese Characteristics: Entrepreneurship and the State* (Cambridge: Cambridge University Press, 2008).

123. For recent calls to arms for both terms, see Gerald Allan Cohen, *Why Not Socialism?* (Princeton, NJ: Princeton University Press, 2009); and Jason Brennan, *Why Not Capitalism?* (London: Routledge, 2014). For recent attempts to rethink political economy, see, among others, George A. Akerlof, Olivier Blanchard, David Romer, and Joseph E. Stiglitz, eds., *What Have We Learned? Macroeconomic Policy after the Crisis* (Cambridge, MA: MIT Press, 2014); Stephen S. Cohen and J. Bradford DeLong, *Concrete Economics: The Hamilton Approach to Economic Growth and Policy* (Boston: Harvard Business Review Press, 2016); and Dani Rodrik, *Economics Rules: The Rights and Wrongs of the Dismal Science* (New York: W. W. Norton, 2016).

124. St. Augustine, *Confessions,* trans. R. S. Pine-Coffin (New York: Longman, 2005), 264.

125. Bevir, *Making of British Socialism,* 12

126. Karl Marx and Friedrich Engels, *The Communist Manifesto,* ed. Gareth Stedman Jones (London: Penguin, 2002), 223, 236, 243.

127. Ibid., 245–247, 252–253.

128. See, among many others, Mansour Shaki, "The Social Doctrine of Mazdak in Light of Middle Persian Evidence," *Archiv Orientální* 46, no. 4 (1978): 289–306; and the broad trajectory delineated in Erik van Ree, *Boundaries of Utopia: Imagining Communism from Plato to Stalin* (London: Routledge, 2015).

129. George Orwell, *Homage to Catalonia* (London: Penguin, 2000), 84.

130. John William Mackail, *Socialism and Politics: An Address and a Programme* (London: Hammersmith Publishing Society, 1903 [1902]), 6.

131. Antonio Gramsci, *Prison Notebooks*, ed. Joseph A. Buttigieg, 3 vols. (New York: Columbia University Press, 1992), 1:197; emphasis added. His source was the recently published Adolfo Zerboglio, "Il ritorno di padre Facchinei," *Rivista d'Italia* 30, no. 1 (15 January 1927): 22–30, which did not explain or problematize Facchinei's use of the term at all.

132. Antonio Gramsci, "Socialism and Italy [originally published in *Il grido del popolo*, 22 September 1917]," in Gramsci, *Pre-Prison Writings*, ed. Richard Bellamy (Cambridge: Cambridge University Press, 1994), 27–30, at 28–29.

133. Ibid. For an argument about "internal strife" and "foreign domination," "socialism" and "unification," in Italy that might have influenced him, see Friedrich Engels, "Preface to the Italian Edition of 1893," in Marx and Engels, *The Communist Manifesto*, 215–217.

134. Though this does not shed much light on the eighteenth century, it is noteworthy regarding the extent to which more recent champions of "socialism" have focused on the belief that "it is possible to make significant changes in the world through conscious human agency" as a core aspect of the doctrine; see, for example, Michael Newman, *Socialism: A Very Short Introduction* (Oxford: Oxford University Press, 2005), 2–3, 136–137; and Axel Honneth, *The Idea of Socialism: Towards a Renewal* (Cambridge: Polity Press, 2017), presumably inspired by Karl Marx's eleventh thesis on Feuerbach: "The philosophers have only *interpreted* the world in different ways; the point is to *change* it," in "On Feuerbach," in Marx, *Early Political Writings*, 116–118, at 118. Though, as Gareth Stedman Jones has demonstrated, a vast chasm separated the historical Marx from his legacy, this aspect of his fame was, at least, true to form; see Jones, *Karl Marx: Greatness and Illusion* (Cambridge, MA: Harvard University Press, 2016), 5.

135. See, similarly, Hont, *Politics in Commercial Society*, 70.

136. See, for example, the agenda in *Manifesto of English Socialists* (London: Twentieth Century Press, 1893).

137. Léon Say, *Le socialisme d'état: Conférences faites au Cercle Saint-Simon* (Paris: Lévy, 1884), esp. 111–112. On Bismarck, see Jonathan Steinberg, *Bismarck: A Life* (Oxford: Oxford University Press, 2011); and, for a very brief yet penetrating summary

of Bismarck's policies, see Stephen Kotkin, *Stalin*, esp. 1:6–7. The founder of the British Labour Party, James Ramsay Macdonald, for one, believed Bismarck's plan had been to "kill the menace of Socialism by kindness"; see his *The Socialist Movement* (London: Thornton Butterworth, 1911), 166.

138. Albert Métin, *Le socialisme sans doctrines: Australie et Nouvelle Zélande* (Paris: Félix Alcan, 1901). For a representative example of presocialist social policies, see Anne-Lise Seip, *Sosialhjelpstaten blir til: Norsk sosialpolitikk, 1740–1920*, 2nd ed. (Oslo: Gyldendal, 1994), esp. 1–64.

139. See, for a similar point, Jacob Viner, "The Intellectual History of Laissez Faire," in Viner, *Essays on the Intellectual History of Economics*, ed. Douglas A. Irwin (Princeton, NJ: Princeton University Press, 1991), 200–225, 224–225.

140. Ferdinand Lassalle, "Arbeiterprogramm," in *Reden und Schriften* (Bremen: Europäischer Hochschulverlag, 2010), 124–155, 152. Stuart K. Hayashi has argued, "I see pure capitalism and a pure night watchman state as ultimately the same set of rules"; see his *The Freedom of Peaceful Action: On the Origin of Individual Rights* (Lanham, MD: Lexington Books, 2014), 294. Robert Nozick, *Anarchy, State, and Utopia* (New York: Basic Books, 2013), esp. 26–27, remains a fundamental reference point on minimal and night watchman states.

141. Ferdinando Facchinei, *Note ed osservazioni sul libro intitolato "Dei delitti e delle pene"* ([Venice]: n.p., 1765), 84–85.

142. In this, Beccaria came quite close to Albert Einstein's argument for socialism based on individual rights in his "Why Socialism," *Monthly Review* 61, no. 1 (1949): 55–61. See, for a similar distinction, also Anthony Pagden, "Human Rights, Natural Rights, and Europe's Imperial Legacy," in *The Burden of Empire: 1539 to the Present* (Cambridge: Cambridge University Press, 2015), 243–262, at 252. On Beccaria's individualist focus, see also Renato Pasta, "Beccaria 'philosophe': Alle origini del diritto penale come 'scienza sociale integrate,'" *Quaderni fiorentini per la storia del pensiero giuridico moderno* 44, no. 2 (2015): 897–909, at 901.

143. See, similarly, John Robertson, *The Case for the Enlightenment: Scotland and Naples, 1680–1760* (Cambridge: Cambridge University Press, 2005), 32. In a similar vein, Martti Koskenniemi has argued that "when natural law finally knew what it wanted to be—and needed to be in order to fulfil its programme—it became economics." Although the tradition of natural law certainly influenced the emergence of political economy, in many ways culminating in it, it is not clear why it would follow that "the increase of wealth, that is to say, the management of the balance of one's advantage, could no longer however be undertaken by regulatory means." See Koskenniemi, "International Law and *raison d'état*: Rethinking the Prehistory of International Law," in *The Roman Foundations of*

the *Law of Nations: Alberico Gentili and the Justice of Empire,* ed. Benedict Kingsbury and Benjamin Straumann (Oxford: Oxford University Press, 2010), 297–339, at 337, 339.

144. Facchinei to Zaccaria, addendum to letter of 17 April 1763, Archivo Histórico de la Casa de Loyola, Sanctuary of Loyola, Azpeitia, Spain, *Fondo Zaccaria,* b. 19, IV. Again, for the importance of differentiating between the politics of *this* and the next world at the time, see Robertson, *Case for the Enlightenment,* esp. 8.

145. Arthur E. Bestor, "The Evolution of the Socialist Vocabulary," *Journal of the History of Ideas* 9, no. 3 (1948): 259–302, at 277.

146. Morris Hillquit, *Socialism in Theory and Practice* (New York: Macmillan, 1909), 11.

147. J. Ramsay Macdonald, *The Socialist Movement* (London: Thornton Butterworth, 1911), 195.

148. Hont, *Jealousy of Trade,* 139. On this later form of "market socialism," see David Ramsay Steele, *From Marx to Mises: Post Capitalist Society and the Challenge of Economic Calculation* (La Salle, IL: Open Court, 1999), 177; and, for an intriguing perspective, Włodzimierz Brus and Kazimierz Laski, *From Marx to the Market: Socialism in Search of an Economic System* (Oxford: Clarendon Press, 1991). For a pugnacious critique of recent "market socialism," see Andrei Shleifer and Robert W. Vishny, "The Politics of Market Socialism," *Journal of Economic Perspectives* 8, no. 2 (1994): 165–176.

149. Daniel Peris, *Storming the Heavens: The Soviet League of the Militant Godless* (Ithaca, NY: Cornell University Press, 1998); Vilfredo Pareto, *Les Systèmes socialistes . . . ,* 2 vols. (Paris: Giard et Brière, 1902–1903), 1:229; Gareth Stedman Jones, introduction to Marx and Engels, *The Communist Manifesto,* 1–187, at 10. Marx maintained in his Paris notebooks that "socialist man understands the *whole of what is called world-history* as nothing but man's creation through human labour," concluding that "socialism is man's *positive self-consciousness,* a *self-consciousness* no longer mediated through the negating of religion." See Karl Marx, "From the Paris Notebooks (1844)," in *Early Political Writings,* 71–96, at 82–83; emphasis in original.

150. Albert Renger-Patzsch, *Eisen und Stahl* (Berlin: Hermann Seckendorf, 1931). On Renger-Patzsch, see Donald Kuspit, *Albert Renger-Patzsch: Joy before the Object* (Oxford: Oxford University Press, 1993). On the history of socialism and architecture, see also Owen Hatherley, *Landscapes of Communism: A History through Buildings* (London: Allen Lane, 2015). On how, in the twentieth century, both "socialist realism" and "capitalist realism" similarly saw "industrial action as a force that will humanize the universe," paradoxically to the point of becoming inhuman, see Adam Weiner, *How Bad Writing Destroyed the World: Ayn Rand and the Literary Origins of the Financial Crisis* (New York: Bloomsbury, 2016), 206.

151. Quentin Skinner, "Meaning and Understanding in the History of Ideas," in *Visions of Politics*, 3 vols. (Cambridge: Cambridge University Press, 2002 [1969]), 1:57–89, at 65. The history of "socialism" may be particularly prone to what Skinner warned against as the "mythology of prolepsis," and generally of precursorism. For a similar point, see Sophus A. Reinert, "The Empire of Emulation: A Quantitative Analysis of Economic Translations in the European World, 1500–1849," in *The Political Economy of Empire in the Early Modern World*, ed. Sophus A. Reinert and Pernille Røge (Basingstoke, UK: Palgrave Macmillan, 2013), 105–128, at 123–124.

152. See, among others on such charges, Stephen Eric Bronner, *Reclaiming the Enlightenment: Toward a Politics of Radical Engagement* (New York: Columbia University Press, 2004), 96; Robertson, *Case for the Enlightenment*, 1.

153. Pietro Verri, "Pensieri sullo spirito della letteratura d'Italia," in *"Il Caffè,"* 1764–1766, ed. Gianni Francioni and Sergio A. Romagnoli (Turin: Bollati Boringhieri, 1993) (hereafter cited as *Il Caffè*), 211–222, at 211.

154. See, among others, Luigino Bruni, *The Genesis and Ethos of the Market* (London: Palgrave Macmillan, 2012); Gary S. Becker, "Crime and Punishment: An Economic Approach," *Journal of Political Economy* 76 (1968): 169–217, at 209; and Richard A. Posner, "An Economic Theory of the Criminal Law," *Columbia Law Review* 85, no. 6 (1985): 1193–1231, at 1193, discussed in Harcourt, *Illusion of Free Markets*, 57.

155. On assumptions in economics, see Jonathan Schlefer, *The Assumptions Economists Make* (Cambridge, MA: Harvard University Press, 2012).

156. See, for a similar argument, Hont, *Jealousy of Trade*, 4.

157. Pietro Verri, "Le parole," in *Il Caffè*, 451–453, at 452.

158. Cesare Beccaria, "[Risposta alla Rinunzia]," in *Il Caffè*, 104–106, at 104.

159. See, for a very similar argument, David Armitage, *Civil Wars: A History in Ideas* (New York: Alfred A. Knopf, 2017), 21.

160. Bevir, *Making of British Socialism*, 3, 12. For particularly striking examples of such a dichotomic approach to political economy, see Von Mises's still-best-selling critique of socialism, in *Socialism: An Economic and Sociologial Analysis*, trans. Jacques Kahane (Indianapolis: Liberty Fund, 1981 [1922]), 16–17, chastising even avowed "enemies of Socialism" who allowed themselves to "compromise" and make any concessions at all to "government interference" or to "the various 'social-political' and 'social-reform' movements," as well as Ayn Rand's marginalia to Friedrich Hayek's *The Road to Serfdom*; when Hayek wrote, of his own influential yet cautious attack on socialism, "it is important not to confuse opposition against this kind of planning with a dogmatic laissez faire attitude," Rand angrily attacked him: "The God damned abysmal fool!." See *Ayn Rand's Marginalia: Her Critical Comments on the Writings of Over 20 Authors*, ed. Robert

Mayhew (New Milford, CT: Second Renaissance Books, 1995), 149, annotating Friedrich A. Hayek, *The Road to Serfdom* (London: Routledge, 1944), 37, and similarly her "Doesn't Life Require Compromise?," in *The Virtue of Selfishness*, 79–81, as well as Ayn Rand to Rose Wilder Lane, 21 August 1946, in *Letters of Ayn Rand*, ed. Michael S. Berliner, intro. by Leonard Peikoff (New York: Plume Books, 1997), 307–309. For caveats regarding these letters, see Jennifer Burns, *Goddess of the Market: Ayn Rand and the American Right* (Oxford: Oxford University Press, 2009), 291–293. On the problems of such dichotomies generally, see Timothy Mitchell, "Everyday Metaphysics of Power," *Theory and Society* 19, no. 5 (1990): 545–577, which is discussed also in Johanna Bockman, *Markets in the Name of Socialism: The Left-Wing Origins of Neoliberalism* (Stanford, CA: Stanford University Press, 2011), 4–5. For a different perspective on the need to overcome the dichotomy of "socialism" and "capitalism," see Hyun Ok Park, *The Capitalist Subconscious: From Korean Unification to Transnational Korea* (New York: Columbia University Press, 2015), esp. 293. It seems useful to keep in mind Gregory Claeys's argument that "utopia and dystopia evidently share more in common than is often supposed," in Claeys, *Dystopia: A Natural History* (Oxford: Oxford University Press, 2017), 7.

161. Italo Calvino, *Invisible Cities,* trans. William Weaver,(Orlando: Harcourt, 1974), 82.

162. Oscar Wilde, "The Soul of Man under Socialism," in Wilde, *The Soul of Man under Socialism and Selected Critical Prose,* ed. Linda Dowling (London: Penguin, 2001), 125–160, at 160. For a longer meditation of a mature "socialist" on the tension, see Morris Hillquit's *Socialism in Theory and Practice* (New York: Macmillan, 1909), 29–35.

163. See, for example, Vincenzo Ferrone, *Storia dei diritti dell'uomo* (Bari: Laterza, 2014), 234; and Jay M. Bernstein, *Torture and Dignity: An Essay on Moral Injury* (Chicago: University of Chicago Press, 2015), 54.

164. On a central such Scottish friendship, see now Dennis C. Rasmussen, *The Infidel and the Professor: David Hume, Adam Smith, and the Friendship That Shaped Modern Thought* (Princeton, NJ: Princeton University Press, 2017).

Afterword

1. On the political economy of this institution, see, among others, Francesca Lidia Viano, *La Statua della libertà: Una storia globale* (Rome: Laterza, 2010), 142–145. On its Italian story in particular, see Cristina della Coletta, *World's Fairs Italian Style: The Great Expositions in Turin and Their Narratives, 1860–1915* (Toronto: University of Toronto Press, 2006).

2. It is worth noting that "global village" originally was conceptualized as a space of incessant disagreement and conflict; see Marshall McLuhan, *The Gutenberg Galaxy: The Making of Typographic Man* (Toronto: University of Toronto Press, 1962). For something like a manifesto of the Expo, however mystical, see Agostino Traini's charming *Che buono, signor Acqua!* (Casale Monferrato: Piemme, 2015). For meditations on the event, see Raffaele Nurra and Marilena Lualdi, eds., *Expo, nessuno uscirà uguale da qui* (Milan: ExpoVillage, 2016).

3. Fernando Mazzocca, ed., *Angelo Inganni, 1807–1880: Un pittore bresciano nella Milano romantica* (Milan: Skira, 1998), 101, 206.

4. On the incongruence of combining McDonald's and Slow Food, see, among others, Carl Honoré, *In Praise of Slow: How a Worldwide Movement Is Challenging the Cult of Speed* (London: Orion, 2005). On Italy's decline, see now Emanuele Felice, *Ascesa e declino: Storia economica d'Italia* (Bologna: Il Mulino, 2015); and, for Lombardy in particular, Giuseppe Berta, *La via del nord: Dal miracolo economico alla stagnazione* (Bologna: Il Mulino, 2015).

5. George Orwell, *Animal Farm* (New York: Houghton Mifflin, 1990), 118.

6. Compare Pietro Verri, "Meditazioni sulla economia politica," in *Edizione nazionale delle opere di Pietro Verri*, ed. Carlo Capra et al., 8 vols. in 10 to date (Rome: Edizioni di storia e letteratura, 2003–2014), vol. 2, pt. 2, 341–570, at 544 to Cesare Beccaria, "Sistema annonario della Lombardia Austriaca [Consulta e minuta di relazione]," 16 January 1793, in *Edizione Nazionale delle Opere di Cesare Beccaria*, ed. Luigi Firpo and Gianni Francioni, 16 vols. in 17 (Milan: Mediobanca, 1984–2015), 15:26–33, at 29, 32. For a rather evident example, see John Connell, "Nauru: The First Failed Pacific State?," *Commonwealth Journal of International Affairs* 95, no. 383 (2006): 47–63.

7. See, among others, Marco Bettiol, *Raccontare il Made in Italy: Un nuovo legame tra cultura e manifattura* (Venice: Marsilio, 2015). For an up-to-date list of such markets in Lombardy, see https://www.dati.lombardia.it/Commercio/Mercati -su-aree-pubbliche/68zx-njaw/data.

8. On East Timor's history, see, among others, Irena Cristalis, *East Timor: A Nation's Bitter Dawn*, 2nd ed. (London: Zed Books, 2009); and for the UN sovereignty, see Jarat Chopra, "The UN's Kingdom of East Timor," *Survival: Global Politics and Strategy* 42, no. 3 (2000): 27–40. For an eminently readable popular account of the country, see Gordon Peake, *Beloved Land: Stories, Struggles, and Secrets from Timor-Leste* (Melbourne: Scribe, 2013). On its colonial past, see Hans Hägerdal, *Lords of the Land, Lords of the Sea: Conflict and Adaptation in Early Colonial Timor, 1600–1800* (Leiden: KITLV Press, 2012). For an overview, see also Sophus A. Reinert and Dawn H. Lau, "East Timor: Betting on Oil," *Harvard Business School Case* 9-716-003 (Boston: Harvard Business School Publishing, 2017).

9. Interview with Cosme da Costa Araujo, Petroleum Unit, Ministry of Finance, Dili, East Timor, 10 August 2015; interview with Farrukh Moriani, United Nations Development Programme, Dili, East Timor, 11 August 2015. See also Alynna J. Lyon, "The East Timorese Church: From Oppression to Liberation," in *The Catholic Church and the Nation-State: Comparative Perspectives,* ed. Paul Christopher Manuel, Lawrence C. Reardon, and Clyde Wilcox (Washington, DC: Georgetown University Press, 2006), 131–148, at 133; R. Michael Feener, *Shari'a and Social Engineering: The Implementation of Islamic Law in Contemporary Aceh, Indonesia* (Oxford: Oxford University Press, 2013), esp. 110.

10. Interview with Young-Hun Lee, Seoul, South Korea, 14 June 2016. On the political economy of North Korea, see Hyun Ok Park, *The Capitalist Unconscious: From Korean Unification to Transnational Korea* (New York: Columbia University Press, 2015); and, on its "marketization from below" in particular, see Hazel Smith, *North Korea: Markets and Military Rule* (Cambridge: Cambridge University Press, 2015).

11. Xanana Gusmão, "Speech Delivered at the International Business Forum and Region Issues on The 'Growth of Trade and Investment Opportunities in Timor-Leste'" (2002), in Gusmão, *Timor Lives! Speeches of Freedom and Independence* (Alexandria: Longueville Books, 2005), 162–168, at 165; interview with Paulo Calhau, Timor Telecom, Dili, East Timor, 15 August 2016.

12. Iqbal Z. Quadir, "Adam Smith, Economic Development, and the Global Spread of Cell Phones," *Proceedings of the American Philosophical Society* 157, no. 1 (2013): 67–91, at 75; emphasis added. On the relationship between communication and cooperation, see the studies discussed in Yochai Benkler, "From Greenspan's Despair to Obama's Hope: The Scientific Bases of Cooperation as Principles of Regulation," in *The Perspectives on Regulation,* ed. David Moss and John Citernino (Cambridge, MA: The Tobin Project, 2009), 65–87, at 69.

13. Interview with José Ramos-Horta, Dili, East Timor, 11 August, 2015; interview with Mari Alkatiri, Dili, East Timor, 11 August 2015. See also Tarun Khanna and Krishna G. Palepu, *Winning in Emerging Markets: A Road Map for Strategy and Execution* (Boston: Harvard Business Press, 2010).

14. Xanana Gusmão, "On the Occasion of the Third Summit of African, Caribbean and Pacific Heads of State and Government in Nadi, Republic of Fiji Island [18–19 July 2002]," in Gusmão, *Timor Lives!,* 170–176, at 176.

15. On the Central African Republic, see the essays in *Making Sense of the Central African Republic,* ed. Tatiana Carayannis and Louisa Lombard (London: Zed Books, 2015); as well as the remarkable guerrilla documentary *The Ambassador,* dir. Mads Brügger (Hvidovre: Zentropa, 2011). I am here also grateful for an interview with Mads Brügger, Cambridge, MA, 8 December 2015. For an eye-opening introduction to the nature of Africa's integration into the world

economy, see Tom Burgis, *The Looting Machine: Warlords, Tycoons, Smugglers and the Systematic Theft of Africa's Wealth* (London: William Collins, 2015).

16. Interview with Mira Mehta, Tomato Jos, Kaduna, Nigeria, 18 July 2017.

17. On some of the challenges of "capitalist" incorporation along such frontiers, see Tania Murray Li, *Land's End: Capitalist Relations on an Indigenous Frontier* (Durham, NC: Duke University Press, 2014), esp. 4. For a global visualization of them, see Jimmy Nelson's stunning *Before They Pass Away* (Kempen: teNeues, 2013).

18. Interview with Farrukh Moriani, United Nations Development Programme, Dili, East Timor, 12 August 2015.

19. Charles Taylor, *Sources of the Self: The Making of the Modern Identity* (Cambridge: Cambridge University Press, 1989), 285–286.

20. Lisa Herzog, *Inventing the Market: Smith, Hegel, and Political Theory* (Oxford: Oxford University Press, 2013), 159–160.

21. See, for a similar point, Johann Gottfried Hoffman, *Die Lehre von den Steuern* (Berlin: Nicolaischen Buchhandlung, 1840), 2–3; quoted in Gustav Cohn, *The Science of Finance*, trans. Thorstein Veblen (Chicago: University of Chicago Press, 1895), 60; discussed in Erik S. Reinert, "Austrians and the 'Other Canon,'" in *Modern Applications of Austrian Thought*, ed. Jürgen G. Backhaus (Milton Park, UK: Routledge, 2005), 253–298, at 285. Or, as Margaret C. Jacob has put it, "When our contemporary theorists privilege a cosmopolitan allegiance over that accorded to the modern national state, we should not forget the historical role played by governmental authority in making any larger, cosmopolitan identity possible"; see Jacob, *Strangers Nowhere in the World: The Rise of Cosmopolitanism in Early Modern Europe* (Philadelphia: University of Pennsylvania Press, 2006), 66.

22. For an intelligent meditation on the concept, see Jacob Viner, "The 'Economic Man,' or the Place of Economic Self-Interest in a 'Good Society,'" in Viner, *Essays on the Intellectual History of Economics*, ed. Douglas A. Irwin (Princeton, NJ: Princeton University Press, 1991), 69–77.

23. Joseph Henrich et al., "In Search of Homo Economicus: Behavioral Experiments in 15 Small-Scale Societies," *American Economic Review* 91, no. 2 (2001): 73–78.

24. Again, Beccaria here drew on Hobbes, *On the Citizen* (see Thomas Hobbes, *On the Citizen* [*De Cive*], ed. Richard Tuck and Michael Silverthorne [Cambridge: Cambridge University Press, 1998], 25), and, for the commercial inflection of sociability, particularly Samuel von Pufendorf, *Of the Law of Nature and Nations*, ed. Jean Barbeyrac, trans. Basil Kennett, 4th ed. (London: Carew, 1729), 625. On the limits of Hobbes's commercial vision, see Istvan Hont, *Jealousy of Trade: International Competition and the Nation-State in Historical Perspective* (Cambridge, MA: Harvard University Press, 2005), esp. 21. On the importance of "culture"

for capitalism and economic development, see Sophus A. Reinert, "The Way to Wealth around the World: Benjamin Franklin and the Globalization of American Capitalism," *American Historical Review* 120, no. 1 (2015): 61–97; and, from a different perspective, Joel Mokyr, *A Culture of Growth: The Origins of the Modern Economy* (Princeton, NJ: Princeton University Press, 2017). For broader critiques of even learned economic values, see a number of works published in the wake of the 2008 economic crisis, including Daniel Cohen, *Homo Economicus: The (Lost) Prophet of Modern Times* (Cambridge: Polity Press, 2014).

25. Thorstein Veblen, "Professor Clark's Economics," *Quarterly Journal of Economics* 22, no. 2 (1908): 147–195, at 160. For a rather different perspective but with similar results, see Sven Beckert, "The New History of Capitalism," in *Capitalism: The Reemergence of a Historical Concept,* ed. Jürgen Kocka and Marcel van der Linden (London: Bloomsbury, 2016), 235–249, at 248.

26. The literature on this phenomenon is now almost endless, and impossible to divorce from many of the great political changes that currently are affecting the world economy. For brief introductions, see Thomas Piketty, *The Economics of Inequality,* trans. Arthur Goldhammer (Cambridge, MA: Harvard University Press, 2015); Joseph E. Stiglitz, *Great Divide: Unequal Societies and What We Can Do about Them* (New York: W. W. Norton, 2016); and Branko Milanovic, *Global Inequality: A New Approach for the Age of Globalization* (Cambridge, MA: Harvard University Press, 2016).

27. Samuel Moyn, *Not Enough: Human Rights in an Unequal World* (Cambridge, MA: Harvard University Press, 2018), 5, 212–213.

28. See, for example, Deirdre N. McCloskey, *The Bourgeois Virtues: Ethics for an Age of Commerce* (Chicago: University of Chicago Press, 2006), 38, 438, 462. On the related role of Providence in early social science, see Jacob Viner's classic *The Role of Providence in the Social Order: An Essay in Intellectual History* (Princeton, NJ: Princeton University Press, 1977).

29. Kevin D. Dougherty et al., *The Values and Beliefs of the American Public: Wave III Baylor Religion Survey* (Waco, TX: Baylor University, 2011), on which see its co-author Paul Froese, quoted in Cathy Lynn Grossman, "Baylor Religion Survey Reveals Many See God Steering the Economy," *USA Today,* 20 September 2011. See similarly Chrystia Freeland, *Plutocrats: The Rise of the New Global Super Rich and the Fall of Everyone Else* (New York: Penguin, 2012), 248–249.

30. On the increasing statelessness of the upper echelons of contemporary capitalism, see, among others, Freeland, *Plutocrats,* esp. 38; Gabriel Zucman, *The Hidden Wealth of Nations: The Scourge of Tax Havens,* trans. Teresa Lavender Fagan (Chicago: University of Chicago Press, 2015), 103–113; Brooke Harrington, *Capital without Borders: Wealth Managers and the One Percent* (Cambridge, MA: Harvard University Press, 2016), esp. 275–278, 290–293. Smith himself, of course,

had argued that "a merchant, it has been said very properly, is not necessarily the citizen of any particular county. It is in a great measure indifferent to him from what place he carries on his trade; and a very trifling disgust will make him remove his capital, and together with it all the industry which it supports, from one country to another"; see Adam Smith, *An Inquiry into the Nature and Causes of the Wealth of Nations*, ed. Edwin Cannan, new pref. by George J. Stigler (Chicago: University of Chicago Press, 1976), compare 1:444–445 and 477–478.

31. Noo Saro-Wiwa, *Looking for Transwonderland: Travels in Nigeria* (Berkeley: Soft Skull Press, 2012), 300; on the complex source of this religiosity, mixing Pentecostal forms and "traditional African animist religion, which has always sought material gain from the gods," see 65–70.

32. Axel Honneth, *The Idea of Socialism*, trans. Joseph Ganahl (Cambridge: Polity Press, 2017), vii–viii.

33. Boyd Hilton, *The Age of Atonement: The Influence of Evangelicalism on Social and Economic Thought, 1785–1865* (Oxford: Oxford University Press, 1986), esp. 189. On this issue, see further Paolo Prodi, *Settimo non rubare: Furto e mercato nella storia dell'Occidente* (Bologna: Il Mulino, 2009), 310–311; Robert H. Nelson, *Economics as Religion: From Samuelson to Chicago and Beyond*, with a new epilogue (University Park: Pennsylvania State University Press, 2014), 346; Giorgio Agamben, *Il regno e la Gloria: Per una genealogia teologica dell'economia e del governo* (Milan: Bollati Boringhieri, 2009); and Viner, *The Role of Providence*.

34. John Kenneth Galbraith, *The Culture of Contentment* (Boston: Houghton Mifflin, 1992), 134–135.

35. Fritz Redlich, "The Business Leader as a 'Daimonic' Figure," *American Journal of Economics and Sociology* 12, no. 2 (1953): 163–178, at 171, on which see Robert Fredona and Sophus A. Reinert, "The Harvard Research Center in Entrepreneurial History and the Daimonic Entrepreneur," *History of Political Economy* 49, no. 2 (2017): 267–314. On the Harvard Research Center generally, see Arthur H. Cole, "The First Blooming of Economics at Harvard [Cambridge, MA 1970]," Baker, ms. HUG 4290.509; Walter A. Friedman, "Leadership and History," in *Handbook of Leadership Theory and Practice: A Harvard Business School Centennial Colloquium*, ed. Nitin Nohria and Rakesh Khurana (Boston: Harvard Business Press, 2010), 291–205. For a relevant framework for studying people like those described by Redlich, see Aaron James, *Assholes: A Theory* (New York: Anchor Books, 2012).

36. On the timelessness of this question, see Pail Taçon, "Australia's Ancient Warriors: Changing Depictions of Fighting in the Rock Art of Arnhem Land, N.T.," *Cambridge Archaeological Journal* 4, no. 2 (1994): 211–248.

37. On institutional voids, see Khanna and Palepu, *Winning in Emerging Markets*.

38. For a recent history of socialism even in the United States, see John Nichols, *The "S" Word: A Short History of an American Tradition . . . Socialism* (London: Verso, 2011), perhaps challenging Werner Sombart, *Warum gibt es in den Vereinigten Staaten keinen Sozialismus?* (Tübingen: J. C. B. Mohr, 1906). See also Sophus A. Reinert, Dawn H. Lau, and Amy Macbeath, "Going Rogue: Choson Exchange in North Korea," *Harvard Business School Case* 9-717-015 (Boston: Harvard Business School Publishing, 2017).

39. Lee Kuan Yew, *Lee Kuan Yew: The Grand Master's Insights on China, the United States, and the World,* ed. Graham Allison and Robert D. Blackwill with Ali Wyne, foreword by Henry A. Kissinger (Cambridge, MA: MIT Press, 2013), 82–83.

40. For introductions to the history of Singapore's economic policies, see Richard H. K. Vietor, "Singapore, Inc.," in *How Countries Compete: Strategy, Structure, and Government in the Global Economy* (Boston: Harvard Business Review Press, 2007), 39–56; and more broadly on all of the East Asian "miracles," including Singapore, see Ian Patrick Austin, *Common Foundations of American and East Asian Modernisation: From Alexander Hamilton to Junichero Koizumi* (Singapore: Select, 2009). On the importance of making haste slowly in eighteenth-century reformism, see Gilbert Faccarello, "'Nil repente!' Galiani and Necker on Economic Reforms," *European Journal of the History of Economic Thought* 1, no. 3 (1994): 519–550; and see Chapter 2, this volume.

41. Suetonius, *Life of Augustus,* 25.4. See also Henk Th. Van Veen, *Cosimo I de' Medici and His Self-Representation in Florentine Art and Culture* (Cambridge: Cambridge University Press, 2006), 24. On Cosimo's developmental state, see Sophus A. Reinert, "Introduction" to Antonio Serra, *A Short Treatise on the Wealth and Poverty of Nations (1613),* trans. Jonathan Hunt (London: Anthem, 2011), 1–93, at 40–43.

42. For an adumbration of this, see Judith C. Brown, "Concepts of Political Economy: Cosimo I de' Medici in a Comparative European Context," in *Firenze e la Toscana dei Medici dell' Europa del '500,* 3 vols., ed. Gian Carlo Garfugnini (Florence: Leo S. Olschki, 1983), 279–293. On more recent "developmental states," see the essays in Meredith Woo-Cumings, ed., *The Developmental State* (Ithaca, NY: Cornell University Press, 1999).

43. Kevin Cullinane, Wei Yim Yap, and Jasmine S. L. Lam, "The Port of Singapore and Its Governance Structure," in *Devolution, Port Governance and Port Performance,* ed. Mary R. Brooks and Kevin Cullinane (Oxford: Elsevier, 2007), 285–311, at 299.

44. Compare Shawna Tang, *Postcolonial Lesbian Identities in Singapore: Re-Thinking Global Sexualities* (London: Routledge, 2016), 162, to the anonymous North Korean quoted in Geoffrey K. See and Andray Abrahamian, "Making Training

More Effective for North Koreans by Separating Ideation from Capacity-Building," *International Journal of Korean Unification Studies* 23, no. 1 (2014): 25–48, at 26.

45. For similar operational conclusions from rather different foundations, particularly with regard to the need for "small steps" that favor "reversibility," see James Scott, *Seeing Like a State: How Certain Schemes to Improve the Human Condition Have Failed* (New Haven, CT: Yale University Press, 1998), 345.

46. Daron Acemoglu, "Capitalism," in *Economic Ideas You Should Forget*, ed. Bruno S. Frey and David Iselin (Cham: Springer, 2017), 1–3, at 2–3.

47. See, similarly, Rawi Abdelal, *Capital Rules: The Construction of Global Finance* (Cambridge, MA: Harvard University Press, 2007), 223. On the making and breaking of the first grand period of "globalization," see, among others, Maurice Obstfeld and Alan M. Taylor, *Global Capital Markets: Integration, Crisis, and Growth* (Cambridge: Cambridge University Press, 2004), 28; and, more generally, Jeffry A. Frieden, *Global Capitalism: Its Fall and Rise in the Twentieth Century* (New York: W. W. Norton, 2007); Kevin H. O'Rourke and Jeffrey G. Williamson, *Globalization and History: The Evolution of a Nineteenth-Century Atlantic Economy* (Cambridge, MA: MIT Press, 1999); and, more broadly, Harold James, *The Creation and Destruction of Value: The Globalization Cycle* (Cambridge, MA: Harvard University Press, 2009).

48. Jacob Viner, "The Intellectual History of Laissez Faire," in *Essays*, 200–225, at 224.

49. Interview with José Ramos-Horta, Dili, East Timor, 11 August, 2015.

50. A plethora of publications emphasize Beccaria's "relevance," going back centuries, but see, for a recent example, Luigi Ferrajoli, "L'attualità del pensiero di Cesare Beccaria," *Materiali per una storia della cultura giuridica* 45, no. 1 (2015): 137–162.

51. For a recent primer, see Hugo Adam Bedau and Paul G. Cassell, eds., *Debating the Death Penalty: Should America Have Capital Punishment? The Experts from Both Sides Make Their Case* (Oxford: Oxford University Press, 2004). See also, more recently, Carol S. Steiker and Jordan M. Steiker, *Courting Death: The Supreme Court and Capital Punishment* (Cambridge, MA: Harvard University Press, 2016), emphasizing Beccaria's importance at esp. 10.

52. See Roger Hood and Carolyn Hoyle, *The Death Penalty: A Worldwide Perspective*, 5th ed. (Oxford: Oxford University Press, 2015). On development and capital punishment, see David T. Johnson and Franklin E. Zimring, *The Next Frontier: National Development, Political Change, and the Death Penalty in Asia* (Oxford: Oxford University Press, 2009), 293–295.

53. As evident, for example, from the evocative cover of Cesare Beccaria, *Dei delitti e delle pene* (Milan: Feltrinelli, 2014), inspired by one of the most iconic photo-

graphs to emerge from the events described in Karen J. Greenberg and Joshua L. Dratel, eds., *The Torture Papers: The Road to Abu Ghraib* (Cambridge: Cambridge University Press, 2009).

54. Beccaria has been intimately connected to variations of "humanity" since his earliest publications, but see, for this particular phrase, [Thomas Byerly], *The Percy Anecdotes: Original and Select*, 20 vols. (London: T. Boys, 1821–1823), 1:145, fittingly pretending to be the work of the fictitious Benedictine brothers Sholto and Reuben Percy, appropriately named after the Percy Coffeehouse in Fitzrovia. On this, see William Ukers, *All About Coffee* (New York: Tea and Coffee Trade Journal Co., 1922), 583.

55. On the recent, and rapid, "normalization" of torture, see among others Henry A. Giroux, *Zombie Politics and Culture in the Age of Casino Capitalism* (New York: Peter Lang, 2011), 140.

56. Franco Venturi to Alexander Gerschenkron, 2 June 1965, HUA, Cambridge, MA, HUG (FP) 45.10, Alexander Gerschenkron, General Correspondence (1948–1949–1975), Box 20 of 21, T (1966) to W (1956–1957), 2r, referencing Cesare Beccaria, *Dei delitti e delle pene*, ed. Franco Venturi (Turin: Einaudi, 1965). On Gerschenkron, see Nicholas Dawidoff, *The Fly Swatter: Portrait of an Exceptional Character* (New York: Vintage, 2003).

57. On the resulting League of Nations, see Susan Pedersen, *The Guardians: The League of Nations and the Crisis of Empire* (Oxford: Oxford University Press, 2015).

58. Thorstein Veblen to Manley Hudson, 31 December 1917, 1v, as well as Veblen, "Memorandum: Suggestions Touching the Working Program of an Inquiry into the Prospective Issue of Peace," both in Manley O. Hudson Papers, *Correspondence A. Period 1: Early Corr.* Aisle 2 Section 19 MS Box 4, 4–19, HLSL, "Veblen, Thorstein B." For Veblen's longer treatise on perpetual peace, see his *An Inquiry into the Nature of Peace and the Terms of Its Perpetuation* (New York: Macmillan, 1917). On Veblen and the problem of peace, see also Stephen Edgell, "Veblen, War and Peace," in *Thorstein Veblen: Economics for an Age of Crises*, ed. Erik S. Reinert and Francesca Lidia Viano (London: Anthem, 2012), 239–256.

59. For eminently readable different perspectives on these atrocities, see Mark Mazower, *Dark Continent: Europe's Twentieth Century* (London: Allen Lane, 1998); and Niall Ferguson, *War of the World: Twentieth-Century Conflict and the Descent of the West* (London: Penguin, 2007).

60. Elton Mayo, *The Social Problems of an Industrial Civilization* (Boston: Division of Research, Graduate School of Business Administration, Harvard University, 1945), dedication to Wallace B. Donham, xi–xvi. On Mayo, see Richard Trahair, *Elton Mayo: The Humanist Temper*, foreword by Ahramah Alezni (Piscataway, NJ: Transaction, 2005).

61. The question of "perennial problems" lies at the core of one of the central po-
    lemics in the historiography of intellectual history in the twentieth century.
    See, principally, Quentin Skinner, "Meaning and Understanding in the His-
    tory of Ideas," in *Visions of Politics*, 3 vols. (Cambridge: Cambridge University
    Press, 2002 [1969]), 1:57–89, esp. 88. For thoughtful meditations on the con-
    temporary relevance of the history of political economy in particular, see,
    from different perspectives, Steven L. Kaplan, *The Stakes of Regulation: Perspec-
    tives on "Bread, Politics and Political Economy" Forty Years Later* (London: Anthem,
    2015), 385–399, and Hont, *Jealousy of Trade*, 156.

62. On the quote, see Garson O'Toole, "History Does Not Repeat Itself, but
    It Rhymes," http://quoteinvestigator.com/2014/01/12/history-rhymes/. The
    first variation of the quote may have been in "Art. I. [Review of A. N. Moura-
    vieff's *A History of the Church in Russia*]," *The Christian Remembrancer*, October,
    1845 [vol. 10, London: Burns, 1845], 245–331, 264: "history repeats her tale uncon-
    sciously, and goes off into a mystic rhyme; ages are prototypes of other ages, and
    the winding course of time brings us round to the same spot again."

63. Alessandro Verri, "Di alcuni sistemi del pubblico diritto," in *"Il Caffè," 1764–1766*,
    ed. Gianni Francioni and Sergio A. Romagnoli (Turin: Bollati Boringhieri, 1993),
    725–739, at 729.

64. Giacomo Giuliani, "Corso di scienze politiche dell'anno 1817–1818," Antoniana,
    Scafale 36, Coidce 772, fasc. 1, 17r–17v.

65. Friedrich Engels to Nikolai Danielson, 29–31 October 1891, in Karl Marx and
    Friedrich Engels, *Collected Works*, 50 vols. (London: Lawrence and Wishart,
    1975–2005), 49:280. On Danielson's political economy, see, among others, An-
    drzej Walicki, *A History of Russian Thought from the Enlightenment to Marxism*
    (Stanford, CA: Stanford University Press, 1979), 432–434.

66. See, for a similar argument, Robert Fredona and Sophus A. Reinert, "Introduc-
    tion: History and Political Economy," in *New Perspectives on the History of Po-
    litical Economy*, ed. Robert Fredona and Sophus A. Reinert (Cham: Palgrave Mac-
    millan, 2018), xi–xxxiii, particularly xx–xxii.

67. On these early uses of socialism as an "idéhistorisk kuriositet," see Dag Einar
    Thorsen, "Liberalisme, konservatisme og sosialisme," in *Den dannede opprører:
    Bernt Hagtvet 70 år*, ed. Nikolai Brandal and Dag Einar Thorsen (Oslo: Dreyer,
    2016), 37–57, at 48.

68. John Maynard Keynes, *The General Theory of Employment, Interest and Money*
    (London: Palgrave Macmillan, 1936), 383–384. For a longer philosophical echo
    of this argument, see Herzog, *Inventing the Market*, 159–160; and for a rather more
    colorful way of saying roughly the same thing, Paolo Barnard, *La Storia
    dell'economia (che ti dà da mangiare) spiegata a Lollo del mio bar* (Rome: Andromeda
    Edizioni, 2013), 13.

69. Verri, "Meditazioni sulla economia politica," in *Edizione nazionale delle opere di Pietro Verri*, ed. Carlo Capra et al., 8 vols. in 10 to date (Rome: Edizioni di storia e letteratura, 2003–2014), vol. 2, pt. 2, 556–558.

70. There are few clearer symptoms of the present incarnation of such a crisis than the unprecedented publishing success of Thomas Piketty, *Capital in the Twenty-First Century*, trans. Arthur Goldhammer (Cambridge, MA: Harvard University Press, 2014), on which see the excellent essays in Heather Boushey, J. Bradford Delong, and Marshall Steinbaum, eds., *After Piketty: The Agenda for Economics and Inequality* (Cambridge, MA: Harvard University Press, 2017), and particularly Arthur Goldhammer, "The Piketty Phenomenon," 27–47. For a mere handful of increasingly popular alternative paradigms "legitimized" in growing circles, see the vast arc spanning from Osama Bin Laden, *Messages to the World: The Statements of Osama Bin Laden,* ed. Bruce Lawrence, trans. James Howarth (London: Verso, 2005); to Aleksandr Dugin, *The Fourth Political Theory,* trans. Mark Sleboda and Michael Millerman (London: Arktos Media, 2012); to James Lovelock, *A Rough Ride to the Future* (New York: Overlook Press, 2015); to Xi Jinping, *The Governance of China* (Shanghai: Shanghai Press, 2015).

71. In his *Jealousy of Trade,* 4, Istvan Hont asked, "should we assume that a plurality of political visions might suit the integration of politics and the market economy, or should we accept the idea that there is just one privileged state form, the modern representative republic, that has an elective affinity with markets?" Recent history makes the second position harder to defend. See, among countless examples discussing nondemocratic market societies, Kellee S. Tsai, *Capitalism without Democracy: The Private Sector in Contemporary China* (Ithaca, NY: Cornell University Press, 2007), and Michael Puett, "Who Is Confucius in Today's China?," in *The China Question: Critical Insights into a Rising Power,* ed. Jennifer M. Rudolph and Michael Szonyi (Cambridge, MA: Harvard University Press, 2018), 231–236, at 233. See, similarly, Sophus A. Reinert, *Translating Empire: Emulation and the Origins of Political Economy* (Cambridge, MA: Harvard University Press, 2011), 287–288.

72. For a beautiful history of courting Utopia, see Gregory Claeys, *Searching for Utopia: The History of an Idea* (London: Thames and Hudson, 2011).

73. See, for a reminder, Jonathan Crary, *24 / 7: Late Capitalism and the Ends of Sleep* (London: Verso, 2014); and, from a different perspective on the preciousness of time in our current situation, Thomas Hylland Eriksen, *Øyeblikkets Tyranni: Rask og langsom tid i informasjonssamfunnet* (Oslo: Aschehoug, 2001); and Eriksen, *Overheating: An Anthropology of Accelerated Change* (London: Pluto Press, 2016), esp. 12–15, 79.

ACKNOWLEDGMENTS

In times such as these, it is perhaps fitting that I incurred debts during the writing of this book that I know full well I can never hope to repay. The original stint of research for this project was funded many moons ago by the South-South Exchange Programme for Research on the History of Development (SEPHIS) of the Dutch Ministry of Foreign Affairs and by the Other Canon Foundation of Norway, but it could not have been concluded in its current form without the uniquely generous moral and financial support of Harvard Business School (HBS). Particularly, I would like to thank my research director, Cynthia Montgomery, for her encouragement and, importantly, for her plentiful patience. I am furthermore grateful for the invaluable help of my faculty support specialists, Anja Goethals, Lauren Pacifico, Kaitlyn Tuthill, Sarah Zeiser, and particularly the tireless Kate Jenkins, who has gone well beyond conceivable calls of duty. I would furthermore like to recognize the assistance of my former research associate, Stefano Calonaci, and the personal support of Debra Wallace and Laura Linard of HBS's Knowledge and Information Services. And I remain always thankful to Kenneth E. Carpenter for foundational inspiration early on. Additionally, at HBS's Hong Kong Asia-Pacific Research Center, I am ever grateful to Dawn H. Lau for helping me explore the final frontiers of capitalism and, memorably, for her grace under fire, in the literal sense of the phrase. Indeed, though the Harvard economist John Kenneth Galbraith once lamented to his friend and intellectual opponent Milton Friedman about "the basic university custom of substituting movement for thought," I have found the two activities—moving and thinking—to be remarkably synergetic, and I am indebted to HBS for the duty and the opportunity to do research on, and write cases about, recent and often far-flung moments in the winding and endlessly intriguing history of global capitalism.

The book could not have been written without the assistance of libraries and librarians across Europe and in the United States, and I would specifically like to thank the staff at the George F. Baker Library and Bloomberg Center at HBS and its Kress Collection of Business and Economics, and specifically Julia Brav and Melissa Murphy, and of course at the Harry Elkins Widener Memorial Library of Harvard University, "a true dream," as Franco Venturi once wrote to Alexander Gerschenkron, "for an Italian scholar," or, in my case, for a sometime historian of Italy. In the United States, I am furthermore indebted to the New York Public Library; in Britain, to the British Library and the Cambridge University Library; in France, to the Bibliothèque Nationale de France in Paris; in Italy, to the Biblioteca Nazionale Centrale and the Archivio di Stato in Florence, the Archivio di Stato in Genoa, the Biblioteca Ambrosiana and the Archivio di Stato in Milan, the Biblioteca Nazionale and the Archivio di Stato in Turin, and the Archivio di Stato in Venice. The Fondazione Luigi Einaudi in Turin is my academic home away from home, and I am greatly indebted to the wonderful staff and frequenters of that unique institution. For invaluable archival help I am, furthermore, personally grateful to the Countess Luisa Sormani for permission to reproduce materials from the Collezione Sormani-Andreani-Verri; to the Countess Barbara Baldasseroni Corsini for graciously allowing me access to the Archivio Baldasseroni Corsini in Florence and for permitting me to quote from its holdings; to Barbara Costa at the Fondazione Raffaele Mattioli in Milan, home of the Archivio Verri; to Luca Guaschetti at the Biblioteca Civica Angelo Mai in Bergamo; to Luigi Mantovani at the Archivio Storico Comunale di Casale Monferrato; to Nicholas Robinson at the Fitzwilliam Museum's Founder's Library in Cambridge; to Olatz Berasategui at the Santuario de Loiola in Loyola; to Fr. Antonio Poppi and Fr. Alberto Fanton for extraordinary access to the Pontificia Biblioteca Antoniana at the Basilica of St. Anthony in Padua; to Guido Mones at the Fondazione Luigi Einaudi in Turin; to Helga Ernestine Fichtner at the Österreichisches Staatsarchiv in Vienna; and to the late Pierangelo Garegnani for permitting me to quote from Piero Sraffa's manuscripts in the Wren Library at Trinity College, University of Cambridge, as well as to Jonathan Smith for facilitating my work there. Finally, for enabling my bibliophilia, special thanks are due to Ian Smith, now of Peter Harrington, Massimo Gilibert of Galleria Gilibert, and particularly Lelia and the late Giorgio Vaccarino, whose generosity, during a very particular period in my life, I will never forget.

My unit in Business, Government, and the International Economy (BGIE) at HBS has proven to be a galvanizing work environmente over the past several years, and I am deeply grateful to Rawi Abdelal, Laura Alfaro, Kristin Fabbe, Jeremy Friedman, Reshmaan Hussam, Akshay Mangla, David Moss, Aldo Musacchio, Laura Phillips-Sawyer, Vincent Pons, Forest Reinhart, Meg Rithmire, Dante Roscini, Jesse Schreger, Rafael di Tella, Gunnar Trumbull, Dick Vietor, Matt Weinzerl, and Eric Werker for their camaraderie. At the HBS Business History Initiative, I would further like to thank Geoffrey Jones, Tom Nicholas, and Walter Friedman, and I remain deeply grateful for the personal support of Francis Frei, Rakesh Khurana, Youngme Moon, and Nitin Nohria. I also owe much to David Bell, Rohit Deshpande, Anita Elberse, Sunil Gupta, Paul Healey, Rebecca Henderson, Jan Rivkin, and, for enlightening discussions about more recent frontiers of capitalism, Tarun Khanna. Similarly, I have greatly enjoyed discussing the many facets of global capitalism, economic development, and commercial society with students in my courses, particularly my elective course "Globalization and Emerging Markets" as well as in the core "Business, Government, and the International Economy" for MBA students and in the executive General Management Program.

Though much has changed since we first met in Ithaca, Steven L. Kaplan's ruthless support for me has never wavered. He remains my most critical and encouraging interlocutor, and has given me new reasons to look forward to layovers in Paris and, more recently, academic boot camps in Biarritz. For fruitful discussions and insights regarding different aspects of this book, from Lombard history to global capitalism, I am furthermore indebted to David Abulafia, Doohwan Ahn, Mari Alkatiri, Rolv Petter Amdam, David Armitage, Jürgen Backhaus, Sven Beckert, Silvio Berlusconi, Christopher Brooke, Angus Burgin, Carlo Capra, Paul Cheney, Michael Chu, Chris Clark, Graham Clure, D'Maris Coffman, Will Deringer, Christine Desan, Wolfgang Drechsler, Hugo Drochon, Gianni Francioni, François Furstenberg, Martin Giraudeau, Bernard E. Harcourt, Anna Hont, Tom Hopkins, Andrea Iacona, Joel Isaac, Béla Kapossy, Rainer Kattel, James T. Kloppenberg, Jan Kregel, Michael Kwass, James Livesey, Ian MacDaniel, Lavinia Maddaluno, Janni Marjanen, John Marshall, Mira Mehta, Farrukh Moriani, Renaud Morieux, Craig Muldrew, Isaac Nakhimovsky, Eric Nelson, John Ngo, Edgardo Novick, Arnaud Orain, Alexandra Ortolja-Baird, Gabriel Paquette, Renato Pasta, Rosario Patalano, Eva Piirimäe, Steve Pincus, Emília Pires, Iqbal Z. Quadir, José Ramos-Horta, Anna Maria Rao, Giuseppe Ricuperati, John Robertson, Emma Rothschild, Philipp Robinson Rössner, Joan-Pau Rubiés, Roberto Scazzieri, Geoffrey See, Richard Serjeantson, Quinn Slobodian, Daniel Lord Smail, Daniel Smith, Michael Sonenscher, Koen Stapelbroek, Philippe Steiner, Irene Yuan Sun, Jomo Kwame Sundaram, Anoush Terjanian, Mikko

Tolonen, Keith Tribe, John Tsang, Richard Tuck, Andre Wakefield, Carl Wenner-lind, Eric Werker, Richard Whatmore, Kerry Yang, and Christine Zabel. Jacob Soll has long been a steadfast ally, and I will never forget our first rabbit under La Mole. John Brewer, Melissa Calaresu, Carlo Capra, Vincenzo Ferrone, Peter Garnsey, John Shovlin, and Corey Tazzara kindly took the time to read the entire manuscript, and saved me from many an embarrassment.

I deeply regret, however, that some of my closest friends and mentors did not live to see the book in print. Pier-Luigi Porta, with whom I had so many warm conversations about the Lombard Enlightenment, was an early inspira-tion, and my work and life would not have been the same without Michael O'Brien's dry chuckles and splendid critiques. Julio Rotemberg took me under his wing at HBS, ever willing to discuss minutiae about balances of payments before dawn, and took the time to read my entire manuscript when he knew that time rapidly was running out. The present work was, however, most directly inspired by my *Doktorvater* Istvan Hont. He first put me on the problem of Enlightenment Socialism, and for a while even thought we should write an article on the subject together. His illness, debilitating in body only, cut those ideas short, but his admo-nition to write this book during our last meeting at Costa Coffee on Mill Road in Cambridge is what ultimately convinced me to do so. I am grateful for their examples, and cherish the time I was allowed to spend with them.

The book builds on some of my previous work over the past decade, and parts of the following articles have been developed with permission: "'One Will Make of Political Economy . . . What the Scholastics Did with Philosophy': Henry Lloyd and the Mathematization of Economics," *History of Political Economy* 34, no. 4 (2007): 643–677; "Patriotism, Cosmopolitanism, and Political Economy in the *Accademia dei pugni* in Austrian Lombardy, 1760–1780," in *The Rise of Economic Societies in the Eighteenth Century: Patriotic Reform in Europe and North America,* ed. Koen Stapelbroek and Jani Marjanen (Basingstoke: Palgrave Macmillan, 2012), 130–156; "Guerra senza sangue e l'aroma dei lumi: La cultura del Caffè tra politica e commercio internazionale nella Lombardia austriaca," in *L'illuminismo delle riforme civili: Il contributo degli economisti Lombardi,* ed. Pier Luigi Porta and Roberto Scazzieri (Milan: Istituto Lombardo di scienze e let-tere, 2014), 255–293; "Achtung! Banditi! An Alternate Genealogy of the Market," in *Economic Growth and the Origins of Modern Political Economy: Economic Reasons of State, 1500–2000,* ed. Philipp Robinson Rössner (London: Routledge, 2016), 239–295; "Enlightenment Socialism: Cesare Beccaria and His Critics," in *Commerce and Peace in the Enlightenment,* ed. Béla Kapossy, Isaac Nakhimovsky, and Richard Whatmore (Cambridge: Cambridge University Press, 2017), 125–154.

I first discussed this project's publication with Michael Aronson at Harvard University Press, and I remain grateful for his early encouragement. Likewise,

I would like to thank Ian Malcolm for believing in the project since our very first meeting and for his invaluable help in bringing it to fruition, and Olivia Woods for cheerful editorial assistance. Antonella Emmi, John Donohue, and Wendy Nelson additionally offered expert copyediting. Scott Walker of Harvard's Map Collection has been of extraordinary help on this and numerous related projects, and I would like to thank Isabelle Lewis for the beautiful maps. Finally, I am much indebted to the three anonymous readers at the Press for helping me improve the book in numerous ways.

Through thick and thin, Robert Fredona has been my best man throughout the gestation of this book; words cannot express my debt to his generosity, friendship, and erudition. In Italy, Carlo Augusto and Giorgia Viano have treated me like a son, and provided shelter from many a storm over the years. In Norway, I remain grateful to my parents, Erik and Fernanda, and to my brother Hugo for their unwavering support across time and space as well as for first instilling in me a love of Lombardy and the mist-shrouded Po Plain. *Dulcis in fundo,* however, I couldn't imagine this project or much else without the love and pugnacity of Francesca and our son Erik August, brigands of their own sort, who, among so many other things, helped me traverse old contraband routes into Lombardy through the "Swiss cliffs of doom." The book is dedicated to Erik August, for, as he often asks, isn't it his turn soon? Yes, it is.

ILLUSTRATION CREDITS

Page xi: Europe at the Time of the Academy of Fisticuffs. © Sophus A. Reinert.

Page xii: Northern Italy at the Time of the Academy of Fisticuffs. © Sophus A. Reinert.

Page 9:   Jean-Baptiste-François Bosio (1764–1827), *Portrait of Cesare Bonesana, Marchese di Beccaria,* n.d. Artokoloro Quint Lox Limited / Alamy Stock Photo.

Page 21:   Anonymous Portrait, *Ritratto giovanile di Pietro Verri che addita una massima politica delle Filippiche,* Milano, Collezione Luisa Sormani Andreani Verri. Saporetti Imagini d'Arte. Reproduction courtesy of Harvard University Libraries.

Page 28:   Jacques Callot (1592–1635), *The Wheel* from the series *The Miseries and Misfortunes of War,* 1633. Collection Albright-Knox Art Gallery, Buffalo, New York, 1905:21.97. Bequest of Miss Maria L. Wilkeson, 1905.

Page 30:   Giovanni Battista Piranesi (1720–1778), "The Pier with Chains," Plate XVI from *Le Carceri d'Invenzione (The Imaginary Prisons),* 1761. Princeton University Art Museum, Princeton, New Jersey. Gift of Frank Jewett Mather Jr., 1938.

Page 30: Milanese Confraternity Seal. Anonymous print, from the collection of Giancarlo Beltrame, reproduced in Italo Mereu, *La Pena di Morte a Milano nel Secolo di Beccaria* (Vicenza: Neri Pozza Editore, 1988).

Page 36: Capital Sentences in the Duchy of Milan, 1738–1767. *Data Source:* Italo Mereu, *La Pena di Morte a Milano nel Secolo di Beccaria* (Vicenza: Neri Pozza Editore, 1988), p. 44.

Page 44: Antonio Perego, *L'Accademia dei pugni, 1766.* Collezione Sormani-Andreani Verri, Milan.

Page 51: Giovanni Battista Tiepolo (1696–1770), *Allegory of Merit Accompanied by Nobility and Virtue,* 1757. Ca' Rezzonico, Venice. ART Collection / Alamy Stock Photo.

Page 61: Google Ngrams of économie / économique / economy / oeconomy / economic / economia / economico. Generated by the author via Google Books Ngram Viewer.

Page 140: Alessandro Magnasco (1667–1749), *Gerichtsszene (Court Scene),* c. 1710–1720. Kunsthistorisches Museum, Vienna. Gemäldegalerie, GG 9037. KHM-Museumsverband.

Page 144: Giovanni Lapi, engraving, in Cesare Bonesana-Beccaria, *Dei Delitti e Della Pene (On Crimes and Punishments),* Third Edition (Lausanne [Livorno], 1765). Frontispiece. Reproduction courtesy of Historical & Special Collections, Harvard Law School Library.

Page 160: Nathaniel Hone (1718–1784), *General Lloyd,* The Fitzwilliam Museum, Cambridge, UK, Accession No. 457, Record ID 3415. © The Fitzwilliam Museum, Cambridge.

Page 216: Giotto, "Justice." Giotto di Bondone (1267–1337), *Justice,* Scrovegni Chapel, Padua, c. 1303–1305. ART Collection / Alamy Stock Photo.

Page 217: Giotto, "Injustice." Giotto di Bondone (1267–1337), *Injustice,* Scrovegni Chapel, Padua, c. 1303–1305. ART Collection / Alamy Stock Photo.

Page 220: Ambrogio Lorenzetti (c. 1290–1348), "The Effects of Bad Government on the Countryside," panel (detail), *The Allegory of Good and Bad Government,* c. 1338–1339. Fondazione Musei Senesi, Palazzo Pubblico, Siena. Paul Fearn / Alamy Stock Photo.

Page 221: Ambrogio Lorenzetti (c. 1290–1348), "Timor" [Fear], panel (detail), *The Allegory of Good and Bad Government,* c. 1338–1339. Fondazione Musei

Senesi, Palazzo Pubblico, Siena. Reproduction from D. Skelector, *Streets in Turmoil,* December 9, 2016, streetsinturmoil.com.

Page 221:   Ambrogio Lorenzetti (c. 1290–1348), "The Effects of Bad Government on the City," panel (detail), *The Allegory of Good and Bad Government,* c. 1338–1339. Fondazione Musei Senesi, Palazzo Pubblico, Siena. Web Gallery of Art/www.wga.hu.

Page 222:   Ambrogio Lorenzetti (c. 1290–1348), "The Allegory of Good Government," panel, *The Allegory of Good and Bad Government,* c. 1338–1339. Fondazione Musei Senesi, Palazzo Pubblico, Siena. Fondazione Musei Senesi.

Page 222:   Ambrogio Lorenzetti (c. 1290–1348), "The Effects of Good Government in the City," panel, *The Allegory of Good and Bad Government,* c. 1338–1339. Fondazione Musei Senesi, Palazzo Pubblico, Siena. Fondazione Musei Senesi.

Page 224:   Ambrogio Lorenzetti (c. 1290–1348), "The Effects of Good Government in the Countryside," panel (detail), *The Allegory of Good and Bad Government,* c. 1338–1339. Fondazione Musei Senesi, Palazzo Pubblico, Siena. The Print Collector / Alamy Stock Photo.

Page 226:   Ambrogio Lorenzetti (c. 1290–1348), "Securitas" [Security], panel (detail), *The Allegory of Good and Bad Government,* c. 1338–1339. Fondazione Musei Senesi, Palazzo Pubblico, Siena. ART Collection / Alamy Stock Photo.

Page 229:   Salvator Rosa (1615–1673), *Rocky Landscape with a Hunter and Soldiers,* c. 1670. Musée du Louvre, Paris, INV586. Franck Raux / © RMN–Grand Palais / Art Resource, NY.

Page 230:   Thomas Cole, American (born in England), 1801–1848. *Salvator Rosa Sketching Banditti,* about 1832–1840, Oil on panel, 17.78 × 24.13 cm (7 × 9½ in.). Gift of Maxim Karolik for the M. and M. Karolik Collection of American Paintings, 1815–1865, inv. 62.268, Museum of Fine Arts, Boston. Photograph © 2018 Museum of Fine Arts, Boston.

Page 246:   Giovanni Michele Graneri (1708–1762), *Piazza San Carlo con Mercato,* 1752. Palazzo Madama, Museo Civico d'Arte Antica, Turin, Inventory No. 0543 / D. © DEA / A DE GREGORIO / De Agostini Editore Collection / age footstock.

Page 248:   Alessandro Magnasco (1667–1749), *Il Mercato del Verziere,* 1733. Pinacoteca Castello Sforzesco, Milan, Raccolte d'Arte Antica, Inventory No. 228. Copyright © Comune di Milano—All rights reserved.

Page 273:   Anonymous Portrait, *Anselm Desing,* c. 1770. Ensdorf, Germany. Paul Fearn / Alamy Stock Photo.

Page 292:   Pietro Verri (1728–1797), marginalia drawing, *Ferdinando Facchinei,* c. 1765. Archivio Verri, Milan. Sophus A. Reinert, by arrangement with Archivio Verri, Milan.

Page 294:   Joshua Reynolds (1723–1792), *Portrait of Joseph Baretti,* 1773. Private Collection. Olga's Gallery/www.abcgallery.com.

Page 303:   [Andrea Appiani (1754–1817)?], *Ritratto di Giulia Beccaria e suo figlio Alessandro Manzoni bambino,* c. 1790. Villa Manzoni, Brusuglio. Wikimedia Commons / Moloch981 (CC-PD-Mark).

Page 381:   Albert Renger-Patzsch (1897–1966), photograph, in *Eisen und Stahl* (Berlin: Verlag Hermann Reckendorf, 1931). Reproduction courtesy of Special Collections, Fine Arts Library, Harvard University.

Page 383:   [Unidentified photographer / manufacturer], "Tripoli—Caserma Pietro Verri," c. 1933. Postcard. Reproduction from the author's collection.

Page 386:   Google Ngrams of capitalism / socialism / socialista / socialismo / socialisti / capitalismo / capitalista / capitalaisti. Generated by the author via Google Books Ngram Viewer.

Page 391:   Angelo Inganni (1807–1880), *Veduta del Verziere,* 1852. Private Collection. Reproduction courtesy of Milàn l'era inscì Urbanfile/Flickr.

Page 395:   Open-air market near Dili, East Timor. © Sophus A. Reinert.

Page 403:   Cesare Beccaria, *Dei delitti e delle pene* (Milan: Feltrinelli, 2014), cover. © 2014, Giangiacomo Feltrinelli Editore, Milano.

Page 404:   Flavio Costantini (1926–2013), *Cesare Beccaria,* 1987. Photo / Scan Credit: Flavio Costantini, *Cesare Beccaria,* 1987. Courtesy Archive Flavio Costantini, Genoa.

INDEX